341.23
C79

W9-BXG-260

From the Library
of

 CALDWELL COLLEGE

Caldwell, New Jersey 07006

Public Papers of
the Secretaries-General of
the United Nations

VOLUME VII

U THANT

1965–1967

Public Papers of
the Secretaries-General of
the United Nations

VOLUME VII

U THANT
1965–1967

Selected and Edited with Commentary by

ANDREW W. CORDIER
AND
MAX HARRELSON

COLUMBIA UNIVERSITY PRESS
1976
NEW YORK

341.2308
C79p
v. 1

ANDREW W. CORDIER served as Dean of the School of International Affairs at Columbia University from 1962 to 1972 and as president of the university from 1968 to 1970. From the beginning of the United Nations until 1962 Dr. Cordier was Executive Assistant to the Secretary-General with the rank of Under-Secretary. During the entire period he also had the top Secretariat responsibility for General Assembly affairs.

MAX HARRELSON served as a United Nations correspondent from 1946 until 1972, the last twenty-two years as chief correspondent of the Associated Press. Later he became a research associate in the School of International Affairs, Columbia University.

CALDWELL COLLEGE LIBRARY
CALDWELL, NEW JERSEY

Library of Congress Cataloging in Publication Data (Revised)

Cordier, Andrew Wellington, 1901–1975 comp.
  Public papers of the Secretaries-General of the
United Nations.

  Vols.   by A. W. Cordier and M. Harrelson.
  Includes bibliographical references.
  CONTENTS: v. 1. Trygve Lie: 1946–53.—v. 2.
Dag Hammarskjöld: 1953–1956.—v. 3. Dag Hammarskjöld: 1956–1957. [etc.]
  1. United Nations—Collected works. I. Foote,
Wilder, joint comp. II. Harrelson, Max. III. Lie,
Trygve, 1896–1968. IV. Hammarskjöld, Dag, 1905–
1961. V. Thant, U, 1909–1974. VI. Title.
JX1977.C62   341.23'08   68-8873
ISBN 0-231-04098-9

Copyright © 1976 Columbia University Press
All rights reserved
Printed in United States of America

89433

THIS VOLUME is dedicated to Andrew W. Cordier, whose idea it was to publish this series and who worked tirelessly with the late Wilder Foote and with me in editing the public papers of Trygve Lie, Dag Hammarskjöld, and U Thant. He died on July 11, 1975, after completing his work as co-editor. I want to take this opportunity to express my gratitude for his wisdom, his patience, and his understanding during our collaboration.

Max Harrelson

May 14, 1976

Editors' Note on the Series

THE ROLE OF THE Secretary-General in the political life and constitutional development of the United Nations since 1945 has far exceeded the expectations of those who wrote the Charter. This has enhanced the historical significance of the public papers of the Secretaries-General. These include many texts that are valuable and often indispensable as source materials in study of the Organization as a whole, of the office of Secretary-General in particular, and of the place of both in world affairs.

It is important that such papers be readily available to scholars and specialists in international affairs. In practice their accessibility has been severely limited. Some of the public papers of the Secretaries-General are included in the official documentation and some are not. In the former category are periodic and special reports to United Nations organs, proposals, and statements at meetings of the General Assembly, the Security Council, the other councils, committees, and commissions, and certain communications to governments. Not included in the official records are various other communications to governments, the Secretary-General's addresses outside the United Nations, statements to the press, press conference transcripts, radio and television broadcasts, and contributions to magazines and books. Most of the texts in this second category were issued as press releases, none as official documents.

More or less comprehensive collections of the official documents are maintained by depository libraries designated by the United Nations and located in most of the countries of the world. After more than twenty-five years it is not surprising that the volume of this documentation is immense. The record of what successive Secretaries-General have spoken or written in the official proceedings is widely dispersed throughout a great mass of records. Furthermore, it is necessary to go to the press releases for the public papers in the second category described above. The Dag Hammarskjöld Library at

United Nations Headquarters maintains a comprehensive collection of press releases but it has not been the practice to include them in the deposit of official documentation in the depository libraries. Yet the press releases are usually the only source of a very important part of the public record—the Secretary-General's speeches to other groups and organizations and his press statements and press conferences. Successive Secretaries-General have frequently used these for historically significant and revealing statements.

Thus the present series of volumes of the public papers of the Secretaries-General has been undertaken to meet a real need. The project has been made possible by a grant from the Ford Foundation to the School of International Affairs of Columbia University. The series will include all texts believed by the editors to be essential or most likely to be useful in study and research about the United Nations. These have been assembled from official, semiofficial, and nonofficial sources. The texts selected for the printed series are reproduced in full except where otherwise indicated. The styles of spelling and capitalization, which were variable in the official documents and press releases, have generally been reproduced as they were in the originals. Dates have been conformed throughout to the month-day-year style. The texts are arranged for the most part in chronological order corresponding to the sequence of events to which they are related. Commentary recalling the contemporary context and giving other background for the texts is provided whenever this seems useful.

It should also be explained that the official records of the United Nations include many reports issued in the name of the Secretary-General that may more correctly be classified with the records of the organs requesting them. Such reports are factual accounts of developments or programs without personal commitments of policy or principle by the Secretary-General. There are a few borderline cases, but in general reports of this nature have not been considered as belonging with the public papers of the Secretaries-General.

Acknowledgments

PUBLICATION of the *Public Papers of the Secretaries-General of the United Nations* was made possible by a grant from the Ford Foundation to the School of International Affairs of Columbia University. The editors are deeply grateful for this financial assistance.

Our editorial and research assistant, Charlotte Carpenter, and her predecessor, Alice Smith, rendered indispensable and devoted service in assembling texts, researching the background of events for use in the commentary, finding and checking sources and references, reading proof, and supervising the reproduction of both texts and commentary.

The task of collecting the papers of U Thant included in this volume was greatly facilitated by the cooperation of the United Nations Secretariat, especially officers of the Dag Hammarskjöld Library and the Public Inquiries Unit at United Nations Headquarters.

The editors are especially grateful for the personal assistance of the late U Thant and other officials close to him in providing background material essential for the commentary. They also wish to acknowledge with appreciation the help given by the late Wilder Foote, former Research Associate in the School of International Affairs and coeditor of the preceding volumes in this series. His comments and suggestions were invaluable.

Contents

Contents

Public Papers of
the Secretaries-General of
the United Nations

VOLUME VII

U THANT

1965–1967

Introduction to This Volume of
the Public Papers of U Thant

I

The middle period of U Thant's ten years as United Nations Secretary-General was full of frustrations both for him and for the United Nations. These were the years—1965, 1966, 1967—in which the Vietnam war cast a dark shadow over the world, stifling the trend toward a détente between the superpowers and undermining public confidence in the United Nations because of its inability to end the fighting. They were years of violence and bloodshed around the globe: the United States military intervention in the civil strife in the Dominican Republic, new outbreaks of fighting in Cyprus, a war between India and Pakistan over Jammu and Kashmir, and the Six-Day War in the Middle East. It is not surprising that many of Thant's public pronouncements during this period reflected gloom and pessimism and that he accepted a second five-year term only with the greatest reluctance. His faith in the United Nations never flagged, but he was deeply disturbed by the failure of the Member states to adhere to the principles of the Charter, to eschew the use of force to settle disputes, and to find solutions to such vital problems as the financing of future peace-keeping operations and the liquidation of debts remaining from past operations.

From the standpoint of Thant's personal role, the middle years will be the best remembered. Throughout this period he persisted in his private efforts to bring the parties to the Vietnam war to the conference table. Sometimes he was criticized by one side or by the other for his initiatives, but he felt that it was only through his good offices that the United Nations was in the Vietnam picture at all. Perhaps the most important decision—and the most controversial—in his two terms as Secretary-General was the withdrawal of the United Nations Emergency Force (UNEF) from Gaza and the Sinai in May 1967. Some critics believed he acted too hastily and that UNEF might have been saved and the war averted if he had exhausted all possible appeals, both personally and through the General Assembly. This conclusion he vigorously challenged. A more detailed commentary on the UNEF controversy will be found elsewhere in this volume (pp. 416–23) together with the pertinent documents (pp. 423–89). Although much of his Vietnam effort was private, he spoke out frankly and frequently on this subject. Many of his press conferences were dominated by questions on the Vietnam war. This volume contains the transcripts of these conferences, in full or in part, as well as his statements and speeches, which also contain many comments on Vietnam. No subject commanded Thant's attention during his middle years as Secretary-General as did this conflict and his attempts to assist in a settlement.

II

At the time Thant took office in 1961 the Vietnam problem was not among the paramount issues of the day. With only 2,000 United States troops in South Vietnam, the conflict was still basically a Vietnamese affair. There was sufficient concern over the situation in Southeast Asia, however, for the subject to be raised at Thant's first press conference on December 1, 1961. The question was whether the United Nations could do anything to alleviate "the tense situation in Southeast Asia, particularly in Laos and Vietnam." The Acting Secretary-General (as he was then) replied cautiously that the question had not come up for discussion in the General Assembly, and in the absence of action by Member states to inscribe the item on the agenda he did not think he "should make any observations."

It was almost two years later before Thant made a substantive statement on Vietnam or took any personal initiative. His first intervention was on behalf of Buddhists who allegedly were being mistreated in the Republic of Vietnam. On June 28, 1963, the Secretary-General disclosed at a press conference that he had taken "certain steps, very discreetly, to see that this alleged discrimination is remedied." On August 31, he made a formal appeal to President Ngo Dinh Diem on the subject. Although Thant never made any secret of his disdain for the Diem government—or the succeeding Saigon régimes, for that matter—he surprised correspondents at a press conference on September 12 by denouncing the undemocratic nature of Diem's administration. He declared that "one of the great virtues

of democracy is its ability to change governments by peaceful constitutional processes and without resort to force—a feature which is
completely absent in the Republic of Vietnam." He said the situation
in South Vietnam was chaotic and that it was going from bad to
worse. He disclosed, in response to a further question, that he had
been in constant contact with United States Ambassador Adlai E.
Stevenson in an effort to enlist the assistance of the Kennedy administration on behalf of the Buddhists.

These were the beginnings of Thant's efforts which were to continue until the peace talks finally got under way in Paris at the end of
1968. By the spring of 1964, he was enunciating principles which
formed the foundation for his later approaches to the problem. In a
press conference in Paris on April 29, 1964, he said the problem in
Southeast Asia "is not essentially military; it is political, and therefore political and diplomatic means alone, in my view, can solve it."
In another press conference in Ottawa on May 26, he expressed
doubts for the first time as to the competency of the United Nations to
deal with the situation in Vietnam, an undertaking which at the time
was being demanded with increasing frequency. In a press conference
in New York on July 8, he went a step further by suggesting that the
Geneva conference of 1954 be reconvened to seek an end to the
fighting. This was a procedure that he never ceased to urge.

By this time Thant was pursuing his peace efforts in private talks
with Ambassador Stevenson. One of his first suggestions was for a
broader-based government in Saigon to ease the way toward negotiations. The United States, however, wanted to maintain the Diem
régime and Thant's suggestions did not strike a happy note. This was
a prelude to the Secretary-General's first major attempt to initiate
peace talks. It should be pointed out here that Thant was fully aware
of his own limitations as a mediator on the Vietnam problem. He had
reason to believe that Washington did not trust him because of his
known opposition to United States policy. He was aware also that
both President Lyndon B. Johnson and Secretary of State Dean Rusk
regarded him as a meddler. On the other hand, neither North Vietnam, the People's Republic of China, nor the National Liberation
Front (Vietcong) would deal with the United Nations or with him as
Secretary-General. His contacts with them had to be in a nonofficial
capacity as a fellow Asian. Furthermore, they were not fully convinced that he was not acting as a tool of the United States. It was

with complete awareness of these handicaps that he set off for talks with Chairman Nikita Khrushchev, President Charles de Gaulle, and President Johnson in the summer of 1964. On his return to United Nation's Headquarters, the Secretary-General told a press conference that he had exchanged views with the three leaders on the situation in Southeast Asia, but that he "did not present any formulae or any proposals." He added: "I just thought aloud, because in my position as Secretary-General of the United Nations, I do not think it would be proper for me to come up with any proposals regarding the solution of the crisis in Southeast Asia."

Actually Thant had suggested during his August 6 talks with Johnson and Rusk that a start might be made by secret discussions between Washington and Hanoi. Believing that Rusk had indicated interest in the idea, Thant passed the proposal on to Ho Chi Minh by way of Moscow. By the end of the month Hanoi had indicated it was agreeable on the understanding that the talks be kept secret. This information was transmitted to Washington by Ambassador Stevenson, but Stevenson was told that nothing could be done until after the November presidential election in the United States. Late in November, Stevenson reported to Thant that the Johnson administration had made inquiries through its own channels and had not received the impression that Hanoi was ready to talk. The Secretary-General, however, was convinced that his information was more accurate than anything available in Washington. On November 29, Soviet Foreign Minister Andrei A. Gromyko arrived in New York for the General Assembly. After talking with him Thant was more certain than ever that Hanoi was indeed willing to meet with a United States representative. It was clear, however, from Washington's reaction that the Johnson administration was not ready for negotiations.

Thant's first effort as Vietnam peacemaker seemed to have reached a dead end, but early in January 1965, Ambassador Stevenson surprised the Secretary-General by suggesting that Thant try to arrange a meeting place for talks between United States and North Vietnamese representatives. It is not necessary to go into detail on the ensuing series of developments here, since they are recounted elsewhere in this volume (pp. 38–41). In brief this is what happened: Thant approached the Burmese government on the Stevenson suggestion and was able to inform the United States representative within a few days that Burma would be happy to have the secret talks in Rangoon;

Stevenson told Thant on January 30 that he had encountered strong opposition in Washington because it was felt that if word of the talks leaked out it would demoralize the Saigon government; on February 6, Hanoi received Thant's message that Washington had rejected a meeting in Rangoon; and on February 7, the United States bombed North Vietnam in retaliation for a Vietcong raid on an American military barracks at Pleiku.

The public had no inkling of these behind-the-scene exchanges that preceded the bombing and was to know nothing of them until many months later. This is convincing evidence that not even President Johnson was aware of the Rangoon arrangements, although he did list in the chronology of Vietnam peace initiatives, produced as an appendix to his memoirs *The Vantage Point,*[1] Thant's report in September 1964 that Hanoi was willing to hold secret talks with a United States representative. Johnson's comment was that the offer had been rejected by the United States, since information from Blair Seaborn, the Canadian representative on the International Control Commission, indicated that Hanoi was not prepared for serious talks. The President added that North Vietnam "later denied that it had suggested any negotiations to U Thant." It should be pointed out that Thant never claimed that Hanoi had suggested negotiations, but had simply given a positive response to his own soundings. It should also be noted that Paul Martin, Canadian Minister for External Affairs, told Thant privately that Seaborn at the time had no access to any member of the Ho Chi Minh cabinet and would not have been in a position to know its thinking. At any rate the presidential press secretary, Bill D. Moyers, said he could find no evidence that the Rangoon matter had come to Johnson's attention. Johnson himself told the Secretary-General in October 1966 that he had never been informed of the Rangoon aspects of the initiative and that the arrangements had been rejected without his knowledge.

Several authoritative accounts of the Rangoon episode have since been published, indicating that Ambassador Stevenson had approached the Secretary-General on the proposed site for the talks without authorization from Washington. Mario Rossi first reported this in an article in the *New York Review of Books* in November 1966.

---

[1] Lyndon B. Johnson, *The Vantage Point* (New York: Holt, Rinehart and Winston, 1971).

It was also reported by Richard J. Walton in his 1968 book on the last years of Stevenson, *The Remnants of Power,*[2] and by David Kraslow and Stuart H. Loory in their book, *The Secret Search for Peace in Vietnam.*[3] Just before his death in July 1965, Stevenson told Eric Sevareid about the Rangoon incident. In an article in the November 30, 1965, issue of *Look* magazine, Sevareid quoted Stevenson as blaming Defense Secretary Robert McNamara for blocking the proposed Rangoon talks. Stevenson was also quoted as saying that Thant was furious over the rejection of his efforts. There is no doubt that the Secretary-General was shaken by this setback. He was firmly convinced that chances for peace talks in the immediate future had been all but eliminated by the United States bombing of North Vietnam and that the war had entered a phase of accelerating escalation. He was determined, however, to continue his efforts even at the risk of further damage to his already poor relations with the United States.

Indeed, Thant never paused. On February 21, during a visit to the White House, he told President Johnson that he had received an indication from unofficial sources that North Vietnam would be willing to begin talks if the United States stopped the bombing. Recalling the conversation in his memoirs, Johnson commented:

Thant's report was interesting but hardly conclusive. We considered it encouraging if in fact Hanoi was ready to talk "immediately" after a bombing halt. We still had no assurances, however, that Hanoi would not take advantage of a complete pause. I asked Rusk to investigate the matter further and to report back anything he discovered. A few days later, on February 26, we received an intelligence report quoting a North Vietnamese contact as saying: "President Ho is waiting, but has insisted that the bombing be stopped first." This was only a straw in the wind, but it suggested that the idea of negotiations was alive in Hanoi.[4]

It was in the midst of these developments that Thant's February 24 press conference took place. He did not mention his Washington conversations, but he stated that during the course of his contacts with the parties directly involved he had presented some "concrete ideas and proposals." In response to a question as to whether the

[2]Richard J. Walton, *The Remnants of Power* (New York: Coward-McCann, 1968).
[3]David Kraslow and Stuart H. Loory, *The Secret Search for Peace in Vietnam* (New York: Random House, 1968).
[4]Johnson, *The Vantage Point*, p. 395.

proposals had been presented to the United States, he replied: "Yes." This created a stir in Washington and brought a denial from George Reedy, Johnson's press secretary, that Thant had presented any proposals to the United States. Top-level Washington officials were even more annoyed by another statement by the Secretary-General at the press conference. This was a suggestion that the American people were being kept in the dark about decisions which were needlessly prolonging the war (pp. 42–50). Although this and other remarks in his February 24 press conference reflected Thant's growing impatience with United States policy, it was here that he expressed the belief "that arrangements could be devised under which a dialogue could take place between the principal parties with a view, among others, to preparing the ground for wider and more formal discussions." He received no positive response, however, from any of the parties involved.

This is where matters stood until spring. Encouraged by President Johnson's Baltimore statement on April 7 that the United States was ready for "unconditional discussions" and by an apparent softening of Hanoi's stand, Thant drafted an appeal for a cease-fire which he proposed to issue if his private soundings indicated the time was ripe for such an appeal. He gave Stevenson a copy of the text, but there was no reply from Washington. Without disclosing details of this rebuff, Thant told a luncheon of the United Nations Correspondents Association on April 15 that he had been thinking for some time about a possible cease-fire appeal but he said, "in the absence of any definite indication from some of the parties directly concerned regarding the compliance with such an appeal, I feel that it is not yet time to launch such an appeal." He added that any cease-fire proposal "eliciting a negative response from some of the parties primarily concerned will not only defeat the purpose of the appeal, but it is likely to compromise the future effectiveness of the one who makes such an appeal." The Secretary-General also disclosed that he had been under pressure from many delegates to visit Peking and Hanoi to discuss peace steps but that he had not actually approached either the People's Republic of China or North Vietnam directly about such a visit. He had requested Algerian President Ahmed Ben Bella, in March, to sound out Peking's views on peace negotiations and had been told that the People's Republic did not want the United Nations involved in any way. In view of Peking's reaction, Thant said, "I do not see any point in discussing the possibility" of a visit to mainland China.

Thant's next major Vietnam initiative did not come until March 1966, when he began pressing for a three-point plan to bring the warring parties to the conference table. He first disclosed the proposal during a visit to Europe at the end of April (pp. 215–23). He felt then as he did during the following months that a cessation of the United States bombing of North Vietnam was an essential first step. So it was natural that this should be point number one in his proposal. The second point was the de-escalation of all military activities, and the third was the inclusion of all the actual combatants in the peace negotiations—meaning the National Liberation Front along with North Vietnam, South Vietnam, and the United States. As he himself put it, the proposal did not meet "with a positive response." He continued to urge this approach, nevertheless, in virtually every press conference and on numerous other occasions. He did submit to the parties in March 1967 a supplementary three-point proposal, but he insisted that his earlier plan still offered the best way to negotiations. His 1967 proposal called for (1) a general standstill truce, (2) preliminary talks, and (3) reconvening of the Geneva Conference. This plan was quickly shelved because, he said, "neither side had fully and unconditionally accepted" it.

These were the major Vietnam peace efforts made by the Secretary-General. There is no way to gauge how much effect they had in finally bringing the combatants to the conference table. Thant was one of many who essayed the role of peacemaker during these tragic years. Although he worked under severe handicaps, he felt that the only way to keep the United Nations from sitting out the war on the sidelines was through his personal activity. One of his major contributions was to help to some degree to limit the loss of prestige suffered by the Organization. His frequent statements and initiatives served to remind the public that the United Nations was interested and concerned even though helpless to deal with the Vietnam war. Although his peace proposals were not accepted, his 1966 three-point plan seems appropriate and sound in retrospect. In fact, the bombing halt proposed as his first point did precede the Paris talks. So did agreement to include the National Liberation Front in the negotiations—his third point. The other point was de-escalation of military activities, which did not precede the Paris talks but which later took place. Many of his public statements ruffled the feelings of the parties concerned, but they also exerted pressure and reminded the public that there were ways other than force through which disputes could be settled. He was convinced from the beginning that the Vietnam war could be ended by diplomatic means alone. Few would dispute today his appraisal made in 1964 in which he said military methods did not solve the Vietnam problem in 1954, "and I do not see any reason why they would succeed ten years later."

III

The outlook for the United Nations was dark as it prepared to observe its twentieth anniversary. In addition to the decline of public confidence over its inability to deal with the Vietnam war, it was in deep financial trouble, and the General Assembly was all but paralyzed by the Article 19 controversy,[5] which might at any moment bring disaster for the Organization. As Thant himself said later in the Introduction to his 1965 Annual Report, no one could deny that serious damage had been done to its "effectiveness and dignity" by the abnormal procedures to which the Assembly was forced to resort.[6] It was only through the personal efforts of the Secretary-General and the President of the Assembly, Alex Quaison-Sackey, that the nineteenth session was able to take any action whatsoever. In order to prevent a showdown vote on Article 19, they had to determine in advance through delicate consultations whether approval of essential housekeeping resolutions could be obtained without a formal vote. Agreement had to be reached separately on each proposal. Any one Member state could have thwarted the "consensus" arrangement by demanding a return to normal procedure. Despite the efforts of Thant and Quaison-Sackey, Albania came dangerously close to forcing a confrontation between the United States and the Soviet Union at the resumed nineteenth session. A showdown was averted only by a quick United States parliamentary maneuver (pp. 26–27). As the following pages will show, the Article 19 threat was lifted by the United States a few months later but the financial difficulties of the Organization continued to be a major problem for

[5]See vol. VI of this series, pp. 681–684, and pp. 26–38 of the present volume.
[6]See vol. VI of this series, p. 135.

the Secretary-General. Despite Thant's urgent appeals for voluntary contributions, it was necessary for him to borrow funds temporarily from special funds in his custody to meet the payroll and other day-to-day expenses. He estimated the Organization's deficit in September 1965 at some $100 million.

During this period Thant also gave serious thought to a number of additional problems of a constitutional nature. One of these was the decision of Indonesia to withdraw from the United Nations. This was the first and only time a Member state had quit the Organization. After consultation with a number of delegates and with his own legal advisers, Thant concluded that there was nothing to prevent the withdrawal of any state which wanted to leave. Although he regretted the withdrawal of Indonesia, he was not greatly disturbed by it. He did not agree with those who believed President Achmed Sukarno's action would start a series of withdrawals in the pattern of the League of Nations. He not only proved to be right, but also saw Indonesia take its seat again on September 19, 1966, eighteen months after leaving.

Thant was more concerned with the broader question of universality of membership in the United Nations, which had long been one of his objectives. In the Introduction to his 1965 Annual Report he said that both the Vietnam situation and the disarmament *impasse* had pointed to "the imperative need" for universality of United Nations membership, but he noted at the same time the existence of "political and other difficulties" in achieving this goal. As an alternative, he renewed his earlier proposal—one made originally by Trygve Lie—that all nonmembers be encouraged to establish observer missions at United Nations Headquarters so they would be "more directly exposed to the views of the rest of mankind." He had in mind especially East Germany, North Korea, North Vietnam, and the People's Republic of China. At the time observers were already being maintained in New York by Monaco, South Korea, South Vietnam, Switzerland, and West Germany, as well as the Vatican. The communist countries, however, were not prepared to accept observer status; so nothing came of Thant's invitation.

Thant was further worried over the revival of the cold war and the possibility that disagreements among the superpowers might "disrupt and stultify" the Organization. He referred to this problem in his speech at the *Pacem in Terris* convocation (pp. 51–55) and also to the effect of big-power differences on the functioning of the Security Council. The Secretary-General, like many others, was disappointed in the performance of the Council—which often was unable to act because of the big-power veto—and was pleased to see the growing influence of the General Assembly. "Account will have to be taken," he said, "of the fact that in the General Assembly are represented, in addition to the big powers, all the other states, the smaller powers, whose understanding, assistance and cooperation are nevertheless essential in regard to decisions involving issues of international peace and security." The functions and relationship of the two principal organs of the Organization were being debated primarily in connection with the question of peace-keeping, but the discussions had focused wide attention on emergence of the small nations as a force to be reckoned with. As this is being written, the debate is still going on and the distribution of functions between the Council and the Assembly remains undefined, with the result that the deadlock over future United Nations peace-keeping procedures continues as tight as ever. Neither the Soviet Union nor France has shown any signs of altering its position that the Security Council must have exclusive responsibility for international peace and security.

The Secretary-General was perturbed by another problem, a possible conflict between the peace-keeping responsibilities of the United Nations and the efforts of regional organizations to deal with disturbances within their own area. Despite his statements during his earlier years as Secretary-General that there was no cause for alarm, Thant was not at all happy about the situation that developed in the spring of 1965 when both the Security Council and the Organization of American States (OAS) were carrying out simultaneous efforts to end civil strife in the Dominican Republic. The major new element in the Dominican conflict was the introduction of an OAS military force. This was a significant step beyond the past regional attempts to deal with the Cuban and Guatemalan problems, a step which many believed to be an encroachment on the responsibilities of the Security Council. Several members of the Council took the position that the establishment of the inter-American force was an enforcement action and was therefore a violation of Article 53 of the United Nations Charter, which states specifically that regional organizations shall not take such action without specific authorization by the Council. Among the Council members who challenged the legality of the OAS military force were the USSR, France, Jordan, and Uruguay. The United States and Bolivia said the inter-American force was created solely to establish an atmosphere of conciliation and could in no way be considered as an enforcement measure. Thant did not enter this debate directly, but he did call for a study of the whole question of regional organizations and their relationship to the United Nations. He saw dangers ahead if regional organizations were recognized as competent to take enforcement measures, noting in one speech (pp. 70–71) that if the OAS could do it, the same principle would apply to other regional organizations such as the Organization of African Unity and the League of Arab States. His main concern was that this would eventually undermine the position of the United Nations as the primary agency for maintaining peace and security.

IV

If Thant was worried by the low estate of the United Nations and by the world outlook in 1965, he was even more pessimistic as his first term neared its end in 1966. He was deeply concerned by the growing tendency of governments to ignore or bypass the Organization and by their use of force in violation of the Charter. His paramount concern was the continued escalation of the Vietnam war and the rebuffs his own peace efforts had encountered, but he saw other signs that the world was drifting away from the objectives of the Organization. One example was the United States military intervention in the Dominican Republic. Another was the fighting between India and Pakistan in the late summer of 1965. His thinking was reflected most clearly, perhaps, in the Introduction to his 1966 Annual Report (pp. 311–40) in which he commented that the "disappointments will seem to have outweighed once more the modest gains" made during the year since his previous report.

It was against this background that Thant pondered the question of whether or not to offer himself for a second term. There was no question but that the decision was his to make. Not only was there no opposition; he was under strong pressure to remain. Yet for him the decision was not easy. He was torn between a strong personal inclination to step down and an equally strong sense of duty to serve. As he himself said, he made up his mind only "after a prolonged inner struggle." But even after he had announced that he would not be

Secretary-General, "fully respect his position and his action in bringing basic issues confronting the Organization and disturbing developments in many parts of the world to their notice. . . ." In his statement Thant noted "with particular appreciation that, for its part, the
Security Council respects his position and his action in bringing to the
notice of the Organization basic issues confronting it, and disturbing
developments in many parts of the world." This formula, worked out
in private negotiations, was considered by Thant as a formal extension of the rights defined in Article 99 of the Charter, which says:
"The Secretary-General may bring to the attention of the Security
Council any matter which in his opinion may threaten the maintenance of international peace and security." In his speech to the
General Assembly, accepting the second term (pp. 304–5), Thant
declared that his decision to stay on stemmed both from a sense of
duty and from his conviction that the United Nations remained the
best instrument by which nations might cooperate for the peace and
development of their people. He also declared that he would seize
every opportunity to press for an end of the Vietnam war and would
continue to regard it as his duty to seek a peaceful solution in every
way possible.

V

There can be little doubt that the most debated decision taken by U
Thant as Secretary-General was his compliance with President Gamal
Abdel Nasser's request for the withdrawal of the United Nations
Emergency Force from the Sinai and the Gaza Strip. Responsible
public figures questioned the decision both at the time and in retrospect, some even suggesting that the 1967 war might have been
averted if he had taken a different approach. Thant was both surprised and angered by the criticism, which he felt was based mainly
on a lack of understanding of the problem. He responded to the
criticism with a vigorous defense of his action. Not only did he go to
great pains in his several reports to the Security Council and the
General Assembly to justify his decision, he took the extraordinary
step of issuing through the Office of Public Information a detailed
defense of his action under the title "Notes on Withdrawal of United

available for a second term, this inner struggle
indicated his willingness to stay on an additiona
November 3, when his term expired, until the end
bowed to the heavy pressure and agreed to accep

What was behind his reluctance to continue? His
nations were somewhat vague. Involved in his cons
were "questions of principle, questions of conscien
personal, official and political" questions. Althoug
edly to elaborate, he did not fully define the question
conscience or the other considerations. He felt that a
so might give the impression that he was trying to im
on the membership. Students of his numerous sta
subject—with some help from his associates—can p
fairly good picture of his reasoning. For one thing, l
that no one should aspire to serve more than one term
"killing nature of the work imposed on him." This un
one of the principles he referred to in his statements,
the overriding issue. His main reasons were his frustra
feeling that his actions were being hampered by Memb
sought to make the Secretary-General "a glorified c
Trygve Lie and Dag Hammarskjöld had fought against
and had succeeded in broadening the office vastly, but Th
encountering difficulties whenever he took political and
initiatives. At the time he was considering the question c
term, his principal critic was the Johnson administration,
being made uncomfortable by his Vietnam peace efforts.
conference on September 19, 1966, Thant said candidly
found it increasingly difficult to function as Secretary-Gen
manner in which I wish to function." Those close to Tha
time say this one sentence was the key to his desire to quit

This is borne out to some extent, at least, by the formula v
to his agreement on December 2, 1966, to accept a secor
Although the exchange of statements between Thant and th
dent of the Security Council, Pedro P. Berro of Uruguay (pp.
was partly a device to enable the Secretary-General to rever
self gracefully, it does contain a concrete acknowledgment of
which Thant and his predecessors had not only claimed but pra
What the Berro statement said specifically was that members
Council, whatever their views may be on observations made t

Nations Emergency Force." This document (pp. 443–53), dated June 3, 1967, stated candidly that it was intended to meet the "widespread . . . and determined misunderstanding on this matter. . . ."

The withdrawal of UNEF and the Secretary-General's explanations are dealt with at length in another part of this volume (pp. 416–89), but the editors believe it would be useful to review here some of the questions raised by Nasser's May 18 request and Thant's response. Did the Secretary-General, for example, act too hastily? Did he act without adequate consultations? What alternatives, if any, did he have? Israel and some Western leaders said he did act in undue haste, that his consultations were too perfunctory, and that he should have left the decision to the Security Council or the General Assembly.

Thant had anticipated criticism from Israel, but he was upset by the adverse comments of some others, including President Johnson and Prime Minister Lester B. Pearson of Canada. Both Johnson and Pearson—the man who in 1956 had proposed the establishment of UNEF—expressed the belief that Thant should not have ordered the withdrawal without first putting the question before the Security Council or the General Assembly. Israeli Foreign Minister Abba Eban called the Thant decision one of the major diplomatic blunders of all time. Influential United States political figures joined in the criticism. The Republican leader of the Senate, Everett Dirksen, said: "We have heard a good deal from U Thant about effective peace-keeping forces. But now he has slipped the troops out like a thief in the night at the request of one man." Senator Jacob K. Javits of New York called the withdrawal order "most deplorable" and "precipitate." "You don't run at the first sign of a breach in the peace," he said. "You shouldn't run for the nearest foxhole at the first boo." One of the most severe indictments came much later from George Lord Brown, who was British Secretary for Foreign Affairs during the Six-Day War. In his memoirs, as published in the London *Sunday Times* of October 25, 1970, Lord Brown called Thant's action "extraordinary." He came close to charging Thant directly with responsibility for starting the war. Here is the key passage from the former British official's comment, as it appeared in the *Sunday Times* (this entire passage was omitted when Lord Brown's memoirs appeared in book form):

To everybody's surprise, and, as I know now, certainly to President Nasser's, the Secretary-General promptly recalled the force. I shall never understand how he was advised to come to this ill-considered and, I feel absolutely sure, totally unnecessary and unexpected decision. Certainly at that moment, if at no other, the need for a very different character at the head of this vital organization, already so weakened by big power conflicts and the growth of the so-called Afro-Asian group, became very apparent. He did not wait for a meeting of the Security Council; he did not give any of us a chance to discuss the matter; he just said that the rules of the game were that the force could stay there only by permission of the host country (in this case Egypt) and that if the host country withdrew permission he was bound under terms of the Security Council resolution, which set up the peace-keeping force, to recall it. [This reference to the Security Council was in error. It was the General Assembly which authorized the establishment of UNEF.] All of this was legalistically true, but wise men, faced with big events whose possible consequences are immeasurable, shouldn't in my view act as though they were working in a solicitor's office conveying property. The withdrawal of the UN force at once increased tension and prompted the Egyptian closure, to Israeli ships, of the Strait of Tiran, leading to the Israeli port of Eilath on the Gulf of Aqaba. That put us firmly under notice that either we, in the United Nations, carried out what we said we would do after the previous war and let Israel see that she could put her trust in the United Nations, or that the Israelis would act for themselves with their pre-emptive strike.

One of the major points at issue in the controversy is whether or not Nasser had wanted or expected the swift acceptance of his request for the immediate withdrawal of UNEF. Lord Brown said in the above comment that he knew for a fact that Nasser had been surprised by Thant's response. President Johnson said in his memoirs two years later that the Egyptian Ambassador to Washington, Dr. Mostafa Kamel, had told United States officials the Nasser government had thought and hoped that Thant would play for time. Some United Nations diplomats attributed such statements also to Amin Hilmy II, a member of the Egyptian Mission to the United Nations. The reasoning behind this theory was that Nasser had made his request because of persistent charges in Syria, Jordan, and other Arab countries that Egypt was hiding behind the "glass curtain" of UNEF while they faced Israeli threats alone. It was said that Nasser had hoped that, after making the gesture of trying to get rid of UNEF, he would be able to bow graciously to some sort of United Nations appeal and withdraw his request. Another version of Nasser's thinking was given by Anthony Nutting, former British Minister of State for Foreign Affairs. In his book *No End of a Lesson,*[7] Nutting says Nasser told him on June 3, 1967, that he had requested the withdrawal of UNEF in order to make effective his deterrent threat against an Israeli attack on Syria but that he had not expected UNEF to pull out of Sharm el Sheikh and the islands guarding the Strait of Tiran. Nasser is said to have told Nutting that he did not want them to leave the strait but that he could not insist that they remain there while pulling out elsewhere to suit his convenience.

It is difficult to evaluate these reports with any degree of accuracy, since doubts are raised by other developments at the time. To begin with, one must wonder how Nasser could have been surprised by Thant's prompt compliance with his request when he had been notified by the Secretary-General on May 16, two days before the formal withdrawal request was delivered, exactly what Thant's intentions were. In an *aide-mémoire* handed to Ambassador Mohammed el-Kony, the Secretary-General made it clear that he would order the withdrawal immediately upon receipt of a request from Nasser, "simultaneously informing the General Assembly of what he was doing and why" (pp. 426–30). As for the Nutting-Nasser conversation about leaving UNEF units at Sharm el Sheikh, Thant also made his position clear in the May 16 *aide-mémoire*. He said a request for a temporary withdrawal from the armistice demarcation line and the International Frontier, "or from any part of them," would be considered by the Secretary-General as tantamount to a request for the complete withdrawal of UNEF from Gaza and the Sinai. Furthermore, Nasser's own actions in advance of Thant's May 18 withdrawal order seemed to have anticipated the Secretary-General's decision. On May 18, some ten hours before Thant's reply was handed to the Egyptian Ambassador, the Foreign Ministry in Cairo was informing the representatives of countries having troop contingents in UNEF that the force had terminated its tasks and must leave forthwith. At the same time Egyptian military units had begun taking over UNEF camps and observation posts, including those manned by Yugoslav troops at Sharm el Sheikh.

Thant himself was convinced that Nasser's request was serious and that appeals or delays would not only have been useless but would

[7] Anthony Nutting, *No End of a Lesson* (New York: Clarkson N. Potter, 1967).

also have endangered UNEF personnel. In his report to the General Assembly on June 26, he tells of his meeting with the Egyptian United Nations representative on May 18, when Nasser's withdrawal request was delivered. The Secretary-General says he expressed deep misgiving "about the likely disastrous consequences of the withdrawal of UNEF" and indicated his intention to appeal urgently to Nasser to reconsider. Later in the day, the report states, Ambassador el-Kony informed Thant that Foreign Minister Mahmoud Riad had telephoned his urgent advice that no appeal should be made to Nasser and that if the Secretary-General should do so his request would be sternly rebuffed. If this was not enough to convince Thant that an appeal would be useless, he had grave doubts as to whether he could prevent the disintegration of UNEF during any kind of diplomatic maneuvers. Both India and Yugoslavia, whose governments maintained close relations with Egypt, had decided that their units would comply immediately with any request from Nasser and withdraw their forces. The combined contingents of the two totaled 1,557 men, or almost one-half of the 3,378 men in UNEF at the time. Nasser himself said in a speech to the Egyptian armed forces on May 22 that Thant had had no choice but to comply with the withdrawal request. In a statement that sounded anything but surprised or unhappy with the Secretary-General's action, Nasser praised Thant for refusing to succumb to political pressures. If he had permitted UNEF to become an instrument of neo-imperialism, Nasser said, "we would have regarded it as a hostile force and forcibly disarmed it."

What alternatives did Thant have? In addition to the course he took, namely, compliance with the request, there were two other obvious courses: rejection of the request or a deliberate delay in the response either by seeking discussions with Nasser or by referring the question to the Security Council or the General Assembly. It was Thant's firm conviction that the buffer functions of UNEF had already been terminated by the infiltration of Egyptian troops even before the withdrawal request came. Without the consent of the Egyptian government and its cooperation, Thant felt, the United Nations Force was in fact dead. He never really considered taking the problem to either the Council or the Assembly because he believed the responsibility belonged to the Secretary-General, since it was Dag Hammarskjöld who had made arrangements with the Egyptian government for UNEF's presence on Egyptian soil. In any event Thant was convinced that any consultation with Council members would produce sharply divided advice, because of the big-power division on the Middle East, and that the Assembly could have done nothing except comply with Nasser's request once his consent for UNEF's presence was withdrawn.

One of the key issues in the controversy, one which comes up repeatedly, is the question of consent of the host country. Thant maintained from the beginning that this was the deciding issue and that there was no way to get around it. Some critics of the Secretary-General, including responsible government officials, have failed to make a distinction between peace-keeping forces, such as UNEF, and enforcement actions. The United Nations had never, up to this writing, sent a military force into any country without the consent of the host country. In the case of UNEF, the General Assembly specifically recognized the principle that it could not station a United Nations force on the territory of a given country without the consent of that country. Only the Security Council has that authority.

Some of the disagreement stems from the varied interpretations given the so-called "good faith" accord and from Hammarskjöld's *aide-mémoire* of August 5, 1957, in which he told of his exchanges with Egyptian officials on the terms for the stationing of UNEF on Egyptian territory. The "good faith" agreement is set forth in a United Nations document in which the Cairo government declared that "when exercising its sovereign rights on any matter concerning the presence and functioning of UNEF, it will be guided, in good faith, by its acceptance of General Assembly resolution 1000 (ES-I) of November 5, 1956." The resolution referred to is the one establishing UNEF "to secure and supervise the cessation of hostilities" in the Suez area. Some of those who criticized Thant contended that Egypt had agreed to continue to accept the presence of UNEF until the task of the Force was completed. The Hammarskjöld memorandum of August 5, 1957, is not an official document and it was never made public by Hammarskjöld.[8] The text was released on June 19, 1967, by Ernest A. Gross, former United States representative at the United Nations. It added fuel to the debate because it said the Egyptian government had accepted Hammarskjöld's view that the reasons for Cairo's consent to UNEF's presence remain valid until its task is

[8] See vol. III of this series, pp. 377–382, and the commentary thereon, pp. 371–372.

completed and that withdrawal of this consent before completion of the task would run counter to the acceptance by Egypt of the decision of the General Assembly. It was Hammarskjöld's understanding also that Egypt had agreed that if a difference should develop as to whether or not the reasons for UNEF's presence were still valid, the matter should be negotiated with the United Nations. Thant took the position that neither the "good faith" agreement nor any understanding reached during this period was relevant, since the task they referred to was the supervision of the cease-fire and not the new mandate given UNEF in the Assembly resolution of February 2, 1957 "to maintain the armistice agreement." Furthermore, the Egyptian government denied it had limited its right to withdraw its consent for UNEF's presence either in the "good faith" undertaking or in any other way. Egypt also insisted it had no knowledge of the agreement reported in Hammarskjöld's August 5 *aide-mémoire*.

In a statement to the press on June 19 Thant minimized the importance of the *aide-mémoire*. "The plain fact," he said, "is that there is little that is new in the memorandum and it makes no revelations which would warrant the special significance being attributed to it in some quarters. In any case, such a paper could not alter the basis for the presence of UNEF on the soil of the United Arab Republic, as set out in the official documents." In this statement and in another made to the General Assembly on the following day, the Secretary-General raised another question which should be noted in considering the issue of "consent." This was the fact that Israel had refused to permit the stationing of UNEF units on the Israeli side of the demarcation line either in 1956 or in 1967, when the Secretary-General explored such a possibility in connection with the Egyptian withdrawal request. The Israeli policy was first laid down by Prime Minister David Ben-Gurion on November 7, 1956, in these words: "Israel will not consent, under any circumstances, that a foreign force—called whatever it may—take up positions whether on Israeli soil or in any area held by Israel."

In his statement in the General Assembly, in reply to criticism from Israeli Foreign Minister Abba Eban (pp. 456–59), Thant said in part:

The Foreign Minister of Israel, I note, made no mention in his critical analysis of my decision of certain decisive facts and factors with which he is certainly very well acquainted. Mr. Eban must know, for example, that the indispensable basis for the effective buffer function exercised by the United

Nations Emergency Force for more than a decade was the voluntary decision of the government of the United Arab Republic to keep its troops away from the line, with only United Nations troops in the buffer zone which was exclusively on the United Arab Republic side of the line.

On the other hand, the Foreign Minister also knows, I am sure, that Israel extended no such cooperation on the United Nations Emergency Force to the United Nations; that, despite the intent of the General Assembly resolution that United Nations troops should be stationed on both sides of the line, Israel always firmly refused to accept them on Israeli territory on the valid grounds of national sovereignty. There was, of course, national sovereignty on the other side of the line as well.

There can be no doubt that it would have been a helpful factor of considerable importance if Israel had at any time accepted the deployment of the United Nations Emergency Force also on its side of the line. I may report in this connection that prior to receiving the United Arab Republic request for withdrawal and prior to giving my reply to it, I had raised with the permanent representative of Israel to the United Nations the possibility of stationing elements of the United Nations Emergency Force on the Israel side of the line. I was told that the idea was completely unacceptable to Israel.

The editors hope that these commentaries and the documents in this volume will help bring into perspective the decision which Thant took on May 18, 1967. There are too many unanswered questions to permit one to say with absolute certainty whether he was right or wrong. Was Nasser really looking for a way to back down? Would an appeal either by Thant or by the General Assembly have led to a reversal of Egypt's request? What would have happened to UNEF personnel if Thant had flatly refused to withdraw them? The answers to these questions will never be known. It can be said, however, that Thant was fully aware of all the alternatives open to him, that he was conscious of the possible grave consequences of his decision, and that he did what he believed to be right and necessary. The one thing that determined his action more than any other was his firm conviction that Egypt and Israel were headed on a collision course and that the usefulness of UNEF had been terminated.

VI

Despite the controversy over the withdrawal of UNEF and his setbacks on Vietnam, Thant began his seventh year as Secretary-General confident that the United Nations would survive the "crisis of confidence" it was facing. He noted in the Introduction to his 1967

Annual Report that the international political situation had continued to deteriorate and that the internal problems of the Organization, including finances and peace-keeping, remained unsolved, but the year ended on a positive note with the unanimous adoption of a Security Council resolution laying down principles for peace in the Middle East. It seemed that perhaps, at long last, stability in the area was in sight. Thant himself was given an important role, through a special representative, in trying to initiate new peace negotiations. He had also succeeded in getting the approval of the Israeli and Egyptian governments—and the Security Council—for the re-establishment of a United Nations presence along the Suez Canal in the form of an observation group. This obviously was not the same as UNEF, but it did help fill the vacuum. Thant could not help but be pleased by these developments. They were not enough, however, to expel his gloom completely. In a year-end message to the United Nations staff, the Secretary-General said: "In the past twelve months I have seen more crises and greater international tension than I can recall at any time during the eleven years that I have spent at and with the United Nations." And he added: "As the festive season approaches, we may look around the world in vain for manifestations of either goodwill or good cheer." He expressed the hope, however, that the United Nations staff would "never falter in their confidence in the United Nations and their faith in its ultimate success."

June 1976   MAX HARRELSON

❧ *1965* ❧

Message to President Sukarno on Indonesia's Withdrawal from the United Nations

NEW YORK   JANUARY 1, 1965

ONE OF THE FIRST PROBLEMS to confront U Thant at the beginning of the new year was Indonesia's threat to withdraw from the United Nations. Actually he learned of the threat on the last day of 1964 when the permanent representative of Indonesia informed him of a statement made earlier in the day by President Achmed Sukarno to the effect that his country would quit the Organization if the Federation of Malaysia was seated as a member of the Security Council. The Secretary-General sent a personal appeal to Sukarno immediately, but the message was little more than a gesture, since it did not touch upon the substance of Indonesia's grievance nor upon the broader implications of the withdrawal on the future of the United Nations. The condition laid down by Sukarno had, in fact, left no room for reconsideration. The seating of Malaysia in the Security Council was a certainty. On December 29, the General Assembly had agreed without objection that, in accordance with a 1963 understanding, Malaysis would complete Czechoslovakia's two-year term ending on December 31, 1965. The former British territory took its seat in the Council on January 7.

Indonesia's First Deputy Prime Minister and Minister for Foreign Affairs, Dr. Roden Subandrio, notified the Secretary-General by letter on January 20 that "Indonesia has decided at this stage and under the present circumstances to withdraw from the United Nations." The letter said Malaysia had been forced into the United Nations on September 17, 1963, by deliberate avoidance of voting although Indonesia and some other "anti-colonial" countries had opposed the action as a "maneuver of neo-colonial powers." It said further that Malaysia's selection as a member of the Security Council was the result of another colonial maneuver. Indonesia had remained silent at the time, the communication said, because it did not wish to obstruct the work of the United Nations at a time when it was faced with a possible breakdown over the Article 19 controversy. Subandrio added that Indonesia's withdrawal, effective January 1, 1965, might serve as a catalyst to reform the Organization and might have a beneficial effect on a speedy solution of the Malaysian problem.

The permanent representative of Malaysia replied in a letter dated January 22, asserting that Malaysia had already been a Member of the United Nations for six years and that in 1963 the General Assembly had simply noted the change of name from the Federation of Malaya to the Federation of Malaysia. He added that the inclusion of Singapore, Sabah (North Borneo), and Sarawak in the state had not changed the international personality of the Federation. This, however, was precisely the issue behind Indonesia's decision to withdraw. U Thant himself had played a role in the 1963 dispute among Indonesia, the Philippines, and Malaya which led to the expansion of the latter and to the ensuing intensification of the controversy. At the request of the three neighbors, he had conducted an opinion survey in which he found that Sabah and Sarawak wanted to join Malaya. The Philippines and Indonesia rejected his findings and refused to recognize the Federation of Malaysia. Singapore, not a major issue in Indonesia's withdrawal, quit the Federation on August 9 and was admitted to the United Nations on September 21, 1965.

Thant did not reply to the Indonesia letter until February 26, after a careful legal study of the situation and extensive consultations with Member states. Although there was no express provision in the Charter for the withdrawal of Members, those who drafted it foresaw such a possibility and stated in a formal declaration that it was not the purpose of the Organization to compel a Member "to continue its cooperation" in the United Nations if that Member, "because of exceptional circumstances," desired to withdraw. Thant concluded that he had no choice but to implement Indonesia's decision. He told Subandrio that the content of his letter had been noted and, while expressing profound regret, he said that arrangements had been made for the Indonesian Mission to "maintain its official status" until March 1, 1965.

Many considered Indonesia's action to be a serious blow to United Nations prestige, especially as the Organization was preparing to observe its twentieth anniversary, but the withdrawal was accepted without any official acknowledgment by either the Security Council or the General Assembly. In the Introduction to his Annual Report, issued on September 20, 1965, Thant noted the concern over Sukarno's decision. "Inevitably," he said, "there were comparisons with the history of the League of Nations, but subsequent events have shown that some of those gloomy prognostications reflected undue pessimism. I sincerely hope that Indonesia's withdrawal from the United Nations is only a temporary phase and that, before long, Indonesia will find that its long-term interests can best be served by resuming its membership and by participating fully in the Organization's constructive activities."

This chapter was closed when Indonesia resumed its place in the United Nations without fanfare on September 19, 1966, after Sukarno was toppled by a military coup.

Excellency, I have just been informed orally that your permanent representative has been instructed to withdraw from the United Nations and that a public announcement to this effect will be made by you. As you may be aware the United Nations has inaugurated International Cooperation Year this very day and we count upon the cooperation of all our Member governments to make it a complete success. I would sincerely hope that your Excellency's government would not think of withdrawing its cooperation from the world Organization. Highest consideration.

SOURCE: UN Press Release SG/SM/212.

THE FINANCIAL SITUATION

JANUARY AND FEBRUARY 1965

As THE GENERAL ASSEMBLY resumed its crucial nineteenth session on January 18, 1965, U Thant's main concern continued to be the threat of a confrontation over Article 19 (see volume VI of this series, pp. 681–84). His plan to have the Assembly approve essential and noncontroversial measures by consensus had averted such a confrontation during the first part of the session, but this segment had been devoted mostly to general debate. He and the President of the General Assembly, Alex Quaison-Sackey of Ghana, had accepted the major responsibility for working out agreements behind the scenes on such questions as the operating budget, admission of new Members, and elections to fill vacancies in the major organs. The Assembly faced a continuous threat, however, that some Member might upset the tenuous arrangement by demanding a vote on one of the questions requiring action.

The Secretary-General addressed the Assembly immediately after it reconvened following the year-end recess. He dealt mainly with the financial situation and the pressing problem of providing funds for the day-to-day operating costs. He appealed to all delegations to cooperate in urgent efforts to end the need for improvisation, but did not refer specifically to the Article 19 controversy. He was followed, however, by Quaison-Sackey who did urge that every effort be made to avoid a confrontation on the issue of Article 19.

Thant himself made a separate statement on this question on February 1 after the conclusion of the general debate. He said *inter alia* that "all Members of the Organization are agreed that, in the best interests of this Organization, a confrontation on the applicability of Article 19 should be avoided at the present session of the General Assembly." In another intervention on February 8, the Secretary-General noted that he and Quaison-Sackey had been engaged in further consultations with various delegations and that the general feeling was favorable to a recess if and when agreement could be reached on machinery for reviewing the whole question of peacekeeping operations. Meanwhile, he proposed action on a number of proposals upon which agreement had been reached. These included interim financial arrangements for 1965, extension of the mandate of the United Nations Relief and Works Agency for Palestine Refugees in the Near East, preliminary approval of plans for a new building for the International School, and confirmation of the appointment of Raúl Prebisch as Secretary-General of the United Nations Conference on Trade and Development. These and other proposals were approved without formal voting. It appeared that the nineteenth session would end without a confrontation on Article 19.

On February 16, however, Halim Budo of Albania rose on a point of order to challenge the legality of the procedure which had been followed during the session. He declared that the Assembly could not permit itself to be blackmailed any longer by United States threats to deprive certain Member states of their voting rights under Article 19. In an attempt to force a showdown, he presented a formal request that the Assembly embark at once upon its normal work under its rules of procedure. He demanded an immediate roll-call vote on his proposal. Despite appeals from a substantial number of delegations, Budo refused to yield. Quaison-Sackey averted a vote by adjourning the meeting for forty-eight hours. On February 18, Budo was back, taking the floor without recognition by the Chair, shouting his demands for a vote even after his microphone was cut off. When Quaison-Sackey ruled that his motion was out of order, Budo challenged the ruling. But the stage was set for a vote on the challenge to the President's ruling rather than on Budo's original motion to return to normal procedures. When Quaison-Sackey recognized United States Ambassador Adlai E. Stevenson on a point of order Budo challenged his right to speak, then heckled him from the floor. Stevenson, however, headed off a confrontation by taking the position that the challenge to the President's ruling was purely a procedural matter and declaring that, in order to prevent the will of the majority from being "frustrated by one Member," the United States would not invoke Article 19. Only Mauritania voted with Albania. The Soviet Union and the United States were among the ninety-seven nations voting to uphold Quaison-Sackey's ruling. The nineteenth session of the Assembly ended on February 18 with no solution in sight for the Article 19 controversy.

---

1. Statement in the General Assembly

NEW YORK   JANUARY 18, 1965

MR. PRESIDENT, in view of various reports and speculations concerning the financial position of the United Nations, I feel it is incumbent upon me to try to set out the factual position. In doing so, I am conscious of the fact that the issues confronting this Assembly cannot be viewed—still less resolved—solely in their monetary context. At the same time, it has to be recognized that political accommodations and compromise formulae, necessary though they are, are not of themselves a substitute for the financial stability of this Organization.

SOURCE: General Assembly Official Records, Nineteenth Session, 1315th plenary meeting.

It is true that the record shows that, despite repeated threats of crisis, the United Nations has somehow managed until now to meet its financial obligations and to survive. In the face of this record, unduly alarmist prophecies are certainly not warranted. But those who profess to believe that the Organization's present financial position and prospects are not so serious must believe me when I say that the problem is serious and merits the urgent attention and concern of its membership. What, then, are the essential facts in the light of which action must urgently be taken? I submit they are as follows:

First, as of today, the Organization's total net cash resources, in respect of the regular budget, the United Nations bond account, and the UNEF and ONUC [United Nations Force in the Congo] special accounts, amount to the equivalent of $14.6 million. Of this amount, $9.3 million represents collections of contributions from Members during the past two weeks. A cash reserve of some $14.5 million, moreover, is little more than the amount required to maintain minimum bank balances throughout the world for the purpose of meeting day-to-day expenditures at the levels currently authorized.

Second, although as of today the accounts show $136 million as the total amount of assessed contributions outstanding, past experience provides no grounds for anticipating payment of more than $6 or $7 million of this amount within the next several weeks. In the meantime, the Organization's current payrolls and other normal expenses on all accounts may be estimated as requiring average monthly cash disbursements of not less than $9 million. Nor do these requirements take account of any growth in 1965 in the Organization's responsibilities, notably in connection with trade and industrial development, responsibilities to which so many delegations have rightfully attached considerable importance.

Third, as of today, the Working Capital Fund, to which recourse would otherwise be had pending receipt of assessed contributions, has been virtually depleted. Of the Fund's paid-up advances of almost $40 million, $39.7 million have been expended to finance past budgetary appropriations. It is imperative, if normal operations and services are not to be seriously disrupted, that the Working Capital Fund be quickly and adequately replenished.

Fourth, as of today, the United Nations owes, mainly to governments for goods and services previously supplied, an estimated total of approximately $45 million. This, of course, is exclusive of indebtedness to governments in respect of the unamortized principal of outstanding United Nations bonds amounting to $154.8 million. The existence of this long-term debt and the consequences, in terms of the United Nations regular budget, of its annual servicing cost, must, I believe, be taken duly into account in the formulation of longer-range proposals for placing the finances of the Organization on a more secure and satisfactory footing.

The more immediate problem, however, is to ensure that in the weeks and months ahead, the United Nations is in a position to keep faith with those who have kept faith with it. No one, surely, can responsibility maintain, in the face of the facts I have presented, that the Organization is now in that position.

It is not my purpose, in making this statement at this time, to seek to persuade any Member state to change, still less to abandon, any position of principle to which it feels itself committed under the provisions of the Charter. It is my firm conviction, nevertheless, as I have said before, that it is not beyond the capacity of reasonable men to reach reasonable accommodations, if there is a will to reach them. By one expedient or another, the Organization has so far managed to meet its obligations and thus to maintain its financial integrity. But experience has shown all too clearly that what I have previously described as a policy of improvisation, of *ad hoc* solutions, of reliance on the generosity of a few rather than the collective responsibility of all—that such a policy cannot much longer endure if the United Nations itself is to endure as a dynamic and effective instrument of international action. That, too, is my firm conviction.

I feel I have done my duty in placing the true facts before the Assembly. I appeal to all delegations, as a matter of urgency, to cooperate in devising ways and means of remedying the situation.

2. *Statement in the General Assembly*

NEW YORK   FEBRUARY 1, 1965

I SHOULD LIKE to recall the statement that I made at the 1286th meeting on December 1, 1964. I mentioned then that there was "an understanding to the effect that issues other than those that can be disposed of without objection will not be raised while the general debate proceeds." Now that the general debate is over, the Assembly has to decide on the procedure to be followed from now on.

During the last several weeks I, like you, Mr. President, have been in consultation with many delegations on this very question. At the 1315th meeting, I made a statement on the serious financial situation which the Organization faces. The financial problem has been so much on my mind that in the course of 1964 I took every available opportunity to bring home the seriousness of this problem in my discussions with various delegations and with Heads of State and Heads of Government, and also in my public statements. I crave your indulgence to reiterate what I said in the course of my address to the African Summit Conference in Cairo on July 17, 1964:[1]

I cannot help referring on this occasion to a problem which has been a matter of serious concern to me ever since I assumed my present responsibilities: I refer to the grave financial position of the United Nations. The Organization finds itself in such straits at the present time mainly because, four years ago, it was called upon to undertake a major peace-keeping operation in the very heart of Africa. After four long years that operation was concluded just a few days ago with the fulfillment of the major objectives laid down by the Security Council and the General Assembly. The serious financial difficulty which has ensued in consequence threatens to impair, not only our ability to undertake future large-scale peace-keeping operations, but our very effectiveness as a world body. This is a problem to which I would like to draw your urgent attention as I believe that all Member states would

SOURCE: General Assembly Official Records, Nineteenth Session, 1326th plenary meeting.

[1]First session of the Assembly of Heads of State and Government of the Organization of African Unity, held at Cairo, July 17–21, 1964.

wish to cooperate in finding ways and means by which the Organization could be enabled to tide over the crisis which looms ahead, and in due course to solve the entire problem on a mutually satisfactory basis.

The Conference, in its final communiqué, endorsed my appeal in the following words:

The Assembly of Heads of State and Government meeting in its First Ordinary Session in Cairo, U.A.R., from July 17 to 21, 1964,

Noting with concern that the United Nations is faced with a serious financial situation arising mainly from its peace-keeping operations, which, if not resolved may affect the very survival of the Organization,

Deeply conscious of its desire to support and strengthen the United Nations to enable it to fulfill its noble objectives among which is to maintain international peace and security,

Recalling the resolution adopted at the Conference of Heads of State and Government in Addis Ababa in May 1963, which, among others, expressed acceptance of all obligations contained in the Charter of the United Nations, including financial obligations,

1. *Earnestly appeals* to Member states of the United Nations to meet their obligations and to render assistance necessary for the Organization to fulfill its role in maintaining international peace and security; . . .

Mr. President, I, like you, have tried my best to obtain agreement on a course of action for the future. I believe that, in spite of our best efforts, we have to recognize that up to now, while there has been some movement, a meeting of minds has not yet been achieved; and there are many specific issues of procedure and timing in regard to which a serious difference of opinion still persists.

While this is true, I have been encouraged by the fact that, to my knowledge, a consensus exists among the entire membership of the Organization regarding certain general principles. First, I believe that all Members are agreed that they should, without prejudice to the position they have hitherto taken on the question of the financing of the peace-keeping operations, put aside their differences in the interests of the Organization, in order to help relieve it of the present situation.

Second, I think that all Members of the Organization are agreed that, in the best interests of this Organization, a confrontation on the applicability of Article 19 should be avoided at the present session of the General Assembly.

Third, it is my impression that Members agree that the financial situation of the Organization should be brought to solvency by voluntary contributions by the entire membership of the Organization—on the understanding that this arrangement shall not be construed as representing any change in the basic position of any individual Member—and should be accepted as a cooperative effort by all Member states aimed at the strengthening of the United Nations, with a view to creating a climate in which the future may be harmoniously planned.

Fourth, there appears to be agreement that contributions should be made as early as possible and that Members, particularly the highly developed countries, should make such substantial contributions as would result in the solution of the financial situation of this Organization.

Finally, there seems to be a consensus that a comprehensive review of the whole question of peace-keeping operations, including the authorization of operations, the composition of forces and their control, and the financing of such operations, should be taken in hand as soon as possible.

In regard to the last question, namely, the comprehensive review of the whole question of peace-keeping operations in all their aspects, I believe it would be necessary, either to set up a new body for this purpose, or to enlarge the mandate of the Working Group of 21,[2] set up under General Assembly resolution 1854 B (XVII) of December 19, 1962. This body could be requested to report to the General Assembly as soon as it has been able to reach a substantial measure of agreement on the points at issue.

I need hardly add that my good offices, and the assistance of the entire Secretariat, will be wholly at the disposal of this body in the discharge of its responsibilities.

In this connection, I should also like to draw the attention of the Assembly to some of the important items which are included in the provisional agenda of the nineteenth session, and in regard to which the Assembly needs to take an early decision in the interest of the proper functioning of this Organization. I have in mind such questions as the election of six members of the Economic and Social Council, the supplementary estimates for 1964 and the budget estimates for 1965, the vacancies on subsidiary bodies of the General

[2]Working Group on the Examination of the Administrative and Budgetary Procedures of the United Nations.

Assembly, the extension of the mandate of the United Nations Relief and Works Agency (UNRWA) at least up to December 31, 1965, and the United Nations International School.

Of course there are also many important questions before the Assembly which I know delegations are anxious to discuss.

I hope that all delegations will give very careful thought to these questions and also to the procedures to be followed.

---

3. Statement in the General Assembly

NEW YORK   FEBRUARY 8, 1965

AT THE 1326th meeting I reviewed briefly the financial position of the Organization and the consensus that existed among the entire membership of the Organization regarding certain principles. I, like you, Mr. President, have since been in consultation with various delegations and I believe that all Members are considering the question of the machinery to be set up for undertaking "the comprehensive review of the whole question of peace-keeping operations in all their aspects" to which I referred at the last meeting. I also suggested that the machinery to be set up could be requested to report "as soon as it has been able to reach a substantial measure of agreement on the points at issue." At the same meeting I also drew attention to some of the important items in regard to which "the Assembly needs to take an early decision in the interests of the proper functioning of this Organization."

I believe, Mr. President, that at the present stage, the general feeling among delegations is favorable to the Assembly recessing once it has agreed upon the machinery for the comprehensive review of the whole question of peace-keeping operations in all their aspects, and after having disposed of the important items to which I referred at the last meeting. The Assembly could, of course, be reconvened as

SOURCE: General Assembly Official Records, Nineteenth Session, 1327th plenary meeting.

soon as the machinery thus set up for the review of peace-keeping operations has been able to report a substantial measure of agreement on the points at issue.

Today I would like to place before the Assembly certain proposals regarding four items in the form of four separate statements, if the Assembly would so agree. These items are:

(1) Interim financial arrangements and authorization for 1965;

(2) Extension of the mandate of the United Nations Relief and Works Agency for Palestine Refugees in the Near East;

(3) United Nations International School;

(4) United Nations Conference on Trade and Development.

I would suggest that in order that delegations may be able to give these proposals the time and attention that they deserve, decisions be taken on these proposals only at the next meeting of the General Assembly and not today. If these suggestions are acceptable to the Assembly, I am ready to proceed with the statements that I have in mind.

I will first deal with the interim financial arrangements and authorizations for 1965.

At its 1314th meeting, on December 30, 1964, the Assembly authorized the Secretary-General, pending decisions to be taken at the resumed session in 1965, to enter into commitments and to make payments at levels not to exceed, subject to statutory requirements, the corresponding commitments and payments for the year 1964 and furthermore, pending such decisions, to continue existing arrangements and authorizations with respect to unforeseen and extraordinary expenses and the Working Capital Fund. It was understood that this authorization was without prejudice to the basic positions and objections of certain countries with respect to certain sections of the budget and to the budget as a whole.

It is my assumption, Mr. President, that, should a further adjournment be decided on, you would wish to continue this authorization of the Secretary-General pending such budgetary decisions as the General Assembly may take when it next meets.

If, however, certain new priority programs, notably in the field of trade and industrial development, are to be effectively carried forward, requirements in the next few months of 1965 will obviously vary somewhat from last year's pattern of estimates. I therefore venture to assume that, within the overall limits of the authorization he has been granted, the Secretary-General is permitted to transfer funds between categories of expense and to enter into such minimum commitments as may be required for the purpose of such programs and supporting services.

I would further request that pending decisions by the General Assembly on the level of appropriations and the scale of assessments for 1965, and subject to such retroactive adjustments as may then be called for, Member states be urged to make advance payments toward the expenses of the Organization in amounts not less that 80 percent of their assessed contributions for the financial year 1964.

There is just one other special problem of a policy as well as budgetary character, concerning which I feel duty bound, as Chief Administrative Officer of the United Nations, to seek this Assembly's understanding and support. I refer to the proposal of the United Nations Joint Staff Pension Board as endorsed by the Executive Heads of participating organizations and by the Advisory Committee on Administrative and Budgetary Questions, that the remuneration of the staff for pension purposes should be on a "full-gross" basis. While I had seriously considered the possibility of deferring action on this proposal, I must take into account the fact that any such postponement would affect the reasonable and just expectations not only of United Nations staff members but also those of all the sister organizations in the United Nations common system. The pension fund itself, for which I have a custodial responsibility, would also stand to lose a potential benefit of some significance. I hope, therefore, that under the same terms of authorization given to the Secretary-General, the Assembly can approve the draft resolution contained in annex IV, parts I and II of the Board's report [A/5808], relating to pensionable remuneration of the staff and its application to future and current benefits. My request is subject, however, to a change in the effective date from January 1 to March 1, 1965, with a consequent reduction of $100,000 in the additional budgetary credits that will be required. The draft resolution in question, in parts III and IV, contains other proposals which, since they are of a less urgent nature, could be deferred for consideration by the General Assembly at a later date.

In the light of the consultations that have taken place during this past week I have been led to conclude that, under prevailing circumstances, the interim financial arrangements and authorizations I have ventured to put forward, represent the only generally acceptable basis on which the Organization can function in the coming weeks and months. I would be less than frank, however, if I did not admit to some misgivings as to the ability of the Secretariat, under strict limitations thus imposed, to respond to the requests of principal and subsidiary organs as fully and as readily as in the past. May I therefore say again what I have said on previous occasions—that the limited resources thus made available to me must be matched by a measure of forbearance and restraint on the part of the principal and subsidiary organs; for it is quite certain that not all the plans for 1965 by way of new and expanded programs, conference services and facilities, etc. will be possible of fulfillment. But we shall continue, as always, to try and do our best.

I will now deal with the question of the continuation of the United Nations Relief and Works Agency for Palestine Refugees in the Near East (UNRWA).

In its resolution 1856 (XVII) of December 20, 1962, the General Assembly extended the mandate of the United Nations Relief and Works Agency until June 30, 1965. Accordingly, the General Assembly at this session, in its consideration of the annual report of the Commissioner-General of UNRWA, would normally have decided whether to extend the mandate of UNRWA and, if so, for how long.

In the statement I made at the 1326th meeting held on February 1, 1965, I referred to the need for "the extension of the mandate of the United Nations Relief and Works Agency (UNRWA) at least up to December 31, 1965" [para. 12]. Since then I have been in touch with the delegations principally concerned, and I believe it is generally agreed that the General Assembly extend the mandate of UNRWA for a further year up to June 30, 1966. This would be without prejudice to existing resolutions on the subject or to the positions of any of the interested parties, and would afford time for a substantive discussion of the matter at the twentieth session if this is then the wish of the Members.

On the above understanding, I would propose that the Assembly agree to the extension of the mandate of UNRWA up to June 30, 1966.

Now I want to deal with the item concerning the United Nations International School. I wish to call attention to three points from my report to the General Assembly on the subject of the United Nations

International School, contained in document A/5834 dated December 9, 1964.

First of all, I would like to draw the attention of the General Assembly to the generous offer of the Ford Foundation to build and equip the school, up to a total cost of $7.5 million, provided the question of the site can be satisfactorily settled and an endowment or development fund can be established adequate to ensure the School's independence.

Second, I would like to invite special attention to my proposal that the School should be built at the north end of the Headquarters site. Schematic plans for the building and a model indicating its position on the United Nations site, as prepared by the architects, Harrison and Abramowitz, will be available for the information of the General Assembly on Tuesday or Wednesday morning. These plans will offer reassurance to those who may have been concerned about encroachment of the School on the gardens or interference with United Nations activities. I am convinced that this solution is the best available in the circumstances, in addition to the consideration that it will provide important facilities for United Nations delegations and Secretariat staff.

If the General Assembly should agree in principle with this proposal it is my intention to submit in precise form to the Advisory Committee on Administrative and Budgetary Questions, the legal and administrative arrangements to be entered into between the United Nations and the School.

Third, I would like to draw attention to my proposal that a significant part of the Development Fund, which I believe should be set at the level of $3 million, should come from governments; to ensure the international character of the School and to give further tangible evidence of the responsibility of governments for the education of children of their nationals serving the United Nations abroad, I propose new and vigorous action by governments to make voluntary gifts and pledges as early as possible in the current year, so that Ford Foundation funds for the construction of the School may be released and work begun in late spring 1965.

These proposals require that the following actions should be agreed to by the General Assembly:

(1) That the General Assembly approves in principle the use of the north end of the Headquarters site for the construction of the United

Nations International School, subject to a review of the legal arrangements by the Advisory Committee on Administrative and Budgetary Questions.

(2) That the General Assembly, noting the establishment of a $3 million Development Fund for the United Nations International School, calls on governments to take prompt action to fulfill the intent of General Assembly resolution 1982 (XVIII).

(3) On the basis of the actions taken on points 1 and 2, that the General Assembly notes that the Secretary-General intends to accept, under Financial Regulation 7.2, the generous offer of the Ford Foundation to make a grant up to $7.5 million to build and equip the School.

Lastly, I want to deal with the United Nations Conference on Trade and Development (UNCTAD). I should like to say a few words regarding the establishment of the United Nations Conference on Trade and Development.

In adopting, on December 30 last, resolution 1995 (XIX), the General Assembly established the United Nations Conference on Trade and Development as an organ of the Assembly, and laid down the provisions for its future operations. In pursuance of this decision, the Trade Conference is now in existence. As the General Assembly has been informed, the first session of the Trade and Development Board will take place early in April 1965.

I propose to appoint Dr. Raúl Prebisch as Secretary-General of UNCTAD. I hope that at its next meeting the General Assembly will confirm this appointment.

The General Assembly has also been informed that it is proposed to convene the Conference of Plenipotentiaries for the adoption of the draft Convention on Transit Trade of Land-locked Countries, pursuant to recommendation A.VI.1 of the Trade Conference[1] in August 1965. It is my hope that at its next meeting the General Assembly will concur with this proposal.

---

[1]*Proceedings of the United Nations Conference on Trade and Development,* vol. 1, *Final Act and Report* (United Nations publication, Sales No.: 64.11.B.11), annexes.

THE SITUATION IN VIETNAM

FEBRUARY 1965

U THANT had made a number of public statements on the Vietnam conflict during 1964, but not until February of 1965 did he acknowledge that he had been involved in private efforts to bring about a negotiated peace. He told a news conference on February 24 that he had "presented concrete ideas and proposals" to some of the principal parties directly involved in the Vietnam conflict. In response to a question, he confirmed that the United States was one of the parties to whom his proposals had been presented. The White House spokesman, George Reedy, promptly denied that Thant had offered any proposals to the United States government, but this apparently was a question of semantics. In his memoirs former President Lyndon B. Johnson says that the United Nations Secretary-General came to the White House on February 21 (three days before the news conference) and reported he had received an indication from unofficial sources that the North Vietnamese would be willing to begin peace talks if the United States halted the bombing of North Vietnam.[1] He quoted Thant as saying that the talks could begin immediately if the United States government notified Hanoi officially that there would be a bombing halt. President Johnson commented that "Thant's report was interesting but hardly conclusive." A few days earlier, on February 12, Thant had issued a statement expressing the belief "that arrangements could be devised under which a dialogue could take place between the principal parties with a view, among others, to preparing the ground for wider and more formal discussions."

It was in his February 24 news conference that Thant suggested the existence of an information gap in the United States on the possibilities for a negotiated peace. "I am sure," he said, "the great American people, if only they know the true facts and background to the developments in South Vietnam, will agree with me that further bloodshed is unnecessary. And also that the political and diplomatic method of discussions and negotiations alone can create conditions which will enable the United States to withdraw gracefully from that part of the world. As you know, in times of war and of hostilities the first casualty is truth." The full implications of his statement were not known until much later when details of his unsuccessful initiatives in the last half of 1964 finally started to leak out.

These efforts began with a visit to Washington on August 6, 1964, two days after the United States retaliatory raids for the Gulf of Tonkin incidents. At a luncheon attended by Dean Rusk, Averell Harriman, William Bundy, Adlai

---

[1]Johnson, *The Vantage Point*, p. 395.

Stevenson, Charles W. Yost, and Ralph Bunche, Thant told Rusk he had been formulating an idea for bringing together representatives of the United States and North Vietnam for private talks. After his return to New York, the Secretary-General decided to make an approach to Hanoi through the Soviet Union. The word came back in late September that Hanoi was interested. President Johnson noted in his memoirs that Thant reported through Stevenson at that time his belief that North Vietnam was willing to talk to an American emissary. Johnson said the offer was rejected by the United States, since Blair Seaborn, the United States' Canadian contact, said Hanoi was not prepared for serious talks. Johnson noted further that Hanoi later denied it had suggested any negotiations to Thant. Stevenson finally advised Thant to shelve the idea until after the November presidential election.

Early in January 1965, Stevenson suggested privately to Thant that he arrange a meeting place, and Thant narrowed the choice to four countries: Cambodia, France, Pakistan, and Burma. On January 16, Thant went to the Burmese Ambassador, James Barrington, and asked him to approach the Burmese government on the question. Two days later the Ne Win government replied that it would be happy to host a private meeting if both sides agreed to the talks. Thant told Stevenson that a site had been arranged but, on January 30, Stevenson advised the Secretary-General that Washington would not send a representative to Rangoon because it felt that if news of such a meeting leaked out it would demoralize the Saigon government. Hanoi received word of the United States rejection on February 6. That was partly what Thant had in mind when he made his statement on February 24 about the United States information gap.

Two years later, on June 19, 1967, Rusk told a group of American educators (on a background basis but later put on the record by Senator J. William Fulbright of Arkansas): "You've heard about the end of '64 beginning of '65 business when peace was about to break out in Rangoon. The only contact there was a Russian member of the Secretariat. During that period, I had several long talks with Mr. Gromyko. So it is not surprising that I would consider Mr. Gromyko more relevant than anything that came from a relatively junior member of the Secretariat. In any event Hanoi denied there was ever any such contact and other denials came into the picture."[2]

This version reflected the United States feeling at that time that Thant was a meddler and that he was not to be trusted. The fact is that Thant had conferred with Gromyko in New York on November 29, 1964, and the Soviet foreign minister had verified the report that Hanoi was interested in establishing a contact with the United States. Despite the rebuffs from the Johnson administration, Thant continued his efforts to bring the parties together.

He remained convinced over the years that the only hope for a Vietnam settlement lay in negotiations. He said repeatedly that it would not be practical to seek a solution in the Security Council because of the fact that

[2]The Secretariat member involved was Vladimir Suslov, Under-Secretary-General for Political and Security Affairs.

some of the principal parties to the conflict—the People's Republic of China, North Vietnam, and South Vietnam—were not Members of the Organization.

---

1. Statement to the Press

NEW YORK   FEBRUARY 12, 1965

I AM GREATLY disturbed by recent events in Southeast Asia, and particularly by the seriously deteriorating situation in Vietnam. My fear, frankly, is in regard to the dangerous possibilities of escalation, because such a situation, if it should once get out of control, would obviously pose the gravest threat to the peace of the world.

I have stated my views on this problem many times before. Only last year, when I was interviewed in Paris in July, I said that "military methods have failed to find a solution of the Southeast Asian problem for the last ten years and I do not believe the same methods will bring about a peaceful settlement of the problem. I have always maintained that only political and diplomatic methods of negotiation and discussion may find a peaceful solution. I have suggested some time ago that a return to the conference table might produce some results. That means, in effect, that a revival of the Geneva Conference may perhaps achieve some results. I am convinced of this because of the very critical situation in that area."

I am conscious of course of my responsibilities under Article 99 of the Charter. I am also aware that there are many difficulties in the way of attempting a United Nations solution to the problem, in view of its past history and the fact that some of the principal parties are not represented in the United Nations. Many world leaders who, I know, share this concern and anxiety have made other suggestions. At the present time it is not possible for me to say what would be the best means of discussing this serious situation in an atmosphere conducive to a positive solution; but I do feel very strongly that

SOURCE: *UN Monthly Chronicle,* vol. II, March 1965, p. 21.

means must be found, and found urgently, within or outside the United Nations, of shifting the quest for a solution away from the field of battle to the conference table. In this connection, I believe that arrangements could be devised under which a dialogue could take place between the principal parties with a view, among others, to preparing the ground for wider and more formal discussions.

Meanwhile I would like to appeal most earnestly to all the parties concerned for the utmost restraint in both deeds and words, and I would urge them to refrain from any new acts which may lead to an escalation of the present conflict and to the aggravation of a situation which is already very serious.

I make this appeal most earnestly in the interest of the peace and well-being of the people of Vietnam and of the world at large.

---

2. From Transcript of Press Conference

NEW YORK　　　　　FEBRUARY 24, 1965

THE SECRETARY-GENERAL: Mr. President, Ladies and Gentlemen: I just wanted to say a few words by way of introduction.

As you all know, I am always happy to have an opportunity of meeting with you—this time, after a lapse of almost four months, since we have established a long tradition of not having press conferences during the General Assembly session.

Of course, as I said last Saturday at the Convocation of *Pacem in Terris,* there are some features of the nineteenth session of the General Assembly which are both depressing and heartening—depressing for the damage done to the effectiveness and dignity of the United Nations, and heartening for the loyal and unceasing efforts of the Member nations to preserve the Organization by finding a solution.

I do not want to elaborate on this. I share the general disappointment about the developments at the nineteenth session of the General

SOURCE: UN Note to Correspondents No. 3075.

Assembly. But, as I see the situation in the last two months or so, there was no sensible alternative course to adopt without bringing up a direct confrontation, with unfortunate consequences in its wake.

. . . QUESTION: After the failure of the General Assembly, what are the alternatives? What do you expect, concretely? What do you foresee? Do you have any specific action in mind?

THE SECRETARY-GENERAL: In my view, the most positive action taken by the nineteenth session of the General Assembly has been the projected constitution by the President of the Assembly of a Special Committee which has been requested to look into all aspects of peace-keeping operations—past, present, and future. I believe that this is the most significant and positive action taken by the nineteenth session of the General Assembly.

As regards the functions of the projected Special Committee, as I see it they have to be divided into two parts: questions relating to the past and the present, and questions relating to the future. In my view, it will be relatively easier for the Committee to devote its attention to the past and present aspects of peace-keeping operations, including, of course, the financial aspects. I feel that it will be much more difficult to arrive at a satisfactory formula for future peace-keeping operations. I am not a pessimist, but I doubt whether the Special Committee will be able to find an agreed formula regarding the future aspects of peace-keeping operations in the contemplated time. I am hopeful, however, that the Special Committee will arrive at a satisfactory formula regarding the past and present aspects in the contemplated period.

QUESTION: Along what lines do you envisage a possible solution of the Vietnam situation? Have you any positive proposals in mind?

THE SECRETARY-GENERAL: As you know, I have been consistently advocating the necessity and the advisability of resort to political and diplomatic methods of finding a solution. I have felt all along that military methods will not produce the desired result, they will not produce an enduring peace in Vietnam.

In my view, there was a very good possibility in 1963 of arriving at a satisfactory political solution. In 1964, the situation deteriorated still further, and the prospects for a peaceful solution became more remote. Today, of course, the situation is much more difficult.

Although opinions may differ on the methods of bringing about a satisfactory solution in Vietnam, there is, I believe, general agreement on one point: that the situation in the Republic of Vietnam has gone from bad to worse. I do not think that there is any difference of opinion on that.

I have always maintained the view that the prospects for a peaceful settlement of this problem will be more and more remote as time goes on and as the aggravation develops. But still I do not believe it is too late to try diplomatic and political methods of negotiation and discussion. Of course I have never advocated the immediate withdrawal of United States troops from the Republic of Vietnam. I am fully conscious of the fact that such a step will naturally involve questions of face and prestige, and questions of the abrogation of previous commitments, and so forth. But I feel that once the diplomatic and political methods have been tried and if there is any perceptible improvement in the situation, if an agreed formula is at hand, if some sort of stability can be restored in the country, then at that time, of course, the United States can withdraw its troops with dignity.

As I said on a previous occasion, one prerequisite for peace in any country is the existence and functioning of a stable government. As you all know, this element is completely absent in the Republic of Vietnam.

. . . QUESTION: You speak of the best way of attaining an enduring peace in Vietnam. In view of the fact that the last negotiated agreements failed to maintain a secure and enduring peace in Vietnam and in view of the fact that the agreements reached at that time were broken, what would your comment be in answer to this argument, which I think is the main one put up against negotiations, that it did not work in the past and therefore it will not work in the future? They were abrogated.

THE SECRETARY-GENERAL: I doubt the correctness of your hypothesis. Let me elaborate a little on this theme.

When I was in Burma, prior to my departure for New York about eight years ago, I studied the situation in Southeast Asia very closely. To my knowledge, there was not a single instance—let me repeat— there was not a single instance of North Vietnamese providing military assistance or arms to the Vietcong in South Vietnam in 1954 and 1955. So far, no evidence has been adduced to prove that the authorities in North Vietnam provided matériel and military assistance to the Vietcong in the Republic of Vietnam in 1954 and 1955. After the developments in the next few months and the next few years, I am sure that there must have been involvement by the North Vietnamese in the affairs of the Republic of Vietnam.

While on the subject, at the risk of its being deemed a digression, let me say this: as you all know, I was very much involved in the affairs of my country, Burma, for many years, since independence in January 1948 until I left Rangoon in 1957. Immediately after Burma's independence in January 1948, the Burmese communists went underground and started a widespread insurrection. This fact is known to everybody. The Burmese government dealt with this internal problem by its own means, without asking for any outside military assistance or outside military arms or outside military advisers—or whatever you call them. The Burmese government dealt with this internal insurrection by its own means. As you know, the Burmese Communist Party is still underground after seventeen years and still illegal. But let me tell you: there has not been a single instance of outside help to the Burmese communists inside Burma in the last seventeen years; there has not been a single instance of one rifle or one bullet supplied to the Burmese communists inside Burma in the last seventeen years. And Burma has maintained and still maintains the friendliest relations with all its neighbours: with Thailand, with Laos, with mainland China, with India, and with Pakistan. As you know, Burma has over 1,000 miles of land frontier with mainland China. If only the Burmese government had decided at some stage to seek outside military assistance to suppress the internal insurrections and revolts, then I am sure that Burma would have experienced one of the two alternatives: either the country would be divided into two parts or the whole country would have become communist long ago. This proves one point: that Burma's attitude and policies in regard to both domestic affairs and foreign affairs have been very appropriate in the circumstances prevailing in Southeast Asia.

Not one American life has been lost in Burma. Not one American dollar has been spent in Burma in the form of military assistance in the last seventeen years. We should ask the great question: Why? I just present these facts to you just to set about thinking: Why?

QUESTION: Have you any indication from the United States government that it might under certain conditions consider a negotiation of the Vietnamese dispute? Also have you any indication that the United States might withhold further reprisals against North Vietnam in order to see whether such negotiations could get under way?

89433

CALDWELL COLLEGE LIBRARY
CALDWELL, NEW JERSEY

THE SECRETARY-GENERAL: I have been conducting private discussions on this question of Vietnam for a long time, as you all know. Of course, it will not be very helpful at this stage to reveal even some parts or some features of the negotiations I have conducted. I just want to say that I have the greatest respect for the great American leader, President Johnson, whose wisdom, moderation, and sensitivity to world public opinion are well known. I am sure the great American people, if only they know the true facts and the background to the developments in South Vietnam, will agree with me that further bloodshed is unnecessary. And also that the political and diplomatic method of discussions and negotiations alone can create conditions which will enable the United States to withdraw gracefully from that part of the world. As you know, in times of war and of hostilities the first casualty is truth.

QUESTION: You said that the first prerequisite is for a stable government. Perhaps you have some ideas and suggestions for the creation or the composition of an inclusive and popular régime in Saigon which might be stable.

THE SECRETARY-GENERAL: Of course, I have certain ideas on this aspect of the problem. I have communicated these ideas to some of the parties primarily concerned in the last two years. As I said a moment ago, I do not think it will be helpful if I reveal some of these ideas publicly at this moment.

QUESTION: Will you permit me to interrupt for a moment this debate on Vietnam? I feel that my question is linked to what you said at the beginning of the press conference. Last Saturday in your address to the *Pacem in Terris* convocation you said that you should say in all frankness that in the circumstances—you meant the different interpretations of the Charter—the United Nations Charter provisions—and you meant the provisions about peace-keeping—are somewhat out of date. "It is this anachronism in the Charter"—you said—"that is partly responsible for the present constitutional and political crisis in the United Nations."

Mr. Secretary-General, this remark is certainly accepted by everybody. But what means are you suggesting? How do you think that this "anachronism" can be overcome? You know better than we that a revision of the Charter is a very difficult undertaking. What have you in mind? I think this problem is important because it is linked directly to the efforts which will be undertaken by the new Committee.

THE SECRETARY-GENERAL: This is primarily, as you have rightly said, Mr. Beer,[1] the concern of the projected Special Committee to be formed by the President of the General Assembly. The General Assembly has authorized the Committee to look into all aspects of peace-keeping. The Special Committee may, if it wishes, even recommend certain necessary amendments of the Charter, as I understand it. As you all know, the present crisis is due to two factors. One is whether the expenses for the peace-keeping operations should be regarded as part of the normal expenses of this Organization. That is the first aspect. The second aspect is whether the Security Council or the General Assembly should be considered as competent, not only in launching peace-keeping operations, but also in allocating financial responsibility on the membership. This is the second aspect.

The first aspect of this question was referred to the International Court of Justice, as you all know. The International Court of Justice, by a vote of 9 to 5, forwarded an Advisory Opinion to the General Assembly, and the General Assembly in turn accepted that recommendation.

But the second aspect of the problem, whether the Security Council or the General Assembly should be considered as competent to allocate financial responsibility on the membership regarding the expenses for the peace-keeping operations, has never been thrashed out in full in any organ, nor has it been referred to the International Court of Justice for an Advisory Opinion. Therefore, in my view, out of these two basic questions, only one has been referred to the International Court of Justice. Consequently, the International Court of Justice has been asked for an Advisory Opinion on only half the problem. I feel that it would be very desirable for the Special Committee to be constituted by the President of the General Assembly to look into this question again. And there may be a clue to the solution, I believe, in Article 24 of the Charter which says that the Security Council shall have "primary responsibility for the maintenance of international peace and security."

As I see it, the word "primary" is important. Does "primary" mean exclusive? Perhaps this might be a clue.

QUESTION: Mr. Secretary-General, going back to Vietnam, you seem to be suggesting that it would be very desirable if the United

---

[1]Max Beer, correspondent for *Neue Zürcher Zeitung*.

States troops got out of South Vietnam, if South Vietnam had a stable government and if there were negotiations to possibly neutralize the whole area. There seems to be something concrete missing in this series. How are you going to achieve that? Can you pin this thing down for us a little more?

THE SECRETARY-GENERAL: As I have been saying, I have presented certain ideas on my own to some of the principal parties directly involved in the question of Vietnam. I have even presented concrete ideas and proposals. But up to this moment the results of these consultations and discussions have not been conclusive. And I do not think it would be in the public interest for me to reveal these ideas publicly at this moment.

QUESTION: Have they been presented to the United States among the other interested parties?

THE SECRETARY-GENERAL: Yes.

QUESTION: May I come back to the question of Vietnam again? If no progress is made toward negotiations, might you feel compelled unilaterally to step into the breach and bring the matter to the Security Council?

THE SECRETARY-GENERAL: I do not think that is a practical proposition, for reasons that are obvious and well known to you. The government of North Vietnam has all along maintained that the United Nations is not competent to deal with the question of Vietnam since, in its view, there is already in existence an international machinery established in 1954 in Geneva. They have all along maintained that position and, as you all know, it is a position that is also maintained by the People's Republic of China. As far as the United Nations is concerned, I think the greatest impediment to the discussion of the question of Vietnam in one of the principal organs of the United Nations is the fact that more than two parties directly concerned in the question are not Members of this Organization. I therefore do not see any immediate prospect of a useful discussion in the Security Council.

QUESTION: Coming back to the question of the competence of the organs of the United Nations in peace-keeping, on which you have just answered a question, I want to draw your attention to a third factor in this whole dispute, which is the Secretary-General, and I want to refer to what General de Gaulle said at his recent press conference. I quote from the official translation:

The then Secretary-General—who was Mr. Hammarskjöld—was led to set himself up as a superior and excessive authority. Continuing these abuses, the Organization involved itself directly in the internal affairs of the Congo. . . . This intervention has ceased, thanks to the wisdom of the present Secretary-General.

Do you agree with this judgment on your predecessor, and do you hold the view expressed by General de Gaulle on the office of the Secretary-General? And what role does this play in the question of the competence of the organs of the United Nations in peace-keeping operations?

THE SECRETARY-GENERAL: I do not think I am competent to make observations on those remarks of President Charles de Gaulle. As you all know, opinion has been divided for a long time regarding the activities of the United Nations: one school maintains that the United Nations has been doing too much, the other school maintains that the United Nations has been doing too little. In the face of those two opposing attitudes and interpretations, I think it is only advisable for the Secretary-General to withhold any comment on these attitudes.

QUESTION: Do you still hold to your previous view that the 1954 Geneva Conference on Indochina should be reconvened in terms of the Vietnam question, and do you think that such a conference should try to find means to carry out the provision in the armistice agreement regarding Vietnam whereby elections would be held in both North Vietnam and South Vietnam for the establishment of a united Vietnam?

THE SECRETARY-GENERAL: As I have been saying, it may be rather belated to expect the same results as one could have expected, say, two years ago. But I think that it is worth trying.

On the twelfth of this month I advocated publicly that, if there are still difficulties on the part of some of the large powers as regards the immediate convening of a Geneva-type conference, it could be worthwhile exploring the possibilities of informal, private, and confidential dialogues between some of the parties directly involved, as a preliminary step toward the convening of a more formal conference. That was my appeal. Of course, I have no way of knowing what will happen if these dialogues take place or if a formal conference takes place. I do not know what will be the result of such discussions; I do not think that anyone knows. But it is worth trying. And let me repeat what I said a moment ago: the longer we delay, the more difficult will be the achievement of an enduring peace in Vietnam.

QUESTION: Could I come back to the question of the elections in North Vietnam and South Vietnam, leading to the unification of the two Vietnams? Do you advocate that?

THE SECRETARY-GENERAL: I do not want to go into the substance of the agreements arrived at in Geneva in 1954. I do not know the practical difficulties in the way of conducting free elections, both in North Vietnam and in South Vietnam. I do believe, however, that elections were possible at some stage.

QUESTION: Have you had any positive or favorable responses from any of the parties, and particularly from Peking and Hanoi, to the proposal you just mentioned—that is, the proposal for preliminary contacts?

THE SECRETARY-GENERAL: I do not think that it would be in the public interest to reveal any information at this stage on that aspect of my discussions. . . .

From Address to Pacem in Terris Convocation

NEW YORK   FEBRUARY 20, 1965

ALTHOUGH the United Nations had left the Congo problem behind in 1964, U Thant's statements during the early months of 1965 reflected increasing gloom as the Vietnam conflict, the United Nations financial crisis, ideological and economic divisions and other problems, new and old, plunged the Organization into what he called "the dark valley of discord and enmity." In his address before the *Pacem in Terris* convocation, he cited the emergence of the superpowers, the new political alignments, and the vastly increasing number of small states as some of the factors responsible for "the present constitutional and political crisis" facing the Organization. The divisions had to be discussed with reason and determination, he said, for if they were allowed to persist they would "unleash, as they already show signs of doing, darker forces of bigotry, fear, resentment, and racial hatred than the world has ever seen." He did not mention his deep concern over the escalation of the Vietnam war, but this was very much in his mind during this time.

. . . WE HAVE ACCEPTED the idea of the United Nations as a representative instrument for promoting and maintaining international order. This is an important step away from the old and narrowly nationalistic attitudes. We are, however, still a long way from showing that confidence in each other and in the great instrument itself, which alone can make it work for us and give practical reality to the ideals to which all nations have subscribed in the Charter. The fact is that, though our desire for peace is undeniable, our approach to peace is often old-fashioned and more attuned to former times than to our present state. Even the United Nations Charter itself provides a good example of this. Chapter VII, for instance, on action with respect to threats to the peace, breaches of the peace and acts of aggression, plainly stems from the experience of the aggressions of the Axis powers in the thirties, a kind of situation which is unlikely to recur in our world of superpowers armed with hydrogen bombs amid a vastly increased number of smaller independent states. To be candid, some

SOURCE: *UN Monthly Chronicle,* vol. II, March 1965, pp. 41–46.

provisions of the Charter, like Chapter VII, were framed with an eye on the potential re-emergence of the Axis powers as a threat to international peace and security. Memories of the war and the ruthlessness of its perpetrators were still very fresh in the minds of the founding fathers of the United Nations when they met in San Francisco. This state of mind explains the concept behind big-power unanimity in taking preventive or enforcement measures against aggression, potential and real. This mood was responsible for the formation of the Military Staff Committee and for the ideas behind its composition and functions.

However, the course of history took a new turn. Alignments changed; old enemies became new friends; old comrades-in-arms found themselves in opposite camps, and the United Nations could not function in the way it was intended to function. The provisions of the Charter relating to action with respect to threats to peace and acts of aggression were subjected to various interpretations. I must say in all frankness that in these circumstances the Charter provisions are somewhat out of date. It is this anachronism in the Charter—the kind of anachronism which is inevitable in our rapidly changing world— that is partly responsible for the present constitutional and political crisis in the United Nations.

We have to work toward a world order in which aggressive nationalism or expansionism is banished as a means of promoting or protecting national interests, where fanaticism is no longer necessary to support a different point of view, and where diversity can be preserved without resort to prejudice and hatred. We have seen how the great religions of the world, after lamentable periods of bigotry and violence, have become accommodated to each other, without losing their influence or spiritual independence, by a mutual respect for, and understanding of, the spiritual and moral aims which are common to them all. We must try, both earnestly and urgently, to extend that process of accommodation to the political, ideological, economic, and racial alignments of the world. All of our high aims, our vaunted technology, our skill, and our real desire to cooperate and to help one another will be of no avail if this adaptation to new circumstances, this general accommodation, this real change of heart, does not come about.

The realignment of political power in the world is a process whose changing outlines frame the political enigma of our times. The forces likely to be released by this process, benign and otherwise, can, however, be foreseen and cannot be ignored. They can, and must, be channeled and directed by a positive effort of all nations working together in the United Nations, if we are to grasp our destiny and mold our future rather than be swept away into a new and appalling age of strife and hatred. It is not enough to be active only when a dire international emergency breaks about our heads. We need to make a constant effort, year in and year out, to strengthen by practice the theory of a peaceful and cooperative world.

Beneath the present political realignments, the world *is* in fact divided in a number of ways. It is divided economically; it is divided racially; and it is divided ideologically, although this latter division may prove to be less basic than the first two. These divisions must be faced and discussed with reason and determination. We ignore them at our peril, for if they are allowed to persist and grow larger they will unleash, as they already show signs of doing, darker forces of big-otry, fear, resentment, and racial hatred than the world has ever seen. We cannot agree to live in such a nightmare, still less to bequeath it to our children.

Though its current problems are great and its present authority uncertain, the United Nations does provide a forum in which these divisions can be discussed and gradually reduced within the frame-work of the common interest in peace and justice, and with the safeguards that only an organization representative of all peoples, all interests, and all motivations can provide. The United Nations has also, on numerous occasions, furnished a machinery through which countries can cooperate to deal with threatening situations and to keep the peace.

As the respect for it grows, the Organization should also serve as a center for the harmonizing of national policies within the wider interest. We must eventually arrive, in the affairs of the world, at a state of political maturity in which it will be considered statesman-like, rather than weak, for even a great country to alter its course of action or to change its national policy in the common interest or in deference to the will of the majority. I hasten to add that we are certainly nowhere near such an idyllic situation today.

These, to my mind, are the compelling reasons why the United Nations must be preserved and strengthened and why the disagree-ments of the greatest powers, however justified they may be, must not be allowed to disrupt and stultify the Organization. We have seen, in the crisis over arrears in payments to the United Nations budget, an episode that is both depressing and heartening—depressing for the damage done to the effectiveness and dignity of the United Nations, heartening for the loyal and unceasing efforts of the Member nations to preserve their Organization by finding a solution. There is no doubt that the relationship between, and the role of, the Security Council and the General Assembly are issues of great importance. These issues will surely continue to occupy the minds of most of us, since they are basic to the great debate now going on. As I have said earlier, the writers of the Charter envisioned complete agreement among the five permanent members of the Security Council, who would be collectively responsible for keeping the peace by supplying arms and men, in certain contemplated situations. These situations, however, did not come about. History took a new turn; the Security Council could not act in the manner it was intended to act, and the General Assembly assumed, or had to assume, certain functions not originally contemplated in the Charter.

We are now witnessing the beginning of the great debate: whether the big powers in unison, through the agency of the Security Council, should take exclusive responsibility for maintaining international peace and security while the General Assembly functions as a glorified debating society in political matters, or whether an attempt should be made to secure a fair, equitable, and clearly defined distribution of functions of the two principal organs, in the light of the changing circumstances, and, particularly, bearing in mind the increase in the membership of the Organization, from fifty in 1945 to one hundred fourteen in 1965. Account will have to be taken of the fact that in the General Assembly are represented, in addition to the big powers, all the other states, the smaller powers, whose understanding, assistance and cooperation are nevertheless essential in regard to decisions involving issues of international peace and security. These issues are serious, and the manner in which they are resolved will affect profoundly the organic growth of the Organization in the years to come. They can only be resolved by a will to compromise and accommodate, in the overriding interest of maintaining peace. The smaller powers are playing, and must play, an essential role as the spokesmen of moderation and common interest in this process and, if a solution is found, much credit will be due to their steadfastness and determination.

Governments, however well and sincerely they may cooperate in the United Nations, cannot by themselves face the great and shifting problems of our age in isolation. The peoples they represent must also give life and reality to the aims and ideals of the Charter, toward which we strive. Here again, we now have the means to achieve a great objective, an enlightened world public opinion. One of the revolutions of our age, the revolution in communications of all kinds, has made a well-informed world public opinion technically possible for the first time in history. Our problem is to ensure a beneficial use of these means of communication. This is a challenge to leaders both temporal and spiritual, to intelligent and creative men and women everywhere. Without real knowledge and understanding and without a determination to learn from the past, to rid ourselves of outmoded prejudices and attitudes, and to face the future together with both hope and wisdom, we shall not succeed in making our aims and ideals a working reality. The encyclical *Pacem in Terris* gives us an inspiring lead toward that change of heart which our great aims so urgently require.

THE SITUATION IN CYPRUS

IN HIS FOURTH REPORT to the Security Council on the United Nations operation in Cyprus, U Thant said the continued tense situation on the island made it impossible either to withdraw the United Nations Force in Cyprus (UNFICYP) or to make any substantial reduction in its strength. The Force, with a total strength of slightly over 6,000 men, had been in Cyprus for twelve months at the time of the Secretary-General's report. He said that, while the last few months had been relatively peaceful, "this should not blind anyone to the equally significant fact that both sides in Cyprus are now better prepared to fight, from a military point of view, than before, and consequently the results of any renewal of fighting are likely to be more severe than heretofore."

There was also trouble over the mandates both of the United Nations Force and the United Nations mediator, Galo Plaza Lasso. Thant pointed out that the Force could not extend its authority but could only do its best to halt violence between the Greek and Turkish communities. The question of Galo Plaza's mandate was raised by Turkey after publication of his report on March 26 on his activities since September 28, 1964. Turkey protested that he had exceeded his mandate by expressing his personal views in analyzing the positions of the parties. For this reason, the Turkish government said, the functions of the mediator had come to an end. In a letter to the permanent representative of Turkey on April 1, Thant declared that it was for the Security Council to interpret its own resolutions, but he added that he himself had found nothing in the mediator's report which he considered going beyond the Council's resolution of March 4, 1964. He stated that he did not consider any action was called for affecting the status of the mediator. He also appealed to the Turkish government not to insist "on the extreme position that the services of the mediator have come to an end."

1. From Report to the Security Council

NEW YORK   MARCH 11, 1965

. . .

271. When I recommended in my last report to the Security Council the extension of UNFICYP for a further period of three months, until March 26, 1965, I had some hope that this might be the last such recommendation that I would find it necessary to make. UNFICYP has now been established for about a year, and, despite the effort of all concerned and the very creditable results achieved thus far, I now see no alternative but to recommend another extension of the Force for a further three months, that is, until June 26, 1965. This, if approved, will be the fourth extension of the Force.

272. In making this recommendation, I am aware that it will become increasingly difficult to maintain UNFICYP because of the special burden on those providing contingents and also because of the growing difficulty of financing UNFICYP by voluntary contributions, particularly since these contributions have, so far, come only from a small number of states, a number of whom have contributed for each period. I wish to express my appreciation to the governments of the contributing states, without whose generosity the Force could not have been maintained.

273. Consideration is being given to the possibility at some stage of reducing the size of UNFICYP, but the Commander naturally sees great difficulties in any substantial reduction in strength, owing not only to the continuing heavy commitments which the Force has to meet with its present strength, but also to recent indications of increasing tension and frustration in the island. Although UNFICYP has had remarkable success since August 1964 in keeping the peace in Cyprus, there can be little doubt, as I pointed out in my last report, that the law of diminishing returns will almost inevitably apply in time

SOURCE: Security Council Official Records, Twentieth Year, Supplement for January, February, and March 1963, document S/6228.

to its effectiveness in keeping the peace. One indication of this probable trend which deserves brief mention is the attitude of some sections of the local Press, which has, on several occasions in the past three months, engaged in tendentious and fanciful campaigns against UNFICYP. Such campaigns, though short-lived and unsubstantiated, cannot fail to have an adverse effect on the attitude of the population and the armed forces toward UNFICYP and have led, in some cases, to incidents and misunderstandings.

274. Another indication of the present situation of the United Nations Force in Cyprus is the renewed vigor with which, in recent weeks, a number of questions have been raised about its mandate. These questions, which have been advanced before, arise from the inevitable fact that UNFICYP by its very nature cannot wholly satisfy the aspirations and aims of either community in Cyprus. On the one hand, it cannot act as an instrument of the government in helping it to extend its authority by force over the Turkish Cypriot community in the areas now under its control. On the other hand, it cannot assume responsibility for restoring the constitutional position which existed prior to the outbreak of hostilities in 1963 and early 1964, nor to contribute to the consolidation of the present stalemate in the island. Both of these courses would basically affect a final settlement of the country's problems, a matter which is the province of the Mediator and not of UNFICYP. The Force's action is limited to doing its best to halt violence, to promote a reduction in tension, and to restore normal conditions of life, thus creating an atmosphere more favorable to the efforts to achieve a long-term settlement.

275. The fact that the anticipated debate on Cyprus in the General Assembly during its nineteenth session did not take place has undoubtedly been one factor which has added to prevailing feelings of frustration and uncertainty in Cyprus. While the last months have been relatively peaceful, this should not blind anyone to the equally significant fact that both sides in Cyprus are now better prepared to fight, from a military point of view, than before, and consequently the results of any renewal of fighting are likely to be more severe than heretofore.

276. In recommending the extension of UNFICYP for a further three months, I once again appeal to the parties concerned to make the most sincere and determined effort, by negotiations, both among themselves directly and through the mediator, to find an agreed basis

for long-term solutions of their intercommunal problems. Only this can afford real assurance against a renewal of violence in Cyprus with all of its disastrous consequences. . . .

---

2. Letter to the Representative of Turkey

NEW YORK   APRIL 1, 1965

I HAVE THE HONOR to refer to your letter of March 31, 1965, by which you conveyed to me the observations of the government of Turkey on the report of the United Nations Mediator on Cyprus which was circulated as a Security Council document [S/6253]. I have, of course, shown this letter to the Mediator and have invited him to submit to me his comments upon it, particularly with regard to matters of fact.

It is not my purpose here to discuss the various points made in your letter. However, I note that your government states that during the conversations which were held with the mediator in Ankara on February 23–25, he "had agreed to refrain from inserting in his report any recommendations or suggestions as to substance and to confine himself to the procedure of mediation by observing that there no longer seemed to be any prospect in mediation by individual contacts and that from now on joint and multilateral negotiations with the mediator might be advisable." Since this is a question of fact concerning discussions which took place between your government and the mediator under the authority and responsibilities conferred upon him by the Security Council's resolution 186 (1964), you will appreciate that I am in no position to comment upon it from personal knowledge. The mediator, however, at my request, has given to me his own understanding of the purport of the conversations in question. He informs me that what is referred to as an agreement about the content of his report would more accurately be described as a statement of the Turkish government's own views on what the report should contain,

SOURCE: Security Council Official Records, Twentieth Year, Supplement for April, May, and June 1965, document S/6267.

and that while he felt able to agree that his report would not present formal recommendations for a solution, he could not and would not agree that he should confine himself solely to what the Turkish government refers to as the "procedure of mediation," in the limiting sense of not dealing with matters of substance. He states that, in fact, he made it clear that his report would include a detailed analysis of the positions of the various parties, from which would inevitably flow certain ideas which might lead the way to an agreed solution, and that he prepared his report accordingly.

I also note that it is the view of the Turkish government that the mediator's report "contains sections which go beyond his terms of reference as specified in the resolution of March 4, 1964"; that "it is obvious that those sections cannot be taken into consideration, cannot be entertained as a mediation effort and cannot therefore constitute in any manner a basis for future efforts"; and that "this creates a situation whereby it must be deemed that Mr. Galo Plaza's functions as a mediator have come to an end upon the publication of his present report."

It is, of course, for the members of the Security Council themselves to make authoritative interpretations of the provisions of resolutions of the Council. But I feel bound to say here that I have found nothing in the mediator's report which I could consider as going beyond, or being in any other respect incompatible with, the functions of the mediator as defined in paragraph 7 of the resolution of March 4, 1964, which consist of "promoting a peaceful solution and an agreed settlement of the problem confronting Cyprus."

While I note with regret the view of your government that the functions of the mediator "have come to an end upon the publication of his present report," I would like to inform you that I do not consider that any action by me at this juncture affecting the status of the mediator is called for.

Indeed, I seize this opportunity to appeal most earnestly to your government not to insist on the extreme position that the services of the mediator have come to an end. I take this liberty only because I fear that this might well mean the end, for all practical purposes, of the mediation effort itself, thus greatly diminishing hopes for a peaceful solution of the Cyprus problem. This appeal, of course, does not apply in any way to the attitude of the government of Turkey toward the substance of the mediator's report.

From Remarks at Luncheon of
United Nations Correspondents Association

NEW YORK   APRIL 15, 1965

IN AN EXCHANGE with United Nations correspondents on April 15, U Thant welcomed President Johnson's statement of April 7 endorsing "unconditional discussions" on the Vietnam conflict as a heartening development, but he indicated that his own personal initiatives had been far from encouraging. He disclosed that he had decided against either making an appeal for a cease-fire or undertaking a peace mission to Hanoi and Peking, despite pressure from some Member states. His rejection of a cease-fire appeal was based on his conviction that it would get a negative response under existing circumstances and that this would compromise his own effectiveness in the future. He said he had never indicated any intention to visit either Peking or Hanoi, but had requested Algerian President Ben Bella in March to sound out the views of the People's Republic of China on Vietnam peace steps. The word came back that Peking had ruled out any United Nations role. "In the face of Peking's reaction to my soundings in Algeria," Thant said, "I do not see any point in discussing the possibility of my visit to Peking." The Secretary-General received an additional setback when Peking criticized him by name for endorsing President Johnson's April 7 statement. Although he was clearly frustrated, he told the correspondents, "I shall continue my efforts to find a peaceful solution of the Vietnamese problem, as I have been doing all along. I feel that my usefulness has not ended." He then added a sentence which many correspondents interpreted as a threat to step down as Secretary-General: "If ever I believe that my usefulness has ended, I shall not hesitate to request the Security Council to recommend to the General Assembly a new man to take my place." In response to a barrage of questions, the Office of Public Information issued a statement making it clear that the Secretary-General was not referring to Vietnam when he spoke of his usefulness, but "to the performance of his over-all functions as Secretary-General."

. . .

THE SECRETARY-GENERAL: . . . Although the threat to the peace of the world is no less grave today, I may say that I find some recent developments to be heartening. As you know, I have welcomed and

SOURCE: UN Note to Correspondents No. 3104.

endorsed the appeal of April 1, of the seventeen heads of state or government of nonaligned countries for the start of negotiations on the Vietnam situation without any pre-conditions. I consider this to be a sound approach because I believe that the only way to get discussions started which would lead to serious negotiation would be without any conditions.

I would very much hope that this appeal will be responded to soon by all of the parties directly concerned. I also trust that the seventeen nations will continue their efforts to achieve a peaceful solution of the problem of Vietnam. I feel that the door to discussion and negotiation has at least been partially opened by President Johnson's statement of April 7 endorsing "unconditional discussions," and by the indication reported in the Press that Premier Pham Van Dong of North Vietnam would be willing to undertake discussions, although under certain stated conditions. I strongly hope that there will be a prompt follow-up on the stated willingness of the parties directly involved to enter into discussions and that no effort will be spared to get discussions started with a minimum of delay. The world, which is gravely threatened by this conflict, is certainly due this much.

Now, Mr. President, I shall be glad to answer questions that may be posed.[1]

QUESTION: Mr. Secretary-General, in the Cyprus and other international conflicts since the United Nations was founded the effort has been first to get a cease-fire. Why do you not appeal for a cease-fire in Vietnam?

QUESTION: Mr. Secretary-General, after the statement of the President of the United States on a solution of the Vietnam conflict, you expressed your deep satisfaction. I think that it would be of utmost interest to all of us, and to the world, to have your reaction to the recent statement of the North Vietnamese government.

QUESTION: Do you intend to make any contact, direct or indirect, with the Peking and Hanoi authorities with a view to obtaining clarification of their recent statements on the possibility of negotiations on Vietnam? In your opinion, would any new initiative by the group of seventeen nonaligned countries in approaching Hanoi and Peking be useful at this present period of the crisis?

---

[1]Questions on this occasion were submitted in writing and were grouped by the Chairman according to subject matter.

THE SECRETARY-GENERAL: Regarding the need for a proposal from somewhere for a cease-fire or a temporary cessation of military activities, I think the important point to take into account is the prospective reaction to such an appeal from the parties directly concerned.

I have been thinking along these lines for some time, as some of you are no doubt aware. But in the absence of any definite indication from some of the parties directly concerned regarding the compliance with such an appeal, I feel that it is not time yet to launch such an appeal. In my view, such an appeal for a cease-fire eliciting a negative response from some of the parties primarily concerned will not only defeat the purpose of the appeal, but it is likely to compromise the future effectiveness of the one who makes such an appeal. I believe that timing is a most important factor in the consideration of such a step.

Regarding the two further questions, I believe I have dealt with them, though briefly, in my introductory remarks. I welcome President Johnson's speech of April 7, for certain features of the President's speech, in my view, are positive, outward-looking, and generous, as I stated through a United Nations spokesman on the next morning. I feel that President Johnson has opened the door for further steps to be taken. I also feel that Premier Pham Van Dong's statement of April 13 also opened the door to some extent for future steps to be taken.

As I see the situation and attitudes, there appears to be a general consensus, at least between Hanoi and Washington, on the need to return to the essentials of the 1954 Geneva Agreements. You will no doubt recall that President Johnson, in one of his recent speeches—if I remember correctly, on March 25—stated the willingness of his government to return to the essentials of the 1954 Agreements. And Premier Pham Van Dong, in his statement of the day before yesterday, also reiterated his government's long-standing position that the North Vietnamese government would be in favor of returning to the essentials of the 1954 Geneva Agreements. I think this is the clue to the settlement of the Vietnamese problem.

While on this subject, I want to make one further observation. In dealing with the problem of Vietnam, I think the most important consideration should be to be clear about our objectives. What should be our objectives regarding an enduring solution of the Vietnamese problem? As I see the situation, there are two or three possible end results of the Vietnamese situation, but the most desirable and, I think, the most sensible objective for all of us to have is to return to the essentials of the 1954 Geneva Agreements, which President Johnson last stated in his speech of March 25, and which the Prime Minister of North Vietnam reiterated the day before yesterday.

QUESTION: Would you go to Peking and Hanoi to explore the chances of a peaceful settlement in Vietnam? Have you asked to go?

QUESTION: Have you contemplated a trip to Hanoi and/or Peking, and, if so, could you give us your present thoughts on such a trip?

QUESTION: Do you have plans, either concrete or in the planning stage, to visit Asia, including countries involved in the Vietnam situation?

THE SECRETARY-GENERAL: I have no plans to visit either Peking or Hanoi. But in the last couple of months, many well-meaning friends have advised me—privately of course—that it might be helpful if I could think of visiting Peking and Hanoi in order to explore the possibilities of achieving a peaceful solution of the Vietnamese problem. I have never discussed this possibility with anyone. I have never indicated my intention to visit either Peking or Hanoi to anyone, but many well-meaning friends, including of course delegates, maintained that it could be useful if I could explore the viewpoints of Peking and Hanoi on certain next steps to be taken toward the achievement of the objectives in Vietnam.

Of course, as you all know, I requested President Ben Bella of Algeria, early in March, through Ambassador Tewfik Bouattoura, to sound out the views of Peking regarding the next steps Peking feels should be taken toward the achievement of a peaceful solution of the Vietnamese problem. As you all no doubt know, Ambassador Bouattoura went over to Algiers and President Ben Bella of Algeria had long and useful meetings with Premier Chou En-lai of the People's Republic of China. And Premier Chou En-lai's views—at least some of the important points transmitted to me through Ambassador Bouattoura—have been covered by the Press, both local and international, and I do not think I should elaborate on these views.

As I have stated all along, the attitude of Peking toward the United Nations is well known. The People's Republic of China is not here. The United Nations has not been involved in the Geneva Conferences of 1954, nor in the Geneva Conference of 1962 regarding Laos, and

Peking felt and still feels that the United Nations should not and cannot be involved in the problem of Vietnam. In the view of Peking, there is already in existence an international machinery to deal with that matter. We may or may not agree with that, but that is the viewpoint of Peking. I am fully aware of this viewpoint. But now, in the face of Peking's reaction to my soundings in Algeria, I do not see any point in discussing the possibility of my visit to Peking. And of course I have no plans to visit Asia in the near future too.

QUESTION: Do you now have any initiative under way in connection with the war in Vietnam?

QUESTION: Have you had any information about the willingness of North Vietnam and China to participate in negotiations to end the war in Vietnam?

QUESTION: Could we ask for your evaluation of the "new stage" of the Vietnam crisis? And can we take this last development as a "new stage" at all? And second, could you evaluate specifically the last Hanoi proposal of four points?

QUESTION: In view of the recent reaction of Hanoi in stating its position in regard to possible negotiations, do you see a particular role that you might be able to play to encourage further development leading toward formal negotiations on Vietnam and possibly on the whole Indochina peninsula?

THE SECRETARY-GENERAL: I think that I dealt with most of those questions in my previous remarks. But I do want to say this: I shall continue my efforts to find a peaceful solution of the Vietnamese problem, as I have been doing all along. I feel that my usefulness has not ended. If ever I believe that my usefulness has ended, I shall not hesitate to request the Security Council to recommend to the General Assembly a new man to take my place.[1]

QUESTION: Do you consider that the publication of your reactions to President Johnson's statement on Vietnam immediately after it was made was the cause of the Chinese and North Vietnamese position against your visit to those countries? I ask that question because for the first time Peking criticized you by name.

QUESTION: You were accused in an authoritative Asian newspaper the other day of setting out to serve United States imperialism in its

[1]Immediately after the press conference, the following oral statement was made by a United Nations spokesman: "The Secretary-General's reference to his usefulness pertained to the performance of his over-all functions as Secretary-General."

designs for negotiations for peace. What is your comment on that accusation?

THE SECRETARY-GENERAL: I think that it is worth reminding ourselves that one of the primary functions of the Secretary-General—who is really the number one servant of this Organization—is to see that the United Nations serves as a center to harmonize the actions of states, with a view to the achievement of common ends. That is clearly provided for in the Charter. I therefore feel very strongly that one of my primary functions is to harmonize the viewpoints of 114 Member states. Of course, that is a very difficult task. I have never deluded myself into thinking that all my statements and all my actions will be endorsed by all the 114 Members. It is far from my belief that all 114 Members will endorse every word I say or every action I take. However, as I have said before, so long as I am performing the functions of Secretary-General it shall be my constant endeavor to harmonize the thinking and action of all Member states toward the achievement of the common ends, as explicitly laid down in the United Nations Charter.

QUESTION: You said in your Introduction to the Annual Report that "countries not at present represented in New York should be enabled to maintain contact with the world body. . . ." In the light of North Vietnam's indispensability with regard to aid for Southeast Asia, would you now wish to comment?

THE SECRETARY-GENERAL: I do not see any early prospect of getting the North Vietnamese government involved in United Nations activities one way or the other. What I suggested in my Introduction to the Annual Report was to focus world attention on the need for exposure and contact with regard to those outside the sphere of the United Nations. My attitude toward all such problems is this: If we have more opportunities for exposure, contact, and communication, that will be a very desirable first step toward the more important second step of involving all nations of the world in United Nations activities.

As you are no doubt aware, I believe in the universality of the United Nations, which is, of course, implied in the Charter. Before that principle of universality can be applied, I believe in the concept of greater contact and greater communication with all states, the concept of greater exposure, whether in the United Nations or outside the United Nations.

QUESTION: Can the United Nations go ahead with plans for

expanded economic development in the Mekong Basin while the Vietnam war is in its present "hot" phase? If so, to what extent?

THE SECRETARY-GENERAL: With regard to President Johnson's stated intention to enlarge the economic development of the Southeast Asian region, I had preliminary consultations with Mr. Eugene Black. Those consultations were very useful. Mr. Black and I agree that there are so many factors involved—some of them very delicate—that we should hasten slowly.

Of course, there is already in existence international machinery in the area—the Mekong Coordination Committee, which was set up by ECAFE [Economic Commission for Asia and the Far East] and has been in operation for the past eight years, with meager means at its disposal.

I think that one of the practical steps to be taken—provided, of course, that the countries concerned agree to the project—is to involve the Mekong Coordination Committee, which is already in existence, to expand its activities in the economic and social fields.

Of course, there are also projected programs in the area, such as the Asian Development Bank, which is coming into being very soon. Perhaps President Johnson's ideas can be usefully utilized within the framework of the projected Asian Development Bank also.

Those steps will take time. I believe—and Mr. Black agrees with me—that we have to be very careful in formulating our plans and arrangements to give effect to the ideas presented by President Johnson on April 7.

QUESTION: In 1949, President Truman's inaugural speech, with its implied support of United Nations technical assistance, electrified the Secretariat at Lake Success. What kind of reaction has there been in this house to President Johnson's proposal to substitute economic development for war in Southeast Asia?

THE SECRETARY-GENERAL: To my knowledge, President Johnson's reference to the need for an expanded program of economic assistance in that area has been widely welcomed. I believe that, if the conditions are conducive to the implementation of those ideas, it will mean a very great deal to the people of the area. As you know, most of the countries in the area are very much underdeveloped, and the development of the economic and social conditions of the peoples in that particular area will be a boon to them; indirectly, of course, it will contribute to the creation of peaceful conditions also.

QUESTION: Do you think that the proposal by Cambodia, endorsed by the Soviet Union, for a Cambodian conference could be of use, particularly in order to have behind-the-scenes talks on Vietnam?

QUESTION: Would you consider a Cambodian neutrality conference an acceptable vehicle for starting exploratory talks on Vietnam? Do you think that the major parties in Vietnam might agree?

QUESTION: Did you discuss with Mr. Harold Wilson the question of reconvening the Geneva Conference on Cambodia? Are you in favor of such a conference, and do you believe it could lead to negotiations on Vietnam?

THE SECRETARY-GENERAL: The government of Cambodia proposed—I believe in early March—the convening of the International Conference on the Neutrality of Cambodia. That proposal was endorsed by Peking and France; the other day the government of the Soviet Union endorsed it. I have been informed that this will be among the items to be discussed today by President Johnson and Prime Minister Wilson in Washington. Of course, I have no means of knowing what Washington and London will decide on this. However, I believe that if the international conference takes place it will serve as a useful forum for the discussion of other matters not directly related to the question of Cambodia.

. . .

THE CIVIL STRIFE IN THE DOMINICAN REPUBLIC

THE UNITED STATES government announced on April 28, 1965, that United States troops had been ordered to land in the Dominican Republic to protect American lives as the result of political turmoil following the overthrow of the three-man junta headed by Donald Reid Cabral. Since April 25 there had been heavy fighting in Santo Domingo between two factions, one consisting of supporters of former President Juan Bosch, headed by Colonel Francisco Caamano Deno, and the other, calling itself the National Reconstruction Government, led by General Antonio Imbert Barreras. U Thant was in Geneva when the Soviet Union, on May 1, requested an urgent meeting of the Security Council to consider what it described as the armed intervention of the United States in the internal affairs of the Dominican Republic. He cut short his Geneva visit and rushed back to attend the Council meetings.

From the standpoint of the United Nations and the Secretary-General, the Dominican problem was significant primarily because it raised once more, as it had previously in cases involving Cuba and Guatemala, the question of regional organizations—in this instance the Organization of American States (OAS)—and the United Nations. The situation was especially delicate because for the first time both the United Nations and a regional organization had peace missions operating in the same country simultaneously. Two days before the Security Council took up the question, the OAS decided to send a five-nation commission to the Dominican Republic to help restore peace. After a series of meetings, the Council unanimously adopted on May 14 a resolution calling for a strict cease-fire and asking the Secretary-General to send a special representative to the Dominican Republic to report on the situation. On May 15, Thant informed the Council that he had appointed Jośe Antonio Mayobre, Executive Secretary of the Economic Commission for Latin America, as his representative, and that an advance party, headed by Major-General Indar Jit Rikhye, had already arrived in Santo Domingo. Mayobre reached the Dominican capital on May 18. His first task, under the direction of the Security Council, was to seek an immediate suspension of hostilities so that the International Red Cross might carry on the humanitarian work of searching for the dead and wounded.

The arrival of Mayobre and the expansion of his original mandate brought a complaint from the Special Committee of the OAS that the United Nations was obstructing its peace efforts and a request that the Security Council suspend all United Nations action until every regional procedure had been exhausted. The Special Committee also asked that it be relieved of further responsibility. The OAS decided to accept the resignation of the Committee and to reassign the peace mission to its Secretary-General, Jośe A.

Mora, who was asked to coordinate his efforts with those of the United Nations representative. The situation was further complicated by the presence of a newly created Inter-American Peace Force, an *ad hoc* military body whose purpose was to guarantee the security of the public and to create an atmosphere of conciliation. Although there were no open clashes between the United Nations and OAS missions, the issue was the subject of an extended debate in the Security Council, where the Soviet Union challenged the right of the OAS or any regional organization to take enforcement action.

On May 21 Thant informed the Security Council that his representative had reported an agreement between the two Dominican factions to suspend hostilities for twenty-four hours. He reported later the same day that the temporary cease-fire was fully effective. Although General Imbert refused to extend the truce, it did in fact end the fighting except for sporadic outbursts. The Security Council, however, continued to deal with the problem at a series of meetings in June and July. The Soviet Union and Cuba pressed for the withdrawal of the 1,700-man Inter-American Peace Force as well as the 12,400 United States troops in the Dominican Republic. France, Jordan, and Uruguay also questioned the legality of the military intervention by the OAS, while the United States maintained that the OAS action could in no way be regarded as an enforcement measure since its aim was simply to restore normal conditions and establish an atmosphere of conciliation. The Council faced a companion issue as to whether or not Mayobre's staff should be enlarged to enable him to supervise the cease-fire and investigate complaints of violation of human rights. The Secretary-General took issue with the view that Mayobre's mandate was broad enough to permit such inquiries. His mandate, Thant said, was limited to observing and reporting. In the end, however, the Council remained divided and no decisions were taken clarifying the relationship between the United Nations and regional organizations.

In the Introduction to his Annual Report (pp. 151–52), Thant noted that "some special and unfamiliar problems" had been raised by the parallel peace efforts of the OAS and the United Nations. This, he said, "led inevitably to difficulties in relationship." Thant added that the developments in the Dominican Republic "should stimulate some thought by all of us concerning the character of the regional organizations and the nature of their functions and obligations in relation to the responsibilities of the United Nations."

The Secretary-General dealt with this question more specifically in a speech before the Annual Conference of Non-Governmental Organizations in New York on May 27 (p. 77), sounding a warning of future dangers if regional organizations should expand their functions to include enforcement action. "If the Organization of American States is recognized as competent to take certain enforcement action in a particular country in its own region," he said, "then we have to admit that the Organization of African Unity is also competent to take certain definitive action by way of enforcement in its region. The same considerations naturally apply to the League of Arab

States, if the League decides to take certain enforcement action in its region." He did not mention the socialist countries, organized under the Warsaw Pact, but his warning proved to be prophetic in the case of Czechoslovakia and the Soviet Union's defense of its military intervention in August 1968. When the Security Council took up the question, the representatives of the USSR, Bulgaria, Poland, and Hungary insisted that the situation in Czechoslovakia was entirely a matter for that country and the socialist group of states and was of no concern to the United Nations.

1. From Transcript of Press Conference

GENEVA   MAY 2, 1965

AS YOU ALL KNOW, Ladies and Gentlemen, I have to cut short my stay in Geneva because of the reasons I mentioned in my statement issued last night. I am very sorry to have to leave Geneva much earlier than I had planned. The Security Council . . . is meeting tomorrow morning and I feel that I have to be present when the Security Council meets. So I will be very happy to answer any questions.

QUESTION: What is the main reason for your recall?

THE SECRETARY-GENERAL: Actually it is not a recall. I got a report last night from Headquarters in New York that the Security Council has to meet on Monday morning, as you know, on the question of the Dominican Republic. And the question of Southern Rhodesia is also to be discussed, because that question was discussed on Friday and a second meeting of the Security Council was scheduled for Monday morning. So, since both these questions are very important, I have been advised that I should come back.

QUESTION: Sir, how do you feel about the situation in the Dominican Republic?

THE SECRETARY-GENERAL: Well, according to newspaper reports, the situation seems to be very serious. I understand that many Latin American countries also view the situation with serious concern. I

SOURCE: UN Note to Correspondents No. 3130, May 12, 1965.

hope that the Security Council, which has the primary responsibility to maintain peace and security, will be able to contribute to the solution of the problem there. Of course, with due regard to the wishes of the people of that country.

QUESTION: Sir, do you feel that the whole problem could be taken out of the Security Council and dealt with by the Organization of American States?

THE SECRETARY-GENERAL: I believe the Organization of American States can play a very useful role as is evident from the constitution of the OAS. There are precedents, of course. In the case of the Congo, as you know, the Organization of African Unity has also been very much involved in seeking a peaceful solution to the problem of the Congo. In the same way I believe that the Organization of American States can play a very useful part. I understand that a delegation of the OAS is proceeding to the Dominican Republic this morning.

QUESTION: What if the Dominican Republic does not agree to have the problem taken over by the OAS?

THE SECRETARY-GENERAL: Well it is very difficult, you know, to make any observation on this aspect, since I am not clear myself which government, or which section of the authorities in the Dominican Republic, can legitimately speak for the country.

. . .

QUESTION: Do you think the developments in the Dominican Republic will affect the situation in South Vietnam?

THE SECRETARY-GENERAL: I am not sufficiently familiar with the background of events in the Dominican Republic, so I don't think I can justifiably comment on this.

QUESTION: What do you think about American intervention in the Dominican Republic?

THE SECRETARY-GENERAL: I will have to study the question much more closely to be able to give a fair reply to this.

QUESTION: Is it possible for the United Nations to send a police force to the Dominican Republic?

THE SECRETARY-GENERAL: The question is now before the Security Council, as I have just said. The Security Council has the primary responsibility for the maintenance of peace and security. I very much hope the Security Council will be able to adopt a resolution which will contribute toward a peaceful solution to this problem.

. . .

2. Statement in the Security Council

NEW YORK   MAY 13, 1965

MR. PRESIDENT, in the light of the statement just made by you, I would like to submit a report to the Security Council regarding the recent developments concerning the representation of the Dominican Republic in the United Nations.

On May 5, 1965, a telegram signed by Dr. Jottin Cury, "Minister for Foreign Affairs of the Dominican Republic," was received by me informing me that the "Constitutional Government" of the Dominican Republic had designated Dr. Moisés de Soto [Martines], alternate representative of the Dominican Republic to the United Nations, as representative *ad interim* until a replacement for Dr. Guaroa Velázquez, who had been relieved of his functions, was appointed.

Then on May 10, 1965, I received a telegram from the "Government of National Reconstruction," confirming the appointment of Ambassador Guaroa Velázquez as representative of the Dominican Republic to the United Nations. The message was signed by: General Antonio Imbert Barreras, President; Mr. Carlos Grisolía Poloney, Member; Mr. Alejandro Zeller Cocco, Member; Colonel Pedro Bartolomé Benoit, Member; and Mr. Julio D. Postigo, Member.

Then on the same day, that is May 10, 1965, I received a communication signed by Ambassador Guaroa Velázquez informing me that on May 7, 1965, a "Government of National Reconstruction" had been established in the Dominican Republic as follows: General Antonio Imbert Barreras, President; Mr. Carlos Grisolía Poloney, Member; Mr. Alejandro Zeller Cocco, Member; Colonel Pedro Bartolomé Benoit, Member; and Mr. Julio D. Postigo, Member. The communication further informed me that Dr. Horacio Vicioso Soto had been appointed by the above-mentioned government as "Secretary of State for Foreign Affairs," and that the government had confirmed Ambassador Velázquez as "permanent representative of the Dominican Republic to the United Nations."

Also on May 10, 1965, I received a telegram signed by Dr. Jottin

SOURCE: Security Council Official Records, Twentieth Year, 1207th meeting.

Cury, "Minister for Foreign Affairs of the Dominican Republic," referring to his earlier cable of May 5 and informing me that the "Constitutional Government" had appointed Mr. Ruben Brache as permanent representative of the Dominican Republic to the United Nations and requesting that this telegram be accepted as provisional credentials for Mr. Brache.

Again on May 10, a telegram was received by me, signed by Dr. Horacio Vicioso Soto, "Secretary of State for Foreign Affairs," informing me that the "Government of National Reconstruction" of the Dominican Republic had confirmed Mr. Guaroa Velázquez as permanent representative of the Dominican Republic to the United Nations and requesting that Mr. Velázquez be recognized as such until the receipt of formal credentials. The message also informed me that Mr. Guaroa Velázquez had been appointed and authorized to represent the Dominican Republic before the Security Council of the United Nations in the discussions concerning the present situation in the Dominican Republic.

Now in addition, of course, there is the telegram dated today, addressed to you, Mr. President, which you referred to in your statement just now.

From the statements which have been made in the Security Council and the communications received from the Organization of American States concerning the Dominican Republic, it is apparent that the situation in that country is far from clear as to which of the contending authorities constitutes the government of the country. Furthermore, there is no information available as to which of the contending authorities is regarded as the government by a majority of states Members of the United Nations.

In the light of the circumstances mentioned above, I feel that at this stage I do not have sufficient information to formulate any opinion as to the adequacy of the provisional credentials which have been submitted.

3. Statement in the Security Council

NEW YORK   MAY 14, 1965

IN ACCORDANCE with the resolution which has just been adopted by the Security Council, I need to say only that I will carry out the wishes of the Council as quickly as possible. I shall, of course, keep the Council informed about the steps which I will be taking. The difficulties in carrying out this mandate are apparent, and I need not elaborate upon them. I expect to receive full cooperation from all those concerned in carrying out the task entrusted to me by the Security Council.

SOURCE: Security Council Official Records, Twentieth Year, 1208th meeting.

4. Appeal to the Parties Involved

NEW YORK   MAY 18, 1965

ON MAY 14, 1965, the Security Council adopted a resolution concerning the situation in the Dominican Republic, expressing deep concern at the grave events in the country; calling for strict cease-fire; inviting the Secretary-General to send, as an urgent measure, a representative to the Dominican Republic for the purpose of reporting on the present situation; and calling upon all concerned in the Dominican Republic to cooperate with the representative of the Secretary-General in the carrying out of this task.

My representative, to whom I have entrusted the message, will arrive in the Dominican Republic today, May 18, 1965, and I have

SOURCE: UN Press Release SG/SM/309.

asked him, as a first and most urgent step, to notify formally all the parties concerned of the Security Council's call for strict cease-fire.

Peaceful means are the only ones which can bring about a lasting settlement of the conflict now besetting the Dominican Republic, and no effort should be spared, by those concerned, to put an end to the fighting which has caused already so much bloodshed and destruction.

I wish, therefore, to convey to all those involved in the conflict in the Dominican Republic my most pressing and earnest appeal to heed the call of the Security Council for an immediate cessation of hostilities as an essential step in bringing about a propitious atmosphere in which a solution may be found to the grave difficulties facing the Dominican Republic.

5. *Report to the Security Council*

NEW YORK　　　　　MAY 18, 1965

1. THE ADVANCE PARTY led by Major-General I. J. Rikhye, which, as indicated in my report of May 15, 1965 [S/6358], had reached Santo Domingo on that date, contacted the parties concerned in the Dominican Republic and made the necessary preparations for the arrival of my representative in the Dominican Republic, Mr. Jose Antonio Mayobre.

2. Mr. Mayobre arrived at New York from Mexico on May 16. After holding discussions with me at Headquarters he departed on May 17 for Santo Domingo, where he is scheduled to arrive in the morning of May 18.

3. I have asked Mr. Mayobre as a first and most urgent step to notify formally all the parties concerned of the Security Council's call for a strict cease-fire. I have also asked him to convey to all those involved in the conflict in the Dominican Republic my most pressing

SOURCE: Security Council Official Records, Twentieth Year, Supplement for April, May, and June 1965, document S/6365.

and earnest appeal to heed the call of the Council for an immediate cessation of hostilities [resolution 208 (1965)] as an essential step in bringing about a propitious atmosphere in which a solution may be found to the grave difficulties facing the Dominican Republic.

[ANNEX OMITTED.]

---

6. From Remarks at Conference of Non-Governmental Organizations

NEW YORK   MAY 27, 1965

. . . I HAD HOPED that 1965 would be a better year, in the sense that the pertinent provision of the Charter relating to the need to practice tolerance and live with one another as good neighbors would be applicable in our relationships. That was our hope at the end of last year. Unfortunately, as I have said on a previous occasion, the first few months of 1965 have not given any ground for optimism—not only in relation to the future functioning of this Organization, but also in relation to the general picture of international relations in terms of the provisions of the Charter. I do not think that I need to go into the details or the circumstances that have led to this situation. But it is a fact—I am convinced of it—that the first five months of 1965 represent a definite set-back, as compared with the very favorable atmosphere that we witnessed in 1963, particularly.

While on that subject, I wish to share with you a very brief thought on the functioning of regional organizations vis-à-vis the United Nations.

Of course, it is far from my intention to question the jurisdiction or the competence of regional organizations in performing certain functions, in accordance with the constitutions laid down by those organizations. But, from the point of view of the functioning of the United

SOURCE: UN Note to Correspondents No. 3140.

Nations in accordance with the Charter, I think that recent developments should stimulate some thought by all of us regarding the character of the regional organizations, the nature of their functions and obligations in relation to the responsibilities of the United Nations under the Charter.

If a particular regional organization considers itself competent to perform certain functions by way of enforcement action in its own region, I am afraid that the same principle should be applicable to other regional organizations too. At present, there are many regional organizations all over the world. I shall mention three in particular: the Organization of American States, the Organization of African Unity, and the League of Arab States. Those three organizations have been formed, not on the basis of political ideologies, but on the basis of geography. If a particular regional organization, under the terms of its own constitution, deems it fit to take certain enforcement action in its own region, it naturally follows that other regional organizations should be considered competent, because of the precedent, to take certain enforcement action in their own regions. If the Organization of American States is recognized as competent to take certain enforcement action in a particular country in its own region, then we have to admit that the Organization of African Unity is also competent to take certain definitive action by way of enforcement in its region. The same considerations naturally apply to the League of Arab States, if the League decides to take certain enforcement action in its region.

Although, as I have said, it is far from my intention to question the competence or the jurisdiction of any regional organization to take any action in conformity with the terms of its own constitution, I feel that all of us and all of you, who have so sincerely and honestly dedicated yourselves to the cause of the United Nations Charter, should do some heart-searching. I am sure that those brief observations of mine will stimulate some thought.

. . .

THE CHAIRMAN: To bring forward our efforts, particularly during the next few months, the Secretary-General has offered to answer three questions this morning that would be pertinent.

QUESTION: I should like to ask one question with reference to regional organizations. Is it not true, and perhaps pertinent to what you said, Mr. Secretary-General, that under the Charter, if any other treaty is in conflict with the Charter, the Charter must prevail?

THE SECRETARY-GENERAL: That is a very pertinent question. So far, I have not expressed any public opinion on this very current topic, which has been one of the aspects of the recent debate in the Security Council. I do not think that it would be in the public interest for me to come out with a public statement on this issue, because it is very contentious.

What I have said, however, is this: Without passing judgment on the competence or jurisdiction of the regional organizations vis-à-vis the jurisdiction of the United Nations, I appeal to you to give some thought to the consequences of the recognition of the competence of the regional organization in taking enforcement action in its particular region, because such a precedent might have very significant, I would say, repercussions in other regional organizations.

Beyond that I do not think it would be in the public interest for me to go in expressing any opinion.

. . .

7. Statement in the Security Council

NEW YORK   JUNE 11, 1965

MR. PRESIDENT, as stated in my report of June 3, 1965, I have provided my representative in the Dominican Republic with the staff and facilities necessary for the discharge of the mandate set forth in operative paragraph 2 of Security Council resolution 203 (1965) of May 14, 1965. My representative has himself reassured me to this effect. The extent of the personnel requirements and other ancillary facilities required by my representative is under constant review.

The present mandate involves observation and reporting. This does not, in my view, or that of my representative, include the actual

SOURCE: Security Council Official Records, Twentieth Year, 1223rd meeting.

investigation of complaints and charges about specific incidents and the necessary verification of information concerning them which involves investigation, other than incidents of overt firing which constitute clear breaches of the cease-fire. For my representative to undertake formally the added function of investigation and verification of complaints, would, by my understanding, require specific clarification by this Council. Such action would provide the necessary sanction for my representative to undertake investigations. It would also require a substantially enlarged staff and increased facilities. Even with this, under prevailing circumstances in the Dominican Republic, I can give no assurance to the Council that an added responsibility of investigation and verification could receive that cooperation from the parties on the spot necessary to ensure effective discharge by my representative.

On the other hand, I may assure the Council that my representative is keeping a "watchful eye" on all such matters and is reporting to me what he sees. A good example of this is to be found in the report [S/6432] which has just been circulated to the Council.

As I have stated above, the level of the staff required by my representative is under constant review and I will provide him with the necessary assistance as the circumstances may demand. Should the Security Council decide to enlarge the terms of reference laid down in the above-mentioned resolution, I would, of course, in the exercise of my responsibilities, take adequate measures to make available to my representative such additional staff and facilities as would be required.

---

8. *Statement in the Security Council*

NEW YORK   JUNE 18, 1965

AT THE MEETING of the Security Council this morning, several matters were raised on which I will comment briefly. One of these dealt with the enlargement of the staff of my representative in Santo

SOURCE: Security Council Official Records, Twentieth Year, 1227th meeting.

Domingo. As I had occasion to inform the members of the Security Council at the Council's meeting on June 11, 1965, "the level of the staff required by my representative is under constant review and I will provide him with the necessary assistance as the circumstances may demand." I wish to assure the members of the Council that in the exercise of my responsibilities I will provide my representative with all possible assistance that he may require in the performance of his duties, both as regards staff and ancillary facilities.

The question of communications between my representative and the United Nations Headquarters in New York is also a subject under close examination by me, and the competent services are now looking into the possibility of either ensuring a more reliable link for the transmission of messages from the Dominican Republic through existing facilities, or, alternatively, the establishment of our own system of communications, which, naturally, would require substantial expenditures. The paramount consideration is, of course, the need to ensure prompt and undisturbed communication between my representative and the United Nations Headquarters here.

The provision of a map to the members of the Security Council was also mentioned this morning. While it was not clear whether the suggestion referred to a map of the Dominican Republic or to one of the City of Santo Domingo, I assume that the Council would wish to have both and I have taken the necessary steps to have these maps prepared and circulated to the members of this Council. For the convenience of the members of the Council, provisional maps of the Dominican Republic and of the City of Santo Domingo have just been distributed to the members of the Security Council. I should also wish to draw to the attention of the members of the Council that a map of the City of Santo Domingo appeared in the annex to the report transmitted by the letter dated May 12, 1965, addressed to me by the Assistant Secretary General of the Organization of American States, which was circulated as document S/6364 on May 18, 1965. This map shows the "safety zone" and the corridor at the date of issuance of that report.

I also wish to inform the Council that I have requested my representative to report to me on the present deployment of the Inter-American Force in the area where the fighting took place on June 15 and 16. This report is expected shortly, and I will, of course, circulate it as soon as it has been received.

From Report of the Secretary-General and the President of the General Assembly to the Special Committee on Peace-keeping Operations

NEW YORK   MAY 31, 1965

ONE OF THE PROPOSALS made by U Thant near the end of the nineteenth session of the General Assembly—and approved by the Assembly—was that the Special Committee on Peace-keeping Operations carry out a comprehensive review of the entire question of peace-keeping. During the intervening months, the Secretary-General and Alex Quaison-Sackey, President of the Assembly, had been engaged in extensive consultations with the permanent representatives of Member states but, as the following report shows, had been unable to find a formula to prevent a continuation of the abnormal voting situation which had all but paralyzed the nineteenth session. The threat still remained that the United States would invoke Article 19 of the Charter and thereby force a confrontation with the Soviet Union. Thant and Quaison-Sackey suggested that the Special Committee give this question its immediate attention. Of more lasting interest, perhaps, were the ten guidelines presented for the use of the Special Committee in drafting plans for future peace-keeping operations. This was a pragmatic approach, attempting to find a workable solution within the terms of the Charter.

. . .

46. THE NECESSITY for the development and strengthening of the United Nations as a really effective instrument for the preservation and maintenance of international peace and security is an accepted fact. Needless to say, in order to achieve this objective, it is necessary to observe strict compliance with the provisions of the Charter, which has been described as the starting point and the common denominator among all the Members of the Organization. It has been suggested that a complete solution, acceptable to all, of all the problems confronting the Organization in its main purpose of maintaining international peace and security might necessitate a revision

SOURCE: General Assembly Official Records, Nineteenth Session, Annex No. 21, document A/5915, annex II.

of various provisions of the Charter. But it is evident that the vast majority of the Members of the Organization are confident that with goodwill and cooperation it should be possible to find some acceptable formula, within the terms of the Charter, to overcome the difficulties that face the Organization.

47. It would be correct to say that the problems that confront the United Nations have largely been due to the fact that the Organization has been, over the last decade or so, called upon to deal with situations in a manner not explicitly spelled out in the Charter. It is a fact that the concept of collective security, which is embedded in the Charter, has undergone significant changes over the last twenty years. This is not to deny the primary responsibility of the Security Council for maintaining international peace and security, nor is any attempt being made or contemplated to minimize the responsibilities of the permanent members of the Security Council.

48. What would appear to be necessary is for the Members of the United Nations, and particularly the permanent members of the Security Council which have a major responsibility in this regard, to face up to the realities of the situation and, in keeping with their obligations under the Charter and their common desire to enable the Organization to fulfill its objectives, take practical measures for overcoming the difficulties that confront the Organization.

49. The Charter of the United Nations contains numerous provisions aimed at dealing with situations involving the maintenance of international peace and security. It is contended by some that these provisions are incomplete and inadequate. At the same time it is a fact that the situations involving the restoration or maintenance of international peace and security vary so considerably that it would be very difficult to attempt to rewrite the Charter to include absolutely clear and precise provisions to deal with every given situation to the satisfaction of all Members. Much of the controversy seems to be at times somewhat academic in nature and one is led to wonder if there are in fact such serious differences in interpreting the Charter. In fact, there is a great deal of merit in the view that wider use of peaceful means of settling disputes, as provided for in the Charter, should be encouraged.

50. The circumstances that led to the establishment of the Special Committee and the general concern of the Members of the Organization to avoid a repetition of the unfortunate experience of the first

part of the nineteenth session have understandably highlighted the need for ensuring the normal functioning of the General Assembly when it resumes its work in September. During the consultations undertaken by the Secretary-General and the President of the General Assembly, the view was repeatedly expressed that there should not be a recurrence of the situation that prevented the General Assembly from functioning normally when it met last. This undoubtedly is one of the immediate tasks before the Committee and must necessarily deserve special attention.

51. Another equally important and pressing question relates to the present financial difficulties facing the Organization. There appears to be substantial support for the view that it is of prime importance to restore the solvency of the Organization by voluntary contributions by the entire membership of the Organization, it being understood that this arrangement shall not be construed as any change in the basic positions of any individual Members and should be accepted as a cooperative effort by all Member states, aimed at the strengthening of the United Nations with a view to creating a climate in which the future may be harmoniously planned. If this view is generally acceptable, it is expected that the members of the Special Committee may wish to authorize the Secretary-General to take appropriate steps, in consultation with Member states, toward this end.

52. There remains the wider question of the comprehensive review that the Special Committee has been asked to undertake of the whole question of peace-keeping operations in all their aspects, including the authorization of operations, the composition of forces and their control, and the financing of such operations. It is accepted that such a review, the scope and importance of which are considerable, cannot be completed by June 15, by which date the Special Committee is required to submit a report to the General Assembly. The comprehensive review must necessarily begin with a clear definition of the term "peace-keeping operations," at present interpreted in several different ways which cannot be reconciled to the satisfaction of everyone without further study. Undoubtedly, there has already been some noticeable progress in this matter, inasmuch as the views have become clearer and do not appear to be so far apart. It would, however, seem appropriate and advisable for the Special Committee to agree at this stage upon certain guidelines, within the terms of the Charter, which could apply to future peace-keeping operations. It

must be borne in mind, in this connection, that peace-keeping operations vary so much in so many ways that a considerable degree of flexibility will be required in dealing with each individual situation. However, the following broad guidelines may be found useful and practical:

(*a*) The Members of the United Nations have conferred on the Security Council primary responsibility for the maintenance of international peace and security.

(*b*) The General Assembly also bears its share of responsibility in maintaining international peace and security. The general functions and powers of the Assembly relating to the maintenance of international peace and security are contained in Articles 10, 11, 12, 14, 15, and 35 of the Charter.

(*c*) The functions and powers of the Security Council and of the General Assembly should be understood as complementary and not as contradictory.

(*d*) In view of the primary responsibility for the maintenance of international peace and security conferred upon the Security Council by the Members of the United Nations for the purpose of ensuring prompt and effective action by the Organization, any question which involves or may involve peace-keeping operations should be examined, in the first instance, by the Security Council in order that appropriate action may be taken as promptly as possible by that organ.

(*e*) If the Security Council is unable for any reason whatever to adopt decisions in the exercise of its primary responsibility for the maintenance of international peace and security, there is nothing to prevent the General Assembly from considering the matter immediately and making appropriate recommendations in conformity with its responsibilities and the relevant provisions of the Charter.

(*f*) According to Article 11, paragraph 2, of the Charter, the General Assembly may choose to refer the question back to the Security Council with appropriate recommendations. If the General Assembly resolves by the required two-thirds majority to make such recommendations, it is to be expected that the weight of such recommendations, supported by a substantial majority of the membership of the United Nations, will have a very significant effect upon the subsequent action by the Security Council. It is likewise to be expected that the General Assembly will duly take into account and give the most serious weight to the views expressed and positions taken in the Security Council when the Council was previously seized of the matter at issue.

(g) The financing of peace-keeping operations should be done in conformity with the provisions of the Charter, and the General Assembly and the Security Council should cooperate in this respect.

(h) In each case involving a peace-keeping operation by the United Nations, various methods of financing may be considered, such as special arrangements among the parties directly involved, voluntary contributions, apportionment to the entire membership of the Organization, and any combination of these various methods.

(i) If the costs of a particular peace-keeping operation, involving heavy expenditure, are to be apportioned among all the Members of the Organization, this should be done according to a special scale, due account being taken of, first, the special responsibility of the permanent members of the Security Council; second, the degree to which particular states are involved in the events or actions leading to a peace-keeping operation; and third, the economic capacity of Member states, particularly of the developing countries.

(j) No decision involving heavy expenditure on a peace-keeping operation shall be taken without advice of the financial implications involved in the operation. The Secretary-General shall, in conformity with regulation 13.1 of the Financial Regulations of the United Nations, submit a report on the administrative and financial implications of the proposal.

53. It is obvious that the guidelines indicated above are neither comprehensive nor fully adequate to meet the varying needs that may arise. There is no doubt that these questions need more detailed study.

54. The Secretary-General and the President of the General Assembly sincerely hope that this report may help the members of the Special Committee in carrying out successfully the mandate given to them by the General Assembly.

"The United Nations—A Twenty-Year Balance Sheet"
Address at Commemorative Meeting

SAN FRANCISCO   JUNE 26, 1965

REFERENCE HAS BEEN MADE earlier to U Thant's growing concern over what he saw as a steady deterioration of the world situation and the inability of the United Nations to cope with a number of major problems. As mid-1965 approached, his gloom deepened.

The San Francisco ceremonies, observing the twentieth anniversary of the signing of the United Nations Charter, found him voicing his concern over "the deeply disturbing situation" confronting the United Nations. He said: "We have witnessed, and are still witnessing, certain tendencies for the cold war to intensify and also to extend to areas which have so far been relatively immune." The greatest obstacle to the realization of the objectives of the United Nations Charter, he said, "is the inescapable fact that power politics still operates, both overtly and covertly, in international relations."

TWENTY YEARS is a long time in the life of an individual, but a short one in the development of a great political institution.

With our human tendency to impatience, we find it hard to accept the time-lag between the formulation of an idea and its practical realization, and we are sometimes inclined to question the validity of an idea before it has had time to prove itself, or even to reject it impatiently before it has had the chance to take root and grow. Our experiences of international relations in the past twenty years may sometimes tempt us to react in this way about the Charter of the United Nations.

It is a merciful fact of life that time diminishes and dims the memories of misery and horror. Time has also blunted that sense of danger and of urgency which produced the Charter. Thus we hear a good deal of talk now about the adaptation of the Charter to the

SOURCE: *UN Monthly Chronicle,* vol. II, July 1965, pp. 141–145.

modern world—talk which sometimes evades the central issue of
making the Charter a working reality.

There is no doubt that the world has changed in many ways, some
of them unexpected, since 1945, and that corresponding adjustments
in the United Nations are desirable. On a previous occasion I have
myself referred to the anachronistic character of certain provisions of
the Charter. But defeatist thinking about the possibility or the necessity of world order merely turns a blind eye to the perils of the future
because of the difficulties of the present. Should we succumb to such
facile arguments, we would stand convicted by future generations of
gross irresponsibility.

I believe, therefore, that the most important thing we can do at this
twentieth anniversary of the signing of the Charter of the United
Nations is to think back to the tragedies and agonies which made the
Charter possible and, in resolving that humanity shall never be so
afflicted again, rededicate ourselves to its aims and ideals. Having
done this, we must look to the future with statesmanship, as well as
realism.

The danger is not, it seems to me, that the Charter will prove
inadequate or unsuited to our purposes and policies. It is, rather, that
our purposes and policies are inadequate, and in some cases inimical,
to the fulfillment of the purposes and principles to which the United
Nations enthusiastically subscribed twenty years ago. It is this inadequacy, which we think we can afford in relatively peaceful times, that
we must guard against.

It was never realistic to suppose that sovereign governments
would, in a short period of time, be able to accept and act on all the
practical implications of the ideals and aims to which they subscribed
in signing the Charter. On the other hand, if we want some better
system for peace and security than an unsteady balance of nationalistic power and aspiration, we have got to work long and hard to
remove the many obstacles in the way, and in that process develop a
new system of relationships between states which really corresponds
to present needs and conditions.

During that arduous task, we must look to the Charter as an
inspiration and a goal, without any illusions as to the ease with which
its objectives can be attained. If we need to assure ourselves that the
goal is worth attaining, we need only turn our thoughts for a moment
to the probable alternative.

I do not wish today to look back at the past twenty years either to applaud what has been done or to regret what has not. I do not propose to refer in detail to our current situation except to say that it demands an urgent and serious effort by all nations to make a reality of the aims of the Charter before we revert in disunity to the helpless conditions which preceded the Second World War. It is all too clear that the unsolved problems within the United Nations over Article 19 and peace-keeping, combined with various ominous conflicts in the world at large, present us with a deeply disturbing situation. In spite of this, I would like, rather, to speak of the future, with its problems and its possibilities.

In 1946, Sir Winston Churchill said of the League of Nations:

The League of Nations did not fail because of its principles and conceptions. It failed because these principles were deserted by those States which had brought it into being. It failed because the Governments of those States feared to face the facts and act while time remained. This disaster must not be repeated.

We are luckier than our fathers were in the twentieth year of the League of Nations, because we still have time to face the facts. It is, however, essential that a sense of false security should not lull us once again into the belief that somehow war can be avoided in a world where the unbridled rivalry of nations is the dominant factor of international life. That is the condition in which the drift to war almost imperceptibly gathers momentum until it becomes irresistible and inescapable. That is what we have, by a conscious and concerted effort, to avoid.

Disturbing developments in various parts of the world today have, of course, direct repercussions all over the world, and for that matter on the United Nations, which is in many ways a mirror of the world. There is a danger that we may become so preoccupied with the immediate crises in Southeast Asia, in the Caribbean, in the Middle East, and elsewhere that we are apt to ignore the larger crisis that looms behind them. That wider crisis must be understood and assessed.

The most serious casualty of the present conflict will be the precarious détente between East and West that has been built and nurtured so laboriously and patiently in the last ten years or so. The United Nations has contributed significantly toward that détente by serving as a catalyst; a forum and an agency for the peaceful settlement of disputes and the relaxation of East-West tensions.

I had hoped that this détente, to be meaningful, would extend to other areas of the globe, since peace is indivisible. But we have witnessed, and are still witnessing, certain tendencies for the cold war to intensify, and also to extend to areas which have so far been relatively immune. This trend must be arrested and reversed if humanity is to be saved from the scourge of war, the primary motivation behind the founding of the United Nations.

The international community on this small planet should comprise all men and women, irrespective of race and creed. As Pierre Teilhard de Chardin had observed, life should move toward a higher plane of consciousness than this one on which we now live. He was undismayed by the ideological clashes men must pass through before they achieve a world community. He saw a great evolution leading toward "a common soul in this vast body"—mankind.

I believe that we are increasingly conscious of the need to harmonize our thoughts and actions toward that end. We have an increasing fear and hatred of war throughout the world, based partly upon the new destructive power of weapons, and partly upon a moral revulsion against violence. The voices of peoples all over the world are raised, as never before, against war and actions likely to lead to war. We have the balance of terror between the nuclear powers, but the proliferation of nuclear weapons may end the nuclear monopoly of the major powers while greatly increasing the risks involved. We have a general agreement, in principle at least, that the domination of one nation or group of nations by another is intolerable, and that mutual aid and cooperation are the best basis for the relationship between nations.

We have the possibility of raising standards of living and opportunity through international cooperation—an immense incentive to peace. We can, if we work together, provide, within a generation or so, a much higher standard of living and reasonable opportunities for all men. We have the possibility of great advances in science, technology and in as yet unexplored realms of the human mind, as well as in outer space—advances all of which will be more rapid and less risky if the skill and talent of all nations can be combined in an organized effort. Finally, we have an agreed framework, the United Nations system, within which, if we wish, we can pursue our aims and bring about an orderly development in international life. This all adds up to a considerable balance sheet of positive assets.

Our problems and liabilities are also considerable, and we sometimes tend to be more impressed by them than by our assets. The greatest obstacle to the realization of the Charter is the inescapable fact that power politics still operates, both overtly and covertly, in international relations. The concept of power politics, whether as the instrument of nationalism or of ideological extremism, is the natural enemy of international order as envisaged in the Charter. It is also an expensive, and potentially disastrous, anachronism.

Patriotism, national pride, or ideological conviction can and must take new and more creative forms than the old concepts of political domination or material power. This is a challenge to statesmanship and political genius in all regions of the world. The basic ideas and machinery are all there—they await the national policies and actions which will put life and strength into them. Such policies will not, in the beginning, be easy for governments, especially powerful ones, to adopt. The larger interests of world peace, the will or opinion of the majority of nations or the accommodation of national prestige to international order will initially often prove hard to accept. But some governments have already found such acceptance possible without suffering disaster, and their example should encourage others.

Even if the problem of power politics were solved, we have to face other basic facts. It is now commonplace to refer to the gulf between developed and underdeveloped nations, to the population explosion, to the conservation of natural resources, to the world food problem or to the social consequences of material development. All of us know the statistics of world poverty and the frustration of the developing countries. We are also aware in all countries that material progress brings with it a host of complications and tensions. And yet, obsessed as we are with our other apprehensions, we still tend to think in small and old-fashioned terms about these fundamental challenges. Our plans to meet them are fragmentary and our resources, both human and material, pitifully inadequate—and, meanwhile, the clock ticks inexorably on. These are problems which never present the kind of dramatic ultimatum that questions of peace and war present. They slowly build up their crushing weight of misery until it becomes an overwhelming human tragedy. We know all of this, and we can together do something about it. We need new approaches and new ideas for our new world. To produce them requires both genius and cooperation. The machinery for cooperation awaits us in the Charter.

We also have a basic problem in our varied heritage of prejudice, resentment, and nationalistic feelings. These are relics from a slower, more isolated, less populated age. They have no place in a liberal and dynamic world of change and progress. Nonetheless, they are frequently exploited or artificially preserved to sustain other struggles. At our best, we know how outmoded and irrelevant these national and racial prejudices are, but we still need a strong and conscious effort to overcome them.

The key to these problems, and many more besides, is to be found in the Charter, and with it we can open the door to an order and a world society worthy of this remarkable century. Only the sovereign Member governments and their peoples, working together in the world and in the United Nations, can open that door, and it is imperative that they should do so urgently.

Is it really only the scourge of war or the lash of terror that can move us toward the goal of peace and justice in the world? Can we not make the effort to advance, out of our own sense of responsibility and knowledge, rather than be driven like refugees before a storm which may be unleashed by our own inability to take hold of the future? I believe not only that we can, but that we must, make the effort.

Twenty years ago, to this very day, the founding fathers signed the Charter of the United Nations. Today I appeal to all Member governments to consider again these simple facts, and to renew their efforts toward the realization of the great objectives prescribed for them in this city, twenty years ago.

From Transcript of Press Conference

GENEVA   JULY 7, 1965

U THANT held the firm view that there should be no change in the United Nation's Charter provision that each state, regardless of size, should have one vote in the General Assembly. Although he had made his position clear on numerous occasions, the question was raised again at his July 7 press conference in Geneva and once more he voiced his opposition to any sort of weighted voting. While no Member state had ever made a formal proposal for such a change, the question was inspired by widespread public demands in the United States for action to offset the growing influence of the small nations in the United Nations. At the time special attention was drawn to the issue by the Article 19 controversy and the fears of some that the United States could not find support for any attempt to suspend the voting rights of the Soviet Union and other Members in arrears in paying peace-keeping assessments. There also was some concern over the continued admission of so-called mini-states to United Nations membership. In 1964, the Organization had admitted three new members—Malawi, Malta, and Zambia—bringing the total membership to one hundred fifteen as compared with its original membership of fifty-one. Three more small states were awaiting admission in 1965: Gambia, the Maldive Islands, and Singapore. Thant was fully aware of the issues, but he maintained that the one-country, one-vote system was based on the "soundest and most democratic principle" and that it should be retained.

. . .

CORRESPONDENT *(Spectator of London):* At the United Nations World Trade Conference last year, there was a proposal to change the voting system at present used in the United Nations by introducing a blocking vote for major industrialized countries. This proposal was not retained in the final institutional arrangements. However, recently, I read in an official document of a certain developed country who was perhaps the most strongly in favor of the blocking vote that they considered that the United Nations voting system should be

SOURCE: UN Note to Correspondents No. 3162, July 9, 1965.

changed, and I quote "to reflect the economic power realities." If I am not mistaken, votes would be given to countries on the basis of their gross national products. I believe that in this particular developed country they still have the system of one man, one vote. However, do you think that such a change might in any way, as this country would think, enhance the effectiveness of the United Nations either in peace-keeping or in economic and social development?

THE SECRETARY-GENERAL: Many views have been expressed by some Member states from time to time in the last two or three years advocating the need to change the voting pattern in the United Nations; in other words, to replace the present system of one country, one vote. Personally, I don't think it is realistic. I believe very strongly, as I have stated on several previous occasions, that the present system of one country, one vote, irrespective of the size and wealth of the Member state, is the soundest and the most democratic principle, as is evident in many countries of the world today. In the same way as the richest man in Geneva has one vote, in the same manner as the doorman in one of the hotels here has one vote, I think this has been accepted as the basic concept of democracy. So I am very much in favor of retaining the present system of one country, one vote.

. . .

URSULA WASSERMAN (*National Guardian,* New York and Montevideo): Mr. Secretary-General, I would like to have some information on the present situation in Santo Domingo, on the continued effort of your representatives in Santo Domingo and also on what is being done to send any relief to the population of Santo Domingo. Thank you.

THE SECRETARY-GENERAL: Thank you. In Geneva, I have been receiving reports from my representative, Mr. Mayobre, every day. According to his assessment, the situation is quiet, relatively speaking, and the cease-fire truce, as ordered by the Security Council, has been in force, but, of course, there are minor violations from time to time, and he has been reporting to me every day. I propose to submit a comprehensive report to the Security Council as soon as I get back to New York. That will be early next week.

About the relief measures for the Dominican Republic—as you know, the United Nations has not been involved and is not involved—and I am very glad to be able to tell you that the Red Cross, the International Red Cross, is doing a magnificent job in this field in the Dominican Republic, and I understand that the Organization of American States has also been involved very usefully in this matter.

. . .

Statement at Memorial Ceremony for Adlai E. Stevenson

NEW YORK   JULY 19, 1965

U THANT was a close friend of Adlai Stevenson and was genuinely moved by his death. Like others who shared Stevenson's confidences, Thant was aware of his frustrations over the Vietnam war and his unhappiness during the final weeks of his life. In his eloquent tribute to the former permanent United States representative, the Secretary-General took the occasion to deplore the "devastating effects of the cold war on humanity." He said that he believed Stevenson, in his innermost thoughts, realized that "the weapons of the cold war contaminate our moral fiber, warp our thinking processes, and afflict us with pathological obsessions." He said he was impressed repeatedly by Stevenson's "dedication to the basic concepts of peace, justice, and freedom."

WHEN I FIRST was told last Wednesday, a little before 1:00 P.M., that Ambassador Stevenson had died in London, I could not believe my ears. I had seen him only recently, in Geneva, less than a week before and he was so alive, and looked so well. When the news was confirmed, it took me some time to accept the fact that Adlai Stevenson had really passed away.

My first thought was to send a message of condolences to President Johnson. In my message I referred to the respect, admiration, and affection of all of his colleagues at the United Nations which Ambassador Stevenson had earned over the last four and a half years by reason of his extraordinary human qualities.

The same afternoon I referred, in a public statement, to my sense of grief and shock because, suddenly and without warning, death had struck and we had lost a good friend and a highly esteemed colleague. As I stated in that tribute, in his years at the United Nations, Ambassador Stevenson had demonstrated with rare distinction how it

SOURCE: UN Press Release SG/SM/338.

was possible to combine the highest form of patriotism with loyalty to the idea of international peace and cooperation.

When on December 8, 1960, it was announced that Mr. Stevenson was to be permanent representative of the United States of America to the United Nations, it seemed to everybody to be such a natural and right appointment. He was, in truth, one of the founding fathers of the United Nations, having been present at the signing of the Charter in San Francisco in June 1945, and also having been closely associated with the negotiations leading up to that historic event.

Thereafter, he was the head of the United States Delegation to the Preparatory Commission and Executive Committee of the United Nations in London, and I believe his offices were located in Grosvenor Square, close to the very spot where he collapsed last Wednesday.

Subsequently, of course, he had entered domestic politics and his direct association with the United Nations was only intermittent. But I have no doubt in my own mind that his presence at the birth of the United Nations was an important factor in the evolution of his own political thinking and in his own dedication to the noble principles and purposes of the Charter.

I remember how many tributes were paid to him when he took over his duties at the United Nations. There were so many encomiums, both within and outside these walls, that they could have turned the head of a lesser man. Not so with Ambassador Stevenson. On one occasion he observed: "Flattery is like smoking—it is not dangerous so long as you do not inhale."

During the four and a half years that he served at the United Nations, he stood as the embodiment of dedication to the principles of the United Nations. His many speeches, which expressed so well his whole mental and intellectual approach, in the championship of fundamental rights, in defense of the dignity and worth of the human person, in support of the equal rights of nations large and small, were cheered and applauded by all sides of the house. He not only spoke with a rare gift of phrase, but with such an obvious sincerity that his words carried conviction.

My first contact with Ambassador Stevenson came about in 1952 when I was one of the members of the Burmese delegation to the seventh General Assembly. This was at the time when he was the Democratic candidate for the presidential election. His speeches were naturally fully reported in the newspapers, and I followed his campaign closely. His speeches were not only masterpieces of oratory, they were also the incisive reflections of a great man and of a great mind, in line with the best traditions of American liberal thought.

There were some during his lifetime, of course, who rated him as too liberal and too far ahead of the times. Others sought to discount his effectiveness on the score that he was too much the idealist and therefore not practical enough. This does him injustice.

The line of distinction between idealism and vision is obscure at best. Vision, certainly, is an essential attribute of statesmanship, and he was a fine statesman. In any case, what a dismal world it would be, and how unpromising its future, without spiritual lift given to mankind by the idealists who, in the courage of their conviction, chart the course and mark the goals of man's progress!

At that time I did not have any personal acquaintance with Mr. Stevenson. For me the chance came a year later when he visited Burma in 1953. On that occasion I had the opportunity to talk to him and to discuss with him many issues of current interest. Again I was greatly impressed, not only by the depth of his intellect, but equally by his breadth of vision.

From the time that Mr. Stevenson became the permanent representative of his country at the United Nations and while I was still the permanent representative of Burma, we developed very close ties of friendship. These ties became even closer toward the end of the year when I assumed my present responsibilities, and continued to be so during the last three and a half years. I found it easy to discuss with him any current issue of importance with complete freedom, and in full frankness and friendliness.

No one can serve his country in the United Nations for long without having his moments of frustration. Ambassador Stevenson had his share of such moments, and on such occasions he confided to me his innermost thoughts, and I was struck by his completely human approach to our common problems. He seemed not only to think about them, but also to feel about them as a human being. In all such discussions I was repeatedly impressed by his dedication to the basic concepts of peace, justice, and freedom.

So many tributes have been paid to Mr. Stevenson since his sudden and tragic passing away. So many of his friends and admirers have eulogized his fine intellect, his modesty and humility. Many have praised his felicitous style and his ready wit. Tributes have been paid to his great learning, which he carried so lightly because he was truly an educated man, a cultured man, a civilized man.

Speaking in San Francisco on June 26, 1965, on the twentieth anniversary of the United Nations, Ambassador Stevenson said:

Some of us here today who were midwives at the birth of the United Nations can never forget those days here in San Francisco in the twilight of the war, when an old world was dying and a new world was coming to birth.

We shared an audacious dream—and launched a brave enterprise.

It seemed so easy then—when all was hope and expectation. I remember my own sense of pride, of history, of exultation. . . .

He went on to reflect:

In the bright glow of 1945, too many looked to the United Nations for the full and final answer to world peace. And in retrospect, that day may seem to have opened with the hint of a false dawn.

Certainly we have learned the hard way how elusive is peace—how durable is man's destructive drive. . . .

We have learned, too, how distant is the dream of those better standards of life in larger freedom—how qualified our capacity to practice tolerance— how conditional our claims to the dignity and worth of the human person— how reserved our respect for the obligations of law.

He then proceeded to restate, on behalf of himself, his government, and the vast bulk of his countrymen, his faith in the United Nations in the following words:

We believe in the United Nations; we support the United Nations; and we shall work in the future—as we have worked in the past—to add strength, and influence, and permanence to all that the Organization stands for in this, our tempestuous, tormented, talented world of diversity in which all men are brothers and all brothers are somehow, wondrously, different—save in their need for peace.

And he concluded by saying:

We have the United Nations. We have set it bravely up. And we will carry it bravely forward.

Unfortunately, Adlai Stevenson is no longer with us to keep step with us in the march forward to the goals he had stated so well.

On this occasion when we are paying homage to the memory of one who has left us so large a legacy, it is fitting, I believe, to give some thought to the momentous questions of war and peace which were so close to his heart.

In my view, many governments, while unwilling to wage war, and at the same time unable to make peace, seem to have resigned themselves to the prospect of an interminable cold war. While admittedly the cold war cannot bring down the physical holocaust on our heads, it has nevertheless already inflicted on us a tremendous moral and psychological injury which is intangible but equally destructive. The long, uneasy cold war has destroyed and mutilated not our bodies, but our minds. Its weapons are the myths and the legends of propaganda.

It has often been said that in war the first casualty is truth. The cold war is also capable of inflicting the same casualty. The weapons designed and utilized to crush and mutilate the human mind are as potent as any of the weapons designed for physical destruction. The weapons of the cold war contaminate our moral fiber, warp our thinking processes, and afflict us with pathological obsessions. These are the invisible but, nevertheless, the most devastating effects of the cold war on humanity. I believe Adlai Stevenson, in his innermost thoughts, realized these truths.

There is no doubt that Adlai Stevenson has earned a place in history—not only a place in the history of his own country, but a place in the history of this world Organization. He brought to international diplomacy, in his dignity, his gentility, and his style, a special dimension. Even more, he has earned the admiration and affection of millions of people to whom he was but a name and a legend.

This was so, I think, because so often his voice rang true as the voice of the people, his eloquence expressed the hopes and aspirations of the common man the world over. He was, in our times, in a quite unique way, the people's friend. Equally, he has earned a permanent place in the hearts of all those who knew him, and today I mourn his passing, not just as a great historical figure, a famous man, but as a true and trusted friend. As the poet says:

> Friendship is a nobler thing;
> Of friendship it is good to sing.

Letter to President Lyndon B. Johnson
concerning the Situation in Vietnam

NEW YORK   JULY 29, 1965

THERE WAS LITTLE movement in the Vietnam situation during the spring and early summer of 1965. On July 28, however, two weeks after the sudden death of Adlai Stevenson, President Lyndon B. Johnson informed the Security Council that the United States had again invited all Member states, individually and collectively, to use their influence to bring the Vietnam problem to the conference table and that the United States remained ready to enter into negotiations unconditionally. Arthur J. Goldberg, newly appointed to succeed Stevenson as permanent United States representative, also delivered to Thant a personal letter from the President praising the Secretary-General for his Vietnam peace efforts. The following note is a reply to the Johnson communication. Although the exchange produced a brief flurry, the situation remained basically unchanged except for the continued military escalation.

In the Introduction to his Annual Report, issued on September 20 (p. 162), the Secretary-General noted that the Vietnam conflict had "cruelly set back" the trend toward a thaw in the cold war and was casting its shadow on almost every area of international cooperation. He mentioned once more that he had devoted considerable personal effort in the realm of quiet diplomacy to getting the parties to stop fighting and to start the discussions which alone, he felt, could lead to a solution. He added: "I remain as fully convinced as ever that total victory or total defeat for one side or the other is out of the question and that military action cannot bring peace and restore stability to the area."

IT WAS MY GREAT PLEASURE yesterday afternoon to receive Ambassador Goldberg and welcome him to the United Nations, and at the same time to have from his hand the letter which you addressed to me, for which I thank you most warmly.

Your letter gives me much satisfaction and encouragement, not only as evidence of the very great personal confidence which you

SOURCE: UN Press Release SG/SM/342.

have in Ambassador Goldberg, but also as reassurance that your government attaches highest importance to the work of the United Nations and will continue to give the United Nations its utmost support.

It is particularly gratifying to know that you have instructed Ambassador Goldberg especially to maintain close contact with me on the situation in Vietnam. For my part, of course, I will keep closely in touch with him on all important issues relating to international peace. Knowing the very great importance which I attach in the present circumstances to the question of Vietnam, you may rest assured that I look forward to continuous mutual consultation on this issue.

In this connection, Mr. President, please allow me to thank you for your kind words about my efforts in the past to find some way to remove the dispute over Vietnam from the battlefield to the negotiating table. I am heartened by your wish that my efforts should be continued, and I gladly assure you of my determination to pursue them by all the means at my disposal, since I believe most strongly that concerted efforts should be made to put an early end to all further hostile military activities.

I shall, of course, be pleased to communicate to you through Ambassador Goldberg, in accordance with your wish, any further suggestions which I would consider helpful in bringing peace to Southeast Asia.

THE SITUATION IN KASHMIR

THE QUESTION of Jammu and Kashmir first came before the Security Council on January 1, 1948, when India complained that Pakistan was assisting tribesmen in an invasion of the Indian princedom which borders on the two countries. Under the Indian Independence Act of 1947, Jammu and Kashmir became free to accede to either India or Pakistan but had taken no decision at the time the fighting began a few months later. The Maharajah, however, requested accession to India after the outbreak of fighting and India accepted with a promise to submit the question to a referendum as soon as normal conditions were restored. Pakistan challenged the accession as illegal and accused India of carrying out a program of genocide against the Muslim inhabitants of Jammu and Kashmir. The so-called Kashmir dispute has been before the Security Council intermittently ever since.

The first United Nations action was the creation of a three-member Commission, later enlarged to five members, to assist in halting the fighting and in creating proper conditions for an impartial plebiscite. The Council instructed the Commission—composed of Argentina, Belgium, Colombia, Czechoslovakia, and the United States—to proceed immediately to the Indian subcontinent. After protracted talks with Indian and Pakistani authorities a cease-fire agreement was finally reached, effective January 1, 1949, and military observers from a number of countries were assembled by the Commission to report on observance of the cease-fire. These observers, formally named the United Nations Military Observer Group in India and Pakistan (UNMOGIP), remained to become one of the oldest United Nations military missions in point of service. It is still functioning at this writing. During late 1948 and early 1949, the commission believed—somewhat prematurely, as it turned out—that the situation was improving and that India and Pakistan were nearing agreement on a plebiscite. On the recommendation of the Commission, Secretary-General Trygve Lie nominated Fleet Admiral Chester W. Nimitz of the U.S. Navy as plebiscite administrator in March 1949. He was to be formally appointed by the government of Jammu and Kashmir when details of the plebiscite were settled. The plebiscite was never held.

There is no need to recount here the various incidents, the continuing charges and countercharges, the proposals for settlement rejected by one side or the other, or the long debates in the Council. In March 1950, the Council decided to terminate the two-year-old-Commission and to transfer its responsibilities to a United Nations representative. It appointed Sir Owen Dixon of Australia to the post. After almost six months of talks with representatives of India and Pakistan, Sir Owen concluded that no progress had been made and asked to be relieved of his position. In April 1951, the Council named Frank P. Graham of the United States as Sir Owen's successor.

Graham was equally unsuccessful, but he continued to make recommendations to the two parties as late as 1958. In 1957, the Council requested its President, Gunnar V. Jarring of Sweden—who later became special representative of U Thant in the Middle East—to consult with officials of India and Pakistan, but he was unable to report any prospect of agreement.

This was the situation in substance until August 1965. The new crisis dated from August 5, when cease-fire violations began accelerating at an unprecedented rate. There was heavy and prolonged artillery fire from the Pakistani side on August 15–16. Between these dates and September 1, Indian Army troops crossed the cease-fire line at several points and occupied Pakistani positions. Major-General Robert H. Nimmo, chief of the forty-five-man military observer group, warned Thant that the situation was deteriorating rapidly. In a statement on August 24, the Secretary-General disclosed that he had been in "earnest consultation" with the permanent representatives of India and Pakistan and had proposed that he send Under-Secretary Ralph Bunche as his personal representative to seek an end to the violence. Both sides, however, had laid down conditions which led him to conclude that such a mission was not feasible. Instead he summoned General Nimmo to Headquarters for consultations.

The Secretary-General on September 1 sent urgent appeals to Mohammed Ayub Khan, President of Pakistan, and Sri Lal Bahadur Shastri, Prime Minister of India, for a restoration of the cease-fire. By that time, however, the cease-fire had collapsed completely and regular army forces of both sides were engaged in heavy fighting. The Council met on Saturday, September 4, and quickly adopted a resolution sponsored by six countries—Bolivia, Ivory Coast, Jordan, Malaysia, Netherlands, and Uruguay—calling on India and Pakistan to restore the cease-fire and requesting the Secretary-General to report within three days on the implementation of the resolution. When the Council met again on September 6, it had before it reports from General Nimmo that rather than ending, the conflict was becoming more intense. After listening to statements by India and Pakistan, both of which defended their refusal to agree to a cease-fire, the Council unanimously adopted a resolution calling upon the parties to cease hostilities in the area immediately and to withdraw all armed personnel to the positions they held before August 5. It further requested the Secretary-General "to exert every possible effort to give effect to this resolution and the resolution of September 4. . . ." Although the new resolution did not say so specifically it was understood, as a result of private consultations, that the Council expected Thant to undertake a personal peace mission to the Indian subcontinent. It was the first such mission given him by the Council and he readily agreed. In a brief statement to the Council he announced that his efforts would include "an early visit to the area."

The Secretary-General left New York on September 7 for a nine-day visit to Rawalpindi and New Delhi. After private talks with the leaders of Pakistan and India, he sent a formal appeal to both parties on September 12 calling for an unconditional cease-fire at 6:00 P.M. Rawalpindi time and 6:30 P.M. New

Delhi time on September 14. In their replies both laid down conditions which Thant had no authority to accept under the Council's resolution. Pending consideration of the conditions by the Council, the Secretary-General proposed a new cease-fire time, effective at the same hours on September 16. Although he still had not won their agreement, Thant left on September 15 for New York to report urgently to the Council. In a final communication to President Ayub Khan and Prime Minister Shastri, the Secretary-General proposed a face-to-face meeting between the two leaders and offered his own assistance in any role desired by the parties. Nothing came of this proposal immediately, but the two leaders did meet four months later at Tashkent, in the USSR, at the invitation of the Soviet Union and reached agreement that all their armed forces would be withdrawn not later than February 25, 1966, to the positions held by them before August 5.

Meanwhile, the Security Council had met following Thant's return from the Indian subcontinent and on September 20 adopted a resolution fixing a cease-fire deadline for September 22 at 7:00 A.M. GMT. This time both India and Pakistan accepted the cease-fire order and it became effective on September 22, some six weeks after the major fighting began. Despite the acceptance of the cease-fire, United Nations observers continued to report numerous violations. The cease-fire remained in danger of collapse during the remaining months of 1965.

---

1. Statement to the Press

NEW YORK   AUGUST 24, 1965

As ALREADY INDICATED, I am greatly concerned about the situation in Kashmir. It poses a very serious and dangerous threat to peace.

Therefore, in the course of the past two weeks, I have been in earnest consultation with the permanent representatives of the two governments with a view to stopping the violations of the cease-fire line which have been reported to me by General Nimmo, Chief Military Observer of UNMOGIP,[1] and effecting a restoration of normal conditions along the cease-fire line.

SOURCE: *UN Monthly Chronicle*, vol. II, August-September 1965, p. 17.

[1]Major-General Robert H. Nimmo, Chief Military Observer of the United Nations Military Observer Group in India and Pakistan (UNMOGIP).

In the same context I have had in mind the possibility of sending urgently a personal representative to the area for the purpose of meeting and talking with appropriate authorities of the two governments and with General Nimmo, and conveying to the governments my very serious concern about the situation and exploring with them ways and means of preventing any further deterioration in that situation and restoring quiet along the cease-fire line.

Should such a mission materialize I had it in mind to ask Dr. Ralph J. Bunche, Under-Secretary for Special Political Affairs, to undertake it. The idea was broached to the two parties informally on August 20. The subsequent responses of the two governments, while not negative, involved in each case conditions which, in my view, would make the mission not feasible at this time and therefore I have abandoned it.

As a further and immediate step, however, I have asked General Nimmo to come quickly to United Nations Headquarters for consultation with me about the situation in Kashmir, and he is expected to arrive from Srinagar before the end of the week. I shall give consideration to other efforts that I might make in the light of the discussions with General Nimmo.

---

2. Identical Messages to the Prime Minister of India and the President of Pakistan

NEW YORK   SEPTEMBER 1, 1965

I HAVE THE HONOR, Excellency, to address you about the current grave situation in Kashmir. That I approach you directly in this urgent way reflects the depth of my fears about recent developments there. You are, of course, aware of my mounting concern over the deterioration of the cease-fire and the cease-fire line, which I have been conveying to Your Excellency's government over the past three

SOURCE: Security Council Official Records, Twentieth Year, Supplement for July, August, and September 1965, document S/6647.

weeks. Since August 5, 1965, there has been an unprecedented number of acts of violence along or in the vicinity of the cease-fire line in Kashmir. Without any attempt to apportion blame, it may be said that such actions now come from both sides of the line, involve an increasingly large number of armed men on each side, and take place in the air as well as on the ground. Most serious of all, it is my understanding that regular army troops from both countries are now engaging in military actions along and across the line.

India and Pakistan freely entered into a cease-fire agreement at Karachi in July 1949 and agreed upon a cease-fire in Kashmir. Observance of that cease-fire has been assisted by the United Nations Military Observer Group in India and Pakistan. That agreement is now being so widely disregarded as to be reduced to little consequence. An outright military confrontation between the armed forces of India and Pakistan is threatened and may be imminent, which can have only the gravest implications for the peace of the world, and for the lives and well-being of the inhabitants of Kashmir and the peoples of India and Pakistan. It also seems to me that the quiet which would result from mutual observance of the cease-fire would afford the most favorable climate in which to seek a resolution of political differences.

I fully realize the very great complexities of the Kashmir problem for your government. I cannot believe, however, that it poses problems which could not be solved ultimately by peaceful processes, or that these problems can ever be really solved by military action. In this latter regard, I must point out that resort to force in the settlement of a dispute of this kind is contrary to both the spirit and the letter of the Charter of the United Nations and the obligations undertaken by your country as a Member of the Organization.

Because I believe firmly that you and your government would wish a peaceful solution of the problem of Kashmir, I appeal to you most earnestly, in the interests of peace in your area and in the world, to indicate immediately your intention henceforth to respect the cease-fire agreement. Essential, of course, to the restoration of the cease-fire would be a cessation of crossings of the cease-fire line by armed personnel from one side of the line to the other, the withdrawal of armed personnel of each side that have occupied positions on the other party's side of the line, and a halt to all firing across the cease-fire line from either side of it. Effective observance of the cease-fire, as you know, requires cooperation on both sides of the line with the United Nations Military Observer Group, and freedom of movement and access for the United Nations observers in the discharge of their duties.

I give you assurance, Excellency, of my fullest possible assistance in the restoration of peace in Kashmir and the solution of its problems.

I make this appeal because I am confident that you believe in peace, as I do, and that you would wish to take any action which would help preserve the peace of the world. I am hopeful, therefore, about your response to my appeal.

3. From Report to the Security Council

NEW YORK   SEPTEMBER 3, 1965

. . .

9. ON THE MORNING of August 9, 1965, a telegram was received from General Nimmo warning that the situation was deteriorating along the CFL [cease-fire line]. On the basis of this report, I saw the representative of Pakistan at 1230 hours on that day, and asked him to convey to his government my very serious concern about the situation that was developing in Kashmir, involving the crossing of the CFL from the Pakistan side by numbers of armed men and their attacks on Indian military positions on the Indian side of the line, and also my strong appeal that the CFL be observed. That same afternoon I saw the representative of India, told him of the information I had received from General Nimmo and of the *démarche* I had made to the government of Pakistan, and asked him to convey to his government my urgent appeal for restraint as regards any retaliatory action from their side. In subsequent days, I repeated these appeals orally for transmission to the two governments, asking also that all personnel of

SOURCE: Security Council Official Records, Twentieth Year, Supplement for July, August, and September 1965, document S/6651.

either party still remaining on the wrong side of the line be withdrawn to its own side. I have not obtained from the government of Pakistan any assurance that the cease-fire and the CFL will be respected henceforth or that efforts would be exerted to restore conditions to normal along that line. I did receive assurance from the government of India, conveyed orally by its representative to the United Nations, that India would act with restraint with regard to any retaliatory acts and will respect the cease-fire agreement and the CFL if Pakistan does likewise. In the meantime, reports from UNMOGIP as of September 2 indicate a continuation of violations of the cease-fire and the CFL from both sides.

10. In view of the continuing deterioration in the situation as of August 16, I gave consideration to a further step in the form of a draft statement about the cease-fire violations which was designed for public release. The draft was handed to the two representatives to be transmitted for the information of their governments. Both governments reacted promptly. The government of India had no objection to the release of the statement but at first wished certain modifications which in part at least I regarded as unacceptable. The government of Pakistan was strongly negative about the statement in general on the grounds that it favored India in that it dealt only with the current cease-fire situation without presenting the political background of the broad issue and thus was lacking in balance, since a cease-fire alone supports the status quo to India's benefit.

11. Weighing carefully all considerations I came to the conclusion that a public statement by the Secretary-General at that time would serve no constructive purpose and might well do more harm than good. My first and primary objective had to be to see the fighting end rather than indicting or denouncing any party for starting and continuing it. I thought it might be helpful to make another quiet effort toward achieving observance of the cease-fire through a new approach to the two governments. Consequently I gave thought to the possibility of sending urgently to the area a personal representative of the Secretary-General for the purpose of meeting and talking with appropriate authorities of the two governments and with General Nimmo; conveying to the governments my very serious concern about the situation; and exploring with them ways and means of preventing any further deterioration in that situation and regaining quiet along the CFL. If such a mission had materialized, I had it in

mind to ask Mr. Ralph J. Bunche, Under-Secretary for Special Political Affairs, to undertake it. The idea was broached by me informally to the two parties on August 20. The subsequent responses of the governments, while not negative, involved in each case conditions which, in my view, would make the mission not feasible at that time and therefore I abandoned it.

12. As a further and immediate step, however, on August 23, I asked General Nimmo to come promptly to the United Nations Headquarters for consultation with me about the situation in Kashmir, and he arrived in New York from Srinagar on August 26. Consideration of other efforts that I might make was then undertaken in the light of the discussion with General Nimmo.

13. General Nimmo's reports on incidents continue to be received as the military observers carry out their investigations of specific actions. The procedure that has been followed is for General Nimmo to submit the reports of the investigations of each incident and the observers' findings fixing blame, to each party, confidentially, and to send copies to me, without any public disclosure. This procedure, which has been found to be in the best interest of the effective functioning of UNMOGIP, is being continued.

14. In view of alarming reports indicating a steady escalation of the fighting in the air and on the ground, involving regular army forces on both sides, I addressed on September 1 an appeal to the Prime Minister of India and the President of Pakistan which was circulated to the Council [S/6647].

15. Restoration of the cease-fire and a return to normal conditions along the CFL can be achieved only under the following conditions:

(*a*) A willingness of both parties to respect the agreement they have entered into;

(*b*) A readiness on the part of the government of Pakistan to take effective steps to prevent crossings of the CFL from the Pakistan side by armed men, whether or not in uniform;

(*c*) Evacuation by each party of positions of the other party now occupied and withdrawal of all armed personnel of each party to its own side of the line, which would include the withdrawal once more of Indian troops from Pakistan positions in the Kargil area;

(*d*) A halt by both parties to the firing across the CFL that has been occurring from both sides in some sectors with artillery and smaller guns;

(*e*) Allowing full freedom of movement and access to the United Nations observers by both parties on both sides of the line.
. . .

---

4. Statement in the Security Council

NEW YORK   SEPTEMBER 6, 1965

I DEEPLY DEPLORE the continuation and broadening of the fighting between India and Pakistan over Kashmir, which has made necessary this meeting of the Council and the resolution just adopted. The situation grows graver by the hour. I accept, therefore, with utmost seriousness the responsibility entrusted to me by this resolution. I shall exert every effort toward the ends we all seek, including a very early visit to the area, in the light of consultations with the two parties.

SOURCE: Security Council Official Records, Twentieth Year, 1238th meeting.

---

5. Statement at Kennedy International Airport

NEW YORK   SEPTEMBER 7, 1965

As I HAVE STATED to the Security Council, I am going to India and Pakistan in connection with the resolution adopted unanimously by the Council yesterday. In it, I was requested to exert every effort to give effect to the Council's resolutions of September 4 and 6, relating to the conflict between India and Pakistan over Kashmir.

Both of these resolutions call for an end to the fighting in which those two countries are now so tragically engaged.

SOURCE: UN Press Release SG/SM/359.

I have accepted this responsibility without hesitation because of the enormity of the threat to the peace of the world in this raging conflict between two of the great countries and peoples of Asia. I have no illusions about this mission: the issues are infinitely complicated and difficult and the situation out there is extremely grave.

Kashmir has posed a baffling problem for the United Nations for seventeen years. I need, then, say only that I will do my very best and hope that my mission will prove helpful. On its completion, I will, of course, report to the Security Council, and will have nothing public to say about it until then.

6. Appeal to the Prime Minister of India and the President of Pakistan

NEW YORK   SEPTEMBER 12, 1965

THE ACUTE SUFFERING of the peoples of India and Pakistan resulting from the existing tragic conflict situation between the two countries, the grave implications of the fighting for the economies of the two countries and for their future relations, and the potential threat which that conflict poses to world peace, afford compelling reasons for pursuing vigorously the search for an enduring solution to the mutual problems of India and Pakistan.

Under prevailing conditions, the first essential step in that search, and an indispensable prerequisite to further efforts, must be an immediate and unconditional cessation of hostilities in the entire area of the conflict. The call for an immediate cease-fire in the Security Council resolutions of September 4 and 6 is in line with the well-established tradition of the United Nations, which invariably requires fighting to cease unconditionally as a necessary prelude to further measures toward the restoration of lasting peace. The immediate objective must be to give effect to these resolutions.

SOURCE: Security Council Official Records, Twentieth Year, Supplement for July, August, and September 1965, document A/6683, pp. 296-297.

In the light of the frank and useful talks I have had in Rawalpindi and New Delhi in the last few days, I now request Your Excellency to order a cease-fire without condition, and a cessation of all hostilities in the entire area of the current conflict between India and Pakistan to take effect on Tuesday, September 14, 1965, at 1800 hours Rawalpindi time, 1830 hours New Delhi time. I have addressed an identical request to Prime Minister Shastri [to President Ayub Khan]. I assume, of course, that all of your commanding officers in the field would be given their orders by you considerably in advance of this time. I have heard in the course of my talks, and understand, the difficulties on both sides to a simple cease-fire, but I make this request to you, nevertheless, because of my strong conviction that it is just and right—for your country and your people as well as for the world at large. I have no doubt that your positive response would win for you the gratitude of the world.

As soon as this request has been acted upon positively, I am confident that the Security Council will wish to provide the necessary assistance in ensuring the supervision of the cease-fire and the withdrawal of all armed personnel on both sides back to the positions held by them before August 5, 1965, as called for by the Security Council resolution of September 6.

I am sure also that the Council will wish to explore, as a matter of urgency, methods for achieving enduring peace between India and Pakistan. On the basis of my talks with Your Excellency, I am confident that, with the well-being of your own country and people at heart as well as the peace of the world, you will find it possible to respond favorably to this appeal to carry out the Security Council resolutions of September 4 and 6. I would ask you to be good enough to communicate your response to me urgently, and in any case, not later than 0730 hours New Delhi time, 0700 hours Rawalpindi time, on Tuesday, September 14, 1965. This message will be held private and confidential until your reply has been received.

In conclusion, may I assure you of my earnest wish to be of continuing assistance in the solution of the outstanding problems and of my warmest good wishes.

7. Identical Messages to the Prime Minister of India and the President of Pakistan

NEW YORK   SEPTEMBER 14, 1965

I HAVE RECEIVED Your Excellency's reply to my message of September 12, in which, in pursuance of the mandate given to me by the Security Council, I requested you to order a cease-fire without condition and a cessation of all hostilities in the entire area of the current conflict. I appreciate the positive attitude toward a cease-fire expressed in your reply, an attitude which has also been expressed by Prime Minister Shastri [President Ayub Khan].

I note, however, that both governments, to their replies to my request for an unconditional cease-fire, have added conditions and qualifications upon which I have no right under the Security Council resolutions to give firm undertakings. These aspects of the replies of the two governments must be referred to the Security Council for its urgent consideration, and they will be so referred immediately by me.

Pending the Security Council consideration of the conditional parts of the replies, I would again ask you in all sincerity, in the interests of the two countries and of world peace, to order a cease-fire and cessation of all hostilities in the entire area of the current conflict.

Since certain delays have transpired, I would set the effective time and date of such cease-fire for 0630 hours New Delhi time, 0600 hours Rawalpindi time on Thursday, September 16, 1965.

I would ask Your Excellency to be good enough to send me an immediate response to this message.

SOURCE: Security Council Official Records, Twentieth Year, Supplement for July, August, and September 1965, document A/6683, pp. 301-302.

8. Identical Messages to the Prime Minister of India and the President of Pakistan

NEW YORK   SEPTEMBER 15, 1965

THE DESPERATE NATURE of the situation brought about by the intensification of the war between India and Pakistan impels me to make a further effort to help your two countries to find a path to peace. The Security Council within a three-day period, from September 4 to 6, has twice called for a cease-fire. I have made two direct appeals to the same end. And a number of governments and heads of state have also made direct appeals to you, as well as offers of good offices, with a view to bringing this tragic conflict to an end.

The replies from both governments to my message of September 12 have shown clearly the desire of both for a cease-fire, but both pose conditions which make the acceptance of a cease-fire very difficult for the other side. For this reason, to my profound regret, it has so far been impossible to obtain a cease-fire as required by the Security Council resolutions of September 4 and 6.

It is worth again considering why such unusual efforts on a world scale have been made to end this conflict. Clearly it is because there is almost universal recognition that war between India and Pakistan can lead only to disaster for the two countries themselves and for the world at large.

I have just completed a round of very frank and open talks with you and President Ayub Khan [and Prime Minister Shastri]. I have implored Your Excellency for the sake of your own people and in the interests of the broader peace, to agree as a first step, to stop the fighting, which in the circumstances of today can solve nothing and lead nowhere but to common disaster. I fully realize the extreme difficulty for both governments of the situation which has led to the present crisis. I do not underestimate for a moment the strength of the

SOURCE: Security Council Official Records, Twentieth Year, Supplement for July, August, and September 1965, document A/6683, pp. 302-304.

feelings involved on both sides or of the intricacy and seriousness of the problems underlying them. I know very well that these problems may take years of patient efforts to tackle and to solve. I have found, however, that both sides have in common a genuine desire for peace, and it must be on that common desire that they must base themselves if they are ever to be able to advance from the present mutually disastrous situation.

It follows that the first step must be to stop fighting and to cease all forms of active hostility on both sides. Since it became clear that my appeal to both sides for a cease-fire has failed to have an effective result, I have been searching for some other approach that might be acceptable to both sides. In my search, I remembered another period, when the eyes of the world were turned in anxiety and fear upon the developments in this part of the world, the period of late 1962. On that occasion, the President of Pakistan and the Prime Minister of India issued, on November 29, 1962, the following joint statement on behalf of their governments:

The President of Pakistan and the Prime Minister of India have agreed that a renewed effort should be made to resolve the outstanding differences between their two countries on Kashmir and other related matters, so as to enable India and Pakistan to live side by side in peace and friendship. In consequence, they have decided to start discussions at an early date with the object of reaching an honorable and equitable settlement. These will be conducted initially at the ministerial level. At the appropriate stage, direct talks will be held between Mr. Nehru and President Ayub.

This was an act of statesmanship which did much to bring calm to the situation in the two countries themselves and to ease the anxieties felt in the world at large. If the subsequent talks did not bring a solution of the basic problems, at least the immediate crisis was weathered and the storm avoided.

I have referred to this statement because I believe that the abatement of the present crisis might now best be achieved by a new effort by the two governments themselves to reach an honorable and equitable settlement. I have so far refrained from making a specific proposal for a meeting of the heads of the two governments at this time, either with or without my presence, because I know well the often expressed reservations of both sides with regard to such a meeting. However, I wish now to suggest, in a situation as grave as or graver than the one which faced both governments in November 1962, that Your Excellency should give urgent consideration to such a meeting.

For my part, I am at your disposal for any role which may assist the two governments in their efforts to stop the fighting and to take the first steps upon the path of mutual accommodation. In this regard, I may remind you of the number of offers you have had from world leaders who are willing to be available to you for any conciliatory assistance you may wish. Indeed, if you seek the ways of peace, most of the world stands ready to assist you.

I am now obliged to return to New York urgently to report to the Security Council, but I hope to receive an early reply to this suggestion, and I wish to make it clear that I am available at any time to assist in efforts to attain the goal of peace and harmony, which, despite all the difficulties, I firmly believe we all have at heart. I have addressed a similar message to President Ayub Khan [to Prime Minister Shastri].

May I be so frank as to say that this appeal is made also because I cannot believe that the leader of either country would wish to bear responsibility for the catastrophe that will visit upon your countries and the world if there is any other reasonable course open to you. What I here propose to Your Excellency clearly is such a course, and I make bold to say that you owe it to your countries and to all the peoples of the world to follow it.

With warmest personal regards and my prayers that the leaders of both countries may find it possible to choose the way of peace.

---

9. *Statement at New Delhi Airport*

NEW DELHI   SEPTEMBER 15, 1965

ON LEAVING the subcontinent for United Nations Headquarters in New York, I wish, first of all, to pay my respects to the governments

SOURCE: UN Press Release SG/SM/363.

and peoples of India and Pakistan and to express my sincere thanks to the two governments for the warm hospitality extended to me and my aides. I also want to restate my deep concern, both as Secretary-General of the United Nations and as a citizen of a sister Asian country, for their present troubles and my desire to assist in the resolution of their problems. I need hardly reiterate the fact that happier future relations between the two nations are vital to the welfare of both countries and the peace of the world.

I am now returning to New York to report to the Security Council. As I stated at the outset of my mission, that will be the first public statement of substance which I shall make on this critical situation. I would, however, like here to say that even if an end to the fighting has not yet been achieved, that is no reason for any cessation of the efforts of all men of goodwill to achieve it. I believe that in the last week the desire of both sides to stop fighting and find a peaceful solution to their problems has become stronger. I find evidence of this in the replies of both governments to my appeal and to that limited extent I am encouraged.

For myself, I shall continue to work toward a cease-fire and a peaceful solution to this tragic problem in the light of the very frank and useful talks I have had in both countries in the last few days. I look forward to the cooperation and support of both governments and of public opinion in this effort and I dare to express the hope and the belief that we may soon see better days.

---

10. *From Report to the Security Council*

NEW YORK   SEPTEMBER 16, 1965

. . .

3. THE FOLLOWING brief account of my own observations of the present situation will serve as a prelude to certain thoughts which

SOURCE: Security Council Official Records, Twentieth Year, Supplement for July, August, and September 1965, document S/6686.

may, I hope, be helpful to the Council in its further consideration of this critical situation. In this tragic war two closely associated nations find themselves locked in a destructive struggle. Regardless of the merits of the case, the present situation is crippling and potentially disastrous for both nations. Each nation feels that it has been abused by the other, and each is convinced that the other has committed aggression. In common they have a feeling of having been let down to some extent by their allies and by the United Nations, whose Members, for the most part, watch in bewilderment and anxiety the spectacle of two sister nations, with both of which many countries have close links, engaged in a fratricidal struggle.

4. Inherent in this situation are all of the phenomena—the aroused emotions, misunderstandings, long pent-up resentments, suspicions, fears, frustrated aspirations, and heightened national feelings—which throughout history have led to needless and futile wars. These are factors which also make it difficult for the leaders on both sides to respond to the unconditional cease-fire appeals of the Security Council. The present war is clearly to the ultimate disadvantage of both nations and can bring no lasting good to either. Both countries have vast economic and social problems which they have been facing courageously and with considerable success. The war will slow down, or even bring to a halt, these vital efforts toward economic and social development.

5. The present crisis has inevitably served to harden even further the previous positions taken by the two governments, since both find it impossible to make concessions under the threat of force. Each has the feeling that only outside support has made it possible for the other to commit what it believes to be aggression.

6. The Security Council is thus faced with a paradoxical situation. It has passed urgently and unanimously two resolutions [209 (1965) and 210 (1965)] requiring an immediate cessation of hostilities. It has authorized me to exert every possible effort to give effect to these resolutions. Before and during my mission, I have received messages of support and offers of assistance from leaders in all parts of the world. Both sides have expressed their desire for a cease-fire and a cessation of hostilities in the entire area of the current conflict. Nevertheless, up to now, I have not succeeded in securing an effective practical measure of compliance by the two sides with the Security Council's resolutions.

7. What further courses of action may be open to the Security Council? In older and less interdependent times, the international community could perhaps have now washed its hands of the matter, leaving the parties to fight it out, heedless of the ruin which such a course must certainly bring to millions of innocent people in both countries. Such a course is inconceivable today. Moreover, it is not only the fate of the peoples of India and Pakistan which is at stake. Both states are linked in a peculiarly intricate way with the mainstream of world affairs. The very unanimity of the Security Council on this matter and the direct appeals from so many governments are indications of how serious a threat this crisis poses to world peace. Quite apart from the well-being of the two nations concerned, there can be little doubt that a real danger to world peace is now imminent.

8. Before advancing some ideas, I feel that I should also state my own views about the role of the United Nations, and of the Security Council in particular, in the present crisis. The Council is faced, as I have said, with a situation of the greatest difficulty and complexity. It has acted with both speed and unanimity. If success has not yet been achieved in securing compliance with the Council's resolutions, that is all the more reason for making further strenuous efforts for a cease-fire as well as for long-term solutions. I feel strongly that in this situation, when the hopes of the world are focused on the Security Council which has the primary responsibility under the Charter for maintaining international peace and security, the Council faces not only an exceptionally difficult task but also a rare opportunity to show that peace can be restored and international harmony promoted by the concerted efforts of the international community. In saying this I am thinking not only of the well-being and future of the governments and peoples of India and Pakistan, but also of the hopes of mankind for a more peaceful world which are centred on the United Nations.

9. With the above impressions in mind, and being convinced—as I stated in my second message to the two heads of government on September 14, and in my statement at the airport in New Delhi on my departure for New York—of the fundamental desire of both parties to end the fighting, I am taking the liberty of expressing the following thoughts in the hope that they may be helpful to the Council and to the two governments themselves in facing the immediate necessity of obtaining an effective cease-fire.

(*a*) The Security Council might now do what it has done once before, and successfully, in another dangerous conflict situation: it could order the two governments concerned, pursuant to Article 40 of the Charter of the United Nations, to desist from further hostile military action and to this end to issue cease-fire orders to their military forces. The Council might also declare that failure by the governments concerned to comply with this order would demonstrate the existence of a breach of the peace within the meaning of Article 39 of the Charter.

(*b*) The Security Council may wish to consider what assistance it might provide in ensuring the observance of the cease-fire.

(*c*) The Security Council resolution of September 6 also calls for a prompt withdrawal of all armed personnel back to the positions held by them before August 5, 1965, and the Council may wish to study means of assisting in the carrying out of this requirement.

(*d*) The Council could request the two heads of government to meet together at the earliest possible time to discuss the current situation and the problems underlying it as a first step in resolving the outstanding differences between their two countries and in reaching an honorable and equitable settlement. Such a meeting might take place in a country friendly and acceptable to both. In this connection, I might draw the attention of the Council to my message of September 15 to Prime Minister Shastri and President Ayub Khan, the text of which is set forth in my preliminary report. The Council could also consider the possibility of creating and making available a small committee to assist in such talks, should its services seem useful and desirable to the two parties.

(*e*) Finally, I may again assure the Council of my availability and of my desire to continue to be of assistance in this matter in any way which may commend itself to the Council and to the two governments.

10. Since the Security Council resolution of September 6 also requested me to take all possible measures to strengthen the United Nations Military Observer Group in India and Pakistan [UNMOGIP], I wish to inform the Council that, as a matter of course, I had consultations with Lieutenant-General R. H. Nimmo, the Chief Military Observer, during my mission. While in the present situation the role of UNMOGIP is obviously even more difficult than usual, I have benefited much from the knowledge and experience of General

Nimmo. I have taken immediate steps to obtain extra transport and communications equipment to facilitate UNMOGIP in its task. I have also made provisional arrangements to increase the number of military observers in UNMOGIP at short notice, should developments make this increase necessary.

11. In its resolution of September 6, the Security Council asked me to keep it informed on the situation in the area. The military situation will be covered in a separate report to be issued shortly.

12. I would not wish to let this occasion pass without expressing my warm appreciation and gratitude to the many statesmen and governments from whom I have received, both before and during my mission to India and Pakistan, messages of support and encouragement as well as practical measures of assistance.

13. Finally, I wish to express my appreciation to the governments of India and Pakistan both for their kindness and hospitality to me and my party and for their frankness and helpfulness in their talks with me. I hope and believe that these talks will eventually contribute to a peaceful solution of the present crisis.

---

11. Statement on His Return from the India-Pakistan Mission

NEW YORK   SEPTEMBER 16, 1965

As I INDICATED on my departure from New York nine days ago, I will have nothing substantive to say about my mission to India and Pakistan until I have reported to the Security Council. My preliminary report has been given to the Council today and I shall be making a further report when the Council meets tomorrow morning.

I would, however, like to say that, even if an end to the fighting has not yet been achieved, that is no reason for any relaxation of all efforts to achieve it. Furthermore, my talks in the past week have convinced me of the basic desire of both sides to stop fighting and find

SOURCE: UN Press Release SG/SM/364.

peaceful solutions to their difficulties. To that extent I am encouraged to continue to work toward a full compliance with the Security Council call for a cease-fire.

The very frank and useful talks I have had in India and Pakistan will be most valuable to me in this continuing effort. The very fact that the Security Council has been able to adopt two unanimous resolutions, on September 4 and 6, leads me to the conviction that it can, this time, contribute effectively toward the peaceful solution of the problem.

As I said on leaving New Delhi, I dare to express the hope and the belief that, on this problem at least, we may soon see better days.

12. From Report on His Initial Steps

NEW YORK   SEPTEMBER 21, 1965

1. THIS REPORT is submitted in pursuance of paragraph 5 of Security Council resolution 211 (1965) of September 20, 1965, which requests me to exert every possible effort to give effect to that resolution and to report to the Council on my efforts.

2. Immediately upon adoption of the resolution in the early morning of September 20, it was transmitted to the governments of the two parties via three channels: by United Nations telegraph facilities, by commercial telegram, and by notes to the two Permanent Missions to the United Nations. The notes were handed to the two representatives at 0205 hours, Eastern United States Daylight Time (EDT), while they were still at the Security Council table. The telegraphic messages were sent from the United Nations at 0250 hours. The message to the Foreign Minister of Pakistan was delivered at 1430 hours, Rawalpindi time (0530 hours EDT), on September 20. The message to the Foreign Minister of India was delivered at 1630 hours, New Delhi time (0700 hours EDT), on the same day.

SOURCE: Security Council Official Records, Twentieth Year, Supplement for July, August, and September 1965, document S/6699.

3. In the afternoon of September 20, I sent identical telegraphic messages to the governments of India and Pakistan through their Permanent Missions to the United Nations as follows:

I refer to resolution 211 (1965), adopted by the Security Council on September 20, 1965, which was immediately transmitted to your government with particular attention called to paragraph 1 of the resolution. In paragraph 5 the Council requests me "to exert every possible effort to give effect" to the resolution and to report to the Council on my efforts. Paragraph 1 of the resolution demands that there be a cease-fire to take effect on Wednesday, September 22, at 0700 hours GMT, and calls upon both governments to issue orders for a cease-fire at that hour and subsequently to withdraw all of their armed personnel to the positions held by them before August 5, 1965.

I am proceeding on the assumption that the governments of both countries will accede to the Security Council's demand, and therefore,

(1) I request you to inform me as quickly as possible that orders have been or will be issued for the cease-fire;

(2) I request your plan and schedule for the indicated withdrawal of your troops;

(3) I have taken steps to determine the availability of a number of military observers to ensure the supervision of the cease-fire and the subsequent withdrawals, and have alerted them to be prepared for early departure;

(4) I have set in motion the necessary logistical arrangements for the maintenance of a team of observers in the field.

I should much appreciate it if this message would be given most urgent consideration.

4. In the above message I have dealt only with operative paragraph 1 of the resolution, because of the pending deadline at 0700 hours GMT on September 22. I am mindful, however, of the explanation given in the Council [1242nd meeting] by the author of the draft resolution that the elements of the resolution are "closely interwoven."

5. On the night of September 20, I received from the Permanent Mission of India to the United Nations a telegram conveying the reply of Prime Minster Shastri to me with regard to the Security Council resolution of September 20. This was not, however, in reply to my telegraphic message of September 20, since the Prime Minster's message had been sent before my message was received. The Prime Minister's message reads as follows:

As already communicated to you in my letter of September 15, 1965 [see S/6683, para. 11], I am willing to order a simple cease-fire and a cessation of hostilities on being informed of Pakistan's agreement to do likewise. To carry into effect such a cease-fire from 7:00 A.M. GMT on Wednesday, September

22, as provided in the Security Council resolution, it would be necessary for me to arrange for the issue of necessary orders to field commanders by 12 noon GMT on September 21. I would, therefore, request you kindly to inform me of Pakistan's agreement to a cease-fire before this hour.

6. On the morning of September 21, I addressed the following message to the Permanent Representative of India to the United Nations:

The Secretary-General of the United Nations presents his compliments to the Permanent Representative of India to the United Nations and has the honor to acknowledge receipt, on the night of Monday, September 20, of the telegram dated September 20, from the delegation of India conveying the reply of Prime Minister Shastri to the Secretary-General with regard to Security Council resolution 211 (1965) of September 20, 1965, relating to the cease-fire which is to take effect from 0700 hours GMT on September 22.

The Secretary-General notes that the Prime Minister of India is 'willing to order a simple cease-fire and a cessation of hostilities on being informed of Pakistan's agreement to do likewise' and also his statement that to carry into effect the cease-fire at the time requested by the Security Council resolution it would be necessary for him to arrange for the issue of the necessary orders to the field commanders by 1200 hours GMT on September 21.

As of 1000 hours EDT on September 21 no word had been received by the Secretary-General from the government of Pakistan concerning its intention with regard to Security Council resolution 211 (1965).

The Secretary-General takes the liberty to call to the attention of the Prime Minister of India that the Security Council resolution in its operative paragraph 1 demands that the cease-fire take effect at the specified time and date. To be fully consistent with that resolution, therefore, each party should instruct its forces to cease fire as of 0700 hours GMT on September 22, without condition, although it would be understandable if in issuing these orders the troops were instructed to fire only if fired upon, that is, if there would be a breach of the cease-fire by the other side.

7. A copy of this note was handed on the same morning to the representative of Pakistan for his information.

8. As of 1900 hours EDT, when this report was sent for reproduction, no word concerning the intention of the government of Pakistan had been received from that government. It is expected that a message concerning the resolution will be brought by the Foreign Minister of Pakistan who is en route to New York and is scheduled to arrive early on the night of September 21. Any message from the government of Pakistan concerning the resolution will be circulated to the members of the Council immediately upon its receipt.

. . .

13. Letter from the Permanent Representative of Pakistan concerning Pakistan's Acceptance of the Cease-fire

NEW YORK   SEPTEMBER 22, 1965

I HAVE THE HONOR to transmit the following message from the President of Pakistan which I have received from Rawalpindi today at 0200 hours, Eastern [United States] Daylight Time (1100 hours Rawalpindi time).

Pakistan considers Security Council resolution 211 (1965) of September 20, as unsatisfactory. However, in the interest of international peace, and in order to enable the Security Council to evolve a self-executing procedure which will lead to an honorable settlement of the root cause of the present conflict, namely, the Jammu and Kashmir dispute, I have issued the following orders to the armed forces of Pakistan:

(1) They will stop fighting as from 1205 hours, West Pakistan time, today;

(2) As from that time they will not fire on enemy forces unless fired upon; provided the Indian Government issues similar orders to its armed forces.

AMJAD ALI
Permanent Representative of
Pakistan to the United Nations

SOURCE: Security Council Official Records, Twentieth Year, Supplement for July, August, and September 1965, document S/6699/Add. 1.

14. *Identical Telegrams to the Prime Minister of India and the President of Pakistan*

NEW YORK   SEPTEMBER 22, 1965

I HAVE THE HONOR to inform Your Excellency that the formal acceptance of the cease-fire demanded in the Security Council resolution of September 20, 1965, has now been confirmed by both governments. The Security Council, at its meeting in the early hours of the morning of September 22, has agreed that the President of the Council should inform the parties that the hour at which the cease-fire is to take effect is 2200 hours GMT on Wednesday, September 22 (September 23 at 0300 hours, West Pakistan time, and 0330 hours, New Delhi time). This postponement is in order to give time for the governments to issue the necessary cease-fire orders to the commanders in the field.

U THANT
Secretary-General of
the United Nations

SOURCE: Ibid., Add. 2.

15. *Identical Telegrams to the Prime Minister of India and the President of Pakistan*

NEW YORK   SEPTEMBER 23, 1965

I HAVE THE HONOR, Excellency, to refer to resolution 211 (1965), adopted by the Security Council on September 20. In view of its acceptance by both parties, the cease-fire became effective at 2200 hours GMT on Wednesday, September 22. This means a cessation of

SOURCE: Ibid.

all hostilities between the armed forces of India and Pakistan and that any hostile military action by either side against the other henceforth would constitute a breach of the cease-fire. I am confident that both sides will scrupulously observe the cease-fire to which they have agreed.

You will permit me, I am sure, to express to you my personal gratification at the action on your part which has made this cease-fire possible.

The resolution of September 20, as also the resolutions of September 4 and 6 [209 (1965) and 210 (1965)], calls upon the parties to withdraw all armed personnel to the positions held by them before August 5, 1965, that is to say, behind the international borders and the Kashmir cease-fire line. As indicated in my message of September 20 to your permanent representative to the United Nations [S/6999, para. 3], it is my duty to inform you that I expect to receive from you at a very early date your plan and schedule for the required withdrawal of any of your troops that are now on the wrong side of these lines.

In pursuance of operative paragraph 2 of the resolution of September 20, as announced in my report of September 21 to the Security Council [S/6999], I have been taking steps to provide the necessary assistance to ensure the supervision of the cease-fire and the withdrawal behind the lines of all armed personnel. In this connection, I have dispatched a number of military observers to the area, and more will soon be coming, to provide the necessary assistance in the discharge of this supervisory function. I am confident that you will instruct your appropriate officers and authorities to afford full cooperation and assistance to these United Nations personnel. Because of the difference in origin of the two operations, I am separating the supervision of the cease-fire and the withdrawals in areas outside of Kashmir from United Nations Military Observer Group in India and Pakistan (UNMOGIP), the existing cease-fire operation in Kashmir. The team of observers operating outside of Kashmir will be known as the United Nations India-Pakistan Observation Mission and will be directed by an officer of appropriate rank and experience. Pending the appointment of such an officer, the new operation will be under the direction of Lieutenant-General Robert H. Nimmo, the Chief Military Observer of UNMOGIP. The two operations, however, will be closely coordinated, administratively and operationally.

With regard to operative paragraph 4 of the resolution of September 20, I shall keep the Council fully informed about the implementation of the cease-fire and withdrawal provisions, it being for the Council itself then to determine its next steps.

U THANT
Secretary-General of
the United Nations

16. From Report to the Security Council

NEW YORK   NOVEMBER 25, 1965

1. THIS REPORT is submitted in pursuance of paragraph 3 of Security Council resolution 215 (1965) of November 5, 1965, in which the Secretary-General is requested to report within three weeks of that date on the progress achieved with regard to carrying out the withdrawals called for by the Security Council.

2. I am now able to report that after helpful consultations with both parties, I have appointed as my representative Brigadier-General Tulio Marambio of Chile, who is to meet with representatives of India and Pakistan for the purpose of formulating an agreed plan and schedule for the withdrawals, as envisaged in paragraph 3 of resolution 215 (1965). I am advised by both parties that they will receive and cooperate with General Marambio.

3. General Marambio, who is fifty-four years of age, is Director of the War Academy in Chile.

4. General Marambio will be proceeding to the two capitals shortly with the objective of arranging an early meeting at a mutually agreed place with the representatives to be designated by India and Pakistan in order to formulate an agreed plan and schedule for the mutual withdrawals, within an agreed time-limit.

. . .

SOURCE: Security Council Official Records, Twentieth Year, Supplement for October, November, and December 1965, document S/6719/Add. 4.

ADMISSION OF NEW MEMBERS

THE ADMISSION of Gambia, Singapore, and Maldive Islands to the United Nations at the twentieth session of the General Assembly came at a time when voices were being raised increasingly in the United States and elsewhere against the growing number of so-called mini-states being accepted for United Nations membership. U Thant had spoken out a number of times in favor of universal membership and had vigorously opposed efforts to introduce weighted voting in the Assembly. In the two statements below, the Secretary-General came to the defense of small states. Such states, he said, are important to the United Nations and the United Nations is important to them.

1. From Statement at Flag-raising Ceremony for Gambia and Singapore

NEW YORK   SEPTEMBER 22, 1965

. . . THE ADMISSION of a new Member into the United Nations is an important step both in the development of that new Member state and in the development of the United Nations itself; and, consequently, it is an important step in the growth of the world as a community of nations. The fact that all three new Members admitted on the opening day of the twentieth session are small states emphasizes the unique significance of the United Nations as the framework within which a small state may develop its own distinctive way of life on a basis of full equality with larger and more powerful states.

The increase in the number of small states in the United Nations reflects the feeling of the small states that they have a vital stake in the strengthening of the United Nations as an instrument for the maintenance of international peace and security, and for the develop-

SOURCE: UN Press Release SG/SM/369.

ment of international cooperation in the economic, social, cultural, and humanitarian spheres of life. It is to the direct interest of the small states to help the United Nations develop as a center for harmonizing the actions of nations in the attainment of their common ends.

. . .

2. From Statement at Flag-raising Ceremony for Maldive Islands

NEW YORK   OCTOBER 12, 1965

. . . THE STATE of the Maldive Islands is surely among the smallest of the Members of the United Nations, in terms of both area and population. This does not, however, affect in any way the significance of this occasion. On the contrary, the admission of this small state recalls once again the fact that the strength of the United Nations resides not exclusively in its commanding the confidence of its large or powerful Members, but equally in the support of its smaller and less powerful Members. And, in turn, the fact that the smaller states need the United Nations to safeguard and make effective their independence and to register their equality in this interdependent world makes it necessary for the great and powerful states to participate in the activities of the United Nations and to support its development.

. . .

SOURCE: UN Press Release SG/SM/379.

Statement of Welcome to Pope Paul VI

NEW YORK   OCTOBER 4, 1965

As MENTIONED EARLIER, U Thant maintained close and friendly relations with both Pope John XXIII and Pope Paul VI. The high spot, of course, was the visit of Pope Paul to United Nations Headquarters on October 4, 1965, and his address to the General Assembly. The visit was Thant's idea and was regarded by his associates as a great personal achievement as well as a badly needed lift for the Organization at a time when its prestige was on the decline. In his statement of welcome, reproduced below, the Secretary-General tells how the idea for the invitation was born, many months before the visit.

IT IS THE CAUSE of peace which brings His Holiness into our midst. It was the cause of peace—universal peace, for all men on earth, without distinction as to race, religion, nationality, or political belief—which led me, many months ago, to explore with His Holiness the possibility of his being present at a meeting of the General Assembly such as this, so that he might join his efforts for peace to those of the representatives of the states Members of the United Nations.

May I briefly recall the origins of this journey which is now reaching its felicitous climax. On December 4 last, in Bombay, His Holiness voiced a special appeal which moved me and many others deeply, as reflecting the aspirations of mankind and as being closely in keeping with the purposes and objectives of the United Nations— an appeal for an end to the armaments race and for the alleviation of human suffering—an appeal to all the governments of the world to undertake, in the words of His Holiness, a "peaceful battle against the sufferings of their less fortunate brothers."

Shortly afterward, on January 15, 1965, His Holiness entrusted to me, as Secretary-General of the United Nations, the text of his appeal. I accepted it, as I stated then, as an invaluable source of

SOURCE: General Assembly Official Records, Twentieth Session, 1347th plenary meeting.

inspiration for me and for the Organization which I serve. That appeal, and the desire of His Holiness to place it at the service of the United Nations, prompted me, with the full support of the then President of the General Assembly, to seek the agreement of His Holiness to appear before, and address, the General Assembly of the United Nations.

That historic occasion has now arrived. It is taking place at a time when there is a renewal of confidence in our Organization. It is a time also of grave dangers to the peace of the world. In adding my words of welcome to those of the President of the General Assembly, and in expressing my deep gratitude to His Holiness, I do so in the conviction that all of us who work for the purposes of the United Nations will draw from his presence here, now and long afterward, inspiration for our continued struggle to attain those goals of peace and human well-being which are also the goals His Holiness so devotedly believes to be within our reach.

Introduction to the Twentieth Annual Report

NEW YORK SEPTEMBER 20, 1965

THE INTRODUCTION to the twentieth Annual Report, issued by U Thant on the eve of the 1965 General Assembly opening, was the most comprehensive of the four submitted by him since he took office. Reference has already been made to various parts of the report elsewhere in this volume, in connection with specific subjects. It was a troubled year and a busy one for the Secretary-General. In addition to the perennial financial crisis and the Article 19 controversy, he was preoccupied with the Vietnam war, the internal strife in the Dominican Republic, the flare-up of the long-standing conflict between India and Pakistan over Jammu and Kashmir, and the continuing United Nations operation in Cyprus. The Secretary-General reviewed these problems, and many others. He also called attention to several questions which in his opinion required study by the Member states. One was the role of the United Nations and regional organizations in the field of peace-keeping and the possibility of conflicting actions in cases where both were involved. This question was raised by the dual intervention of the United Nations and the Organization of American States in the Dominican Republic. Another was the tendency to dispatch a peace-keeping mission to a trouble area and leave it there indefinitely without pursuing a settlement of the underlying conflict. He mentioned especially the missions in Cyprus, the Middle East, and Kashmir. Member states, he said, would do well to study the possibility of strengthening the machinery for peace-making (good offices, mediation, conciliation, arbitration, etc.) to operate parallel to United Nations peace-keeping missions.

I

DURING THE PERIOD of approximately ten months since the introduction to my last annual report on the work of the Organization was published in November 1964, there have been many developments on the international scene, which have inevitably had their repercussions on the United Nations. The postponements of the opening date of the nineteenth session of the General Assembly, and its inability,

SOURCE: General Assembly Official Records, Twentieth Session, Supplement No. 1A (A/6001/Add. 1).

when it met, to follow the normal rules of procedure on account of the controversy over the applicability of Article 19 of the Charter, constituted the prime cause of concern. When the Assembly recessed on February 18, 1965, a mood of frustration and dissatisfaction prevailed. There was no disputing the damage which had been done to the effectiveness and dignity of the United Nations. Nevertheless, as I remarked at the time, the episode had its heartening aspect in the loyal and unceasing efforts of the Member states to preserve their Organization by finding a solution.

Another regrettable development of direct concern to the United Nations was the announcement by Indonesia of its decision to withdraw from the Organization as from January 1, 1965. Inevitably there were comparisons with the history of the League of Nations, but subsequent events have shown that some of those gloomy prognostications reflected undue pessimism. I sincerely hope that Indonesia's withdrawal from the United Nations is only a temporary phase and that, before long, Indonesia will find that its long-term interests can best be served by resuming its membership and by participating fully in the Organization's constructive activities.

The desire of the Members to resolve the crisis in which the Organization had found itself was reflected in the decision of the General Assembly, before it recessed in February, to establish the Special Committee on Peace-keeping Operations with the task of conducting a comprehensive review of the question of peace-keeping operations in all their aspects, including ways of overcoming the financial difficulties of the Organization. During the subsequent months, strenuous efforts were made in the Special Committee to find at least an interim solution to the constitutional and financial problems covered by its terms of reference. That these efforts did not altogether succeed before June 15, by which date the Committee was due to submit a report to the General Assembly, was only an indication of the serious differences of interpretation and opinion which continued to prevail among the Member states. In the circumstances, it was a substantial achievement that the Committee was able to reach a consensus by which the members agreed that the United Nations should be strengthened through a cooperative effort and that the General Assembly, when it reconvened, must conduct its work normally, according to its rules of procedure.

The Special Committee resumed its work in mid-August and was able on August 31 to reach a further consensus which unquestionably represented considerable progress and gave rise to a new feeling of encouragement and hope. The consensus was as follows:

(a) That the General Assembly will carry on its work normally in accordance with its rules of procedure;

(b) That the question of the applicability of Article 19 of the Charter will not be raised with regard to the United Nations Emergency Force and the United Nations Operation in the Congo;

(c) That the financial difficulties of the Organization should be solved through voluntary contributions by Member states, with the highly developed countries making substantial contributions.

A tribute is due to the patient and constructive work of the Committee and to the cooperation of all delegations, which made this result possible. Much, of course, remains to be done. The actual financial situation of the Organization, to which I refer elsewhere in this introduction, remains precarious at the time of writing. In addition, I wish to address an appeal to all Member states to cooperate with the Special Committee in completing its work and finalizing its recommendations on all points covered by its terms of reference. In my view it is essential for the successful conduct of peace-keeping operations in the future that we should have well-established ground rules and guidelines to govern them. This is particularly true of the financing of peace-keeping operations. As I have pointed out in connection with the United Nations Force in Cyprus, the policy of piecemeal extension of peace-keeping operations, to be financed by voluntary contributions which may or may not be forthcoming, makes their efficient planning and economical running almost impossible. I hope that this problem will receive some attention at the twentieth session of the General Assembly and that the discussions on the subject may assist the Special Committee on Peace-keeping Operations in evolving and formulating its own recommendations on this urgent question.

The difficulties of the Organization proper were overshadowed through this period by adverse developments in international relationships, to which I shall make further reference in the pages that follow. Yet, although a review of the last ten months may leave behind it a general feeling of lack of achievement, much constructive work, in the whole range of activities from peace-keeping operations to technical assistance, has been carried out during the period. For example, the United Nations Force in Cyprus has made a significant contribution to the maintenance of peace in the area and to bringing quiet to Cyprus, even though the political problems remain unsolved. There have been accomplishments of particular satisfaction in such other fields as economic and social development and decolonization. Our work in the economic and social field has, in my view, been accurately assessed by the Administrative Committee on Coordination in the report on its meeting in Vienna in the last week of April:

As this session of the Administrative Committee on Coordination is being held during International Cooperation Year, which marks the middle of the United Nations Development Decade, the members of the Administrative Committee on Coordination deem it fit, on this occasion, to place particular emphasis on the steady progress achieved in the building of peace through cooperative action in the economic, social, and cultural fields and to lay stress on the indisputable value of the results to which this international cooperation has already led.

They are unanimously convinced that such cooperation, which the agencies of the United Nations system are empowered and equipped to promote and to assist, and the essentially technical character of which is a prerequisite for its success, must be further considerably strengthened and intensified, so as to respond more adequately to the increasing needs of the developing countries and to the promotion of peace and progress in the world as a whole.

I must add that it is the feeling of the Executive Heads of all the organizations that a pre-condition for the continued success of economic, social, and cultural cooperation on an international plane is the preservation to the greatest possible extent of the essentially technical character of such action. I have previously had occasion to observe that it would be a matter for regret on the part of the entire international community if important meetings dealing with these questions, and depending for their success on the vital element of international cooperation, were to fail to yield solid results because of the introduction of highly contentious political issues into the discussions and deliberations. The admitted difficulty of drawing a clear line between what is political and what is not must not be allowed to distract the Member states from their specific duty to respect the Charter, the conventions, and the constitutional procedures of the agency concerned and from their general obligation to safeguard, in the common interest, the future of international order itself.

A development of note in recent years is an increasing movement toward seeking solutions to international problems within the United Nations by way of consensus rather than by reliance upon majority votes. Thus, for example, detailed procedures of conciliation have been developed for the United Nations Conference on Trade and Development. There has also been a growing interest in methods of peaceful settlement of international disputes, and there are at least three items on the provisional agenda of the twentieth session of the General Assembly which may lead to a comprehensive review of the whole question of pacific settlement, both through the United Nations and through general diplomacy.

Alongside these developments, I have noted, there has been a most welcome trend—on the part, in particular, of newly independent African states—to accept, often without extensive reservations, the compulsory jurisdiction of the International Court of Justice. I very much hope that this trend will be continued, and that states will also have more frequent recourse to the Court as a means of settling their legal disputes. I would like to take this opportunity to draw attention once more to the resolution adopted by the General Assembly in 1947 calling upon Member states to accept the compulsory jurisdiction of the Court under Article 36, paragraph 2, of its Statute. The Court has already established that it merits universal confidence, and if real progress is to be made in the peaceful settlement of disputes, I feel that the Court should increasingly come to play the vital role envisioned for it in the Charter as the principal judicial organ of the United Nations.

A different aspect of the question of the extent of participation by countries in organized international activities is raised by the recent phenomenon of the emergence of exceptionally small new states. Their limited size and resources can pose a difficult problem as to the role they should try to play in international life. In one or two cases, such states have decided to restrict their membership to one or more of the specialized agencies, so that they may at any rate receive the fullest possible assistance from the United Nations system in advancing their economic and social development. I believe that the time has come when Member states may wish to examine more closely the criteria for the admission of new Members in the light of the long-term implications of present trends.

One of the important events of 1965 was the celebration of the twentieth anniversary of the United Nations in San Francisco. Our thanks are due to the City of San Francisco, to its Mayor, and to its distinguished citizens for their dedication to the United Nations, for the fitting way in which they arranged the celebration, and for their heartwarming hospitality. The occasion provided an appropriate and timely reminder both of the achievements of the international community and of the distance that still lies between us and the goals we set ourselves two decades ago.

II

The deterioration in the international situation generally, as well as the inability of the nineteenth session of the General Assembly to function normally, have made an adverse impact in the field of disarmament. No substantial progress has been achieved since my last report, and the high hopes engendered by the agreements reached in 1963 have been greatly diminished.

Yet the danger to world peace looms larger all the time. The past year has been marked by increasing concern over the evident intensification and extension of the nuclear arms race. The nuclear tests conducted by the People's Republic of China have raised the number of nuclear powers to five. Other nations possess or are close to possessing a nuclear capacity which any worsening of global or regional relations may tempt or force them to explore. There is real reason for anxiety that, unless steps are taken quickly to halt the proliferation of nuclear powers and weapons, the nations of the world may within a very few years find the problem of proliferation beyond control. A world containing ten, fifteen, and perhaps even more nuclear powers could well be a world confronting itself finally with the question of its survival.

A recognition of the sheer necessity of finding some way to cope with the dangers of the arms race and of nuclear proliferation has at least led to a renewal of disarmament discussions and negotiations. The Disarmament Commission, composed of all the Members of the United Nations, undertook a comprehensive review of the whole range of disarmament problems and reached some significant decisions. One resolution welcomed the proposal for a world disarmament conference and recommended that the General Assembly should consider the proposal at its next session. A second resolution specifically recommended that the Conference of the Eighteen-

Nation Committee on Disarmament should give priority to agreement on preventing the proliferation of nuclear weapons and extending the partial test-ban treaty to underground tests. The Commission indicated that in seeking new approaches to disarmament, all States, large and small, nuclear and non-nuclear, could make a contribution. It also recognized that partial measures and limited steps offered the best prospects for early agreement. The two measures singled out for urgent action were viewed as the first concrete steps necessary to halt the further expansion of the nuclear arms race.

Detailed and expert negotiations were taken up in the Conference of the Eighteen-Nation Committee, which resumed its work at the end of July and is still in session at the time of writing. The very resumption of the Conference was of political importance in a period of increasing international tensions. The continuation of negotiations should provide opportunities to narrow the gap between opposing positions and to seek new areas of agreement on disarmament itself. At the same time, however, in disarmament as in other political questions, concessions are needed from all sides if agreements are to be reached. It is a matter not only for regret but also for grave concern that there is not yet sufficient evidence of a readiness to make such concessions or accommodations in the form either of new proposals or of acceptable modifications of old ones.

The prevention of the further proliferation of nuclear weapons is the most urgent question of the present time and should remain at the very top of the disarmament agenda. It is of prime importance that both the nuclear and non-nuclear powers give first priority to this problem and devote their concentrated and unceasing attention to solving it. The emergence of additional nuclear powers threatens to have a contagious and cumulative effect, which may produce its own chain reaction. Both the nuclear and non-nuclear powers must exercise the highest degree of responsibility and restraint to prevent that from happening.

One hopeful development that indicates a practical recognition of this need for responsibility and restraint is to be found in the efforts of States of Latin America. Since the adoption of General Assembly resolution 1911 (XVIII) of November 27, 1963, on the denuclearization of Latin America, they have made good progress toward an agreement to keep their territories free of nuclear weapons. Success in their endeavors will not only be an achievement of great benefit to the States of Latin America, militarily, politically, economically, and socially; it can, indeed, be of great importance to the world at large. It may well have a catalytic effect on other initiatives for denucleariza-tion, for preventing the further spread of nuclear weapons, and for other measures of disarmament.

The year 1965 marks not only the twentieth anniversary of the founding of the United Nations; it signals also the twentieth anniver-sary of the explosion of the first atomic bomb. It is not by the force of nature but by his own will that man finds himself engaged in a race between building a better world and destroying an imperfect one. And it is in the power of man alone to determine how that race will end. A growing awareness that the decisive moment may be close should lead to a more insistent demand, and a more persistent search, for new ideas and new methods for bringing about disarmament and lasting peace. The search for solutions can go on simultaneously in many ways—multilaterally and bilaterally, on a universal basis and at regional levels. It must go on.

III

There has been some further progress in the area of international cooperation in the peaceful uses of outer space. Several international programs, such as the International Year of the Quiet Sun, the International Indian Ocean Expedition, the World Magnetic Survey and others, have developed successfully during the period.

On the basis of unanimous opinion within the Committee on the Peaceful Uses of Outer Space, it was decided that the Scientific and Technical Sub-Committee need not meet in 1965, but that the Com-mittee, with the assistance of the Secretariat, should continue to fulfill the objectives in the field of science and technology which were outlined in its previous report. In response to the Committee's request, the Secretariat has been compiling information for a report on the possibility of establishing a civil worldwide navigational satel-lite system. The Secretariat has also continued to compile informa-tion on facilities for education and training in basic subjects related to the peaceful uses of outer space, as well as to compile reviews of national and cooperative international space activities on the basis of information voluntarily submitted by Member states. These compila-tions are to be published every other year.

The Secretariat has continued to receive from Member states literature on the goals, tools, applications, and results of space technology. The Member states have been given information on various space conferences and symposia open to their scientists. Consultations have proceeded with the specialized agencies and the Committee on Space Research on the question of the possible need for material which would enhance popular understanding of space activities and also on the question of the distribution of technical literature.

It is now to be hoped that further steps in international cooperation in this field may result from the decision, to which I referred in the introduction to the last annual report, by the Committee on the Peaceful Uses of Outer Space to establish a working group of the whole to examine the desirability, organization, and objectives of an international conference or meeting to be held in 1967 on the exploration and peaceful uses of outer space. The working group, which is due to meet in September, will report to the Committee at its next session.

The Committee's Legal Sub-Committee has meanwhile continued to work on the drafting of the international agreements on assistance to and return of astronauts and space vehicles and on liability for damage caused by objects launched into space. The completion of the two agreements would contribute substantially to the development of the law of outer space, and it is to be hoped that the Committee will address itself to further subjects in respect of which legal rules are essential.

Taking this question as a whole, we can claim that there has been very significant progress in the past few years in the United Nations in seeking to ensure that the exploration and use of outer space would be confined to peaceful purposes. General Assembly resolution 1884 (XVIII) of October 17, 1963, which endorsed and broadened the understanding reached between the United States of America and the Union of Soviet Socialist Republics to refrain from stationing in outer space any objects carrying nuclear weapons or other weapons of mass destruction, and resolution 1962 (XVIII) of December 13, 1963, containing the Declaration of Legal Principles Governing the Activities of States in the Exploration and Use of Outer Space, were very important steps. They helped significantly to meet the increasingly insistent demand for ensuring that outer space should be used exclusively for peaceful purposes. I had myself expressed the hope on the occasion of the adoption of resolution 1884 (XVIII), that its implementation should assist in placing necessary restrictions on the military uses of scientific and technological developments. I should like once again to express my sincere hope that the positive trend that has developed in the United Nations in the peaceful uses of outer space will not be halted or reversed.

IV

Some consolation may be drawn from the fact that neither the sharpening of international political problems nor the financial crisis within the United Nations seriously affected the momentum of existing international action in the economic and social fields. Yet here, too, a disturbing shadow has been cast, in the form of a worsening of the relative economic position of the developing countries. Since my last report there has been a deterioration in market conditions for exports from those countries, after improvements which proved short-lived. The year 1965 opened with export prices at a lower level than twelve months previously, and still falling. Once again, therefore, it has to be recorded that the terms of trade are moving against the developing countries. The danger of this trend in world trade is accentuated by problems of external financial imbalance in leading industrial countries, causing them to adopt restrictive measures and to hold back on programs of development assistance.

This situation gives added significance to the results of the first United Nations Conference on Trade and Development and to the action which has followed it. The work started by the Geneva Conference was carried an important step further when the General Assembly gave its unanimous approval to the establishment of the new institutional machinery of the Conference. The machinery is endowed with an instrument that is new to the United Nations system—a mechanism consisting of special procedures with which to formularize conciliation between various interests before voting takes place. The primary objective of these procedures is to maintain the fundamental principle of equality of vote while at the same time taking into account the fact that specific recommendations for action may substantially affect the economic and financial interests of particular countries. Recommendations which do not reflect the common will of all parties concerned run a grave risk of remaining without effect on national policies, since they cannot be assured of the positive support and cooperation of the various Governments to which they are addressed. The conciliation mechanism, which will no doubt give a new dimension to international cooperation within the United Nations by recognizing the different requirements of the contemporary world, will represent an important tool in the continuing process of adjustment through negotiation and mutual accommodation. It is equally important, however, that we should be aware that this mechanism is only part of what is needed to arrive at satisfactory and practical agreements. The success of the new procedure must depend largely on the will to arrive at solutions.

The main objective during the past year has been the administrative and organizational consolidation of the new institutional machinery. A solid foundation for future work has now been established. The first session of the Trade and Development Board established four specific committees, all of which will bear important responsibilities and will become centers for the formulation of policies in their respective fields, with an appropriate institutional basis. They will thus be capable of contributing efficiently and expeditiously to the implementation of the work program of the Conference.

Despite the progress made in the organizational and administrative field, however, the year has not fulfilled the hopes generated in developing countries by the agreements, reached in Geneva. Many of the Geneva recommendations, adopted either unanimously or by large majorities, still remain to be implemented. That the implementation of these recommendations is necessary and that the time for it is ripe is, I believe, hardly open to question. Such action would not only assist economic development in the developing regions and thus strengthen the world's economy, but it would also have a positive and far-reaching effect on the international climate in general. The new trade machinery is not just another forum for exerting pressure. It should be a center for formulating new policies and for achieving specific solutions of trade problems. More specifically, it is an indispensable instrument for the adoption, by both developed and developing countries, of new approaches to international economic problems within the context of a new awareness of the needs of developing countries. I am confident that answers to those problems will be found if all parties continue to show the same patience and the same spirit of conciliation they have shown during this first year of the United Nations Conference on Trade and Development.

Aside from trade, this year of political and financial difficulties has been one of intensified activity in all sectors of the economic and social field. The fact that twenty years after the signing of the Charter we find ourselves at the midpoint of the United Nations Development Decade, as well as the realization that, so far, progress toward the objectives of the Decade has been disappointingly slow, has led Member states to look to the United Nations for greater assistance in their efforts to achieve more rapid progress and to sharpen and multiply the tools available to the Organization for this purpose. This is clear from the recent records of the Economic and Social Council and its subsidiary bodies.

Among the problems to which a new emphasis has been given are the relationship of population growth to development and the phenomenon of migration toward cities. Research programs have been launched to give Governments more insight into these problems and into the ways of solving them. There is also a greater awareness of the importance of social policies—of the role of human resources and factors, especially those represented by the younger generation, in the shaping of a better life for all. In the economic field, United Nations activities aimed at fostering industrial development are gaining a new momentum, and there has been a strengthening of the Secretariat in this area. Throughout the economic and social field, work has been stimulated by the energy with which the Advisory Committee on Science and Technology of the Economic and Social Council has set about its task.

Particularly noteworthy is the increasing attention given to development planning and, with it, the desire of the growing number of governments which resort to it to obtain through the United Nations a better knowledge of the methods which can help them to organize their development efforts in the most coherent and purposeful manner. I regard this as significant and promising, and I welcome the support given by the Economic and Social Council to the idea of having a group of high-level experts assist the Secretariat in this field.

More research has been undertaken over a broader range of problems and more assistance is being provided to governments by the Organization through its technical assistance programs and through its work as an executing agency of the Special Fund. The latter is entrusting to the United Nations an increasing number of projects, especially in the area of the development of natural resources.

The ability of the Organization to provide guidance to those shaping national development policies and to promote international cooperation for narrowing the gap between rich and poor countries has owed much, and more this year than in the past, to the dynamism of the regional economic commissions. This is reflected in the increased number of meetings held and projects carried out at the regional level. Together with the creation of the United Nations Institute for Training and Research and the steps taken to continue and enlarge the World Food Programme, the launching of the African Development Bank and the measures aimed at the establishment of an Asian Development Bank must be considered as major advances on the institutional front.

The Economic and Social Council has reaffirmed the objectives of the United Nations Development Decade and stressed the importance of increasing the quantity and quality of international aid and cooperation. It is to be hoped that the interest shown in better planning at the national level will lead to those objectives being translated into a coherent set of interrelated goals and targets providing a framework for the development efforts of the world community over the next five or ten years, as well as a better means of measuring the progress achieved. This should enhance our ability, in the years to come, to improve upon the performance in the first half of the United Nations Development Decade, during which shocking disparities in conditions and levels of living have persisted.

The two large United Nations development assistance programs supported by voluntary contributions—the Expanded Programme of Technical Assistance and the Special Fund—have had another year of vigorous activity. I may mention that in July 1965 the Expanded Programme observed a notable anniversary by completing its first fifteen years of operation. In a special review marking the occasion, the Executive Chairman of the Technical Assistance Board recalled that assistance had been given to more than 120 developing countries. This assistance took the form of 32,000 man-years of advice and the award of 31,700 fellowships for study abroad, as well as seminars and training courses and the provision of equipment for demonstration, training, and investigation purposes. To make these services and facilities available, a total of almost $500 million was spent by the participating organizations in the fifteen years, all of it derived from the voluntary contributions of governments. I am sure that those Governments will share with the organizations a justifiable feeling of satisfaction, indeed of pride, in the accomplishments of this unprecedented enterprise, which has amply demonstrated both the feasibility and the value of concerted action in meeting some of the most pressing needs of the developing countries in a disinterested manner free from political considerations.

In the current Expanded Programme, field operations are continuing at the record level of $101 million for the biennium 1965–1966. A new element in the Programme is the use of its funds to assign to several countries a small number of experts with formally defined operational and executive responsibilities, pursuant to a decision made by the Economic and Social Council in 1964. The greater part of the Programme, however, consists as before of the supply of advisory experts, consultants, instructors, and fellowships. Such work has continued in a number of cases to open the way to larger projects qualifying for support from the Special Fund; at the same time, there has been no slackening of the demand by Governments for the great range of services which the Expanded Programme is uniquely suited to provide. On the whole, greater attention has been given by Governments to gearing their demands to development needs and to the use of the facilities of the Programme as a fully integrated element of their development strategy. There remains no doubt that the scale of assistance could substantially and usefully be increased.

During 1965 the Special Fund also set a new pace in its development assistance activities. The Governing Council approved a record level of 111 new projects with an overall cost of $265.5 million. This brought the total program to 522 projects costing $1,151 million, 58 percent of which is being provided by the recipient Governments and the remainder by the Fund. There was also an impressive growth in the level of operations: disbursements of Special Fund resources are expected to rise to between $70 million and $75 million in 1965, compared with $48.7 million in 1964. Particular credit for this large increase in field work is due to the ability of the executing agencies to gear themselves to carry out operational activity on an entirely new scale.

The number of Special Fund-assisted pre-investment projects

reaching completion also rose steeply. With projects averaging four years in duration, field work will have been completed on some forty of them in 1965 compared with forty-two over the previous five years. These and other projects at present in operation have already yielded a harvest of significant returns. Surveys and feasibility studies have provided much useful data on natural resources and industrial and agricultural potentialities in scores of developing countries. Projects supporting applied research have brought science and technology to bear on economic growth in hundreds of practical ways, and advanced education and technical training have continued apace.

Some of these results can be given in statistical terms, and these are impressive and gratifying. By July 1, 1965, nineteen projects had directly or indirectly led to the investment of over $1,026 million in domestic and external capital. Over 70,000 senior and middle-level engineers, technicians, instructors, managers, supervisors, and administrators had been trained under Special Fund auspices. Besides building up supplies of knowledge, capital, and manpower, the Fund-assisted projects had helped to establish or strengthen, in all developing regions, vital training, research, planning, and service institutions from which future growth will spring. Still greater results from this pre-investment assistance may be confidently forecast as the program continues to expand in scope and effectiveness.

Increased resources are needed by both the Expanded Programme and the Special Fund if they are to meet a larger proportion of the rising requests for their services. That is why I have urged that the General Assembly raise to $200 million the annual target for the two programs together. I am happy to note that this suggestion has received the support of a number of governments. It is my hope, moreover, that the Assembly will shortly be able to consider and expeditiously approve the Economic and Social Council's proposals for combining the Expanded Programme and the Special Fund in a new United Nations Development Programme. I have expressed the view on other occasions that this consolidation has now become a matter of some urgency; it should help to rationalize the efforts and considerably to strengthen the capacity of the United Nations family of organizations to help meet the urgent needs of the developing countries for accelerated economic and social advance in the second half of the United Nations Development Decade.

I have mentioned earlier that the first half of the Development

Decade has seen an awareness of the necessity to invest more in human resources in order to achieve economic growth and social progress. This investment must logically begin with the child. The phenomenon of children growing to adulthood unhealthy, uneducated, and unprepared for the demands of life can only retard progress. The grave problems facing children in developing countries are still, however, insufficiently recognized. It is virtually impossible for countries with a very low national income to provide all the services necessary to protect the child through his vulnerable years and prepare him for life in an era of change. There is a need for far greater outside resources specifically directed to helping developing countries meet the needs of the rising generation.

In ensuring a useful and productive future for children and youth in developing societies, an essential task accordingly falls to the United Nations Children's Fund: but the requests for aid from the Fund are outpacing its resources. The current annual expenditures of about $35 million must be spread over 118 countries and territories for programs in aid of children in the fields of health, nutrition, education, vocational training, and social services. These programs are cooperative ventures with the technical agencies of the United Nations family. Because of the need to meet continuing projects, less than 10 percent of the program allocations made by the Executive Board of the Fund in June 1965 could be devoted to new projects. While aid from the Fund continues to be highly effective in many areas, it clearly does not yet have sufficient resources to carry out fully its vital role in the Development Decade.

V

I think it is appropriate to recall that, despite difficulties within the membership over the financing of United Nations peace-keeping operations, all of the actual operations of this nature have been maintained according to plan. Peace-keeping action was in fact extended, in a limited form, by the mission undertaken by the United Nations in the Dominican Republic. In all cases these operations continued to vindicate the importance which most Member states attach to the valuable function which the United Nations is capable of carrying out in situations which are by common consent judged dangerous to international peace.

Among the present United Nations peace-keeping operations, that in Cyprus continues to be a major concern of the Organization. The duration of the United Nations Force in Cyprus, which was established on March 27, 1964, for three months, has repeatedly been extended under its original mandate, the last time for a period of six months ending on December 27, 1965.

The repeated extension of the Force by the Security Council, involving the agreement of the parties directly concerned in the Cyprus problem, attests abundantly to the helpful if not indispensable role of the Force. The explosive situation prevailing in the island has been contained remarkably well and there have been no major outbreaks of fighting since August 1964. With the cessation of active hostilities, it has been possible to make some progress toward the relaxation of prevailing restrictions and a return to normal conditions. There is no doubt that this general improvement has been due in large measure to the efforts of the United Nations Force. While the Force has been successful in these respects, the underlying causes of the conflict remain without change. The Government of Cyprus, on the one hand, and the Turkish Cypriot leadership, on the other, have maintained their basic positions regarding the future of the country and their relations continue to be marred by suspicion and mistrust. The continuance of the armed confrontation between the two sides makes the present quiet little more than an uneasy truce. I am convinced that there would be an imminent danger of violence breaking out anew and quickly if the United Nations Force were to be withdrawn from the island.

In the light of this situation, I had no sound alternative but to recommend that the Security Council extend the Force once more. But I did so with some misgivings. As time goes by, the Force may find that it will have to make greater efforts to obtain smaller results, while the United Nations will find the responsibility of financing the operation increasingly difficult, particularly since the financial burden is being borne by the generous voluntary contributions of only a handful of Member states. An indefinite prolongation of the Force contains also the danger of perpetuating the present stalemate by providing the parties concerned with an excuse for not exerting all possible efforts toward a settlement.

The need therefore becomes all the more urgent to achieve a

political solution to the Cyprus problem. To help the parties find this solution, the United Nations Mediator on Cyprus, Mr. Galo Plaza, devoted his best efforts from September 1964 to March 1965. On March 26, he submitted to me a report on the mediation activities, which I found encouraging because it envisaged a reasonable basis for a settlement of the problem. In view of the importance which I attach to the Mediator's report, I decided to transmit it immediately to the parties concerned as well as to the members of the Security Council.

Unfortunately, two of the parties reacted negatively to the report, to such an extent that the Mediator has been unable actively to continue his endeavors since the publication of the report. While I deeply regret this turn of events, I believe that it should not preclude a continuation of efforts by all possible means to bring about direct discussions and negotiations between the parties concerned, as recommended by the Mediator and in the light of his analysis of the situation. It is my earnest hope that, in the interest of the well-being of the people of Cyprus and the cause of international peace and security, these parties will soon find it possible to meet together in the search for a peaceful solution and an agreed settlement of the Cyprus problem, in the true spirit of the Security Council resolution of March 4, 1964. At my request, the Mediator remains available to the parties for the continuation of the mediation effort, in accordance with the provisions of that resolution.

VI

A new United Nations mission in the peace-keeping category was established in the Dominican Republic following the adoption by the Security Council of resolution 203 (1965) of May 14, 1965, which called for a strict cease-fire in that country and invited me to send a representative there for the purpose of reporting to the Council on the prevailing situation. In pursuance of that resolution, I appointed Mr. José Antonio Mayobre as my Representative in the Dominican Republic.

The situation in the Dominican Republic arising from the civil strife which broke out in Santo Domingo at the end of April 1965 was of unusual complexity. It had considerable international repercussions, reflected in numerous Security Council meetings, particularly with regard to the unilateral military involvement of the United States in the initial stage and, later, to the actions of the Organization of American States, including the establishment and deployment in Santo Domingo of a force designated as the Inter-American Peace Force. The violent struggle between contending parties in the Dominican Republic generated deep-seated feelings of hatred and mistrust. The rapidly deteriorating economic situation resulting largely from the crisis added another disturbing dimension to the problems confronting the country.

While the mandate of my Representative in the Dominican Republic is a limited one, the effect of his role has been significant. When he arrived in Santo Domingo on May 17, fighting between the two Dominican contending parties had flared up despite a cease-fire agreement reached on May 5 under the auspices of the Organization of American States. My Representative played a major role in bringing about a cessation of hostilities on May 21. Since then the situation has remained generally quiet, although there have been a number of isolated incidents. My Representative, assisted by a small but efficient staff, has kept me informed as to the situation both in Santo Domingo and in the interior of the country, regarding not only the observance of the cease-fire but also serious cases of violations of human rights and the prevailing economic conditions. I have transmitted this information to the Security Council at frequent intervals, thus keeping the Council informed of all important events and developments.

It bears mentioning that for the first time a United Nations peace mission has found itself operating in the same area and dealing with the same matters as an operation of a regional organization, in this instance the Organization of American States. Apart from its deeper implications, this circumstance has given rise to some special and unfamiliar problems in the way of relationships and liaison, which have, however, been progressively surmounted.

The presence of my Representative in the Dominican Republic has undoubtedly been a moderating factor in a difficult and dangerous situation which, at the time of writing, holds promise of being peacefully resolved.

VII

The newer peace-keeping efforts of the United Nations in Cyprus and in the Dominican Republic have naturally tended to overshadow those of much longer standing: the United Nations Truce Supervision Organization in Palestine, the United Nations Emergency Force and, until the recent renewal of conflict over Kashmir, the United Nations Military Observer Group in India and Pakistan. To the extent that any generalization can be valid, these three operations, like the United Nations Force in Cyprus, have often seemed to possess the limitations of their own success, namely, that they have helped over long periods to contain and isolate explosive situations without really affecting the basic causes of conflict. Two of the three have lasted for sixteen years and one for nearly nine years; all have been indispensable for most of that time to relative peace and order in the areas in which they operate, and their withdrawal would without question have had far-reaching consequences. On the other hand, the very fact that they have become an accepted and semi-permanent part of the way of life in the areas has tended to some extent to reduce the sense of urgency which might stimulate a search by the parties concerned for a basic and peaceful solution of their conflicts. This state of affairs is no reflection on the conduct and competence of the officers, men, and Secretariat officials of these three missions; on the contrary it is perhaps the best testimony to their effectiveness, good judgment, courage, and vigilance. It is, nonetheless, a dilemma which Member states would do well to study carefully in relation to both present and future operations of a peace-keeping nature, with a view to strengthening the machinery for peace-making (good offices, negotiation, mediation, conciliation, arbitration, etc.) parallel to that of peace-keeping.

While the foregoing considerations apply to the Military Observer Group in India and Pakistan in a general sense, its position warrants further comment. There is no doubt in my mind that over a long period the presence of the Group acted to some extent as a deterrent to the renewal of hostilities; however, as I pointed out in my report to the Security Council of September 3, 1965, on the situation which had by that time developed in Kashmir, it must be recognized that the mandate of the mission had been strictly limited in scale and scope.

The mission had consisted simply of a group of forty-five officers stationed along a cease-fire line almost 500 miles in length; it had been given the quite limited function of observing and reporting and of investigating complaints of violations received from either party; it had no authority or function entitling it to enforce or prevent anything, or to try to ensure that the cease-fire was respected. Since the Security Council is, at the time of writing, actively seized of the crisis over Kashmir, I do not think it appropriate for me to go further in the present context than to ask that those limitations should be properly understood.

One operation of a peace-keeping nature, the United Nations Yemen Observation Mission, was terminated on September 4, 1964, having been established by the Security Council on June 11, 1963. This operation was both limited in scope and small in size. Its function was to observe and report on the implementation of the disengagement agreement in Yemen between the United Arab Republic and Saudi Arabia in the effort to ensure against any developments in the situation that might threaten the peace of the area. As I reported to the Security Council on July 2, 1964, the Mission observed only a disappointing measure of disengagement, in particular with regard to the withdrawal of the troops of the United Arab Republic, and I appealed most urgently to the parties concerned to meet at the highest level with a view to achieving full and rapid implementation of the disengagement agreement. I also warned the Council that in my opinion the Mission should be terminated in September 1964, if no improvement in the situation was by then evident. The parties concurred in the termination of the Mission on September 4. Since that time there have been favorable developments, culminating in consultations and agreement at the highest level among the parties, which I had always felt to be essential to a solution of the situation in Yemen.

As far as the United Nations Mission was concerned, its mandate was so limited, being restricted to observation and reporting only, that inevitably the results achieved were widely interpreted as disappointing. There is little doubt that the Mission could have accomplished much more if its functions had been broader and stronger. Yet, in the circumstances, I believe that the Mission actually accomplished more than could have been expected of it and that, during its fourteen months of existence, it exercised an important restraining influence on hostile activities in the area. The problem continued inevitably to rest between the two principal countries involved, the United Arab Republic and Saudi Arabia, whose Heads of State have now successfully brought their statesmanship to bear on finding an agreed settlement.

VIII

In the introduction to the annual report last year, I recalled the continued efforts of the United Nations in the field of decolonization and referred to the major questions in that field for which solutions had to be found through peaceful means and which therefore called for attention by the General Assembly.

In the intervening period, another former dependent territory, the Gambia, acceded to independence, and constitutional progress toward self-government and independence was made in some of the remaining dependent territories. However, the problems to which I referred last year remain without any positive movement toward peaceful solution. The Special Committee on the Situation with regard to the Implementation of the Declaration on the Granting of Independence of Colonial Countries and Peoples, which continued to discharge its mandate as established by the General Assembly in resolution 1956 (XVIII) of December 11, 1963, accordingly gave priority in its work to examining the situation in those territories which continued to give cause for serious concern.

With regard to Southern Rhodesia, the United Kingdom Government found it necessary, in view of its concern about the possibility of unconstitutional action by the Government of the Territory, to reiterate its warning of the serious consequences which would flow from a unilateral declaration of independence by that Government. It also reaffirmed its intention of pursuing the search for a political settlement based on general consent. However, no progress can yet be recorded in this regard and it is to be hoped that a basis for early independence, acceptable to the majority of the population, will soon be found which, in conformity with United Nations resolutions, will embody full democratic freedom and recognition of the equal rights of all the inhabitants.

In the case of the territories under Portuguese administration, there was no change in Portugal's position of noncompliance with United

Nations resolutions and in its refusal to cooperate with the Organization in implementing them. Far from recognizing the right of the inhabitants to self-determination, as laid down by the General Assembly, it pursued its policy of closer political and economic integration of the territories with Portugal.

Likewise, South Africa has maintained its disregard of United Nations resolutions concerning South West Africa and its attitude of noncooperation in this respect. In addition to continuing the application of apartheid policies in the territory, it has taken preliminary steps to implement some of the recommendations of the Odendaal Commission which, in the view of the Special Committee, would lead to the partition of the territory and its absorption into South Africa.

In regard to the territories mentioned above, the Special Committee gave increasing attention to the implications of the activities of foreign economic and other interests and their mode of operation in order to assess their economic and political influence. It is the hope of the Special Committee that a study of these activities will result in greater appreciation of some of the factors impeding the implementation of the Declaration.

At its nineteenth session, the General Assembly, following a recommendation by the Special Committee and in response to an invitation by New Zealand as the administering power, authorized the supervision by the United Nations of the elections in the Cook Islands, including observation of the proceedings concerning the Constitution in the Legislative Assembly to be elected. The report of the United Nations Representative appointed for the purpose remains to be considered by the General Assembly. It is hoped that the Assembly's deliberations and those of the Special Committee will lead to increased cooperation between administering powers and the Organization in regard to dependent territories.

Another development of note was the decision of the Special Committee to hold meetings in Africa during May and June 1965 in order to establish direct contact with peoples under colonial rule in the continent and to acquire a deeper knowledge of their situation as well as of their aspirations.

In the resolutions adopted by the Special Committee during its meetings in Africa, emphasis was placed on the legitimacy of the struggle of colonial peoples to secure the effective exercise and enjoyment of the rights set forth in the Charter, the Universal Declaration of Human Rights, and the Declaration embodied in General Assembly resolution 1514 (XV). In one of these resolutions, the Special Committee recommended that the Security Council and the General Assembly should take the positive measures laid down in the Charter to ensure respect for the rights of the African populations in Southern Rhodesia, in Territories under Portuguese administration, in South West Africa, and in Basutoland, Bechuanaland and Swaziland. At the same time, the Special Committee requested all states and all international institutions to refuse assistance of any kind to the Governments of Portugal and South Africa and the minority settler régime of Southern Rhodesia, so long as the latter failed to renounce their policy of colonial domination and the practice of apartheid.

I am hopeful that the Special Committee's work in Africa will have served to demonstrate further the concern of the United Nations for the position of the dependent peoples and to enable the Special Committee to increase its contribution to the speedy emergence of their countries from dependence.

It may be timely to recall, in a year proclaimed as International Cooperation Year, that the Declaration contained in General Assembly resolution 1514 (XV) was adopted nearly five years ago. In it, the General Assembly declared:

Immediate steps shall be taken, in Trust and Non-Self-Governing Territories or all other territories which have not yet attained independence, to transfer all powers to the peoples of these territories, without any conditions or reservations, in accordance with their freely expressed will and desire, without any distinction as to race, creed, or color, in order to enable them to enjoy complete independence and freedom.

It is my earnest hope that all Member states and in particular the administering powers will, in a spirit of constructive cooperation, do their utmost to assist the dependent peoples to achieve their aspirations in conditions of peace and harmony.

IX

The situation in the Republic of South Africa presents no less dark and disturbing a picture than previously. As a result of further study by the United Nations organs, it was also revealed in clearer detail than ever before. The Expert Committee established under the Security Council resolution of June 18, 1964, submitted its report at the end of February 1965. The Special Committee on the Policies of Apartheid of the Government of the Republic of South Africa continued to follow the situation constantly and submitted two reports to the General Assembly and the Security Council, with a number of recommendations for action.

It is to be regretted that the South African Government has failed to respond to the invitation of the Security Council to accept the main conclusion of the Group of Experts that "all the people of South Africa should be brought into consultation and should thus be enabled to decide the future of their country at the national level." Such consultations are crucial to any efforts to find a solution which would take into account the legitimate rights and concerns of all the people of South Africa. Attempts to impose solutions by force, when a great majority of the people do not have representation in the sovereign Parliament, can only lead to increased bitterness, tension and conflict.

The Security Council and the General Assembly are due to consider the situation soon in the light of the most recent developments, which have in no way diminished its seriousness. The overwhelming feeling among Member states is clearly that it is essential to secure an abandonment of the policies of apartheid and a resolution of the situation through the full, peaceful, and orderly application of human rights and fundamental freedoms to all the inhabitants of South Africa, regardless of race, color, or creed, in order to forestall serious dangers to peace and to fulfill the objectives of the United Nations. I would hope, therefore, that earnest efforts will be made to overcome differences about procedures and specific measures and that effective action commanding the widest support in the Organization will be taken.

Such action, in my opinion, should make it clear that the solution sought by the United Nations is one which takes full account of the legitimate rights and concerns of all the people of South Africa, and which emerges through free discussions among representatives of all the people. It should express the readiness and willingness of the United Nations to assist those people in the search for such a solution. In view of the grave dangers of tension and conflict, the United Nations should give the utmost attention to political and humanitarian measures which would not leave violence as the only means of fulfilling legitimate aspirations, and which would help counteract the growth of racial bitterness and tension. In this connection, I wish to express my appreciation to several Member states who have responded to the appeal in General Assembly resolution 1978 B (XVIII) of December 16, 1963, for assistance to families of persons persecuted for their opposition to apartheid.

Meanwhile I have been taking steps, in consultation with the appropriate specialized agencies, to establish a program for the education and training of South Africans abroad. A few fellowships and grants have been awarded for the academic year 1965–1966, and the full program is expected to come into operation next year. I hope that this program will receive the generous support of Member states.

X

I feel bound to emphasize that the actual financial crisis, in which the Organization has for too long found itself placed, has by no means been dispelled by the consensus reached by the Special Committee on Peace-keeping Operations and, in effect, accepted by the General Assembly on September 1, 1965. As I write these words, our financial difficulties remain serious, and it seems appropriate for me to restate them here in factual terms.

During the first eight months of this year the Organization's cash outgo to meet its current operating expenses and to settle some of its most pressing debts from prior years exceeded its cash income. As a result it was necessary on several occasions during this period to borrow money temporarily from special funds and accounts in my custody, in order to meet the payroll and other day-to-day expenses.

Between January 1 and August 31, 1965, the Organization received a total of approximately $73.6 million from governments consisting of advance payments toward the regular budget and United Nations Emergency Force expenses for 1965 ($35.4 million); payments of assessed contributions to the regular budget, and to the accounts of the Emergency Force and the United Nations Operation in the Congo for 1964 and prior years ($18.5 million); voluntary contributions to assist the Organization out of its present financial difficulties and voluntary contributions to the Emergency Force and Congo accounts ($18.5 million); and deferred payment for a United Nations bond ($1.2 million). During the same period miscellaneous income, other than from staff assessment, was received in an amount estimated at $4.3 million in respect of the regular budget and Emergency Force accounts.

The Organization's expenses for the same eight-month period in respect of the regular budget and the Emergency Force are estimated as having totaled approximately $72 million. Since, in addition to paying current operating expenses, it was necessary to settle some of the more pressing debts from prior years, all the income received in the first eight months of 1965 was disbursed, the relatively modest cash balances which the Organization had available at the beginning of this year were drawn down, and it became necessary to resort to the borrowings referred to above.

My estimate is that, as of the beginning of September, an amount of approximately $100 million would be required to enable the Organization to liquidate in full the obligations currently outstanding against the special accounts of the United Nations Emergency Force and the United Nations Operation in the Congo; to meet in full the additional obligations that will be incurred, in the case of the Emergency Force, between September 1, 1965, and such time as a decision will have been reached at the twentieth session of the General Assembly on the future of that operation and its financing; to restore the Working Capital Fund to its authorized level of $40 million; and to cover amounts due to Member states as adjustments on assessed contributions for the costs of the two peace-keeping forces.

It has been agreed, in the terms of the consensus referred to earlier, that these financial difficulties should be solved through voluntary contributions by Member states. At the time of writing, such contributions paid or pledged total somewhat less than one fifth of the amount required. I have already made an urgent appeal to all who have not yet done so to come forward with contributions. I should like to reiterate this appeal; and I do so with some confidence that, on reflection, governments will see the clear and pressing need to enable the Organization to solve its financial difficulties, in view of the stake they have in its survival and the value they attach to its present and potential usefulness.

XI

I was gratified to be able to announce, just before September 1, 1965, the date recommended by the General Assembly in resolution 1991

(XVIII), that the amendments to the Charter approved under that resolution had been ratified by more than two thirds of the Members of the United Nations, including all the permanent members of the Security Council.

The amendments enlarge the Security Council and the Economic and Social Council, and alter the number of votes necessary for decisions by the Security Council. In order to give effect to the amendments, elections will be held during the twentieth session of the General Assembly to fill both the new seats and those which will become vacant on December 31, 1965, in the two Councils. This procedure is consistent with Assembly resolution 1991 (XVIII), which provides that elections to fill both old and new seats should be held at the same time. In accordance with rule 140 of the rules of procedure of the General Assembly, the term of office of the members of the Councils will begin on January 1, 1966.

It will be a matter of general satisfaction that the wish of the Organization to see the composition of two of its principal organs reflect more adequately the present membership will thus be fulfilled with a minimum of delay.

XII

I referred at the beginning to certain developments on the international scene which have inevitably had their repercussions on the United Nations. Of these, perhaps the most important is the escalation of the conflict in Vietnam, even though, paradoxically, the problem of Vietnam is one in regard to which the Organization has not been able to take any constructive action. This of course is to some extent understandable. The settlement reached at Geneva in 1954 prescribed no role for the Organization in the settlement that was to follow. Neither North Vietnam nor South Vietnam is a Member of the United Nations, and most recently the parties directly interested in the Vietnam conflict have openly voiced the view that the United Nations as such has no place in the search for a solution to the problem of Vietnam. This last factor, of course, cannot by itself prevent the United Nations from discussing the problem, but it does militate against the Organization being able to play a constructive role at this stage.

It is because of the profound effect that the Vietnam situation is having on problems of global as well as regional importance, and the shadow it casts on almost every area of international cooperation, that I have devoted considerable personal effort in the realm of quiet diplomacy to getting the parties concerned to stop the fighting and to start the discussions which alone, in my view, can lead to a solution. I remain as fully convinced as ever that total victory or total defeat for one side or the other is out of the question and that military action cannot bring peace and restore stability to the area. The only way to those goals is the way of discussions; and it is clear, as I have stated previously, that those discussions can yield fruitful results only if there is a willingness by all sides to make major concessions.

I cannot emphasize too strongly the profound and dangerous effect which, however paradoxical the circumstances, the present situation in Vietnam is having on the atmosphere in the United Nations, reflecting in turn the impact of the dispute upon the relations between East and West. Patient and persistent efforts over several years, within the United Nations as well as outside it, had brought East and West closer together than at any other time in the past decade and had opened up many real possibilities of fruitful collaboration. Signs at last were present of a thaw in international affairs which could be encouraged not only to endure but also to spread around the world. The conflict over Vietnam has cruelly set back that trend and has served to revive, to intensify, and even to extend some of the attitudes of the cold war. The conflict engages not only the lives of the soldiers and civilians who are caught up in the present fighting. It threatens also to affect the peace of the world and the fate of all mankind. It must be stopped.

One of the issues before the United Nations on which the situation in Vietnam has had a noticeable impact is disarmament, on which I have made some comments elsewhere in this introduction. The lack of substantial progress, both in the discussions of the Disarmament Commission in New York and the subsequent meetings of the Conference of the Eighteen-Nation Disarmament Committee in Geneva, is one obvious result of the intensification of the cold war. I feel most strongly, however, that the time has come when the nuclear powers must agree on the total banning of nuclear tests, including underground tests, and take at least the first positive steps toward the prevention of the proliferation of nuclear weapons. I am convinced that progress in these two directions is in the interest of all countries—whether they be large or small, nuclear or non-nuclear—and I very much hope that the deliberations of the twentieth session of the General Assembly will help toward progress in these two directions.

I also venture to hope that at its twentieth session the General Assembly will approve the recommendations of the Disarmament Commission to hold a world disarmament conference. In this connection, I cannot help observing that progress in disarmament, whether general or nuclear, can hardly be made if all the major military Powers of the world, in terms of both conventional and nuclear weapons, are not enabled to participate in the deliberations. I would regard it as essential, therefore, that the world disarmament conference should be held under conditions which would make it possible for all countries, if they so wished, to participate in it.

Both the Vietnam situation and the disarmament *impasse* point once again to the imperative need for the United Nations to achieve universality of membership as soon as possible. Being aware of the political and other difficulties involved in bringing this about, I should like to renew the suggestion which I made in the introduction to my last annual report to the effect that, in the meantime, the countries not at present represented at United Nations Headquarters should be enabled to maintain contact with the world body and listen to its deliberations, and thus be more directly exposed to the views of the rest of mankind. I feel, indeed, that the experience of the last ten months has reinforced the view I expressed on this matter last November. I have no doubt that the true interests of peace would be better served if non-Member states were to be encouraged to maintain observers at United Nations Headquarters so that they may be in a position to sense the currents and cross-currents of world opinion which are so uniquely concentrated in the Organization. Meanwhile, it is to be recorded that last year the General Assembly admitted three new Members—Malawi, Malta, and Zambia—and that applications are now pending on the part of Gambia, the Maldive Islands, and Singapore.

The importance of the universality of membership applies not only to the political work of the United Nations, but also to its economic and social activities. In this connection, I feel that it is very important that the governments of all Member states should be enabled to participate in the work of at least one of the regional economic commissions. The excellent record of cooperative endeavor and positive results which the regional economic commissions have been able to achieve is no doubt responsible for the desire of some Member states, now denied such participation, to be enabled to join in this constructive effort. Inasmuch as the regional commissions have so far been able to get on with their work in the interests of the economic benefits of the countries involved, avoiding as far as possible political considerations, I hope that this widening of participation may be possible.

In addition to making progress toward universality of membership, we have also striven very hard to achieve the participation of nationals of all Member states in the Secretariat of the United Nations. Special efforts have been made to secure an adequate place in the Secretariat for nationals of those countries which, for one reason or another, have continued to be underrepresented during recent years. These special efforts have included the dispatch of special missions for the recruitment of suitable candidates from countries of Africa and Eastern Europe. I hope that, thanks to their efforts, we shall be able to obtain a larger number of qualified candidates for service not only at Headquarters but also with the economic commissions and in the field offices.

The events in the Caribbean which have been the subject of discussion in the United Nations in recent months have focused attention once again on the role of regional organizations in the maintenance of peace. In the case of the Dominican Republic, the regional organization concerned assumed virtually full responsibility for both a peace-keeping operation and the mediation of a political settlement, and the United Nations undertook only the limited—although, as it turned out, very important—function which I have described earlier. As I have stated, the fact that the United Nations operation had to function in parallel with that of the regional organization led inevitably to difficulties in relationships. Without wishing to comment further on this specific situation, and without intending to question the competence of any regional organization to take action in conformity with the terms of its own constitution, I maintain the view which I expressed at the time, that the developments in the Caribbean should stimulate some thought by all of us concerning the character of the regional organizations and the nature of their functions and obligations in relation to the responsibilities of the United Nations under our Charter. I believe that a good deal of thinking has in fact been applied to this question in a number of quarters, and I should like now to suggest that it is one which deserves some concerted study within the United Nations.

In very recent weeks the international situation has again been deeply disturbed, in this case by the armed conflict which broke out between India and Pakistan over the long-standing problem of Kashmir. At the time of writing I am, in compliance with resolutions adopted by the Security Council, actively engaged in the endeavor to bring the fighting to an end; and, in accordance with the decisions which the Council has so far taken, I shall continue to exert every effort to bring about a return to peaceful conditions in the area. Under the circumstances it would be inappropriate for me to comment here on the situation as it now stands. One thing already clear, however, is the danger, which the Kashmir conflict has once more brought home, of leaving without a solution grave problems affecting relations between states, in the hope that the mere passage of time may solve them. We must draw from it a warning of the ever-present danger of an explosion, in any part of the world, if long-standing sources of conflict are not dealt with in a purposeful manner, and when any incident is capable of raising national emotions to fever-pitch. Such warnings may, I feel, increase our recognition of the importance of having an effective international machinery which can intervene in such difficult situations. From this it follows that, if the United Nations is to be an effective instrument for the maintenance of peace and security, it should not continue to have to contend with financial and other inadequacies. The Organization, to be strong and effective, must also be solvent.

The ten months that have passed have without doubt been difficult ones in the history of the United Nations. On the other hand, the situation in the world today has brought home, I believe, to all Member states how important it is that the United Nations should function effectively. I should like to believe that the Organization is emerging from its recent crisis with a new spirit of confidence and determination that will be reflected, in the first instance, in the work of the twentieth session of the General Assembly. A heavy responsibility now lies on all Members to translate revived hopes into those measurable achievements that can only be attained by far-sighted initiatives and by a will to find and agree on common measures and programs of action.

All Member states have a stake in the maintenance of international peace and security, which is, in fact, the condition of their own survival. In the common task of preserving peace, there is no better instrument available to them than the United Nations. If the Organization is a fragile instrument, and still insufficiently universal in its nature, it rests with the Member states to make it more durable in substance and all-embracing in scope. It is understandable that the United Nations should mirror the difficulties and dissensions which we see in so many parts of the world today; but in reflecting these distortions of peace the mirror itself should not be allowed to distort the image further. The image, however disturbing, must be clearly seen, so that in full awareness of the realities we may continue to move patiently but purposefully toward the goal of peace.

U THANT
Secretary-General

September 20, 1965

Statement in the General Assembly on Financial Problems

NEW YORK   SEPTEMBER 1, 1965

UP TO THE TIME the Special Committee on Peace-keeping Operations resumed its meetings on August 16, little progress had been made in finding a way to avoid a repetition of the abnormal voting situation which had brought the proceedings of the General Assembly to a near standstill at its nineteenth session (see volume VI of this series, pp. 681–684). At his first news conference after assuming his duties as permanent representative of the United States, Ambassador Arthur Goldberg acknowledged that the Johnson administration had not arrived at any final position as to what it would do when the Special Committee reconvened. Between this news conference on July 28 and the resumption of the discussions in the Special Committee, however, the United States decided to withdraw its threat to invoke the voting penalties provided in Article 19 of the Charter, thus removing the likelihood of a confrontation with the Soviet Union at the closing of the nineteenth session on September 1 or the twentieth session opening on September 21.

Goldberg's statement before the Special Committee is worth quoting at some length because of its historical significance. Following is a key section of the statement:

"The United States regretfully concludes, on ample evidence, that at this stage in the history of the United Nations, the General Assembly is not prepared to carry out the relevant provisions of the Charter in the context of the present situation. From private consultations, from statements by the principal officers of the Organization, from the statements and exhaustive negotiations within and outside this Committee, from an informal polling of the delegations—indeed from the entire history of this affair—the inevitable conclusion is that the Assembly is not disposed to apply the loss-of-vote sanction of Article 19 to the present situation.

"We regret that the intransigence of a few of the Member states, and their unwillingness to abide by the rule of law, has led the Organization into this state of affairs.

"The United States adheres to the position that Article 19 is applicable in the present circumstances. It is clear, however, that we are faced with a simple and inescapable fact of life which I have cited. Moreover, every parliamentary body must decide, in one way or another, the issues that come before it; otherwise it will have no useful existence, and soon no life.

"Therefore, without prejudice to the position that Article 19 is applicable, the United States recognizes, as it must, that the General Assembly is not prepared to apply Article 19 in the present situation and that the consensus of the membership is that the Assembly should proceed normally. We will not seek to frustrate that consensus, since it is not in the world interest to have the work of the General Assembly immobilized in these troubled days. At the same time, we must make clear that, if any member can insist on making an exception to the principle of collective financial responsibility with respect to certain activities of the Organization, the United States reserves the same option to make exceptions if, in our view, strong and compelling reasons exist for doing so. There can be no double standard among the Members of the Organization.

"Some Members may believe that in not applying Article 19 no important decision is being made. The United States believes that no one can or should overlook the fact that the exercise of important prerogatives of the Assembly granted it under the Charter is being impaired. The United States wishes to strengthen, not weaken, the United Nations by adhering to rather than departing from basic, sound principles. Therefore we must disclaim responsibility for the Assembly's attitude, which has developed contrary to the views we still hold to be valid, and place the responsibility where it properly belongs—on those Member states which have flouted the Assembly's will and the Court's [International Court of Justice] opinion."[1]

Although Goldberg's statement in effect ended the Article 19 crisis, the termination was formalized in the report of the Special Committee on August 31 and by the Assembly itself on September 1. The Committee's report contained a three-point declaration, later approved by the Assembly, to the effect that (1) the Assembly should carry on its work normally in accordance with its rules of procedure; (2) the question of the applicability of Article 19 of the Charter would not be raised with regard to the peace-keeping operations in the Congo and the Middle East; and (3) the financial difficulties of the Organization should be solved through voluntary contributions by Member states, with the highly developed countries making substantial contributions.

Thant took note of the consensus both in a statement before the Assembly on September 1 and later in the Introduction to his Annual Report which was issued on September 20 (p. 136). He did not refer in either statement to the United States action in withdrawing the threat to invoke Article 19 penalties, but paid tribute to the patient and constructive work of the Com-

[1]The summary record of this statement is given in Official Records of the General Assembly, Nineteenth Session, annex No. 21, p. 86.

mittee and "to the cooperation of all delegations." He called the consensus a "substantial achievement." He took the occasion to make an urgent appeal to all Member governments to follow through with voluntary contributions, as provided in the consensus, so that the Organization might finally pull out of the financial crisis which continued to plague it.

ON THIS OCCASION, and before the nineteenth session of the General Assembly comes to a close, I wish to make a brief statement.

I believe there will be general agreement that the nineteenth session, which began in an atmosphere of crisis, is ending on an encouraging and hopeful note. So much of the credit for this change of atmosphere is due to the leadership of the President of the nineteenth session of the General Assembly, His Excellency Mr. Alex Quaison-Sackey, Foreign Minister of Ghana, to the patient and constructive work of the Special Committee on Peace-keeping Operations, and to the cooperation of all delegations. I wish to take this opportunity to pay my tribute to you, Mr. President, and to the representatives of Member states gathered here today.

I am very glad that the Special Committee on Peace-keeping Operations was able to reach a consensus on some of the questions referred to it for consideration, and that the Assembly had adopted the reports of the Committee. I welcome, in particular, the proposal that Member governments should make voluntary contributions to help solve the present financial difficulties of this Organization. As the Assembly is aware, some Member governments have already taken the lead in pledging voluntary contributions for this purpose, and I have expressed my deep appreciation to these governments. I take this opportunity to make an urgent appeal at the present time to all Member governments to make voluntary contributions so that the financial difficulties of the Organization may be solved and the future may be faced with renewed hope and confidence.

In this connection, I have been asked by many delegations to give an estimate of the amount of funds that would be needed to accomplish this purpose. I did make available, earlier this year, on a

SOURCE: General Assembly Official Records, Nineteenth Session, 1331st plenary meeting.

confidential basis, certain estimates in this regard to the members of the Special Committee on Peace-keeping Operations. Naturally, those estimates now need some revision, in the light of subsequent developments. I feel that it would be helpful, therefore, if I were to give an up-to-date estimate of the financial situation of the Organization and of its needs, as of today, September 1, 1965. In order not to take up the time of the Assembly, I propose to circulate very soon, as a General Assembly document, a revised and up-to-date statement of the estimated financial needs of the Organization. I hope that all Member governments will take note of the continuing seriousness of the financial situation of the Organization and respond urgently and generously to my appeal for voluntary contributions.

PROPOSAL FOR A WORLD DISARMAMENT CONFERENCE

THE FOLLOWING STATEMENT by U Thant on proposed action to call a world disarmament conference was made some two months before the General Assembly's First (Political and Security) Committee began its discussion of the question. Approval of the proposal was assured, however, by a vote of 89 to none, with 16 abstentions, in the Disarmament Commission on June 11. The idea had been advanced by the Second Conference of Non-Aligned Countries meeting in Cairo in October 1964. One of the objectives of the sponsors was to bring the People's Republic of China into the disarmament talks, which so far had been limited to members of the United Nations or its specialized agencies. Thant's statement, read to the Inter-Parliamentary Union by United Nations Under-Secretary C. V. Narasimhan on September 9, endorsed the proposed provision for inviting all countries to take part in the world conference. He said such a move would be a significant step forward in the relaxation of international tension. Although the Assembly approved the idea on November 29 by a vote of 112 to none, with only France abstaining, and called for the establishment of a preparatory committee to convene a world disarmament conference not later than 1967, the conference was never held, largely because of the negative reaction of Peking. During earlier discussions in the Disarmament Commission, Albania had warned that the People's Republic of China would not attend such a conference under United Nations auspices as long as it was refused a seat in the Organization. When this was confirmed by Peking, plans to organize the preparatory committee were shelved quietly and the question was not raised again until the Soviet Union revived it in 1971. It was postponed once more when the United States and the Peking government, finally given China's seat, joined in urging that the question be put over until 1972.

In a statement before the Assembly on December 3, the Secretary-General alluded to the approved proposal for a world disarmament conference, but he simply noted that this was among a number of disarmament resolutions adopted by near unanimous votes. Commenting that the votes would seem to indicate the existence of a consensus, at least on goals and guidelines, he urged "the highest levels of government" to demonstrate their desire to reach specific agreements. Nothing could more quickly and surely improve the prospects for agreement, he said, than the restoration of peace in Vietnam.

1. From Address at the Fifty-fourth Conference of the Inter-Parliamentary Union

OTTAWA   SEPTEMBER 9, 1965

[IN THE ABSENCE of the Secretary-General this address was read by C. V. Narasimhan, Under-Secretary for General Assembly Affairs and Chef de Cabinet.]

. . .

The General Assembly will also have before it the proposal for the convening of a world disarmament conference to which all countries would be invited. This idea is not incompatible with the current Geneva negotiations, whose utility has been repeatedly reaffirmed by the Members of the United Nations. While the convening of such a conference under the aegis of the United Nations may not be enough to bring about agreement on general disarmament, it could serve to focus attention in all parts of the world on the common predicament that is shared by mankind. Differences between nations have not in the past prevented an exchange of views on how to curb the arms race, nor should they in the future. While the major powers in the United Nations have still far to go before they exhaust the partial measures open to them as a result of their unique situation in the arms race, we must begin to plan seriously for a later stage, knowing the problems but conscious also of the opportunity inherent in this idea. Sometime, somehow, we must finish the job of building a world community under the United Nations consisting of all nations, regardless of ideology, regardless of size, so that all nations may be moved by the same impulse on behalf of peace, freedom, and justice.

If this should be our goal, it is obvious that we should strive to bring about, as soon as possible, universality of membership of the United Nations. Progress in disarmament, whether general or nuclear, can hardly be made while one of the major military powers of the world in terms of conventional weapons, which has recently become a nuclear

SOURCE: *UN Monthly Chronicle*, vol. II, October 1965, pp. 118–122.

power in its own right, does not participate in the deliberations on such a serious subject. It seems to me essential, therefore, that when the world disarmament conference is held, it should take place under conditions which would make it possible for all countries, if they so wished, to participate in its deliberations. This would be, in my view, a very significant step forward in the relaxation of international tension and the reduction of the feeling of insecurity which prevails in various parts of the world.

. . .

2. Statement in the General Assembly

NEW YORK   DECEMBER 3, 1965

TODAY, with the adoption of the resolutions on the agenda items on the urgent need for the suspension of nuclear and thermonuclear tests, on the Declaration on the denuclearization of Africa, and on the question of general and complete disarmament, the Assembly has completed consideration of the disarmament items. The various aspects of the disarmament problem have, quite understandably, been a dominating feature of the twentieth session of the General Assembly. The deliberations have resulted in virtually unanimous resolutions; only a single negative vote has been cast against one of the disarmament resolutions adopted. These votes would seem to indicate the existence of a consensus, at least on goals and guidelines, for the coming year.

The Members of the Assembly have earlier this session expressed their clear support for the idea of convening a world disarmament conference. This was accomplished in a manner intentionally designed, as I understand it, to make possible the participation of all major powers in such a conference. Today, the General Assembly has once again clearly expressed its support for the continuing mandate

SOURCE: General Assembly Official Records, Twentieth Session, 1388th plenary meeting.

of the Eighteen-Nation Disarmament Committee to proceed with the immediate negotiating task. Once again the Members of the United Nations have indicated a desire to move forward simultaneously on every possible road to disarmament.

Unfortunately, the Eighteen-Nation Disarmament Committee will resume its work against the background of a war[1] that seems to be gathering fresh and dangerous momentum. Nothing could more quickly and surely improve the prospects for agreement on disarmament than bringing an end to this conflict. Nevertheless, the world will doubtless experience some feeling of reassurance when the disarmament talks resume.

The substantive results of your deliberations are clear. The General Assembly has taken the steps that are feasible for it to make the prevention of the direct or indirect proliferation of nuclear weapons the paramount objective of immediate disarmament efforts. The goal of nonproliferation has been buttressed by the most recent resolutions calling for the suspension of all nuclear tests and by the Declaration on the denuclearization of Africa.

I note with satisfaction that the resolution on nuclear testing alludes specifically to the improved possibilities for international cooperation in the field of seismic detection. Nations must ask not only what is already possible by way of detection and identification techniques to sustain confidence in a test-ban treaty, but also—and perhaps more immediately—what they can do together to develop still better means so as to facilitate a treaty acceptable to all.

Once again the Members of the United Nations have called on the nuclear powers to suspend all nuclear weapon tests. Difficult as it may be for sovereign states to abstain voluntarily from testing, producing, or deploying nuclear weapons which are technically feasible for them, their willingness to do so may be decisive in halting the arms race.

The disarmament negotiations in Geneva cannot but benefit from regional efforts in Latin America and Africa. The initiative taken by the countries of these geographical areas is a most heartening recent development in the field of disarmament. The countries of Africa and Latin America, if they succeed in their great endeavor, may provide real stimulus and leadership in concrete disarmament achievements.

[1]The conflict in Vietnam.

It is, of course, my intention to comply fully with the request of the Assembly, and to make available to the countries of these regions all possible facilities and assistance.

The resolutions adopted point the way to progress through the sharing of initiative and responsibility in the field of disarmament among nuclear and non-nuclear, among small and large powers, among Members and nonmembers of the United Nations. But the main responsibility for the curbing of the arms race throughout the world remains with the great powers. The international atmosphere is quick to respond to positive initiatives of the great powers.

I am sure that we all derive great satisfaction from the overwhelmingly favorable votes which the resolutions on disarmament have received this year. Certainly this demonstration of agreement on objectives and machinery for their attainment is most welcome.

The main task now is to turn the overwhelmingly positive votes into concrete acts that will help stem the spiraling trend of fear and of armaments. For this, it is essential that all powers, and first of all the great powers, give evidence of a real desire to make the mutual concessions and accommodations that are necessary for agreements to be achieved. In the field of disarmament, perhaps even more than in other areas of international action, agreements can be reached only if governments are convinced that such agreements are in their interest, and if there is a real will on the part of governments to agree. As I have indicated on previous occasions, it would help to achieve such agreements, and at the earliest possible time, if the highest levels of government were to demonstrate once again their active and continuing interest in the negotiations and their desire to reach specific agreements.

Mr. President, I should like to conclude by thanking you and the Members of this Assembly for affording me this opportunity and by expressing the fervent hope that the forthcoming year will be marked by concrete achievements. The dangers of failure and the need for success are very great.

Statement in the General Assembly on the Establishment of the United Nations Development Programme

NEW YORK   NOVEMBER 22, 1965

THE CREATION of the United Nations Development Programme (UNDP) brought together two successful United Nations operations—the Expanded Programme of Technical Assistance and the Special Fund[1]—thereby laying the foundation for the most ambitious international effort ever undertaken in the economic field. Almost immediately it was receiving more money through voluntary contributions than the United Nations was receiving through its annual assessments. U Thant called the founding of UNDP "a truly significant step" in the global war on want. By the end of 1970, UNDP had approved more than 1,200 major pre-investment projects and several thousand smaller technical assistance undertakings which, upon completion, cost UNDP some $1,870 million and the recipient countries $2,120 million. The total amount pledged to UNDP for 1971 was $240 million, more than four times the combined pledges of the Special Fund and the Expanded Programme of Technical Assistance in 1959.

THE GENERAL ASSEMBLY of the United Nations has just taken a truly significant step. In establishing a new United Nations Development Programme it has moved to put our world Organization in the very front line of the global war on want—a struggle that is perhaps the most critical of these times, and surely the most creditable in which men have ever engaged themselves. You have reaffirmed one of the basic purposes of the United Nations and reinforced its ability to carry out that purpose.

It is not my intention to comment now on the many specific benefits that are sure to flow from the creation of the United Nations Develop-

SOURCE: General Assembly Official Records, Twentieth Session, 1383rd plenary meeting.

[1]See Economic and Social Council resolution 222 (IX) of August 14 and 15, 1949; and see General Assembly resolution 1240 (XIII) of October 14, 1958.

ment Programme. Delegates of both industrialized and low-income nations have warmly testified to the effectiveness of its predecessors—the Expanded Programme of Technical Assistance and the Special Fund. They have also expressed strong confidence in this dynamic new partnership for progress—a confidence which I fully share. It is, of course, a great privilege to extend the Secretariat's appreciation for their generous words and—far beyond that—for the effective action of all governments in supporting the efforts of the United Nations family to stimulate peaceful progress.

This Assembly is a world forum whose actions attract world attention. Thus we share here today an opportunity to focus the eyes of the world once again on the need for all nations to act, with greater urgency and unity, against the plague of poverty that sorely afflicts so many of their number. That opportunity must not be missed.

It is no doubt true that the Secretariat of the United Nations is the servant of Member governments. Yet if a major world crisis were imminent, it would be my imperative duty to express my viewpoint on it and strongly to urge all steps that could lead to a successful solution. I feel this duty no less incumbent because the crisis of the world poverty is a quiet, almost a creeping crisis, or because the prospects of a final solution may be distant.

On this occasion there is no need for me to recite in detail the tragic litany of hunger and homelessness, ignorance and ill-health, destitution and despair with which this Assembly is so familiar. Little would be accomplished by parading a vast array of somber statistics. Statistics cannot, by themselves, arouse the world's conscience, nor effectively appeal to its common sense for remedy. Yet the mathematics of misery are so massive, the totals so stark and staggering, as to demand at least summary mention.

Thus, while I will be brief, I must also be blunt. We must, at least, recall that two thirds of the world's population is subsisting on less than one sixth of the world's income, that one and one half billion people in a hundred developing lands are desperately beset by every kind of deprivation, and that millions upon millions are clinging to survival itself by a thin and fraying lifeline. Realism requires us to speak of the global war on want in terms ordinarily reserved for the most serious international conflicts, and to recognize the heavy casualties incurred by our failure to make swifter progress in this struggle. For global poverty quite literally kills tens of thousands of human beings every single day. It cripples hundreds of millions more through malnutrition, chronic disease, enforced idleness, total illiteracy, and a host of other attendant evils. No one can accurately assess the losses which the world community suffers from the inability of so many of its members to realize their productive potential. But, in terms of money alone, the cost must be hundreds of billions.

Our present progress in the war on want is clearly inadequate when matched against what must and can be done. The developing nations are not receiving the modest but essential amounts of assistance they need to solve their most pressing problems and realize their most promising potentials. It is, for example, quite unrealistic to ask that low-income nations formulate long-range development programs without offering these countries adequate assurance of the necessary support. Thus, not only should development assistance be progressively increased, as the ability to make good use of it progressively grows; there should also be concrete forward projections of that aid.

Yet, even now, in many quiet ways, the crisis of worldwide want is being faced up to and dealt with. Today's action by the General Assembly is a seemingly undramatic but certainly significant milestone. Establishment of the United Nations Development Programme opens the way for a fuller mobilization of international resources and a fuller coordination of international efforts on a most important front in the battle for a better world. It provides our United Nations family with greatly increased ability to fulfill the basic mission of pre-investment assistance. That mission is to help developing countries make fuller use of their own resources for strengthening their economies, for enriching the lives of their people, and for contributing to the greater well-being of the entire world community.

One cannot fail to find encouragement in the symbolism of this step, freely taken by governments of developed and developing countries alike. It indicates that essential pre-conditions exist for making greater progress in the future than we have thus far achieved in the past. It demonstrates a high unity of purpose: an alliance between moral obligation and practical action, between conscience and common sense, between vision and realism. There are, of course, legitimate disagreements on the strategy and tactics of the global war on want. We should not try to suppress them, since confrontation of different ideas is essential to speeding progress.

But on our final aims, there is no real disunity. The nations have long since declared their common purpose to banish poverty from the face of this small planet they all share. From the beginning, the United Nations and all of its related agencies have striven to serve as ever more effective instruments in the implementation of that common purpose.

The United Nations family has met this charge, placed upon it by governments, with steadily growing competence. On this occasion I have no hesitation in appealing to governments for the increased but still modest resources essential for swiftly fulfilling the new promise proclaimed here just now.

Exchange of Messages with
President Charles de Gaulle

THE FOLLOWING EXCHANGE of messages between U Thant and President de Gaulle of France reflects the continuation of the cordial relations between the two and of de Gaulle's support for the United Nations as Thant began his fifth year in office.

Letter to President de Gaulle, December 22

Mr. President,

Allow me to offer you my warm congratulations on your re-election to the Presidency of the French Republic and to reiterate my wishes for the continuation of the task you have undertaken in the cause of cooperation between nations and world peace. At a time when serious threats are gathering over the world, I very sincerely hope that the achievement of the objectives you have set yourself in the international field may advance the hour when conditions for ending the armed conflict which is spreading in Asia will prevail.

Allow me also, on this occasion, to thank you for your interest in the United Nations and for your kind feelings toward me. I need hardly say what an indispensable support they are to me in my efforts to develop the capacity of the United Nations to serve the cause of peace.

Letter from President de Gaulle, December 23

Mr. Secretary-General,

I am particularly appreciative of your kind message, which has just been communicated to me by the representative of France to the

SOURCE: UN Press Release SG/SM/417.

United Nations. Like yourself, I place the maintenance of peace and cooperation among nations above every other goal. I appreciate the great distinction with which you are discharging your difficult mission, and request you to accept, Mr. Secretary-General, the assurances of my highest consideration.

❦ 1966 ❦

Messages on the Tashkent Declaration

BEFORE HIS DEPARTURE from the Indian subcontinent on September 15, 1965, U Thant had appealed to Indian Prime Minister Lal Bahadur Shastri and to President Mohammed Ayub Khan of Pakistan to meet face to face to seek a settlement of the Kashmir conflict (see pp. 115–17). The time was not ripe for such a meeting, but the two leaders did accept a Security Council demand for a cease-fire, effective September 22. There was no immediate agreement on the withdrawal of troops to their August 5 positions, however, and the whole question of the future of Jammu and Kashmir remained as far from solution as it had been in 1948. Shastri and Ayub Khan finally were brought together at Tashkent, in the USSR, at the initiative of Aleksei N. Kosygin, Chairman of the Council of Ministers of the Soviet Union. The meeting began on January 4, 1966, and ended with the Tashkent Declaration on January 10, in which the two leaders stated their firm resolve to restore normal relations between their countries and to settle future disputes by peaceful means. They also agreed to withdraw their respective forces by February 25 to the positions they held on August 5, Thant sent messages immediately to the Foreign Minister of India, Sardar Swaran Singh, and Ayub Khan, noting with satisfaction the terms of the Declaration, and to Kosygin, praising his "timely initiative" in bringing the parties together.

FOLLOWING ARE TEXTS of cables sent January 10, 1966, to the Chairman of the Council of Ministers of the Union of Soviet Socialist Republics, Aleksei N. Kosygin, to the Minister for External Affairs of the Republic of India, Sardar Swaran Singh, and to the President of the Republic of Pakistan, Mohammed Ayub Khan.

SOURCE: UN Press Release SG/SM/431, January 11, 1966.

Cable to Chairman Kosygin

May I express my deep satisfaction with the measures agreed upon in the course of the Tashkent meeting and embodied in the Tashkent Declaration. Your timely initiative in bringing the parties together to discuss their problems and your efforts to create a propitious atmosphere greatly facilitated the progress made toward the peaceful settlement of the serious conflict between them. The Tashkent Declaration, I hope, will constitute an effective step toward the establishment of a stable peace in the area.

Cable to Indian Foreign Minister

I have just received the tragic news of the sudden and untimely death of Prime Minister Lal Bahadur Shastri. Please accept my deepest condolences, which I have also conveyed to His Excellency the President.

The sense of loss which is felt at the United Nations is all the more acute because the Prime Minister's death followed so soon after the talks at Tashkent. I had learned with great satisfaction of the measures agreed upon and embodied in the Tashkent Declaration. I am gratified by the conciliatory spirit and determined efforts applied by both sides to the attainment of these points of agreement. I attach special importance to the fact that in accordance with the United Nations Charter, the parties to the Tashkent Declaration renounce the use of force in the settlement of disputes, and that, in conformity with the appropriate resolution of the Security Council, they have agreed to the withdrawal of all armed personnel.

The measures agreed upon in Tashkent are an important step toward establishing a stable peace between India and Pakistan. I also note with great satisfaction the willingness of the governments to continue meetings on matters of direct concern to your country and Pakistan, and express the hope that this continued contact will lead to a lasting settlement of the problems involved and thus help the cause of peace between India and Pakistan and in the region as a whole.

Cable to President Ayub Khan

I have learned with great satisfaction of the measures agreed upon and embodied in the Tashkent Declaration. I am gratified by the conciliatory spirit and determined efforts applied by both sides to the attainment of these points of agreement. I attach special importance to the fact that, in accordance with the United Nations Charter, the parties to the Tashkent Declaration renounce the use of force in the settlement of disputes, and that, in conformity with the appropriate resolution of the Security Council, they have agreed to the withdrawal of all armed personnel.

The measures agreed upon in Tashkent are an important step toward establishing a stable peace between Pakistan and India. I also note with great satisfaction your willingness to continue meetings on matters of direct concern to your country and India, and express the hope that this continued contact will lead to a lasting settlement of the problems involved and thus help the cause of peace between Pakistan and India and in the region as a whole.

From Transcript of Press Conference

NEW YORK   JANUARY 20, 1966

ON JANUARY 20, U Thant held his first formal press conference at United
Nations Headquarters since February 24, 1965. The interval was so long that
Milt Freudenheim, President of the United Nations Correspondents Association (UNCA), took note of it in his welcoming remarks after the opening
statement of the Secretary-General. Freudenheim expressed the hope "that
today's conference will resume your series of more or less regular monthly
meetings with correspondents." Actually Thant had never met correspondents that frequently, but during 1962, 1963, and 1964 he had held at least
three press conferences a year in New York and that many or more away
from Headquarters. In 1965, he had held a single press conference in Geneva
on July 7 in addition to the February 24 meeting in New York. Thant himself
did not refer to the reduced number of press conferences, but those who
knew him well discounted any suggestion that his relations with the press
corps were cooling. From August until the end of the year he had been
involved personally in the Kashmir peace efforts—in addition to the usual
heavy load of work connected with the General Assembly—and he had felt
that it would not be wise for him to subject himself to a general press
conference.

When he did meet the press on January 20, it was the Vietnam situation, as
usual, which dominated the questioning. He made no new disclosures about
his own private peace efforts, but did make a number of statements on
various aspects of the problem, including his own view that the political
climate for negotiations had been improved by the temporary halt in the
United States bombing of North Vietnam.

As he had done on a number of occasions, Thant stated that at the moment
he saw no role which the United Nations could usefully play, but that he
himself was still doing his utmost to bring the parties to the conference table.
Meanwhile, he acknowledged that the image of the United Nations "must
have been somewhat tarnished by its seeming impotence in dealing with the
greatest crisis facing mankind since the Second World War."

For many, the most interesting development during the press conference
was his reply to a question as to whether he would be a candidate for another
term as Secretary-General when his current term expired at the end of the
year. Although he indicated he had not yet made up his mind, he clearly did
not rule out the possibility of another term. He said he would "decide one
way or the other perhaps before the end of June" so that the Security Council
would have ample time to recommend a successor if his decision was in the
negative. He told the correspondents his thinking about the job had not
changed since 1962 when he laid down three main objectives: (1) to try to

bring about a relaxation of world tensions, (2) to try to bring about a rapprochement between the big powers, and (3) to do his best to see that the United Nations developed into a really effective instrument to carry out the functions outlined in the Charter.

THE SECRETARY-GENERAL: We are meeting today, as you know, after we have had some rest following a strenuous session of the General Assembly. I think that we can look back on that twentieth session as one of special interest: not only because it marked, if not the end, at least the easing of the crisis which had prevented the General Assembly from functioning properly since 1963, but also because the Assembly came back into action, so to speak, with renewed vigor and, in my opinion, with some hopeful signs that new achievements in international cooperation are possible.

In my view, the twentieth session of the General Assembly is one of the most productive sessions in the life of the United Nations— productive in the sense that it has been able to decide on a great many issues. Many of the decisions are of a far-reaching character although their immediate impact will not be readily discernible. The visit of Pope Paul VI to the United Nations and his historic message of peace were among the highlights of the session.

The session has its debit side too. Its seeming lack of enthusiasm to take a closer look into the peace-keeping functions of the United Nations is far from gratifying. My repeated appeals for voluntary contributions drew generous response only from a few Member states. I am afraid some of the existing United Nations peace-keeping operations like the United Nations Emergency Force (UNEF) and the United Nations Force in Cyprus (UNFICYP) are in danger of being curtailed in the near future owing to lack of funds. Our only hope now lies in the work of the Special Committee of Thirty-three[1] and the newly created Committee of Fourteen[2] which, I understand, will meet in the next one or two weeks.

SOURCE: *UN Monthly Chronicle,* vol. III, February 1966, pp. 33–43.

[1]Special Committee on Peace-keeping Operations.
[2]*Ad Hoc* Committee of Experts to Examine the Finances of the United Nations and the Specialized Agencies.

The world scene today is dominated by the conflict in Vietnam. As you are all aware, there have been, during the past few weeks, a number of developments in that conflict. A halt has been brought in the United States air raids against North Vietnam, and the parties to the conflict have stated anew their positions on a negotiated settlement. I do not feel that it would be appropriate for me to comment now on these developments, because the situation is not entirely clear. The parties may still be considering what their decisions should be. When there were raids against North Vietnam, the prospects for negotiations were certainly more remote than at present, and, in such a complex and fluid situation, when trends have a possibility of being reversed, extraordinary patience is much needed and one has to take a longer view of the conflict.

Looking at the evolution of the conflict over the last year, it must be observed that, in spite of the horrors of the war and however grim the situation still remains, there has been an undeniable rapprochement between the positions of the parties. All agree now that Geneva offers the most appropriate framework for discussions; in other words, all sides now recognize that any lasting settlement must have the unanimous support of all the great powers, including, naturally, China. This indicates a considerable progress. In addition, certain basic principles of a negotiated settlement seem to have already been agreed upon, namely, that both parts of Vietnam will not enter into military alliances or seek foreign military assistance, and that both parts of Vietnam will be free to decide between themselves the question of reunification.

Everyone recognizes that the people of South Vietnam should be free to settle their own affairs without foreign intervention and in accordance with democratic principles. But, behind these common principles, there seems to exist much divergence of view, the extent of which it is difficult to assess, concerning the implementation of these principles. However, I have been wondering whether the time has come to raise such practical questions as what type of government in South Vietnam, representative, as far as possible, of all the sections of the South Vietnamese people, could take over the responsibility of organizing the exercise by the people of their right to decide their own affairs. If the parties were to make concrete proposals on this issue, I think a refusal to negotiate would be difficult to justify, particularly if, as I have already said, discussions to bring about an end to the fighting must be held with those who are fighting there.

Now I would invite questions.

QUESTION: As the first question following your statement, I wonder whether you could comment on your indications, from your many contacts with governments, of the prospects for continued de-escalation of the Vietnam war.

THE SECRETARY-GENERAL: As I stated in my opening remarks, the situation today, during the cessation of bombing, is more congenial for fruitful discussions than the situation of a few weeks ago when the bombings were taking place. I very much hope that the situation will continue to improve so that the parties to the conflict will be in a position to come to the conference table with clear ideas, not only about the items to be discussed, but also about the objectives of the discussions.

QUESTION: Have you, in the course of your contacts, had any indication directly or indirectly from anyone else that the communists in that part of the world are beginning to look favorably upon negotiation either at Geneva or in any other part of the world?

THE SECRETARY-GENERAL: As you know, the approach to the problem of Vietnam and the assessment of the background to the developments in Vietnam, and, of course, the assessment of the present situation in Vietnam, varies from person to person and from country to country. My understanding of the developments leading toward the present crisis in Vietnam and my assessment of the situation in Vietnam are different from the understanding and assessment of most of you, I believe. But, with regard to the specific question just posed, I am conscious of the fact that in my position as Secretary-General of the United Nations, I have very severe limitations with respect to my actions or my statements. I am sure you will understand that I have to be very discreet. But, I want to say that the political climate for negotiations today is more favorable than the political climate of, for instance, last year.

QUESTION: Mr. Secretary-General, do I understand from your first statement to us that it is your belief that the National Liberation Front should be included as a party to the peace negotiations, as well as in a coalition government that must succeed the present situation in Vietnam? Would you be more explicit on this idea?

THE SECRETARY-GENERAL: My views on the nature of discussions, and even on the composition of certain delegations attending such discussions, have been stated several times.

I felt very strongly, and I still feel very strongly, that if realistic discussions are to take place, there must be participation in them by, among others, those who are actually fighting. In my view, that is the only sensible approach.

With respect to the second part of the question, concerning the composition of some sort of government in South Vietman, I think that I have dealt with that aspect adequately in my opening statement.

QUESTION: On February 24 last year—I think that that is the correct date—you said, if I remember rightly, that you thought that these Asian problems were best settled by Asians. Do you still hold to that belief, and would you expand on it in the light of the present situation?

THE SECRETARY-GENERAL: I have never said that Asian problems must be settled exclusively by Asians. In this particular instance, the problem of Vietnam has involved many countries, both Asian and non-Asian. My view is that both Asians and non-Asians were involved in trying to settle the Vietnam problem in 1954 at Geneva. I have maintained all along, and I still maintain, that the Geneva Agreements of 1954 should be the basis for future discussions. I have maintained all along, and I still maintain, that future discussions should focus attention primarily on the modalities of implementing the Agreements arrived at in Geneva in 1954. I do not think that it would be realistic to confine the participants in such discussions to Asians.

QUESTION: Do you base your statement that the situation in Vietnam is more favorable today on the four points of Hanoi and the fourteen points of the United States? Do you feel that within the four points and the fourteen points there is some basis, some hope, for compromise?

THE SECRETARY-GENERAL: When I say that the political climate today is more congenial for discussions than the political climate of, say, a few weeks ago, I am thinking primarily of the psychological climate generated by the cessation of the bombing of North Vietnam. Of course, I have no comment to make publicly on the four points and the fourteen points, but I feel that all those points adduced by the parties primarily concerned in the conflict should receive very serious consideration at any conference table.

QUESTION: Have you any reason to believe, or even to hope, that the present cease-fire might be continued indefinitely and/or that the present cessation of bombing might be continued indefinitely?

THE SECRETARY-GENERAL: I have no means of knowing what the plans of the United States government are, but I very much hope that the present psychological climate generated by the cessation of bombing will be further improved by all measures possible, so that the parties involved in the conflict may be brought to the conference table as soon as possible.

. . .

QUESTION: Let us suppose for a moment that there was some magic formula which resulted in the United States accepting the Vietcong as a party to the negotiations and the Vietnamese accepting the withdrawal of all United States forces in South Vietnam through a step-by-step process over a period of two or three years; let us suppose that military operations then stopped and that this was followed by negotiations and the constitution of a provisional government and elections throughout South Vietnam; and, finally, let us suppose that all that was done under the supervision of the United Nations. I should think that the problem then would be tremendous, with difficulties that were sometimes insurmountable. Have you some thoughts on that subject to share with us?

THE SECRETARY-GENERAL: The steps you have just outlined are very sensible. With respect to a possible United Nations involvement in the implementation of all those steps, I have made my views very clear on many previous occasions. I felt, and I still feel, that at least at this stage the United Nations cannot be involved in the Vietnam conflict. The reasons I have adduced are well known to all of you. As I have said on many previous occasions, I believe that, at some stage, the United Nations can be usefully and effectively involved in seeing that the agreements arrived at in a future peace conference are implemented. It all depends on the circumstances. It all depends on the attitudes of the parties primarily involved. It all depends on the changing circumstances at that time. For the moment I do not see any possibility of United Nations involvement in the Vietnam conflict.

. . .

QUESTION: Mr. Secretary-General, would you personally favor a meeting of the Security Council to at least debate the Vietnamese war?

THE SECRETARY-GENERAL: I do not believe that a useful purpose will be served by an open debate in the Security Council.

QUESTION: On your statement that at some stage you believe the United Nations will play an effective role in Vietnam, and in connection with what you answered just now, well, we have a war and there are killings and there is a threat to international peace. Mr. Secretary-General, do you not believe that it is the primary duty of the United Nations, according to the Charter, to see that there is an immediate cease-fire, at least a stoppage of the killings? Isn't it the duty of the United Nations to act immediately as these things are going on daily?

THE SECRETARY-GENERAL: I understand the motivations of your question. Of course, it is true that the United Nations has a primary responsibility to maintain international peace and security. It was true in 1954, as it is true in 1966. Now, look at the situation in 1954. The parties to the conflict decided to resolve their differences in Geneva, outside the framework of the United Nations. Of course, a lot of thought was given to the prospective United Nations involvement even at that time. But the big powers, plus the parties to the conflict, decided that the discussions should take place outside the framework of the United Nations, for the obvious reason that some of the parties to the conflict were not Members of the United Nations. That was the simple explanation.

If it was true that the discussions on the Vietnam situation could take place in Geneva in 1954, outside the framework of the United Nations, the same considerations still apply today, because some of the parties primarily involved in the conflict are still not Members of the United Nations. This is the greatest impediment to any United Nations involvement in finding a peaceful solution to the Vietnam conflict.

QUESTION: Mr. Secretary-General, you have recently seen both Mr. Goldberg and Mr. Fedorenko.[3] What is your assessment of the current status of relations between the giants?

THE SECRETARY-GENERAL: I think on this I know as much as you

[3]Arthur J. Goldberg, permanent representative of the United States, and N. T. Fedorenko, permanent representative of the USSR.

do. As I have stated on a previous occasion, there has been some rapprochement between the big powers in 1963. There was a considerable setback in 1964, in terms of chronology. My feeling is that although the trend toward rapprochement is slowly developing, the crisis in Vietnam is one great single impediment, which is likely to reverse this trend.

QUESTION: Mr. Secretary-General, when you said that the Geneva Accords of 1954 should form the basis of future discussions, do you have in mind discussions for the implementation of that accord or are you trying to suggest that that Accord should be reopened for fresh negotiations on the basic elements of the settlement?

THE SECRETARY-GENERAL: The ideal situation would be for the parties primarily involved in the conflict to agree on the Geneva Agreements of 1954 and to try to find modalities for the implementation of these Agreements. That would be the ideal situation. But, of course, I am aware of the fact that this is not very realistic. So I would be happy also if the discussions could be based on the Geneva Agreements of 1954 without a prior commitment regarding the acceptance of the Agreements arrived at in 1954. I would be equally happy.

QUESTION: Mr. Secretary-General, have you decided whether or not you will be a candidate again when your term expires at the end of the year?

THE SECRETARY-GENERAL: It is a very difficult question to answer. You will perhaps recall that when I accepted the present assignment in November 1962, I said, among other things, that nobody would like to accept the position of the Secretary-General knowing as he does what it means, but only out of a keen sense of duty. That has been my thinking all along. I also said on that occasion, if I remember right, that I would try my best to settle the Congo problem, that I would try my best to bring about the relaxation of tensions in the world, that I would try my best to bring about a rapprochement between the big powers, and that I would try my best to see that this world Organization develops into a really effective instrument for the performance of the functions outlined in the Charter. These were some of my observations made in November 1962.

So when the time comes for me to decide one way or the other, whether I should offer myself for the second term or whether I should not offer myself for the second term, I have to take into consideration all these factors which I have just stated. Of course, as far as the

Congo is concerned, as you all know, the United Nations has disengaged itself militarily, although, of course, six months later than I had proposed. You will recall that I had proposed that the United Nations military operations in the Congo should be withdrawn at a certain date. The General Assembly, however, decided to withdraw the United Nations military forces from the Congo six months later. If only my recommendation were accepted by the General Assembly, it would, in terms of financial obligations alone, have effected a saving of at least $50 million.

I am saying this not in a spirit of any dissatisfaction with the steps taken by the General Assembly. The General Assembly, comprising as it does all the Member states, is the supreme body in these matters. But as far as the question of the United Nations developing into a really effective instrument for the maintenance of international peace and security is concerned, I have dealt with that aspect of the problem very briefly in my opening statement. In my view, the General Assembly at its twentieth session should have taken a more energetic position on the United Nations peace-keeping operations, particularly the financial aspects of the peace-keeping operations.

I should like to take this opportunity of expressing my thanks to some governments, particularly the government of Ireland, for taking the initiative in trying to put the financial aspect of the peace-keeping operations on a firmer basis. As I have said in my opening remarks, the future of some of the peace-keeping operations like the United Nations Emergency Force and the United Nations Force in Cyprus is rather gloomy. In spite of my repeated appeals for contributions, the response has been far from encouraging.

Of course, in many other areas of activities the United Nations has been able to achieve tremendous results, particularly in the economic and social fields. And even in the peace-keeping area, I think, the United Nations has achieved a very great success in bringing about a cease-fire between India and Pakistan. These are achievements—not insignificant.

But when I have to decide about my future, of course, I have to do justice to the United Nations by informing the Security Council, for instance, very well in advance of the expiry of my present term. I think I should decide one way or the other perhaps before June, so that the Security Council will be in a position to nominate someone to succeed me—if I decide not to offer myself for a second term—and to make a recommendation to the General Assembly. Of course, if the Security Council were in a position to find someone to be recommended to the General Assembly to succeed me, in the course of the next few months, I believe it would facilitate my decision.

. . .

QUESTION: Mr. Secretary-General, do you feel that the prestige of the United Nations as an Organization is being damaged by its not trying a more active role in settling the Vietnamese war?

THE SECRETARY-GENERAL: I must confess that the image of the United Nations as such must have been somewhat tarnished by its seeming impotence in dealing with the greatest crisis facing mankind since the Second World War. But, as you know, in my private capacity I have been doing my utmost to bring about a peaceful solution for the last two and one half years or so. Without, of course, revealing the substance of the steps I took, I can say without fear of contradiction that in 1963 my efforts were directed primarily toward the stability of South Vietnam. In 1964, my efforts were directed primarily toward the holding of informal private dialogues between the parties primarily concerned. In 1965, my efforts were directed primarily toward the cessation of hostilities and the holding of informal conferences with the participation of the big powers, including, of course, Peking. All these efforts have not been successful so far, but I can assure you that I am still continuing my efforts to bring about a peaceful solution of the problem.

. . .

THE SITUATION IN CYPRUS

IN MARCH 1966, the United Nations Force in Cyprus began its third year of operations without any prospect of being withdrawn. On March 4, U Thant sent a note to the Security Council stating that he had not yet been able to restore the mediation function which had been suspended since Turkey's refusal a year earlier to deal further with the United Nations mediator, Mr. Galo Plaza, because of comments made by the mediator in a report to the Security Council. The post of mediator had actually been vacant since December 22 when Galo Plaza resigned. The purpose of Thant's March 4 note was to inform the Council that he was asking his special representative, Carlos A. Bernardes, to take on at least part of the mediator's peace-making functions. Specifically, he asked Bernardes to use his good offices in any way he could to get discussions started again. In a statement to the Council on March 16, after that body had voted a new six-month extension of the Cyprus force, the Secretary-General once more expressed his unhappiness over "uncertain and inadequate" financial support for the operation.

1. Note to the Security Council

NEW YORK   MARCH 4, 1966

I WISH TO INFORM the members of the Security Council that, on March 2, 1966, after having informed the parties directly concerned, I sent the following message to Mr. Carlos A. Bernardes, my special representative in Cyprus:

As you know, my efforts to bring about a resumption of the mediation function in Cyprus have not as yet met with success. I am, of course, continuing these efforts. At the same time, I do not believe that there should be any interruption in the exploration of all possibilities which might prove helpful in the Cyprus situation.

Therefore, having in mind the fine rapport you have established and

SOURCE: Security Council Official Records, Twenty-first Year, Supplement for January, February, and March 1966, document S/2180.

maintain with all of the parties directly concerned, I authorize you, in your capacity as my special representative in Cyprus, to employ your good offices and make such approaches to the parties in or outside the island of Cyprus, as may seem to you to be likely to be productive, in the sense of achieving in the first instance discussions at any level of problems and issues of either a purely local or a broader nature.

I feel confident that this added responsibility will not unduly burden you under prevailing conditions in Cyprus.

It goes without saying that your activities under these broader instructions are without prejudice to the mediation function as envisaged in the Security Council resolution.

You will, of course, keep me informed as usual. I have informed the representatives of Cyprus, Greece, and Turkey of my intention to broaden your responsibilities as indicated above, and I am sure that we may count on the cooperation of those governments in your forthcoming efforts.

It is my intention to inform the Security Council of this step, possibly by including the text of this message in my next report.

---

2. Statement in the Security Council

NEW YORK   MARCH 16, 1966

THE ACTION just taken by the Security Council again extends the Force in Cyprus. This is a desirable and, indeed, an essential action in the light of the continuing circumstances in the island. But once again the resolution just adopted by the Council, in extending the Force, has ignored the financial situation affecting it. Quite frankly, I am disappointed that the resolution makes no effort to strengthen the financial support for the Force, which, as the members of the Council are aware, has been uncertain and inadequate. While, thanks to the public-spirited generosity of some Member states, the financial outlook is better than it was, there is still a substantial deficit which can be met only by more and greater contributions than are in sight at this time.

The Council, I am sure, will readily understand this expression of disappointment when I point out that it is one thing to vote to extend

SOURCE: Security Council Official Records, Twenty-first Year, 1275th meeting.

the Force and quite another thing to have to maintain and support that Force in the field from day to day and to meet the obligations it incurs, which is the continuing responsibility of the Secretary-General.

Thus I feel that I have no choice but to repeat what I said in paragraph 149 of my report to the Council, namely that I must put on notice the governments providing contingents to the Force that unless unforeseen financial support is forthcoming I will not be in a position to honor fully previously made commitments for reimbursement of the extra costs that have been, and are likely to be, incurred.

Message to the United Nations Association of South Africa

NEW YORK   MARCH 24, 1966

U THANT spoke out frequently, both as Burma's permanent representative at the United Nations and later as Secretary-General, against South Africa's policies of apartheid. Although the South African government had taken him to task for what it called his meddling in South Africa's internal affairs, he considered he was within his rights, since he was voicing opinions in line with United Nations resolutions. One of his sharpest statements on apartheid was contained in a message to the United Nations Association of South Africa, sent on March 24 at the invitation of that organization. He called South Africa's racial policies a "distorted and dangerous but passing phase in the adjustment and evolution of human attitudes" and expressed the hope that governmental policy and public practice in South Africa were "capable of being corrected, and corrected peacefully."

I AM GLAD to be able to accept the invitation extended to me to send a message to the United Nations Association of South Africa. I have already done so in the case of a number of other national associations, for I have always attached great importance to their efforts to promote support for international cooperation and for the United Nations itself. The United Nations can only benefit from these activities. Its effectiveness depends critically upon public awareness—and more than that, upon realistic understanding—of its functions and its possibilities and the extent to which they have been and can be realized.

In most parts of the world, a basis of such understanding has been established. There cannot be a single Member state whose people and government do not recognize the United Nations, as far as its authority and the evolution of international relationships allow, to be an indispensable instrument for the maintenance of peace and the promotion of international cooperation.

SOURCE: UN Press Release SG/SM/473.

In the two decades of its existence the Organization has made some crucial contributions, for which no other practical means existed, to promoting the pacific settlement of disputes, to containing and resolving conflicts, and to assisting the peaceful evolution to independence of peoples in colonial territories. It has also become in a very real sense a center for directing and providing the resources for substantial programs of international cooperation in the economic, social, and cultural fields. If it has not yet had enough direct influence in resolving the basic issues which divide the great powers and which therefore leave the whole world insecure, there can be no question but that the United Nations has at least begun—and made a more substantial beginning than any previous attempt—to create that climate of experience and understanding in which further cooperation is possible.

South Africa, as a founder Member of the Organization, made a significant contribution to the formulation of the United Nations Charter. And I am convinced that South Africa and its people, who have it within themselves to combine for the common good a great variety of cultural and economic backgrounds, experience, and skill, can play an even more substantial part in fulfilling the ideals upon which the Charter is based.

I express this conviction in full knowledge of those present circumstances which may seem, from other points of view, to contradict it. I do not seek to minimize the differences which exist between South Africa and most of its fellow Member states over the questions, in particular, of apartheid and South West Africa, both of which are accepted by the United Nations as a whole as being matters of legitimate international concern. Nor would I wish to minimize the gravity of the situation which has given rise to those differences, or the profound anxiety which exists about those present manifestations of it in southern Africa which are disrupting relations among states, as well as disturbing the conscience of most of mankind.

I have never concealed my own belief that racial discrimination in any form and in any corner of the world is an odious aberration. I continue to hope, however, that the aspects of governmental policy and public practice in southern Africa which have aroused particular alarm in the United Nations are capable of being corrected, and corrected peacefully. I believe that they represent a distorted and dangerous but passing phase in the adjustment and evolution of human attitudes. And I believe that the resolution of these problems will come about more quickly and more calmly if all of the peoples concerned make a genuine effort to respect one another's legitimate rights, as well as the concern of humanity at large. In doing so, they will contribute to the fulfillment of the principles and purposes of the United Nations Charter in the world as a whole and lay the basis for the more fruitful role which they can play in international relations and particularly within the United Nations system.

With these reflections I send my best wishes that constructive results will be forthcoming from your discussions.

Statement at Unveiling of Portrait of Dag Hammarskjöld

NEW YORK   APRIL 5, 1966

THE PORTRAIT of Dag Hammarskjöld by Bo Beskow was hung in the lobby of the United Nations Secretariat building some four and one half years after Hammarskjöld's death. In his statement at the unveiling of the portrait on April 5, U Thant made no reference to the widespread comments among staff members that the painting did not reflect accurately the personal magnetism of Hammarskjöld and that it therefore did not do justice to him. On the contrary, Thant said his impression was that the artist had been "very successful indeed" in putting on canvas the essential character of Hammarskjöld.

IN THIS HEADQUARTERS complex there are memorials to the late Secretary-General, but none as yet which presents a likeness of him. Mr. Hammarskjöld is known to have had some strong reservations about the display of portraits or likenesses of himself, and it is a fact that very few portraits of him, other than photographic ones, exist.

Nonetheless, we have felt that there should be in the United Nations Headquarters a suitable painting of the man who, with rare distinction, carried out the taxing duties of chief officer of this Organization for eight years, and died serving it. We are fortunate in having gained possession of a splendid portrait of him by Bo Beskow, who is not only an eminent artist but was also a close friend of Mr. Hammarskjöld. In the light of these circumstances, I am sure that Mr. Hammarskjöld would understand and even concur in our desire to obtain and display this fine likeness.

A portrait of the first Secretary-General, Mr. Trygve Lie, also hangs in this building, on the thirty-eighth floor.

Mr. Beskow devoted work and thought over many years to this picture in the effort to portray on a few square feet of canvas not only the features but the essential character of a most remarkable and

SOURCE: UN Press Release SG/SM/480.

many-sided man. As we live with this picture day by day, we shall better be able to judge how successful Mr. Beskow has been, but it is my early impression that he has been very successful indeed. The painting grows on one and conveys life and vitality.

It was originally intended that the portrait should be hung in the Hammarskjöld Library. After extensive exploration, however, it was decided that there was no wall in the Library Building which was fully suitable to its strength and size. We have, therefore, chosen this wall, where the picture has the necessary space to be seen properly and where many of those who work here, as well as members of the general public, will view it in the course of their daily comings and goings. It thus will hang, appropriately enough, in this building where Mr. Hammarskjöld, in the course of his eight arduous years here, spent more of his time than anywhere else, including his home.

The generosity of the Ford Foundation and of the Swedish publishing house of Bonniers has made it possible to acquire this portrait for the United Nations, and to them I express our earnest thanks and appreciation.

I now unveil this portrait of Dag Hammarskjöld.

From Transcript of Press Conference

NEW YORK   APRIL 6, 1966

U THANT's April 6 press conference was his second of the year. It was accepted by correspondents as evidence that the long gap between his January 20 meeting with the press (see p. 185) and his previous one was due to circumstances rather than policy. He said he was unable to add anything to his January 20 statement as to whether or not he would be a candidate for another term as Secretary-General. He repeated that he hoped to make his decision known by June, but that he had been telling delegates who sought his views that he would be happy if the Security Council could find someone to succeed him in November.

. . .

QUESTION: In January you told us that you would have to decide before June of this year whether to make yourself available for re-election for another term as Secretary-General. It is now April; have you yet made your decision?

THE SECRETARY-GENERAL: I do not think I have anything more to add to what I told you on January 20. As you have rightly pointed out, we have about two and a half months to go, and my feelings remain the same. As I have stated on previous occasions, if the Security Council were in a position to find someone to recommend to the General Assembly to succeed me in November of this year, I would be happy. I have expressed these views again and again to those representatives who sought my private views on this. Of course, it is still too early yet to make an official decision on this, for reasons which you understand. But, in any case, to do justice to this world Organization, if I decide not to stand for re-election, I have to make my decision known—I believe, some time in June.

QUESTION: Mr. Secretary-General, to what extent do you believe the war in Vietnam has become a contest for strategic position among the United States, China, and the Soviet Union? What steps could

SOURCE: UN Press Release SG/SM/482.

these three powers take to try to end the suffering of the Vietnamese people?

THE SECRETARY-GENERAL: It is difficult to assess the Vietnam crisis in the context of the strategic interests of the big powers. Of course, the term "strategic interests" is not a very happy one, since it has connotations of military strategy. But I understand that some big powers have strategic interests in the area as in other parts of the world. To be frank about it, the United States has certain strategic interests in the South Pacific; at the same time, the People's Republic of China must have similar interests.

My feeling is that the Vietnam problem could have been solved earlier if there had been a basic acceptance of some fundamental facts. As I have stated on previous occasions, I have all along believed that Vietnam could be an independent and nonaligned country as it was envisaged in the Geneva Agreements of 1954. Of course, when I say "independent and non-aligned" it should be preferably guaranteed by the big powers, including, of course, Peking and Washington. That has been my approach to this problem for the last eleven years. I believed all along that Vietnam could be made an independent and nonaligned country. That is the reason why, when General de Gaulle came out three years ago with his proposal to make Southeast Asia nonaligned or to have a conference to consider the question of nonalignment of Southeast Asia, comprising not only Vietnam but also Laos and Cambodia, I was among the first to endorse that proposal. I think there were missed opportunities in this regard, if I may say so. What was possible, for instance, in 1964 is, I am afraid, no longer possible today, as I have been saying all along. But I think we should keep on trying.

But of one thing I am sure. In order to bring peace to Vietnam, to find an enduring peace for that very unfortunate country, its independence and nonalignment should be the objective of all parties primarily concerned in the conflict, and this concept of independence and nonalignment should preferably be guaranteed by the big powers, including Peking and Washington.

. . .

QUESTION: To go back to Vietnam—there seems to be a great upheaval in the country today, politically, which is, of course, directly connected with the war. Do you feel that the situation there affords an opportunity for a renewed initiative of some kind in the way of a peace effort, as it appears to me that there has been something of an unhealthy lull in this initiative, as the war is getting more and more bitter? Do you feel that there is room here for a turning point?

THE SECRETARY-GENERAL: I think one lesson we can draw from the Vietnamese crisis, and for that matter from developments in many parts of the world today, is the fact that nationalism is still the most potent force in the life of a people. Whether you assess the situation in Vietnam or Syria or Ghana or Indonesia or elsewhere, I think historians may draw one conclusion: that nationalism, more than any political belief or political ideology or political conviction, is the most potent force in the life of a people. This applies equally to Africa or to Latin America or even to Europe. I think it is misleading to think primarily in terms of political ideologies in the context of the newly emerging nations.

If my reading of history is correct, the peoples in these newly independent countries are much more obsessed with their economic development and their national identity than they are with their feelings regarding political ideologies or political beliefs. That is my assessment. I think that in all these countries the leaders are more obsessed with economic matters than with political matters. First of all, they are devising ways and means of advancing the economic and social progress of their own peoples—how to feed their people, how to house their people, how to clothe their people. Man is essentially an economic animal, and only secondarily is he a political animal. I think this basic fact must be understood in any approach to the problems of the newly independent countries.

I should like to make one further observation. After twenty-five years of war and strife and struggle, no people in the world wants peace more, and deserves peace more, than the people of Vietnam.

QUESTION: What might be the conditions for a possible Indonesian re-entry into the United Nations? Would it require formal readmission by the General Assembly?

THE SECRETARY-GENERAL: While, so far, I have been following the newspaper reports on this subject with, of course, very close interest, I have not received anything official from the government of Indonesia. But of one thing I am sure: if the government of Indonesia decides to come back to the United Nations, the entire membership will be very delighted to take it back in this family of nations. With respect to procedure, I believe that I have to go through the same motions as those I went through when Indonesia decided to withdraw from the United Nations. As you know, there are no specific provisions in the Charter regarding the withdrawal of membership and, for that matter, there are no specific provisions in the Charter regarding re-entry. But I feel that the same motions have to be gone through.

QUESTION: If Indonesia applies for readmission, will it be made a condition under Article 4 of the Charter that she renounce aggression against Malaysia?

THE SECRETARY-GENERAL: Of course, the very fact that a country applies for membership or applies for readmission implies acceptance of the obligations provided for in the Charter. I do not think any special requests or conditions should be made in any particular case.

QUESTION: Mr. Secretary-General, at the Congress of the Soviet Communist Party some important statements were made directly concerning the United Nations. For example, in the report of the Central Committee to the Congress, [Chairman Leonid] Brezhnev said that the Soviet Union strives persistently to facilitate the unity of all states in the United Nations which are against aggression and, thus, to enhance the role of this Organization in the struggle for peace and the independence of peoples. The report also points out that the USSR considers the United Nations as an arena of active political struggle against aggression and for the cause of peace and the security of all peoples. I would like to know your opinion of that statement.

THE SECRETARY-GENERAL: I read Mr. Brezhnev's report to the twenty-third Congress with very close attention. I noticed that he made, for the first time to my knowledge, some very important references to the United Nations and, if I may interpret them, a rededication to the Charter principles and a reaffirmation of faith in the future of the United Nations. These statements, in my view, are very positive and very useful, and I want to take this opportunity of expressing my very sincere thanks to Mr. Brezhnev for his references to the United Nations, which I believe are very significant in the context of the present day realities.

QUESTION: Mr. Secretary-General, Ambassador Muhammad El-Farra of Jordan, on behalf of the Arab states, yesterday presented you with an invitation to visit the Palestine Arab refugee camps. Might you tell us what your initial reaction was to that invitation and whether any decisions have been made in this context?

THE SECRETARY-GENERAL: Ambassador El-Farra transmitted to me the invitation of the Arab governments to visit the refugee camps in the Middle East. I have not replied to him officially. I am still studying the implications of this invitation. As you know, Mr. [Laurence] Michelmore, the head of the United Nations Relief and Works Agency for Palestine Refugees in the Near East has been directly involved in these matters on behalf of the United Nations and on behalf of the Secretary-General. I have been in contact with him, as you know, and I am still weighing the pros and cons of my visit to the area vis-à-vis the visits which have been made by Mr. Michelmore on behalf of the United Nations. If I see any indication of more positive results by my visit, of course I will be very glad to accept the invitation. If not, I am afraid I will have to decline the invitation with thanks. As you all know, the plight of the refugees is most pathetic.

QUESTION: Mr. Secretary-General, last fall the Security Council took certain action against Southern Rhodesia, the rebellious government of Ian Smith. To date, those actions have not been very effective in bringing that government into line. Do you have any recommendations to make to the Council or to the General Assembly to bring the Ian Smith government into line? And if these actions are not successful, do you think this is going to hurt the prestige and the effectiveness of the United Nations as a peace-keeping body?

THE SECRETARY-GENERAL: I am increasingly concerned about the developments in Southern Rhodesia. Only yesterday I had occasion to discuss this question with the Chairman of the Committee of Twenty-four,[1] and I understand that the Committee of Twenty-four is taking up this matter today. I believe the Committee as a whole will take more vigorous action. I also understand that the British government is actively considering further measures to give effect to its policies, and even economic sanctions under Chapter VII [of the United Nations Charter] cannot be ruled out.

. . .

QUESTION: You have said some things about Vietnam. If you were to suggest one immediate and specific thing which might lead toward peace in Vietnam, what would it be?

THE SECRETARY-GENERAL: I have been suggesting more than one

[1]The Special Committee on the Situation with regard to the Implementation of the Declaration on the Granting of Independence to Colonial Countries and Peoples.

specific thing for the last three years, unfortunately so far without success, and it is rather difficult to summarize the steps I have proposed in the last two years. I think many of you are aware of the steps I have taken, and for the moment I still feel that the two sides are speaking two different languages. If the objectives and the methods to be applied can be defined more clearly, I think there will be some proximity of positions. For the moment, I am sorry to say, I do not see any immediate prospect of a reconciliation of viewpoints.

QUESTION: In the same report made by Mr. Brezhnev to the twenty-third Communist Party Conference in Moscow, it was suggested that such steps as the signing of a nonproliferation treaty, the creation of areas free from nuclear weapons in different parts of the world, pledges by the nuclear powers not to use nuclear weapons, and the banning of underground nuclear tests should be undertaken to solve the problem of disarmament. Could you give us your opinion concerning these problems?

THE SECRETARY-GENERAL: As I have said before, the question of nonproliferation of nuclear weapons is the most pressing issue before the Eighteen-Nation Disarmament Committee (ENDC), which is still meeting in Geneva. Of course, the ENDC has been running into some snags, and one of them is, as you know, the nature and the character of the participation by one of the members of NATO [North Atlantic Treaty Organization] in the matter of control of nuclear weapons. To my knowledge, this is still a stumbling block, but I very much hope that common sense will prevail on all sides and that we will have the benefit of an agreed text on the nonproliferation of nuclear weapons. On the banning of underground nuclear tests, I am very much interested in the latest formula submitted by Sweden the other day in the ENDC in Geneva. I believe that the Swedish proposal deserves very close attention.

QUESTION: Regarding the war in Vietnam, the consensus among the 18,000 or 20,000 Vietnamese living in Europe, among them about 4,000 doctors, professors, and lawyers, mostly residing in Paris, is as follows: they see no immediate, no possible end to the tremendous sufferings of their countrymen at home, and they feel immensely proud to be able to show to the world how a brave small nation can resist victoriously against the first military power on earth. Even those who were most well known as very pro-American have the strong feeling that while the United Nations is just watching the killing, the United States is conducting an unjust and immoral war with the utmost savagery, with the use of napalm, gas, B-52 airplanes, killing old people, women, and children indiscriminately and that the Vietnamese people are serving just as guinea pigs for the Pentagon experiments. They are convinced that, in the end, in a desperate effort, the United States would not hesitate to use atomic and nuclear weapons in case of necessity. Since President [Lyndon B.] Johnson stated last week that, during the last three months, 50,000 Vietnamese have been killed or wounded, they think that at that rate of killing the Vietnamese race will be totally exterminated.

Now, since they believe that the United States government would never accept free elections in South Vietnam, because there is no doubt that no régime could ever have more than 10 per cent—

(Interruption by the President of UNCA): Mr. Ky,[2] please state your question. Your statement is—

THE SECRETARY-GENERAL: Yes—please make your question as brief as possible, because of the limited time at our disposal.

QUESTION: My question is this: Should a neutralist régime composed in part of a number of this refugee group—a kind of government-in-exile—demand the immediate withdrawal of American troops from South Vietnam, and should the United States government refuse to comply—as Ambassador [Henry Cabot] Lodge has already said—can the matter be brought to the Security Council by a Member such as the Soviet Union, France, Albania, or Cambodia, or could this government-in-exile request from the Security Council the right to be heard?

THE SECRETARY-GENERAL: On the human aspects of the war, I have on many previous occasions expressed my views and my assessments, and I do not think I should go over these again. On the question of Security Council involvement, I am sure my views are well known and I would wish only to give reasons additional to those I have already given on previous occasions.

As you know, I have consistently been opposed to Security Council involvement in the Vietnam question for reasons which you know. One of these reasons is that in 1954 the parties directly involved in the conflict decided that the matter should be brought to Geneva outside the framework of the United Nations because of the simple fact that

[2]Tran Van Ky, correspondent for *La Vérité* of Cambodia.

only France, of all the participants, was a Member of the United Nations. The same consideration should apply today; of the parties primarily involved in the conflict in Vietnam today, only one, the United States, is a Member of the United Nations. I think the same consideration should apply today as applied twelve years ago.

But it is not only for the reason that Hanoi is not a Member of the United Nations or that Peking is not a Member of the United Nations. There are other reasons too. As I see the situation, one basic reason is that if the matter is brought before the Security Council, Hanoi, particularly, is afraid that the Geneva Agreements of 1954 might be diluted. Another reason is that from the point of view of Peking—rightly or wrongly; I am not trying to identify my position with that of Peking, or against that of Peking—rightly or wrongly, Peking feels, as you all know, that in the Security Council there is a usurper. So, if Peking is asked to appear before the Security Council and plead its case, rightly or wrongly, it feels that it would be in a position somewhat like that of an accused being summoned before a jury where, among the important members of the jury, there is somebody whom the accused considers to be inimical to its interests. That is their position.

Of course, my attitude regarding Security Council involvement is guided by one single consideration: If the Security Council has to take any action on any dispute, the first prerequisite is that it must be in a position to hear both sides of the question; this is a must.

As in the case of the Arab-Israel dispute or the Indo-Pakistan dispute, the Security Council, before coming to a decision on a particular issue, must be in a position to hear both sides of the case. If both sides were to come and plead their respective case before the Security Council, I will be the first to advocate immediate Security Council involvement. But, as you know, this is not the case; there are no prospects of Peking or Hanoi coming to the Security Council, because of the reasons I have just stated.

QUESTION: Mr. Secretary-General, as you know, it has been reported that Peking of late has been warning its people of the imminence of a war with the United States. Could you assess the seriousness of the threat?

THE SECRETARY-GENERAL: With respect to the statements by Peking, I am, of course, in the same position as you; I do not think I have any means of assessing the motivations behind such statements.

QUESTION: Could you give us an evaluation of how you regard

efforts to use the International Control Commission (ICC) to bring about an end to the war in Vietnam?

THE SECRETARY-GENERAL: This matter was discussed by me with some of the delegations that posed this problem in January. At that time, two or three possible means of bringing about a conference were discussed. One was the Security Council involvement; the other was involvement by some of the neutral countries; and the third was the possible involvement by the International Control Commission.

In the context of these discussions in January, my personal feeling at that time was that it was worth exploring the possibilities of a useful ICC involvement in contributing toward the peaceful settlement of the Vietnam problem, in preference to the Security Council involvement or the involvement of neutral countries.

QUESTION: Do you consider that military alliances, such as NATO or SEATO [Southeast Asia Treaty Organization] or the Warsaw Pact, in their present form, now constitute a hindrance to peace in Europe or in Asia?

THE SECRETARY-GENERAL: In the Charter of the United Nations there are specific provisions permitting regional military alliances or pacts for the purpose of common defense. Therefore, strictly speaking, these military pacts, like NATO or SEATO or CENTO [Central Treaty Organization] or the Warsaw Pact, do not contravene the provisions of the United Nations Charter. But, of course, the political assessment regarding their effectiveness or necessity or utility is a different matter.

In my view, it would be wise to review the character and functioning of these military alliances from time to time, in the light of the changing circumstances.

QUESTION: It has been taken for granted, in the first part of the discussion of the expected Indonesian request to return to this house, that it would come off. However, the morning paper brings the report that President Achmed Sukarno said yesterday that Indonesia would return to the United Nations only when changes were made in the Organization; and he went on to say: "We will only return to the United Nations if changes have been made. If conditions remain as they are at the present, then Indonesia prefers to stay outside the United Nations."

Do you attach great importance to this statement of President Sukarno?

THE SECRETARY-GENERAL: It is difficult to pass judgment on newspaper reports of that kind and, personally, I do not think that it will help if I make any public judgment or assessment of such statements which appear from time to time in the Press.

QUESTION: Do you feel that the application of East Germany is somewhat in the light of a step toward the realization of your own statement made in the Introduction to your Annual Report, in which you thought that divided countries, and all countries, should have posts of observation here at the United Nations?

THE SECRETARY-GENERAL: I have stated in my two Introductions to the Annual Reports the need for universality in this world Organization. Regarding the specific case which you mentioned, I have acted in a manner from which it is clear that I refuse to define whether any part of a divided country is a state or is not a state. So, that is why I refuse to invoke rules 58 and 59 of the rules of procedure of the Security Council; I do not think that it would be proper on my part to attempt to define whether a part of a divided country is a state or is not a state. I will adopt the same attitude if I receive applications from any part of a divided country, whether Germany, or Korea, or Vietnam, if the application is for admission and I am convinced that what I have done is correct.

. . .

QUESTION: I have just a question of clarification. In one of your earlier answers, you said that Vietnam should become a nonaligned and independent country. Did you mean South Vietnam, or did you mean a united Vietnam?

THE SECRETARY-GENERAL: If we accept the Agreements arrived at in Geneva in 1954, it means a united Vietnam.

QUESTION: You are aware, of course, of the military takeovers that have occurred in Africa during the last few months. I wonder if you would give us your views on whether or not the United Nations has a role in that situation.

THE SECRETARY-GENERAL: I do not really see how the United Nations can be involved in these matters which, strictly speaking, are internal matters. So long as developments in any part of the world do not threaten international peace and security, I do not think that the Security Council can be involved. Of course, if any Member state wishes to bring this to the attention of either the General Assembly or the Security Council, these organs have to take them up; but so far as the Secretary-General is concerned, under the Charter provisions he is empowered to bring to the attention of the Security Council only such matters as threaten international peace and security.

. . .

QUESTION: Mr. Secretary-General, the Members of the United Nations agreed last September that when the work of the Assembly was normalized, as it was later, they would all make voluntary contributions to remove the financial difficulties of the Organization, including substantial contributions from developed countries. Now, the Special Committee on finances[3] has arrived at an estimate of the financial difficulties which allows countries to decide what would be substantial contributions in their cases. How soon do you expect that the developed countries generally, and the Soviet Union and France in particular, will make pledges of such contributions?

THE SECRETARY-GENERAL: In the light of the preliminary report submitted by the Committee of Fourteen, I had discussions with some of the members of the Committee of Fourteen. They seem to be optimistic about the prospective outcome in regard to voluntary contributions toward filling the deficit. Of course, the final report of the Committee of Fourteen is expected to be out only perhaps in July, and I do not know whether these gestures from Member states, in the form of voluntary contributions, will be made in the coming weeks or coming months. But from my talks with some of the delegations, they seem to be optimistic about the outcome.

QUESTION: Mr. Secretary-General, could you say something about the talks you have had with countries which are providing peace-keeping forces in Cyprus, whether any other countries look as if they are going to withdraw their forces there, and whether this is discouraging news in any plan that there may be for putting a United Nations presence in South Arabia in the next two years before independence, as has been suggested?

THE SECRETARY-GENERAL: The financial aspects of the United Nations Force in Cyprus (UNFICYP), of course, have been disappointing as I have stated before the Security Council. As you will recall, I recommended to the Security Council that the financial aspects of UNFICYP should also be considered in their decisions. My recommendation was not taken into account in the resolution that was adopted.

[3]The Special Committee to Examine the Finances of the United Nations and the Specialized Agencies.

Immediately after the adoption of the resolution, I also expressed my disappointment at the absence of any reference to the financial aspects of UNFICYP. As a result, as you all know, the government of Ireland has informed me that it has decided to withdraw its contingent from Cyprus when the rotation time comes on April 18. Only yesterday I wrote to the Foreign Minister of Ireland asking him to reconsider that decision, and at the appropriate time, of course, I will make that correspondence public.

In connection with this financial aspect, the system of voluntary contributions that has been introduced in regard to the United Nations Force in Cyprus, has been very unsatisfactory, as I have been saying all along; and I think the membership should take a closer look into the financial aspects of future peace-keeping operations. As you all know, the Committee of Thirty-three[4] is seized with this problem, among others, and I very much hope that the Committee of Thirty-three will come up with very useful and worthwhile recommendations to the next session of the General Assembly.

[4]Special Committee on Peace-keeping Operations.

VISIT TO EUROPE

AT THE END of April 1966, U Thant visited London and Paris where he had the opportunity for private talks with Prime Minister Harold Wilson and President Charles de Gaulle. Although he had traveled to Geneva several times, this was the first time in two years that he had held discussions with the British and French leaders on the Vietnam problems and other issues that were on his mind at the time. As usual, he had little to say about the substance of the talks. However, in the course of a press conference and a television interview in London, a statement on French radio and television and speeches before the United Nations Association of the United Kingdom and the Consultative Assembly of the Council of Europe held in Strasbourg, he touched on some of the questions discussed and gave his own thinking on them. In his Paris broadcast, for example, he outlined the three conditions which later became known as the Thant formula for getting negotiations started on the Vietnam conflict. This was his first public mention of his three-point proposal, although a United Nations spokesman had disclosed the proposal on March 9. The "conditions" he set forth were, first, "the cessation of bombing of North Vietnam; second, the de-escalation of all military activities in South Vietnam . . . by all the parties involved in the fighting in South Vietnam; and third, the willingness on the part of some of the parties primarily concerned to speak to those who are fighting, to discuss with those who are fighting." The latter point referred to the reluctance of the United States and the Saigon government to negotiate with the National Liberation Front. The Secretary-General stressed these points in discussing the Vietnam question with British and French leaders.

One of the important results of his European visit was the strengthening of his rapport with President de Gaulle. This was reflected in the exchange of toasts which took place at a dinner given by the President. De Gaulle was lavish in his praise of the Secretary-General and said of his qualities of conscience and intelligence, judgment and impartiality, equity and wisdom, "these qualities are recognized as being yours everywhere, and particularly in France." The French President said he had wanted to talk with Thant "in order to prepare in advance the joint action of the forces of common sense" when the course of events opened up the possibilities of peace in Asia. Thant, in turn, lauded de Gaulle for his efforts "to achieve a thaw in the cold war." Although the Secretary-General did not refer to de Gaulle's belief that the United Nations could not play a useful role in a Vietnam settlement—other than the role being played by Thant—he fully agreed with it, mainly because none of the parties to the conflict except the United States was a Member of the Organization. The Secretary-General took the trouble to explain his own views on this both in his London press conference and in his

May 1 interview carried by the British Broadcasting Corporation. He also stressed during his visit that he remained strongly committed to the principles of the Geneva Agreement of 1954 and to the belief that the best way to deal with the problem would be to reconvene that conference. At one point, when asked about a possible new initiative by the Soviet Union and the United Kingdom as co-chairmen of the Geneva Conference, he expressed the belief that "it would be difficult for the two co-chairmen to come out with a fresh initiative at this moment."

Another problem which Thant discussed with British officials during his three days in London was the situation in Southern Rhodesia and the British efforts to work out a settlement with the government of Prime Minister Ian Smith, whose white minority régime had been under attack in the United Nations since its unilateral declaration of independence of November 11, 1965. It was natural that this subject should be taken up, since African states at the time were consulting on United Nations action to prod Britain to take stronger steps to quell the rebellion, and new negotiations were beginning to open up between the British government and Rhodesian officials. In his public statements Thant carefully avoided any disclosure of the views expressed by himself and Prime Minister Wilson, but he did say that the United Nations as a whole felt that "further stronger measures are necessary on the part of the British government." He added, "In the view of the majority of the membership, further, closer cooperation between London and the United Nations is called for, and I am confident that the British government, in its wisdom, will take further measures to bring about the implementation of the resolutions adopted by the General Assembly and the Security Council" (p. 232). These resolutions, adopted immediately after the Smith régime's declaration of independence, called on the United Kingdom to use all necessary steps, including the use of force, to put an end to the illegal government in Rhodesia. The British government has supported United Nations demands for an economic boycott of the Smith régime, including an embargo on oil and petroleum products, but had insisted that the illegal government could be ended without the use of force. Thant did not mention the possibility of enforcement action, under Chapter VII of the Charter, in connection with the Rhodesian situation, although he did suggest that this was the next step needed to end apartheid in South Africa, explaining that what he had in mind was the use of binding economic sanctions against the South African government. However, when the Security Council imposed mandatory selective economic sanctions for the first time in history, the action was not against South Africa but against the Ian Smith régime. This action was taken on December 16 by a vote of 11 to none, with Bulgaria, France, Mali, and the Soviet Union abstaining. The resolution was presented by the United Kingdom.

1. *From Address to the United Nations Association of the United Kingdom*

LONDON   APRIL 28, 1966

. . . THE PROCESS of granting independence to former colonies and other non-self-governing territories, in which the United Kingdom has been a pioneer and leader, has naturally had profound effects upon the United Nations, as upon the world at large. One of its more obvious results has been to increase greatly the membership of the United Nations and thus, if I may say so, to give the United Nations the benefit of the presence of many new nations with fresh ideas as well as fresh problems. The Organization would have lost touch with the reality of the world itself if it had failed to accept this salutary injection of new blood and new attitudes.

It is important to understand the process through which the new countries have to go in order to take their place in the world. These new nations must first establish their national roots if they are to survive internationally, and in growing those roots they are bound at times to show a high and even hypersensitive degree of nationalism. This is a phase which older and more fortunate nations have for the most part already gone through; the fact of their established nationalism has given them the freedom and confidence to go beyond it into internationalism. At the same time, it is to the advantage of the new nations that they have come to independence in an era of relatively strong international organization, which indeed has played a significant part in the emergence of many of them. They do not, therefore, find their attachment to the principles of international cooperation incompatible with the need to assert their national identities and aspirations. It becomes, in fact, one of the important functions of the United Nations to help the new countries in the initial phases of nationalism to find their footing and their place in the world, and to give them that feeling of security which unquestionably derives from

SOURCE: UN Press Release SG/SM/491.

membership in an international community. The pressures of the modern world demand that they mature in this sense far more rapidly than older countries had to do, and this rapidity of adjustment will sometimes give rise to attitudes and reactions which may seem unreasonable. I am sure that you in the United Kingdom are very much aware of the necessity for patience and for understanding of the points of view of the newer countries during this very difficult and crucial phase of their development. Most of the older countries, as I have said, have had similar experiences.

It is sometimes forgotten, especially by those who are not very enthusiastic about international cooperation through the United Nations, that almost all the peace-keeping operations of the United Nations have been made necessary by the aftermath of European colonialism. Moreover, all of the current peace-keeping operations in the Middle East, in Kashmir, and in Cyprus, pertain to problems which arose from the process of British decolonization. In fact, one of the most useful achievements of the United Nations has been to stand watch over the power vacuums created by the lapse of European influence and the subsequent process of decolonization in areas such as the Middle East or the Congo, and thus to diminish the risks of a power confrontation between East and West in these areas. Those who still delight in asserting that the United Nations Operation in the Congo was unnecessary, misguided, or ineffective would do well to ponder this fact. In several areas where the burden has proved too heavy or too complex for a single government to bear alone, the United Nations has provided a vital relief to the former colonial powers, as well as to the inhabitants of the disturbed areas themselves.

Another function of the United Nations is to provide means through which governments may reconcile their various world commitments. I believe that here too the United Nations has been of considerable assistance to many countries, including the United Kingdom, in a number of situations over the past twenty years, most recently in the conflict between India and Pakistan last September (see pp. 103–29).

I would like to take this opportunity to mention the British contribution to the United Nations operations which, by and large, has kept the peace in Cyprus two full years. You will recall that the United Nations undertook the task at a time when the strife in Cyprus between the Greek Cypriot and Turkish Cypriot communities was giving rise to communal violence, bloodshed, tensions, and great hardship, as well as to a serious threat to the wider peace. As yet, regrettably, no long-term solution for Cyprus is in sight, but the fighting has been largely stopped and some of the tensions have been reduced. Much of the credit for this success of the United Nations Force in Cyprus must go to the ready and generous cooperation of the British government, which had, early in 1964, deployed a peace-keeping force in the island, and to the fine performance of the successive British contingents in the United Nations Force. I may add that the British participation in this operation is the unique exception to the firm, if unwritten, rule that United Nations peace-keeping operations should not include the forces of the permanent members of the Security Council. The exception was made, of course, in the light of the wishes of the parties mainly concerned and of the fact that British troops were already on the ground, and it has, I know, proved to be of benefit to all.

The government of the United Kingdom has always supported the peace-keeping role of the United Nations, and many people in this country, in unofficial as well as official circles, have shown a keen interest in the future of international peace-keeping. I therefore feel bound to say here that the present prospect for making the peace-keeping role of the United Nations more effective and reliable for the future is, for political and constitutional reasons of which you are well aware, extremely uncertain. However, I must add that the efforts of a number of governments, including your own, in the sphere of ear-marking contingents for future United Nations use, are a constructive and welcome initiative. In spite of these efforts, I am afraid that in the near future the United Nations may be less able to respond effectively to threats to the peace than hitherto. To give one practical example, I regard the present method of voluntary and optional financing for the Cyprus operation, quite apart from the serious practical difficulties it creates, as a retrograde step in the general development of United Nations peace-keeping capacity. I sincerely hope that this setback is only temporary.

I have stated on previous occasions my own reservations about the idea of a standing international peace-keeping force in the present stage of development of the international organization. I believe that a continuing study of the idea is a valuable investment for the future, but we should not underestimate the difficulties of such a major innovation in international relations, nor the obstacles which have to be overcome. There will have to be major developments in concepts of national sovereignty and international responsibility, in law and in the relations of states to each other, not to mention methods of financing international efforts, before such an advanced idea can begin to come into the realm of practical politics. I point out these difficulties not to discourage those—and they are many—who are working for progress in peace-keeping, but to show what great and continuous efforts will be needed to improve on the present situation. It is fortunate that the peace-keeping operations in which the United Nations has engaged up to now have not been impaired in any significant degree by the lack of a standing force.

. . .

---

2. From Transcript of Press Conference

LONDON   APRIL 29, 1966

. . .

QUESTION: How do you assess a new peace initiative with Vietnam, either by the United Nations or by you personally?

THE SECRETARY-GENERAL: I have been involved in private informal discussions and negotiations for the last two and a half years, with a view to bringing about a peaceful settlement of the problem. So far my endeavors have been inconclusive.

About the United Nations involvement, I have expressed my view on previous occasions. I do not think for the moment that the United Nations could be involved, or should be involved. If the Security Council is to be involved in the discussion of any issue, one prerequisite is that it must be in a position to hear both sides of the question. This is a "must." In the present circumstances, I do not see any reason to believe that either Hanoi or Peking will be willing to appear

SOURCE: UN Press Release SG/SM/496.

before the Security Council and plead their case. In 1954, when the question of Vietnam was discussed, there was general agreement that the discussions should take place outside the framework of the United Nations, because of all the participants in the dispute, only one, France, was a Member of the United Nations.

I think the same considerations should apply today. Of all the parties directly involved in the conflict in Vietnam, only one, the United States of America, is a Member of the United Nations. The others are not Members of the United Nations. This is a very important consideration. If the Security Council is to be involved usefully in any problem representing a threat to international peace and security, it must be in a position to hear both sides of the question. As you all know, neither Peking nor Hanoi will appear before the Security Council and plead its case. Peking, particularly, feels—whether we agree with its point of view or not—that if she were asked to appear before the Security Council, she would be more or less in the position of an accused, and she would be asked to appear before a jury among whom there was somebody who was inimical to the interest of that particular accused. From the point of view of Hanoi my understanding is that Hanoi will never wish the United Nations to be involved in the question of Vietnam, because Hanoi is afraid that any United Nations decision on this problem would dilute the Geneva Agreements of 1954.

QUESTION: What are your views on recent developments on Rhodesia? Do you think that the decision reached to resume talks is in conformity with United Nations decisions so far?

THE SECRETARY-GENERAL: The Secretary-General has to be guided by the resolutions or decisions of the principal organs of the United Nations. He cannot speak or act outside the framework of those resolutions. Since 1962, both the General Assembly and the Security Council have, from time to time, taken up this question. They have adopted certain resolutions, including the resolution rejecting the Constitution of 1961, considering Mr. Smith's government illegal and describing Southern Rhodesia as a non-self-governing territory, and calling upon the British government to take certain measures. These are the resolutions of the General Assembly and the Security Council. Now I understand that some of the Member states, particularly the African Members of the United Nations, are meeting almost daily in New York, and, according to my latest information, they are going to request a meeting of the Security Council on or around May 10. I do not think it would be proper for me to assess the actions or statements of the British government on this issue.

. . .

QUESTION: Can you say whether you have in mind any new ideas or any early new action for a Vietnam settlement?

THE SECRETARY-GENERAL: I think that the Vietnam problem is getting more complex and more difficult as time goes on. What could have been done in 1964 is not possible of accomplishment this year. In my view, there were many cases of missed opportunities. The basic need is that the parties directly involved in the conflict should come out with clearer objectives. They should define their objectives in clearer terms than they have done before. There are some basic issues which are of primary importance for discussions at any conference table. For instance, whether the parties primarily involved in the conflict would agree to define the modalities for the implementation of the Geneva Agreements of 1954. As you all know, the government of Hanoi has maintained, and still maintains, that it cannot deviate from the Agreements arrived at twelve years ago in Geneva. It will be very helpful for anybody who is interested in taking some initiative to bring about negotiations to be conversant with the attitudes of the parties primarily concerned. The Geneva Agreements of 1954 envisaged elections in North Vietnam and South Vietnam. In a way, the elections were a plebiscite to ascertain the views of the people of North Vietnam as well as South Vietnam in regard to a united Vietnam. This is one of the issues which has to be thrashed out.

QUESTION: In this context would you welcome an initiative by the two co-chairmen of the 1954 Agreements, Great Britain and the Soviet Union, if they approached the parties directly concerned and asked them to define their views?

THE SECRETARY-GENERAL: Certainly I would welcome any initiative by countries or a country.

QUESTION: By these two in particular?

THE SECRETARY-GENERAL: Yes. I welcomed the initiative of the two co-chairmen some time ago, but for obvious reasons I feel it would be difficult for the two co-chairmen to come out with a fresh initiative at this moment.

. . .

QUESTION: Are you hopeful that at the forthcoming General Assembly any progress can be made to end a situation in which one state, by its attitude, has been able over all these years to exclude the largest state in the world, namely, China?

THE SECRETARY-GENERAL: As you know, this question was taken up by the General Assembly and has been taken up at every session for the last several years. On this, as Secretary-General of the United Nations, I have no personal views. On this, as I have explained before (see volume VI of this series, p.39), you should treat U Thant as two U Thants, one as the permanent representative of Burma to the United Nations up till November 1961, and the other the U Thant who can speak and act only as the Secretary-General of the United Nations within the framework of the decisions and resolutions of the principal organs. In my second capacity I have no views of my own, except in the context of the General Assembly resolutions.

QUESTION: If you overcome perhaps the industrial disease of the Secretary-General of the United Nations and the schizophrenic situation, surely you must have a view whether it is a good thing or not that, in view of the principle of universality in the United Nations, such a state continues to be excluded?

THE SECRETARY-GENERAL: As the permanent representative of Burma, I expressed certain views. As Secretary-General of the United Nations, I cannot express any views, except in the context of the decisions of the General Assembly or the Security Council. On this question, of course, there are two approaches. One section of the Member states maintains that the question is one of admission of the People's Republic of China to the United Nations. The other section maintains that it is not a question of admission, but it is a question of representation—who should represent China at the United Nations. The matter was taken up at the last session of the General Assembly and the voting was 47 to 47. It is difficult to assess what the voting will be at the forthcoming session of the General Assembly, but, in the context of the implied universality of membership, of course, it will be very desirable for a great country such as the People's Republic of China to be at the United Nations.

. . .

3. Statement on French Radio and Television

PARIS   APRIL 30, 1966

NEEDLESS FOR ME to say, I am very happy to be back in Paris once again. I want to take this opportunity of expressing very sincere thanks to the government of France, and particularly the President, for his kind invitation to me to visit Paris on my way to Strasbourg to address the Council of Europe.

As you all know, I spent three days in London before I came here. While I was in London, I had very useful talks with leaders of the British government on matters of common interest to the United Kingdom and to the United Nations. Of course, inevitably we discussed important problems like Rhodesia, Vietnam, and Cyprus. On these questions, as you all know, I have expressed my views on previous occasions. Particularly, the problem of Vietnam is getting more and more complex and more and more difficult as days go on. As I have been saying all along, what was possible in 1964 or even 1965 is no longer possible today. I have presented my views in my personal capacity from time to time to the parties concerned and unfortunately without success. I have made certain proposals, both procedural and substantive, but unfortunately all these proposals are still inconclusive. I find that the situation has gone from bad to worse. I still maintain that there are three conditions necessary for opening the way to useful negotiations by the parties primarily concerned. These conditions are: the cessation of bombing of North Vietnam; second, the de-escalation of all military activities in South Vietnam. When I say de-escalation of all military activities, I mean de-escalation by all the parties involved in the fighting in South Vietnam; and third, the willingness on the part of some of the parties primarily concerned to speak to those who are fighting, to discuss with those who are fighting. I still maintain that these are the prerequisites for a successful contact toward negotiations. I very much hope the parties

SOURCE: UN Press Release SG/SM/495.

primarily concerned will realize the gravity of the situation and show a spirit of give-and-take, not only for the sake of peace in that part of the world, but also for the sake of world peace.

Once again, Ladies and Gentlemen, let me reiterate my very sincere thanks to the government and people of France for making my visit possible. I look forward to very fruitful discussions with the President and with the Foreign Minister, among others, tomorrow. I wish the people of France all the best. Thank you.

---

4. Exchange of Toasts with President Charles de Gaulle

PARIS   APRIL 30, 1966

President de Gaulle made the following toast to U Thant:

Mr. Secretary-General, your visit here is most gratifying. First, because of the very high responsibilities you discharge and which have the exceptional character of international hope. As Secretary-General of the United Nations, you are in a position to see the world situation as a whole, and it so happens that you see it lucidly and impartially.

So, we greatly appreciate your presence here which enables us to exchange our views. The war developments in Asia do not fail to give rise, in particular here, to growing feelings of concern and disapproval. Doubtless, one cannot yet visualize what could be done for the time being to put an end to the extending drama. But how could we fail to believe that some day the course of events and the turning of human minds will open again possibilities to peace? With this in view, we wished to talk with you in order to prepare in advance the joint action of the forces of common sense.

Finally and foremost, we appreciate this contact because of your personality. It is a fact that, after four years in office, no enlightened

SOURCE: UN Press Release SG/SM/497.

person in the world is reluctant to pay a fair tribute to you. The qualities of conscience and intelligence, judgment and impartiality, equity and wisdom—these qualities are recognized as being yours everywhere, and particularly in France. And let me tell you that they lead us warmly to wish that you pursue your task in a world where, and at a time when, the cause of man is in dire need of being well served.

I drink this toast to His Excellency U Thant, Secretary-General of the United Nations.

Responding, the Secretary-General said:

Mr. President, I am overwhelmed by your gracious words, especially as to my task as Secretary-General of the United Nations. As you are well aware, my conception of the Secretary-General's functions is very clear. I consider the United Nations, in conformity with the Charter, as a center for the harmonizing of actions by states with a view toward their common aim.

I am a catalyst and I consider myself as somebody who must do everything to promote better understanding and relations between states.

You, Mr. President, are a source of great inspiration for many of us at the United Nations because of your ceaseless endeavors to bring about international understanding and a détente, and because of your efforts to achieve a thaw in the cold war. Your endeavors are in conformity with the Charter, which states that all Members must exercise tolerance and live together in peace as good neighbors. This provision is one of the most significant and your action conforms with it. We, at the United Nations, and especially the small countries, have great admiration for your noble efforts to bring about new conditions in the light of the changing circumstances in the world. We all wish you to succeed in these efforts, and we are guided by your wisdom and vision, because you consider the future instead of the past.

I think that we, too, in the United Nations, should consider the future, because without vision, man perishes. For the last million years which represent history, man has accomplished many things in art, science, literature, music, religion. All these creations are in danger of being annihilated in the second half of the twentieth century by the atom bomb.

I think that we all should see to it that conditions for peace are secured and that all the tensions which lead mankind from one crisis to another are eliminated. In this quest for peace, we are led by your courage, determination, and vision.

---

5. From Transcript of Television Interview by the British Broadcasting Corporation

LONDON   MAY 1, 1966

ERSKINE CHILDERS [writer and broadcaster on international affairs]: U Thant, Secretary-General of the United Nations since November 1961, former school teacher and diplomat of Burma.

ROBERT MCKENZIE [Professor, London School of Economics]: Mr. Secretary-General, there's great uneasiness about the condition of the United Nations, partly because you have had to stand aside in great crises like that in Vietnam; partly because of differences and difficulties over peace-keeping activities. Now, is there a danger that the Organization will degenerate into a kind of debating society?

U THANT: Well, I think this fear, this general concern about the future of the United Nations, is widely shared by most of the membership. In my view, the United Nations is now passing through a very crucial stage, particularly in regard to the future of the peace-keeping operations. As you will recall, the General Assembly at its last session had formed a Special Committee of Thirty-three to look into all aspects of peace-keeping operations. The Committee of Thirty-three is now in session in New York. . . .

MR. CHILDERS: This problem of peace-keeping, Mr. Secretary-General, is it the cause of the present uncertainty, the present situa-

SOURCE: *UN Monthly Chronicle,* vol. III, May 1966, pp. 57-66.

tion the United Nations is in, or is it a symptom of something larger?

U THANT: I would say it is more or less a symptom. To launch effective peace-keeping operations, in my view, the first requisite is some sort of understanding among the big powers, which is a necessary prerequisite to launch a peace-keeping operation. As I have been saying all along, the necessary prerequisite for the successful launching of a peace-keeping operation is some degree of détente or understanding between the East and West, which, as you know, is still lacking.

MR. MCKENZIE: Mr. Secretary-General, what is surely even more worrisome than the difficulty there has been over peace-keeping operations, such as those in the Congo and so on, is where you get the greatest single threat to the world's peace since the war, namely Vietnam, and here you and your Organization have been able to play almost no part. Now, why not?

U THANT: Well, on this question I have made myself very clear on several previous occasions. First of all, it is worth recording what happened in 1954, when the question of Vietnam was brought to the attention of the international community. At that time, a lot of thought was given regarding the possibility of the United Nations involvement, in finding a solution to the problem of Vietnam, and it was decided, twelve years ago, that among the participants directly involved in the war in Vietnam, only one—France—was a Member of the United Nations. Others were not Members. So there was general agreement that the question should be dealt with outside the framework of the United Nations and, thus, the Geneva Conference took place in 1954. I think the same considerations should apply today. Among the parties principally concerned in the conflict in Vietnam only one—the United States of America—is a Member of the United Nations. Others are not Members of the United Nations. So, since there was general agreement in 1954 that the Vietnam question should be dealt with outside the framework of the United Nations, I believe the same considerations equally hold true today.

MR. MCKENZIE: But, surely, Mr. Secretary-General, the problem here is that for thirteen or fourteen months a war, really a major war, has been going on in this area. The Geneva Agreement has not worked, they have not been prepared to reassemble under that aegis outside the United Nations, and yet you stood by, your Organization stood by, apparently impotent, in the face of this really appalling destruction. Now, is there nothing more that the United Nations could do here?

U THANT: Well, as I see the situation, I think this feeling is shared by the vast majority of the membership. If the Security Council is to be usefully involved in finding a solution to any problem threatening international peace and security, one prerequisite is that the Security Council must be in a position to hear both sides of the question.

In my view, this is a must. Without this prerequisite I do not believe that the Security Council should be involved in any question. So, since the Security Council should hear both sides of the question, let us look into the matter rather closely. As I see it, I am sure everybody will agree with me that Peking or the North Vietnamese government will not, under any circumstances, appear before the Security Council. Not only because of the fact that they are not Members of the United Nations, but for another additional reason. Peking, for instance, feels very strongly—rightly or wrongly—of course, I am not identifying myself with that particular point of view—Peking feels, it has felt all along, that there is someone in the Security Council who is a usurper. As in the case of an accused who has been summoned to appear before a jury and in the view of that particular accused there is someone among the jury who is inimical to the interests of that particular accused.

MR. MCKENZIE: This is the Formosa government?

U THANT: Yes, in the view of Peking. So, particularly because of this reason, I believe Peking will never appear before the Security Council to plead its case. I think that is the most important factor which we all should take into consideration. These are the practical difficulties of why, in my view, the Security Council cannot be involved usefully in finding a solution to the Vietnam question.

MR. CHILDERS: Then in terms of the voice of the United Nations, Sir, this leaves you almost alone being able to do something. Now, what are the essential conditions, in your view, toward moving toward negotiations?

U THANT: It is generally known, particularly in United Nations quarters, that I have been involved in private and very informal negotiations and discussions with the parties principally concerned for the last three years or so, and so far, of course, my attempts, my efforts, are not conclusive. I had made, from time to time, various proposals, some procedural in nature, some substantive in nature, but unfortunately one party or the other could not find itself in a position to accept my proposals. But, of course, I am still continuing with my efforts. But as I see the situation today, what is necessary is that the parties directly involved in the conflict should come out with very clear objectives as to what they want done about the Vietnam question.

In my view, this clear definition of the objectives is lacking.

MR. MCKENZIE: Lacking on both sides?

U THANT: On both sides. I think what is necessary today is for the parties principally concerned to come out with very clear objectives. Whether, for instance, they can go along with the modalities to implement the Geneva Agreements of 1954. Or whether they want some sort of a deviation from the Agreements arrived at in 1954. This I am citing as an instance. I think, in my view, there is no clear definition of objectives by both sides.

MR. MCKENZIE: May we bring you back for a moment, Mr. Secretary-General, to your comment on China. Now, if as seems obvious to many of us, the greatest potential threat to a world war is an American-Chinese clash, surely then, if your point was well taken a moment ago, the only possibility of the United Nations playing a decisive role in that kind of situation is if we can ensure Communist China becoming a full Member of the United Nations. Now, how is that going to happen?

U THANT: Well, regarding this question I think the responsibility is on the entire membership. As I have stated on a previous occasion, on such questions there are two U Thants. One U Thant as the representative of Burma to the United Nations—I have some definite views on this—reflecting the views of the Burmese government. Another U Thant, as the Secretary-General of the United Nations, cannot speak or act except in the context of the General Assembly resolutions, except through the decisions of the principal organs of the United Nations.

In the latter category, in the second category, my view is that the General Assembly has discussed this question from year to year, and last year, also, it discussed this. My feeling is that the entire membership believes in the principle of universality. But the question is one of definition—whether this question is the question of admission of China to the United Nations or the restoration of the lawful rights of the People's Republic of China at the United Nations. In other words, the question is whether it is one of admission of China, admission of a new Member state to the United Nations, or the question of representation. This question, I believe, will again be dealt with very comprehensively in the forthcoming session of the General Assembly. But the indications for the moment are that the question will not be solved in the coming twenty-first session of the General Assembly.

MR. CHILDERS: Do you at all share the view, Sir, that we are unlikely to know what Chinese policy would really be, as long as Peking feels ostracized and encircled?

U THANT: Yes, on this also, I have expressed some views on a previous occasion. When a country is regarded as an outcast, as an outlaw, as the villain of the piece, if I may say so, I think that particular country is apt to act in a rather strange way. I feel that countries and states, like individuals, have to undergo certain tensions, certain emotional upsets and even be subject to emotional breakdowns, or nervous breakdowns. From time to time, if you assess the statements of the Chinese leaders coming out from Peking, I get the impression that the Chinese leaders from time to time speak in a rather strange way, even at times with hysteria, with a certain degree of arrogance. I think we have to understand their state of mind in the context of the circumstances in which China has been ostracized for so long. I think that is the explanation. But, in my view, the Chinese leaders' actions are different from the Chinese leaders' statements.

I do not think we should attach very great importance to the statements coming out from Peking from time to time which are characterized by a certain degree of arrogance, a certain degree of even hysteria.

MR. CHILDERS: There have been suggestions in this atmosphere from time to time from Peking, and at one stage from Indonesia, about forming another international organization. Do you think there are any grounds for such fears?

U THANT: I think this idea is as dead as a dodo.

MR. MCKENZIE: Could we bring you, Mr. Secretary-General, to another crisis in which the United Nations has been rather more involved, but by no means decisively involved yet, and that's Rhodesia. Now, what kind of settlement of the Rhodesian problem—and the negotiations are beginning to reopen now—what kind of settlement would be acceptable, in your view, to the majority of the United

Nations membership which is, of course, primarily an Afro-Asian membership?

U THANT: The United Nations has been seized of this question since 1962, both in the General Assembly and in the Security Council. These two principal organs of the United Nations have passed several resolutions, among them, of course, are resolutions relating to the declaration of Southern Rhodesia as a non-self-governing territory: the United Nations has rejected the Constitution of 1961; the United Nations has called upon the British government to conduct elections on the basis of adult universal suffrage; and the United Nations, through the Security Council, has also called upon the United Kingdom government to take certain drastic measures to bring about the restoration of justice and fair play. Of course, there is a general consensus among the entire membership that the present Ian Smith government is illegal.

MR. MCKENZIE: Well then, Sir, if this government were allowed to remain in power, and Rhodesia did not get majority rule, which by definition would mean obviously African rule, you are suggesting perhaps that the United Nations would not be satisfied with this as a settlement?

U THANT: No, the United Nations, as a whole, in my view, feels that further stronger measures are necessary, on the part of the British government. In the view of the majority of the membership, further, closer cooperation between London and the United Nations is called for, and I am confident that the British government, in its wisdom, will take further measures to bring about the implementation of the resolutions adopted by the General Assembly and the Security Council. Of course, on these questions, I have no private views of my own. I have to speak simply within the four corners of the resolutions adopted by the General Assembly and the Security Council.

MR. CHILDERS: Looming behind the Rhodesia issue is the question surely of apartheid in South Africa. Now, you yourself, and the whole United Nations membership, long ago took a clear stand in principle on the question of apartheid, but the plight of the African majority remains very much the same there, Sir; what now can the United Nations do?

U THANT: Yes, on the question of apartheid there is general unhappiness, if I may say so, distress among the Members of the United Nations regarding the ineffective measures so far taken by the

United Nations. On this, in my view, I think substantial progress can be made only on the basis of the agreement between the big powers. I do not think the small powers, or medium powers, can effectively contribute toward the improvement of the conditions in South Africa. I think one prerequisite for bringing about a satisfactory solution of the problem is the unity in any case, some general consensus among the big powers, regarding the methods to be adopted.

MR. MCKENZIE: Mr. Secretary-General, surely on that point they have all formally condemned apartheid. All the big powers, as far as I know, have. What remains to be done, what kind of action, in fact, in your view, could alter the apartheid policy in South Africa?

U THANT: The next step, in my view, is enforcement action, of the resolutions adopted by the two organs of the United Nations. This enforcement action can be implemented only with the agreement of the big powers.

MR. CHILDERS: These would be economic sanctions? The range of measures of this kind required?

U THANT: Yes.

MR. MCKENZIE: Now, as many people see it, Mr. Secretary-General, this kind of intervention by the United Nations, in what some would argue is a domestic policy, in South Africa, really stretches far beyond the original intention of the Charter—the idea of a threat to the peace. In other words, this was thought to be, by many people, simply international threats, inter-nation conflicts. Now, you seem to be defining the right of the United Nations to move into domestic situations of this kind. If into South Africa, why not concern for Mississippi race policy? Where is the limit?

U THANT: Well, on this, of course, there is a division of opinion, but in the view of the majority of the Member states, the situation in South Africa poses a threat to international peace and security, inasmuch as it involves a question of race, the question of racial inequalities and discriminations, which are sure to have repercussions beyond the frontiers of South Africa. For instance, more than thirty countries in Africa, as you know, are black, their interests are very much involved in the situation in South Africa. It involves problems which go beyond the national frontiers. In the case of Mississippi, of course, these are Americans, whether the Americans are white or black, they are all Americans. But in South Africa the situation is different—the whites belong to a certain sector of society and the blacks are regarded in the rest of the African states—African populations in Africa—as belonging to their races and to their regions. So there is a distinct difference between the two situations.

MR. CHILDERS: When you speak about the necessity of enforcement action, over the question of apartheid, Sir, behind that, again there is the fear that this entire situation is going to degenerate into a very bloody racial war eventually. This would pose the greatest single challenge so far to the United Nations peace-keeping capacity. Now again, is that dependent then on great-power agreement?

U THANT: Yes, I would say so. As I see the whole situation today, tensions are generated by two or three causes. One reason for tensions is based on political differences in political ideologies. Another cause of tensions is based on economic disparities between the "haves" and the "have-nots." I think the third cause of tension is based on racial discrimination. In my view, the tensions generated by racial discrimination or disparity in treatment among the whites and the blacks, is much more dangerous—I think, in the long run, much more explosive than the division of the world on ideological grounds. This is, in my view, potentially one of the most serious threats to international peace and security.

MR. CHILDERS: As you have said yourself, a great many of the smaller countries in Africa—small countries everywhere—are involved and concerned in this kind of danger. You have spoken of the situation as far as the great powers are concerned over peace-keeping and the whole financial problem; is there anything you feel that the smaller and the medium-sized countries could do to contribute to a solution to this that they are not doing now?

U THANT: Yes, I feel that smaller powers and medium powers can and should contribute much more significantly toward a solution of problems of this nature. In my view, they have done their best, but because of the circumstances—I mean the financial situations, the economic situations—the small powers and the medium powers have not been able to contribute as adequately as they would have wished, because of the limitations in their economic and financial resources.

MR. MCKENZIE: Mr. Secretary-General, when you place the onus, understandably, on the big powers in this kind of situation, does it not raise a danger which is bound to cause uneasiness abroad if you look back, for example, to the debates last November in this country on Rhodesia. The Prime Minister here did make the remark that there was a danger of the Red Army in blue berets showing up in Africa, presumably implying the possibility of the involvement of the Soviet Union in some kind of United Nations operation. So is it not—does it not rouse anxieties when you place the onus on the big powers to take the lead in settling these racial disputes in Africa?

U THANT: Well, in the matter of peace-keeping operations launched by the United Nations, in about twenty-one years there has not been one single instance of the big powers contributing fighting forces or contingents in any of the United Nations peace-keeping operations, except one. That is in the Cyprus operation. The British forces are there, because the British were more or less involved in the situation in Cyprus for many years, and they are legitimately very much concerned about the situation there. So the United Nations, through the Security Council, has agreed that the British contingents should also be stationed in Cyprus along with other forces. This is the only one single exception, but throughout the history of the twenty-one years of the United Nations, there has not been a single instance of any big power providing fighting forces or contingents in any other United Nations peace-keeping operations. So the prospect of the Soviet forces being involved in the Rhodesian situation, for instance, is, in my view, out of the question.

MR. CHILDERS: Sir, you have described this problem between the great powers over peace-keeping as a function of their own tensions among themselves, the lack of a détente. Now, here we come obviously to disarmament between these great powers. We have had the partial test-ban treaty; do you see signs of further progress along that kind of road now?

U THANT: Yes, as you know, the Eighteen-Nation Disarmament Committee is still meeting in Geneva. So far, unfortunately, the progress has been very slow. Understandably they are dealing first of all with the question of nonproliferation of nuclear weapons, and secondly, of course, on the test-ban treaty. On the test-ban treaty, I have endorsed publicly the proposal of the Swedish government, but so far the progress has been slow. But it seems with a spirit of "give and take," particularly on the part of the United States and the Soviet Union, there is likely to be some progress in the field of a test-ban treaty, including, of course, the underground tests.

MR. MCKENZIE: But again, Mr. Secretary-General, as long as Communist China is outside this operation, too, the situation is slightly ludicrous—they are proceeding with their bomb tests and so on; they are still in this field, too, an outcast nation. Can we hope to make real progress in this matter till they are in?

U THANT: That is definitely a very important factor, in any discussion on disarmament, so that is why the General Assembly at its last session has decided to have a universal worldwide disarmament conference, obviously meant to involve the People's Republic of China also. But on this I think there are several factors to be taken into consideration; the feeling of the small powers—the feeling of the nonaligned countries particularly—will be very significant in getting the People's Republic of China involved in such discussions.

Without China's participation, I think the progress of disarmament will be very slow.

. . .

MR. MCKENZIE: Mr. Secretary-General, could we ask you finally a few questions about your own role in all these events. You used the extremely challenging sentence when you said that you want to be impartial, but not necessarily neutral as Secretary-General. What exactly did you mean?

U THANT: Well, that is my concept of the role of the Secretary-General. I said this before I was appointed as the Secretary-General of the United Nations four and a half years ago. I do not think a Secretary-General of the United Nations should be neutral on questions involving moral issues. He can be impartial, he must be impartial like a judge, but I do not think he should be neutral, particularly on issues involving moral questions. Of course, these are nuances which have certain significance. To illustrate my point, if I am asked, for instance, to join the Communist Party or the John Birch Society, I think I will be neutral, because there are only two choices before me.

But if I am asked to opt for one or the other involving moral questions, or moral issues, I do not think I can be neutral. Of course, I have to be impartial, as far as my understanding of the Charter provisions is concerned. On this, I want to remind you about the proposal of the late President Roosevelt before the United Nations was formed. He suggested, I believe in 1944, that the Chief Executive Officer of the United Nations should be called Moderator. I think it is a very accurate description of the job I am in.

. . .

MR. MCKENZIE: But, Mr. Secretary-General, your predecessor,

Dag Hammarskjöld, spoke of the intense loneliness of the job—presumably meaning there was no cabinet, there was no country on which you can fall back directly. Have you found it that kind of job?

U THANT: Yes, I agree with him entirely on this. It is not only the loneliest job in the world; in my view, it is sometimes the most frustrating job in the world.

. . .

---

6. *From Address to the Consultative Assembly of the Council of Europe*

STRASBOURG, FRANCE   MAY 3, 1966

. . . IT IS UNTHINKABLE that we may need a third world war to teach us how to co-exist on this richly endowed planet, but sometimes events in the world seem to be pointing in this direction. There is thus a desperate need to bring the forces of enlightened public opinion to bear firmly on problems which threaten, or are likely to threaten in the future, the welfare of all. If we are not to slide helplessly toward total disaster, or even toward the lesser calamities which our carelessness may bring on us, a conscious effort must be made, not just by a few visionary and remarkable men struggling amid the apathy and inattention of the majority, but by whole peoples guided and encouraged by leaders and governments to turn their thoughts to the future rather than to the past. Freedom and prosperity for some are no longer enough. We must also try to grasp and direct our fate.

In this effort, the harmonizing function of the United Nations, which is also an important aspect of the work of the Council of Europe, is vital for future peace in the world. If our pursuit of the effort to harmonize the actions of nations could be more closely concerted, the effectiveness of both organizations in terms of the future might be considerably strengthened. Obviously, such concerted action applies to economic and social activities, but I believe it

SOURCE: *UN Monthly Chronicle,* vol. III, June 1966, pp. 51-60.

should also apply to the great political problems which affect peace and security in the world and which increasingly affect all nations.

Tension is now a common affliction both for individuals and for nations, and in both cases it can lead to serious consequences. The present tensions in the world arise from four main, but related, sources. They arise from the rivalry of political ideologies—although this I believe to be a passing phase. They arise from economic disparity, which is our greatest practical problem. They arise from still unresolved colonial issues which deeply strain international relations. And, finally, these tensions arise from racial feelings exacerbated by a long history of discrimination. Each of these four sources of tension contributes in some degree to the malign influence of the others, and it is not possible therefore to deal with any of them in isolation.

With their long history of political experiment, the countries of Europe have, since the Second World War, given a lead in political tolerance and have played an important role in the process of tempering the violence of ideological differences. It is inconceivable to me that any country or group of countries would wish to push their ideological differences to such a point of fanaticism that they could be resolved only by a global war. I referred earlier to the fact that Europe was the starting point, and the main battleground of two world wars within living memory. It is hardly necessary for me to expatiate to you, as Europeans, on the magnitude of the losses sustained in these two wars, both human and material. We know that the next global war, wherever it may start, will be a thermonuclear war and you are all well aware of the consequences of such a war to human civilization and, in fact, to human existence. The risk of a nuclear war becomes increasingly serious with the proliferation of nuclear weapons, a subject which has received considerable attention during the last session of the General Assembly and in recent meetings of the Eighteen-Nation Disarmament Committee.

While many statesmen and politicians the world over are engaged in the unending quest for peace, I sometimes wonder whether the world is fully aware of the calamitous effects which a nuclear war would have. While scientists may dispute the exact degree or magnitude of devastation and destruction, they no doubt recognize that the nuclear bomb itself is the potential tragedy of our times. Perhaps, even at this late stage, the United Nations should be asked to undertake a thorough study of the probable effects of a nuclear war and its report could be distributed in several languages as widely as possible so that common people the world over may understand what is involved. I believe that a wider understanding of this problem may help to mobilize more widespread and popular support to leaders of men and of thought such as you are, in your greater endeavors for nuclear disarmament and world peace.

It is, in my view, the growing economic disparity of the nations of the world which faces us with our most serious source of tension and with the direct possibility of future calamity. Despite international programs for economic development and bilateral aid agreements, the plain fact is that the rich industrialized countries of the world are growing steadily richer and the less developed countries are—at best—standing still. Taken in conjunction with the probable growth of population over the next thirty or forty years, this trend opens up a most distressing prospect. The reports of famine from various parts of the world and the evident and increasing difficulties of many of the less developed countries are only harbingers of the coming storm.

It is essential that our preoccupation with our own immediate problems, or with more spectacular and short-term crises, should not make us deaf to these warnings. If we do not pay heed to them there can be little doubt that we are courting a disaster in which even the most prosperous and stable countries may eventually be swept away. We cannot allow it to be said of us by history that, with all our knowledge and technological skill, we allowed this long foreseeable, and foreseen, calamity to overwhelm us.

We must now concert and vastly strengthen our efforts to bridge this gap, no matter what the discouragements, the frustrations of the problems may be. Together the countries of Europe assembled here represent, both politically and economically, a great concentration of power, wealth, and tradition. Their long and often violent history has finally brought them to a maturity and a detachment which others may well envy. The countries of Europe, united in this and other organizations, have a particularly favorable position from which to promote the concerted action which the world so urgently needs and to mobilize expertise and resources on the scale which the size and seriousness of the problem demand.

It is largely the great progress of decolonization during recent years—the emergence of peoples from dependence to nationhood and thus to a position where they can make known through their own voices their aspirations, wants, and needs—that has sharpened the focus of the attention we are now giving to these problems of economic disparity. The process of decolonization has been perhaps the most striking phenomenon of our time, and certainly of the past decade: it may also prove in the long run to have been one of the most fundamentally important changes affecting the condition of mankind as a whole. However, the fact that the liquidation of colonialism has been so widespread, that it has so spectacularly transformed the national and political configuration of so large a part of the world, cannot be allowed to blind us to the truth that the process is not yet complete. Indeed, in Africa particularly, there remains a hard, dangerous residue of colonialism that not only suppresses the right of many millions of human beings to dignity and opportunity but also menaces, directly or indirectly, the security and the well-being of us all. The repression of human rights which colonialism represents is not only all the more unwarranted, but also all the more cruel, when it persists in an era characterized otherwise by the liberation of peoples on an unprecedented scale and by their sharply rising expectations of a peaceful, dignified, and prosperous life. And by the same token, the dangers to the peace of the world inherent in these situations are all the more serious. They constitute an anachronism which the international community as a whole must set about bringing peacefully and rapidly to an end.

I have referred, as another source of tension, to the problem of racial discrimination. In my view this is inherent in the colonial problems I have just mentioned, but it also extends well beyond them and has proved capable of surviving, like an evil weed, even in industrially advanced and prosperous societies. It is true that the racial conflict is not, at present, a prominent feature of the European scene. It must not be forgotten, however, that certain colonial attitudes have left an unhappy legacy in many parts of the world, a smoldering resentment which can all too easily be fanned into a conflagration that can be disastrous to all concerned. Europeans should also not forget that the strictest form of racial discrimination is still the official policy of the white government of a large and important African country, and that discriminatory practices are prevalent also in other areas of the African continent. Only a determined attitude to these problems and a firm reassertion of higher values and principles can remedy this situation and can finally extinguish the resentment caused by racial discrimination, be it deliberate or unwitting. This is a problem in which we are all involved, whether we like it or not.

I do not for a moment believe that the leaders and peoples of Europe have any intention either of sinking into a kind of prosperous provincialism or of reverting to the aggressive nationalism of the past. What I wish to emphasize today is the urgent need for leadership and concerted action in the world. Such leadership can only be effective if the older nations show understanding and tolerance toward the new nations of Asia and Africa. Europe, itself the seed-bed of all kinds of revolutions and new ideas, has been through many vicissitudes in the last thousand years. The stages of development which most of its peoples have gone through over a period of centuries must now be traversed by the new countries in the space of a generation or so if they are to aspire ever to take their place in the modern world. The new countries for the most part start this race with many handicaps, not the least of which are their consciousness of the opportunities which they are missing and the pressures of time and population which make their present situation desperate. These conditions must be appreciated and viewed sympathetically if the resentments, fears, and frustrations of yesterday are to become the friendships and partnerships of tomorrow.

The fortitude, ingenuity, and imagination of Europe have again placed its countries, despite two world wars, in a fortunate and strong position. Europe may no longer be the political or economic arbiter of the world—indeed, that can now hardly be said of any country or continent in our developing planet. But the genius and spirit of Europe applied with vision to new situations is a natural resource of which the world has great need. I am sure that the Council of Europe, representing the European spirit at its best, will show increasingly how Europe, which used to be called the Old World, can be among the leaders of the New.

From Statement at Annual Conference
of Non-Governmental Organizations

NEW YORK   MAY 12, 1966

IN THE FOLLOWING statement to representatives of non-governmental organizations, U Thant took note of the widespread public disappointment over the fact that the United Nations had no role in Vietnam peace efforts. Thant had explained frequently why the Organization was unable to deal with the problem of Southeast Asia despite the damaging effect this conflict was having on many United Nations endeavors such as disarmament. The Secretary-General acknowledged that the dissatisfaction was legitimate, but he took this occasion to elaborate at some length on the reasons why the United Nations could not become effectively involved. These reasons, he said, were accepted by a vast majority of the Member states. Basically, the usefulness of the United Nations was nullified by the fact that only one of the parties to the Vietnam conflict was a Member of the United Nations—the same situation that had led to the calling of the Geneva Conference in 1954 rather than bringing the question to the United Nations. In 1954, France was the only Member state involved; a decade later it was the United States. Neither South Vietnam, North Vietnam, nor the National Liberation Front (Vietcong) was prepared to take part in any discussions under United Nations auspices. The People's Republic of China, while not a direct party to the conflict, also strongly opposed a United Nations role. In the Security Council itself, Thant noted, both France and the Soviet Union were against United Nations involvement of any type in Vietnam, and the United Kingdom was cool toward the idea. It was recognition of these facts, he said, which accounted for the general agreement by the Member states that no good would come of bringing the Vietnam problem to the United Nations. This, of course, did not rule out the use of his own good offices to do whatever he could and he promised to continue his attempts in all ways possible.

. . . TURNING TO the very explosive and tragic situation in Vietnam, I have stated my position on many previous occasions. The reasons I have given are well known to all of you, I am sure. Among the participants directly involved in the conflict, only one, the United

SOURCE: UN Press Release SG/SM/504 Rev. 1

States, is a Member of the United Nations. The same situation prevailed twelve years ago when the question of Vietnam was brought to Geneva, outside the scope of the United Nations, for the simple reason that among the parties directly involved in the conflict, only one, France, was a Member of the United Nations. The others were not Members of the Organization. The same considerations apply today as applied twelve years ago. This is one reason.

Another reason, which in my view is more basic, is the disagreement among the big powers regarding the projected United Nations involvement in Vietnam in the field of peace-keeping. Everybody knows that the Soviet Union and France are against United Nations involvement in peace-keeping of any type, of any character, in Vietnam. Their attitudes are known to everybody, and I have very good reason to believe that the United Kingdom would be very reluctant to get the United Nations involved in any sort of peace-keeping operation in Vietnam. So the situation is much more complex, much more difficult, than the situation the United Nations faced two years ago in the Dominican Republic. In the case of the Dominican Republic, as I said a moment ago, among other reasons one of the big powers was opposed to United Nations involvement in peace-keeping operations there. Now, in the case of Vietnam, more than two big powers will not agree to any type of United Nations involvement by way of peace-keeping operations in that country. I think this is a basic fact.

So, with the full knowledge of the attitudes of these big powers, how can the Secretary-General say that the United Nations must be involved in Vietnam, that the United Nations should be involved in Vietnam? As I have to reflect the views of the Member states in my statements and my actions, if my interpretation of my functions is correct, I have to say that at least for the moment the United Nations cannot and should not be effectively involved in peace-keeping operations or in operations of the nature of the maintenance of international peace and security or law and order in Vietnam, because of the very plain facts:

(1) That the United Nations was not involved in the Vietnam situation twelve years ago and, therefore, the same considerations do apply today and the United Nations cannot be involved in any peace-keeping operations in Vietnam today;
(2) That at least two big powers were opposed to any United Nations involvement in Vietnam.

So, when I have been saying for the last three years that, in my view, the United Nations cannot be and should not be usefully involved in peace-keeping operations of any character in Vietnam, I am just reflecting the views of the Member states, particularly the big powers.

If I may say so, I am in a position to assess the views of other Member states also. I have come to the conclusion that the vast majority of the Members, large and small, agree that, at least for the moment, the United Nations cannot be usefully involved in the settlement of the very tragic and very distressing developments in Vietnam.

I just want to take this opportunity of elaborating my thesis which I have presented to you and to others publicly on previous occasions.

Now the question arises which is the big question, naturally, in the minds of most people. The United Nations, as the primary organ for dealing with breaches of peace, for dealing with situations threatening international peace and security, is for the moment impotent in regard to Vietnam. Of course, quite legitimately, a lot of dissatisfaction has been expressed regarding the inability of the United Nations to be involved in the most serious crisis which has ever faced the world since the end of the Second World War. But, as I have explained to you, I have to be guided in my statements and actions by, and reflect, the views of the membership, particularly the views of the big powers. However, although the United Nations is not able to perform a very significant role in Vietnam, as you all know, in my private capacity I have endeavored my utmost in the last three years to bring about a peaceful settlement. Some of my attempts and endeavors were known to the public, and some are not yet known. For reasons which I hope that you will understand, it is not time for me to reveal all the steps I have taken in the last three years to bring about dialogues, to bring about peaceful discussions, to bring about pre-conference conferences, and even to bring about a formal conference. So far, my endeavors have not been crowned with success, but I am not giving up my attempts to find a peaceful solution, a just solution. I am still continuing with my endeavors to bring about a just and fair and equitable solution of the problem of Vietnam.

As I said on a previous occasion, my understanding of the developments in Vietnam and my assessment of the present situation there are different from the understanding and assessment of most people, if I may say so. So, my approach to the problem of Vietnam is, in a way, different from the approach of some governments. But I hope in due course, at the proper time, I shall be able to disclose some of the important steps I have taken and how and why those attempts were still inconclusive.

I can assure you, Ladies and Gentlemen, that I will not give up my attempts to find a peaceful solution to the Vietnam problem, and at the proper time, perhaps, I may be in a position to reveal at least some of the salient points of my attempts in the last three years.

. . .

"Democracy and Peace"
Speech to the Amalgamated Clothing Workers of America

ATLANTIC CITY, NEW JERSEY   MAY 24, 1966

U THANT said frequently that as an Asian his understanding of the Vietnam war was different from that of many other people. In the following speech before the Amalgamated Clothing Workers of America, he gave his views in some detail. Among other things, he challenged the basic American belief that this was a war to prevent the spread of communism in Southeast Asia. "Twenty years of outside intervention and the presence of a succession of foreign armies," he said, "have so profoundly affected Vietnamese political life that it seems illusory to represent it as a mere contest between communism and liberal democracy. Indeed, recent events have shown that the passion for national identity, perhaps one should say national survival, is the only ideology that may be left to a growing number of Vietnamese." He repeated his belief that at least two preliminary steps were essential to bring the parties to the conference table: (1) a scaling down of military operations and (2) an agreement that any peace talks must include the "actual combatants"—meaning the inclusion of the National Liberation Front (Vietcong) along with the United States, South Vietnam, and North Vietnam. Thant said a majority of the Members of the United Nations were convinced that military methods would not restore peace in Vietnam and that the war must be stopped on the initiative of the participants themselves.

IT IS BOTH a pleasure and an honor to be with you here today in Atlantic City. For me this is also a most stimulating occasion. My duties as Secretary-General of the United Nations bring me into contact, for the most part, with diplomats, statesmen, and politicians. It is to some extent true of all of us that we live in a world of our own, and, of course, the world of any profession has its own atmosphere and its own preoccupations. It is, nonetheless, most valuable to be with people who are engaged in a different type of activity and to try

SOURCE: *UN Monthly Chronicle,* vol. III, June 1966, pp. 61–70.

to see problems through their eyes. That is why I welcome the opportunity to be with you here today to share some of my thoughts with you, the representatives of one of the most important elements of the labor movement in the United States. Although our spheres of activity differ, our two basic objectives are the same—peace and human advancement.

I want to talk today about two words which many of us take very much for granted—democracy and peace—and their relationship to each other. In these two words is bound up much of the future which we hope to build for ourselves and our children. There is a danger, however, that words so frequently used may easily begin to lose some of their importance and meaning. In examining them in relation to each other I hope to shed some light on the present world situation and on our hopes for the future.

Democracy is the most difficult of all forms of government, and yet it is the one to which most nations now aspire. This is because it seems to most people to be the form of government which provides the best hope of making both peace and justice the birthright of all men—of making a world in which privilege, good fortune, or the accidents of history or heredity will no longer determine the horizons of opportunity and in which, therefore, the human spirit will flourish best.

A successful democratic system requires a number of pre-conditions, most of them difficult in themselves to establish. It requires popular acceptance of certain standards of behavior and certain common objectives. It requires the active cooperation of the community for the common good. It requires institutions which can ensure that those who obey the law will not become the victims of those who do not. It requires mutual respect and a shared pride in the objectives and traditions of the community as a whole. It requires the absence of any form of discrimination based on race, sex, belief, or opinion. It requires the fully equal treatment of minorities. It requires freedom of expression and tolerance of diversity. It requires, especially from those who have power and influence, restraint and patience. It requires a system of laws which are at the same time effective enough to ensure peace and justice and not so restrictive as to hamper enterprise or strangle opportunity. It requires political vitality and broad popular participation. It requires a constant reassertion of the place, worth, and dignity of the individual. In fact, it requires a combination of the highest human qualities with the most carefully developed institutions and traditions.

Democracy is certainly not a system for the timid, the lazy, or the insecure. Difficult as it is, this is the system of government to which most peoples in the world now aspire. The establishment of a democratic society is an ambitious goal for the emerging nations. It has been achieved, if only imperfectly, in the older democratic countries only after centuries of trial and error, not infrequently accompanied by periods of violence and injustice. It should be no surprise, therefore, that the achievement of political independence has not, in many cases, also led immediately, in newly independent countries, to the degree of individual liberty so highly prized in the older democratic countries. But if it is clear that the will to achieve democratic government is there, the older countries should show patience and understanding, remembering their own histories. There is more than one road to democracy, and in choosing the road much will depend on where a nation is starting from.

The principles of democracy also underlie the concept of world order outlined in the Charter of the United Nations. The requirements for the establishment of such a world order are similar in terms of the community of nations to those which I have outlined above for national communities. We must ask outselves, therefore, how best we can hope to provide the conditions in which democratic practices and institutions are most likely to flourish, and how we can strengthen their development both in nations and in the world community at large. We should also ask, from time to time, what sort of alternatives we have and what their consequences are likely to be.

It is a truism—and no less important for that—that peace is essential to the growth of democracy and the proper working of democratic institutions. Our experience in two world wars shows clearly not only that insecurity, tension, and war tend to foster authoritarian and tyrannical régimes and practices, but that even in well-established democratic countries the stresses and strains of war, or the threat of war, inevitably curtail and endanger in many ways the process and tradition of democratic liberty. Wars cannot be run democratically. Truth, the essential basis of all free institutions, is usually one of the first prisoners of war. It follows that as long as we have either actual wars, or situations and relationships among the nations of the world which can easily deteriorate into war, we shall not achieve the flowering of democracy or realize its full possibilities even at the national level, let alone in the community of nations. If this sounds unrealistic or over-idealistic, I put it to you that our present situation is unrealistic without even the benefit of being idealistic. In fact, we could go further and say that in continuing to accept our present situation we are being not only unrealistic, but cynical.

Let us for a moment consider our present position in very general terms which can apply to most governments and peoples. There is not a government in the world, perhaps for the first time in history, which does not profess, in its own way, to be peace-loving. One hundred and seventeen governments have ratified the United Nations Charter, which sets out the rights and obligations of peace-loving nations. There is hardly a government in the world which is not committed to work for the peace and prosperity of its people. There is a view universally held—although its formulations vary widely—that the future of mankind lies in cooperation rather than conflict. Certainly the interdependence of nations is now a fact which even the greatest must recognize. There is a vast and growing body of expert knowledge, available to all, which points the way to cooperative solutions of mankind's greatest problems.

But then we turn the coin and see the obverse—the cynical side. The greatest powers are locked in an ideological struggle and in a balance of terror based on the most destructive—and most expensive—arsenal of armaments ever known. The lesser powers survive in this precarious balance either through alliances with either side or in the more complex position of nonalignment. The majority of the world's people live in poverty and backwardness, the helpless spectators of this spendthrift struggle of giants. And by far the greatest efforts and expenditures are still for wars which no one can win—not for the human problems and possibilities which it is within our power to solve and to realize if we have the vision, the patience, and the will to cooperate. Is not this gap between stated ideals and actual practice truly cynical? And yet we all in some degree connive in the vast self-deception.

We need to wage a determined and broadly based struggle to extricate ourselves from this self-deception, which could easily be suicidal. The labor movement both here and abroad is no stranger to such efforts, for it has, in the last hundred years, waged a struggle which has radically changed the economic and social order and extended the horizon of opportunity in numerous countries, including all the most advanced ones. In doing this, despite strong and well-entrenched opposition and the direct prophecies of chaos and disaster, it has, in effect, vastly strengthened the countries and societies in which it has succeeded.

Many of the obstacles which the labor movement has faced in its great struggle were similar to those we face now in our efforts to make a better and safer world. It faced, and at times even to this day still faces, outmoded thinking, entrenched power in the hands of small groups, a social and economic system firmly based on the status quo, and the fear of change expressed in a widely felt reluctance to face the future. It faced selfishness and rapacity in the guise of conventional and respectable customs and attitudes. It faced the dangers of extremism both within and outside its own ranks. Above all, it faced the inertia inherent in the belief that the old way of doing things should somehow go on, despite the technological, political, and social changes which had already made it obsolete.

Those who wish to establish a better world order face, in general, somewhat similar problems. In particular, the last obstacle is very much in evidence—the belief that the old way of doing things can, and should, go on. It is all too clear, whether we examine the goals we have set ourselves or the dangers that beset us, that it cannot. How, for example, can we reconcile our democratic ideals or our desire for social justice, either in one nation or in the world community, with the persistence of the gap between rich and poor or with large-scale racial discrimination? How can we—and by "we" I mean all the people in the world—reconcile our professed love of peace or our knowledge of the fearful risks of modern war with policies whose ultimate sanction is war and whose practical result is a vast and continuing arms race?

The answers are, of course, anything but simple. But one fundamental reason for the tension and the lack of confidence in the world is that most governments and peoples, despite the revolutionary changes of the past century, have not yet relinquished some of the habits of thought of a hundred or more years ago. They tend still to see the outside world as hostile and treacherous, or as a happy hunting ground for the pursuit of national interest. They tend still to believe that force can solve problems when all else has failed, that purely nationalistic aims can still be pursued with impunity in a world of increasing interdependence, and that ideological controversies or international disputes can, if necessary, still be fought out on the battlefield. And how, they ask, and with some justification, can one government or people take the risk of changing its ways if all the others have not already done so? Thus, despite all the earnest professions of devotion to peace and progress, we are still in the vicious circle of the arms race, of mutual fear and hatred, of the fight for spheres of influence, of the perpetuation of historic grievances and disputes, and the competitive and cutthroat economic system of opportunism and "the devil take the hindmost." It is this series of vicious circles that we must break somehow, if we really wish to achieve the peace and justice which we so often invoke.

I have mentioned nationalism. Nationalism is a fact of contemporary life and the binding force of the most advanced form of political and social organization which has so far gained a firm footing in the world—the nation state. As such it is an indispensable element in the scheme of world order outlined in the United Nations Charter, which is based on the sovereign equality of its Member states. Indeed, I sometimes think that the older nations are guilty of an unwitting hypocrisy when they express pained surprise at nationalistic manifestations in the new countries. Basic nationalism is the foundation in all countries of a sense of identity and security. Without it nations will be unlikely to be able to venture successfully into the next stage of internationalism. We must understand that the effort to establish this basic identity under the pressures of the modern world may well temporarily produce attitudes and actions which appear unreasonable. Growing up politically is a complex and painful process, especially when it coincides, as it does in most emerging countries, with the necessity of trying to catch up in all sorts of other ways as well.

Aggressive nationalism in international relationships, however, whether it be in pursuit of ideological aims or of more immediate and concrete objectives, is an anachronism which the world can no longer afford. Aggressive nationalism, albeit in transmuted and disguised forms, is still a potent factor in the world, and is found both in the older and the newer countries. Only twenty-seven years ago it was the basic cause of the Second World War, and in new forms it is still the source of the most dangerous tensions in the world. It feeds on fear, on the propaganda of hate and ideological antagonism, and on the intolerable presumption that the world should be remade in its own image. Aggressive nationalism produces a breakdown of understanding and communication which is perpetuated by a powerful mythology. It is not confined to any one nation or group of nations and it smolders beneath many conflicts, both great and small, many of which can at any moment burst into a wider conflagration. Aggressive nationalism is the political disease which still, more than any other factor, infects the relations of states. Its elimination is indispensable to any reasonably reliable system of world order.

I have not referred to specific cases, for the truth is that most nations are in various degrees afflicted by the vicious circle of tension, lack of confidence, and the belief in the notion that attack may ultimately be the best form of defense. It is an additional tragedy that, all too often, small and inoffensive countries are ground under the wheels of these giant forces. But if the giants live in fear of each other, what chance is there that the fears and aspirations of the small countries of the world will be seriously heard or heeded?

It is not enough to say that confidence and understanding are the keys to the vicious circle. The question is how to begin to prepare the ground in which confidence and understanding can grow. The world is not clearly divided between good and evil, as many leaders would have us believe, and the confusion is increased by the fact that all powers, the great powers included, are unanimous in expressing in their different ways the highest motives and the best intentions. In most countries there is no serious question any more of ignoring the masses of the people or of pursuing a course designed only for the benefit of a tiny and fortunate minority. The idea is now taking hold, both nationally and internationally, that the fortunate have a responsibility for the less fortunate and that we are all members of one human race on one small planet and must sink or swim together. The true basis for this idea is enlightened self-interest rather than altruistic humanitarianism. Men, nations, and institutions are in a constant process of growth and change, not infrequently for the better. We see, here in the United States and everywhere else, that the revolutionaries and firebrands of yesterday are the moderates of today and the conservatives of tomorrow. Between good and evil, left and right, reactionary and reformer there is no clear-cut distinction any more in a world of tumultuous change and development.

In fact, we live now in a highly mobile society in which many of the old barriers and stratifications have been swept away. That is why we must look earnestly for new ideas, and even new political forms, to contain the forces we have unleashed and to channel them into constructive and peaceful pursuits before they tear us to pieces. Certainly the days of national self-sufficiency are gone. Imperial domination, as history has known it, is also a thing of the past, a phenomenon of the age in which greed and power could endlessly exploit ignorance, servility, and weakness. It seems probable also that the conflict of global ideologies is a transient phenomenon, for ideologies tend rapidly to be blurred and made obsolete by the present pace of historic change. Nonetheless, it is the residual effects of these phenomena which perpetually distract us from facing our real problems—misery, poverty, starvation, overpopulation, and the preservation and enhancement of human dignity—and from reaping the harvest of our extraordinary inventiveness.

Certain simple and related propositions are becoming increasingly clear. Total war is unthinkable. No one nation, even the most powerful, is now capable of policing the world or imposing a pattern upon it. Most of our gravest problems can best be solved by the orderly cooperation of sovereign states, and some cannot be solved in any other way. The less developed countries require much from the advanced countries, and without such help, given freely and without political or other pressures, the current economic and social gap will widen to the extent where it threatens the stability of all nations. I would add that multilateral aid would seem in the long run to be superior, in meeting this challenge, to bilateral aid which tends to give rise to political strains and stresses both for the giver and the receiver. And, finally, no problem is too great for us to tackle, and probably to solve, if we wish to use adequately the resources and knowledge which we have in common. If we can conquer the atom or outer space, it is absurd that we cannot conquer urban misery or the problem of producing and distributing an adequate food supply. These simple propositions should provide a basis on which all nations should be able to start to come to terms with the world in which we actually live.

I, for one, do not think that any government or people is likely to lose in stature or dignity or worldly advantage from an all-out effort to come to terms with such questions. On the contrary, it is highly probable that the future leaders of the world will be those who first can bring themselves to make the attempt. There have been already, in the past twenty years, governments which had the vision and the courage to throw away the outmoded trappings of a glorious past and which have gained nothing but advantage from doing so. Let us hope that they are merely the forerunners of a more general and forward-looking movement.

We have now come to a stage where all ideological concepts or national aims, however high-minded, will become meaningless if their pursuit involves a third world war. On the other hand, an abject surrender of principles and aims cannot be an acceptable answer for any nation. The answer must therefore lie, for governments and peoples, in an effort more difficult and less spectacular—the effort to come to terms with the world in which they live. Reliable ways will have to be found, as they have been found in the brief history of the labor movement, to replace strife, harmful, if not disastrous, to all parties, with organized bargaining mediation and reconciliation of divergent interests. This is only a first step towards the next and more important stage of active cooperation in pursuit of common aims. To effect this change will require patience, courage, and the self-confidence to face inevitable risks. In a democratic country it will also require the active participation and understanding of the mass of the people.

The United Nations Charter is, of course, in terms of practical politics, far ahead of its time. But if governments and peoples will persevere in the effort, both private and public, to come to terms with the world as it now is, they will begin to find in the Charter a most useful mechanism for their protection and for the regulation of their affairs, rather than what it sometimes seems to be now—a catalogue of good intentions and, sometimes, a useful last resort in times of trouble.

This process must start at the grass-roots level, with the thinking and the will of the peoples of the world whose instruments their governments and their world Organization should be. If they persevere in coming to terms with realities, concepts like peace and democracy will begin to have a fuller meaning, which may well produce a real revolution in the human condition.

You will expect me, I believe, to mention one specific problem which is very much on all our minds—I refer to Vietnam. Let me say at once that I have no answers to this problem, nor do I wish to pronounce any judgments as to where right or wrong, responsibility or culpability, reality or myth, may lie in what is a tragic situation for all the peoples and governments involved. The situation is far too serious for that. It is more important and relevant, I believe, to search objectively and without rancor for ways to end this historic tragedy.

The world has been watching the inexorable escalation of the war in Vietnam with increasing anxiety. Little by little, larger forces and more powerful armaments have been introduced, until an anguished and perplexed world has suddenly found that a limited and local conflict is threatening to turn into a major confrontation. And though the fear of a much larger conflict may still have a restraining influence upon the demands of military strategy, the temptation to win a military success may still prove stronger than the more prudent call to reason.

As the war worsens, its justification in terms of a confrontation of ideologies is becoming more and more misleading. For democratic principles, which both sides consider to be at stake in Vietnam, are already falling a victim to the war itself.

In Vietnam there is growing evidence that the so-called fight for democracy is no longer relevant to the realities of the situation. Twenty years of outside intervention and the presence of a succession of foreign armies have so profoundly affected Vietnamese political life that it seems illusory to represent it as a mere contest between communism and liberal democracy. Indeed, recent events have shown that the passion for national identity, perhaps one should say national survival, is the only ideology that may be left to a growing number of Vietnamese. Thus, the increasing intervention by outside powers in the conflict—involving their armies, their armaments and, above all, their prestige—has tended to alienate the people of Vietnam from their own destiny. And if, therefore, the issue in Vietnam is not a struggle between two different views of democracy, what is really at stake, unless an early end to the hostilities is brought about, is the independence, the identity, and the survival of the country itself.

Apart from the loss of life, destruction, and human suffering which this war is causing, the war in Vietnam has also to be judged by the halt which it has imposed on the great enterprise of cooperation and understanding between nations which had barely made a modest start in recent years. The much larger international efforts, which should have been undertaken during this decade to relax world tensions and to improve the miserable conditions of the more unfortunate countries, have already been postponed and may be made infinitely more difficult by the continuation of this war. It would also be unrealistic to believe that significant progress in international relations can be achieved while so much tension and hatred are accumulating in Asia.

In these grave circumstances, it would appear normal to entrust a world Organization such as the United Nations with the task of bringing the parties together to negotiate. Unfortunately, the United Nations is not, at present, so constituted that it could play this role. I have explained on various occasions why this is so. But, although the United Nations cannot act in a conflict which is beyond its scope, nonetheless, the majority of Member states is increasingly concerned by its development. They are convinced that military methods will not restore peace in Vietnam and that this war must be stopped on the initiative of the participants lest it get out of hand. To give effect to these convictions, and also because it represents my firm belief, I have undertaken, in my personal capacity, to make a number of suggestions to the parties. In particular, I have said that peace can only be restored by a return to the Geneva Agreements and that, as a preparatory measure, it would be necessary to start scaling down military operations, and to agree to discussions which include the actual combatants. Perhaps, under these conditions, it will still be possible to arrive at an agreement between all powers concerned, and, among them, the five major powers, including the People's Republic of China. But those who are genuinely troubled today by the great problems of war and peace should not delude themselves that action by the United Nations or its Secretary-General can resolve this problem. The solution lies in the hands of those who have the power, and the responsibility, to decide. If they seek a peaceful solution, the United Nations and many of its Members stand ready to help them in all possible ways. Of course, it must be recognized that a sincere effort to reach a diplomatic settlement is a most arduous and frustrating task. That is why all the forces of peace must join together to make their influence felt by the leaders of the countries engaged in this war, so that they may find a way to reverse its fateful trend and to restore peace before it is too late.

May I conclude by a direct appeal to you, representatives of the labor movement in one of the most advanced countries of the world. The labor movement in the United States, though it still has much unfinished business, is now a very weighty part of the national establishment. It is a measure of your success that your movement, which within living memory was an embattled newcomer battering on the doors of the old order, is now the most powerful single organized group in the country. Your own great leader and founder, Sidney Hillman, was a champion not only of the labor movement in the United States but of the cause of democracy throughout the world. He was a great leader because, in the words of his epitaph, he not only demanded justice *for* labor, but also demanded greatness *from* labor.

I urge you now, in your great success, to devote much of your energy and your organization to new and equally vital objectives—to the great problems of establishing a world order in which peace and democratic principles really prevail, and to the application in the world community of those great ideals for which you have been and are fighting in your own country. Peace and order in the world are not the exclusive business of statesmen, diplomats, and international officials. They are the urgent personal business of all men and women who are capable of wishing for a better world for their children and their fellow men. It is the will and the informed preference which they evince, which can put governments and the United Nations firmly into the path of progress and peace and can rescue mankind from hopelessness and cynicism. It is their support which alone can sustain governments in the risks and uncertainties which they are bound to encounter.

It will be a long and hard struggle. Old prejudices, habits, and ideas die hard, and fear and hatred, though they are bad advisers, are also persuasive ones. Men and nations, especially the well-established ones, are wary of change and lazy about facing the future. But in the matter of peace and justice we can no longer afford to rely on muddling through. The risks are too great, and what we have to gain from success is too important to be thrown away through careless-ness or inertia. We would be foolish, however, to underestimate the effort required to reverse the collision course on which the great nations of the world seem sometimes to be set or the work involved in developing our political institutions to match our technological prog-ress. Learning to live in peace may well prove, initially at any rate, to be more difficult and more exasperating than muddling through with the threat of war, just as democracy requires far more of the average

citizen than despotism or authoritarian government. The labor movement, with its vast influence and prestige, can be a very powerful
force in producing the changes of attitude which will be required.

The task is great and the time is certainly short. The choice may
well be between ruin and the fulfillment of all we have dreamed of in
the name of peace and democracy. It is a choice in which all must
participate if it is to be correctly and firmly made.

From Address at the University of Windsor

WINDSOR, ONTARIO   MAY 27, 1966

U THANT often stressed the urgency of United Nations efforts to devise peace-keeping machinery and breaking the big-power deadlock on financing such operations. At the time he delivered the following remarks at the University of Windsor, the Special Committee on Peace-keeping Operations—functioning as a working group—had resumed its discussions but no signs of progress were visible. Thant dealt at length with the situation underlying the continuing deadlock on peace-keeping and the possible tragic consequences. It was inconceivable, he said, that the United Nations "could be rendered impotent by a failure to agree on satisfactory arrangements for the control and financing" of peace-keeping operations, but, he added, "that is the kind of risk which we are now running."

. . . I FIND IN the present situation a great paradox, and I venture to warn that it runs the risk of proving to be a tragic paradox. On the one hand, there is very wide agreement among the governments as to both the necessity and the effectiveness of the peace-keeping operations of the past and the present. As you know, these activities constitute a function for the Organization which was not clearly foreseen by the founders of the United Nations—no doubt because they have responded to situations which could not easily have been predicted in advance, but which nevertheless have seriously disturbed the peace, or threatened to do so, in many parts of the world. They are situations which have largely been due to the changes in human and international relations following from the process of decolonization. Although these changes have generally been, in my view, inevitable, necessary, and beneficial to mankind as a whole, they have often been so radical as to have had turbulent effects, and it is these turbulences that the United Nations has been called upon to quiet.

In proving itself able to do this by lending its physical presence to the areas of dispute, the United Nations has, in my view, immeasura-

SOURCE: UN Press Release SG/SM/511.

bly strengthened its practical usefulness to mankind. It is well to recall that in most of these situations the United Nations has served as a life-saving last resort, called upon in circumstances, sometimes desperate, when the efforts of individual states, or combinations of states, or regional organizations or alliances have all failed. It is well to ponder, too, the likely consequences in many of these situations if the United Nations had not existed or had felt unable to act.

There are other aspects of the peace-keeping operations from which the world, as a whole, ought to have been able to take heart and draw confidence in the potential power for good of organized international action. In varying degree, for example, each such operation has required one or more of the states concerned voluntarily to liberalize its conception of national sovereignty, if not sometimes in effect to yield temporarily a part of that sovereignty, in order to allow an international operation to function on its territory. Another aspect of these operations is the entirely new phenomenon of the development of impartial, disinterested, multinational teams and forces, and the evolution of a new breed of soldier of peace.

In all these respects the peace-keeping operations of the United Nations have constituted, in my view, a great step forward in international cooperation and a great promise of the capacity of men and nations to turn away from violence and toward international action and assistance as the means of resolving their disputes.

Yet, on the other hand, the chances of the United Nations being able in the future to continue to carry out this kind of operation are being seriously jeopardized by the lack of agreement so far in regard to one or another of the constitutional, financial, and administrative aspects of the operations. This lack of agreement is made all the more serious by what I can only describe as a certain measure of apathy, to which the absence of agreement has perhaps given rise.

To all those who are pledged to further the interests of the United Nations, it should be inconceivable that the demonstrated need for and ability of the Organization to play a direct part in reducing tensions, in calming passions, and in helping nations and peoples dangerously at odds with one another to find acceptable paths to the peaceful settlement of their disputes, could be rendered impotent by a failure to agree on satisfactory arrangements for the control and financing of those activities. I have said that such a situation should be inconceivable: nevertheless, that is the kind of risk which we are now running.

I know very well, of course, that from the viewpoint of some governments, there are, in this matter, issues of national interest, of principle and of legality which they regard as being of the highest importance. I am no less aware that broader considerations of national policy and international relations—indeed, the condition of the international political climate as a whole—tend quite often to override the practical, as distinct from the philosophical, concern of governments for the solution of problems that directly embroil the fate of peoples other than their own.

I venture to suggest, however, that all of us must take care not to delude ourselves into thinking that these problems can be isolated from the whole course of human development, and that their solution—or lack of solution—has no consequences for those other aspects of this development which may seem of more direct concern to us. From the beginning of history, mankind has been carried forward by a steady evolution in all fields—political, economic, social, scientific, and cultural. From time to time in certain societies it happened that this great process of evolution or change was resisted too long by those in power, and then social explosions occurred. If there is one lesson we can learn from history, it is that attempts to maintain a static concept of society, purportedly insulated from changes taking place around it, have always failed.

The human situation may be likened to a stream which starts gently at the source but gathers speed and becomes more turbulent as it flows on. In the earliest stages of man's development he adapted himself as best he could to his wild environment and took from it sufficient to meet his needs, which were few. With time, however, he began to attempt to transform his environment. He succeeded, and his needs grew. His society did not just change slowly and gently as in the beginning; the change became faster as time went on.

Although man has been on the earth about a million years, it was perhaps only during the last six or seven thousand years that he began to create a civilization as we know it. Different forms of civilization have come and gone in many parts of the world, but there has been a continuing thread of progress. For thousands of years, the rate of progress was not very spectacular; suddenly it accelerated at a tremendous pace. Most historians who have studied the progress of human culture agree that it was around the end of the eighteenth century that the accelerating pace of human progress reached the point at which it began to be revolutionary. Changes that used to be gentle, like the flow of a stream at its source, are today rapid, turbulent, and widespreading. Changes that used to be imperceptible over many generations now take place within a decade, and they spill irresistibly over every natural and man-made barrier.

A realization of this change in the character of change itself is essential in the conduct not only of national affairs, but also of international affairs. Human ingenuity must match the accelerated pace of this extraordinary evolution and the complex problems such an evolution generates. Here the United Nations, representing the human society in an organized form, must have a role to play. One of its main concerns should be how to keep pace with man's accelerating evolution and society's accelerating and universal change, and to fashion its tools to cope with its accelerating tasks. Otherwise the United Nations, too, will run the risk of becoming an anachronism.

It may well be, of course, that the United Nations will never be able to move closer toward the objectives it set for itself twenty years ago until the world it inevitably—and deliberately—mirrors is fundamentally a better and saner world than it is now. In other words, it may well be that, before the United Nations can be relied upon to keep the peace even in places that may seem secondary in the geopolitical order of things, we shall have to see larger progress made by the great powers toward the resolution of the conflicts that still exist between them.

But can we really afford to wait for a resolution of these conflicts before we try, through the United Nations as it now exists, to provide more effective and dependable help to governments and peoples which already want and need that help?

I do not think so. Ours is not a world populated solely by Americans, Chinese, Russians, and Vietnamese. There are others among us, Europeans, Africans, Asians, the people of the Middle East and Latin America—and if I may say so, Canadians as well. All of us have a stake in the success or the failure of the United Nations. All of us have a responsibility to put the Organization to work, and to try to make it work effectively, wherever in the world its work is needed and wanted, and regardless of the areas, political or geographical, in which it cannot yet be given a part to play.

This is true, if I may put things in simple terms, because all of us have a place in humankind. Wherever the United Nations fails, it is humanity as a whole that fails. Wherever it succeeds, humanity succeeds. And we just cannot afford to fail, if humanity is to survive.

THE SITUATION IN VIETNAM

JUNE AND JULY

BEGINNING WITH his remarks at a luncheon of the United Nations Correspondents Association on June 20 and continuing through a press conference at Kennedy International Airport on his return from Moscow, July 30, U Thant referred frequently to the three steps he had proposed as a preliminary to Vietnam peace negotiations. As previously mentioned (p. 224), these were: (1) the cessation of the bombing of North Vietnam; (2) the scaling down of all military activities in South Vietnam; and (3) the willingness of all sides to enter into discussions with those who were actually fighting (including the Vietcong). In his June 20 luncheon remarks, Thant confirmed that he had been presenting his proposals "to some of the parties principally concerned." He did not say just when he had first begun presenting his proposals, but it became known subsequently that he had submitted them early in March. He told the luncheon that he had not made any new proposals in the last few weeks, "since I feel that these proposals are still as applicable today as they were six months ago." At a press conference in Geneva on July 6, the Secretary-General said he felt very strongly about the three steps which he had proposed, "but so far these have not met with a positive response from several quarters." He added, however, that in his view his three steps alone could "create an atmosphere congenial for discussions and negotiations." He repeated his proposals in a statement to the press on July 16 together with his comment that they alone could open the way for peace talks. Later in the month Thant paid a five-day visit to Moscow, his first since August 1963. "Inevitably," he said in an airport press conference in New York on July 30, "the Vietnam war dominated our talks." He added, however, that he had not brought up his three-point peace plan in Moscow, since he did not believe it had "any relevancy to the government of the Soviet Union." In fact, he came away from the Soviet capital more apprehensive than ever that the Vietnam war might spill over the frontiers. "My fears were confirmed after my talks with the Soviet leaders," he said. "If the present trend continues, I feel that the Vietnam war is likely to develop into a major war."

1. From Remarks at Luncheon of
United Nations Correspondents Association

NEW YORK   JUNE 20, 1966

. . .

THE SECRETARY-GENERAL: You will recall that at our last press conference on April 6, I stated that I might have to make my decision known one way or the other about my availability for the second term before the end of June (p. 203). The same considerations which prompted me to make that statement are still in order, but I feel that as I have to visit Europe toward the end of this month, I should defer the announcement of my decision until I return to Headquarters.

I would be very glad to answer questions.

QUESTION: We have some questions regarding your plans which might bear on what you have just told us, Mr. Secretary-General. Do you feel that the three months' advance notice is sufficient? What is your appraisal of the importance of the timing with respect to the amount of time between the end of your term and the time of your announcement?

THE SECRETARY-GENERAL: Some friends and colleagues with whom I have discussed this question felt that perhaps a four months' advance notice was too long. They have suggested, of course with the best of intentions, that perhaps a couple of months' prior notice would be quite ample for the Security Council to take the necessary action in case I decided not to offer myself for a second term. This is also one consideration in my decision to defer my announcement.

QUESTION: In making your decision about another term as Secretary-General, will you take into consideration the needs of your own country? The questioner refers to a report in today's newspaper about economic plans and the need in the government there for people with experience in these and other matters.

THE SECRETARY-GENERAL: No. My decision, of course, will neces-

SOURCE: UN Press Release SG/SM/524.

sarily be governed by several considerations, both official and personal. As most of you are aware, for the past four or five months I have given a good deal of thought to these problems. My decision will be guided not by two or three considerations, but by many considerations, including political and official considerations and personal considerations. The substance which is brought out in this question does not apply to my considerations.

. . .

QUESTION: We now have a number of questions on Vietnam. The first one points out that when Prime Minister Jens Otto Kraag of Denmark was here in April, he said that he had encouraged you, on behalf of his government, to make concrete proposals for the cessation of hostilities in Vietnam when the time was right. Have you submitted such proposals, and could you comment on this question of the timing, when the time is right in terms of developments in the Vietnam situation?

THE SECRETARY-GENERAL: As you will recall, the Prime Minister of Denmark had very kindly endorsed my proposals, even publicly. I think it is worth reiterating some of the proposals which I have been presenting to some of the parties principally concerned and which, of course, have been made public.

I feel very strongly that without a spirit of give-and-take on the part of the parties primarily concerned, there will be no negotiations leading to the return to the Geneva Agreements of 1954, on which everybody seems to agree now. As you all know, I have been proposing three steps to bring about a situation congenial for discussions and negotiations. First, the cessation of the bombing of North Vietnam; second, the scaling down of all military activities in South Vietnam, which alone could lead to the bringing about of a cease-fire; and third, the willingness by all sides to enter into discussions with those who are actually fighting. I think these three steps alone can create conditions conducive to the holding of a conference and to the creation of conditions for a peaceful settlement of the problem of Vietnam. I have not made any new proposals in the last few weeks, since I feel that these proposals are still as applicable today as they were six months ago.

QUESTION: With respect to the question of timing, are you suggesting that these de-escalation steps should begin immediately?

THE SECRETARY-GENERAL: As for the timing, the sooner the better, of course. As I have been saying all along, the longer we wait the worse will be the war situation. What was possible in 1964 was no longer possible in 1965, and what was possible of achievement in 1965 is no longer possible today. Therefore, the situation is very urgent and very critical. People are being killed by the hundreds every day and, if I may say so, the war in Vietnam is one of the most barbarous wars in history. I think the sooner the parties involved sit down at the conference table after these conditions have been met, the better it will be not only for Vietnam but for the rest of the world also.

QUESTION: Have delegates from Asian countries in which there is strong Buddhist influence discussed with you the possibility of again sending a United Nations fact-finding mission to South Vietnam to check on the violation of human rights?

THE SECRETARY-GENERAL: There have been no discussions between me and any delegation of the Buddhist groups in any part of the world.

QUESTION: Recently you had a private conversation with Secretary of State Dean Rusk at the White House. Is that conversation likely to lead to new initiatives in the Vietnam situation?

THE SECRETARY-GENERAL: During my last visit to the White House, I had a few moments with the Secretary of State. Of course, with the background of the reception, our conversation was more or less very informal and, if I may say so, even casual. We covered a lot of ground, including the problem of Vietnam. Nothing of substance was discussed. We just exchanged views on our respective understanding of the developments.

QUESTION: Do you expect the Vietnam case to come before the General Assembly—in whatever form?

THE SECRETARY-GENERAL: To my knowledge, there has been no move by any Member state to bring this item before the twenty-first session of the General Assembly.

. . .

QUESTION: Following up on your announcement at the beginning, one of our members would like to know exactly when you are planning to return to Headquarters and whether you intend to make the statement about your future plans in the middle of July, or do you leave the timing open?

THE SECRETARY-GENERAL: For the moment I would prefer to leave the timing open. I have to take into consideration many aspects and many factors. Of course, as I have said on many previous occasions, I will be very happy if the Security Council is in a position to find somebody to succeed me. I do not agree with those who maintain that it will be very difficult for the Security Council to find somebody if I do decide not to offer myself for a second term. I think this is not an insurmountable problem. Of course, I do not mean to imply that I have decided one way or the other. But in case I decide not to offer myself for a second term, I am confident that the Security Council will be able to find somebody to succeed me. If necessary, I will be very glad to help the Security Council in finding someone, provided, of course, the Security Council so desires. But I do not think it is a very big problem.

. . .

2. From Transcript of Press Conference

GENEVA   JULY 6, 1966

. . .

THE SECRETARY-GENERAL: In my statement before the Economic and Social Council yesterday I tried to focus attention on two major themes. I just want to make a very brief reference to these two themes by way of an opening remark.

First, the crisis in international aid. I would recall that the developed countries, in 1961, in a General Assembly resolution, and again in 1964 at the first United Nations Conference on Trade and Development (UNCTAD), pledged themselves to provide annually at least 1 percent of their national income for the development of the developing countries. How has the pledge been made good? Despite the fact that developed countries are now considerably richer than in 1961, despite the fact that developing countries are today in a much better position to make fruitful use of an increased volume of aid, and despite the fact that we have now evolved increasingly effective

SOURCE: UN Press Release SG/SM/531.

mechanisms such as the International Development Association, the regional development banks, and the United Nations Development Programme (UNDP) for channeling aid into productive development, we are face to face with a very paradoxical situation. While the needs of developing countries for increased amounts of aid have never been greater, the developed countries are now providing a smaller, a considerably smaller, percentage of the national wealth to development than when the Development Decade was first proclaimed five years ago. This state of affairs will almost certainly lead to a slower growth in the developing countries and sometimes will mean complete stagnation, or even regression.

Second, I tried to show yesterday that the Economic and Social Council has a highly important role to play in providing the world community with an overall perspective of the economic and social development of the developing countries—a perspective that has become strategically important with the recognition that planning is an indispensable discipline. The process of development is a complex one, as you all know, and it presents a picture that might be compared to a jigsaw puzzle. It is the role of the Council to see that all the pieces do fit together and to draw attention to gaps and, even in some cases, to areas where too much emphasis is perhaps being given. I think that the Council is now able to carry out this task more effectively than hitherto.

I attach great importance to this session of the Council as it provides an opportunity for developed and developing countries to cooperate in finding solutions to the major economic and social problems facing the world today. It is also a forum where suspicions and fears can be brought out in the open and freely discussed. I think that we have already made significant progress in this direction during the recent joint meetings of the Special Committee on Coordination and the Administrative Committee on Coordination, where a real dialogue developed and both committees were able to gain a better understanding of each other's points of view.

I would now invite any questions which you may wish to ask.

QUESTION: In connection with your statement yesterday in the Economic and Social Council, may I ask you three questions. Will you be kind enough to tell us whether you are satisfied with UNCTAD after three years of its existence?

Second, what is the need of the new Industrial Development Organization? In this connection, would you be kind enough to tell us whether you believe that it is necessary to have a number of organizations working in the same field, especially in the development field, since more and more time must be devoted to the coordination of work of this Organization?

THE SECRETARY-GENERAL: Regarding your first question, I must say that it is very difficult to assess the work of an organization or a specialized agency in the context of its achievements or lack of achievements in the first few years of its existence. As I said yesterday, and on previous occasions, the functions assigned to UNCTAD have been viewed by some countries in a rather perfunctory manner, if I may say so. As regards the flow of trade and aid, the progress so far achieved in the last three or four years has been far from satisfactory. I have made this plain in my statements, not only yesterday but on previous occasions. But for this lack of perceptible progress, I do not think we should put the blame on UNCTAD. If the blame is to be laid somewhere, I think the entire membership of the United Nations should be jointly responsible. I tried to assess the situation rather comprehensively in my statement yesterday, and I do not wish to go beyond that.

With regard to your second question about the prospects of the usefulness or the utility of the new Industrial Development Organization, at the joint sessions of the Special Committee on Coordination and the Administrative Committee on Coordination in the last few days, we have reached some conclusions, and I am sure that the Secretariat will make available to you its report on the findings of these joint sessions, perhaps in the next few days.

Regarding your third question, on the proliferation of specialized agencies, I do not believe that the Secretary-General is competent to pass judgment on their necessity or otherwise. It is for the entire membership to decide whether a particular specialized agency is necessary or not.

QUESTION: Have you already taken a decision as to whether you will accept a new mandate as Secretary-General and, second, can this decision be influenced by the development of the situation in Vietnam?

THE SECRETARY-GENERAL: On the question of my availability for the second term, similar questions have been posed from time to time, and I have made my position known on previous occasions. I believe, first of all, that nobody should aspire, generally speaking, to serve as Secretary-General of the United Nations for more than one term because of the very difficult and killing nature of the work imposed on him. Second, I do not believe in the concept of indispensability of any person for any particular job. I have said on previous occasions that if the Security Council is able to find someone to succeed me when my present term expires in November 1966, I shall be very happy to leave my present assignment. I believe that the Security Council will be able to find someone agreeable to all parties and, of course, acceptable to the big powers. I do not think it is an insurmountable problem.

Regarding the second part of your question, I do not wish to give a reason or reasons which may guide my decision because giving at least a few reasons is likely to be misleading. There are, of course, many reasons which govern my decision: personal reasons, official reasons, and political reasons. I do not want to give the impression that if certain conditions are not met I will leave. I do not want to put myself in such a position as to impose any conditions of the membership. As a matter of fact, I have not made up my mind definitely, although I have expressed my desire to be relieved of my duties at the end of my term. Many friends and well-meaning government representatives advise me that if I decide one way or the other I should not announce it three or four months ahead of the expiry of my term. They feel it will be in order if I decide, say, a couple of months ahead of the expiry of the term. So I am thinking of making a public announcement about the end of August.

. . .

QUESTION(interpretation from French): At the beginning of this week you had a meeting with the Minister for Foreign Affairs of Greece. How does the Cyprus situation appear to you at this time?

THE SECRETARY-GENERAL: Regarding the question of Cyprus, I have expressed my views in my latest report to the Security Council just before it met last month. Apart from that, I have no additional remarks to make. But, as you all know, on the basis of my recommendation, the Security Council has extended the life of the United Nations Force in Cyprus (UNFICYP) until December 26, 1966. Apart from other considerations, the most serious problem confronting UNFICYP is the financial problem. As I have stated on previous occasions, the principle of voluntary contributions to finance peace-keeping operations has been very unsatisfactory. So I am not sure whether the United Nations will be able to maintain UNFICYP in Cyprus beyond the end of this year. Of course, it is up to the Security Council to decide on this.

As regards the political settlement, I have been doing my utmost to contribute toward a just and peaceful settlement of the problem. So far, the results of our endeavors have not been conclusive. My special representative, Mr. Carlos A. Bernardes, is also continuing with his efforts to bring about a peaceful solution in Cyprus and to contribute toward the finding of a just solution.

QUESTION: Would you care to reiterate your attitude on the Member nations that are in arrears in their financial obligations to the United Nations?

THE SECRETARY-GENERAL: On this question the General Assembly took certain action, as you all know, at the nineteenth session. At the twentieth session it created a Special Committee of Thirty-three to look into all aspects of peace-keeping operations, including the financial aspects. That Committee has been in session for the last few months, and I understand it will meet again in August. The matter is purely one for the Committee of Thirty-three to assess.

As regards the financial situation of the United Nations, I have expressed my views from time to time on that subject. The situation is very distressing, and the future prospects of the United Nations peace-keeping role are not very bright if the present financial situation continues to be bad; but I very much hope that the Committee of Thirty-three will be able to submit a positive and useful report to the twenty-first session of the General Assembly, particularly in respect of the financial position of the United Nations, so that the twenty-first session of the General Assembly will be able to bring back into solvency the whole of the Organization, as was the wish of the twentieth session.

QUESTION: What, in your view, are the prospects for bringing China into the United Nations?

THE SECRETARY-GENERAL: I have no means of anticipating what may be the attitude of the twenty-first session of the General Assembly when the question of China comes before it. It is for the Member states to discuss and decide. Up to the present I have no indication of what the outcome of the discussions may be.

QUESTION: Is there at present any indication as to when Indonesia will return to the United Nations?

THE SECRETARY-GENERAL: I have no official word from Djakarta about its attitude toward returning to the United Nations, but I believe that should Indonesia decide to come back to the United Nations, the entire membership would be very delighted to receive it once more into the family of nations.

QUESTION: Can you give any information about the items you are going to discuss in Moscow?

THE SECRETARY-GENERAL: I have accepted the kind invitation of the Soviet government to visit Moscow at the end of this month, as you all know. I have no set agenda to discuss. I have of course indicated to the Soviet government that I shall be happy to discuss any matter or matters that may be brought up by the Soviet government. So far there is no set agenda.

QUESTION: Has there been any recent development with regard to a peace conference on Vietnam? Everything goes on behind the scenes.

THE SECRETARY-GENERAL: There have not been any new developments, to my knowledge, likely to lead toward a peace conference on Vietnam. As you all know, during the last few months I have made certain proposals but so far these have not met with a positive response from several quarters. I feel very strongly about the three points which I proposed: that is, the cessation of the bombing of North Vietnam, the scaling down of all military operations in South Vietnam by all parties, and willingness on the part of all parties to enter into discussion with those who are actually fighting. These are the three points I have proposed, and, in my view, they alone can create an atmosphere congenial for discussions and negotiations.

As to the general question of Vietnam, as most of you are aware, my understanding of the developments and my assessment of the situation of Vietnam are different from the understanding and assessment of many people. For instance, there are two divergent views regarding the origin of the conflict in Vietnam. One view is that the whole trouble started with the so-called aggression from the North. The other view is that the war was a civil war like the Spanish civil war of the 1930s, resulting in the introduction of massive foreign elements into the area. I feel that both those viewpoints are oversimplifications and apt to be misleading. My assessment of the origins of the Vietnam conflict is related to the innermost yearnings of the long-suffering people for political independence and their determination to fashion their own future without foreign interference. Coming, as I do, from a country which has experienced strife and struggles for national independence, I know what it is to fight for independence, to fight for real national independence. In these fights for independence, communists, noncommunists, and anticommunists have all participated, but the fact is that if the struggle intensifies, if the situation deteriorates, the more extreme elements are likely to come to the surface and dominate the scene. That has been the case in many parts of the world. If the granting of independence is too long delayed, or if the struggle for independence has to intensify for a variety of reasons, extreme forces come to the surface and dominate the scene, making the problem far more difficult to solve. That is my assessment.

---

3. Statement to the Press

NEW YORK   JULY 16, 1966

THE SECRETARY-GENERAL believes that human life is sacred. Based on this belief, he views all forms of violence and all wars as evil. This conviction, among others, has prompted him to exert his utmost to contribute toward the cessation of all hostilities in Vietnam and a search for a just and peaceful solution of the Vietnamese conflict. When the news of the impending trial of American prisoners in North Vietnam was brought to his notice, he expressed his concern over the possible fate of those prisoners. In addition to humanitarian grounds, he feels that the possible trial of American prisoners is certain to generate still more intense escalation of the war. The Vietnam war already has potentialities of developing into the Third World War.

The Secretary-General has noted the statement of several United States senators, made yesterday, that the trial and execution of

SOURCE: *UN Monthly Chronicle,* vol. III, August-September 1966, pp. 32–33.

American prisoners would lead to "new levels of suffering and sorrow, and fixing more firmly still the seal of an implacable war."

The Secretary-General wishes, therefore, to appeal to the government of North Vietnam to exercise restraint in its treatment of American prisoners. He also appeals to all parties to comply with the provisions of the Geneva Convention of August 12, 1949, irrespective of various conflicting interpretations. In conclusion, the Secretary-General wishes to take this opportunity to reiterate the three points which he has repeatedly proposed regarding the Vietnam conflict, namely:

1. The cessation of the bombing of North Vietnam;
2. The scaling down of all military operations by all parties in South Vietnam;
3. The willingness of all parties to enter into discussion with those who are actually fighting.

The Secretary-General feels very strongly that these steps alone can create an atmosphere congenial for discussions and negotiations.

---

4. From Transcript of Remarks to the Press at Kennedy International Airport

NEW YORK   JULY 30, 1966

THE SECRETARY-GENERAL: As you know, I just came back from Moscow after a five-day visit there at the kind invitation of the Soviet government. I had very useful and frank and friendly exchanges of views with the Soviet leaders, including the General Secretary of the Central Committee, Mr. Brezhnev, Premier Kosygin, and the Acting Foreign Minister. Of course, there were no set items for discussions but we dealt with matters of common interest to the Soviet Union and the United Nations. Of course, developments affecting international peace and security were brought up.

SOURCE: UN Press Release SG/SM/543.

Inevitably, the Vietnam war dominated our talks. The talks were very useful and I will be glad to answer some questions, if you have any.

QUESTION: After your visit, Sir, do you now feel that the Soviet Union is going to . . . Do you expect the Soviet Union to make any voluntary contribution to the United Nations financial crisis?

THE SECRETARY-GENERAL: Well, in the course of our talks, this question was raised. I was given to understand that the Soviet government is studying the reports of the Committee of Fourteen which, as you know, has been dealing with the financial situation of the United Nations and, so far, they have not come to any decision regarding action based on the recommendations of the Committee of Fourteen.

QUESTION: Do you have any indication from the Soviet Union about peace talks over Vietnam?

THE SECRETARY-GENERAL: Well, I assessed their views and their attitudes toward the Vietnam war, and the views of the Soviet government are well known. I have nothing new to add to what you have known already. Of course, they told me they are prepared to render all possible assistance to the government of North Vietnam.

QUESTION: Did your trip help you to make up your mind, Sir, whether or not to be available for another term as Secretary-General?

THE SECRETARY-GENERAL: Well, my trip was not related to my prospective decision regarding my availability for a second term, and it was not my purpose in making the trip to Moscow or, for that matter, to any other capital of Member states.

QUESTION: Did the Soviet leaders give you any indication that they might intercede with Hanoi on behalf of the captured American pilots?

THE SECRETARY-GENERAL: I don't think the Soviet government would intercede in this question. As you well know from the reply of President Ho Chi Minh to some of the leaders—replies which have been made public—I don't think the captured American pilots will get the extreme penalty, and I believe that they will receive a very lenient treatment, from the public statements of the authorities in Hanoi.

QUESTION: Do you think a trip to Hanoi at this point by yourself would be useful?

THE SECRETARY-GENERAL: I don't think so.

QUESTION: Why?

THE SECRETARY-GENERAL: Because, as you know, North Vietnam is not a Member of the United Nations. As Secretary-General of the United Nations, the attitude of Hanoi has been made very clear. Hanoi has nothing to do with the United Nations as far as the question of the Vietnam war is concerned. I have been exerting efforts to contribute toward a solution of the Vietnam war as an individual—as U Thant—not as the Secretary-General of the United Nations.

QUESTION: You have been quoted from Paris as saying that you fear that the Vietnam war may spill over the frontiers. What did you mean by that?

THE SECRETARY-GENERAL: I have all along felt that if the Vietnam war develops in the way it has been developing, it is likely to develop into a major war, and my fears were confirmed after my talks with the Soviet leaders. If the present trend continues, I feel that the Vietnam war is likely to develop into a major war.

QUESTION: You mean with Russia and China perhaps involved?

THE SECRETARY-GENERAL: No, I don't want to go into specifics. My feeling is that the fighting might spill over the frontiers.

QUESTION: Sir, did you find agreement by the Soviet leaders with your three-point program on lessening and finally ending the Vietnam war?

THE SECRETARY-GENERAL: I did not bring up the question of my three-point proposal with the Soviet leaders, as I do not believe that they have any relevancy to the government of the Soviet Union.

QUESTION: Was there any discussion with the Soviet Union concerning disarmament?

THE SECRETARY-GENERAL: Yes.

QUESTION: Can you tell us anything about that?

THE SECRETARY-GENERAL: Well, you know the Vietnam war has repercussions in all fields of discussion, including disarmament. I think, in the disarmament talks which are going on in Geneva, the atmosphere is not very propitious, but I very much hope—and I have expressed this hope in all the capitals I have visited—that some perceptible advance would be made on both items: nonproliferation of nuclear weapons; and the banning of all tests before the twenty-first session of the General Assembly.

QUESTION: Sir, what was it about your discussions with the Soviet leaders that made you come back with the same pessimism about this expansion, this possible expansion of the Vietnam war? Was it anything specifically that they said, or was it something that they didn't say?

THE SECRETARY-GENERAL: Yes, they told me, as I said a moment ago, that they are prepared to render all possible assistance to North Vietnam. Of course, as you know, the conceptions are different and the attitudes are different. For instance, to put it in plain terms, the United States views North Vietnam as aggressors. The Soviet Union views the United States as aggressors. With these very differing viewpoints, it is very difficult to reconcile the attitudes.

. . .

THE QUESTION OF A SECOND TERM

THROUGHOUT THE YEAR 1966, U Thant was under pressure both from Member states and from the press to make known his intentions regarding a second term as Secretary-General. It will be recalled that he originally had been appointed Acting Secretary-General on November 3, 1961, and that a year later, on November 30, 1962, he had taken the oath of office as Secretary-General with the understanding, at his own request, that his five-year term should date from the time he became Acting Secretary-General. The expiration of his term was thus due on November 3, 1966. As the date approached it was clear that he could have a second term if he wanted one. Despite the fact that he had stepped on the toes of some Member states, including the United States and the Soviet Union, he was being urged by almost everyone to stay on. The question came up at his first press conference of the year on January 20: Had he reached a decision? He replied that he had not yet made up his mind, but that he probably would let the Security Council know one way or the other by June. In June he said he still was not ready. On July 6, he told a press conference in Geneva that he had been advised by many friends not to make any announcement until about two months before the expiration of his term. Anyway, he said, he still had not made up his mind definitely, although he had told Security Council members he would like to be relieved of his duties if a successor could be found. He added that he was thinking of making a public announcement about the end of August. He declined to go into the reasons which were causing his hesitation beyond saying they were both personal and political. "I do not want to give the impression," he said, "that if certain conditions are not met I will leave."

In a public statement, circulated to all permanent representatives on September 1, he made known his decision. "I have decided not to offer myself for a second term," he said. He gave no explanation for his decision, although he did mention his disappointment in the failure of the Member states to solve the financial problems of the Organization, their lack of progress in devising peace-keeping machinery, and his deep concern over the continued escalation of the Vietnam war. He insisted, however, that he had an unshakable faith in the United Nations and in its ultimate success. On September 15, he told a luncheon of the United Nations Correspondents Association that "the decision involved questions of principle, questions of conscience and, of course, personal, official, and political considerations." He elaborated further at a press conference on September 19. He said there were personal reasons, which he did not want to reveal, family considerations, and the urge to return to his own country of Burma after an absence of some nine years. Then he gave what almost everybody knew to be the real reason: the effort on the part of some governments to limit the functions of the Secretary-General to administrative matters or, as he put it, to make him "a glorified clerk." "I do not accept this concept of the Secretary-General," he said. He did not identify these countries, but the attitude of the USSR toward the Office of Secretary-General was well known. At the moment Thant's principal concern was with United States objections to his intervention in the Vietnam war. "To be candid," he declared, "I feel that I have found it increasingly difficult to function as Secretary-General in the manner in which I wish to function." What he wanted particularly was a clear understanding that political and diplomatic initiatives are "an essential part of the functions of the Secretary-General."

It was at this press conference that Thant disclosed his willingness to extend his term at least temporarily. He said he might consider serving an additional two months, until the end of the General Assembly session, if the Security Council was unable to agree on a successor. The Council quickly took him up on the offer. After a private meeting on September 29, it was announced that Council members welcomed Thant's press conference statement and further considered that, if he should agree to serve another term, this would fully meet the desires of the Council. On October 28, the Council adopted a resolution at a private meeting recommending to the General Assembly that it extend Thant's appointment until the end of the Assembly's twenty-first session. The Assembly approved the extension unanimously on November 1. In expressing his personal satisfaction for the extension, Thant indicated that the door had not been closed irrevocably on a second term. Permanent representatives noted the following: " . . . my *final decision* will have to take into account a variety of considerations, to which I have referred previously, including, of course, the long-term interests of the Organization and the outlook for peace in Asia and elsewhere in the world."

The issue was resolved in the end when members of the Security Council publicly accepted Thant's position that the Secretary-General had the right to bring to their attention basic issues confronting the Organization as well as disturbing developments anywhere in the world. In a statement read by the President of the Council, Ambassador Pedro P. Berro of Uruguay, on December 2, the members also appealed to Thant to serve for another full term in the higher interests of the Organization. In a separate statement, also read by Berro, Thant took note of the Council's agreement to respect his position and declared that, in view of this, he would accede to the appeal addressed to him by the Council. The Council then proceeded to adopt a resolution recommending that the Assembly appoint Thant for a new term ending December 31, 1971. Later in the day the Assembly unanimously approved the appointment.

The matter was concluded when Thant, in his acceptance speech, declared that his decision to stay on stemmed from a deep conviction that the United Nations remained the best instrument by which nations might cooperate for the peace and development of their people.

1. From Transcript of Press Conference

MEXICO CITY　　　AUGUST 26, 1966

. . .

QUESTION: Do you have any objections to announcing your decision as to continuation of your duties as Secretary-General of the United Nations?

THE SECRETARY-GENERAL: My first obligation regarding the announcement of my availability, or not, for the second term is to the entire membership of the United Nations, particularly to the Security Council. I am obligated to inform the Security Council and, for that matter, other Members of the United Nations first, before I make an announcement elsewhere. As I have indicated earlier in New York, I propose to inform the members of the Security Council, as well as the entire membership of the United Nations, on September 1, on my return to New York. So, before that date, I don't think it will be very proper for me to reveal my decision.

QUESTION: What action is the United Nations planning to adopt in order to avoid the expansion of the Vietnam war and its development into a wider conflict:

THE SECRETARY-GENERAL: Regarding the conflict in Vietnam, I have stated my position on several occasions in the past and I have stated the reasons also why the United Nations cannot and should not be involved in this conflict, at least for the present. My feeling is that the vast majority of the Members of the United Nations agree with me that the United Nations, as it is at present constituted, is not in a position to contribute materially toward the solution of the Vietnam problem, since there is already an international machinery, constituted twelve years ago in Geneva. This view has been shared by the vast majority of the Member states. But, although the United Nations has not been involved in seeking a solution to the conflict in Vietnam, I have been trying in my private capacity to bring about a peaceful settlement of the problem in the last three years. I think it is common

SOURCE: UN Press Release SG/SM/556, August 30, 1966.

knowledge that the various steps I have taken in the last three years have not been conclusive so far, but I can assure you, as I have assured the leaders of the government of Mexico, that I will continue with my endeavors to contribute toward a peaceful solution of the problem in my private capacity.

. . .

QUESTION: Is there any project that may render the United Nations operative and effective in the solution of conflicts like this one of Vietnam?

THE SECRETARY-GENERAL: According to the Charter, the United Nations has the primary responsibility to maintain peace in any part of the world. Of course, one of the primary purposes of the United Nations when it was constituted was, according to the language of the Charter, "to save succeeding generations from the scourge of war, which twice in our lifetime has brought untold sorrow to mankind." So I think it is very legitimate for anybody to ask this question: Why is the United Nations impotent to deal effectively with the very serious crisis in Vietnam? I have, on many previous occasions, explained why the United Nations has not been able to contribute significantly toward a solution of this problem. As I indicated a moment ago, of all the participants in the conflict, only one, the United States of America, is a Member of the United Nations; others are not Members of the United Nations. Second, for the solution of the Vietnam problem there is already machinery set up by the Geneva Agreement of 1954. This machinery is outside the scope of the United Nations. And third, many important members of the Security Council today would not view with favor any attempt by any Member state to bring the matter to the Security Council. They are opposed to the Security Council being involved in the discussions of this question for reasons, some of which I have stated earlier. So the question is not concerned with the modification of the Charter of the United Nations or amending the Charter of the United Nations. It is concerned with the realities of the situation today. These are among the reasons why the United Nations cannot and should not be involved in finding a solution to the Vietnamese conflict.

QUESTION: We all wish you to be re-elected, Sir, but should you not decide in this direction, would you favor having a Latin American or, particularly, a Mexican, appointed?

THE SECRETARY-GENERAL: Well, this is a matter first of all for the

Security Council to take the initiative. I must make it very clear that I have not informed the Security Council so far of my decision. As I indicated a moment ago, I will inform the members of the Security Council and simultaneously all the Members of the United Nations on September 1. In case I decide not to offer myself for the second term, the procedure is for the Security Council to meet and discuss and deliberate on a suitable successor. I have no means of knowing, in such an eventuality, whom the Security Council will recommend to the General Assembly for acceptance. It is not for the Secretary-General to indicate his desire or his thinking on who the next Secretary-General should be. It would be very improper on my part to venture an opinion on this question.

. . .

QUESTION: Has Indonesia taken any concrete steps toward returning to the United Nations?

THE SECRETARY-GENERAL: So far, there has been no official communication from the government of Indonesia to the United Nations regarding the possibility of resumption of all activities in the United Nations by Indonesia, but there are indications that some leaders of Indonesia are desirous of coming back to the family of nations. If the government of Indonesia decides to come back to the United Nations, I am sure that the entire membership will be delighted to welcome her back to the family of nations. Of course, Indonesia has come back, as you all know, to UNESCO [United Nations Educational, Scientific and Cultural Organization], and to some of the other specialized agencies of the United Nations.

QUESTION: You have stated, Sir, that the Security Council considers that the United Nations should not enter the Vietnam conflict and that you, in your personal capacity, have tried to bring about some solution. How can this be accepted, when the functions of the United Nations should be to avoid conflicts and suffering for the people?

THE SECRETARY-GENERAL: I think I made it clear earlier that many members of the Security Council feel that the United Nations, as it is at present constituted, cannot be involved in a solution of the Vietnam conflict. I also said that in my private capacity I have been trying my best to bring about a peaceful solution. I think the two statements do not conflict. To give you some background, I must say that I belong to that part of the world—as you all know, I come from Burma, very close to the scene of the conflict. Apart from that, I

know personally some of the leaders involved in the conflict. I have
studied the situation in Vietnam very closely for a number of years,
even long before I came to New York as Ambassador from my
country. Most people in Burma with experience of war and struggle
for independence, as you have experienced the struggle for independence many years ago, know what it means to fight for independence.
So my assessment of the situation and my understanding of the
background of the Vietnamese conflict are different from the assessment and understanding of many people. As I see the situation, the
Vietnam conflict primarily should be related to the longings of the
long-suffering people of Vietnam for independence and their desire to
fashion their own future by their own means, without interference
from outside. When the people have to struggle for independence so
long and so violently, it is inevitable that extreme forces come to the
surface and dominate the scene. That is one of the great lessons of
history, as far as I am concerned. If the people have to struggle for
independence too long, causing tremendous sacrifices, then it is
inevitable that very extreme forces come to the surface and dominate
the scene. Such a situation does not contribute toward the cause of
peace or the cause of democracy. That is why in my private capacity,
as a man coming from that part of the world, as one who has been
obsessed with peace throughout his life, I have been trying my utmost
to contribute toward a peaceful solution of the problem.

QUESTION: Since, as you have said, the Vietnam dispute is outside
the competence of the United Nations, is it one of your missions, one
of your purposes as a man of peace and as a democrat, to seek the
good offices of Mexico and other Latin American countries to
mediate this dispute outside the United Nations?

THE SECRETARY-GENERAL: In my travels to the various capitals of
Member states in the last few months and, for that matter, in the last
few years, inevitably the question of Vietnam came up for discussion.
It was not my intention to try to influence Member states to mediate
in the Vietnam conflict; it is for the Member states themselves to take
the initiative. As regards my present trip to Mexico also, I have had
very useful exchanges of views on the Vietnam situation, with both
the Foreign Minister and His Excellency the President. These discussions were very useful, but it was not my intention to try to influence
the Member states to use their good offices or to offer to act as

mediators in this dispute because I know that any mediation effort at this stage—let me stress, at this stage—would not be realistic.

QUESTION: What is your opinion on the contemplated denuclearization treaty for Latin America, and is it your feeling that the nuclear powers will support such a treaty?

THE SECRETARY-GENERAL: As you all know, many Latin American countries, particularly your country, Mexico, have been exerting efforts in the last few years toward the denuclearization of Latin America. Of course, Mexico, in particular, has initiated some studies on the subject and I have been most gratified to be able to contribute to these studies by the provision of some technical experts to cooperate with the government of Mexico and to assist the government in these studies. They are in a very preliminary stage now, as you all know. It is too early now to assess whether there are immediate prospects of the denuclearization of Latin America. Regarding the attitude of the big powers on this problem, their attitude has been made known, particularly in the General Assembly debates. So I do not want to summarize, or give the substance of their view—they are well known.

. . .

QUESTION: What are the prospects for the admission of Communist China to the United Nations, and if so, what should be the contribution of that country toward the settlement of the question of Vietnam and its contribution to world peace?

THE SECRETARY-GENERAL: I have stated my position on previous occasions regarding my concept of the United Nations. I believe in the principle of universality of membership of the United Nations which is, of course, implied in the Charter. Regarding the question of the representation of China in the United Nations, I think it is very necessary for you to know that there are two U Thants. One U Thant, as representative of Burma, has certain definite views on this subject, as I have made known on previous occasions. Another U Thant, as Secretary-General of the United Nations, has to be guided in such matters by the decisions of the principal organs of the United Nations, such as the General Assembly and the Security Council. So, in my capacity as the Secretary-General of the United Nations, I do not wish to make any statement on this question. But I believe personally that if the concept of universality of membership is fulfilled, the United Nations will be in a much stronger position to settle many problems which it cannot settle now, particularly the problem of Vietnam.

---

2. *Letter to All Permanent Representatives*

NEW YORK   SEPTEMBER 1, 1966

IN PURSUANCE OF the undertaking I have given in public to inform the members of the Security Council by the end of August 1966 of my decision in regard to my willingness to serve for a further term as Secretary-General of the United Nations, I transmit herewith, at the same time as I am sending it to the members of the Security Council, a copy of my statement.

(Signed) U THANT
Secretary-General of
the United Nations

Statement by the Secretary-General

Members of the Organization are aware that my term as Secretary-General of the United Nations expires on November 3, 1966. During recent months I have had exchanges of view with many of them, including, in some instances, heads of state and government. I believe that it would be proper for me and helpful to the governments of Member states to make my own decision known at the present time.

In this connection it may be pertinent to recall that, in the first instance, I was appointed Acting Secretary-General of the United Nations for the unfinished term of Dag Hammarskjöld from November 3, 1961, to April 10, 1963. In November 1962, when the question of the extension of my term was under consideration, many members

SOURCE: General Assembly Official Records, Twenty-first Session, Annexes, agenda item 18, document A/6400.

of the Security Council as it was then constituted asked me to accept a further term of five years from the date of expiry of that mandate, until April 10, 1968. I expressed my preference to serve a term of five years from November 3, 1961, the date of my appointment as Acting Secretary-General, to November 3, 1966. In taking this attitude I had two considerations in mind. One was to reinforce the practice already established that the normal term of the Secretary-General should be five years. The other was my reluctance to accept a commitment to serve as Secretary-General for a longer period than five years.

I should also like to avail myself of this occasion to refer briefly to some of the problems which the Organization has had to face since I was first appointed to this office. Though I am making these observations at this time, I do not wish to relate them to the variety of considerations—personal, official, and political—which, as I have explained more than once, have influenced my own decision.

Members of the Organization may remember that, on November 30, 1962, when I accepted the extension of my term to November 3, 1966, I referred to a statement I had made earlier that my decision to accept the position of Secretary-General for a longer term would "be governed primarily by a few considerations, including the prospects of an early settlement of the Congo problem, the prospects of the stability of this world Organization as a potent force for peace, and the prospects of my playing a humble part in bringing about a more favorable atmosphere for the easing of tension . . ." (1182nd plenary meeting, para. 19).

Looking back over the work of the United Nations during the last fifty-eight months I feel justified in saying that a measure of progress has been made in some of these respects.

In particular, while the financial solvency of the Organization has not yet been assured, there is no longer the same sense of crisis and anxiety about it. I am still hopeful that, in line with the decisions taken earlier by the Special Committee on Peace-keeping Operations and the General Assembly, and in the light of the recent report of the *Ad Hoc* Committee of Experts to Examine the Finances of the United Nations and the Specialized Agencies, substantial voluntary contributions will be forthcoming which will place the Organization on a basis of complete solvency, so that it can face the great tasks ahead with confidence.

The need of the United Nations for solvency does not, however, apply to the question of finances alone. A lack of new ideas and fresh initiatives and a weakening of the will to find means of strengthening and expanding genuine international cooperation would have even more serious consequences. In respect of one of its most important activities, that of peace-keeping, the promise held out by the demonstrated usefulness and success of our extensive operations in recent years has remained unfulfilled because of the continuing failure to agree on basic principles. In my judgment it is important that, in conformity with the Charter, the United Nations should be enabled to function effectively in this field.

The task of peace-building is no less important. In this regard it may be claimed that, while the United Nations Development Decade, which was launched with high hopes, has fallen short of its modest objectives, on the positive side it has stimulated the efforts of the United Nations to equip itself with more effective means—the consolidated United Nations Development Programme, the United Nations Conference on Trade and Development, and the United Nations Industrial Development Organization—of tackling some of the basic problems of development.

Speaking still of the situation within this Organization, I may say that, during all these months, I have striven to make the Secretariat more truly international in outlook and approach and a more energetic and efficient servant of the governments of Member states. I believe that, within its limitations, the Secretariat has performed well and that, with further organizational improvements, it is capable of doing even better. I take this opportunity to place on record my deep appreciation of the cooperation I have received from my colleagues in the Secretariat.

I owe a great debt of gratitude to my friends and colleagues in the delegations for their unfailing cooperation and courtesy. The progress made during these fifty-eight months is due in large measure to their friendly counsel and assistance.

Members of the Organization are surely aware of my abiding concern for peace. During the fifty-eight months that I have been in office, hopes and prospects have risen and fallen many times. The world situation appears to me to be extremely serious. The state of affairs in Southeast Asia is already a source of grave concern and is bound to be a source of even greater anxiety, not only to the parties directly involved and to the major powers but also to other Members of the Organization. It is of the deepest concern to me personally. The cruelty of this war, and the suffering it has caused the people of Vietnam are a constant reproach to the conscience of humanity. Today it seems to me, as it has seemed for many months, that the pressure of events is remorselessly leading toward a major war, while efforts to reverse that trend are lagging disastrously behind. In my view the tragic error is being repeated of relying on force and military means in a deceptive pursuit of peace. I am convinced that peace in Southeast Asia can be obtained only through respect for the principles agreed upon at Geneva in 1954, and indeed for those contained in the Charter of the United Nations.

Elsewhere in the world, too, there are signs of growing tension. While the situation in Europe has shown signs of improvement, the state of affairs in many other parts of the world has undergone some deterioration. The increasing imbalance in the world economic situation, to which I have constantly drawn attention, most recently in my statement to the Economic and Social Council (1421st meeting), can only add to the clear and present dangers.

I must also confess to a sense of dissatisfaction with the fact that the Organization has not yet achieved universality of membership. I believe I am not alone in this feeling. Many of the problems facing the world today, be they regional or global, become more intractable because of this circumstance. This is true, for example, of the lack of progress in such vital fields as disarmament.

It thus happens that, owing mainly to the international situation and to circumstances beyond the control of the Organization, no decisive progress has been made by the governments of Member states in the cooperative efforts which are essential if the Organization is to serve effectively the cause of peace and to contribute significantly to the economic development of the poorer regions of the world.

I now come to the question of my own plans for the future. I have been greatly touched, indeed overwhelmed, by the many kind references to my work which have been made at the level of heads of state and government, as well as on an informal and personal basis by my friends and colleagues. If I have not found it possible to accept their urging to be available for a further term of office, it is not for lack of appreciation and gratitude for their sentiments. It is my belief, as I have said more than once in the past, that a Secretary-General of the

United Nations should not normally serve for more than one term. I have similarly made it known that I do not believe in the concept of indispensability of any particular person for any particular job. In the circumstances the conclusion I have reached will, I hope, be understood by all my friends and colleagues: I have decided not to offer myself for a second term as Secretary-General, and to leave the Security Council unfettered in its recommendation to the General Assembly with regard to the next Secretary-General.

I am sure that my own unwillingness to be available for a second term as Secretary-General will not be misconstrued by those who know me. I have an abiding and unshakable faith in the United Nations and in its ultimate success. Despite the difficulties facing the Organization, I believe and hope that the world will continue its efforts to develop the United Nations as an indispensable instrument for the attainment of a peaceful and just world order. In this task, I pledge my personal support and wholehearted devotion.

---

3. From Remarks at Luncheon of United Nations Correspondents Association

NEW YORK   SEPTEMBER 15, 1966

. . . I AM OVERWHELMED by the very gracious words just expressed by my friend and dear colleague Dr. Leichter[1] about me, and I understand that on this occasion Dr. Leichter and his colleagues want me to say something which is likely to be of interest not only to those who are present at the lunch today, but also to those who could not be present here.

One topic which is currently occupying your attention, I believe, is my statement of September 1 which I submitted to the Members of the United Nations. Many friends and well-wishers have asked me if I had anything to add to that statement. As most of you are no doubt

SOURCE: UN Press Release SG/SM/564.
[1] Otto Leichter, Chairman of the Dag Hammarskjöld Scholarship Fund.

aware, I gave a good deal of thought before I came to that decision. As a matter of fact, it took me several months to weigh the pros and cons, and after a prolonged inner struggle I decided not to offer myself for a further term.

The decision involved questions of principle, questions of conscience and, of course, personal, official, and political considerations. I believe that my statement of September 1 is self-explanatory.

Many friends and well-wishers asked me why I had made such a decision in the face of a massive volume of very gracious expressions of trust in me, not only from governments of Member states but also from legislators, leaders in various fields of activities, and private individuals from all over the world. I want to express my very sincere thanks and heartfelt gratitude to all those friends and well-wishers who have very kindly expressed their trust in me and their belief in the need for my continued association with the United Nations. Let me assure you that I would be the last person to show any ingratitude or lack of response to such gracious expressions of trust and confidence in me.

Day after day I have been stricken with a kind of guilt for having to show some insensitivity to all such kindnesses. I have been told by many representatives of governments that they do not wish to give any thought to the question of a suitable successor. I have been told that my departure at this time will create a major crisis in the United Nations. Let me say, with all humility, that I do not agree with such assumptions. As the saying goes, if there is a will there is a way. If the Members have the will to see the United Nations develop into a really effective force for peace and progress, to bring it back to solvency, to see that this Organization is so constituted as to contribute significantly toward the easing of tensions and conflicts and toward enabling the United Nations to perform its harmonizing function, as envisaged in the Charter, then there will be a way to achieve these objectives—with a new man at the helm.

There is a law of diminishing returns, and, as I have said before, nobody should aspire to serve as Secretary-General of the United Nations for more than a term of five years. I have taken this opportunity to restate my convictions on this subject. I continue to believe that the best interests of the Organization would be served if the Member governments would direct their efforts to the finding of a suitable and acceptable successor.

I would also very humbly appeal to all those concerned to avoid any kind of fanfare, either in the search for a successor or in public expressions of their continued trust and confidence in me. I am most grateful to them for their sincere goodwill, but I believe that very discreet and quiet diplomacy alone, in the present circumstances, will serve the common purpose which all of us seek.

---

4. Transcript of Press Conference

NEW YORK   SEPTEMBER 19, 1966

MR. MILT FREUDENHEIM (President, United Nations Correspondents Association): Mr. Secretary-General, before asking a question, it is my duty to inform you of the overwhelming feeling among members of the United Nations Correspondents Association and among the Press generally, as expressed to me, since your announcement that you will not offer yourself for a second term.

Our sentiments are of an impending great loss, both personally and professionally. In our work as reporters and critics, explaining and interpreting the United Nations, we have benefited from your deep understanding of the need of world opinion to be informed. Among your many successes in your high office, this one is appreciated by us acutely, because it is of such immediate professional concern.

On the personal level, I know that I express the feelings of all your many friends in the news media when I repeat what has been said all over the world by the great and by the humble. We have been honored by your friendship. We shall be honored by it always. We hope that your future will be bright in every way. Sharing as we do your own ideals, we hope for your success.

I should now like to ask a question on behalf of the *Chicago Daily News*. Can you tell us whether anything is happening or specifically could happen that would result in your making yourself available to continue as Secretary-General after November 3?

SOURCE: UN Press Release SG/SM/567.

THE SECRETARY-GENERAL: Mr. Freudenheim and friends: I am particularly grateful for the very gracious words just spoken by Mr. Freudenheim on behalf not only of himself but also of his colleagues. I am deeply touched by those very kind words. Of course, I know your feelings for me, and I also know that they are shared by all of your colleagues in the Press corps here. I can assure you that these feelings are mutual. As you all know, my contacts with you in the past few years have been very warm, very friendly and, if I may say so, even affectionate.

As I said on September 15 at your luncheon, I have been overwhelmed by the massive volume of very generous and gracious expressions of trust and faith in me by many people all over the world.

My decision in the face of these overwhelming gestures of appreciation and trust is not due to the fact that I am insensitive to these feelings and sentiments, but to other reasons, as I have explained on previous occasions.

Before I answer your question specifically, I should like to make a few preliminary remarks.

I am happy to have this opportunity to meet with the Press on the eve of the twenty-first session of the General Assembly. The Assembly will have an important agenda to discuss, and I am sure that your coverage of the different points of that agenda will add greatly to public understanding of their significance.

You will recall that in my statement of September 1, as well as in my Introduction to the Annual Report, I have also drawn attention to certain issues, some of which are of primary importance to the continued effectiveness of the Organization in various fields, and some of which are of global significance in relation to world peace. In regard to those issues, although I quite realize that overnight solutions are not feasible, it is my sincere hope that the public debate and the many consultations which take place during the General Assembly will bring a new awareness of the gravity of the problems involved and generate renewed efforts at trying to solve them.

I wish again to express my strong feeling that what is important at the present stage is that attention be directed to these issues.

Coming back to the specific question regarding the circumstances which have led to my decision on whether those circumstances changed since my statement of September 1, I would say this: I believe that I made it very clear in my statement of September 1 that I did not wish to relate my decision to my observations on the situations prevailing in the United Nations or elsewhere. It was far from my intention to connect my decision with those considerations. It was far from my intention to pose those issues as conditions; in other words, it was far from my intention to state that if those conditions, or at least some of them, were met I would be in a position to change my decision. As I have said on previous occasions, my decision was based on personal, official, and political reasons. It took me many weeks, even months, to weigh the pros and cons in coming to that decision.

I realize, of course, that the situation in the United Nations or outside the United Nations will not change in the next few months. That is just plain common sense.

But, I must say that, for the moment, in my view, the attention of the Members of the United Nations, particularly the members of the Security Council, should be directed primarily toward the finding of a suitable and acceptable successor. Of course, if it proves impossible to find an agreed man, somebody acceptable to all, in the course of the next few weeks, I may perhaps consider serving until the end of the present session. In my view, two additional months will be quite ample for the Members, particularly the members of the Security Council, to look for a suitable man. I also feel inclined to the view that it would be undesirable to change secretaries-general in the middle of the General Assembly session.

QUESTION: Mr. Secretary-General, there is a report out of Hanoi that the North Vietnamese government might react positively to your three-point peace plan for Vietnam if the United States accepts that plan. Have you any word on that or any reaction to this report?

THE SECRETARY-GENERAL: I have not received any official reaction from Hanoi to my three-point proposal, either positively or negatively. So from this I have come to the conclusion that my three-point proposal has not been rejected by Hanoi.

QUESTION: Mr. Secretary-General, many of your friends and observers feel that the basic reasons you have given for leaving the post, the three points, are the very reasons, under the present critical circumstances of the world, why you should remain and not leave. Would you care to comment on that?

THE SECRETARY-GENERAL: Yes, I am fully aware of these sentiments expressed in many quarters of the world. It is difficult for me to enumerate the reasons which prompted me to make the decision which I did. You will recall that as early as November 1962, when the members of the Security Council very kindly offered me a further term of five years beyond April 1963, I requested them to make my term five years, inclusive of the previous year which I had served. Therefore, in a way it is obvious that I was inclined even four years ago to leave at the end of the present term. As I have stated, there are personal reasons too and I do not think it would be proper for me to reveal publicly all the personal reasons involved. Of course, there are family considerations and the urge to return to one's own native land after an absence of so many years, and of course, as I have said, there are official and political reasons too.

To be candid, I feel that I have found it increasingly difficult to function as Secretary-General in the manner in which I wish to function, and second, I do not subscribe to the view that the Secretary-General should be just a chief administrative officer, or, in other words, that the Secretary-General should be a glorified clerk. I do not accept this concept of the Secretary-General. As I have said repeatedly on previous occasions, besides the functions of administration, the Secretary-General must take the necessary initiatives in the political and diplomatic fields. These political and diplomatic initiatives, in my view, are an essential part of the functions of the Secretary-General.

Then, coming back to the political considerations, I think I have made myself very clear, both in my statement on September 1 and in my Introduction to the Annual Report. The East-West détente which was developing very well until 1963, received a setback for various reasons; among them, of course, the most important reason was the Vietnam war. The Vietnam war has caused a steady deterioration in East-West relations and caused the stiffening of attitudes by all sides, and, as I have said, the relationship between the big powers has dropped to a new low. To my knowledge, there has not been any meaningful dialogue between Washington and Moscow for a long time. I think it is a very regrettable situation. And, of course, as far as the United Nations functions are concerned, I believe I have made my assessment very clear, particularly in my Introduction to the Annual Report.

QUESTION: Mr. Secretary-General, in your Introduction to the Annual Report you mentioned that you have been increasingly distressed to observe that discussions on Vietnam had by and large been dominated by consideration and analysis of the power politic involved, and that there had been much less concern for the tremendous suffering occurring there. Has there been, from your vantage point, an increase of groups, highly placed and significant to the war, who do not care about the suffering of the Vietnamese people? And if there has been, on what basis do we dare hope for peace?

THE SECRETARY-GENERAL: I do not think any clarification is necessary on my statement on this point. I have made myself abundantly clear. And apart from political and military considerations, I think that what is most significant, what is most important, is the human factor. I have been obsessed with this humanitarian point of view for a long time, as you all know, and apart from the military and strategic and political considerations, these considerations of the human factor, the human element, also should play a very prominent part.

QUESTION: Under what conditions, possibly in the future, do you see any role for the United Nations in taking part in a settlement or in negotiations on Vietnam?

THE SECRETARY-GENERAL: Well, at least for the moment the United Nations as such cannot be involved and should not be involved in the Vietnam conflict or in the search for a peaceful solution. But I still feel that at some stage United Nations involvement cannot be ruled out. I am very hopeful of it.

QUESTION: Mr. Secretary-General, if, unhappily for us all, you do leave the post, can we expect that you will give your leadership on these very issues to the world after you have left the post?

THE SECRETARY-GENERAL: It is very kind of you to pose this question. I have thought of it also very comprehensively, and I am convinced that somebody else can give the same leadership.

QUESTION: Mr. Secretary-General, you said something earlier about there having been no meaningful dialogue between Moscow and Washington for some time. Would you care to comment on the total absence of dialogue between Washington and Peking, and also on the new "low" in dialogue between Peking and Moscow?

THE SECRETARY-GENERAL: I think it is common knowledge that there has been no meaningful dialogue between Washington and

Peking and between Washington and Moscow. In my view, there should be more contacts. My approach to all such problems is, of course, well known to you. In my view, there should be increased contacts between Washington and Moscow, Moscow and Peking, Peking and New Delhi, New Delhi and Rawalpindi, and so forth. This is what the United Nations is here for, and I suppose it is what I am here for.

I think my approach to these problems is based on this considera- tion of increased contact, increased exposure and increased commu- nication; but the developments in many parts of the world have retarded this process. Of course, I am not putting the blame on any country or any government. There are many factors involved; many unpredictable situations and moods are involved. If I may say so, Peking's attitude is also a very great enigma—it is a real Chinese puzzle—and I must say that Peking's statements from time to time indicate that Peking has ceased to distinguish between its friends and well-wishers and its foes. In the view of Peking, anybody who goes to Moscow has something up his sleeve to sell the United States peace plan on Vietnam, and so on. From the point of view of Peking, Moscow is the clandestine headquarters for something very sinister. It is difficult to rationalize its statements, but it is important to make a distinction between what Peking says and what Peking does. I am sure most of you will agree with me that what Peking has done is very different from the very bellicose and irrational statements uttered from time to time by some of its leaders.

QUESTION: I think it is rather welcome news, in this circle anyway, that you might stay on, Mr. Secretary-General, until the end of the Assembly session, particularly—and this is the point of my ques- tion—insofar as it gives you ample time to play, perhaps, an impor- tant role here in whatever "whispering" or "feeler" developments may come out in this Assembly. Could you tell us whether you are prepared to do this, and also, perhaps, what assistance or aid could be secured from the President of the Assembly, who always functions as a potential personality in such an affair?

THE SECRETARY-GENERAL: I do not think I should add to anything I have said before. As I have said—and let me repeat it—if the Mem- bers, particularly the members of the Security Council, cannot find a suitable and acceptable successor in the next few weeks, I would consider accepting a further term up till the end of the present session of the General Assembly—if the Members so desire. I do not think I have anything more to add to this.

QUESTION: If nobody has been found by the end of the year, Mr. Secretary-General, would you agree to stay for a few more months, or would you just walk out?

THE SECRETARY-GENERAL: Well, I do not agree with that assumption. Somebody will be found.

QUESTION: When you say "the present session of the General Assembly," do you mean the debate in the General Assembly, or do you mean the whole session?

THE SECRETARY-GENERAL: The present session of the General Assembly, which is likely to be terminated on December 20—so, roughly, toward the end of this year.

QUESTION: In your statement today, Mr. Secretary-General, you have divorced the reasons for your not seeking a second term from your analysis of the world situation. Public opinion throughout the world has connected the two of them. In these circumstances, even if the big powers are able to find a successor, do you think a successor will be able to function unless some progress is made prior to that on the issues you have raised?

THE SECRETARY-GENERAL: As to the linking of my decision with my assessment of the situation, I am sure I made it very clear in my statement of September 1. It was not my wish to relate my decision to the observations on the developments.

Regarding the second part of your question, I think it is a hypothetical one. A successor who is suitable and who is considered acceptable by all the Members, particularly the big powers, will, in my opinion, be in a position to perform his functions in the manner in which I have been performing them, whether there has been progress or lack of progress in the coming few weeks.

QUESTION: Mr. Secretary-General, a little while ago you referred to your function in the United Nations as that of a "glorified clerk," and you said that the Secretary-General must take the necessary diplomatic and political initiatives. Do you feel that the position of Secretary-General ought to be amended or extended? Were you dissatisfied with the power that you had?

THE SECRETARY-GENERAL: I am not saying that I am dissatisfied. I am saying that the functions of the Secretary-General, in my view, are different from the functions desired by a section of the membership. I have said that I have experienced increasing restrictions on the legitimate prerogatives of the Secretary-General.

QUESTION: Mr. Secretary-General, have you had a chance to read the Pope's encyclical, and if so, would you care to comment on it?

THE SECRETARY-GENERAL: I have not read the Pope's encyclical but have heard it on the radio. It is, I am sure, a historic message, As you know, I have the highest esteem for His Holiness. I consider him not only a great leader of a great religion, but also a great human being with an extraordinary awareness of the problems of war and peace and with a genuine dedication to the cause of peace and progress and human rights. So whatever he says must be studied very closely. His historic visit to the United Nations last year on October 4 was a very significant event in the history of the United Nations. I am glad too that His Holiness has designated the fourth of October—the first anniversary of his visit to the United Nations—as a day for universal prayer. To me, his decision to celebrate October 4 as a universal day of prayer is significant in more ways than one. It is the renewed dedication of the Holy Father to the work of the United Nations and it is his recognition of the importance of the United Nations in trying to perform the functions envisaged in the Charter; and of course it is the recognition by the Holy Father of the universal acceptance of his visit to the United Nations as a truly historic event.

QUESTION: Referring to your earlier remarks that the great powers do not use the United Nations to great advantage as a forum for dialogue, have you any suggestions for improving the machinery here so that they might actually make it function in this way?

THE SECRETARY-GENERAL: I think it is not a question of machinery. It is a question of atmosphere; in other words, it is a question of the political climate in the world, which is of course reflected in the United Nations. If the political climate or the psychological climate in the world is congenial for more contacts and more dialogue among the big powers, then there will be more contacts and more dialogue in the United Nations. I do not think it is primarily a question of machinery.

QUESTION: You spoke of the restrictions put on the office of the Secretary-General. In this respect I want to say that probably many of us have been wondering about the superhuman patience with which you tolerated this during the past few years; it was only in your statement of September 1, and particularly in the Introduction to your report to the General Assembly, that you pointed to these very delicate points. Looking back, do you not think it would have been better if you had warned the membership of the United Nations, and particularly the four big powers a little earlier of what they were doing during the past two or three years—all of them?

THE SECRETARY-GENERAL: On all available occasions whenever I had the opportunity to discuss with the permanent representatives of Member states, I attempted to draw their attention to my conception of the functions of the Secretary-General. The points you raised in your question were also dealt with from time to time—of course, in a very confidential manner.

QUESTION: Going back to this question of linkage, would you go so far as to say that if the world situation had been considerably different from what it is, and better, you still would have made the same decision?

THE SECRETARY-GENERAL: Such a situation might influence to some extent my decision, but not primarily or exclusively. As I have said, the considerations were personal, official, and political. Some improvement in the political field, for instance, might to some extent contribute toward the necessity of my reviewing my decision.

QUESTION: One of the primary subjects on the agenda for 1966 will be, of course, the admission of Red China to membership. The speculation is that there may not be enough votes for its membership this year. In your opinion, if Red China is not admitted what effect will that have on the United Nations as an instrument in obtaining world peace?

THE SECRETARY-GENERAL: On this question of the representation of China, I have on previous occasions made my position known. It is necessary to remember that on such questions there are two U Thants: one representing Burma, as a spokesman for Burma in the United Nations, and the other as the Secretary-General. In the latter capacity, he is not expected to—and he should not—express his views in one way or the other in anticipation of the decision of the principal organs of the United Nations. Of course, I made it very clear that I believe in the principle of universality of membership for this Organization. I know the difficulties are very great. I know that negotiations and discussions on basic issues like disarmament, non-proliferation of nuclear weapons, and the banning of all nuclear tests will be impeded by the absence in this Organization of such a great country as China. But I am just stating the facts. As the Secretary-General I do not wish to project my opinion one way or the other. But I believe very strongly that this Organization must be universal—the sooner the better.

QUESTION: You mentioned the fact that you do not think that the major problems can reach anything like an improvement over the next few weeks. You also said that you are considering staying on toward the end of this session. Do you have even the slightest hope that if you stay on some of these problems may improve immeasurably before the end of the year?

THE SECRETARY-GENERAL: At least I will have some indication of the mood of the General Assembly and the mood of the membership on the basic issues before the United Nations.

QUESTION: I meant it in connection with your decision to stay on.

THE SECRETARY-GENERAL: Yes, I have said that if no suitable successor is found in the next few weeks I may perhaps consider the possibility of extending my term till the end of the present year, if the Members so desire. It does not depend on the improvement or lack of improvement of the world situation.

QUESTION: Mr. Secretary-General, have you had any indications lately that any of the Member countries will come through soon with voluntary contributions or specific pledges to remove the deficit? How soon would you expect such contributions or pledges? Do you think that by the end of this session there will be enough to remove the estimated deficit? Can you tell us how many countries, and perhaps specify their identities?

THE SECRETARY-GENERAL: I have no indication from any quarter regarding the intention to contribute toward the meeting of the deficit. As you know, the two reports of the Special Committee of Fourteen are now before the General Assembly. I very much hope that the consideration of these reports will get priority in the Fifth (Administrative and Budgetary) Committee, first of all, and then the recommendations of the Fifth Committee will go to the plenary session. But I have the feeling that there will be some positive moves after the adoption of these reports by the General Assembly.

QUESTION: I should like to ask a couple of questions on the Vietnam war. One is on the Vietnam elections and the other on what is called an all-Asian peace conference on Vietnam. During the last three or four weeks, as you know, there were many talks about an all-Asian peace conference to try to end the war in Vietnam. The idea has been in the air for years, but some stories attribute it to the Foreign Minister of Thailand. It seems to me rather peculiar that the *New York Times* in a long article two weeks ago praised him as one of the most creative statesmen in Asia. It seems to me rather naïve because both the Philippines and Thailand, and especially Thailand which is a base for United States military attacks on North Vietnam, are among the worst places to talk about initiating an all-Asian conference. In a way the idea now has the strong blessing of the White House and the Republican leaders of Congress.

THE SECRETARY-GENERAL: Will you make this question as short as possible?

QUESTION: May I ask you what you think about that?

THE SECRETARY-GENERAL: Regarding your first question on elections in South Vietnam, I do not think it will be very helpful if I tried to give an opinion on those elections. I just want to say that in my own country, Burma, there were elections for the Constituent Assembly in 1947, a few months before independence, in a sort of a civil war situation. Of course, there were pressures on the voters from all sides, from all quarters. At that time the Burmese government did not bar those directly or indirectly connected with the communists or neutralists from running as candidates. The Burmese government did not bar them; everybody was free to run as candidates. At that time the situation was also very bad in my country. There was an insurrection going on after the war. But I must say that the situation in Burma at that time was not so messy as the situation now prevailing in South Vietnam. Another difference is that in Burma at that time there were no foreign elements.

However, as I have said, the elections did take place, after a great deal of pressure from all sides. I would not say that the elections in Burma for the Constituent Assembly in 1947, a few months before Burma's independence, were free and fair. I would not say that. Of course, I do not want to make any observation on the elections in South Vietnam.

In this connection, I would remind you that in many countries the governments or the parties in power used to announce after elections that 99.9 percent of the eligible voters had cast their votes and that 99.8 percent had voted for the party in power. Of course, different people assess such results in different ways.

With regard to your second question, on the projected Asian conference to try to contribute toward a peaceful solution of the Vietnam problem, I must say that the motivations of the countries that would like to take the initiative are very laudable. I think that it is desirable in a way that regional problems should be settled by regional machinery. In principle, that is desirable. But what is more important are the political factors. In a situation like that prevailing in Vietnam, many political factors are involved, as you all know. Even ideologies are involved. Some participants in the conflict are claiming that this is a holy war for the triumph of one particular ideology and the elimination of another particular ideology. While the issues are framed in that context, I do not think it is realistic for some of the Asian countries that have openly subscribed to a particular political ideology to come out with the proposal to mediate or conciliate. What is important is the question of trust by all sides. If the country or countries that offer to mediate or conciliate have the trust and confidence of all the parties involved in the conflict, I think that the chances for such a conference will be very good. Otherwise, if the parties to the conflict have no trust in these initiators, I do not think that there will be any headway.

Perhaps I may give one illustration. As you know, there is a conflict between the United States and Cuba. If some of the very well-meaning Latin American countries were to come out with a proposal that they should conciliate or mediate between the United States and Cuba, I think that the primary consideration in the minds of both the United States and Cuba would be whether the initiators of such proposals had the trust and confidence of one side or the other. I think that this political consideration is very important.

Of course, I want to take this opportunity of offering my very sincere thanks to those governments that want to contribute meaningfully toward the peaceful solution of the Vietnam problem. But, having in mind the political considerations, I do not think that such steps are realistic.

QUESTION: In a previous reply, . . . you stated that if the world situation had been different, had been better in relation to the human factor, you would have considered a review of your decision. Let us say that a miracle happens during the coming session of the General Assembly. Would that reply still hold good?

THE SECRETARY-GENERAL: I do not want to answer such "iffy" questions. Let me have another opportunity to discuss this with you.

---

5. *Statement in the General Assembly*

NEW YORK   NOVEMBER 1, 1966

MR. PRESIDENT, I am grateful to the Security Council for recommending to the General Assembly, pending further consideration of the question, the extension of my appointment as Secretary-General of the United Nations until the end of the twenty-first session of the General Assembly. I am equally grateful to the General Assembly for the unanimous and heart-warming manner in which it has agreed to the extension of my appointment as proposed by the Security Council. It gives me particular pleasure to accept this extension because, as I have already explained before, I do not believe that it is advisable, under normal circumstances, to change the Secretary-General while the General Assembly is in session. It is a matter of personal satisfaction to me in this case because it assures me of the possibility, pending further consideration of the question, to work closely with you, Mr. President, and indeed the entire membership during the course of the twenty-first session of the General Assembly in cooperative and constructive efforts designed to strengthen the Organization's effectiveness and capacity to serve the cause of world peace and human betterment.

I quite realize that many of my friends and colleagues would wish that this question should be settled finally well before the end of the twenty-first session of the General Assembly. This is a view which I share. At the same time, it will no doubt be appreciated that my final

SOURCE: General Assembly Official Records, Twenty-first Session, 1455th plenary meeting.

decision will have to take into account a variety of considerations, to which I have referred previously, including, of course, the long-term interests of the Organization and the outlook for peace in Asia and elsewhere in the world.

I take this opportunity to place on record once again my gratitude to all of you for your sustained cooperation and goodwill, and to my friends and colleagues in the Secretariat for their unfailing loyalty and support. I also take advantage of this occasion to reaffirm my oath of office, and I solemnly swear to exercise in all loyalty, discretion, and conscience the functions entrusted to me as Secretary-General of the United Nations, to discharge these functions and regulate my conduct with the interests of the United Nations only in view, and not to seek or accept instructions in regard to the performance of my duties from any government or any other authority external to the Organization.

---

6. *Statements by Ambassador Pedro P. Berro of Uruguay, President of the Security Council, and by the Secretary-General*

NEW YORK   DECEMBER 2, 1966

THE PRESIDENT: The Security Council, recalling its consensus of September 29, 1966,[1] concerning the great positive role played by the Secretary-General, U Thant, in the activities of the United Nations, has further examined the question of the appointment of the Secretary-General and, in particular, the situation created by the impending expiration of the present term of Secretary-General U Thant at the end of the twenty-first regular session of the General Assembly.

After taking all considerations into account, the members of the

SOURCE: Security Council Official Records, Twenty-first Year, 1329th meeting.

[1] Security Council Official Records, Twenty-first Year, 1301st meeting.

Council have agreed that the higher interests of the Organization would be best served if U Thant continues in the post of Secretary-General.

They are aware of the Secretary-General's intention not to offer himself for a second term and his desire to leave the Council unfettered in its recommendation. They have weighed the Secretary-General's wish that they examine the possibility of another nominee. Whatever their views may be on the observations he made with his announced expression of intention, they fully respect his position and his action in bringing basic issues confronting the Organization and disturbing developments in many parts of the world to their notice, as he has done in his statement of September 1, 1966[2] to which they accord their closest attention.

The members of the Security Council would like to ask him to recognize with them that the Organization should continue to be served by a Secretary-General who has the demonstrated capacity to evoke the cooperation and confidence of all Members. The wide support for the present Secretary-General among all the Members of the United Nations is an important factor which should be preserved in order to help the Organization continue to face its problems constructively and play its role in maintaining peace and security.

The Security Council therefore, conscious of his proven qualities and his high sense of duty, has unanimously decided to appeal to U Thant's dedication to the Organization and to ask him to continue to serve for another full term as Secretary-General of the United Nations. The Security Council hopes that the Secretary-General will accept its appeal, and thereupon it would be the intention of the Security Council to make the appropriate recommendation to the General Assembly.

The President then read the text of the following statement by the Secretary-General.

The Secretary-General is grateful to the Security Council for the serious consideration it has given to the question of the appointment of the Secretary-General. He is also deeply appreciative of the sym-

[2] See Ibid., Twenty-first Year, Supplement for July, August, and September 1966, document S/7481.

pathetic understanding it has shown of the reasons which impelled him to announce his intention not to offer himself for a second term.

The Secretary-General takes note of the observations made by the Security Council and recognizes the validity of the reasons it has advanced in requesting him to continue to serve the Organization for another full term. He notes with particular appreciation that, for its part, the Security Council respects his position and his action in bringing to the notice of the Organization basic issues confronting it, and disturbing developments in many parts of the world. He hopes that the close attention being given to these issues and developments will serve to strengthen the Organization by the cooperative effort of the entire membership, and promote the cause of world peace and progress. It is in this hope that the Secretary-General accedes to the appeal addressed to him by the Security Council.

---

7. Statement in the General Assembly Accepting a Second Term

NEW YORK   DECEMBER 2, 1966

MR. PRESIDENT, distinguished delegates and friends, I accept today a fresh five-year term as Secretary-General of the United Nations, in response to the wishes of the Security Council and the General Assembly. Ever since I announced, on September 1, my unwillingness to offer myself for a second term as Secretary-General, I have received many insistent requests to reconsider this decision. I have indeed been deeply touched by the warm personal references made to me by heads of delegations in the course of the general debate. I must also acknowledge with gratitude the numerous letters addressed to me from all parts of the world, by people high and low, urging me to stay at my post.

At the same time I can well understand that my final acceptance of

SOURCE: General Assembly Official Records, Twenty-first Session, 1483rd plenary meeting.

a renewed term of office and the prolonged responsibilities it brings may have caused some surprise among those who believe that a change of Secretary-General at this stage would hasten a reappraisal of the issues before the United Nations and other grave international problems and thus help the cause of peace. During these past months, as many of you are aware, I too have shared that belief. Today, however, I am confronted by an overwhelming weight of opinion that, under present circumstances, my continuance as Secretary-General for another term would best serve the higher interests of the Organization and thus represent a positive factor in the current international situation. Not without apprehension, however, and regardless of my personal preferences, I feel I have to accept that evaluation.

At this point, because of the personal stand I have taken, I should like to make it clear that my present decision is not based on any new element which has developed in recent weeks or on any fond hope for the foreseeable future. On September 1, I thought it my duty to draw attention to some of the basic issues before the United Nations and the disturbing developments in many parts of the world. The observations I made then still represent my conviction today. My concern for the lack of advance in international cooperation and in making this Organization more truly representative of the state of the world remains. At the same time, I have noted with particular appreciation that the Security Council respects my position in bringing these issues and developments to the notice of the Members of the Organization, and I earnestly hope that these problems will continue to receive close attention.

I am well aware that, in some respects, the present session of the General Assembly has made some real progress. I have also been encouraged to believe that, in the near future, the financial situation of the Organization will be greatly alleviated by actions under consideration by some Member states. From my private consultations, I am also confirmed in my belief that there is a sincere desire to reach an agreement on a mutually acceptable basis in regard to the main principles of peace-keeping operations.

Mr. President, the threats to peace in many parts of the world, and more particularly in Vietnam, are for me a continuing source of anxiety and even anguish. I was glad to know a few days ago that there is general agreement in regard to a brief pause in the fighting in

Vietnam on the occasion of Christmas and other holidays. Is it too much to hope that what is made possible for just a couple of days by the occurrence of common holidays may soon prove feasible for a longer period by the new commitments that peace requires, so that an atmosphere may be created which is necessary for meaningful talks to be held in the quest for a peaceful solution?

The imperative necessity of undertaking new efforts for peace is being underlined by the continuing intensification of the war. This problem, as you all know, has been uppermost in my mind for a long time, and I need hardly add that it will continue to be so in the months ahead. I shall seize every occasion to recall that this war must be ended, and I will continue to regard it as my duty to make every effort on a personal basis to help promote a solution which will bring peace and justice to the people of Vietnam.

Notwithstanding some hopeful signs, we must all recognize that a difficult, indeed a crucial, period lies ahead for this Organization. All of us must surely realize what a dangerous disillusionment would inevitably follow today's comforting consensus if we were not to give our close attention to the basic problems that the world faces today and if renewed and sincere efforts toward peace and progress were not soon to be undertaken through a revived respect for the high purposes and principles of our Charter.

And yet, although little has happened to brighten the outlook for the months ahead, my conviction stands undiminished that the United Nations remains the best instrument by which nations may cooperate for the development and peace of their people. My acceptance of an extended mandate today stems out of this deep conviction as much as out of a sense of duty; and I assure Members of this Organization that all my faith and all my efforts are unhesitatingly pledged to maintaining and developing this Organization as an indispensable center for harmonizing the actions of nations in the attainment of our common ends and as an increasingly effective instrument for peace and development.

In this task I have the considerable asset represented by the Secretariat which I am proud to head. All the organizational or other administrative improvements that are necessary will be undertaken with the assistance of my colleagues so that all Members may continue to rely upon the efficiency, competence, and integrity of this body of dedicated servants of the Organization.

Fully conscious of the indispensable support which close consultation with members of the Security Council and the General Assembly has brought to me during my last term, I shall continue to seek extended advice and cooperation from them in the discharge of my responsibilities.

I also take this occasion to reaffirm my oath of office, and I solemnly swear to exercise in all loyalty, discretion, and conscience the functions entrusted to me as Secretary-General of the United Nations, to discharge these functions and regulate my conduct with the interests of the United Nations only in view, and not to seek or accept instructions in regard to the performance of my duties from any government or other authority external to this Organization.

Before I conclude allow me, Mr. President, to express my very sincere thanks to you for your gracious words, to the members of the Security Council for their unanimous recommendation, and to the Members of the General Assembly for the unanimous extension of my appointment as Secretary-General.

From Introduction to the Twenty-First Annual Report

NEW YORK   SEPTEMBER 15, 1966

THE INTRODUCTION to the twenty-first Annual Report is of special interest since it was issued fifteen days after U Thant notified Member states that he would not offer himself for a second term as Secretary-General. Like other statements made by him during the year, the Introduction was on the pessimistic side. The disappointments, he said, outweighed the modest gains. He expressed his personal distress over what he called the domination of Vietnam peace efforts by power politics, the happenings in Africa, the India-Pakistan conflict, and the deterioration of the international situation generally during the past twelve months. These were all factors which weighed heavily in his reluctance to accept a second term as Secretary-General. He did not refer to his announced decision to step down, a decision which he later reversed.

I. General

THIS HAS BEEN a year in which, to all those looking and working toward larger international cooperation for the peace and well-being of mankind, the disappointments will seem to have outweighed once more the modest gains made in some directions.

The international political situation has not improved. The cloud over Viet-Nam has grown larger and more ominous. The serious open conflict between India and Pakistan over Kashmir has, with the help of the United Nations, been calmed, but tensions have been heightened and violence has erupted elsewhere. Nuclear as well as conventional armaments have developed apace. Comparatively little has happened to brighten the prospects of those who occupy the two thirds of the world where poverty, disease, ignorance, and lack of opportunity are the most conspicuous facts of daily life. Frustrations have been more dominant than constructive change in respect of such long-standing problems as the situations in South Africa, South West

SOURCE: General Assembly Official Records, Twenty-first Session, Supplement No. 1A (A 6301/Add.1).

Africa, and Southern Rhodesia, and such long-standing disputes as those in Cyprus and the Middle East.

These are conditions which, even if they strongly underline the need for the United Nations, are at the same time not conducive to the most effective action of which the Organization is capable. Generally speaking and as reflected by positions taken in the United Nations, the powerful nations have not during this period shown themselves able to rise above the suspicions, fears, and mistrust that spring from their different ideologies and from their different conceptions of the best interests of the rest of the world; nor the rich nations above their concern for the continuation of their own prosperity; nor the poor nations above the dead weight of their chronic poverty and their anachronistic social structures.

Against such a background the international community, as represented—and still, I regret to say, incompletely represented—by the United Nations, has again made only limited progress in those areas such as peace-keeping, disarmament, economic and social development, decolonization, and human rights where most is expected of it. There can be no doubt how deeply and widely these expectations are felt by people around the world; they have, indeed, seldom been more movingly expressed than by His Holiness Pope Paul VI in his memorable address to the General Assembly on October 4, 1965.

Within the Organization, I must again report with regret that, in spite of the unanimous agreement a year ago that the financial difficulties should be solved through voluntary contributions by Member states, those contributions have still not come forward in an amount sufficient to meet the deficit of the past, which remains substantial. On the other hand, the work of the *Ad Hoc* Committee of Experts to Examine the Finances of the United Nations and the Specialized Agencies, which was established by the General Assembly last December, should, I believe, help to allay the somewhat disquieting degree of concern and uncertainty which many Member states had shown over some of the broader aspects of our financial affairs. To many of the underlying difficulties, notably those arising from constitutional or political differences, the *Ad Hoc* Committee has not been able to suggest ready solutions. It has found equally difficult the problem of relating unlimited global needs to the comparatively limited resources which can in present circumstances be made collectively available for their satisfaction. The *Ad Hoc* Committee was, however, singularly successful in the attainment of its more immediate objectives: the preparation of a clear and complete analysis of the financial situation of the United Nations with a view to the early restoration of its solvency, and the working out of measures to secure better utilization of the funds available through rationalization and more thorough coordination of the activities of the United Nations and the various organizations brought into relationship with it. I trust that the detailed analysis made by the *Ad Hoc* Committee in its first report and the large measure of agreement reached as to the Organization's present financial deficit will provide an acceptable basis for the liquidation of this deficit and the settlement of past indebtedness.

I also believe that Member states will have noted with appreciation, as I have done, the careful and constructive approach taken by the Committee in its thorough review of the budgeting, programming, and coordination processes of the family of international organizations. In the face of unlimited global needs, the most rational and effective utilization of available resources is not merely a desirable objective but also a practical necessity. A large measure of responsibility must, of course, continue to be assumed by Member states themselves, since programs and priorities reflect essentially decisions taken in the various legislative organs. In the execution of these decisions, however, the Secretariat has a no less important duty, and it is ready to make its contribution in whatever direction and by whatever means may be agreed upon after consideration of the many valuable proposals contained in the *Ad Hoc* Committee's second report.

In the Introduction to my last Annual Report on the work of the Organization, I expressed my view that it was essential for the successful conduct of peace-keeping operations in the future that we should have well-established ground rules and guidelines to govern them. At that time, and subsequently as well, I expressed the hope that the Special Committee on Peace-keeping Operations would succeed in evolving and formulating its recommendations on this urgent question. The Special Committee adjourned on the eve of the resumed nineteenth session of the General Assembly on an optimistic note. Although it had not been successful in finding even an interim solution to the constitutional and financial problems covered by its terms of reference, the Special Committee was able, with the cooperation and understanding displayed by its members, to reach a consensus on the need to strengthen the United Nations through a cooperative effort, on the normal functioning of the General Assembly, and on solving the financial difficulties confronting the Organization. This unquestionably represented significant progress and gave rise to encouragement and hope. It was followed by a substantive debate on the subject at the twentieth session of the General Assembly, during which several concrete ideas and proposals were put forward.

It is therefore a matter of regret to me that the report submitted by the Special Committee to the General Assembly is so negative. It not only shows the continuing failure to agree on basic principles, but it also reflects a reluctance to come to grips with the problem. I realize that this may be due to the adverse international situation and perhaps to circumstances beyond the control of the Organization and not to any lack of interest or concern on the part of Member states. I do, however, hope that this problem, which is so closely related to the role of the Organization in the maintenance of international peace, will not be put aside but will receive the attention it deserves.

At this point I should like to refer briefly to the important question, traditionally a somewhat controversial one, of informing the public about the United Nations. It will be agreed, I think, that the ultimate strength of the Organization and its capacity to promote and achieve the objectives for which it has been established lie in the degree to which its aims and activities are understood and supported by the peoples of the world. In this sense, a purposeful and universal program of public information is, in fact, a program of implementation— an essential counterpart of the substantive activities of the Organization. This fact was recognized and formally embodied by the General Assembly in 1946 in resolution 13 (I), section II, which laid down the policies and programs for the information activities of the United Nations. It is also underscored by the essentially public nature of the debates in the Organization.

I believe, however, that it will also be generally agreed that while much has been achieved over the years in promotiong worldwide public awareness and understanding of the work, methods, and objectives of the Organization, this achievement has been neither total nor evenly spread in the various regions of the world. A large task lies ahead, for the Organization itself and for its Member states, not only in adjusting information programs and activities to the altered information needs of today, but also in exploiting more effectively and fully the possibilities presented by the recent technological "explosion" in the means of mass communication. Account has to be taken, as well, of the increasing importance which Member states attach to the widest possible dissemination throughout the world of their activities at the United Nations. New and expanded information needs, coupled with new and expanded technical means and possibilities, make it necessary, I believe, to examine how adequate are the present methods and resources of the United Nations Office of Public Information for the accomplishment of its task. This review is currently being carried out.

It is equally necessary and urgent that since the General Assembly placed the primary responsibility for promoting public understanding and support for the aims and activities of the Organization on the national information services, official and unofficial, Member states should also re-examine and reassess the nature and extent of their own information activities and programs devoted to the discharge of that responsibility. It is in close cooperation between the national media and a strengthened and modernized Office of Public Information that the possibility exists of carrying effectively, to all corners of the globe, the story of the collective purpose and effort represented by the United Nations, at a time when the Organization's success offers hope of a breakthrough from the age-old cycles of poverty, ignorance, and strife and when its failure would spell the risk of total disaster.

II. The Slowdown in Disarmament

The past year has regrettably seen a reversal of the trend of recent years toward some progress in the stabilization and reduction of armed forces and military budgets. The escalating hostilities in Viet-Nam and the deteriorating international situation have inevitably intensified the arms race in both the conventional and the nuclear fields and have no less inevitably had an adverse effect on negotiations for disarmament, above all for general and complete disarmament.

The testing of nuclear weapons has gone on both in the atmosphere and underground. Two countries, France and the People's Republic of China, which are not parties to the partial test-ban treaty of August 1963 prohibiting tests in the atmosphere, under water, and in outer space, continued to conduct tests in the atmosphere, with the evident purpose of developing at least a basic nuclear armament. The three major nuclear powers, the Union of Soviet Socialist Republics, the United Kingdom, and the United States, which are parties to the partial test-ban treaty, conducted tests underground. It is difficult to conceive of any other reason for these underground tests than that they are intended to produce more sophisticated nuclear weapons or, perhaps, to develop antiballistic missile systems. The possible consequences are alarming; if there should be a unilateral technological breakthrough by one of these powers in either offensive or defensive nuclear weapon capability, it could upset the existing uneasy balance of terror and lead at once to a new and greatly accelerated nuclear arms race.

The past year has also witnessed—although, I regret to say, not on the same scale—an intensification of efforts to limit and control the nuclear arms race. The Conference of the Eighteen-Nation Committee on Disarmament has met in almost continuous session at Geneva in an endeavor to fulfill the tasks entrusted to it by the twentieth session of the General Assembly. The Committee's work has focused mainly on the prevention of the spread of nuclear weapons and on the achievement of a comprehensive nuclear test ban.

With regard to the question of preventing the spread of nuclear weapons, which was given the highest priority, the Eighteen-Nation Committee sought to agree on the text of a nonproliferation treaty based on the two draft treaties presented respectively by the Soviet Union and the United States, taking into account the principles laid down in General Assembly resolution 2028 (XX). While these efforts have not yet met with success, it can at least be said that the search for an agreed treaty is continuing. The positions of the parties have been clarified and all of them are aware of the compromises which have to be made if agreement is to be reached. I still hope, and I have continued to urge, that the governments concerned will find it possible to make the necessary adjustments in their positions so that a treaty on nonproliferation can be agreed upon and put into force at the earliest possible date.

The dangers of nuclear proliferation are very real and very grave, more so than may be generally recognized. The use of nuclear reactors produces plutonium which, when processed in a separation plant, can be used to make nuclear weapons by techniques that are no longer secret. According to some estimates, by 1980 nuclear power reactors throughout the world will produce more than 100 kilograms of plutonium every day. It is always possible that cheaper and simpler methods of producing fissionable material may be discovered and that their availability for warlike purposes will increase astronomically. The risks that now exist of the further spread of nuclear weapons hold such peril for humanity that international safeguards should be established not only over nuclear power reactors but also over other nuclear plants which produce, use, or process significant quantities of fissionable materials.

There may already be some countries which may, however misguidedly, hope—or in desperation persuade themselves—to try to improve their security by acquiring nuclear weapons as a deterrent against attack by a hostile neighbor. These countries may well be reluctant to forgo the option of acquiring such weapons unless other means of protection are found. Some countries may also be reluctant to give up the right to acquire such weapons unless the present nuclear powers commit themselves—in the words of resolution 2028 (XX)—to "an acceptable balance of mutual responsibilities and obligations." These preoccupations of the non-nuclear countries raise serious and difficult problems and these problems must be faced. The responsibility for solving them must be shared by all states Members of the United Nations, and it rests as well with states not represented in the Organization.

A comprehensive nuclear test ban, including a ban on underground tests, is an important objective in itself. It would slow down the nuclear arms race and prevent a new race for antiballistic missiles which, in the manner of the relentless progression that takes place in this appalling business, would lead to the competitive development of weapons to counter such antiballistic missiles. It would also be an important step toward preventing the further proliferation of nuclear weapons. Even within the membership of the United Nations, however, agreement on an underground test ban is still deadlocked by the dispute between the Soviet Union and the United States as to whether the latest scientific advances in instrumentation make it possible to detect and identify all underground tests by national detection systems alone. Various compromise suggestions have been put forward. Some of these propose a "threshold" treaty whereby all tests above a certain seismic magnitude would be banned. Others have suggested a moratorium on underground tests below the agreed threshold, together with an exchange of scientific and technical information by the nuclear powers and the progressive lowering of the threshold. Another suggestion that deserves serious consideration is for the suspension of all underground tests—with or without a threshold treaty—for a temporary trial period, to be accompanied by a system of "verification by challenge." Under this system a country suspected of having conducted an underground test would be challenged to prove its innocence; it could do this in a variety of ways, including an invitation to outside observers to make an on-the-spot inspection. This concept of verification by challenge could provide a means of facilitating progress not only in the control and verification of underground tests but perhaps in other disarmament measures as well. One suggestion that has gained some acceptance is for the establishment of a "detection club" whereby a number of countries would agree to develop their seismic detection systems and cooperate in the exchange of information and data obtained from them. Several governments are at present engaged in studying ways and means of implementing this idea. Its application could contribute in an important way to the detection and identification of underground tests and to the practicability of an agreement banning such tests.

In this area where the smallest hope is always worth pursuing, I find some encouragement in the progress made during the past year toward the denuclearization of Latin America. The countries engaged in this effort have broken new ground in elaborating the text of a draft treaty, and if they can agree on a treaty that would eliminate nuclear weapons and avoid a potential nuclear arms race for the whole or a part of their area of the world, it would mark a considerable step forward both in the nonproliferation of nuclear weapons and in disarmament generally. Such a treaty could point the way to, and might perhaps become a model for, the denuclearization of Africa and other areas of the world and, if it received the support of the nuclear powers, would also help to reduce the size of the problem of proliferation and give a much needed impetus to other disarmament measures.

While the disarmament negotiations in the main have concentrated, and rightly so, on nuclear weapons, there remain dangers to the peace and security of the world in the continuation of the conventional arms race. The acquisition and dissemination of conventional weapons are still leading to increased tensions. Wars fought with conventional weapons can cause grievous loss and suffering; moreover, there is always the risk that they may escalate into nuclear war. In the final analysis, only general and complete disarmament can provide an effective guarantee of lasting peace and security. Efforts have been made to prepare the groundwork for the holding of a world disarmament conference, as called for by the General Assembly at its last session. Progress has been slow, but there is some hope that present efforts will bear fruit and that a worldwide conference can be convened before too long.

The search for ways to halt and control the arms race and finally to achieve general and complete disarmament has been long, difficult, and frustrating, and so far it has had relatively few rewards. Paradoxically, disarmament is at one and the same time a recognized condition for the survival, security, and full development of mankind, and a condition which the leaders of mankind appear least able to bring about. During its twenty-one years of existence, the United Nations—born and raised in the nuclear age—has devoted a great deal of time and discussion to disarmament. The results so far are extremely meager—so meager that it is natural to question to what extent governments and people really understand the effects of the nuclear arms race. In all this time no organ of the United Nations has ever carried out a comprehensive study of the consequences of the invention of nuclear weapons. Since they were used for the first and only time on actual targets over twenty years ago, their destructive power, their quantities in stockpile, the manner of their use, and the amount of human and material resources devoted to their manufacture and potential delivery have expanded far beyond the comprehension of most people and, I suspect, of many governments. I believe that the time has come for an appropriate body of the United Nations to explore and weigh the impact and implications of all aspects of nuclear weapons, including problems of a military, political, economic, and social nature relating to the manufacture, acquisition, deployment, and development of these weapons and their possible use. To know the true nature of the danger we face may be a most important first step toward averting it.

. . .

IV. Peace-keeping Operations

Financial and political difficulties notwithstanding, the United Nations peace-keeping activities were maintained and even increased during the year under review. The United Nations Emergency Force, the United Nations Force in Cyprus, and the United Nations Truce Supervision Organization in Palestine continued their assigned functions on the same basis as before. The United Nations Military Observer Group in India and Pakistan was temporarily strengthened and two supplementary operations of a quite temporary character, the United Nations India-Pakistan Observation Mission and the United Nations India-Pakistan Mission on Withdrawals, were established following the new outbreak of fighting between India and Pakistan in August 1965.

The United Nations Mission in the Dominican Republic has continued to inform me and, through me, the Security Council of developments relating to peace in that country. Despite its limited mandate, the Mission, which was established in May 1965 following the eruption of civil war, acted as a stabilizing influence and as a catalyst in helping to prevent the escalation of incidents and the recurrence of fighting and in facilitating reconciliation. It is gratifying that an agreement between the contending parties was finally achieved, which led to the holding of general elections on June 1, 1966, and the establishment of a government one month later. Following the installation of this government, the withdrawal of the Inter-American Peace Force was begun and is expected to be completed shortly.

In view of these events, I feel that it is now possible to envisage the termination in the near future of the United Nations Mission there. Mention may be made here of a unique aspect of this mission, namely, that for the first time in the United Nations peace-keeping experience, one of its missions has found itself in juxtaposition with an operation maintained by a regional organization. This has given rise to some special problems and difficulties of relationship, which fortunately have been worked out satisfactorily. In the light of this experience, I feel it desirable again to call attention to the question of relationships between the United Nations and regional organizations in the hope that the Members of the United Nations will give further study to this matter.

Although the United Nations has continued to be active in peace-keeping, this is a crucial if not a critical time for such efforts or—to put it more accurately—the future of them. This is the case, I feel, not only because of the financial difficulties which have beset some of these efforts in the past and which now increasingly beset all of them,

but even more so because of the fact that the long-standing controversy over the proper nature of, and the "legal" basis for, United
Nations peace-keeping operations has reached an impasse. In these
circumstances, I can only reiterate the hope that the General Assembly at its twenty-first session will devote its most serious and determined attention to the problem of peace-keeping, with a view to
finding a solution to both its constitutional and its financial problems.
The present situation, certainly, has most serious implications for the
United Nations and for its effectiveness as an instrument for peace in
the world. A mere tabulation of the situations of conflict in which the
United Nations has been called upon to intervene and the peace-
keeping operations in which it has engaged in the twenty-one years of
its existence will amply testify to the importance of this subject.

I do not mean to imply and I do not believe that the United Nations,
however deep the constitutional and financial controversies over the
peace-keeping operations may be, would ever find itself totally unable to respond to a need for peace-keeping. On the other hand, it is all
too likely that, in the present circumstances, the United Nations may
respond to situations which call for peace-keeping efforts of an operational kind only when matters have reached the gravest and most
advanced state of crisis.

It is true, of course, that the United Nations has found itself unable
to meet the challenge of the increasingly dangerous war in Vietnam.
But this is because of well-known and overriding political considerations and not because of the issue of peace-keeping itself. As I see it,
should there be other severe crises such as those which occurred in
recent years in Cyprus and the Dominican Republic, the United
Nations would feel bound to take some appropriate type of peace-
keeping action. I am equally certain, however, that any such action—
like that taken with respect to Cyprus, for example—would be of an
ad hoc kind, improvised hastily and without adequate provision for
financing. I have frequently and strongly criticized the inadequacy of
financing the Cyprus peace-keeping operation by means of voluntary
contributions. This criticism is made not because the arrangement
places upon the Secretary-General, in addition to his other responsibilities in connection with the operation, the difficult task of raising
the money; the essential weakness is that it has been an extremely
uncertain way of financing and one that has very definitely placed an
unfair burden upon those Members of the United Nations, as well as a

few nonmembers, who have been cooperative enough to make the contributions necessary to keep the Force going.

On several occasions I have stressed that peace-keeping is a means, not an end; that in the very nature of the case its ultimate purpose in seeking to restore and maintain peace is to provide the time and the atmosphere of calm in which alone efforts to resolve the issues giving rise to the conflict may be hopefully pursued. This is only part of the full story, of course, and in no sense is it to be inferred that to stop the fighting and keep it stopped is not intrinsically important. Obviously, also if in the time and quiet provided by the peace-keeping effort a solution of the issues, for whatever reason, is not found, the continuation of that effort will be much less costly in every respect and for all concerned than a resumption of hostilities. This is, indeed, the dilemma now confronting the United Nations in several areas of its activity.

The two outstanding United Nations observation operations, one in Palestine and one in Kashmir, have been in existence since 1949. They have very limited resources in manpower and facilities and their authority to "observe" is confined to investigating and reporting on incidents after they have occurred, which inevitably means that often only inadequate, if not one-sided, testimony and evidence can be obtained. These operations have nevertheless been remarkably effective, especially in stopping the fighting by arranging cease-fires on the spot. The morale of the observers continues to be high, and their very presence in the areas helps to keep the peace. They are not always able, however, to prevent or to control incidents and, as in the tragic instance of the outbreak between India and Pakistan last autumn, the danger of a recourse to open hostilities is always present.

A peace force, such as the United Nations Emergency Force or the United Nations Force in Cyprus, is, of course, more effective than a team of observers. It is also far more costly. Here, too, the operations tend to assume a semipermanent character: the Emergency Force is now approaching its tenth year of existence and the Force in Cyprus has been deployed for two and a half years.

In such cases as the United Nations Emergency Force, the United Nations Truce Supervision Organization in Palestine, the United Nations Military Observer Group in India and Pakistan, and the United Nations Force in Cyprus, the crux of the matter from the standpoint of the United Nations is the continuing absence of any earnest resolve on the part of the parties direcely involved in the dispute to seek a reasonable way out of it. Indeed, at times it seems, and it may actually be the case, that they tend to take the attitude that the very United Nations presence frees them from any pressing obligation to exert a really serious effort toward a settlement of their differences. It may well be true that the existence of the United Nations peace-keeping operation and the feeling of security that grows with its effectiveness reduce the sense of danger and urgency about the continuing dispute, thus relieving the pressure on the parties to seek a settlement.

There is no readily apparent way out of the dilemma I have described other than for the United Nations to persevere in its peace-keeping wherever it is clearly necessary, and at the same time to intensify its peace-making efforts, seeking always to find new and better means of inducing states to settle their disputes peaceably and of helping them to do so. It seems to me that there is, in this direction, much that could be done by the Security Council and the General Assembly. I have no doubt that there is room for imaginative and forward-looking initiatives by these organs in seeking ways to improve and further develop the capacity of the United Nations to settle disputes instead of trying merely to stop the fighting and to avoid a recurrence of it once it has erupted. Indeed, I submit that much could be gained if Members of the United Nations which are represented in the organs concerned with peace-keeping would undertake the consideration of possible new approaches to the task of solving disputes. This would be much more useful than holding inflexibly to their present positions with regard to peace-keeping, which can only result in inhibiting the capacity of the Organization to deal with threats or actual violations of the peace at the time when this capacity is needed most.

I also believe that individual Members of the United Nations could play an important role in helping to find a settlement of the political problems that lie at the root of international conflicts. In spite of all the efforts of the United Nations, the success of peace-making endeavors rests, in the last analysis, on the parties directly concerned in the conflicts. And here governments which entertain friendly relations with those parties may be able, in certain cases such as Cyprus, to contribute, individually or collectively, to bringing them closer together and to instilling in them the will to make those necessary concessions without which no agreement is possible. Such action could usefully complement what is undertaken through United Nations organs on behalf of peace.

V. *Problems of Economic and Social Development*

In view of the importance of ecomonic and social progress as a foundation for peace and as an area of United Nations activities, it is not surprising that the loss of momentum of international aid has been recognized as one of the most serious problems of the past year. The gravity of the problem has stimulated some fresh thinking about means of remedying it. In particular, an interesting proposal for supplementary financing has been put forward by the staff of the International Bank for Reconstruction and Development in response to a resolution of the United Nations Conference on Trade and Development, and a penetrating survey of the problem of development financing in its various aspects has been placed before the Economic and Social Council.

Nevertheless, the stark fact which emerges intact from all the studies, reports, and discussions devoted to the subject in the course of 1966 is that international aid is stagnating while the capacity of developed countries to provide such aid, measured in terms of an increase in their per capita incomes, has become greater. This fact, together with the feeling that the circumstances warrant exploring what can be done about multilateral food aid, prompted me to add my voice to those already expressing concern about the condition of international assistance. The General Assembly will find in the report of the Economic and Social Council a substantial reflection of these preoccupations.

Another salient feature of the general economic situation, and one from which some solace can be drawn, is the increasing importance attached to devising means of orienting and organizing development activities in a more purposeful and coherent manner. This trend has led to the creation of a Committee for Development Planning under the auspices of the Economic and Social Council. Governments now seem willing to exchange their experiences in both the formulation and the implementation of their development plans, and they are turning to the United Nations for help in meeting their need for a background against which they can project national efforts.

There also seems to be a genuine desire to see the United Nations Development Decade become a framework in which the development objectives of the world community can be set less haphazardly and in which delays or imbalances and their implications can be better assessed, if not anticipated. Whether these new attitudes contain the promise of a more vigorous attack on development problems in the second half of the Decade than in the first remains to be seen. If, however, there is now a sufficiently strong will to ascertain and meet future requirements, the work which has been undertaken on projections and planning can help to set the stage for more effective international cooperation for development in the 1970s.

Another encouraging tendency which has made itself felt in 1966 is the greater attention given to questions which cut across specific areas of work. The effectiveness of all activities in the economic and social fields, moreover, is greatly dependent on the manner in which these questions are tackled. The transfer and adaptation of science and technology, on the one hand, and the development of human resources, on the other, are the subjects of considerable research, discussion, and attempts to accelerate progress on the broadest possible front. The work of the Advisory Committee on Science and Technology to development is having a very stimulating effect on the quest for ways and means of making the inventiveness of man serve the needs of developing countries instead of leaving them out of the mainstream of its preoccupations and unable to reap its benefits. Perhaps as a result of this increased awareness of the complexity and unity of the development process, a larger concern for the interrelationships of the economic and social aspects of development questions is replacing the often invidious distinction previously drawn between economic and social affairs; the approach taken to the study of regional development is an example of this welcome trend.

These factors, together with the desire of developing countries to see development activities multiply, have given a new turn to the cooperation of international agencies within the United Nations family of organizations. Coordination has come to mean something more than dividing labor or avoiding duplication. It has become a dynamic process. More activities than ever before are being undertaken jointly under the inspiration of the two expert groups which I have mentioned above and which possess outstanding competence and a central vantage point: namely, the Committee for Development Planning and the Advisory Committee on Science and Technology. The latter has adumbrated a world plan of action and, to an increasing extent, work programs in the economic and social fields are being shaped in the perspective of the Development Decade, in the sense that they include series of projects or activities to be carried out over a five-year period. Moreover, the Economic and Social Council has reorganized its work in order to cope more effectively with its increased responsibilities at the plexus of the intricate system which now exists of functional bodies, regional commissions, specialized agencies, and institutes of various kinds.

As part of the reorganization of its work, the Council has made progress toward measuring the activities within its purview against the budget of the United Nations. This kind of comparison, however, is limited by the standards of budget presentation. It would be desirable, and it should prove possible, to link programs and costs in such a way as to identify more clearly the requirements and limitations in each main field of work in what may well be called the peace-building activities of the United Nations.

The financial crisis within the Organization has not prevented a remarkable diversification and intensification of these peace-building activities. There has been a gratifying response on the part of governments whenever the fate of a new priority program has depended on voluntary contributions to supplement budgetary resources. It is clear, however, that, in the long run, arrangements of this kind are no substitute for a sound financial policy. Some time ago I advocated a policy of controlled expansion for economic and social affairs. I must now warn that, should the stabilization of the budget become a lasting constraint, a large part of the investment of efforts and resources made in the last few years might well prove to have been wasteful. There might also be a shattering of the hope that the United Nations can help to promote better international cooperation for development—the hope so recently renewed by the start made in such areas as development planning, resources development, housing and building and demography, by the launching of the United Nations Conference on Trade and Development, and by the forthcoming establishment of the United Nations Organization for Industrial Development.

The investment in time, in the evolution of common policies and in the development of institutions which these enterprises represent, and the need for further resources, in will as well as in money, to make the investment bring worthwhile returns, are well illustrated by the history of the United Nations Conference on Trade and Development. The establishment within the United Nations of permanent machinery for cooperation in trade and development was the culmination of a long process aimed at the solution of some of the most substantial and urgent problems confronted by the developing countries. The first year of the experience of the Trade and Development Board in grappling with the issues and questions whose solution had been considered at the Geneva Conference as a joint responsibility of the international community has confirmed beyond any doubt that the political will of governments of Member states is the main factor which will determine in the long run the extent to which the Conference machinery can also constitute an effective mechanism for the adoption of concrete solutions.

Given the compelling necessity to seek adequate formulas and to obtain practical answers to questions relating to commodities, manufactures, development financing, and invisible trade, there is widespread concern over the lack of more rapid progress within the various organs of the Conference in the implementation of the recommendations adopted at Geneva. The intentions expressed there have not yet been translated into positive action to any satisfactory degree, notwithstanding the fact that the Conference lacks neither the ideas nor the technical expertise required to bring about practical decisions with the speed called for by the significance of the Final Act.[1]

Sustained efforts have been made during the past year to overcome critical difficulties in the field of commodities. Two concrete attempts to adopt international agreements on cocoa and sugar failed, although new concepts and technical formulas of commodity trade were considered in order to avoid the kinds of problem that had been encountered in the past in the operation of such arrangements. In the case of cocoa, the failure to reach an agreement was all the more disappoint-

---

[1]The Final Act of the Conference, which was formally adopted on June 16, 1964, consisted of three parts. The first of these was a preamble which described the background, constitution and proceedings of the Conference, followed by a statement of the findings by which the Conference had been guided and of the essential reasons and considerations on which its recommendations had been based. The second part consolidated the recommendations of the Conference, and the third part contained the text of these, together with observations and reservations by groups of countries or individual delegations, and messages from heads of state.

ing because the difficulties involved were considered by all the parties concerned as not being insurmountable. They all remain ready, however, to discuss further what can be regarded as a useful start, and it is my sincere hope that a solution will be reached in the near future.

It is also a matter of record that the Board and its technical bodies have made valuable contributions to the gradual process of building a new policy for development. The conclusions of the expert bodies of the Conference on monetary issues, for instance, have brought to the attention of the world community the need to bear in mind the interests of the developing countries in any reform of the international monetary system that may be under consideration, and before it is carried out. Various concrete proposals have already been put forward and discussed in relation to the expansion of exports of manufactured and semimanufactured products from the developing countries, to invisible trade and maritime transport and to development financing. Upon the basis of one of the recommendations of the Conference, the scheme on supplementary financing prepared by the International Bank, which I mentioned earlier, is being actively considered, and it may well become the first practical application of the new ideas that emerged at Geneva in 1964. To develop these ideas further and translate them into practical undertakings should prove feasible if governments act with a strong conviction about the principles that should inspire policies for international trade and development and with an awareness of the obstacles that have been blocking or retarding the application of these principles.

I am glad to observe that it is in a spirit of mutual understanding and open-mindedness that the Conference is making preparations for its next session. The United Nations can indeed feel gratified if the second session gives further proof not only that economic cooperation based on real solidarity between Member states is possible but also that they are determined to put it into effect in the interests of better living conditions for all peoples.

The evolution of international policies, institutions, and programs for industrial development provides another example of the United Nations equipping itself with the machinery by which, given the further moral and material resources needed, it can play a fuller part in economic and social development. The need for a more appropriate instrument to intensify, concentrate, and expedite international efforts for industrial development has been felt over a number of years, and it is particularly appropriate that the General Assembly should have taken a unanimous decision to establish an autonomous United Nations Organization for Industrial Development at a time when there is a growing concern over the disappointingly slow progress in the development efforts of the newly industrializing countries.

The creation of a central machinery to deal with industrial development is intended to improve the range and direction of international development efforts. It is now generally accepted that soundly based industrialization is essential to the balanced development of all economic activities, including the proper use of the human potential which has remained to a large extent dormant, or at least seriously under-fulfilled, in the less developed areas. Moreover, recent history provides much evidence that sound industrialization can be accelerated, and the present economic and social conditions in the developing countries strongly indicate that it should be speeded up. While in the industrially advanced countries the accumulation of capital and technology provides the basis for a fairly high level of continuing progress, the industrialization of the developing countries has been at best a sporadic process. Only in very few such countries is there any substantial hope of achieving a viable industrial sector in the foreseeable future without some special stimulus. The relatively disappointing results evident in many countries in the early stages of industrialization indicate that efforts in this direction have lacked sufficient intensity. The time appears ripe for a concentrated attack on the problems of industrial development, to be undertaken as a cooperative effort of industrialized and industrializing countries.

The coming into existence of the United Nations Organization for Industrial Development should provide a rallying point for their concerted efforts. Action by the United Nations cannot, of course, be a substitute for national endeavors, but it can play an important role when there is willingness to cooperate in the attainment of common objectives. The industrially advanced countries have a particular responsibility in this field because of the magnitude of their resources of technology and capital. They must show the necessary foresight to be able to give up limited short-term interests in favor of the long-term benefits to be derived by the world as a whole from upgrading the productivity of two thirds of mankind to levels that are now technically possible. The major effort in industrialization, however, will still rest with the developing countries, and they also must exercise a high degree of initiative if the best advantage is to be taken of all existing opportunities.

The importance of industrialization is further recognized by the decision to hold an International Symposium on Industrial Development next year. This will be the first worldwide gathering on the problems of industrial development. It should afford an opportunity to countries at various stages of development and with different economic systems to exchange views not only on the problems that have to be faced but also on the broad strategy of industrialization.

In giving these highlights of our work in the economic and social fields, I feel that reference also should be made to two other recently established institutions—the United Nations Institute for Training and Research and the United Nations Research Institute for Social Development.

The coming into being of the United Nations Institute for Training and Research is an important achievement accomplished at the mid-point of the Development Decade. The purpose of the Institute is to enhance the effectiveness of the United Nations in achieving its major objectives, in particular the maintenance of peace and security and the promotion of economic and social development. Its autonomous position within the framework of the United Nations is intended to enable it to carry out training and research free from the stresses of the demands on the Secretariat for meeting the immediate, day-to-day needs of the Organization. At the same time the Institute, as an arm of the Organization, will be responsive to the requirements of the Secretary-General, the principal organs of the United Nations, and the specialized agencies. Through both its training and research activities, the Institute is expected to make a direct contribution to the development process in its political, economic, and social aspects; to the crystallization of the experiences gained by the United Nations in various types of undertakings; to the formulation of new approaches and the initiation of new techniques with regard to the global operations of the Organization; to the building of highly trained cadres on various levels for national and international service connected with the purposes and work of the United Nations; and to the development of fresh insights into the broad question of international organization and its position and role in the world of the present and the future. I believe that the wholehearted support which the Institute is continuing to receive from the Member states reflects their confidence that its work will have an impact on the great issues of peace and general welfare which confront the United Nations.

The other autonomous institution—the United Nations Research Institute for Social Development—is well engaged in its program of fundamental research into problems and policies of social development and relationships between various sectors of social and economic development during different phases of economic growth. In its first two years of operation, the Institute has made a valuable scientific contribution. It has provided the first extensive field research on methods of inducing change at the local level, which not only contributed to the *1965 World Social Report* but may also lead to qualitative improvement in the operational programs of the United Nations agencies and bilateral assistance. It has undertaken research in methods of social planning and interrelations of economic and social factors in development which will contribute directly to the work of the Committee on Development Planning and is already being utilized in the training programs of the regional planning institutes in Santiago, Bangkok, and Dakar. Its study of social factors affecting agricultural productivity, carried out in collaboration with the Food and Agriculture Organization of the United Nations, is of importance to many Member states. The establishment of the Institute was made possible by the generosity of the Netherlands government, which guaranteed its financing for the first three years. It is important that the work of the Institute, which is of a pioneering character not duplicated by any other international organization and with few counterparts at the national level, should continue for a further three-year period. A goal of $1.5 million for its financing for the period 1968–1970 has been set by the Board. Several projects in the present work program of the United Nations in the economic and social fields will require scientific contributions from the Institute. The Economic and Social Council has requested me to seek ways and means of obtaining further support for the Institute from both governmental and private sources. The goal is potentially 60 percent fulfilled by a grant which requires matching funds, and I urge governments to make pledges at an early date.

. . .

X. Concluding Observations

This review of the most important developments within the United Nations during the last twelve months has the usual contrasts of light and shadow. The continued slow rate of progress in many of our fields of endeavor, and the setbacks which have been suffered in others, can only be a cause of disappointment to the peoples of the world in whose name the Charter of the United Nations was written. For this, however, they must not blame the Charter itself nor the institutions which it created.

The weaknesses and shortcomings of the United Nations lie not in its constitutional purposes, objectives, and procedures but in world conditions at the present juncture of history. The proceedings of the Organization inevitably mirror the state of the relationships between different peoples and different nations and sometimes between the rulers and the ruled; the economic circumstances under which they live; the social conditions that surround them. It is in these realms, and not in the structure of the United Nations, that the roots of the troubles of the world lie.

The troubles arising from present conditions are abundant. They are the prevalence of narrow nationalisms, the periodic reliance on crude power—whether political, military, or economic—to serve or protect supposed national interests, the appalling rise in the quantity and destructive potential of nuclear armaments, the ever more serious gaps in economic development, the persistence of colonial domination over several million people, the continuing prevalence in many parts of the world of racial discrimination and suppression of human rights, and, among populations constantly increasing, the widespread inadequacies of education, food shortages verging on famine, and lack of medical care. These excesses, inequities, and injustices—and the fears, tensions, frustrations, jealousies, and aggressions which they breed among peoples and among nations—still too largely condition the state of the world, still too strongly and adversely influence the national policies which Member states bring to bear on the work of the United Nations, and still too seriously obstruct rather than challenge the capacity of the Organization to fulfill its purposes.

In the present difficult state of international affairs, I believe it to be the first duty of the membership to face up to the fact that the chances of fruitful international cooperation on many crucial issues in which the United Nations has a clear responsibility for decision and action—issues ranging from disarmament to development—have been steadily and seriously impaired over the past two years by a situation over which, for well-known reasons, the United Nations has not been able to exercise any effective control. This situation, of course, is the deepening crisis over Viet-Nam, where the dangerous escalation of armed force has been accompanied, in my view, by an increasing intransigence and distrust among governments and peoples.

For my own part, I have tried my best to help in the efforts which have been made to reduce the escalation of the conflict in Viet-Nam and to move to the conference table the quest for a solution of the problem. In doing so, I have been increasingly distressed to observe that discussions of the matter have by and large been dominated by consideration and analysis of the power politics involved, and that there has been much less concern for the tremendous human suffering which the conflict has entailed for the people of Viet-Nam and also for the people of other countries involved in the fighting. My heart goes out to them. The Viet-Namese people, in particular, have known no peace for a quarter of a century. Their present plight should be the first, not the last, consideration of all concerned. Indeed, I remain convinced that the basic problem in Viet-Nam is not one of ideology but one of national identity and survival. I see nothing but danger in the idea, so assiduously fostered outside Viet-Nam, that the conflict is a kind of holy war between two powerful political ideologies.

The survival of the people of Viet-Nam must be seen as the real issue, and it can be resolved not by force but by patience and understanding, in the framework of a willingness to live and let live. If this approach can be accepted on all sides—and the moral influence of governments and peoples outside the immediate conflict can help to bring this about—I believe it should be possible to reach a settlement which would end the suffering in Viet-Nam, satisfy the conscience of the world at large, and remove a formidable barrier to international cooperation.

Although Viet-Nam represents the most serious manifestation of the unsatisfactory state of international affairs, it is not the only point of open danger. The situation in the Middle East has shown no improvement, and dangerous tensions persist. I sincerely trust that the hopes newly raised for a settlement in Yemen will be fulfilled. I also hope that the involvement of the United Nations in the difficult question of Aden may help to bring about a peaceful solution there. Beyond these questions lies the long-standing conflict between Israel and the Arab states and the continuing need for passions to be restrained and the terms of the armistice agreements to be observed by all concerned.

I shall not conceal my distress at some of the happenings in Africa during the last twelve months—not only those which hardened the colonial and quasi-colonial attitudes still entrenched in large parts of the continent, but also those involving sudden and violent political changes in newly independent states. They have created a sense of instability which can easily be misrepresented or exaggerated to the disadvantage of Africa as a whole and, by causing an increase in tensions among African countries, they have produced a setback to African unity. By no means all of the many problems that the African peoples are facing are of their own making, but few, if any, of them can be solved except by the African countries themselves showing the qualities of maturity and restraint which they have often displayed, and using these qualities to engender the greater spirit of cooperation and willingness to work together, which is essential to the fulfillment of Africa's destiny. This task is so important that governments and peoples must put above everything else a willingness to sink their differences in the higher interests of Africa and of the world as a whole.

The situation in Latin America also gives cause for some concern. Notwithstanding the several factors which should enable Latin America to move forward in its economic and social development, the area as a whole is finding it very hard to consolidate satisfactory growth rates. Many of the difficulties encountered are home-made and must be eliminated by the Latin American countries themselves, while others stem from Latin America's economic relations with the rest of the world and their solution must be sought in an effective and continuous policy of international understanding and cooperation.

At the same time, I must make clear my belief that, while we face up to the existence of national and even international situations which are beyond the control of the United Nations and recognize the harmful effects which they may have on the progress of international cooperation within its sphere of activity, the United Nations should be enabled to act more effectively and decisively than it has done so far on many of the matters before it. We cannot wait for the world to right itself—for the great powers, in particular, to adjust their differences—before applying greater determination and, if necessary, a larger sacrifice of time-honored attitudes to the solution of urgent problems.

It has, of course, been partly because of the deterioration in the international situation that it has not been possible to make greater progress in regard to such basic issues as disarmament. The world disarmament conference still remains a somewhat distant goal. The problem of nonproliferation of nuclear weapons has gained added urgency and there is a greatly increased need for early action on account of the terrible prospect of more countries joining the "nuclear club." It is also, in my view, both necessary and feasible to agree upon a ban of all nuclear tests. I hope that the discussions at the forthcoming session of the General Assembly will demonstrate, above all to the nuclear powers themselves, how essential it is to make speedy progress in regard to these matters.

Moreover, the international situations to which I have referred, the rise of tensions and the emergence of new dangers in so many parts of the world, point to the need for a stronger rather than a weaker United Nations, and one which can be relied upon to undertake peace-keeping operations wherever such action could help in the restoration of stable conditions. Unfortunately, although there seems to be a measure of agreement that these operations have been effective in the past and could prove useful in the future, we are still far from agreement on basic principles. I very much hope that, in the months to come, the general membership and in particular those Members which have a special responsibility with regard to the maintenance of international peace and security, may find it possible, within the Charter, to agree upon the procedures to be followed in launching such operations, the responsibility of the various organs in their actual conduct, and the financial arrangements by which the expenditures involved may be met. I must draw attention to the fact that the peace-keeping activities of the United Nations, perhaps more than any other part of its work, have enabled the Organization to gain a measure of public confidence which is in danger of being lost if the Member states remain deadlocked on the constitutional and financial questions involved.

I should like to add, in this connection, that I believe that regional organizations will have an important role to play in future in reducing tensions within their regions and in promotiong cooperative efforts to attain common ends. The work of the United Nations at the regional level in the economic and social fields has won universal acclaim; the regional economic commissions have become increasingly effective in helping the developing countries not merely through research and studies but also by direct operational activities, including those which have led to the establishment of economic and social planning institutes and development banks. The work of inter-governmental regional bodies outside the United Nations can also, I am sure, contribute to the solution of problems between countries within a region. However, there are certain questions of jurisdiction and competence which arise with regard to the maintenance of international peace and security, especially in the peace-keeping field, and concerning which the role of the regional organizations requires clearer definition. Some time ago, I suggested that a study of the functioning of regional organizations in terms of their respective charters might be useful, and I mention it again in the belief that governments should wish to follow it up.

It is as important for a stronger United Nations to continue the long-term task of building the peace as it is to equip itself for helping countries to keep the peace. It is not enough, in my opinion, for the United Nations to deal where it can, and as the case arises, with each specific problem that threatens world peace. The causes of tension in the world have to be attacked at all of their many roots. We have the means of doing so and we have made a start. While, for example, the international activities in the fields of economic and social development and human rights do not figure in the headlines, the fact is that the greater part of the resources of the United Nations and its family of agencies is devoted to these tasks. The manner in which they are undertaken has a direct relationship to the reduction of tensions. I have said many times that it is essential that the gulf between the rich and the poor countries should be narrowed. I attach the greatest importance to the governments of Member states taking seriously the goals of the United Nations Development Decade and making deliberate progress toward the achievement of these goals.

There are other causes of tension which cannot be left to resolve themselves. In particular, I feel that the United Nations must make a sustained attack on the problems which we might, because of their origin or their nature, describe as the problems of colonialism. While recognizing that substantial progress has been made, we cannot afford to forget that the process of decolonization has not been completed. A hard core of actual colonialism still exists, particularly in Africa. It is coupled with the kindred problem of racial discrimination, and this evil in turn subjects the majority of the population of one of the largest independent states in Africa to conditions akin to the worst type of colonial subjection. I believe that in these situations there lies a great opportunity for statesmanship on the part of the colonial powers—an opportunity which they must seize before it is too late.

It is impossible, moreover, to view some of these outstanding problems—whether it is the position of the United Nations with regard to the crisis in Southeast Asia or the lack of progress in disarmament—without relating them to the fact that the United Nations has not yet attained the goal of universality of membership. In the long run the Organization cannot be expected to function to full effect if one fourth of the human race is not allowed to participate in its deliberations. I know that there are serious political difficulties involved in correcting this situation; but I hope that the long-term advantages may be more clearly seen and the necessary adjustments made.

This process may take some further time. Meanwhile, I feel that all countries should be encouraged and enabled, if they wish to do so, to follow the work of the Organization more closely. It could only be of benefit to them and to the United Nations as a whole to enable them to maintain observers at Headquarters, at the United Nations Office at Geneva, and in the regional economic commissions, and to expose them to the impact of the work of the Organization and to the currents and cross-currents of opinion that prevail within it, as well as to give them some opportunity to contribute to that exchange. Such contacts and intercommunication would surely lead to a better understanding of the problems of the world and a more realistic approach to their solution. In this matter I have felt myself obliged to follow the established tradition by which only certain governments have been enabled to maintain observers. I commend this question for further examination by the General Assembly so that the Secretary-General may be given a clear directive as to the policy to be followed in the future in the light, I would hope, of these observations.

The United Nations is an experiment in multilateral international diplomacy. Governments maintain here permanent representatives who have to carry out instructions understandably designed to promote the political and other interests of the governments concerned. At the same time, however, these governments have subscribed to the principles and ideals of the Charter and they have to recognize that one of its basic purposes is to be "a centre for harmonizing the actions of nations" in the attainment of the common ends for which the United Nations was established. I am glad that in most cases the representatives of Member states do not, in their pursuit of national interests, forget the larger interests of humanity represented by this Organization. I personally believe that it should be possible for the governments of Member states in all cases to use the United Nations as a center for harmonizing their actions so that the interests of humanity may not suffer but may be properly served.

In these observations I have stressed some of the basic beliefs which I have held in the discharge of my functions as Secretary-General over the last fifty-eight months. I feel that this is an appropriate occasion for me to urge that the problems to which I have referred and the suggestions which I have made deserve careful consideration if the Organization is to be strengthened, if peace is to be preserved and promoted, and if we are to make real progress toward the goal of the economic and social advancement of all peoples. There are many ways of reaching these objectives of peace and well-being, and I do not believe that anyone should adopt a dogmatic approach to them. Conditions differ widely from country to country and each has the right, within the broad framework of the principles of the United Nations, to pursue its goals in its own way and by means which it judges most appropriate and fruitful. At the same time I believe that the ideological differences that have divided the world are beginning to show signs of losing their sharp edge, and I approach the end of my term of office with some confidence that, over the years, the United Nations will prove to be the means by which mankind will be able not only to survive but also to achieve a great human synthesis.

U THANT
Secretary-General

September 15, 1966

CORRESPONDENCE WITH POPE PAUL VI

U THANT's great admiration for Pope Paul VI and their cordial relationship is reflected once more in the following messages. At his press conference on September 19 (p. 299), the Secretary-General said he considered Pope Paul "not only a great leader of a great religion, but also a great human being with an extraordinary awareness of the problems of war and peace and with a genuine dedication to the cause of peace and progress and human rights." Noting that the Pontiff had designated October 4, the first anniversary of his visit to the United Nations, as a day of universal prayer, Thant said this was significant because it was "the recognition by the Holy Father of the universal acceptance of his visit to the United Nations as a truly historic event." Thant was particularly pleased by the initiative of Pope Paul in establishing an organism within the Roman Catholic Church to educate and stimulate Catholics in the field of social justice and development and by the Pontiff's promise that the agency would maintain close relations with the United Nations family of agencies.

1. Message from the Secretary-General on the Occasion of the Anniversary of Pope Paul's Visit to the United Nations

NEW YORK   OCTOBER 4, 1966

ON THIS FIRST anniversary of Your Holiness' visit to the United Nations, I wish to recall the enduring inspiration of that day and of Your Holiness' message to the General Assembly.

The presence of a great spiritual leader in our midst and his historic words of wisdom, reason, and compassion had, and continue to have, a profound effect upon those who labor for peace here in the United Nations. That effect has been preserved and reinforced by subse-

SOURCE: UN Press Release SG/SM/577.

quent pronouncements of Your Holiness, including your letter of January 24, 1966, on the occasion of the meeting of the Committee of Eighteen on Disarmament, your message addressed through me to the Governing Council of the United Nations Development Programme on May 26 of this year, and your recent and most moving appeal for peace in the world.

In sending Your Holiness greetings on this day, may I express again, as Secretary-General of the United Nations, my gratitude to you for having brought your great spiritual authority and strength to the support of the efforts of the United Nations for peace and human well-being and my confident hope that your inspiring endeavors and our labors will not prove to be in vain.

I beg Your Holiness to accept the renewed expression of my profound gratitude and homage.

---

2. Letter from the Secretary-General

NEW YORK   NOVEMBER 21, 1966

DURING THE CURRENT SESSION of the General Assembly which is drawing to its close, there has been considerable interest in, and deep appreciation of, the efforts of Your Holiness on behalf of world peace and the economic and social progress of mankind. In particular, the phrase that you have made your own: "Development is the new word for peace" is one which every passing month underlines in importance as the evidence accumulates of faltering food supplies, growing hunger, more uncontrollable urban migration and worklessness, and behind it all, more exasperation and more despair.

The concern shown by Your Holiness for these difficult and chronic issues is a source of great encouragement to me and all my colleagues. Ever since the Bishops gathered at the Vatican Council voted to establish an organism of the universal Church to educate and stimulate the Catholic community in the field of worldwide social justice and development, I have been following with the closest

SOURCE: UN Press Release SG/SM/639, January 13, 1967.

interest the evolution of this proposal and I was delighted to read this summer of the appointment of a committee under His Eminence Cardinal Roy to make practical recommendations for the establishment of the proposed organism for social justice and development. I myself have maintained that the task of peace-building is as important as peace-making. I also believe that we shall never be able to persuade governments to give the tasks of development their essential priority unless we can help to form and encourage a really enlightened public opinion on the vital connection between development and peace. From the standpoint of my own office, I am made to realize every day that the needed scale of education and enlightenment is simply vast. We must try, in season and out of season, to reach the minds and consciences of people, to tell them the facts of hunger and need, to arouse their intelligence, stir their hearts, and confirm their commitment.

It is a great consolation to me to know that a body with such universal influence as the Catholic Church is ready to give a vital lead in this role of worldwide education and stimulus. The progress of this work will be watched with eager interest, not only by the United Nations but also by its family of agencies which, I am sure, would wish to maintain closest and most fruitful cooperation with the instrument you might decide to establish for this great purpose. I look forward eagerly to the news of further developments and I firmly believe that out of your initiative will grow one of the most important educative influences in our evolving international society.

I beg Your Holiness to accept the renewed expression of my profound gratitude and homage.

---

3. Pope Paul's Reply

ROME   DECEMBER 12, 1966

WE ARE COMFORTED by your comments concerning the establishment of an organism of the Catholic Church to educate and to stimulate the

SOURCE: UN Press Release SG/SM/639, January 13, 1967.

Catholic community in the field of worldwide social justice and development. No opportunity has been lost to encourage influential leaders and to impress upon them the urgent need for brotherly cooperation and assistance in a spirit of true respect and understanding.

Only by an awareness of the gravity of the world situation and by a firm commitment to accept necessary sacrifices, can the prosperous and emerging nations take their rightful place in the family of nations and develop in an atmosphere of peace for the general well-being of their citizens. In season and out of season We shall continue to reach people in the confident hope that such fraternal collaboration will become a reality instead of merely a fond desire. Soon this new organism will be established, and it will maintain close relations with all organizations interested in this vast and pressing problem and, in particular, with the family of agencies sponsored by the United Nations.

We avail Ourself of this occasion to express to you, Honorable Sir, Our heartfelt greetings on the forthcoming Feast of Christmas, the Feast of Peace and Love.

THE SITUATION IN VIETNAM

NOVEMBER AND DECEMBER

As 1966, neared its end, U Thant continued to press for his three-point plan for Vietnam peace negotiations. He renewed his proposals in a message to Lord Fenner Brockway, Chairman of the British Council for Peace in Vietnam, on November 11 and in a letter to Ambassador Arthur J. Goldberg, permanent representative of the United States, on December 30. He told Goldberg that he welcomed a request by the United States government that he take whatever steps he considered necessary to arrange a cease-fire, but he added that this was a situation in which a powerful nation like the United States should take the initiative in the quest for peace. He said further that public opinion throughout the world favored a halt in the United States bombing of North Vietnam. If the United States would stop the bombing, he said, "and if the New Year cease-fire could be extended by all the parties, I feel hopeful that thereafter some favorable developments may follow."

---

1. Message to Lord Brockway, Chairman of the British Council for Peace in Vietnam

NEW YORK   NOVEMBER 11, 1966

YOU HAVE ASKED ME what every one of us could do to contribute to bring an end to the war in Vietnam. This is a proper—indeed an essential—question, for the prolongation of this conflict is a source of concern and anxiety for all human beings. The tremendous sufferings engendered by this war cannot be accepted as inevitable. Furthermore, the dangerous escalation of armed force has been accompanied by an increasing distrust among governments and peoples, resulting in a dramatic setback for human development.

This wall of suspicion between the parties as to their final objec-

SOURCE: UN Press Release SG/SM/609 Rev. 1.

tives has become in itself an obstacle to peace. That is why I have drawn attention, some time ago, to three preliminary steps to be taken by the parties as a proof of the sincerity of their peaceful intentions. These initiatives, independent as they are one from the other, could—I still believe—contribute to creating an atmosphere more conducive to negotiations:

1. The cessation of the bombing of North Vietnam;
2. The scaling down of all military activities by all sides in South Vietnam;
3. The willingness to enter into discussions with those who are actually fighting.

If the bombing is to cease, there should be no conditions, no time limit. The scaling down of all military activities by all parties is a preparatory measure toward gradually restoring the problem to its true national framework and it is in this light that the parties, inasmuch as they are concerned, should initiate it. As to the third step, it should not be construed as prejudging in any way the substance of a final settlement.

On the larger issues concerning this settlement, my personal stand has always been clear. There is no other way than a return to the 1954 Geneva Agreements guaranteeing the independence and neutrality of the whole of Vietnam. If there are conflicting views among Vietnamese concerning the future of South Vietnam, these can only be reconciled by the people of South Vietnam and cannot be decided beforehand otherwise than through peaceful processes and without foreign intervention.

A settlement along these lines is not beyond the reach of those who have the power, and therefore the responsibility, to decide. I am convinced that all the forces of peace in the world will stand ready to help them should they be prepared to undertake the renewed efforts to restore peace. Perhaps there may be some limited risks involved in such efforts, but they are nothing compared to the major risks that we all face unless this fateful trend toward a larger war is reversed in time.

2. Letter to Arthur J. Goldberg, Permanent Representative of the United States

NEW YORK   DECEMBER 30, 1966

I HAVE VERY carefully studied your letter to me dated December 19, 1966 [S/7641], on the subject of Vietnam. May I say how appreciative I am of your government's request that I might take whatever steps I "consider necessary to bring about the necessary discussions which could lead to such a cease-fire," and especially of the assurance that "the Government of the United States will cooperate fully . . . in getting such discussions started promptly and in bringing them to a successful completion."

You are, of course, aware of my preoccupation with the question of Vietnam during the last three years. This preoccupation stems not merely from my recognition of the serious risk that the continuation of this war poses to international peace and security. To a very large extent it is influenced even more by my deep sympathy, and indeed anguish, over the untold suffering of the people of Vietnam who have known no peace for a generation, the tragic loss of lives on all sides, the increasing number of civilian casualties, the appalling destruction of property, and the vast and mounting sums being spent on the prosecution of the war.

In this context may I also stress my strong feeling, publicly expressed more than once, that what is really at stake in Vietnam, unless an early end to the hostilities is brought about, is the independence, the identity, and the survival of the country itself.

I have already referred to the serious risk to international peace and security that the continuance of the war in Vietnam poses. There is an ever present danger that the war in Vietnam may spread, and even spill over its frontiers. Already the war has poisoned relations among states and has, as I said earlier, brought to a halt the great

SOURCE: Security Council Official Records, Twenty-first Year, Supplement for October, November and December 1966, document S/7658.

enterprise of cooperation and understanding between nations which had barely made a modest start in recent years.

This is how I see the overall situation. It is a situation in which a powerful nation like the United States should take the initiative in the quest for peace and show an enlightened and humanitarian spirit. I believe that in the circumstances only action deliberately undertaken in such a spirit which, because of its power and position, the United States can afford to undertake, can halt the escalation and enlargement of this war, and thus bring about a turning of the tide toward peace.

Let me take this opportunity of reiterating my three-point program, to which I still firmly adhere:

1. The cessation of the bombing of North Vietnam;
2. The scaling down of all military activities by all sides in South Vietnam;
3. The willingness to enter into discussions with those who are actually fighting.

I strongly believe that this three-point program, of which the cessation of the bombing of North Vietnam is the first and essential part, is necessary to create the possibility of fruitful discussions leading to a just and honorable settlement of the problem of Vietnam on the basis of the Geneva Agreements of 1954.

I also wish to recall that in the course of the twenty-first session, in the debate of the General Assembly, the majority of the delegations have endorsed the three-point program. Many more heads of delegation also specifically pleaded for the cessation of the bombing of North Vietnam. It seems to me that this is a very clear indication of the public opinion of the world at large on this issue.

Leaders of religious faiths all over the world have also expressed their anxiety about the continuance and escalation of the war in Vietnam. Only a few days ago the General Secretary of the World Council of Churches expressed a similar concern.

When His Holiness the Pope made his plea for an extended cease-fire, I endorsed it and I urged all parties to heed his appeal. In my statement in the General Assembly on December 2, I said:

. . . Is it too much to hope that what is made possible for just a couple of days by the occurrence of common holidays may soon prove feasible for a longer period by the new commitments that peace requires, so that an atmosphere may be created which is necessary for meaningful talks to be held in the quest for a peaceful solution?

This is what I have in mind when I refer to the need for a humanitarian approach. If action in such a spirit could be undertaken, even without conditions, by the United States to stop the bombing of North Vietnam, and if the New Year cease-fire could be extended by all the parties, I feel hopeful that thereafter some favorable developments may follow. I am reminded in this context that in 1954 negotiations for a peaceful settlement were conducted even without a formal cease-fire and while fighting was going on. Even though there may be sporadic breaches of the cease-fire on account of lack of control and communication, I believe that this would provide a welcome respite for private contacts and diplomatic explorations so that, in time, formal discussions can take place on the basis of the Geneva Agreements of 1954.

I am writing this letter to you after long deliberation. I would like to close by assuring you and your government that, in my personal and private capacity, I shall continue to exert my utmost efforts and to explore every avenue which may lead to a just, honorable, and peaceful solution of the problem of Vietnam.

As your letter under reply was issued as a Security Council document, I am arranging for this reply also to be issued as a document of the Security Council.

Statement in the Third Committee
on the Twentieth Anniversary of UNICEF

NEW YORK   DECEMBER 9, 1966

ON DECEMBER 9, 1966, U Thant made one of his rare appearances before the Third (Social, Humanitarian and Cultural) Committee to take part in a ceremony observing the twentieth anniversary of the creation of the United Nation's Children's Fund (UNICEF). He told the Committee that of the billion children across the world, 900 million lived in communities still struggling with overwhelming problems of sickness, illiteracy, and poverty. What UNICEF aid did for Europe's children after the Second World War, he said, must now be done for the millions in need in Asia, Africa, the Middle East, and Latin America.

MADAME CHAIRMAN, the Chairman of the UNICEF Executive Board, Members of the Third Committee:

On this occasion it is natural that our minds should go back twenty years to the creation of UNICEF. The Children's Fund flowed from the creation of the United Nations itself in the aftermath of the Second World War. The chain of circumstances leading to its birth was most fitting, since the very first words of the Charter of the United Nations are about children.

The Preamble, adopted only eighteen months before UNICEF's inception, spoke first, you will recall, of how "We the peoples of the United Nations" were "determined to save succeeding generations from the scourge of war." We were thinking then of the children of the world who became the focus of UNICEF's work. They were the "succeeding generations." We felt that it would be an intolerable blot in the record of mankind if war were to engulf and ravage their world, as it had the world of their parents and grandparents. In a very real sense, with those first few words of the Charter, the United Nations became a kind of mirror to the conscience of us all, as we looked at

SOURCE: UN Press Release SG/SM/622. The summary record is given in General Assembly Official Records, Twenty-first Session, Third Committee, 1454th meeting.

our children and contemplated the kind of world we must try to pass on to them. Those children gave us our mandate in the United Nations. And their very condition, amid the ruins of war and the poverty of developing countries, gave UNICEF its mandate for action.

I see the closest connection between the responsibility of the United Nations to create the conditions for peace between nations, and UNICEF's responsibility to care for those "succeeding generations," the young inheritors of the peace we hoped and still hope to build. In this task of peace-building, children can themselves become, so to speak, junior architects. I say this because the receptivity and fresh outlook of children may be a key to understanding among all peoples of the world. Not yet weighed down with artificial prejudices and narrow provincialism, children should have the opportunity to remain free of these stifling handicaps, enfeebling to themselves and dangerous to the world at large. It is through values of universal brotherhood first felt in the hearts of children that the minds of men can open out to the creation of a peaceful world community.

We can bequeath to our children the inertia and mental stagnation of hunger and illiteracy—or the creative energy and open-mindedness of a child properly fed and schooled and cared for by family and community.

Gunnar Jahn, Chairman of the Nobel Committee of the Norwegian Storting, said a year ago during the UNICEF Nobel Peace Award ceremonies that at the heart of the fight for peace is the development of the mind, beginning with the child.

In short, what we are now beginning to recognize as the vital process of human-resource development is also the development of generations that can positively nurture peace between nations. The two processes are surely inseparable. It is enough to consider the stark arithmetic of what we could call "two mankinds" which, like yesterday's "two nations" within one nation, now confront us as a billion children across the world. On one hand, 300 million children born in communities that can give them a relatively healthy, educated, and prosperous life; on the other, 900 million children born into communities still struggling with overwhelming problems of sickness, illiteracy, and poverty. There is our "succeeding generation"—and there, supremely, is the challenge that UNICEF has taken up. Madame Chairman, Members of the Third Committee, all of us who have followed the history of UNICEF may wish to take this opportunity to congratulate this member of the United Nations family for the work of the past twenty years.

But I know that the supporters of the Children's Fund throughout the world would agree that this is not a moment for much time to be spent in retrospective congratulation. As directly engaged in the cause of peace as any other unit of the United Nations family, UNICEF has a monumental task before it.

That task began in Europe twenty years ago and it was done. Now we need to go farther on a journey of the mind and heart to other generations whose lives and future must now be safeguarded in turn.

UNICEF's challenge now lies in Asia, where the Executive Director, Mr. Henry Labouisse, is at this moment looking at the needs of millions of children; and in the villages and cities of Africa, the Eastern Mediterranean, and Latin America. What UNICEF aid did for Europe's rising generation must now be done for these hundreds of millions of children.

Therefore, I would like to repeat the appeal the first Secretary-General of the United Nations, Mr. Trygve Lie, made twenty years ago when he said:

The provision of necessary resources . . . is a matter of the utmost urgency if the lives and future of the rising generation are to be safeguarded.

Statement to the Staff

NEW YORK   DECEMBER 21, 1966

A NUMBER OF CHANGES had taken place in the administration of the Secretariat during U Thant's first term. For one thing, the staff had continued to expand with the creation of new agencies, such as the United Nation's Conference on Trade and Development, the United Nation's Institute for Training and Research, and the United Nation's Industrial Development Organization. It had also achieved wider geographic representation under new policies initiated by Dag Hammarskjöld and implemented by Thant. Since the new recruitment policy, designed to fill posts in the professional category on as wide a geographic basis as possible, became effective in 1962, Thant stated in his Annual Report that only Eastern Europe had not moved up to the desired level, although fifty-one new staff members from Eastern Europe had been added during the year ending August 31.

Since he became Secretary-General on November 3, 1961, Thant had made it a practice, as Hammarskjöld had, to meet with the staff periodically—usually on Staff Day, to review Secretariat problems. Because of the uncertainty of his own status, he did not address the staff until December 21, after the General Assembly concluded its session. He mentioned the subject of geographic distribution in his statement along with some other changes implemented since he took office. For example, he noted that the rate of staff advancement had been increased and that the full amount of the gross salaries payable to staff members had been made pensionable.

As I BEGIN my renewed term as Secretary-General I should like to share a few thoughts with you. In my acceptance speech on December 2 I said, " . . . And yet, although little has happened to brighten the outlook of the months ahead, my conviction stands undiminished that the United Nations remains the best instrument by which nations may cooperate for the development and the peace of their people. My acceptance of an extended mandate today stems out of this deep conviction, as much as out of a sense of duty. And I assure Members of this Organization that all my faith and all my efforts are unhesitatingly pledged to maintaining and developing this Organization as an

SOURCE: UN Press Release SG/SM/631.

indispensable center for harmonizing the actions of nations in the attainment of our common ends, and as an increasingly effective instrument for peace and development. In this task, I have the considerable asset which the Secretariat represents and which I am proud to lead. All the organizational and other administrative improvements that are necessary will be undertaken with the assistance of my colleagues so that all Members may continue to rely upon the efficiency, competence, and integrity of this body of dedicated servants of the Organization. . . ."

My first thought after beginning my second term was to meet with you all personally and individually if possible. Owing to the fact that the General Assembly was in session and owing to my other preoccupations this could not be done. I therefore thought I would meet with you collectively today.

During the five years and more that I have been the Secretary-General of this Organization, many changes have taken place in the world. This is not the occasion to dwell in detail on the various aspects of the international scene. I have dealt with them extensively in my Introduction to the Annual Report every year and most recently in my statement of September 1.

While the world situation today is no doubt dark and gloomy, we must not forget that the prospect facing the Organization in September 1961 was infinitely more bleak. I take this occasion to pay tribute to my distinguished predecessor, Mr. Dag Hammarskjöld, who died in the pursuit of peace. His death plunged the Organization into a crisis from which it took quite some time to recover. In connection with the organizational and administrative improvements of the Secretariat, to which I have referred in my statement of December 2. I have been reading some papers prepared and published in the middle of 1961, and they bring back to my mind the difficult situation that existed at that time.

I said a moment ago that I do not wish to dwell on the various aspects of the international scene. I do believe, however, that it would be appropriate for me to mention a number of new organs that have been set up in the interval in the pursuit of the twin goals of peace and progress. I have in mind particularly the United Nations Conference on Trade and Development, the United Nations Institute for Training and Research, and the Centre for Industrial Development which will become the United Nations Industrial Development

Organization from January 1, 1967. Meanwhile, as you all know, the Special Fund and the Technical Assistance Board have been merged into one single instrument as UNDP [United Nations Development Programme].

The setting up of these new institutions shows how much the international community wishes to rely on the work of the Secretariat in the pursuit of peace and development. It is my conviction that if this pursuit is to make accelerated progress it will depend very much on the dedication, effectiveness, and impartiality of the Secretariat.

The establishment of a Secretariat, international both in composition and in outlook, has been one of the significant events of our time. In the light of the experience of the past five years, I see no workable alternative to the basic principles laid down by the founders of the United Nations for the administration of the Secretariat.

Some of you may recall that five years ago the composition of the Secretariat was a hotly debated issue in the Fifth [Administrative and Budgetary] Committee. The understandable concern of many Member states to see in the Secretariat a true reflection of the membership of the Organization had not yet assumed a workable administrative form. Today, the issue is still debated, but not as much about basic principles. A set of guidelines has now been in operation for four years. It has led to very substantial improvements in the representative character of the Secretariat. The Secretariat has come to be the most diversified body of officials ever assembled under one direction in the service of one organization. Nationals of 112 countries, comprising almost the entire membership, drawn from all parts of the world, and imbued with practically every known culture make up this corps of international civil servants.

The process of broadening the international outlook of the Secretariat is necessarily a continuing one. There is room for further improvement. But there is little reason for disputing the overriding Charter considerations of competence, efficiency, and integrity.

This past year has provided ample evidence that the Member states are anxious to ensure the most efficient use of the limited resources made available for international cooperation. One of the prerequisites of efficiency in any administration is a reasonable measure of continuity and a firm base upon which traditions are established. This is particularly so in an international administration which is denied the benefits of competitive recruitment from among graduates of a single educational system possessing a common cultural background. As in previous years, the task ahead remains how to reconcile the requirements of efficiency with the legitimate demands for as fully international a composition as possible.

In the past five years, several tangible improvements have also taken place in the conditions of service of the staff.

The United Nations has kept pace with the best national systems of compensation for employees engaged in comparable work. I know that a system of four separate categories of staff, which are governed by different principles of pay and therefore may have different adjustments at different times, is not the most felicitous of schemes. But the realities of an international administration cannot be ignored. And the reasons which have led to the distinctions between the categories have lost little of their original validity. So we must continue to make the most effective use of existing arrangements to ensure fair and equitable compensation to all members of the staff.

An important measure of considerable interest to many of you in recent years has now been approved for application with effect from next year, 1967. I am gratified that a solution has been found to the problem faced by staff members who are subject to the higher rate of the United States social security tax. With effect from January 1967 (that is, in respect of the social security tax payable for 1966), the difference between the amount of the tax which a staff member is required to pay as an employee of the United Nations and the amount which he would have paid as an employee of an outside employer will be fully reimbursed.

The rate of staff advancement has been measurably increased. In 1961, there were altogether 114 staff members in the General Service category at Headquarters who were promoted to the two senior levels. By comparison, in the first eleven months of this year, 1966, a total of 189 such promotions were granted, representing a rate of increase which is considerably above the increase in the number of posts. In the professional category, there were 150 promotions for all duty stations in the year 1961, as against 293 in the first eleven months of this year. Arrangements have recently been made for regular reviews of staff, both in the Manual Workers and Field Service categories, as a result of which the first promotion registers for these staff members have already been issued and implemented.

So far as the General Service category is concerned, I reiterate that it is the policy of the United Nations to provide working conditions that truly exemplify the "best prevailing conditions." At the same time you are aware that as part of a long-term plan to provide a more meaningful career for the large group of staff in this category, I have asked the offices concerned to undertake, in consultation with representatives of the Staff Council, an early review of the structure of the category so that there may be a proper restructuring of the General Service category on a suitable basis for establishing the best prevailing conditions, including the question of fringe benefits. This review will have high priority and I hope that at least the consideration of some of the items involved in the review may be completed by the end of March 1967.

Since March of last year the full amount of the gross salaries payable to United Nations staff members has been pensionable. This change in the conditions of service represents one of the more significant improvements in the history of the social security protection provided by the Organization.

Beginning next year, health insurance made available to the staff on a cost-sharing basis between the Organization and the staff participating in the scheme will be extended to cover retired staff members and their families. This additional protection for those who have already left the service of the Secretariat and those who will do so in the years ahead is a further step in the direction of keeping pace with the best practices of national administrations.

The system of legal assistance to any staff member seeking to appeal an administrative decision or subject to disciplinary action has been in effective operation since 1962. Over these past years, many staff members who wished to protect their rights under their letters of appointment were able to avail themselves of the advice and help of a counsel selected in consultation with the Staff Council from among members of the Secretariat. The disposition of the cases brought before the Appeals Board and the Disciplinary Committee, and the judgments of the Administrative Tribunal, bear witness to the value of this unique system of free administration of justice.

The panel of counsel to assist staff members in need of legal advice is not the only product of the close cooperation between the representatives of the staff and the representatives of the Secretary-General concerned with administration. Throughout these past years, conscious efforts have been directed toward enlargement of the area of consultation. Although changes in representation resulting from periodic elections inevitably entail a certain break of continuity in the process, the system has worked well and will, I am sure, continue to do so in the future. I am glad to know that joint efforts to improve the conduct and content of consultation are already under way. I need hardly assure you of my deep interest in this, and of the access your accredited representatives consequently have to me, both directly and through the established channels.

I am confident that recognition of the weight to be attached to the views of the elected organ of the Staff Association, along with recognition of the responsibilities conferred upon the Administration, will remain the two cornerstones of the system of staff relations which has been built up since the earliest days of the Secretariat into a sound and creditable tradition.

Only a few days ago, a special ballot held in the Second [Economic and Financial] Committee of the General Assembly, accompanied as it was by a keen competition for the honor of serving as host to a new organ of the United Nations, the United Nations Industrial Development Organization, provided a timely reminder that the location of an office can be a welcome occurrence. It was also a reminder of the growth and spread of United Nations activities. This expansion means that some of the methods of work which were suitable in earlier years may not be adequate at present. It is my intention in the coming years to ensure that our organizational pattern and administrative procedures are adapted to the new demands placed upon the Secretariat as the executive arm of the Organization.

I would like to take this opportunity to thank each and every one of you for your part in the smooth running of the busy session of the General Assembly which concluded yesterday. Without the extraordinary efforts put in by the various services of the Secretariat, the task facing the Assembly, the Security Council, the Economic and Social Council, and some of the subsidiary organs which have all met during these past three months would have been well-nigh impossible. I hope the coming few days will give you a well-deserved respite.

In accepting my appointment for a further term of office, as I recalled at the very beginning of this address, I had occasion to give expression to my warm feelings about the Secretariat I am privileged to head. I look forward to our continued cooperation.

Inspired by the ideals of the Charter, presenting as we do the image of one human race bound together in countless ways, let us carry on the tradition of a loyal, dedicated, and effective Secretariat engaged in the selfless service of all nations of the world.

May I conclude by wishing you all an enjoyable holiday and a very happy New Year.

❧ 1967 ❧

THE SITUATION IN VIETNAM

JANUARY AND FEBRUARY

IN HIS FIRST PRESS CONFERENCE of 1967, held on January 10, U Thant discussed the Vietnam situation at length, although carefully avoiding any information as to what new steps, if any, he had taken personally to help bring about peace talks. Any premature revelations, he said, might spoil the chances for fruitful results. In response to questions, he declined to acknowledge that either the United States or North Vietnam had rejected his three-point proposal. Washington, he said, had tied a possible halt in the bombing of North Vietnam to reciprocal action by Hanoi. He told correspondents it was for them to interpret whether this was a rejection, an acceptance, or a conditional acceptance. As for Hanoi, he declared, it was well known that both North Vietnam and the National Liberation Front (Vietcong) had taken exception to his second point, which called for a gradual de-escalation of the fighting after the implementation of a bombing halt.

During the conference, Thant spoke out candidly about his differences with the United States on some aspects of the war. First, he challenged the view that the National Liberation Front was "a stooge" to Hanoi. Second, he said he did not subscribe to the so-called domino theory which held that if South Vietnam fell to the communists, then other neighboring countries would suffer the same fate one by one. And, third, he disputed the view that South Vietnam was strategically vital to Western interests and Western security. It was his opinion, he said, that the leaders in Vietnam were obsessed with the principle of nonalignment. He declined to elaborate on the status of his relations with the United States government except to state that "there are basic differences in our approach, in our concepts, and even in our assessment of the situation."

1. Transcript of Press Conference

NEW YORK   JANUARY 10, 1967

THE SECRETARY-GENERAL: Mr. Raghavan[1] and friends: First of all, I should like to congratulate you, Mr. Raghavan, on your very well-deserved election as President of the United Nations Correspondents Association for 1967. You have established your reputation here as a serious, responsible, and untiring correspondent for a number of years. And so your election did not come to me as a surprise. I look forward to a year of very close cooperation with you and your colleagues, as in the past.

To the ladies and gentlemen of the Press, first of all I wish you a very Happy New Year and I can also assure you of my continued personal cooperation, as in the past.

I do not propose to make a long introductory statement. According to tradition, I shall give the floor first to the President.

MR. RAGHAVAN (President, United Nations Correspondents Association): Mr. Secretary-General, I deeply appreciate your very kind words. On this, your first formal meeting with us in your second term, may I convey to you on behalf of the United Nations Press Corps and on my own behalf our sincere good wishes and felicitations, and say how happy we are that our mutual associations are to continue. I am sure I am speaking not only on behalf of all of us here but also of world public opinion when I express the hope that the New Year will see the fruition of your efforts to bring peace to the part of the world you and I come from.

Sir, now I wish to ask you a question in my capacity as correspondent of the Press Trust of India. It is this:

Since your December 30 letter to Ambassador Goldberg,[2] there have been a number of developments: Mr. Goldberg's reply to you and remarks and statements flowing out of Washington, Premier Van

SOURCE: UN Press Release SG/SM/637.

[1]Chakravarti Raghavan, Press Trust of India.
[2]Arthur J. Goldberg, permanent representative of the United States.

Dong's interview with Mr. Harrison Salisbury and Mai Van Bo's remarks to the diplomatic Press in Paris.

In the light of these, could you give us your assessment of the Vietnam situation and the responses of the two sides and the prospects for peace?

THE SECRETARY-GENERAL: First of all, Mr. Raghavan, I thank you for your very kind words about me and your best wishes. Regarding your question, I must say that some matters, like the delicate question of Vietnam, are better kept confidential for some time. What I mean is that the revelation of even some of the steps taken, or some of the actions taken, at the wrong time, that is, prematurely, could spoil the whole thing. I think Harrison Salisbury had a very pertinent piece in last Sunday's *New York Times* when he said, if I remember correctly, that preliminaries must be conducted with skill, tact, and complete absence of publicity or headlines. That is a very wise observation. So, as far as the private discussions and contacts are concerned, I am sure you will agree with me that it is not the right time for me—and, I hope, for anybody else—to disclose any event. As regards the published statements of Premier Pham Van Dong and Mr. Mai Van Bo, if my understanding is correct, there was nothing new as far as the position of the North Vietnamese government is concerned. They are just restating their old well-known positions, perhaps in new language.

QUESTION: Mr. Secretary-General, do you consider that the United States has rejected your first point on unconditional cessation of bombing and, if so, can you reconcile this with the pledge of full American support to do what you consider necessary to bring this crisis to the conference table?

THE SECRETARY-GENERAL: Everybody knows that my proposal involves a three-stage action. First of all, in my view, it is absolutely necessary that the bombing of North Vietnam must stop without conditions. Of course, as you all know, the United States reply is that it would stop the bombing of North Vietnam provided there was some reciprocal reaction from the other side. So it is up to any one of you to interpret whether it is a rejection or an acceptance or a conditional rejection or a conditional acceptance. But I still feel very strongly that there will be no move toward peace so long as the bombing of North Vietnam is going on.

QUESTION: Sir, in your opinion, are the reported political conflicts inside mainland China having any effect upon the present Vietnam situation?

THE SECRETARY-GENERAL: It is very difficult for me to assess the developments in China, as we have to rely on published accounts not necessarily originating in Peking. As you all know, the general assessment is that a very bitter power struggle has been going on in China for a long time, but I do not think anybody can come to any conclusion. Even the China experts, I am sure, will have conflicting interpretations of the developments in China. I am not in a position to assess or forecast what the eventuality will be and what the effects will be on the war in Vietnam. I think it is anybody's guess.

QUESTION: The United Nations has put great effort into the Upper Mekong region, and many countries, including the United States, have contributed funds toward the developments there. Meanwhile, in the very recent past, the United States has escalated the war and dropped many troops into the area of the Lower Mekong. Can life be destroyed so in the Lower Mekong without affecting the United Nations activities in the Upper Mekong?

THE SECRETARY-GENERAL: The war affects everything, not only the projected economic activities in the area but even the functioning of normal human life. So I am sure everybody will agree with me that the war hinders not only the Mekong project but all other economic and social activities contemplated by the governments or by the United Nations or by other agencies. That is one reason why we all should strive in the direction of the achievement of conditions for peace.

QUESTION: Focusing rather narrowly on the statement by Mai Van Bo in Paris—that if, after the definitive and unconditional cessation of the bombardments the American government proposes to enter into contact with the Hanoi government, "I believe this proposal will be examined and studied"—do you consider this a response toward peace?

THE SECRETARY-GENERAL: I have all along interpreted the North Vietnamese position in this way. For the last two years my understanding of North Vietnam's position was the same as stated by Mr. Mai Van Bo on January 5. If there is an unconditional cessation of bombing of North Vietnam, as I have been saying all along, I feel hopeful that there will be a definite move toward negotiations. So, as far as I am concerned, Mr. Bo's statement of January 5 did not come to me as a surprise. I have understood this all along.

QUESTION: In connection with the cessation of bombing, was there any suggestion made to you personally or through any other contact from Washington, either Ambassador Goldberg or anybody else, to arrange for a meeting during one of these cessations of bombing, either Christmas or New Year or maybe even the next New Year that comes up?

THE SECRETARY-GENERAL: As I said a little earlier, I do not think it would be very helpful to disclose any of the moves for private talks and preliminary discussions at this stage.

QUESTION: As you are aware, the Buddhist New Year falls in February. A recent report stated that for the Buddhists, February was an especially good time for peace according to the astrologists. As a Buddhist, would you care to comment, and could you delineate some of the good signs for peace in Vietnam appearing in February?

THE SECRETARY-GENERAL: I do not want to make any observations on the astrological aspects of war and peace, but, as I have stated in my reply to Ambassador Goldberg on December 30, I am all for the extension of the cease-fire, as must be obvious to all of you. Whether it is an auspicious time or not, I have nothing to say.

QUESTION: Discarding astrology, Mr. Secretary-General, in view of the present impasse, on the basis of what we have heard just now in all these questions and your replies, which do not seem too promising, how do you view, on the basis of your knowledge, hope for 1967 on the Vietnam question, which is posing a great danger for mankind?

THE SECRETARY-GENERAL: I do not think I should attempt to forecast events for 1967, but, as I have been saying all along, my assessment of the Vietnam war and my understanding of the developments leading to the war are different from the assessment and understanding of many people and many governments. I have been saying this for the last two years. I think it would be helpful if I elaborated on these differences to some extent.

First of all, I do not subscribe to the generally held view that the National Liberation Front in South Vietnam is a "stooge" of Hanoi. I do not agree with this thesis. In my view, the National Liberation Front, although receiving perhaps very substantial help from the North, is an independent entity in the same way as the National

Liberation Front of Algeria in the late 1950s was receiving very substantial help from Tunisia or Morocco or the United Arab Republic. Of course, there is one difference. In the case of Vietnam, there are the 1954 Geneva Agreements which resulted in the temporary division of the country into two zones with the demarcation line at the seventeenth parallel. In Algeria, that was not the case. Of course, on this I must admit that there are differences of opinion, but I have all along subscribed to the view that the National Liberation Front is not a "stooge" of Hanoi.

Second, I do not subscribe to the generally held view that if South Vietnam falls, then country X, then country Y, then country Z will follow. I do not agree with this so-called domino theory. In my view, the destiny of every country is shaped by its own peculiar circumstances, its national characteristics, its historical background, its own political philosophy. What is true of country X is not necessarily true of country Y or country Z.

Third, I do not subscribe to the view that South Vietnam is strategically vital to Western interests and Western security, whatever its political or ideological pattern may be, in the same way as—to give an extreme example—Yugoslavia for instance does not pose a threat to international peace and security. I think I know the mood of the leaders in Vietnam. I think that the leaders in Vietnam are very independent. They are very obsessed with the principle of nonalignment, which, as you know, is one of the twin objectives of the Geneva Agreements. And, speaking about the Geneva Agreements, it is worth recalling that Sir Anthony Eden, now Lord Avon, was one of their main architects. The twin principal objectives of the Geneva Agreements were independence and nonalignment.

If Vietnam is independent and militarily nonaligned, as I have been advocating, preferably with the guarantee of the big powers, including the United States, then I do not see how this could pose a threat to international peace or security or how Vietnam could be strategically vital to the interests and security of the West.

Those are some of the differences I have had in mind when I have been saying for the last two years that my approach to the problem and my assessment of the situation are different from the assessment and approach of many people and many governments.

QUESTION: You make a distinction between your own private personal diplomacy, and say, the undertakings of the General Assembly or the Security Council. There are reports that Hanoi does not accept this distinction. Would you comment on the possibility that it does not and that this might influence its attitude toward your three points?

THE SECRETARY-GENERAL: To my knowledge, Hanoi has not stated anything in that direction. Hanoi has never said that it accepts or does not accept the distinction between U Thant and the Secretary-General of the United Nations. Of course I know that Peking does not make that distinction.

QUESTION: Having stated so courageously and so sharply your differences—let us be frank, your differences are essentially differences with the United States government which is a party to the war; differences not only on the roots of understanding which you have just outlined but, more pertinently, on the question of the cessation of the war, that is, the cessation of the bombing of North Vietnam. What then remains in your relationship with the United States, which has apparently given you all the latitude—I think that is the word that was used—but is not accepting your premises? Do you feel that you are caught in a painful contradiction there in your negotiations or perhaps even in a crisis of confidence? This is a very sharp question and I hate to put it to you. But I know that you are not afraid of that kind of question.

THE SECRETARY-GENERAL: I do not think that it would be in the public interest if I expressed my feelings regarding the policies and actions of Member states, particularly those of the big powers.

I am grateful to the government of the United States for expressing its confidence in me and for asking me to use my good offices to bring about conditions for the cessation of hostilities in Vietnam. I am very thankful to the government of the United States for this. But of course, as you are aware, there are basic differences in our approach, in our concepts, and even in our assessment of the situation. Apart from that, I do not think that it would be helpful if I commented further.

QUESTION: I should like to ask a question on Rhodesia. You have been asked to report to the Security Council by March 1 and there is a threat implied of Council action at that time against noncooperators in sanctions. In view of the paucity of reports from Members on the actions they are taking, what hopes have you of making a significant statement to the Council by then?

THE SECRETARY-GENERAL: As you know, on the basis of the Security Council resolution of December 16, I have addressed a communication to all Member states as well as all members of the specialized agencies asking them to give me all pertinent information on the basis of the resolution. As you all know, the resolution involved some selective economic sanctions which are mandatory. I am proposing to address a second communication to all Member states and all members of the specialized agencies, with a comprehensive questionnaire on the list of commodities mentioned in the resolution, and asking for full information on the volume of trade in those particular commodities with a view to helping me in preparing my report for the Security Council. On the basis of the information thus received, I shall have to submit a report to the Security Council, which is due not later than March 1.

QUESTION: I have a question on the Israeli-Syrian situation. In your two reports to the Security Council on November 1 and 2 you said that Israel refuses to cooperate with the Mixed Armistice Commission. And then, in the second report, you said that Israel has managed to create a situation whereby Arab villagers in the demilitarized zone have been forced to leave their villages. Now, Israel complains that these villagers who are coming back to cultivate their lands are infiltrators from Syria, and Israel refuses to cooperate with the Mixed Armistice Commission. My question is: What steps will you take in order to force Israel to comply with the articles of the Mixed Armistice Agreement?

THE SECRETARY-GENERAL: On that question the attitude of Israel is well known, as its representatives have repeatedly stated it in the Security Council, and so I do not think I should interpret what the meaning of this statement is. On the question of cultivation in the demilitarized zone, you will remember that this is a time of the year when the rains begin to fall in the area, the grass grows, and cultivation starts. At this time of the year, whenever cultivation starts, there are sporadic shootings and incidents. So I would say that the present phase, in certain sections of the demilitarized zone between Israel and Syria, is more seasonal than anything else.

QUESTION: You have already expressed your views on the danger of escalation in Vietnam itself. In view of the increasing reports of military build-up in Thailand—American forces being somewhere between twenty-five and forty thousand—and the new reports indicating bombing of North Vietnam from Thailand, would you extend your expressions of concern to that phenomenon in Thailand?

THE SECRETARY-GENERAL: I do not think I have any real basis for comment on this particular aspect of the war. Of course, if I have sufficient data upon which to base an assessment or a judgment, I think I may have to express my opinion one way or the other at the appropriate time.

QUESTION: Mr. Secretary-General, you have just outlined the basic difference which exists between you and, primarily, Washington. I wonder if you could perhaps outline the difference, if any, between you and Hanoi, and you and the National Liberation Front?

THE SECRETARY-GENERAL: It is common knowledge that out of my three-point program, both Hanoi and the National Liberation Front have taken exception to my second point. So this is one indication of the difference of approach between me, on the one hand, and Hanoi and the National Liberation Front on the other. Of course, there may be other instances too.

QUESTION: Mr. Secretary-General, last year an invitation was issued to you by the Arab Member states of the United Nations to visit the refugee camps and ascertain the conditions for yourself. In view of the opinions expressed by refugees at the last session, I wonder if there has been any change in that position about not visiting them, as you expressed it at a previous press conference.

THE SECRETARY-GENERAL: I think my statement was perhaps misunderstood. I have accepted the invitation of the Arab states to visit the Middle East and even to visit some refugee camps. I have accepted the invitation. The only thing is that I have not been in a position so far to determine when I could visit the area. So my answer is: I have accepted the invitation of the Arab states to visit the area, and I am looking forward to visiting at least some of the refugee camps at the earliest available opportunity.

QUESTION: You have told us this morning that it would not be helpful to disclose moves for preliminary talks or discussions. May we therefore assume that such moves are afoot and that you probably are hopeful that they may materialize in the near future?

THE SECRETARY-GENERAL: On the basis of my earlier statement, I do not think that I should make any comments on that question. I hope you will understand.

QUESTION: Ambassador Goldberg has suggested that it would be helpful if you would seek to find out from the other side whether there would be any reciprocal response in the event of a cessation of the bombing. Have you made such an effort, and can you give us any indication whether the comments you made earlier are based on responses from the other side to such a query?

THE SECRETARY-GENERAL: As in the case of my previous answer, I do not want to make any statement on this particular aspect. All I want to say is this: I think that it is desirable for all of us to understand the attitude of the other side also. Without in any way wishing to project myself as a "devil's advocate," I must say that the other side maintains a totally different approach from that of, for instance, the United States. Here I am dealing primarily with the bombing of North Vietnam. They maintain that, apart from the peculiar circumstances of the Vietnam question and the background of that question—for instance, the Geneva Agreements of 1954, which resulted in the temporary demarcation of the country into two zones—there are questions of principle involved. They maintain that the United States has no right to bomb an independent, sovereign country. They make the following argument, for instance—if I may bring in a parallel that is not too relevant, that of India and Pakistan: Should India bomb Pakistan on the basis of the accusation that Azad Kashmiris are crossing the cease-fire line? Or should Pakistan bomb India on the basis of the accusation that Kashmiris on the Indian side of the cease-fire line are crossing over that line into Azad Kashmir? That is how they look at this problem. I am not trying to justify their position, or this or that position; I am merely indicating to you how the war—particularly the bombing of North Vietnam—is seen from the other side.

QUESTION: On your third point in connection with Vietnam—that is, the inclusion of the National Liberation Front directly in negotiations—there have been interpretations in the Press recently that the United States has accepted that third point. Do you consider that to be a correct interpretation?

THE SECRETARY-GENERAL: The President of the United States has been saying all along that the participation of the National Liberation Front in any projected conference is not an insurmountable obstacle. I think it is a very wise move on the part of the United States, since in my view a meeting of Washington and Hanoi alone—although, of course, very desirable, as it would be a very big move in the direction of peace—would not solve the whole Vietnam problem. As you know, all of us, I think—many parties, directly or indirectly involved in the conflict—have been trying for so long to bring about a dialogue between Washington and Hanoi. We are trying to create conditions congenial for such a dialogue. I think these are efforts in the right direction. But in my view a meeting between Washington and Hanoi alone, although a very important step, would not solve the problem of South Vietnam. Of course, in such a meeting Washington and Hanoi could deal with problems relating to Washington and Hanoi in the context of the Vietnam war. But the problem of South Vietnam must be solved primarily by the South Vietnamese peoples themselves. This is the basic issue. I think it is the basic and fundamental point which everybody should bear in mind.

QUESTION: How soon do you expect to send a mission to Aden?

THE SECRETARY-GENERAL: I am conducting negotiations with the Administering Authority—the United Kingdom government—and the Committee of Twenty-Four through its Chairman, Ambassador Collier.[3] I hope to organize a mission in the next few weeks.

QUESTION: Could you give us your views on the problem of self-determination for the people of Taiwan?

THE SECRETARY-GENERAL: No—I have not given sufficient thought to it.

QUESTION: To come back to your answer on sanctions. As it is a basic rule of law that nobody can be censured without being heard, and as the Security Council has refused to hear Rhodesia because it is not an independent state, does that not lead to the compelling conclusion in law and logic: (a) that sanctions can only be imposed on independent states; (b) that sanctions imposed on an entity which cannot be heard and defend itself are illegal and void?

THE SECRETARY-GENERAL: As you know, I am not a jurist or a constitutional lawyer. As the Secretary-General I have to comply with the decisions of the principal organs of the United Nations. The Security Council in its wisdom has adopted a resolution—a historic resolution. Whether it is legal or illegal is not my business to argue. I have to comply with the decision of the Security Council. Therefore, I am proceeding on the lines I indicated earlier.

[3]Gershon B. O. Collier, permanent representative of Sierra Leone.

QUESTION: Mr. Secretary-General, last September when you met us you expressed belief that the United Nations would sometime in future be involved in the Vietnam situation. Did you mean then that the United Nations would have a role after the fighting stops?

THE SECRETARY-GENERAL: That possibility cannot be ruled out—of course, with the agreement of the parties directly concerned.

QUESTION: Mr. Secretary-General, a point of clarification. If I understand you correctly, a while ago in talking about the differences between your position and that of Hanoi and the National Liberation Front, you said that the North Vietnamese have taken exception to the second part of your program. If that is true, then they have not really accepted your three-point program. Has this been a recent development?

THE SECRETARY-GENERAL: No. Any compromise proposal, any proposal intended to bridge the gulf and intended to reconcile differences will inevitably run into opposition from both sides. If any proposal is acceptable to only one side, then, in my view, it is not a very helpful proposal.

Coming back to my recommendations and to Hanoi's reactions to my second point, I would draw your attention to the official radio broadcast from Hanoi on October 6, 1966. This is, of course, public knowledge, since it was a broadcast. This was the Hanoi broadcast in reply to my three-point proposal. I shall quote a part of the reply related to my second point:

While the first point proposed by U Thant conforms to the requirements for a settlement of the Vietnam issue, the second point is obviously negative and clashes with the first. It negates the positive character of the first point, since U Thant has failed to make a distinction between the United States imperialists, the aggressors, and the Vietnamese people, the victims of aggression.

It has been the traditional North Vietnamese line that nobody should equate what they call the aggressors with the indigenous fighters for independence.

QUESTION: Mr. Secretary-General, would you say, however, that there is at last a sort of dialogue in process concerning the war in Vietnam?

THE SECRETARY-GENERAL: I would prefer not to answer that question, at least not at this moment.

QUESTION: May I ask a clarification of the statement you just made about Hanoi's reaction to your second point. In your letter of December 30, you referred to the fact that the 1954 Geneva talks took place while fighting was going on. In the light of your present statement about Hanoi's reaction to the second point, does your December 30 letter envisage that, once American bombing ceased, there could be preliminary contacts which might lead to the cessation of hostilities, without the cessation of hostilities necessarily taking place first?

THE SECRETARY-GENERAL: I feel hopeful that it will come about.

QUESTION: May I put a previous question in another form? Do you feel, after having outlined the differences, some of which designate a pretty wide gap, that you still have a constructive and hopeful margin of negotiation left to you, that you can move on from here and that you have not reached a dead end?

THE SECRETARY-GENERAL: As you know, I am an optimist. One reason why I changed my mind and accepted a second term as the Secretary-General of the United Nations was that I felt, rightly or wrongly, that in my present position I would be able to contribute more significantly toward the settlement of the Vietnam war and toward the strengthening of the United Nations as a force for peace. So in this spirit I shall exert my utmost to contribute toward the achievement of peace in Vietnam.

---

2. Statement on the Cease-fire

NEW YORK   FEBRUARY 10, 1967

I HAVE WELCOMED the cease-fire which accompanied the celebrations of the Vietnamese Tet New Year, and have appealed for its extension. I believe that an indefinite and unconditional extension of this cease-fire would help in moving this tragic conflict to the conference table.

In this connection, I wish once again to recall my three-point proposal which, starting with an unconditional end to the bombing of North Vietnam, could, I am convinced, bring about a favorable climate for peaceful talks between the parties.

SOURCE: UN Press Release SG/SM/660.

Statement at the Opening Meeting of the
Ad Hoc Committee for South West Africa

NEW YORK   JANUARY 17, 1967

THE STATUS of South West Africa, a League of Nations mandate administered by South Africa, came under discussion in the United Nations in 1946
when the General Assembly rejected an application for incorporation of the
317,887-square-mile territory into South Africa. Prime Minister Jan Chris-
tiaan Smuts and succeeding leaders of the country stood firm against
demands that the territory be placed under the United Nations trusteeship
system. With the rise of independent countries in southern Africa and their
membership in the United Nations, the issue had become increasingly critical. By 1966, many Member states were demanding that the United Nations
take over the administration of South West Africa and prepare it for independence regardless of South Africa's stand. Fifty-four African and Asian
countries introduced a resolution in the General Assembly to this effect on
September 27, 1966. It was adopted on October 27. The resolution provided
for the establishment of a fourteen-member *Ad Hoc* Committee which would
recommend practical means for achieving the United Nations takeover. The
Ad Hoc Committee was directed to report to the General Assembly at a
special session as soon as possible but not later than April 1967. When the *Ad
Hoc* Committee began its work on January 17, U Thant welcomed the
members but warned that they would face "extraordinary difficulties" in
carrying out the task assigned to them.

I SHOULD LIKE, first of all, to extend a very warm welcome to all the
distinguished representatives on this Committee. The importance of
the task assigned to this Committee is recognized by all Members of
the United Nations, who are no doubt awaiting with keen interest the
outcome of your labors.

As you are aware, this Committee was established by the General
Assembly by resolution 2145 (XXI) adopted on October 27, 1966,
following a historic debate on the question of South West Africa in
the plenary meetings of the General Assembly.

SOURCE: UN Press Release SG/SM/641.

The question of South West Africa, as is well known, has been the subject of consideration at every session of the United Nations General Assembly beginning with the first session in 1946 as well as by several special committees established by the Assembly. During this long period of twenty-one years, the General Assembly has adopted no less than seventy-six resolutions on this question. It has also been the subject of three references to the International Court of Justice; twice for the purpose of obtaining advisory opinions and the third time for a decision on the case submitted by the governments of Ethiopia and Liberia.

All the efforts of the Organization as well as of individual Member states during this period have been directed at persuading the government of South Africa to cooperate with the United Nations in taking necessary measures to enable the people of the territory to exercise their rights, recognized in the Charter of the United Nations, in conditions of peace and harmony. Had South Africa cooperated with the Organization, this Committee would not have been faced today with the task which has now been entrusted to it by the General Assembly. In fact, this Committee would not have been necessary. In this connection it is pertinent to recall that, of the seven territories in Africa which remained under League of Nations mandate at the time of the establishment of the United Nations, all except South West Africa were brought under the trusteeship system by the governments responsible for their administration and all of them have since achieved self-determination and independence.

The United Nations, in its numerous resolutions on the question of South West Africa, has reaffirmed the inalienable right of the people of this territory to self-determination and independence. The Organization therefore has clearly an obligation to assist the people of South West Africa to achieve this inalienable right of theirs.

In resolution 2145 (XXI) adopted by the General Assembly at its twenty-first session, the Assembly decided that South Africa, having failed to fulfill its obligations in respect of the administration of the territory, has no other right to administer it and that henceforth South West Africa comes under the direct responsibility of the United Nations. Further, it resolved that the United Nations must discharge its responsibilities with respect to this territory.

Having thus decided to take over the responsibilities for South West Africa, the General Assembly established this *Ad Hoc* Committee and gave it the task of recommending practical means by which South West Africa should be administered so as to enable the people of the territory to exercise the right of self-determination and to achieve independence and to report to the Assembly at a special session as soon as possible and, in any event, not later than April 1967.

It may be mentioned in this connection that while this Committee has been entrusted with the specific functions to which I have referred, the question of South West Africa also remains the concern of the Special Committee of Twenty-four[1] within the context of the implementation of the Declaration on the Granting of Independence to Colonial Countries and Peoples embodied in General Assembly resolution 1514 (XV).

I am conscious of the historical importance as well as the extraordinary difficulties of the task entrusted to this Committee. I also recognize the fact that, since the Committee is called upon to report to a special session of the General Assembly not later than April 1967, the time at its disposal is limited. However, I am confident that you, the distinguished members of this Committee, conscious of your responsibilities, will spare no effort in drawing up a report which would assist in the taking of concrete and constructive decisions by the appropriate organs of the United Nations for a just and peaceful solution of this problem, which all of us so ardently desire. In conclusion, I wish to extend my best wishes for the success of your endeavors. You may rest assured that you can always count on my full cooperation and assistance.

[1] Special Committee on the Situation with regard to the Implementation of the Declaration on the Granting of Independence to Colonial Countries and Peoples.

Message Sent to President Lyndon B. Johnson, Premier Aleksei N. Kosygin, and Prime Minister Harold Wilson on the Occasion of the Signing of the Treaty of Principles Governing the Activities of States in the Exploration and Use of Outer Space, including the Moon and Other Celestial Bodies

NEW YORK   JANUARY 27, 1967

ONE OF THE GREAT milestones in applying the rule of law to outer space was reached on December 19, 1966, when the General Assembly approved unanimously the text of a draft treaty governing the exploration of outer space, including the moon and other celestial bodies. Work on the treaty had been in progress since the Assembly had adopted the declaration of legal principles governing space exploration. The final draft of the treaty, which incorporated the 1963 principles and expanded upon them, was achieved through discussions in the Legal Sub-Committee of the Committee on the Peaceful Uses of Outer Space and through private negotiations between the United States and the Soviet Union. The following message by U Thant was sent to the heads of government of the United States, the United Kingdom, and the USSR on January 27, 1967, on the occasion of the formal opening of the treaty for signatures in London, Moscow, and Washington, the capitals of the depository governments. The treaty came into force on October 10, 1967, well in advance of the first manned flight to the moon in July 1969.

I WISH IT WERE possible for me to be present in London, Moscow, and Washington at the same time on the auspicious occasion of the signing of the Treaty of Principles Governing the Activities of States in the Exploration and Use of Outer Space, including the Moon and Other Celestial Bodies. May I convey to you my sincere congratulations and express my feeling of deep satisfaction at this historic event

SOURCE: UN Press Release SG/SM/646.

in international relations—a feeling which, I am certain, is shared by all peoples everywhere. I am particularly gratified that the United Nations was able to make a significant contribution toward this major achievement.

The conquest of space gives rise to many new problems, because of the terrifying military potentialities involved and, also, because of the impact of space technology on our physical environment. As man ventures into space, he cannot rely solely on his scientific and technological knowledge, great as it may be. He must equally depend on legally binding universal standards of conduct, progressively developed as science unravels the mysteries of space.

It is both urgent and necessary that the powerful forces generated by human ingenuity be kept under control and utilized for the benefit of humanity and the strengthening of peace. It is most gratifying to see that the problems of exploring outer space are being solved through positive and sustained international action and measures within the framework of the United Nations.

I have no doubt that this Treaty will not only greatly reduce the danger of conflict in space, but also improve international cooperation and the prospects of peace on our own planet. The Antarctic Treaty of 1959, the Test-Ban Treaty of 1963, and the present Treaty are true landmarks in man's march toward international peace and security. I fervently hope that these achievements will be shortly followed by similar agreements on nonproliferation of nuclear weapons and other steps toward general and complete disarmament.

THE SITUATION IN VIETNAM

MARCH

IN MARCH 1967, U Thant launched his most important Vietnam peace initiative since he circulated his three-point proposals just twelve months earlier (p. 224). The military situation had reached a new intensity after a brief truce during the lunar New Year (Tet) observation. The United States not only had resumed its bombing of North Vietnam, but its naval guns were shelling areas north of the demilitarized zone and mines were being laid in North Vietnamese waters. President Lyndon B. Johnson told a press conference he had ordered the new actions to hasten the end of the war. The step-up in the fighting came despite appeals by Pope Paul VI and Thant for an indefinite extension of the Tet cease-fire. On the same day that Johnson made his statement in Washington, it became known that a North Vietnamese diplomatic mission had arrived in Rangoon where Thant was spending a brief vacation. Although the presence of the Hanoi representatives was the subject of widespread speculation, the purpose of the visit was shrouded in secrecy. Thant left on February 28 for a three-day rest at the Burmese seaside resort of Ngapali without having made any contact or having sought any. North Vietnamese officials, however, made a preliminary approach while Thant was at Ngapali, resulting in a secret visit by the Secretary-General to the North Vietnamese consulate in Rangoon on March 2. The meeting was not to be a secret for long. On the day after the talks the North Vietnamese Consul General, Le Tung Son, said: "U Thant came here and I received him as an Asian and we exchanged views on the Vietnamese problem." Taking part in the talks along with the Consul General were Colonel Ha Van Lau, North Vietnam's chief representative on the International Control Commission in Hanoi, and Nguyen Tu Nguyen. The latter two left immediately for Hanoi, and Thant left for New York on March 4. At the Rangoon airport before leaving, the Secretary-General confirmed that he had held talks with the North Vietnamese. Like Le Tung Son, he stressed that he was acting in his "private capacity and not as the Seceretary-General of the United Nations." He declined to go into the substance of the discussions except to say he had a "useful and friendly exchange of views with the consul general as well as the two officials who happened to be in Rangoon." He added that he had presented to them his own assessment of the situation and that they, in turn, presented theirs. Thant confirmed an earlier statement of the Consul General that the Hanoi representatives had brought no message from President Ho Chi Minh. In a pause at the London airport en route to New York, Thant told reporters that his talks had been friendly and "very useful," but he added that "as far as the outlook for peace in Vietnam is concerned, I must say with

regret that the prospects are not very bright—at least, for the moment."
Both at the London airport and later on his arrival in New York, he declared
that he was convinced more than ever that the cessation of the bombing of
North Vietnam alone could create conditions conducive to negotiations.

Not until March 28, at a press conference at United Nation Headquarteres,
did Thant disclose that he had submitted to the parties to the Vietnam war a
revised three-point peace proposal. By that time word of the new proposals
had leaked out and some of the parties had already published their reactions.
Thant said he had already received in writing the replies of the parties
principally involved but that he regarded them as confidential and, therefore,
could not comment on them. The new proposals actually were sent on March
14 as an *aide-mémoire* to the United States, North Vietnam, South Vietnam,
and the National Liberation Front, although he disclosed that he had first
offered them orally during his Rangoon meeting with the Hanoi representatives. Thant insisted that he still regarded his original three-point plan as
representing the most useful first step and that the new proposals were
offered only in the hope of finding common ground among the participants in
the war in view of the known reactions to the 1966 plan.

The Secretary-General's *aide-mémoire* is presented in full in the transcript
of his press conference (pp. 388–89). The main points, however, were brief: (1)
a general standstill truce, (2) preliminary talks, and (3) reconvening of the
Geneva conference. While the proposal for a standstill truce was perhaps the
most important new element and the one which brought a strong reaction
from Hanoi, the *aide-mémoire* contained other provisions which made it
difficult for other parties to accept. Thant's decision to make his proposals
public was based mainly on the sharp criticism which had been coming from
North Vietnam. At his press conference he referred to "certain reactions
which are likely to confuse the general public regarding my sincere desire for
peace." A broadcast from Hanoi Radio on March 19 charged that the United
States government was trying to "use the United Nations to interfere in the
Vietnamese question." On March 27, the day before the Secretary-General's
meeting with the Press, North Vietnam's official news agency broadcast a
statement by a spokesman of the Foreign Ministry, saying: "to call on both
sides to cease fire and hold unconditional negotiations while the United
States is committing aggression against Vietnam and taking serious steps in
its military escalation in both zones in Vietnam is to make no distinction
between the aggressors and the victim of aggression, to depart from reality and
to demand that the Vietnamese people accept the conditions of the aggressors." The reaction from the other side at first seemed more favorable. The
Saigon government did not reject the proposals, but asked for a number of
"clarifications and modifications." The United States accepted the proposals
in principle in a letter dated March 18, but both Washington and Saigon
raised questions about provisions under the second point of Thant's plan
which proposed that preliminary talks be limited to representatives of the
United States and North Vietnam. Actually the Saigon government protested
to the Secretary-General over his failure to include it in the preliminary

talks—an omission made deliberately to avoid the question of inviting also the National Liberation Front. A South Vietnamese spokesman said: "We resent being treated as puppets. It is unthinkable that the recognized government of South Vietnam should not be included in talks which so vitally affect its interests." In more diplomatic language, the United States put it this way: "Of course, the government of South Vietnam will have to be appropriately involved throughout this entire process." Although it was clear that no one was happy with the new Thant proposals, he said he did not consider any of the published reactions to be "a categorical rejection" of his proposals, and he thought that efforts had to be "pursued in the direction of peace." In response to a further question, he said it was his intention "to pursue these ideas." He insisted, however, that his earlier three-point plan still offered "the best possible solution to the conflict" and that it had by no means been discarded. On April 1, four days after his press conference, Thant issued a statement calling on the United States to put the proposed standstill truce into effect by unilateral action. It was clear, he said, that the existing impasse could be broken only if one side or the other would take the initial first step undertaking unilaterally to fire only when fired upon. He declared that the United States could well afford to take such an initiative because of its world position.

---

1. Statement to the Press

RANGOON   MARCH 4, 1967

BEFORE I LEAVE for New York I once again want to express my very sincere thanks to the government of Burma, particularly the Chairman of the Revolutionary Council, General Ne Win, for the very warm hospitality extended to me and Mrs. Thant during our stay in Burma. We had a very pleasant stay here, seeing friends and relatives and particularly my mother.

I had opportunities of exchanging views on matters of mutual interest with the Chairman of the Revolutionary Council, with the Honorable Foreign Minister and the members of the Foreign Affairs Committee of the Burmese government.

In my private capacity, and not as the Secretary-General of the United Nations, I visited the Consul General of the Democratic

SOURCE: UN Press Release SG/SM/668.

Republic of Vietnam on March 2. I had a useful and friendly exchange of views with the Consul General as well as the two officials from Hanoi who happened to be in Rangoon. I presented to them my own assessment of the situation in Vietnam and they, in turn, presented their own assessment of the situation. And, I must say that the talks were very useful. Well, Gentlemen, that is all I have to say.

A question-and-answer period followed U Thant's statement.

QUESTION: Did you receive any message from President Ho Chi Minh of Hanoi regarding the Vietnam problem during your discussions?

THE SECRETARY-GENERAL: No, I did not receive any message from President Ho Chi Minh.

QUESTION: Did the North Vietnamese representatives present the latest views of Hanoi on the subject of peace negotiations to you?

THE SECRETARY-GENERAL: Yes, they did express their latest views on the general situation in Vietnam.

QUESTION: Can you describe what these views were?

THE SECRETARY-GENERAL: Well, it is difficult to do justice to these views in the space of a few minutes, but I am sure their views are well known.

QUESTION: Who were the two representatives who came from Hanoi with whom you spoke after the Consul General?

THE SECRETARY-GENERAL: They are two high officials from Hanoi, I understand. About their names and designations, I think you can get them from the office of the Consul General in Rangoon.

QUESTION: Were these representatives optimistic about the prospects of peace?

THE SECRETARY-GENERAL: It is difficult to assess the mood of any diplomat whom you talk to regarding the situation in Vietnam. It is difficult for anyone to be optimistic.

QUESTION: Any plans to see them again?

THE SECRETARY-GENERAL: No such plans.

QUESTION: Did you receive from the French government any proposal to visit Paris to discuss Vietnam problems?

THE SECRETARY-GENERAL: No. During my stay in Rangoon, I did not receive any message from France. Thank you very much.

2. *Transcript of Remarks at Heathrow Airport*

LONDON   MARCH 5, 1967

THE SECRETARY-GENERAL: I am now on my way back to New York, after a week's visit to Burma. As you are no doubt aware, the primary purpose of my visit to Burma was to rest and to see friends and relatives, especially my aged mother; and I had occasion to discuss with the Chairman of the Revolutionary Council, General Ne Win, and members of the cabinet, on matters of mutual interest to Burma and the United Nations. And in my personal capacity—and not as the Secretary-General of the United Nations—I also had discussions with the Consul General of North Vietnam, and also with two officials from Hanoi, who happened to be in Rangoon at that time. The discussions were friendly, and, if I may say so, very useful. But, as far as the outlook for peace in Vietnam is concerned, I must say with regret that the prospects are not very bright—at least, for the moment. But we all have to carry on with our efforts for peace.

QUESTION: Mr. Secretary-General, you said the talks were useful and friendly. How useful?

THE SECRETARY-GENERAL: Useful in a sense that they have clarified some of the issues which were not very clear to me before I saw them.

QUESTION: Now that you have listened to North Vietnam's views, is it your impression that Hanoi really does want peace, or do you think—not this year?

THE SECRETARY-GENERAL: Well, I think you will get a true picture of the situation if you understand the two opposing views. Hanoi's assessment of the situation is very different from the United States assessment. I think it is very important to understand the differences between the two viewpoints.

QUESTION: Have you been able to sort out the precise terms on which Hanoi would agree to a peace conference? This seems to be the biggest issue: On what terms will they agree to a peace conference?

SOURCE: UN Press Release SG/SM/673, March 15, 1967.

THE SECRETARY-GENERAL: Well, to understand Hanoi's position clearly, it is necessary to recount Hanoi's attitude. Hanoi's attitude toward the whole problem is that the Vietnamese people have been struggling for independence for twenty-five years. They have been struggling against colonialism, against imperialism, against foreign domination for the last twenty-five years—under one single leadership. That is their assessment of the problem. So, for them, it is a question of national independence, national survival. Of course, the United States attitude is different, completely different. As you know, the United States assessment of the situation is that the trouble started with the aggression of South Vietnam by the North Vietnamese, and also certain commitments to honor. So, with these opposing viewpoints, it is very difficult to get a compromise formula, which I am trying to seek.

QUESTION: You said on your way here, Mr. Secretary-General, that the greatest obstacle to peace was the lack of trust on both sides.

THE SECRETARY-GENERAL: Yes, that is true.

QUESTION: What would you like to see both sides do to create that trust?

THE SECRETARY-GENERAL: To take some risk to find out the *bona fides* of the other side.

QUESTION: What would you like to see both sides do to create that trust?

THE SECRETARY-GENERAL: As I have been advocating for some time, in my view the first prerequisite for meaningful talks is the cessation of the bombing of North Vietnam. I have been advocating this for more than a year. I still maintain this view. The first requisite for a move toward peace talks is a cessation of the bombing of North Vietnam.

QUESTION: What about on the other side—on the North Vietnamese side?

THE SECRETARY-GENERAL: Well, that is a question of interpretation, you know. Of course, you are familiar with the United States attitude—there must be some reciprocity, there must be some reciprocal de-escalation on the other side. But the difficulty, in my view, is how to supervise or ascertain whether there is some de-escalation on the other side or not.

QUESTION: (speaking off-mike) But—notion of reciprocity—by the North Vietnamese—?

THE SECRETARY-GENERAL: Well, when you mention the question of reciprocity, the concept of reciprocity on the part of Hanoi is different from the concept of reciprocity in the mind of the United States. Hanoi's idea of reciprocity is, in South Vietnam there has been a civil war, there is a civil war; Hanoi is assisting one side and the United States is assisting the other side. So Hanoi's idea of reciprocity is, if the United States would withdraw its support of one side, Hanoi is prepared to withdraw its support of the other side. That is the idea of reciprocity, which is completely different from the idea of reciprocity of the other side.

QUESTION: Reports out of Rangoon say that you are taking a new position on the North Vietnamese government's attitude to New York. If this is so, Sir, is this new position softer toward the United States?

THE SECRETARY-GENERAL: Well, I do not think it is accurate, you know, to say that I have brought a new position.

QUESTION: No, the position of the North Vietnamese government, Sir. Reports out of Rangoon say that you are taking a new North Vietnamese position back with you.

THE SECRETARY-GENERAL: I don't think it is true.

QUESTION: Do you think, Sir, that the Americans should stop bombing the North, without firm guarantees from Hanoi that they would not take advantage of a stopping of the bombing to build up their forces?

THE SECRETARY-GENERAL: Well, my position has been clear for a very long time. I still maintain this.

QUESTION: But twice when America has stopped the bombing, the North has used this to build up resources and pump more men and more weapons in.

THE SECRETARY-GENERAL: Well, I must say in all fairness that both sides are sending their forces in during the pause—both sides.

QUESTION: But do you think Hanoi would give a guarantee that they would stop taking advantage of this situation?

THE SECRETARY-GENERAL: I do not think Hanoi will guarantee. Well, thank you very much.

3. Transcript of Remarks at Kennedy International Airport

NEW YORK   MARCH 5, 1967

THE SECRETARY-GENERAL: As a matter of fact, Ladies and Gentlemen, there is nothing very much for me to say, since I have said what I should say both in Rangoon and in London. As you know, I had a meeting with the Consul General of the Democratic Republic of Vietnam and two high officials from Hanoi who happened to be in Rangoon while I was there. I met them on March 2. We exchanged views on the situation in Vietnam. I presented to them my own assessment of the situation and they, in turn, presented their own assessment.

I must say that the conflict is going to be prolonged and bloody. Peace is not yet in sight, and the North Vietnamese are convinced that their military supporters will never let them down, whatever the circumstances may be.

I came back more than ever convinced that the cessation of the bombing of North Vietnam alone can create conditions conducive to useful talks and meaningful negotiations.

QUESTION: Simply, Mr. Secretary-General, what would happen if the United States stopped the bombing?

THE SECRETARY-GENERAL: As I said on a previous occasion, I believe that in a few weeks' time after the cessation of the bombing, talks would take place.

QUESTION: Do these words come from the North Vietnamese?

THE SECRETARY-GENERAL: Not necessarily, not directly from them. But I believe that this would be the case.

QUESTION: Do you believe that it would be in the interest of the United States to stop the bombing of North Vietnam?

THE SECRETARY-GENERAL: Definitely.

QUESTION: The United States government requested and author-

SOURCE: UN Press Release SG/SM/669.

ized you, publicly, to take whatever steps you deemed necessary to create an atmosphere in which talks might be possible. As a result of your trip, do you see any possibility at all of even informal, private talks between the United States and North Vietnam?

THE SECRETARY-GENERAL: Yes, there is a possibility of talks between the United States and North Vietnam if the bombing is stopped.

QUESTION: At your last press conference at the United Nations, Mr. Secretary-General, you mentioned that Hanoi had rejected the second point in your three-point peace plan. Do they still stand by that position?

THE SECRETARY-GENERAL: Yes. My position is well known to the North Vietnamese, and the North Vietnamese position is well known to me. As you all know, the North Vietnamese have certain reservations regarding my second point. But I am now dealing primarily with the first point, the cessation of bombing.

QUESTION: The scaling-down?—to put it on the record.

THE SECRETARY-GENERAL: The scaling-down of all military activities by all sides; that is my second point.

QUESTION: Are they suggesting the withdrawal of support from South Vietnam, and the withdrawal by Hanoi of support from the Vietcong? Does this support mean only the bombing, as far as the United States is concerned, or have you indications of other kinds of support that they have in mind?

THE SECRETARY-GENERAL: No; I mean primarily that if the bombing of North Vietnam is stopped, talks would take place. As to the further steps, of course these are matters for negotiations and discussions.

QUESTION: But the first step must be the cessation of the bombing?

THE SECRETARY-GENERAL: The cessation of the bombing.

QUESTION: Have you detected any hardening of Hanoi's position, or is there any more flexibility in their position that you have found in your talks?

THE SECRETARY-GENERAL: I think this is a matter of interpretation. They reiterated the substance of the statement made by Premier Pham Van Dong to Mr. Burchett[1] on January 28. In their view, that

---

[1] Wilfred Burchett, Australian journalist.

statement represents the latest and the most comprehensive résumé of the North Vietnamese attitude toward the war.

QUESTION: Do the North Vietnamese expect you to transmit the gist of their conversations with you to the United States government?

THE SECRETARY-GENERAL: I was not asked to transmit anything.

QUESTION: Do you plan to do so?

THE SECRETARY-GENERAL: Yes—whatever steps I deem necessary toward the creation of conditions for peaceful talks.

QUESTION: You would meet, then, with members of the United States government?

THE SECRETARY-GENERAL: Yes, I will exchange views with representatives of the governments directly involved in the conflict.

QUESTION: Do you think that it is wrong for the United States to demand some reciprocal de-escalation by Hanoi before agreeing to stop the bombing of North Vietnam?

THE SECRETARY-GENERAL: I do not want to say that it is wrong or it is right. But the idea of reciprocity is something which we all should ponder very deeply. To my knowledge, the North Vietnamese understanding of the concept of reciprocity is different from the United States understanding. For instance, in the view of the North Vietnamese, reciprocity means: the United States is bombing North Vietnam, and North Vietnam is bombing the United States. That, in their view, would be reciprocity. Since North Vietnam is not bombing the United States, the United States, in their view, should not bomb North Vietnam. That is their understanding of reciprocity. So these concepts have different connotations and different interpretations by different parties. I do not want to say that the United States concept of reciprocity is right or wrong. I am just trying to interpret the two viewpoints which are poles apart.

QUESTION: You said that you would be conveying to the United States government the ideas of the representatives of Hanoi. Do you have a timetable for this?

THE SECRETARY-GENERAL: No, I have not. I do not think I have any message to be conveyed urgently to the parties primarily concerned.

QUESTION: Would you like to talk personally with President Johnson about your meeting with the North Vietnamese officials?

THE SECRETARY-GENERAL: The President is a very busy man, you know. If there is anything worthwhile, in my view, to be conveyed to the President directly, I shall be very glad to convey it to him. But, in the circumstances, I do not consider that I have any substantive message or messages to be conveyed directly to the President.

---

4. From Transcript of Press Conference

NEW YORK   MARCH 28, 1967

THE SECRETARY-GENERAL: In the interval since my last press conference there have been several developments. As you know, I was able to pay a brief visit to Burma during the interval. Early next week I am leaving for Geneva to preside over the ACC meetings, that is, the meetings of the Administrative Committee on Co-ordination. Thereafter, I shall visit Ceylon, India, Nepal, Afghanistan, and Pakistan. You are already aware of the details of my itinerary.

You may also be interested to know that in the latter half of May I shall be visiting the United Kingdom and Belgium before proceeding to Geneva to address the inaugural session of the *Pacem in Terris* Second Convocation, on May 28. Before returning to New York, I may also pay a brief visit to Vienna to sign on behalf of the United Nations the Headquarters Agreement with the government of Austria relating to the establishment of the United Nations Industrial Development Organization in Vienna.

We are meeting again today at a time when the world, perplexed by recent developments in Vietnam, is looking anxiously for an alternative to the grim reality of the conflict's continuing for an indeterminate future toward an inconclusive end.

Since we last met there has been more death, destruction, devastation, and consequent misery, increasing at a more rapid rate than in any comparable period in the past, and there is an even greater danger of the war spreading beyond the frontiers of Vietnam. While the United Nations at present seems incapable of dealing with the war, many governments and personalities have been trying to bring about

SOURCE: *UN Monthly Chronicle*, vol. IV, April 1967, pp. 67–77.

conditions for the transfer of the conflict from the battlefield to the conference table, so far without success. As Secretary-General of the United Nations I am distressed lest the prolongation of this war bring about a suffocation of this Organization and in the end seriously affect the détente and cooperation among all nations.

Since my return to New York in the first week of March, a good deal of speculation has focused on my reported new proposals to end the Vietnam war. Some capitals have even come out with public reactions to those proposals. When this press conference was arranged for today, it was far from my intention to make those proposals public, but, in view of the widespread interest shown in those proposals, and in view of certain reactions which are likely to confuse the general public regarding my sincere desire for peace, I have now decided to make those proposals public. It is for the world community to judge and assess those proposals against the background of the growing fury of the war, with definite prospects of involving larger areas of Asia. I have already received in writing the reactions of the parties principally involved, which I must continue to regard as confidential, and therefore I cannot comment upon them. My purpose in presenting those proposals was only to try to find, if possible, a common ground among the participants in the conflict, in view of the known reactions to my earlier three-point proposals. However, I would emphasize that I continue to regard my three-point proposals as representing the most useful first steps in preventing further escalation and intensification of the war and in beginning the reverse process of de-escalation and negotiation. In particular, I have never ceased to consider that the bombing of North Vietnam constitutes an insurmountable obstacle to discussions. I also stand by my conviction that Vietnam is a political problem, which no amount of force will solve—and, after all, previous military measures have not succeeded in bringing about any talks.

Therefore, while it is all too clear that the positions of the parties have never been so far apart, I have continued, and intend to continue, my efforts. I wish, particularly, at this stage, to urge all responsible world leaders not to resign themselves to permitting a further aggravation of the situation. The obstacles to peace may be enormous, but it is not true, even at this stage, that negotiations would necessarily fail. A settlement respecting the principles agreed upon at Geneva and the realities of Vietnam and yet safeguarding the long-term interests of all concerned is not beyond reach. Such a settlement would at least open the way for the new, far-reaching initiatives in other fields urgently needed today.

Now I shall read to you the proposals which, on March 14, in the form of an *aide-mémoire* I presented to the parties directly involved in the Vietnam conflict. The text reads as follows:

On many occasions in the past, the Secretary-General of the United Nations has expressed his very great concern about the conflict in Vietnam. That concern is intensified by the growing fury of the war resulting in the increasing loss of lives, indescribable suffering and misery of the people, appalling devastation of the country, uprooting of society, astronomical sums spent on the war, and last, but not least, his deepening anxiety over the increasing threat to the peace of the world. For these reasons, in the past three years or so, he submitted ideas and proposals to the parties primarily involved in the war, with a view to creating conditions congenial to negotiations, which, unhappily, have not been accepted by the parties. The prospects for peace seem to be more distant today than ever before.

Nevertheless, the Secretary-General reasserts his conviction that a cessation of the bombing of North Vietnam continues to be a vital need, for moral and humanitarian reasons and, also, because it is the step which could lead the way to meaningful talks to end the war.

The situation being as it is today, the Secretary-General has now in mind proposals envisaging three steps:

(*a*) A general stand-still truce

(*b*) Preliminary talks

(*c*) Reconvening of the Geneva Conference.

In the view of the Secretary-General, a halt to all military activities by all sides is a practical necessity if useful negotiations are to be undertaken. Since the Secretary-General's three-point plan has not been accepted by the parties, he believes that a general standstill truce by all parties to the conflict is now the only course which could lead to fruitful negotiations. It must be conceded that a truce without effective supervision is apt to be breached from time to time by one side or another, but an effective supervision of truce, at least for the moment, seems difficult to envisage as a practical possibility. If the parties directly involved in the conflict are genuinely motivated by considerations of peace and justice, it is only to be expected that earnest efforts will be exerted to enforce the truce to the best of their ability. Should a public appeal by the Secretary-General in his personal capacity facilitate the observance of such a truce, he would gladly be prepared to do so. Appeals to that effect by a group of countries would also be worthy of consideration.

Once the appeal has been made and a general standstill truce comes into effect, the parties directly involved in the conflict should take the next step of entering into preliminary talks. While these talks are in progress, it is clearly desirable that the general standstill truce should continue to be observed. In the view of the Secretary-General, these talks can take any of the following forms:

(1) Direct talks between the United States of America and the Democratic Republic of Vietnam.

(2) Direct talks between the two governments mentioned in (1) above, with the participation of the two Co-Chairmen of the Geneva Conference of 1954.

(3) Direct talks between the two governments mentioned in (1) above, with the participation of the members of the International Control Commission.

(4) Direct talks between the two governments mentioned in (1) above, with the participation of the two Co-Chairman of the Geneva Conference of 1954 and of the members of the International Control Commission.

The Secretary-General believes that these preliminary talks should aim at reaching an agreement on the modalities for the reconvening of the Geneva Conference, with the sole purpose of returning to the essentials of that Agreement as repeatedly expressed by all parties to the conflict. These preliminary talks should seek to reach an agreement on the timing, place, agenda, and participants in the subsequent formal meeting—the reconvening of the Geneva Conference. The Secretary-General deems it necessary to stress that the question of participants in the formal negotiations should not obstruct the way to a settlement. It is a question which could be solved only by agreeing that no fruitful discussions on ending the war in Vietnam could take place without involving all those who are actually fighting. Since the government in Saigon, as well as the National Front of Liberation of South Vietnam, are actually engaged in military operations, it is the view of the Secretary-General that a future formal conference could not usefully discuss the effective termination of all military activities and the new political situation that would result in South Vietnam, without the participation of representatives of the government in Saigon and representatives of the National Front of Liberation of South Vietnam.

In transmitting these proposals to the parties directly concerned, the Secretary-General believes that he is acting within the limits of his good offices purely in his private capacity. He hopes that the divergent positions held by the parties both on the nature of the conflict and the ultimate political objectives will not prevent them from giving their very serious attention to these proposals. Indeed, he takes this opportunity to appeal to them to give their urgent consideration to his proposals.

QUESTION: Mr. Secretary-General, could you tell us whether you view the reported statement coming out of Hanoi, and published in the newspapers this morning, as a rejection of your *aide-mémoire* proposals, or does the implication in your opening statement that you have received their views give you a contrary impression?

THE SECRETARY-GENERAL: I do not think it would be proper on my part to attempt to interpret the reactions to my proposals of the parties primarily concerned. I think it will be only appropriate for the parties concerned to make their reactions public; and it is for everybody to interpret those reactions.

QUESTION: Mr. Secretary-General, some United Nations representatives believe that you may have impaired your influence with Hanoi by suggesting the "standstill," which, in effect, would require reciprocity from Hanoi in exchange for the end to the American bombing; in other words, they feel that you are siding now with the United States. What comment have you on this?

THE SECRETARY-GENERAL: No, I do not believe that assessment is correct. As I have repeated in the statement I made just now, I still maintain that a cessation of the bombing of North Vietnam is an imperative necessity to create conditions for peaceful talks. My new proposals are in effect an adaptation of my three-point proposal to suit the existing circumstances and prevailing moods of the parties principally concerned. I still regard my proposals as a reiteration and an adaptation and modification of my original three-point proposal, which I presented over a year ago, to suit the existing mood of the parties principally concerned.

QUESTION: Sir, without giving any details at all, have you found any hopeful reaction at all to your initiative from those to whom you sent your proposals?

THE SECRETARY-GENERAL: I have so far received initial reactions from some of the parties principally involved, but since they are in the nature of very confidential responses, I do not think it would be proper on my part to disclose them. It is for them to do so, of course, if they feel like it.

QUESTION: I have in mind your own personal reaction, Sir. Do you find anything hopeful? Do you feel more hopeful now than you did before you began?

THE SECRETARY-GENERAL: I do not want to put myself in the position of predicting the future, but my assessment of the situation in Vietnam is the same as I stated at the earlier press conference in January: the prospects are still far from bright and the intensification of the fighting is something that we all should deplore. I think that, if we really want a peaceful settlement of the war in Vietnam, some necessary concessions have to be made by both sides in a spirit of accommodation.

QUESTION: Sir, I would like to ask you if you still hold to the theory or to the feeling that you so strongly expressed when you returned from Moscow and at other times, when you said that this war was inexorably leading to a world war. These words no longer appear in your press conferences or in your letters and have not appeared, to my knowledge, since January. Can you tell us how you feel about it?

THE SECRETARY-GENERAL: Although I might have omitted these references in my subsequent statements and press conferences, I still hold the view that the trend of the war is leading to more escalation and that the war is likely to spread over the frontiers, as I stated in the previous press conference to which you have referred. The indications are, in my view, ominous, and I am afraid that if no spirit of give-and-take is shown by all sides in the conflict, the war is likely to get out of hand.

QUESTION: Mr. Secretary-General, we understand that, while you were in Burma recently, you did talk with representatives of North Vietnam. That was before you drew up your last proposals. Did you get any optimistic response or any encouragement from the representatives of North Vietnam at that time toward those proposals?

THE SECRETARY-GENERAL: I presented those proposals orally, of course, to the representatives of North Vietnam when we met in Rangoon. It was only on the fourteenth of this month that I put them down on paper. And, of course, even at that time, as I indicated at my press conferences on my return from Rangoon on the way to New York, the positions of the two sides were very far apart. It is very difficult to reconcile those different approaches, as I have stated on previous occasions, because the war as seen from both sides is so different; the perspectives are so different and far apart that it is very difficult to submit a conciliatory proposal. But, in my view, my three-point proposal, which I presented early last year and which I formulated in my new proposals in keeping with the mood of the present time, still offers the best possible solution to the conflict.

QUESTION: Mr. Secretary-General, did you send your *aide-mémoire* to the National Liberation Front of Vietnam as well, and have you received a reply from it?

THE SECRETARY-GENERAL: I attempted to make this *aide-mémoire* available to all participants in the conflict.

QUESTION: Mr. Secretary-General, do you still consider—I am just asking you to interpret what you said—that a cessation of bombing is a necessary pre-condition to peace talks?

THE SECRETARY-GENERAL: Yes, I still maintain this view.

QUESTION: Does the cessation of the military activities mean only the cessation of bombing of North Vietnam, or also the legal and logical corollary of the withdrawal of the North Vietnamese invasion army from South Vietnam?

THE SECRETARY-GENERAL: As all of you must have well understood, the proposal which I presented to the parties early last year, envisaged three steps. The first is the cessation of bombing of North Vietnam. In my view, this alone could lead to fruitful talks and negotiations, and that was, of course, reaffirmed by the Foreign Minister of North Vietnam in his interview with a journalist some time in January, I believe.

QUESTION: Mr. Secretary-General, may I pose two unrelated questions. First, in the event that your new three-point program is accepted and there is a standstill truce, do you not envisage some difficulty on the question of the supervisory role? Will the United Nations play a role in this?

My second question, which is unrelated, is this. I wonder if you can tell us how the talks in the Middle East are progressing over the demilitarized zone, whether General Odd Bull[1] has made any progress.

THE SECRETARY-GENERAL: In reply to your first question, I do not think it is realistic to expect a supervised cease-fire in South Vietnam. I have given a good deal of thought to this. We all remember that in 1954, when the Geneva Conference started, the fighting was still going on; while the fighting was going on, the parties primarily concerned met and talked and came to some agreement. Therefore, my intention was just to appeal to the parties to the conflict to comply with an appeal for a standstill truce. Of course, supervision of the truce is not practical in the circumstances. But my intention is just to bring the parties to the conflict to the conference table. There may be, of course, sporadic fighting here and there, since a truce cannot be supervised. In a war of this dimension, I do not think effective supervision is a practical possibility.

Therefore, we must bear in mind the situation in 1954, when the Geneva Conference was convened while fighting was still going on. In

---

[1]Lieutenant-General Odd Bull, Chief of Staff of the United Nations Truce Supervision Organization in Palestine.

my view, it is not realistic to expect a supervised truce in the situation now existing in Vietnam.

Regarding your second question, General Odd Bull is trying to bring about meetings. He had already conducted three meetings, as you know, and at present, because of health reasons, he has gone on home leave to recuperate in his country. I am sure that, as soon as he comes back to the area, he will try to bring about a meeting of the parties involved in the conflict in the Middle East.

QUESTION: I am sorry; I think I am still a little bit confused. Are you saying to us, in effect, that while you do maintain personally your earlier position that an unconditional cessation of the bombing is essential, at the same time you can now, in order to move something forward a little bit, afford to step away from that and offer this new proposal; and, therefore, the two proposals cannot really exist side by side?

THE SECRETARY-GENERAL: As I see it, my present proposal is an adaptation of my three-point proposal to suit the existing circumstances and the prevailing moods of the parties principally concerned. I do not think it is a deviation from my original three-point proposal.

QUESTION: Given the initial replies you have received from both sides, what is your next step?

THE SECRETARY-GENERAL: I do not think it would be proper for me to reveal the initial reactions of both sides. Of course, some reactions have appeared in the Press. I do not believe them to be a categorical rejection of my proposals, and I think that efforts have to be pursued in the direction of peace.

QUESTION: So you will pursue them?

THE SECRETARY-GENERAL: Yes, it is my intention to pursue these ideas.

QUESTION: Could you say whether your warning about the danger of the spread of war is based on new information about the intentions of China?

THE SECRETARY-GENERAL: I do not want to be specific on this point, for obvious reasons, but my feeling all along has been that, if the war is not brought to a stop, we are in for a wider war, a larger war, and a more intensified war involving other areas which are not yet involved.

QUESTION: We seem to be talking about the war all the time, but

North Vietnam has hammered away at the fact that the Vietnam conflict can only be solved between the Vietnamese people themselves. Can you perhaps address yourself to that aspect of the situation?

THE SECRETARY-GENERAL: The position of the North Vietnamese is well known, and I do not think that I should elaborate on this. Of course, they resent interference by outside forces in Vietnam. That is well known to all of you, and I do not think I am in a position to interpret the attitude of North Vietnam in this respect.

QUESTION: I should like to ask a couple of questions in connection with your forthcoming trip to Asia. First, do you plan to meet with North Vietnamese officials on this trip? Second, we know you are going to be the first recipient of the Nehru Peace Prize for International Understanding. Will this be an occasion for a major speech by you?

THE SECRETARY-GENERAL: First of all, I have no plans to contact representatives of North Vietnam during my projected trip to India and other countries. Second, I am still working on my speech, to which you referred, and so I am not yet very clear about the substance of the speech.

QUESTION: The Pope has today released his encyclical and in it he asks for a world fund for the development of developing countries and speaks of the growing gap. Would you comment on that, particularly in the light of a question which I asked at your last press conference about how the war affects the Mekong project,[2] which is, as we know, a multilateral development about which our news is that the Mekong development cooperation is now seriously impaired by the absence of Cambodia because of the war?

THE SECRETARY-GENERAL: On the Pope's appeal today, which I have just received, my first reaction is that it is a very wise appeal. It is also in line with the various resolutions of the principal organs of the United Nations, particularly the General Assembly and the Economic and Social Council. If my interpretation of His Holiness' appeal is correct, he called for a world fund for undeveloped nations taken from the arms expenditures of the industrialized powers. I believe it is a very wise appeal, and I support it wholeheartedly.

[2]For an explanation of the MeKong project, see vol. IV of this series, pp. 453–454.

About your second question, of course, as you know, the Mekong project is very much affected by the war in Vietnam to the extent that one of the principal parties involved, Cambodia, is still reluctant to participate wholeheartedly in the project.

I have appealed to the government of Cambodia to reconsider its decision, but I do not know what the response will be. The war in Vietnam poisons the atmosphere not only in Vietnam, but also in the neighboring countries. As you all know, that has been my assessment all along. Personally speaking, I would not be surprised if Cambodia decided not to participate in the Mekong project.

QUESTION: Mr. Secretary-General, in connection with your expressed fear of a wider war if the Vietnam conflict continues the way it is going, could you tell us what you feel about the prospects of the Soviet Union and China openly entering this conflict?

THE SECRETARY-GENERAL: I do not think that I am competent to answer this question categorically. As far as the North Vietnamese are concerned, they are confident that their military supporters will never let them down, whatever the circumstances. So I foresee a very prolonged and bloody war.

QUESTION: Mr. Secretary-General, you spoke earlier this morning about the suffocation of the United Nations. Are you intimating that if we cannot arrive at some solution soon to the Vietnam problem, the United Nations might go the way of the League of Nations?

THE SECRETARY-GENERAL: I would not go that far. The United Nations has so far been performing on a very different level from the level of the League of Nations. The United Nations has been involved in many peace-keeping operations in which the League of Nations was never involved. What I am trying to drive home is the fact that the Vietnam war poisons the atmosphere everywhere and has a definite impact on the United Nations. But I would not go so far as to say that the United Nations is going the way of the League of Nations. I do not think that there are omens in that direction.

QUESTION: Does your standstill truce include the prohibition of activities of the South Vietnam government or the United States forces against the Vietcong in the South?

THE SECRETARY-GENERAL: Yes, it is comprehensive.

QUESTION: I have two questions to ask. The first question: the first order of business for bilateral talks will be a total cease-fire and supervision of the conflict. Am I right in saying that once the bombing is suspended, you expect the talks to begin and that the first order of business on the agenda will be how to supervise the elections?

My second question is with regard to the prospects of a nonproliferation treaty. When the threat of escalation continues to dominate the region, and particularly the independence of smaller countries is threatened, how do you view the prospects for a nonproliferation treaty?

THE SECRETARY-GENERAL: Regarding your first question, as I have been saying all along, the cessation of the bombing of North Vietnam is the first prerequiste for the next move, and I feel more convinced than ever that if the bombing of North Vietnam ceases, in a few weeks there will be talks. I think that in this connection it is worth recalling what the Foreign Minister of North Vietnam said to a correspondent on January 28. He made this categorical statement:

It is only after the unconditional cessation of United States bombing and all other acts of war against the Democratic Republic of Vietnam that there could be talks between the Democratic Republic of Vietnam and the United States.

I think that that is a very categorical statement and, as I said on a previous occasion, I am convinced that after the cessation of the bombing of North Vietnam, in a few weeks there will be meaningful talks.

Regarding your second question, as you all know, the Eighteen-Nation Committee on Disarmament has recessed for six weeks, because the participants wanted to clear up some of the misconceptions and misunderstandings which arose out of the preliminary talks in Geneva. There are some differences of approach and differences of emphasis, but I cannot say whether I am hopeful or optimistic about the prospects for the nonproliferation treaty, in the context of the prevailing mood of the big powers today.

QUESTION: The government of North Vietnam keeps talking about the unconditional end of bombing, which is to say an end of bombing without any time limit. You say that, after a few weeks, talks would occur. How can you say that?

THE SECRETARY-GENERAL: I do not think there is a difference between these two approaches. When North Vietnam says "unconditional cessation of bombing," it does not mean that cessation of bombing must last two years or ten years or twenty years. That is unrealistic. In my view, unconditional cessation of bombing implies that the bombing must not be linked with any reciprocity on the part of North Vietnam. In my view—I repeat once again—once the bombing of North Vietnam is stopped there will be meaningful talks in a matter of a few weeks. So the nuances of "conditional" or "unconditional" have no particular significance. I think that if the bombing is stopped for a few weeks there will be meaningful talks.

. . .

THE SITUATION IN VIETNAM

APRIL AND MAY

DURING THE first three weeks in April, U Thant was away from United Nations Headquarters, first stopping in Geneva and then traveling on to Asia with visits to Ceylon, India, Nepal, Afghanistan, and Pakistan. In his talks with heads of state and government the Vietnam problem was dominant. The discussions, however, contributed little to his peace efforts, since these were countries already in agreement with his views that military means could not bring a solution and that the objective should be a return to the Geneva Agreements of 1954. During his visit to New Delhi, the Secretary-General had had an opportunity to talk with the Indian Consul General in Hanoi, whose views on the chances of his latest peace proposals were anything but encouraging. On his return to New York he heard the news that the United States had again bombed the Haiphong area. He was convinced that a similar bombing of Hanoi had led to the breakdown of a Polish peace initiative in December 1966 and therefore feared a new setback. He told his April 21 press conference that any intensification of the war was "very undesirable, especially in the context of this very delicate stage of negotiations and private explorations." He declined to elaborate on his reference to negotiations except to say that it was "more or less common knowledge that private talks have been going on back and forth." Actually, there were several initiatives during the preceding weeks in addition to those of the Secretary-General. These included the appeal by Pope Paul VI for an extension of the lunar New Year truce; efforts by British Prime Minister Harold Wilson during the London visit of Chairman Kosygin; a letter from President Johnson to President Ho Chi Minh on April 6; a proposal by Ceylon's Prime Minister Dudley Senanayake for a meeting of representatives of the Saigon government, Hanoi, and the National Liberation Front to consider a cease-fire; and a proposal by Paul Martin, Canadian Secretary of State for External Affairs, for a progressive four-stage reapplication of the Geneva Agreements.

During the weeks since the circulation of his March 14 *aide-mémoire,* Thant had become convinced that nothing could be achieved until the bombing of North Vietnam ceased. He stressed this in statements to the Speakers Research Committee on May 10 and at a luncheon of the United Nations Correspondents Association on May 11. On both occasions he quoted United States Secretary of Defense Robert McNamara as saying the bombing had not had the desired result of reducing the rate of infiltration from the North and expressed the firm belief that Hanoi would not begin peace talks until the bombing stopped. He acknowledged that a bombing halt might have "certain limited risks" but he added that the alternative was "far more dangerous and more disastrous." There was a risk, he said, that a just and lasting settlement in Southeast Asia would be "definitely jeopardized, as well as the détente between the larger powers. . . ." There was little surprise when he told the press luncheon that his plan for a general standstill truce had been shelved, since "neither side had fully and unconditionally accepted those proposals." For the time being, he would concentrate on trying to get a bombing halt "which alone, in my view, can create conditions for meaningful talks." "The only realistic approach," he said, "is to focus our attention on only one aspect of the problem—that is, the cessation of the bombing of North Vietnam."

1. Statement to the Press

NEW YORK   APRIL 1, 1967

IT IS MY CUSTOM to refrain from public comment on positions taken publicly by officials of any government. This statement, therefore, is most definitely an exception to the practice and is not to be taken as a precedent for the future.

I make this exception because I have been so greatly impressed by the statement made by Senator Joseph S. Clark in his speech to the National Convention of Americans for Democratic Action on March 31. My latest proposal was necessarily directed to both sides in the conflict and implicitly called for simultaneous action with regard to the standstill truce by the two sides. Nevertheless, I recognize the harsh reality of the existing impasse. Indeed, this realization was the sole motivation for my latest proposal. But it becomes ever more clear to me that this impasse can be broken and a halt put to the increasingly horrible slaughter and destruction of the Vietnam war only if one side or the other shows the wisdom and the courage and the compassion for humanity to take the initiative on a first step— that is to say, by undertaking unilaterally to put the standstill truce into effect, and thereafter to fire only if fired upon. The United States, with power and wealth unprecedented in human history, is in a

SOURCE: UN Press Release SG/SM/686.

position to take this initiative. I must say in all frankness that I share Senator Clark's view that the United States can afford to take such a step even though there is an admitted, but, in my opinion, limited risk for the United States in doing so.

2. Transcript of Press Conference

NEW YORK   APRIL 21, 1967

THE SECRETARY-GENERAL: Ladies and Gentlemen, I have been saying almost the same things at every stop, so I do not think I should repeat what I have been saying all along in the last twenty-five hours or so. But I believe there is one thing which ought to be repeated, namely, that in the course of my travels to five Asian countries— Ceylon, India, Nepal, Afghanistan, and Pakistan—I had very useful exchanges of views with the heads of state and heads of government, and I found myself in complete agreement with those governments regarding the basic concepts of the Vietnam problem.

First of all, we agreed that military means cannot bring about a peaceful solution of the Vietnam problem. Only the diplomatic and political methods of discussions and negotiations can bring about a peaceful settlement.

Second, we agreed that the problem of Vietnam should be settled by the people of Vietnam themselves without outside interference.

Third, we agreed that the objective should be a return to the Geneva Agreements of 1954.

Those were some of the areas of agreement between myself and the five governments I referred to. Of course, there are other problems of local interest to each country.

QUESTION: Could you say anything about the latest American escalation, namely, the bombing of Haiphong today?

THE SECRETARY-GENERAL: I was not aware of it. I was just told

SOURCE: UN Press Release SG/SM/694.

when I came into this room. In my view, any act of military escalation or intensification of the conduct of the war is very undesirable, especially in the context of this very delicate stage of negotiations and private explorations.

QUESTION: Do you think the United Nations will take any action as a result of the bombing?

THE SECRETARY-GENERAL: I do not see any possibility of the United Nations acting, at least at this stage—for obvious reasons.

QUESTION: Did you see Mr. Paul Martin in London?

THE SECRETARY-GENERAL: No, I did not see him. I got a telephone call from him at six o'clock this evening, London time.

QUESTION: Could you comment on his peace proposal?

THE SECRETARY-GENERAL: No, he just gave me a little background regarding his latest peace proposals. I did not see him, of course. I talked with him on the telephone briefly.

QUESTION: As a result of your consultations—obviously the theme of Vietnam has come into all your conversations—do you expect that there is going to be a considerable build-up in Asian diplomatic circles for a new strong initiative for peace?

THE SECRETARY-GENERAL: In all the countries I visited the question of Vietnam dominated the thinking of the governments. They are very much obsessed with this tragic problem. Of course, I do not know whether any new initiative or new plans will be forthcoming from that area, but as far as I am concerned this trip was very useful.

QUESTION: You were quoted today as saying that you were convinced that both sides could begin negotiations within weeks if the United States bombing of Vietnam stopped. Has something specific happened on this trip to convince you of that?

THE SECRETARY-GENERAL: No. I have been saying the same thing since January 10. If you will recall, at my press conference on January 10, I said it for the first time. I have been repeating it off and on, because I am convinced of it.

QUESTION: You stated that this escalation is undesirable, especially at this very delicate stage of the negotiations. Is that what you said?

THE SECRETARY-GENERAL: Yes, private negotiations, private contacts.

QUESTION: Could you elaborate?

THE SECRETARY-GENERAL: No, I do not think any elaboration is necessary. I think it is more or less common knowledge that private talks have been going on back and forth.

QUESTION: Would you say that the bombing lessens the chance for peace or will widen the war?

THE SECRETARY-GENERAL: In my view, there are increasing prospects of the war spreading over the frontiers, as I have been saying, and I am afraid that even some of the countries which are not directly involved in the war may be increasingly involved.

QUESTION: I believe the Indian Consul General in Hanoi had come down to New Delhi and participated in your talks. Has he carried any message from you to the North Vietnamese President and Prime Minister?

THE SECRETARY-GENERAL: No, he has not.

---

3. From Transcript of Remarks to Speakers Research Committee

NEW YORK   MAY 10, 1967

CRITICISMS HAVE BEEN leveled at the United Nations for some time with regard to its obvious inability to become involved effectively in the greatest crisis facing mankind since the end of the Second World War. I am referring to the war in Vietnam. I have explained why the United Nations has not been able to be involved in that crisis and I have explained also why the United Nations, at least for the moment, as it is constituted at present, is not in a position to deal effectively with this tragic situation. Of course, I do not want to reiterate the reasons I have adduced on previous occasions, in view of the shortness of time. I just want to say that—taking account of the history of the past few years—the United Nations would not have been able to do anything in regard to the solution of the West Irian problem, for

SOURCE: UN Press Release SG/SM/707.

instance, if either the Netherlands or Indonesia had not been a Member of the United Nations at that time. The United Nations would not have been able to do anything in Kashmir in the past eighteen years if either Pakistan or India had not been a Member of the United Nations. The United Nations would not be able to do anything in the Middle East, through the United Nations Truce Supervision Organization in Palestine or the United Nations Emergency Force, if either Israel or the Arab states were not Members of the United Nations. The explanation is as simple as that.

Another criticism leveled at the United Nations for some time, which has come to my knowledge is that the 122 Member states are spending every year more than $100 million for the United Nations. The question has been posed: Is it worthwhile? My answer is this. If we take into consideration the various activities of the United Nations, not only in the political field, but also in the economic and social fields and in the colonial field, my conviction is that, even if the United Nations had not been able to do anything in the political field in the past twenty-two years, it is still worthwhile. Of course, that is not so. The United Nations has been able to do many things in the political field also. Even if the United Nations had not been able to do anything in the economic and social fields—which is, of course, far from true—again it is worthwhile. Even if the United Nations had not been able to do anything in the colonial field, that is, in facilitating the emergence of nonindependent states to independent status, it is worthwhile. But we have to consider this in the context of other developments.

To cite one very obvious example, we come back to the tragic situation in Vietnam again. I think it worth remembering that what the actual combatants are spending in the Vietnam war in two days is equivalent to what the United Nations has been spending in one whole year. I think it is a very obvious illustration of the need for a real perspective in regard to the expenditure of funds by the Member states vis-à-vis the United Nations and other activities. According to a rough calculation, the amount of money spent by the combatants in the Vietnam war—apart from the tremendous destruction, devastation, and loss of life, and only in terms of the money spent by the actual combatants—for two days is equivalent to the amount of money spent by 122 Members of the United Nations for 365 days. In other words, the money that is being spent in Vietnam for one whole year is sufficient to operate the United Nations for another 185 years. I think we should look at this problem from such relative perspectives.

I believe I would be doing an injustice to this distinguished gathering, particularly to my colleagues, the permanent representatives and the members of this Committee, if I did not make even a brief reference to the war in Vietnam. I have been stating my views for the past three and a half years, as you are all aware, and I still maintain the same views. First of all, I am still convinced that cessation of the bombing of North Vietnam is a prerequisite to meangful talks. I have maintained this since February 7, 1965, when North Vietnam was bombed for the first time—we are told, in retaliation for an attack on Pleiku.

While on this subject, I want to draw a demarcation line in the Vietnam war. I want to divide the Vietnam war into two phases. The first phase is prior to February 7, 1965. The second phase is post-February 7, 1965. In the first phase, as you are no doubt aware and as many governments are no doubt aware now, Hanoi showed a willingness to talk. That was in the first phase, prior to February 7, 1965. In the second phase, post-February 7, 1965, Hanoi has not shown any willingness to talk. So the explanation is obvious. It is not only obvious, it has been reiterated by leaders of Hanoi from time to time, particularly in the Foreign Minister's statement of January 28, 1967, that so long as the bombing of North Vietnam is going on there will be no talks. Of course, the argument against this is that the cessation of bombing of North Vietnam will increase the infiltration rate to the South. That is the argument, but if we consider this problem objectively, in true perspective, we have to come to the conclusion that that is not the case.

You will perhaps recall that, in January 1965, one official estimate of the strength of North Vietnamese regulars in South Vietnam was about 10,000. Two years later, two years after the bombing of North Vietnam—that is, in February 1967—one official estimate of the strength of North Vietnamese regulars in South Vietnam was 50,000. Of course, the government of North Vietnam has never accepted these figures, but that is beside the point. The point I want to bring home is the fact that after two years of bombing of North Vietnam the strength of North Vietnamese regulars in the South is estimated to have increased by five times.

You will also remember that even the Secretary of Defense, Mr. McNamara, said last January—and his statement is in the official records—that the bombing of North Vietnam did not and does not have the desired result of stopping or reducing the rate of infiltration from the North to the South. So my point is that, although the cessation of the bombing of North Vietnam might have certain limited risks, the alternative is far more dangerous and far more disastrous. That is why I have been advocating—and many people and many governments have also been advocating—the taking of that limited risk and the cessation of the bombing of North Vietnam. Of course, "unconditionally" or "indefinitely" do not have any meaning for me. It does not mean that the bombing has to be stopped for one year or ten years or one hundred years. I have been saying for the past three or four months that I am convinced that, once there is a cessation of bombing in North Vietnam, there will be talks in a few weeks' time. So I want to take this opportunity of reiterating my appeal from this platform that the first step to achieve peace in Vietnam is the cessation of bombing of North Vietnam.

I also want to reiterate another point: that the objective of all the combatants in Vietnam should be a return to the essentials of the Geneva Agreements of 1954. On this, of course, there is no dispute. As you will remember, last month I visited five Asian countries, and in the course of my visits I had very useful discussions with the leaders of their governments. Of course, Vietnam dominated our talks, naturally, and all the five governments—of Ceylon, India, Nepal, Afghanistan, and Pakistan—agree with me on certain basic concepts regarding the Vietnam war. First of all, all five of those governments agree that the cessation of bombing of North Vietnam should be the initial step which could lead to meaningful talks. Second, all five of those governments agree that military methods will not bring about a peaceful solution of the problem. Only diplomatic and political methods of discussion and negotiation can and will bring about peaceful solutions. All five governments also agree that in the final analysis the people of Vietnam should solve their problems without foreign interference. All five governments also agree that the objective should be the implementation of the Geneva Agreements of 1954.

I hope that these few remarks of mine will be relevant to the occasion, because I know your sentiments, your approach to the problem, your obsession with this very tragic problem, and I can assure you, Ladies and Gentlemen, that I will never cease to endeavor to contribute toward a peaceful solution of this very tragic conflict.

---

4. From Transcript of Remarks at Luncheon of United Nations Correspondents Association

NEW YORK   MAY 11, 1967

DURING THE six weeks which have elapsed since we last met on March 28, the war in South Vietnam has intensified with increasing casualties on all sides. There has been a new escalation of the airwar against North Vietnam, resulting in the destruction of the few remaining untouched objectives in North Vietnam, with a mounting number of victims. There is no need for me to emphasize that these last steps are fraught with very grave consequences.

The fact that the Democratic Republic of Vietnam, a developing nation, is continuing to withstand the pressure of an enormously superior power has been and still is the essential factor which has prevented an enlargement of the conflict beyond the frontiers of Vietnam. But, in the meantime, further very heavy damage continues to be inflicted upon Vietnam both in the North and in the South, and there is a greater risk that the possibilities of a just and lasting settlement in Southeast Asia will be definitely jeopardized, as well as the détente between the larger powers who carry the major load of responsibility for the maintenance of world peace.

In view of the above events, and others which have followed my proposals of March 14 for a general standstill truce, I wish to put the record straight. You may all be aware by now that neither side has fully and unconditionally accepted those proposals, which must therefore be regarded as being no longer under consideration.

Meanwhile I am convinced that now, as before, the first obstacle to

SOURCE: UN Press Releases SG/SM/708 and 709.

talks remains the continued air bombardments of North Vietnam. On the prerequisite of their cessation, I found myself in agreement with every one of the five Asian governments I consulted during my recent trip. Since January 28, and even recently, members of the government of the Democratic Republic of Vietnam have repeated that if the bombardments were to cease there could be talks. It may be assumed that such a diplomatic stand has been taken by North Vietnam with full knowledge of the positions of its allies, and I regard this as a very important development.

The view has been often advanced that the positions of the parties being what they are, such talks would fail to bring about peace negotiations. However, I personally continue to believe that talks conducted in the spirit of the Geneva Agreements could pave the way for a settlement. But first there must be a reversal of the trend of mounting escalation with its ever present risk of internationalization of the Vietnam war, and a willingness to deal with the problem in its national context, making full use of all the processes for peaceful settlement which are envisaged in the Geneva Agreements.

These Agreements, the first of their kind to be arrived at between all great powers, were probably one of the most important achievements in the field of international relations since the end of the Second World War. If there is a willingness to return to the situation envisaged by these Agreements, then the way would be open for new, imaginative, and constructive steps toward peace.

QUESTION: Mr. Secretary-General, in addition to making statements such as the one you came out with last night, what are you doing to get peace in Vietnam?

It seems that the parties are further apart than ever on Vietnam and that your room to manoeuver is limited. On your latest formal proposals, one side purports to have accepted them and the other is said to have rejected them. Since you have said that the danger of a wider war is greater than ever before, would you give us an assessment of the attitude of the parties to negotiations now and the status of your latest proposals? Do you contemplate any new moves or a greater attempt to publicize the dangers of a far greater war?

THE SECRETARY-GENERAL: I shall answer the second part of the question first. I made it very clear in my introduction that the first prerequisite for moving the conflict to the conference table is the cessation of bombing of North Vietnam. I have been advocating that for quite some time. As I said yesterday, we have to divide the Vietnam war into two phases. The first phase is pre-February 7, 1965, and the second phase is post-February 7, 1965. It will be noticed that Hanoi showed a willingness to talk in the second phase—that is, since February 7, 1965. Therefore, I maintain the view that I have held all along: that the first prerequisite to creating conditions for meaningful talks is the cessation of bombing of North Vietnam.

I also made it very clear in my statement yesterday that, although there may be some limited risks in such a step, the alternative is fraught with very dangerous and indeed disastrous consequences. Hence, in my view, the first alternative, involving perhaps some restricted risks, should be taken up.

I also want to make this very clear: In my view, the bombing of North Vietnam has not produced the expected result. This was made clear even by the Secretary of Defense, Mr. McNamara, in his statement before the Senate late January of this year.

Therefore, with regard to what steps I propose to take in the near future, my answer is simply that I would reiterate my appeal for the unconditional cessation of bombing of North Vietnam, which alone, in my view, can create conditions for meaningful talks. That view is, as I said in my introduction, shared by all the five governments of Asian countries that I visited last month.

QUESTION: Do you fear a confrontation between the United States, on the one hand, and the Soviet Union or China, or both, on the other hand, over the war in Vietnam?

Do you believe the world is now nearer to a third world war than last year, when you mentioned this for the first time?

Are you convinced that the United States has chosen a policy of military victory in Vietnam, and, if so, does this not mean the end of the United Nations as an organization created to keep the peace?

Do you believe that the present course of the war in Vietnam is leading to a third world war and the destruction of the United Nations?

THE SECRETARY-GENERAL: I am afraid that, if the present trend continues, a direct confrontation between Washington and Peking is inevitable. I hope I am wrong. But I am afraid that we are witnessing today the initial phase of a third world war. If you recall the circumstances leading to the First World War and the Second World War, you will realize that the prologues were quite long. I mean that the psychological climate, the creation of political attitudes, took some time to develop. When conditions were ripe, when there was some plausible incident, then the global wars were triggered. In my view, we are today witnessing similar conditions.

You will no doubt agree with me that when A and B are fighting, and when A is fighting more or less on its own and B is receiving or has received quite a substantial volume of physical or military aid from, let us say, C and D, etc., it is inevitable and only logical and rational that, if this fight is prolonged and intensified, A has to confront not only B, but also C and D, etc.. I think that this is the only logical conclusion and the only rational sequence of such actions.

I am really concerned about the potentialities of this war, knowing as I do the moods not only of the parties primarily involved, but also of the parties not directly involved at present. This is why I say that, if the present trend continues, a direct confrontation between Washington and Peking is inevitable and that I am even afraid that we may be witnessing today the initial phase of the third world war. In this context, I must say that the mutual defence pact between Moscow and Peking is still in force.

QUESTION: On April 15, 1965, you stated that you would not hesitate to request the Security Council to recommend a new man in your place if you felt that your usefulness in the search for a Vietnam solution had ended. Since then, your peace-making efforts have been repeatedly rebuffed by both sides. Yet you agreed to serve for another five-year term. Does your warning about your possible resignation still stand?

THE SECRETARY-GENERAL: As you all know, one of the primary reasons for the reversal of my decision late last year was my expectation and belief that, in my present post, I would be in a better position to contribute significantly to the peaceful solution of the Vietnam problem. Of course, it is now some four months since I assumed the post of Secretary-General for a second term. In my view, it is a little too early to assess the possibilities and potentialities. I therefore do not think I can say right now what my position will be. But let me assure you that I will never cease my endeavors to contribute to the peaceful solution of this very tragic problem.

QUESTION: These are questions resulting from your statement yesterday. What is the actual basis for your conviction that, within a few weeks after the cessation of bombing of North Vietnam, there would be talks?

THE SECRETARY-GENERAL: I believe that I first made that statement in my press conference in January this year. I have repeated it several times on appropriate occasions. Although I have not been authorized by Hanoi, or for that matter, any participant, to say so, I am increasingly convinced that, once the bombing of North Vietnam ceased, meaningful talks would take place in a matter of a few weeks.

QUESTION: Have you abandoned your standstill truce plan and reverted to the earlier proposal based on cessation of bombing by the United States, because the United States is unwilling to initiate the standstill truce unilaterally and without prior agreement on details with Hanoi?

THE SECRETARY-GENERAL: I think I referred to that aspect in my introduction. I said that, because of the developments in the last few weeks, my proposals embodied in my *aide-mémoire* of March 14, 1967, must be regarded as being no longer under consideration. In my view, the only realistic approach is to focus our attention on only one aspect of the problem—that is, the cessation of the bombing of North Vietnam.

Among the reasons I have given in the past, I think I should reiterate one—and I gave this reason last night—that is, that the bombing of North Vietnam has not had and is not having the expected result. The fact that, according to one official estimate there were about 10,000 North Vietnamese regulars in South Vietnam in January 1965, before the bombing of North Vietnam began, and that two years later it was similarly estimated that there were about 50,000 regular North Vietnamese troops in South Vietnam, is an obvious illustration of my point that the bombing has not had any effect either in stopping the infiltration or in reducing the infiltration.

I believe all of you are aware that even Secretary of Defense McNamara made an assessment on this aspect during Senate hearings which took place late in January 1967. I may perhaps read out the actual text of his statement. In reply to a senator's question, Secretary of Defense McNamara said:

"I believe it"—that is, the bombing of North Vietnam—"is a penalty and not a restriction, in the sense that I do not believe that the bombing up to the present has significantly reduced, nor any bombing that I could contemplate in the future would significantly reduce, the actual flow of men and material to the South.''

I am sure you will agree with me that subsequent events have confirmed his assessment.

QUESTION: Does your statement of yesterday not freeze the respective positions of both sides—the North Vietnamese not being able to adopt a more flexible attitude after you said ''no talks are possible without a previous cessation of bombing''—and, on the other hand, does it not stiffen the attitude of the present or any other United States President, who might be afraid of appearing to surrender?

THE SECRETARY-GENERAL: I think I have already given an answer in reply to a previous question. I have given many other reasons in support of my contention. I therefore do not think additional comments are necessary.

QUESTION: In the past two years, a wave of highly disquieting upheavals has been sweeping the world: Greece, Ghana, Indonesia, military coups in Africa, authoritarian régimes in many Latin American countries. What do you think is the main factor involved in this backward trend? Can it all be attributed to the moral and political implications of the Vietnam war?

THE SECRETARY-GENERAL: I would not go so far as to link those developments with the Vietnam war. I am sure that most of them have no relevance whatsoever to the Vietnam war. There are peculiar factors and circumstances governing those developments. In some cases the developments are related to consequences in one or another direction of the rising spirit of nationalism than to anything else. I have always maintained—you are, of course, aware of my view in this particular direction—that nationalism, more than any political ideology, has been and still is the most potent force in the life of a people. If you view the developments in many parts of the world, you find that this has something to do with them. In other cases, it is, in my view, a tacit admission of the failure of democracy and democratic processes, as understood in the West. We must realize that democracy is the most desirable but most difficult system of government to operate, and it is not surprising that some may feel that dictatorships or totalitarian systems of government are much easier.

Therefore, in many newly independent countries—and particularly in small, developing countries—they have to dispense with these difficult, delicate, and sophisticated democratic systems and resort to easier systems, which in fact are not democratic, as the word "democratic" is generally understood in the West.

QUESTION: What is your comment on the argument that increasing the military pressure—for example, extending the bombing of Haiphong, MIG bases, and so forth—will induce North Vietnam to negotiate for peace?

THE SECRETARY-GENERAL: In my view, the intensification of the air war against North Vietnam only helps to stiffen North Vietnam's attitude. That is my experience, and that is my conviction.

QUESTION: How do you explain Hanoi's willingness to meet the United States in Warsaw, Poland, last December, even though there was no unconditional halt to the bombing? I ask that question in view of your statement that, so long as the bombing of North Vietnam goes on, there will be no talks.

THE SECRETARY-GENERAL: Regarding that episode, I believe I made a statement a couple of days ago, through my Press Officer, that I have two completely different versions of this particular matter. I, therefore, do not think it would be in the public interest for me to disclose—at least at this stage—the substance of these two versions.

With regard to the question why Hanoi has shown willingness to talk to Washington without insisting on a bombing pause, I think we have to take into account all possibilities, particularly if we distinguish between private contacts and public contacts.

QUESTION: Have you any plan for further direct talks with North Vietnamese representatives during your *Pacem in Terris* Geneva visit, or during other planned trips in the near future?

Do you believe a personal visit to North and South Vietnam might be helpful to all concerned?

THE SECRETARY-GENERAL: In answer to the first question, I have no plans to meet with any representatives of North Vietnam during my projected visit to Geneva or other countries.

With regard to the second question, I do not believe that a personal visit to North or South Vietnam by the Secretary-General, or for that matter anybody else, would help to contribute to a solution of this problem. The views of both South Vietnam and North Vietnam are well known. I do not think a personal visit by anybody would add to that knowledge.

. . .

QUESTION: Would an extension of the forthcoming truce agreed to for Buddha's birthday constitute a *de facto* standstill truce, clearing the way for the second point in your three-step proposals?

Since both sides have been invited to attend the *Pacem in Terris* conference in Geneva, is this not an almost compelling opportunity for those who really want peace to agree to an extended truce and get down to talks?

THE SECRETARY-GENERAL: In the course of my travels to Asia last month, I had occasion to appeal publicly for an indefinite extension of the truce proposed for Lord Buddha's birthday on May 23. So far, the response has not been very encouraging. However, in my view, a truce—irrespective of its duration: one day or two days, or one week or one month—is very desirable. The cessation of fighting, even for a short period, is conducive to the creation of conditions for meaningful talks. I therefore maintain that if the parties primarily involved in the war could find it possible to extend this truce indefinitely, such a step would be in the right direction.

QUESTION: You and many others have expressed sadness and regret over the lowering of the effectiveness and prestige of the United Nations, due primarily to its inability to help end the Vietnam conflict. What in your opinion could give the United Nations the renewed lift it needs presently?

THE SECRETARY-GENERAL: As regards the present state of the United Nations, I am sure that all of you are quite competent to assess it, to analyze it, and to interpret it in different lights. In my view, the present state of this world Organization has some relevancy to the conflict in Southeast Asia. The Vietnam war has repercussions all over the world, in all international activities; it affects the nature of international relationships, it poisons the atmosphere and, so, definitely, since the United Nations holds up a mirror to human society today, the war has, inevitably, repercussions on activities here.

As I have been saying all along, I do not see how the United Nations can be effectively involved in the settlement of this tragic conflict. As I said on a previous occasion, the explanation, at least to me, is very simple. The United Nations would not have been able to contribute toward the settlement of the West Irian problem if either the Netherlands or Indonesia had not been Members of the United Nations at that time. The United Nations would not have been able to perform its functions successfully in Kashmir, for instance, for the last eighteen years if either Pakistan or India had not been Members of the United Nations. The United Nations would not have been able to do what it has been doing for the last seventeen years in the Middle East if either Israel or the Arab states had not been Members of the United Nations. Thus the same considerations do apply today when we consider the United Nations functions vis-à-vis the Vietnam war. To me, the answer is as simple as that.

. . .

QUESTION: There are two questions on the Middle East. There have been recent reports indicating serious difficulty at the borders between Syria, Lebanon, and Israel. Could you give us your assessment of the situation there?

Can you make any further comment regarding what the Israeli Ambassador has called the "rapidly deteriorating situation" on the Israeli-Syrian border?

THE SECRETARY-GENERAL: I must say that, in the last few days, the El Fatah type of incidents have increased, unfortunately. Those incidents have occurred in the vicinity of the Lebanese and Syrian lines and are very deplorable, especially because, by their nature, they seem to indicate that the individuals who committed them have had more specialized training than has usually been evidenced in El Fatah incidents in the past. That type of activity is insidious, is contrary to the letter and spirit of the armistice agreements and menaces the peace of the area. All governments concerned have an obligation under the general armistice agreements, as well as under the Charter of the United Nations and in the interest of peace, to take every measure within their means to put an end to such activities.

. . .

QUESTION: Does the Secretary-General feel any cause for alarm in the recent armed clashes along the border area and waters between North and South Korea? Is the United Nations Command in Korea keeping him directly informed?

THE SECRETARY-GENERAL: I must admit that I have not received one single report from the United Nations Command in Korea.

QUESTION: Your plans to visit Cairo are now public. Since the United Arab Republic [UAR] is heavily involved in Yemen and South Arabia, and, since the United Nations has grave responsibilities there, will you not discuss charges of poison gas, UAR troops in Yemen and so on, with President Nasser. If you do discuss these matters, will you have similar talks in Saudi Arabia and Jordan?

THE SECRETARY-GENERAL: I propose to visit Gaza, that is, the United Nations Emergency Force early in July on my way to attend the summer session of the Economic and Social Council in Geneva. Since the time at my disposal will be very limited, it seems that I can spend perhaps only one day in Gaza. Since Gaza happens to be under UAR administration, I decided that I should also make a brief visit to Cairo, and of course I look forward to exchanging views with the leaders of the UAR on matters of mutual interest to it and the United Nations. For the moment at least, because of the circumstances I have just explained, I cannot make any other trip to the area, at least for some time.

. . .

QUESTION: There have been statements in more or less general terms that the Soviet Union and France will eventually make a voluntary financial contribution, and that the United States "will not be found wanting." Has the Secretary-General had any definite word from the Soviet Union and France—or from the United States—that such payments will in fact be made? If so, how much is indicated and when can the payments be expected?

THE SECRETARY-GENERAL: On this matter I must admit that I know what you all know, and nothing more.

. . .

THE WITHDRAWAL OF THE UNITED
NATIONS EMERGENCY FORCE

PRIOR TO May 1967, U Thant had played no significant role in the Middle East. Although there were numerous incidents along the Israeli-Syrian and Israeli-Jordanian borders, they were dealt with through the established United Nations machinery. The United Nations Truce Supervision Organization (UNTSO) and the mixed armistice commissions, set up under the 1949 armistice agreements, filed their reports and the Secretary-General transmitted them to the Security Council. On the Israeli-Egyptian frontier, the United Nations Emergency Force (UNEF) had stood as a buffer since the end of the 1956 fighting and incidents during the intervening ten years had been minimal. Even though Thant frequently mentioned the Middle East as one of the potentially explosive problems, it happened that his first five years in office coincided with the quietest period since the United Nations became involved in the controversial Palestine question in 1947. Many of his press conferences during the period produced not a single mention of the Middle East and even in some of the Introductions to his Annual Reports there was only the barest reference to the problem. Thant had visited Europe, Asia, Africa, and Latin America, but not the Middle East.

By January 1967, the situation along the Israeli-Syrian border had taken a turn serious enough for the Secretary-General to make a personal appeal to the two governments to exercise restraint and to accept without delay or precondition a proposal by the chief of staff of UNTSO, Lieutenant-General Odd Bull, for an emergency meeting of the Israeli-Syrian Mixed Armistice Commission. Both sides accepted, but the talks were disrupted after a major military clash on April 7. On May 8, the Secretary-General circulated to the Security Council a message he had sent to General Bull asking him to initiate separate talks with each of the parties in an effort to halt the growing crisis.

One of the problems was the emergence of the Palestine liberation movement, made up of militant Palestinian Arabs uprooted by the 1948 war and now becoming increasingly active as saboteurs inside Israel. Thant did not attempt to conceal his concern over the activities of these groups, especially the highly publicized El Fatah. At a press conference on May 11, he noted that "unfortunately" the El Fatah type of incidents had increased and that they seemed to indicate that the individuals had been given more specialized training than had been evident in the past. "That type of activity," he said, "is insidious, is contrary to the letter and spirit of the Armistice Agreements and menaces the peace of the area. All governments concerned have an obligation under the General Armistice Agreements, as well as under the Charter of the United Nations and in the interests of peace, to take every measure within their means to put an end to such activities." At this same press conference, Thant disclosed plans for his first Middle East visit. Surprisingly, it was to be limited to one day in Gaza, headquarters of UNEF, with a brief trip to Cairo where he expected to exchange views with President Gamal Abdel Nasser "on matters of mutual interest" to the United Arab Republic and the United Nations. The visit was to take place early in July just in advance of his usual trip to Geneva for the opening of the summer session of the Economic and Social Council. "I cannot make any other trip to the area, at least for some time," he said. At the time of his statement, the Secretary-General did not have the slightest information pointing to the events of the coming week. Although under attack in Syria and Jordan for sitting securely behind the "glass curtain" of UNEF while they struggled alone against Israel, the United Arab Republic had shown no inclination to open a new front. President Nasser himself said in a speech to the Egyptian armed forces on May 22: " . . . we had no plan before May 13 because we believed that Israel would not dare attack any Arab country. . . ." The sequence of events, as given by Nasser, is as follows: (1) on May 13, he received information that Israel was concentrating on the Syrian border an armed force of about eleven to thirteen brigades; (2) on May 17, he learned that Israel had made a decision to attack Syria; (3) on May 14, the United Arab Republic told Syria that Egypt would enter the war "from the first minute" if Syria were attacked; and (4) that same day Egyptian forces "began to move in the direction of Sinai to take up normal positions."

On the following day, Israeli Premier Levi Eshkol delivered a major policy speech to the Knesset (Parliament) in Jerusalem in which he denied that Israeli forces were concentrating on the Syrian border and gave assurances that Israel had no intention of attacking anyone. "We do not intend launching an attack," Eshkol said. "I want to say this to the Arab states and especially to Egypt and Syria, although we have said it time and time again." He said Egyptian forces in the Sinai had grown from 35,000 to 80,000 within a short time and declared that "the status quo must be restored on both sides of the border."

For the United Nations the crucial period began on May 16. At 10 P.M. (Gaza time) Brigadier Eiz-El-Din Mokhtar handed to Major-General Indar Jit Rikhye, the commander of UNEF, a letter from Lieutenant-General Mohammed Fawzy, Chief of Staff of the United Arab Republic (UAR) armed forces, informing him of the UAR troop movements and requesting the immediate withdrawal of United Nations forces manning the observation posts along the Israeli-Egyptian border. Rikhye replied that he had no authority to withdraw any troops of UNEF but that he would report the request at once to the Secretary-General. On that same day, May 16, Thant replied through the permanent representative of the United Arab Republic asking for clarification of the withdrawal request. A key part of the reply, as summarized by the Secretary-General (p. 428), declared:

"If it was the intention of the government of the United Arab Republic to withdraw the consent which it gave in 1956 for the stationing of UNEF on the territory of the United Arab Republic and in Gaza it was, of course, entitled to do so. Since, however, the basis of the presence of UNEF was an agreement made directly between President Nasser and Dag Hammarskjöld as Secretary-General of the United Nations, any request for the withdrawal of UNEF must come directly to the Secretary-General from the government of the United Arab Republic. On receipt of such a request, the Secretary-General would order the withdrawal of all UNEF troops from Gaza and Sinai, simultaneously informing the General Assembly of what he was doing and why.''

THE SITUATION of UNEF deteriorated rapidly on May 17. Rikhye reported that UAR army units had occupied a UNEF observation post at El Sabha and that Yugoslav UNEF camps at El Sabha and El Qusaima were now behind the positions of UAR forces. Later in the day, Rikhye received a communication from Fawzy requesting the withdrawal of Yugoslav detachments in the Sinai within twenty-four hours and the UNEF detachment at Sharm el Sheikh within forty-eight hours. The UNEF commander also reported that a sizable detachment of UAR troops was moving into the UNEF area at El Kuntilla. Thant called in the permanent representative of the United Arab Republic and handed him an *aide-mémoire* declaring that UNEF could not remain in the field under such conditions. The Secretary-General brought the situation to the attention of the UNEF Advisory Committee, composed of the seven countries contributing troops to the United Nations Middle East force. Attending the informal session were representatives of Brazil, Canada, Denmark, India, Norway, Sweden, and Yugoslavia. Thant told them he had informed the UAR representative, Mohammed Awad el-Kony, that if "there is a request from his government to the Secretary-General for withdrawal of the UNEF, I will comply with it, since it is the legitimate prerogative of the United Arab Republic to make such a request." He said further that he intended to inform the General Assembly immediately of any action he took, but that it was his decision alone to make. "It is not within the competence of the General Assembly," he said. George Ignatieff, permanent representative of Canada, urged Thant to inform the Assembly immediately without waiting for a formal request for the withdrawal. He questioned whether "in view of the very serious results that we know could occur— particularly in the movement of UAR forces in the El Aqaba area—it would be wise to cede to the unilateral request to withdraw UNEF forces before the Assembly has had a chance to consider the matter." José Sette Camara of Brazil and Hans Tabor of Denmark strongly backed Ignatieff's position, but the representatives of Yugoslavia and India favored immediate compliance with any Egyptian request for withdrawal. Indian Ambassador Gopalaswami Parthasarathi said, "If the government of the United Arab Republic requests the removal of UNEF we have to abide by that request. The General Assembly in this case has . . . no authority to deal with the matter."

On May 18, at noon, the permanent representative of the United Arab

Republic delivered to the Secretary-General a message from the UAR Foreign Minister, Mahmoud Riad, formally requesting the withdrawal of UNEF "as soon as possible." Late in the afternoon Thant informed the UNEF Advisory Committee, plus Ceylon, Colombia, and Pakistan—who had provided military contingents for UNEF, but were not members of the Advisory Committee—that he had received the UAR request and that he had informed Ambassador el-Kony that "the force will be withdrawn." His reply to the UAR government was sent during the early evening. As he had indicated, he said he was proceeding to issue the necessary instructions for the withdrawal. He told Riad further that, although he was complying with the request, he had "serious misgivings about it for, as I have said each year in my annual report to the General Assembly on UNEF, I believe that this force has been an important factor in maintaining relative quiet in the area of its deployment during the past ten years and that its withdrawal may have grave implications for peace."

These were the steps culminating in what proved to be the most controversial decision during Thant's two terms as Secretary-General. His immediate concern, however, was to try to halt the brinkmanship which seemed to be plunging the Middle East into almost certain war. Two days after the Secretary-General ordered the withdrawal of UNEF he announced that he would fly to Gaza and Cairo immediately instead of waiting until July. One of his primary objectives was to urge President Nasser to avoid a confrontation with Israel over the Gulf of Aqaba, Israel's water outlet to the Red Sea. Egyptian forces had already occupied Sharm el Sheikh, however, and on May 22—the day Thant left New York for Cairo—Nasser announced he had ordered a blockade of Israeli shipping through the Strait of Tiran. "The Aqaba Gulf," he said, "constitutes our Egyptian territorial waters. Under no circumstances will we allow the Israeli flag to pass through the Aqaba Gulf." By the time Thant arrived in Cairo, Egyptian boats had already planted mines in the gulf to reinforce the blockade. The Secretary-General appealed to Nasser to lift the blockade, but without avail. He broke off his Cairo visit a day ahead of schedule and rushed back to New York where the Security Council had begun urgent debate of the Middle East situation. In a report to the Council on May 26, Thant declared that the closing of the Strait of Tiran represented "a very serious potential threat to peace." He urged all the parties concerned to exercise special restraint during a "breathing spell" to allow the Council to deal with the underlying causes of the crisis.

In his May 26 report, Thant took note of the criticism directed at him in connection with the withdrawal of UNEF. "It has been alleged in some quarters," he said, "that the prompt compliance with the request for the withdrawal of the Force is a primary cause of the present crisis in the Near East." He referred to the "persistence of this misunderstanding" and to "various recent statements of some responsible leaders." During this period and later a number of Western and Israeli leaders actually blamed Thant for opening the way for the Six-Day War which began on June 5. Israeli Foreign Minister Abba Eban called the Secretary-General's action "disastrously swift." In a statement before the fifth emergency special session of the General Assembly on June 19, Eban said in part:

"On May 18, Egypt called for the total removal of the United Nations Emergency Force. The Secretary-General of the United Nations acceded to this request and moved to carry it out, without reference to the Security Council or the General Assembly; without carrying out the procedures indicated by Secretary-General Hammarskjöld in the event of a request for a withdrawal being made; without heeding the protesting voices of some of the permanent members of the Security Council and of the government at whose initiative the Force had been established; without consulting Israel on the consequent prejudice to its military security and its vital maritime freedom; and without seeking such delay as would enable alternative measures to be concerted for preventing belligerency by sea and a dangerous confrontation of forces by land.

It is often said that United Nations procedures are painfully slow. This one, in our view, was disastrously swift. Its effect was to make Sinai safe for belligerency from north and south; to create a sudden disruption of the local security balance; and to leave an international maritime interest exposed to almost certain threat. I will not say anything of the compulsions which may have led to those steps; I speak only of consequences. I have already said that Israel's attitude to the peace-keeping functions of the United Nations has been traumatically affected by this experience. What is the use of a fire brigade which vanishes from the scene as soon as the first smoke and flames appear? Is it surprising that we are resolved never again to allow a vital Israeli interest and our very security to rest on such a fragile foundation?"

Another critic of the Secretary-General was President Lyndon B. Johnson. In a statement on May 23, the President said: "We are dismayed at the hurried withdrawal of the United Nations Emergency Force from Gaza and Sinai after more than ten years of steadfast and effective service in keeping the peace, without action by either the General Assembly or the Security Council of the United Nations. We continue to regard the presence of the United Nations in the area as a matter of fundamental importance. We intend to support its continuance with all possible vigor." Johnson had additional comment in his memoirs, *The Vantage Point,* published in 1971. Referring to the initial Egyptian request on May 16 for the withdrawal of UNEF, the President said: "In action that shocked me then, and that still puzzles me, Secretary-General U Thant announced that UN forces could not remain in the Sinai without Egyptian approval. Even the Egyptians were surprised. Nasser's ambassador in Washington, Dr. Mostafa Kamel, told us that his government had hoped that U Thant would play for time. But he did not, and tension increased."[1]

[1]Lyndon B. Johnson, *The Vantage Point* (New York: Holt, Rinehart and Winston, 1971), p. 290.

As will be seen in the documents below, Thant defended his action as the only feasible course open to him. Beginning with his special report to the General Assembly on May 18, he stressed the principle that the consent of the host country had always been accepted as essential to all United Nations peace-keeping operations. "In the face of the request for the withdrawal of the Force," he said, "there seemed to me to be no alternative course of action which could be taken by the Secretary-General without putting in question the sovereign authority of the government of the United Arab Republic within its own territory." He also took pains to reply to allegations that he acted in haste, that he acted without adequate consultations, and that he should have referred the question to the General Assembly for a decision. Prompt action was essential, he said, because Egyptian forces had overrun UNEF positions, UNEF personnel were in danger of actual bodily harm, they were neither equipped to resist by force nor authorized by their mandate to do so, and because UNEF was on the verge of disintegrating through the threatened withdrawal of the Indian and Yugoslav contingents which made up almost one half of the 3,378-man force at the time of the Egyptian request.

Thant went into this question in some detail on June 3 in a document entitled "Notes on Withdrawal of United Nations Emergency Force." Why did he not at least appeal to President Nasser to reconsider the withdrawal request? "The Secretary-General at the time," he said, "had been made well aware of the high state of emotion and tension in Cairo and in the UNEF area and had the best possible reasons to be convinced that the decision to request the withdrawal was final and that any appeal by him for a reversal of this decision would most certainly be rebuffed." On the question of consultations, he cited a statement by Dag Hammarskjöld on February 26, 1957, that an indicated procedure on a withdrawal request would be for the Secretary-General to inform the UNEF Advisory Committee, "which would determine whether the matter should be brought to the attention of the Assembly." He noted that he had consulted the Advisory Committee before replying to the UAR request on May 18. The records of this meeting show, however, that no vote was taken. In his report to the Security Council on May 26, Thant said, " . . . the Committee did not move, as it was its right to do" to request the convening of the Assembly. As to why he himself did not refer the matter to the Assembly, the Secretary-General said this procedure not only would have been incorrect but unrealistic. He said that UNEF had been stationed on Egyptian territory under terms worked out between Hammarskjöld and Nasser and that there was no "official United Nations document on the basis of which any case could be made that there was any limitation on the authority of the government of Egypt to rescind that consent. . . ." As a practical matter, he said, "It is hard to see what decision other than the withdrawal of UNEF could have been reached by the Assembly once United Arab Republic consent for the continued presence of UNEF was withdrawn."

Thant's reference to the absence of an "official United Nations document" indicating a limitation on the authority of Egypt to rescind its consent passed without notice at the time, but its significance became apparent after the publication on June 19 of the Hammarskjöld *aide-mémoire* of August 5, 1957 (see volume III of this series, pp. 377–382). This document, made public by Ernest A. Gross, former United States representative to the United Nations, was Hammarskjöld's account of the private negotiations between him and the Egyptian government prior to the stationing of UNEF in Gaza and the Sinai. Gross said Hammarskjöld had given him a copy of the *aide-mémoire* two days after its completion and had emphasized that it was not secret, although there was no reason to circulate it at the time. The document described Hammarskjöld's efforts to get Egypt to accept a voluntary limitation on conditions under which it would withdraw its consent for the continued presence of UNEF. His specific objective was to tie the termination of the Egyptian consent to the completion of the task assigned to UNEF— to secure and supervise the cessation of hostilities. In his opinion this was done in the text of the agreement of understanding between him and President Nasser. Egypt had agreed to be guided "in good faith" by its acceptance of the General Assembly resolution of November 5 creating UNEF. .

Publication of the *aide-mémoire* touched off a brief flurry of discussion, but by then the main question had become the aftermath of the Six-Day War. Thant said in a statement that he was "aware of the substance of the paper" when he met Nasser late in May, but insisted that it was not an official document and that it was not relevant to the situation on May 18. The United Arab Republic disavowed the *aide-mémoire* and said it was not binding either legally or politically.

Thant's decision to withdraw UNEF without delay was strongly defended by President Nasser himself as a courageous act in the face of a worldwide campaign opposing the withdrawal. In a speech of May 22, Nasser said:

> "It is obvious that UNEF entered Egypt with our approval and therefore cannot continue to stay except with our approval. . . . . A campaign is also being mounted against the United Nations Secretary-General because he made a faithful and honest decision and could not surrender to the pressure being brought to bear upon him by the United States, Britain and Canada to make UNEF an instrument for implementing imperialism's plans. It is quite natural—and I say this quite frankly— that had UNEF ignored its basic mission and turned to achieving the end of imperialism, we would have regarded it as a hostile force and forcibly disarmed it. We are definitely capable of doing such a job."

The withdrawal of UNEF was not completed until June 17—after the war had come and gone. In his report on July 12 on the liquidation of UNEF, Thant commented:

> "It is only realistic to accept the fact that when a United Nations peace-keeping operation, whether it may be an observation mission or a peace force, is no longer welcome in a country and cooperation with it is withheld, it cannot hope to continue to perform any useful function,

may well soon find itself defenseless and in grave danger, and thus had best be withdrawn as amicably as the prevailing circumstances will permit. If there should be any serious doubt about the wisdom of this latter course, it would be advisable to abandon altogether the notion of a voluntary peace-keeping operation and turn to consideration of enforcement-type actions under Chapter VII of the Charter. The two cannot be mixed. It should be added, however, that it is extremely doubtful that any of the peace-keeping operations thus far mounted by the United Nations would have been acceptable to the governments of the countries in which they have been stationed if they had been originally envisaged in the context of Chapter VII of the Charter. There is no room at all for doubt about this as regards UNEF.''

1. Note to the Security Council

NEW YORK   JANUARY 15, 1967

1. IN VIEW OF disturbing reports received from the Chief of Staff of the United Nations Truce Supervision Organization in Palestine on the morning of January 15, 1967, I have dispatched by telegram to the governments of Israel and Syria through their permanent representatives to the United Nations the following urgent appeal. The appeal reads:

"Reports received by me on the morning of January 15 from General Odd Bull, Chief of Staff of the United Nations Truce Supervision Organization in Palestine, are of such disturbing nature as to impel me to communicate with you urgently. The reports tell of a large build-up of heavy arms, armored vehicles, and military personnel in the area of and within the demilitarized zone on both sides of the line. It is clear that the situation threatens to erupt at any moment into a large-scale clash of military forces in overt violation of the provisions of Security Council resolutions and of the Israel-Syrian General Armistice Agreement.

"I appeal to you in most urgent terms, and I am appealing to the

SOURCE: Security Council Official Records, Twenty-second Year, Supplement for January, February, and March 1967, document S/7683.

other side in identical terms, to restrain your military forces from any action which might result in an armed clash. I also appeal to you to accept without delay or pre-conditions the proposal of the Chief of Staff for an immediate emergency or extraordinary meeting of the Israel-Syrian Mixed Armistice Commission on an agreed agenda, with a view to reaching an understanding on the problems of cultivation in the area which have given rise to the incidents of recent weeks.

"Because of the potential danger implicit in the present situation, I have advised the Chief of Staff to take every step within his authority, including a reinforcement of United Nations military observers on both sides of the line, to secure a halt to the build-up and to avoid a large-scale armed clash. I am also taking the unusual step of immediately informing the members of the Security Council and the Council itself of this message to you.

"I would hope and expect to receive from you a prompt and cooperative response to this appeal."

2. I have also taken the liberty of informing the members of the Council individually of the action I have taken.

---

2. *Special Report to the General Assembly*

NEW YORK   MAY 18, 1967

---

1. This special report is submitted in accordance with paragraph 4 of General Assembly resolution 1125 (XI) of February 2, 1957.

2. On May 18, 1967, at 12 noon, I received through the permanent representative of the United Arab Republic to the United Nations the following message from Mr. Mahmoud Riad, Minister for Foreign Affairs of the United Arab Republic:

Source: Document A/6669; same text as document A/6730 (see General Assembly Official Records, Fifth Emergency Special Session, Annexes, agenda item 5).

The government of the United Arab Republic has the honor to inform Your Excellency that it has decided to terminate the presence of the United Nations Emergency Force on the territory of the United Arab Republic and Gaza Strip.

Therefore, I request that the necessary steps be taken for the withdrawal of the Force as soon as possible.

I avail myself of this opportunity to express to Your Excellency my gratitude and warm regards.

3. I replied to the above message in the early evening of May 18 as follows:

I have the honor to acknowledge your letter to me of May 18 conveying the message from the Minister of Foreign Affairs of the United Arab Republic concerning the United Nations Emergency Force. Please be so kind as to transmit to the Foreign Minister the following message in reply:

"Dear Mr. Minister,

"Your message informing me that your government no longer consents to the presence of the United Nations Emergency Force on the territory of the United Arab Republic, that is to say in Sinai, and in the Gaza Strip, and requesting that the necessary steps be taken for its withdrawal as soon as possible, was delivered to me by the permanent representative of the United Arab Republic at noon on May 18.

"As I have indicated to your permanent representative on May 16, the United Nations Emergency Force entered Egyptian territory with the consent of your government and in fact can remain there only so long as that consent continues. In view of the message now received from you, therefore, your government's request will be complied with and I am proceeding to issue instructions for the necessary arrangements to be put in train without delay for the orderly withdrawal of the Force, its vehicles and equipment and for the disposal of all properties pertaining to it. I am, of course, also bringing this development and my actions and intentions to the attention of the UNEF Advisory Committee and to all governments providing contingents for the Force. A full report covering this development will be submitted promptly by me to the General Assembly, and I consider it necessary to report also to the Security Council about some aspects of the current situation in the area.

"Irrespective of the reasons for the action you have taken, in all frankness, may I advise you that I have serious misgivings about it for, as I have said each year in my annual reports to the General Assembly on UNEF, I believe that this Force has been an important factor in maintaining relative quiet in the area of its deployment during the past ten years and that its withdrawal may have grave implication for peace."

4. Instructions relating to the withdrawal of UNEF were cabled by me to the Force Commander in the evening of May 18.

5. As background, the General Assembly will recall that in resolution 1125 (XI) the General Assembly considered "that, after full withdrawal of Israel from the Sharm el Sheikh and Gaza areas, the scrupulous maintenance of the Armistice Agreement requires the placing of the United Nations Emergency Force on the Egyptian-Israel armistice demarcation line and the implementation of other measures as proposed in the Secretary-General's report, with due regard to the considerations set out therein with a view to assist in achieving situations conducive to the maintenance of peaceful conditions in the area." The General Assembly further requested the Secretary-General, in paragraph 4 of resolution 1125 (XI) "in consultation with the parties concerned, to take steps to carry out these measures and to report, as appropriate, to the General Assembly." Since the eleventh session of the General Assembly the Secretary-General has reported to the Assembly annually on the Force.

6. The general considerations which I have had in mind and the sequence of events leading up to the present situation are set out in an *aide-mémoire* of May 17 which I handed to the permanent representative of the United Arab Republic at 5:30 P.M. on May 17, the text of which reads as follows:

1. The Secretary-General of the United Nations requests the Permanent Representative of the United Arab Republic to the United Nations to convey to his government the Secretary-General's most serious concern over the situation that has arisen with regard to the United Nations Emergency Force in the past twenty-four hours as a result of the demands upon it made by United Arab Republic military authorities and of certain actions of United Arab Republic troops in the area.

2. Before engaging in detail, the Secretary-General wishes to make the following general points entirely clear:

(*a*) He does not in any sense question the authority of the government of the United Arab Republic to deploy its troops as it sees fit in United Arab Republic territory or territory under the control of the United Arab Republic.

(*b*) In the sectors of Gaza and Sinai, however, it must be recognized that the deployment of troops of the United Arab Republic in areas in which UNEF troops are stationed and carrying out their functions may have very serious implications for UNEF, its functioning and its continued presence in the area.

(*c*) The Commander of UNEF cannot comply with any requests affecting the disposition of UNEF troops emanating from any source other than

United Nations Headquarters, and the orders delivered to General Rikhye on May 16 by military officers of the United Arab Republic were not right procedurally and quite rightly were disregarded by General Rikhye.

(*d*) UNEF has been deployed in Gaza and Sinai for more than ten years for the purpose of maintaining quiet along the Armistice Demarcation Line and the International Frontier. It has served this purpose with much distinction. It went into the area and has remained there with the full consent of the government of the United Arab Republic. If that consent should be withdrawn or so qualified as to make it impossible for the Force to function effectively, the Force, of course, will be withdrawn.

3. The following is the sequence of events which have given rise to the present crisis:

(*a*) At 2200 hours local time on May 16 Brigadier Eiz-El-Din Mokhtar handed to General Rikhye, the Commander of UNEF, the following letter:

"For your information, I gave my instructions to all Armed Forces of the United Arab Republic to be ready for action against Israel the moment it might carry out any aggressive action against any Arab country. Due to these instructions our troops are already concentrated in Sinai on our eastern borders. For the sake of complete security of all UN troops which install observation posts along our borders, I request that you issue your orders to withdraw all these troops immediately. I have given my instructions to our Commander of the eastern zone concerning this subject. Inform back the fulfillment of this request. (Signed) M. Fawzy, General of the Army."

(*b*) The Commander of UNEF replied that he had noted the contents of General Fawzy's letter and would report immediately to the Secretary-General for instructions, since he had no authority to withdraw any troops of UNEF, or in any other way to redeploy UNEF troops, except on instructions from the Secretary-General.

(*c*) On learning of the substance of General Fawzy's letter to General Rikhye, the Secretary-General asked the permanent representative of the United Arab Republic to the United Nations to see him immediately. The permanent representative of the United Arab Republic came to the Secretary-General's office at 1845 hours on May 16. The Secretary-General requested him to communicate with his government with the utmost urgency and to transmit to them his views, of which the following is a summary:

(i) The letter addressed to the Commander of UNEF was not right procedurally since the Commander of UNEF could not take orders affecting his command from a source other than the Secretary-General. General Rikhye was therefore correct in his insistence on taking no action until he received instructions from the Secretary-General.

(ii) The exact intent of General Fawzy's letter needed clarification. If it meant the temporary withdrawal of UNEF troops from the line or from parts of it, it would be unacceptable because the purpose of the United Nations Force in Gaza and Sinai is to prevent a recurrence of fighting, and it cannot be asked to stand aside in order to enable the two sides to resume fighting. If it was intended to mean a general withdrawal of UNEF from

Gaza and Sinai, the communication should have been addressed to the Secretary-General from the government of the United Arab Republic and not to the Commander of UNEF from the Chief of Staff of the Armed Forces of the United Arab Republic.

(iii) If it was the intention of the government of the United Arab Republic to withdraw the consent which it gave in 1956 for the stationing of UNEF on the territory of the United Arab Republic and in Gaza it was, of course, entitled to do so. Since, however, the basis for the presence of UNEF was an agreement made directly between President Nasser and Dag Hammarskjöld as Secretary-General of the United Nations, any request for the withdrawal of UNEF must come directly to the Secretary-General from the government of the United Arab Republic. On receipt of such a request, the Secretary-General would order the withdrawal of all UNEF troops from Gaza and Sinai, simultaneously informing the General Assembly of what he was doing and why.

(iv) A request by the United Arab Republic authorities for a temporary withdrawal of UNEF from the Armistice Demarcation Line and the International Frontier, or from any parts of them, would be considered by the Secretary-General as tantamount to a request for the complete withdrawal of UNEF from Gaza and Sinai, since this would reduce UNEF to ineffectiveness.

(d) The Secretary-General informed the Commander of UNEF of the position as outlined above, as explained to the permanent representative of the United Arab Republic, and instructed him to do all that he reasonably could to maintain all UNEF positions pending further instructions.

(e) At 0800 hours Z, on May 17, the Commander of UNEF reported that on the morning of May 17, 30 soldiers of the Army of the United Arab Republic had occupied El Sabha in Sinai and that their troops were deployed in the immediate vicinity of the UNEF Observation Post there. Three armored cars of the United Arab Republic were located near the Yugoslav UNEF camp at El Sabha and detachments of 15 soldiers each had taken up positions north and south of the Yugoslav camp at El Amr. All UNEF Observation Posts along the Armistice Demarcation Line and International Frontier were manned as usual.

(f) At 1030 hours Z on May 17, the Commander of UNEF reported that troops of the United Arab Republic had occupied the UNEF Observation Post on El Sabha and that the Yugoslav UNEF camps at El Qusaima and El Sabha were now behind the positions of the Army of the United Arab Republic. The Commander of UNEF informed the Chief of the United Arab Republic Liaison Service of these developments, expressing his serious concern at them. The Chief ot the United Arab Republic Liaison Service agreed to request the immediate vacation of the Observation Post at El Sabha by troops of the United Arab Republic and shortly thereafter reported that orders to this effect had been given by the United Arab Republic military authorities. He requested, however, that to avoid any future misunderstandings the Yugoslav Observation Post at El Sabha should be immediately withdrawn to El Qusaima camp. The Commander replied that any such withdrawal would require the authorization of the Secretary-General.

(g) At 1200 hours Z, the Chief of the United Arab Republic Liaison Service conveyed to the Commander of UNEF a request from General Mohammed Fawzy, Chief of Staff of the Armed Forces of the United Arab Republic, for the withdrawal of UNEF Yugoslav detachments in the Sinai within twenty-four hours. He added that the Commander of UNEF might take forty-eight hours or so to withdraw the UNEF detachment from Sharm el Sheikh.

(h) At 1330 hours Z, the Commander of UNEF reported that a sizable detachment of troops of the United Arab Republic was moving into the UNEF area at El Kuntilla.

4. The Secretary-General is obliged to state that UNEF cannot remain in the field under the conditions described in the foregoing paragraphs. The function of UNEF has been to assist in maintaining quiet along the line by acting as a deterrent to infiltration and as a buffer between the opposing forces. It can discharge neither of these functions if it is removed from the line and finds itself stationed behind forces of the United Arab Republic. In other words, UNEF, which has contributed so greatly to the relative quiet which has prevailed in the area in which it has been deployed for more that ten years, cannot now be asked to stand aside in order to become a silent and helpless witness to an armed confrontation between the parties. If, therefore, the orders to the troops of the United Arab Republic referred to above are maintained, the Secretary-General will have no choice but to order the withdrawal of UNEF from Gaza and Sinai as expeditiously as possible.

5. The Secretary-General wishes also to inform the permanent representative of the United Arab Republic that as of now, on the basis of the fully reliable reports received from the Chief of Staff of the United Nations Truce Supervision Organization in Palestine, there have been no recent indications of troop movements or concentrations along any of the lines which should give rise to undue concern.

6. The Secretary-General requests the permanent representative of the United Arab Republic to transmit the contents of this *aide-mémoire* with utmost urgency to his government.

7. At the same time the following *aide-mémoire* dated May 17 was handed by me to the permanent representative of the United Arab Republic:

It will be recalled that in an *aide-mémoire* attached to the report of the Secretary-General on basic points for the presence and functioning in Egypt of the United Nations Emergency Force it was recorded that:

"1. The government of Egypt declares that, when exercising its sovereign rights on any matter concerning the presence and functioning of UNEF, it will be guided, in good faith, by its acceptance of General Assembly resolution 1000 (ES-I) of November 5, 1956."

The *aide-mémoire* also records that:

"2. The United Nations takes note of this declaration of the government of Egypt and declares that the activities of UNEF will be guided, in good faith, by the task established for the Force in the aforementioned resolutions; in particular, the United Nations, understanding this to correspond to the wishes of the government of Egypt, reaffirms its willingness to maintain UNEF until its task is completed."

The General Assembly, in resolution 1121 (XI) of November 24, 1956, noted with approval the contents of the *aidmémoire* referred to above.

The Minister for Foreign Affairs of Egypt, in concluding on behalf of the government of Egypt the agreement of February 8, 1957, concerning the status of the United Nations Emergency Force in Egypt, recalled:

". . . the declaration of the government of Egypt that, when exercising its sovereign powers on any matter concerning the presence and functioning of the United Nations Emergency Force, it would be guided, in good faith, by its acceptance of the General Assembly resolution of November 5, 1956. . . ."

8. As a result of the situation described above, I held an informal meeting with the representatives of the countries providing contingents to UNEF in the late afternoon of May 17. I informed them of the situation as then known and there was an exchange of views.

9. Since the first *aide-mémoire* was written the following developments have been reported by the Commander of UNEF:

(*a*) Early on May 18, the sentries of the UNEF Yugoslav detachment were forced out of their observation post on the International Frontier near El Kuntilla camp. At 1220 hours GMT on May 18, 1967, soldiers of the United Arab Republic forced UNEF soldiers of the Yugoslav contingent to withdraw from the observation post on the International Frontier in front of El Amr camp, and later officers of the United Arab Republic visited El Amr camp and asked the UNEF Yugoslav platoon to withdraw within fifteen minutes.

(*b*) At 1210 hours GMT on May 18, officers of the United Arab Republic visited the Yugoslav camp at Sharm el Sheikh and informed the Commanding Officer that they had come to take over the camp and the UNEF observation post at Ras Nasrani, demanding a reply within fifteen minutes.

(*c*) At 1430 hours GMT on May 18, the UNEF Yugoslav detachment at El Qusaima camp reported that two artillery shells, apparently ranging rounds from the United Arab Republic artillery, had burst between the UNEF Yugoslav camps at El Qusaima and El Sabha.

(*d*) At 0857 hours GMT on May 18, a UNEF aircraft carrying Major-General Rikhye, the Commander of UNEF, on a flight from El Arish to Gaza was intercepted west of the Armistice Demarcation Line by two Israel military aircraft which tried to make the UNEF aircraft follow them to the Israel side of the line to land, and went so far as to fire several warning shots. The pilot of the United Nations aircraft, on instructions from the UNEF Commander, ignored these efforts and proceeded to land at Gaza. I have strongly protested this incident to the government of Israel through the permanent representative of Israel to the United Nations. The Chief of Staff of the Israel Defense Forces has since conveyed regrets for this incident to Major-General Rikhye.

10. Late in the afternoon of May 18, I convened a meeting of the UNEF Advisory Committee, set up under the terms of paragraphs 6, 8, and 9 of resolution 1001 (ES-I) of November 7, 1956, and the representatives of three countries not members of the Advisory Committee but providing contingents to UNEF to inform them of developments and to consult them on the situation.

11. The exchange of notes between the Minister for Foreign Affairs of the United Arab Republic and the Secretary-General, quoted at the beginning of this report, explains the position which I have found myself compelled to adopt under the resolutions of the General Assembly and the agreements reached between the Secretary-General of the United Nations and the Egyptian authorities as the basis for the entry of UNEF into the territory of the United Arab Republic in November 1956, and its subsequent deployment in Gaza and Sinai in 1957.

12. I have taken this position for the following main reasons:

(*a*) The United Nations Emergency Force was introduced into the territory of the United Arab Republic on the basis of an agreement reached in Cairo between the Secretary-General of the United Nations and the President of Egypt, and it therefore has seemed fully clear to me that since United Arab Republic consent was withdrawn it was incumbent on the Secretary-General to give orders for the withdrawal of the Force. The consent of the host country is a basic principle which has applied to all United Nations peace-keeping operations.

(*b*) In practical fact, UNEF cannot remain or function without the continuing consent and cooperation of the host country.

(*c*) I have also been influenced by my deep concern to avoid any action which would either compromise or endanger the contingents which make up the Force. The United Nations Emergency Force is, after all, a peace-keeping and not an enforcement operation.

(*d*) In the face of the request for the withdrawal of the Force, there seemed to me to be no alternative course of action which could be taken by the Secretary-General without putting in question the sovereign authority of the government of the United Arab Republic within its own territory.

13. I cannot conclude this report without expressing the deepest concern as to the possible implications of the latest developments for peace in the area. For more than ten years UNEF, acting as a buffer between the opposing forces of Israel and the United Arab Republic on the Armistice Demarcation Line in Gaza and the International Frontier in Sinai, has been the principal means of maintaining quiet in the area. Its removal inevitably restores the armed confrontation of the United Arab Republic and Israel and removes the stabilizing influence of an international force operating along the boundaries between the two nations. Much as I regret this development, I have no option but to respect and acquiesce in the request of the government of the United Arab Republic. I can only express the hope that both sides will now exercise the utmost calm and restraint in this new situation, which otherwise will be fraught with danger.

14. Finally, I must express the highest appreciation to the governments of all the Members of the United Nations which have supported UNEF and especially to those which have provided the military contingents which made up the Force. The appreciation of the United Nations is also due to the many thousand officers and men who have served so loyally and with such distinction in UNEF. The Force at its inception represented an extraordinary innovation in the efforts of the world community to find improved methods of keeping the peace. For more than ten years it has fulfilled its functions with a far greater degree of success than could have been hoped for. It is, in fact, the model upon which many hopes for the future effectiveness of the United Nations in peace-keeping have been based. Its termination at this particular time raises serious anxiety as to the maintenance of peace in the area in which it is operating. In this anxious time, therefore, I feel it my duty to appeal not only to the parties directly affected by the withdrawal of UNEF to do all in their power to keep

the peace, but also to all the Members of the United Nations to intensify their efforts both for the maintenance of peace in this particular situation and for the improvement of the capacity of the organization to maintain peace. It goes without saying that I shall continue to do all within my power toward the attainment of both these objectives.

---

3. Report to the Security Council

NEW YORK   MAY 19, 1967

---

1. I HAVE FELT it to be an obligation to submit this report in order to convey to members of the Council my deep anxiety about recent developments in the Near East and what I consider to be an increasingly dangerous deterioration along the borders there.

2. The members of the Council will be aware of the special report on the United Nations Emergency Force which I made to the General Assembly on May 18, 1967 [A/6669].

3. I am very sorry to feel obliged to say that in my considered opinion the prevailing state of affairs in the Near East as regards relations between the Arab states and Israel, and among the Arab states themselves, is extremely menacing.

4. There has been a steady deterioration along the line between Israel and Syria, particularly with regard to disputes over cultivation rights in the demilitarized zone, since the first of the year. In this regard I may point to my notes to the Council of January 15, 1967 [S/7683] and of May 8, 1967 [S/7877]. In late January the Chief of Staff of the United Nations Truce Supervision Organization in Palestine, General Odd Bull, obtained the agreement of Israel and Syria to attend an emergency and extraordinary meeting of the Israel-Syrian Mixed Armistice Commission on an agreed agenda item on cultivation problems. Three meetings were actually held but the agreed

SOURCE: Security Council Official Records, Twenty-second Year, Supplement for April, May and June 1967, document S/7896.

agenda item was not discussed because both parties insisted on first bringing up broader issues. It has not been possible to achieve a resumption of these meetings owing to an impasse over a position taken firmly by Syria. In consequence, General Bull, on my advice [see S/7877], is now trying to initiate separate discussions with the two parties in order to work out practical cultivation arrangements affecting disputed lands along the line.

5. It was precisely in the effort to avert serious armed clashes such as that which occurred on April 7, 1967, that so much emphasis has been given by the Chief of Staff of the United Nations Truce Supervision Organization in Palestine to the need for discussion and agreement on cultivation arrangements, whether achieved within or outside the Israel-Syrian Mixed Armistice Commission. In the absence of such an agreement, tension along the line continues high and the possibility of new armed clashes in disputed areas is ever present.

6. A number of factors serve to aggravate the situation to an unusual degree, increasing tension and danger.

7. El Fatah activities, consisting of terrorism and sabotage, are a major factor in that they provoke strong reactions in Israel by the government and population alike. Some recent incidents of this type have seemed to indicate a new level of organization and training of those who participate in these actions. It is clear that the functions and resources of the Truce Supervision Organization do not enable it to arrest these activities. Although allegations are often made, to the best of my knowledge there is no verified information about the organization, central direction, and originating source of these acts, which have occurred intermittently in the vicinity of Israel's lines with Jordan, Lebanon, and Syria. All three of the latter governments have officially disclaimed responsibility for these acts and those who perpetrate them. I am not in a position to say whether any or all of the governments concerned have done everything they reasonably can to prevent such activities across their borders. The fact is that they do recur with disturbing regularity.

8. Intemperate and bellicose utterances, by other officials and non-officials, eagerly reported by the Press and radio, are unfortunately more or less routine on both sides of the lines in the Near East. In recent weeks, however, reports emanating from Israel have attributed to some high officials in that state statements so threatening as to

be particulary inflammatory in the sense that they could only heighten emotions and thereby increase tensions on the other side of the lines.

9. There have been in the past few days persistent reports about troop movements and concentrations, particularly on the Israel side of the Syrian border. These have caused anxiety and at times excitement. The government of Israel very recently has assured me that there are no unusual Israel troop concentrations or movements along the Syrian line, that there will be none and that no military action will be initiated by the armed forces of Israel unless such action is first taken by the other side. Reports from observers of the Truce Supervision Organization have confirmed the absense of troop concentrations and significant troop movements on both sides of the line.

10. The decision of the government of the United Arab Republic to terminate its consent for the continued presence of the United Nations Emergency Force on United Arab Republic territory in Sinai and on United Arab Republic controlled territory in Gaza came suddenly and was unexpected. The reasons for this decision have not been officially stated, but they were clearly regarded as overriding by the government of the United Arab Republic. It is certain that they had nothing to do with the conduct of the Force itself or the way in which it was carrying out the mandate entrusted to it by the General Assembly and accepted by the government of the United Arab Republic when it gave its consent for the deployment of the Force within its jurisdiction. There can be no doubt, in fact, that the Force has discharged its responsibilities with remarkable effectiveness and great distinction. No United Nations peace-keeping operation can be envisaged as permanent or semipermanent. Each one must come to an end at some time or another. The United Nations Emergency Force has been active for ten and a half years and that is a very long time for any country to have foreign troops, even under an international banner, operating autonomously on its soil. On the other hand, it can be said that the timing of the withdrawal of the Force leaves much to be desired because of the prevailing tensions and dangers throughout the area. It also adds one more frontier on which there is a direct confrontation between the military forces of Israel and those of her Arab neighbors.

11. It is well to bear in mind that United Nations peace-keeping operations such as the United Nations Emergency Force, and this

applies in fact to all peace-keeping operations thus far undertaken by the United Nations, depend for their presence and effectiveness not only on the consent of the authorities in the area of their deployment but on the cooperation and goodwill of those authorities. When, for example, the United Arab Republic decided to move its troops up to the line, which it had a perfect right to do, the buffer function which the Force had been performing was eliminated. Its continued presence was thus rendered useless, its position untenable, and its withdrawal became virtually inevitable. This was the case even before the official request for the withdrawal had been received by me.

12. It is all too clear that there is widespread misunderstanding about the nature of United Nations peace-keeping operations in general and the United Nations Emergency Force in particular. As I pointed out in my special report of May 18, 1967, to the General Assembly, "The United Nations Emergency Force is, after all, a peace-keeping and not an enforcement operation." This means, of course, that the operation is based entirely on its acceptance by the governing authority of the territory on which it operates and that it is not in any sense related to Chapter VII of the Charter. It is a fact beyond dispute that neither the United Nations Emergency Force nor any other United Nations peace-keeping operation thus far undertaken would have been permitted to enter the territory involved if there had been any suggestion that it had the right to remain there against the will of the governing authority.

13. The order for the withdrawal of the United Nations Emergency Force has been given. The actual process of withdrawal will be orderly, deliberate, and dignified and not precipitate.

14. I do not believe that any of the governments concerned are so careless of the welfare of their own people or of the risks of a spreading conflict as to deliberately embark on military offensives across their borders, unless they become convinced, rightly or wrongly, that they are threatened. Nevertheless, there is good reason to fear that the withdrawal of the Force will give rise to increased danger along the armistice demarcation line and the international frontier between Israel and the United Arab Republic. The presence of the Force has been a deterrent and restraining influence along both lines. There are some particularly sensitive areas involved, notably Sharm el Sheikh and Gaza. The former concerns the Strait of Tiran.

In the Gaza Strip there are 307,000 refugees and the substantial Palestine Liberation Army must also be taken into account.

15. It is true to a considerable extent that the Force has allowed us for ten years to ignore some of the hard realities of the underlying conflict. The governments concerned, and the United Nations, are now confronted with a brutally realistic and dangerous situation.

16. The Egyptian-Israel Mixed Armistice Commission, established by the Egyptian-Israel General Armistice Agreement, remains in existence with its headquarters at Gaza, and could, as it did prior to the establishment of the United Nations Emergency Force, provide a limited form of United Nations presence in the area, as in the case of the other mixed armistice commissions which are served by the United Nations Truce Supervision Organization in Palestine. The government of Israel, however, has denounced the Egyptian-Israel Mixed Armistice Commission and for some years has refused to have anything to do with it. The United Nations has never accepted as valid this unilateral action by the government of Israel. It would most certainly be helpful in the present situation if the government of Israel were to reconsider its position and resume its participation in the Egyptian-Israel Mixed Armistice Commission.

17. Similarly, I may repeat what I have said in the past, that it would be very helpful to the maintenance of quiet along the Israel-Syrian line if the two parties would resume their participation in the Israel-Syrian Mixed Armistice Commission, both in the current emergency session and in the regular sessions.

18. Since the announcement of the decision of the government of the United Arab Republic with regard to the United Nations Emergency Force, tension in the area has mounted. Troop movements on both sides have been observed, but as of the evening of May 19 these do not seem to have attained alarming proportions. Although one brief shooting incident on May 19 has been reported, I believe it can be said that as of this moment there is no indication on either side of the line of any major action of an offensive nature, but the confrontation along the line between the armed forces of the two countries which has been avoided for more than ten years now quickly begins to reappear. Unless there is very great restraint on both sides of the line, one can readily envisage a series of local clashes across the line which could easily escalate into heavy conflict.

19. I do not wish to be alarmist but I cannot avoid the warning to the Council that in my view the current situation in the Near East is more disturbing, indeed, I may say more menacing, than at any time since the fall of 1956.

---

4. *Report to the Security Council*

NEW YORK   MAY 26, 1967

---

1. IN MY REPORT of May 19, 1967 [S/7896], which I submitted to the Security Council following the receipt on May 18, 1967, of the official request of the government of the United Arab Republic for the withdrawal of the United Nations Emergency Force (UNEF), I described the general situation in the Near East at present as "more disturbing, indeed, . . . more menacing, than at any time since the fall of 1956." I can only reiterate this assessment.

2. It has been alleged in some quarters that the prompt compliance with the request for the withdrawal of the Force is a primary cause of the present crisis in the Near East. This ignores the fact that the underlying basis for this and other crisis situations in the Near East is the continuing Arab-Israel conflict which has been present all along, and of which the crisis situation created by the unexpected request for the withdrawal of the Emergency Force is the latest expression. In my special report to the General Assembly, in paragraph 12, I gave the main reasons for the position that I have taken on this issue. In my report to the Security Council on May 19, 1967, I restated the basis for my decision and pointed out that there was a "widespread misunderstanding about the nature of United Nations peace-keeping operations in general and the United Nations Emergency Force in particular." In view of the evident persistence of this misunderstanding and of various recent public statements by some responsible leaders, I feel obliged once again, before proceeding with my report, to restate

SOURCE: Security Council Official Records, Twenty-second Year, Supplement for April, May and June 1967, document S/7906.

briefly the grounds for the position which I have taken on the withdrawal of the Force.

3. The United Nations Emergency Force was introduced into the territory of the United Arab Republic on the basis of an agreement between the Secretary-General of the United Nations and the President of Egypt. The consent of the host country, in this as in other peace-keeping operations, was the basis for its presence on the territory of the United Arab Republic. When that consent was withdrawn, the essential part of the basis of the Force's presence ceased to exist.

4. As stated in my special report to the General Assembly, I consulted with the Advisory Committee of the Force on May 18, 1967. The Committee did not move, as it was its right to do under the terms of paragraph 9 of General Assembly resolution 1001 (ES-I), of November 7, 1956, to request the convening of the General Assembly on the situation which had arisen. It was after this meeting of the Advisory Committee, on the evening of May 18, that I transmitted my reply to the government of the United Arab Republic concerning the withdrawal of the Force.

5. My decision in this matter was based upon both legal and practical considerations. It is a practical fact that neither the United Nations Emergency Force nor any other United Nations peace-keeping operation could function or even exist without the continuing consent and cooperation of the host country. Once the consent of the host country was withdrawn and it was no longer welcome, its usefulness was ended. In fact, the movement of United Arab Republic forces up to the line in Sinai even before the request for withdrawal was received by me had already made the effective functioning of the Force impossible. I may say here that the request received by me on May 18 was the only request received from the government of the United Arab Republic, since the cryptic letter to Major-General Rikhye from General Fawzy on May 16 was both unclear and unacceptable. Furthermore, I had very good reasons to be convinced of the earnestness and the determination of the government of the United Arab Republic in requesting the withdrawal of the Force. It was therefore obvious to me that the position of the personnel of the Force would soon become extremely difficult, and even dangerous, if the decision for the withdrawal of the Force was delayed, while the possibility for its effective action had already been virtually elimi-

nated. Moreover, if the request were not promptly complied with, the Force would quickly disintegrate due to the withdrawal of individual contingents.

6. It may be relevant to note here that the Force functioned exclusively on the United Arab Republic side of the line in a zone from which the armed forces of the United Arab Republic had voluntarily stayed away for over ten years. It was this arrangement which allowed the Force to function as a buffer and as a restraint on infiltration. When this arrangement lapsed United Arab Republic troops moved up to the line as they had every right to do.

7. If the Force had been deployed on both sides of the line as originally envisaged in pursuance of the General Assembly resolution, its buffer function would not necessarily have ended. However, its presence on the Israel side of the line has never been permitted. The fact that the Force was not stationed on the Israel side of the line was a recognition of the unquestioned sovereign right of Israel to withhold its consent for the stationing of the Force. The acquiescence in the request of the United Arab Republic for the withdrawal of the Force after ten and a half years on United Arab Republic soil was likewise a recognition of the sovereign authority of the United Arab Republic. In no official document relating to the Force has there been any suggestion of a limitation of this sovereign authority.

8. In order to discuss the situation with the government of the United Arab Republic, and especially in order to examine with that government the situation created by the withdrawal of the Force, I decided to advance the date of a visit to Cairo which I had planned some time ago for the beginning of July. I arrived in Cairo on the afternoon of May 23, and left Cairo on the early afternoon of May 25, to return to United Nations Headquarters.

9. During my stay in Cairo I had discussions with President Gamal Abdel Nasser and Mr. Mahmoud Riad, the Minister for Foreign Affairs. They explained to me the position of the government of the United Arab Republic, which is substantially as set forth in the speech given by President Nasser to the United Arab Republic Air Force Advance Command on May 22, 1967, which has been reported fully in the Press. President Nasser and Foreign Minister Riad assured me that the United Arab Republic would not initiate offensive action against Israel. Their general aim, as stated to me, was for

a return to the conditions prevailing prior to 1956 and to full observance by both parties of the provisions of the General Armistice Agreement between Egypt and Israel.

10. The decision of the government of the United Arab Republic to restrict shipping in the Strait of Tiran, of which I learned while en route to Cairo, has created a new situation. Free passage through the Strait is one of the questions which the government of Israel considers most vital to her interests. The position of the government of the United Arab Republic is that the Strait is territorial waters in which it has a right to control shipping. The government of Israel contests this position and asserts the right of innocent passage through the Strait. The government of Israel has further declared that Israel will regard the closing of the Strait of Tiran to Israel flagships and any restriction on cargoes of ships of other flags proceeding to Israel as a *casus belli*. While in Cairo, I called to the attention of the government of the United Arab Republic the dangerous consequences which could ensue from restricting innocent passage of ships in the Strait of Tiran. I expressed my deep concern in this regard and my hope that no precipitate action would be taken.

11. A legal controversy existed prior to 1956 as to the extent of the right of innocent passage by commercial vessels through the Strait of Tiran and the Gulf of Aqaba. Since March 1957, when UNEF forces were stationed at Sharm el Sheikh and Ras Nasrani at the mouth of the Gulf of Aqaba, there has been no interference with shipping in the Strait of Tiran.

12. It is not my purpose here to go into the legal aspects of this controversy or to enter into the merits of the case. At this critical juncture I feel that my major concern must be to try to gain time in order to lay the basis for a détente. The important immediate fact is that, in view of the conflicting stands taken by the United Arab Republic and Israel, the situation in the Strait of Tiran represents a very serious potential threat to peace. I greatly fear that a clash between the United Arab Republic and Israel over this issue, in the present circumstances, will inevitably set off a general conflict in the Near East.

13. The freedom of navigation through the Strait of Tiran is not, however, the only immediate issue which is endangering peace in the Near East. Other problems, such as sabotage and terrorist activities

and rights of cultivation in disputed areas in the demilitarized zone between Israel and Syria, will, unless controlled, almost surely lead to further serious fighting.

14. In my view, a peaceful outcome to the present crisis will depend upon a breathing spell which will allow tension to subside from its present explosive level. I therefore urge all the parties concerned to exercise special restraint, to forgo belligerence and to avoid all other actions which could increase tension, to allow the Council to deal with the underlying causes of the present crisis and to seek solutions.

15. There are other possible courses of action which might contribute substantially to the reduction of tension in the area. In paragraph 16 of my report to the Security Council on May 19 [S/7896] I referred to the possibility of the Egyptian-Israel Mixed Armistice Commission providing a limited form of United Nations presence in the area. In that report I stated that "it would most certainly be helpful in the present situation if the government of Israel were to reconsider its position and resume its participation in the Egyptian-Israel Mixed Armistice Commission." I suggest that the Council consider this possible approach also during its search for ways out of the present crisis. This form of United Nations presence could to some extent fill the vacuum left by the withdrawal of the Force.

16. In paragraph 17 of my previous report to the Council I also suggested that "it would be very helpful to the maintenance of quiet along the Israel-Syrian line if the two parties would resume their participation in the Israel-Syrian Mixed Armistice Commission, both in the current emergency session and in the regular sessions," and I would wish on this occasion to repeat that suggestion.

17. It also would be useful for the Council to recall that, by its resolution 73 (1949) of August 11, 1949, the Council found that "the Armistice Agreements constitute an important step toward the establishment of permanent peace in Palestine." And reaffirmed: "the order contained in its resolution 54 (1948) to the governments and authorities concerned, pursuant to Article 40 of the Charter of the United Nations, to observe an unconditional cease-fire and, bearing in mind that the several Armistice Agreements include firm pledges against any further acts of hostility between the parties and also provide for their supervision by the parties themselves, relies upon

the parties to ensure the continued application and observance of these Agreements."

18. In my discussion with officials of the United Arab Republic and Israel I have mentioned possible steps which could be taken by mutual consent and which would help to reduce tension. I shall of course continue to make all possible efforts to contribute to a solution of the present crisis. The problems to be faced are complex and the obstacles are formidable. I do not believe however that we can allow ourselves to despair.

19. It should be kept always in mind that in spite of the extreme difficulties of the situation, the United Nations has played an essential and important role for more than eighteen years in maintaining at least some measure of peace in the Near East. In that task it has encountered many setbacks, frustrations, crises, conflicts, and even war, but the effort continues unabated. We are now confronted with new and threatening circumstances, but I still believe that with the cooperation of all parties concerned the United Nations, and the Security Council in particular, must continue to seek, and eventually to find, reasonable, peaceful, and just solutions.

5. Notes on Withdrawal of UNEF

NEW YORK   JUNE 3, 1967

IN HIS SPECIAL REPORT of May 18, 1967, to the General Assembly (A/6669) the Secretary-General gave the main reasons for his decision to comply promptly with the request of the government of the United Arab Republic for the withdrawal of the United Nations Emergency Force (UNEF). He repeated and amplified these reasons in his reports to the Security Council of May 19, 1967 (S/7896), and May 26, 1967 (S/7906). Since there still seems to be a widespread and, in some quarters, both governmental and public, a determined misunder-

SOURCE: UN Press Release EMF/449.

standing on this matter, the following comments summarize the basis
of and the reasons for the Secretary-General's decision.

I

The question of alternative courses of action

1. The decision on the withdrawal of UNEF was based on both
legal and practical considerations of an overriding nature.

2. Briefly, the legal considerations are that since UNEF was introduced on the territory of Egypt on the basis of the consent of the
government of Egypt and by an agreement between Secretary-General Dag Hammarskjöld and President Nasser, that consent was at
any time basic to its presence on the territory of Egypt. When that
consent was withdrawn—and the United Arab Republic's right to do
this could not be questioned—the basis for UNEF's presence ceased
to exist.

3. As a purely practical matter and apart from legal considerations,
all the United Nations peace-keeping forces depend not only on the
consent, but on the active cooperation, of the host government. The
functions of a peace-keeping force cannot be exercised without that
consent and cooperation. The Security Council, of course, has
authority under Chapter VII of the Charter to take enforcement
measures. In the case of UNEF, its buffer function, which had been
made possible for over ten years only by the cooperation of the
United Arab Republic, had already lapsed before the request for
withdrawal was received by virtue of the decision of the United Arab
Republic to move its troops up to the line. Furthermore, the position
and security of the personnel of the Force would certainly have been
gravely endangered if the Secretary-General had sought to maintain
the Force against the express wish of the government of the United
Arab Republic.

4. Both the legal and the practical reasons for the withdrawal of
UNEF will be examined in more detail later, but with these considerations in mind the Secretary-General had only three possible courses
of action, namely, to comply with the request for withdrawal, to
reject the request, or deliberately to delay the response. In the
considered opinion of the Secretary-General the latter two courses, in

the existing circumstances, would have served no purpose other than to worsen an already explosive situation and might also have had disastrous results as regards the safety of the United Nations Force.

5. The Secretary-General has had, and has expressed, from the very outset of the present crisis his deep misgivings about the consequences which would probably ensue from the withdrawal of UNEF. These misgivings have also been expressed more than once in recent years in the Secretary-General's annual reports to the General Assembly, when the continued existence of UNEF was being threatened through the dwindling and increasing uncertainty of funds. These misgivings, however, could not affect the overriding nature both of the legal and practical reasons for compliance with the request of the United Arab Republic for withdrawal.

II

Regarding assertions that the decision to withdraw UNEF was "hasty," "hurried," etc.

6. The question of the withdrawal of UNEF is by no means a new one. In fact, it was the negotiations on this very question with the government of Egypt which, after its establishment by the General Assembly, delayed the arrival of UNEF, then concentrated in a staging area at Capodichino airbase, Naples, for several days in November 1956. The government of Egypt, understandably, did not wish to give permission for the arrival on its soil of an international force, unless it was assured that a request for withdrawal would be honored. Over the years in discussions with representatives of the United Arab Republic the subject of the continued presence of UNEF had occasionally come up, and it was invariably taken for granted by United Arab Republic representatives that if the United Arab Republic officially requested the withdrawal of UNEF, the request would be honored by the Secretary-General. Thus, although the request for the withdrawal of UNEF came suddenly and as a surprise, there was nothing new about the question of principle nor about the procedure to be followed by the Secretary-General—hence the decision taken by him on May 18, 1967, to comply with the request for the withdrawal of the Force. The actual withdrawal itself, of course, was to

be, and is being, carried out in an orderly, dignified, deliberate, and not precipitate manner. That withdrawal is now under way in accordance with a carefully worked out plan.

7. It has been alleged in some quarters that the United Arab Republic first requested only the withdrawal of UNEF from the line and not from United Arab Republic territory. In a practical sense, this is an academic point, since UNEF, if it was not stationed actually on the line, would have had no useful function anyway. In fact, however, the cryptic letter received by General Indar Jit Rikhye from General Mohammed Fawzy on the night of May 16, 1967, was ignored by General Rikhye and rejected by the Secretary-General as being both incorrectly directed and unclear in meaning. The only official request received by the Secretary-General, therefore, was the one which came from the Foreign Minister of the government of the United Arab Republic on May 18, 1967, and this very clearly called for the complete withdrawal of UNEF. This request from the Foreign Minister of the United Arab Republic was not an "ultimatum," as it has been called, but a request to the Secretary-General that steps be taken to remove the Force as soon as possible.

8. It has been said also that the Secretary-General should have appealed to the government of the United Arab Republic to reconsider this request. The Secretary-General at the time had been made well aware of the high state of emotion and tension in Cairo and in the UNEF area and had the best possible reasons to be convinced that the decision to request the withdrawal was final and that any appeal by him for a reversal of this decision would most certainly be rebuffed. In fact, ominous expressions such as "army of occupation" were already beginning to emanate from Cairo, and they would only have been magnified and justified if UNEF had sought to stay beyond its welcome, with a predictable hostile public reaction to the presence of the Force.

III

The question of adequate consultation by the Secretary-General

9. It has been said that there was not adequate consultation with the organs of the United Nations concerned or with the Members before the decision was taken to withdraw the Force. As stated

above, the Secretary-General was, and is, firmly of the opinion that the decision for the withdrawal of the Force, on request of the host government, rested with the Secretary-General after consultation with the Advisory Committee on UNEF. Secretary-General Hammarskjöld took the following position in reply to a question about the withdrawal of the Force from Sharm el Sheikh on February 26, 1957:

An indicated procedure would be for the Secretary-General to inform the Advisory Committee on the United Nations Emergency Force, which would determine whether the matter should be brought to the attention of the Assembly (A/3563, annex I.B.2).

The Secretary-General consulted the Advisory Committee before replying to the letter of May 18, 1967, from the United Arab Republic requesting withdrawal. This consultation took place within a few hours after receipt of the United Arab Republic request, and the Advisory Committee was informed of the decision which the Secretary-General had in mind to convey in his reply to the Foreign Minister of the United Arab Republic. As indicated in the report to the Security Council of May 26 (S/7906, para. 4):

The Committee did not move, as it was its right to do under the terms of paragraph 9 of General Assembly resolution 1001 (ES-I) of November 7, 1956, to request the convening of the General Assembly on the situation which had arisen.

Before consulting the Advisory Committee on UNEF, the Secretary-General had also consulted the permanent representatives of the seven countries providing the contingents of UNEF and informed them of his intentions. This was what was required of the Secretary-General.

10. Obviously, many governments were concerned about the presence and functioning of UNEF and about the general situation in the area, but it would have been physically impossible to consult all of the interested representatives within any reasonable time. This was an emergency situation requiring urgent action. Moreover, it was perfectly clear that such consultations were sure to produce sharply divided counsel even if they were limited to the permanent members of the Security Council. This sharply divided advice would have complicated and exacerbated the situation, and, far from relieving the Secretary-General of the responsibility for the decision to be taken, would have made the decision much more difficult to take.

11. It has been said that the final decision on the withdrawal of UNEF should have been taken only after consideration by the General Assembly. This position is not only incorrect but also inapplicable and unrealistic. In resolution 1000 (ES-I) the General Assembly established a United Nations command for an emergency international force. On the basis of that resolution the Force was quickly recruited and its forward elements flown to the staging area at Naples. Thus, though established, it had to await the permission of the government of Egypt to enter Egyptian territory. That permission was subsequently given by the government of Egypt as a result of direct discussions between Secretary-General Hammarskjöld and President Nasser of Egypt. There is no official United Nations document on the basis of which any case could be made that there was any limitation on the authority of the government of Egypt to rescind that consent or which would indicate that the United Arab Republic had in any way surrendered its right to ask for and obtain at any time the removal of UNEF from its territory.

12. As a practical matter, there would be little point in any case in taking such an issue to the General Assembly unless that body could be expected expeditiously to reach a substantive decision. It is hard to see what decision other than the withdrawal of UNEF could have been reached by the Assembly once United Arab Republic consent for the continued presence of UNEF was withdrawn.

13. As regards the practical possibility of the Assembly considering the request for UNEF's withdrawal, it is relevant to observe that the next regular session of the General Assembly was some four months off at the time the withdrawal request was made. The special session of the General Assembly which was meeting at the time could have considered the question, according to rule 19 of the Assembly's rules of procedure, only if two thirds, or eighty-two Members, voted for inscription of the item on the agenda. It is questionable, to say the least, whether the necessary support could have been mustered for such a controversial item.

IV

The issue of refusing or delaying response to the United Arab Republic request

14. Consent of the host government to the presence and operation of United Nations peace-keeping machinery is a basic prerequisite of

all United Nations peace-keeping operations. Secretary-General Hammarskjöld in defining the principles of the establishment and functioning of UNEF in his report (A/3302) of November 6, 1956, to the General Assembly stated:

... the force if established would be limited in its operations to the extent that consent of the parties concerned is required under generally recognized international law. While the General Assembly is enabled to *establish* the force with the consent of those parties which contribute units to the force, it could not request the force to be *stationed* or *operate* on the territory of a given country without the consent of the government of that country.[1]

The Secretary-General went on to point out that the situation might have been different had the Force been initiated by the Security Council. In a sentence immediately following the extract just quoted, he said:

This does not exclude the possibility that the Security Council could use such a force within the wider margins provided under Chapter VII of the United Nations Charter. I would not for the present consider it necessary to elaborate this point further, since no use of the Force under Chapter VII, with the rights in relation to Member states that this would entail, has been envisaged.

The General Assembly by paragraph 1 of resolution 1001 (ES-1) expressed its approval of this and the other guiding principles.

15. As recently as May 24, 1967, in relation to the current events, Prime Minister Lester Pearson of Canada said to the House of Commons:

I remember very well the background and I am not being critical of the Secretary-General because I have no doubt that on an examination of the documents one would come to the conclusion that what he did was right in terms of the documentary evidence. There was a special arrangement made between Mr. Hammarskjöld and President Nasser. I objected to that arrangement at the time because I thought it might cause a lot of trouble in the future.

16. The question of the right of a state to obtain the withdrawal of an international force after it has given consent for its presence on its territory touches upon an exceedingly sensitive attribute of sovereign authority. It is extremely unlikely that at this stage in international life any sovereign state would accept an international military force

[1]See vol. III of this series, p. 347.

on its territory if there were to be any suggestion that the force would not be removed when the consent for its presence was withdrawn, or indeed, if there were any uncertainty about the state's right to withdraw that consent or as to what would be required to ensure the removal of the force. In fact, the rule of consent, for good and practical reasons in UNEF extended even beyond the question of the stationing of the Force on Egyptian territory. Informally, the consent of the Egyptian government was obtained also on the national composition of the Force, since it was found that governments were not willing to provide contingents for UNEF unless they could be assured that their troops would be welcome. In the light of such considerations, it is inconceivable that, once the United Arab Republic consent for the presence of the Force was withdrawn, any decision other than compliance with its request for withdrawal could seriously be taken.

17. It has been asserted that the so-called "good faith" accord (A/ 6669 of May 18, 1967, para. 7) implied that Egypt's acceptance of General Assembly resolution 1000 (ES-I) of November 5, 1956, would oblige Egypt to continue to accept the presence of UNEF until the task of the Force was completed. Such a view, which reads more into the "good faith" understanding than is justified, also ignores the fact that this understanding was reached in mid-November 1956 and therefore could relate *only* to General Assembly resolution 1000 (ES-I) of November 5, 1956, which defined the task of UNEF in very general terms as being "to secure and supervise the cessation of hostilities." At that early stage the purpose of the Force in reality was to replace the withdrawing forces of France, Israel, and the United Kingdom, and to be, in fact, the condition for the withdrawal of those forces. Hostilities ceased, automatically in fact, once UNEF was deployed and thus its task at that time was completed. It was not until its resolution 1125 (XI) of February 2, 1957, that the General Assembly broadened the function of UNEF by stating that:

the scrupulous maintenance of the Armistice Agreement requires the placing of the United Nations Emergency Force on the Egyptian-Israeli armistice demarcation line and the implementation of other measures as proposed in the Secretary-General's report. . . .

That broader task, clearly, is not completed, and it would be impossible to say at present when it will or can be completed. The armistice has already endured for over eighteen years. But this was not the task

envisaged or defined for UNEF when Secretary-General Hammarskjöld and President Nasser reached the "good faith"
understanding.

18. Quite apart, therefore, from the almost certain practical consequences for the personnel of UNEF of a refusal or a delay in responding to the United Arab Republic request, there would seem to be no
basis in any agreement or decision of the United Nations for such a
refusal or delay.

V

*The question of continued UNEF operation once the United Arab
Republic consent to its presence was withdrawn*

19. As stated above, the consent and active cooperation of the host
country is essential to the effective operation and, indeed, to the very
existence, of any United Nations peace-keeping operation, and the
sovereign right of the host country to withdraw such consent and
cooperation is not in question. The fact is that UNEF had been
deployed on Egyptian and Egyptian-controlled territory for over ten
and a half years with the consent and cooperation of the government
of the United Arab Republic. Although it was envisaged in pursuance
of General Assembly resolution 1125 (XI) of February 2, 1957, that
the Force would be stationed on both sides of the line, Israel exercised its sovereign right to refuse the stationing of UNEF on its side,
and the Force throughout its existence was stationed on the United
Arab Republic side of the line only.

20. In these circumstances the true basis for UNEF's effectiveness
as a buffer and deterrent to infiltration was, throughout its existence,
a voluntary undertaking by local United Arab Republic authorities
with UNEF, that United Arab Republic troops would respect a
defined buffer zone along the entire length of the line in which only
UNEF would operate and from which United Arab Republic troops
would be excluded. This undertaking was honored for more than a
decade, and Egyptian cooperation extended also to Sharm el Sheikh,
Ras Nasrani, and the Strait of Tiran. This undertaking was honored
although UNEF had no authority to challenge the right of United
Arab Republic troops to be present anywhere on United Arab Republic territory.

21. It may be pointed out in passing that over the years UNEF dealt with numerous infiltrators coming from the Israel as well as from the United Arab Republic side of the line. It would hardly be logical to take the position that because UNEF has successfully maintained quiet along the line for more than ten years, due in large measure to the cooperation of the United Arab Republic authorities, the United Arab Republic government should now be told that it cannot unilaterally seek the removal of the Force and thus be penalized for its long cooperation with the international community in the interest of peace.

22. There are other practical factors relating to the above-mentioned arrangement which are highly relevant to the withdrawal of UNEF. First, once the United Arab Republic troops moved up to the line to place themselves in confrontation with the military forces of Israel, UNEF had, in fact, no further useful function. Second, if the Force was no longer welcome, it could not as a practical matter remain in the United Arab Republic, since the friction which would almost inevitably have arisen with the United Arab Republic government, armed forces and the local population would have made the situation of the Force both humiliating and untenable. The dignity and the reputation of this pioneering force had to be protected. UNEF clearly had no mandate to try to stop United Arab Republic troops from moving freely about on their own territory. UNEF was never designed, moreover, to be a fighting force and was equipped only with personal arms for self-defense. This was a peace-keeping force, not an enforcement action. Its effectiveness was based entirely on voluntary cooperation.

23. Quite apart from its position in the United Arab Republic, the request of that government for UNEF's withdrawal automatically set off a disintegration of the Force, since two of the governments providing contingents quickly let the Secretary-General know that their contingents would be withdrawn, and there can be little doubt that other such notifications would not have been slow in forthcoming.

24. For all of the foregoing reasons, the operation and even the continued existence of UNEF on United Arab Republic territory, after the withdrawal of United Arab Republic consent, would have been impossible, and any attempt to maintain the Force there would without question have had disastrous consequences.

VI

The allegation that the withdrawal of UNEF is the principal cause of the present crisis

25. It has been said that the withdrawal of UNEF is a primary cause of the present crisis in the Near East. As the Secretary-General pointed out in his report of May 26, 1967, to the Security Council (S/7906), this view "ignores the fact that the underlying basis for this and other crisis situations in the Near East is the continuing Arab-Israel conflict which has been present all along, and of which the crisis situation created by the unexpected request for the withdrawal of UNEF is the latest expression." Certainly UNEF has served for more than ten years as a very valuable instrument in helping to maintain quiet, especially between Israel and the United Arab Republic. Its withdrawal reveals once again in all its depth and danger the undiminishing conflict between Israel and her Arab neighbors. It has also made acute the problem of access to the Gulf of Aqaba through the Strait of Tiran—a problem which had been dormant for over ten years only because of the presence of UNEF. But the presence of UNEF did not touch the basic problem of the Arab-Israel conflict—it merely isolated, immobilized, and covered up certain aspects of that conflict. At any time in the last ten years either of the parties could have reactivated the conflict and, had they been determined to do so, UNEF's effectiveness would automatically have disappeared. Now in the context of the whole relationship of Israel with her Arab neighbors, the direct confrontation between Israel and the United Arab Republic has been revived, and UNEF has therefore lost its usefulness. In recognizing the extreme seriousness of the situation thus created, its true cause—the Arab-Israel conflict—must also be recognized. It is merely confusing to seek the cause elsewhere or to indulge in the sophistry that the conflict could have been solved simply if UNEF had stayed on. This, manifestly, it could not have done.

6. *Statement on UNEF Memorandum*

NEW YORK   JUNE 19, 1967

I HAVE NOTED PRESS REPORTS on the morning of June 19 relating to a paper or memorandum which I am told was written by Dag Hammarskjöld in August 1957, setting forth certain of his views about the presence of the United Nations Emergency Force (UNEF) in the United Arab Republic.[1] The plain fact is that there is little that is new in the memorandum and it makes no revelations which would warrant the special significance being attributed to it in some quarters. In any case, such a paper could not alter the basis for the presence of UNEF on the soil of the United Arab Republic, as set out in the official documents. I wish to make the following specific comments on this memorandum:

1. It is not an official document, is not in the official files of the Secretary-General's office, and its existence has never been reported in any way to any organ of the United Nations, including the UNEF Advisory Committee. It was thus of a purely private character and although supposedly secret in nature, is said to have been given by him to one or more of Mr. Hammarskjöld's friends. To say the least, the release of such a paper at this time would seem to raise some question of ethics and good faith.

2. It can be said with full confidence that this paper was never conveyed to President Nasser or to the government of the United Arab Republic, that that government knew nothing about it and was in no way bound by it.

3. I, however, had been made aware of the substance of the paper before my visit to Cairo to talk with President Nasser.

4. The crux of the matters dwelled upon in the Hammarskjöld paper is the understanding between Mr. Hammarskjöld and President

SOURCE: UN Press Release SG/SM/752.

[1]See the *New York Times,* June 19, 1967, or *International Legal Materials,* May-June 1967, vol. VI, no. 3.

Nasser which sometimes has been referred to as the "good faith" accord. There is, in fact, nothing new about this. In my special report to the General Assembly of May 18 (A/6669, para. 7), I gave the text of an *aide-mémoire* which I had immediately sent to the government of the United Arab Republic on the "good faith" accord. No response to it was received.

5. It is puzzling to me, however, that those who attempt to read so much into the Hammarskjöld paper, and particularly into the "good faith" accord, do not see—or do not choose to see—the clear fact that the "good faith" accord, having been reached in November 1956, had a more limited scope and could not possibly have envisaged or have had any relevance to the later function defined for UNEF by the General Assembly in February 1957. In OPI [UN Office of Public Information] background release EMF/449 of June 3, 1967, entitled "Notes on Withdrawal of United Nations Emergency Force (UNEF)," this point was clearly stated in paragraph 17 of that paper in the following words:

It has been asserted that the so-called 'good faith' accord (A/6669 of May 18,1967, para. 7) implied that Egypt's acceptance of General Assembly resolution 1000 (ES-I) of November 5, 1956, would oblige Egypt to continue to accept the presence of UNEF until the task of the Force was completed. Such a view, which reads more into the 'good faith' understanding than is justified, also ignores the fact that this understanding was reached in mid-November 1956 and therefore could relate *only* to General Assembly resolution 1000 (ES-I) of November 5, 1956, which defined the task of UNEF in very general terms as being 'to secure and supervise the cessation of hostilities.' At that early stage the purpose of the Force in reality was to replace the withdrawing forces of France, Israel, and the United Kingdom, and to be, in fact, the condition for the withdrawal of those forces. Hostilities ceased, automatically in fact, once UNEF was deployed and thus its task at that time was completed. It was not until its resolution 1125 (XI) of February 2, 1957, that the General Assembly broadened the function of UNEF by stating that: "the scrupulous maintenance of the Armistice Agreement requires the placing of the United Nations Emergency Force on the Egyptian-Israeli armistice demarcation line and the implementation of other measures as proposed in the Secretary-General's report. . . ."

That broader task, clearly, is not completed, and it would be impossible to say at present when it will or can be completed. The armistice has already endured for over eighteen years. But this was not the task envisaged or defined for UNEF when Secretary-General Hammarskjöld and President Nasser reached the 'good faith' understanding.

6. There is also a failure by many to recognize another central and decisive point which is not touched upon a⁺ all in the Hammarskjöld paper. This point is that from the time of the deployment of UNEF along the line between Israel and the United Arab Republic in pursuance of the General Assembly resolution (1125 (XI))—of February 2, 1957 although only on the United Arab Republic side because of Israel's firm refusal to accept it on the Israel side—UNEF's effective discharge of its buffer function depended completely upon the voluntary action of the United Arab Republic in keeping its troops away from the line, thus leaving UNEF in a buffer position and avoiding a direct military confrontation between the armed forces of Israel and the United Arab Republic. Indeed, Israel has never observed a buffer zone on its side of the line and Israel troops have always patrolled directly alongside it. On the other hand, no one could possibly question the full right of the United Arab Republic to move its troops to the line whenever it might choose to do so. Once its troops began to make such a move, as they did in fact on the morning of May 17— more than twenty-four hours before I received the request from the government of the United Arab Republic for the withdrawal of the Force—UNEF could no longer perform any useful function in maintaining quiet and its continuing presence on United Arab Republic territory lost any real significance.

---

7. Statement in the General Assembly

NEW YORK   JUNE 20, 1967

DURING THE LAST five and a half years I have never had reason to comment upon a statement made to this Assembly by a representative of any government. But I feel it necessary to reply very briefly to certain statements made by the Foreign Minister of Israel [Abba Eban] in his address to the General Assembly on the morning of June

SOURCE: General Assembly Official Records, Fifth Emergency Special Session, 1527th meeting.

19 with regard to my decision to comply with the request of the United Arab Republic for the withdrawal of UNEF.

Mr. Eban's remarks on this subject were highly critical, but it is not for that reason that I speak now. I personally welcome criticism when it is just, based on fact, and does not obscure or ignore essential facts. The concern behind this intervention is that the picture which Mr. Eban gave yesterday can be very damaging to the United Nations with regard to its peace-keeping function, past and present. I seek only to restore in that picture the balance which the facts warrant.

I have to say at the outset that I was rather surprised at the breadth and vigor of the Foreign Minister's dissatisfaction with the withdrawal decision, since in a quite recent meeting we had discussed that issue and at that time I had given a rather full explanation of just why the decision I took had to be taken in the way it was and I heard no such reaction as Mr. Eban projected to the General Assembly yesterday; nothing like it. I wish now to say that I do not accept as having validity Mr. Eban's strictures on this matter.

My position on the decision to withdraw UNEF and the reasons for it have been set forth clearly in reports which I have submitted to the General Assembly and the Security Council.

Beyond this, I need make only the following specific comments.

The Foreign Minister of Israel, I note, made no mention in his critical analysis of my decision of certain decisive facts and factors with which he is certainly very well acquainted. Mr. Eban must know, for example, that the indispensable basis for the effective buffer function exercised by the United Nations Emergency Force for more than a decade was the voluntary decision of the government of the United Arab Republic to keep its troops away from the line, with only United Nations troops in the buffer zone which was exclusively on the United Arab Republic side of the line.

On the other hand, the Foreign Minister also knows, I am sure, that Israel extended no such cooperation on the United Nations Emergency Force to the United Nations; that, despite the intent of the General Assembly resolution that United Nations troops should be stationed on both sides of the line, Israel always and firmly refused to accept them on Israel territory on the valid grounds of national sovereignty. There was, of course, national sovereignty on the other side of the line as well.

There can be no doubt that it would have been a helpful factor of considerable importance if Israel had at any time accepted the deployment of the United Nations Emergency Force also on its side of the line. I may report in this connection that prior to receiving the United Arab Republic request for withdrawal and prior to giving my reply to it, I had raised with the permanent representative of Israel to the United Nations the possibility of stationing elements of the United Nations Emergency Force on the Israel side of the line. I was told that the idea was completely unacceptable to Israel. Moreover, for all of those ten years Israel's troops regularly patrolled alongside the line and now and again created provocations by violating it.

Finally, may I say that Mr. Eban cannot help but know that the government of the United Arab Republic had never accepted any limitation or restriction with regard to the exercise of its sovereign powers concerning the presence of the United Nations Emergency Force on its territory. It can also be emphasized that there was no limitation of any kind on the right of the United Arab Republic to move its troops up to the line at any time with the inevitable result of immediately making academic the question of withdrawal of the United Nations Emergency Force or its continued presence.

In this regard, Mr. Eban referred to the alert order issued to the Egyptian troops on the morning of May 17. He failed to mention, however, that it was on that same morning that Egyptian troops began to move up to the line, thus eliminating the buffer zone, as I have previously reported to this body.

I have noted Mr. Eban's picturesque simile of the "fire brigade which vanishes from the scene as soon as the first smoke and flames appear!" Mr. Eban would agree, I am sure, that for more than ten years the United Nations Emergency Force had been remarkably effective in preventing clashes along the line and in extinguishing the flames of the raids across the line, the terror of the fedayeen. But I am sure that Mr. Eban did not mean what he seemed to imply, namely that the United Nations Emergency Force was on Egyptian territory to stay as long as the United Nations saw fit and to fight against United Arab Republic troops, if necessary, to prevent them from moving up to the line in their own territory.

On the matter of consultation, Mr. Eban should know that I did engage in consultations before taking my decision, to the full extent required of me and even somewhat more.

I conclude these observations by quoting a statement on the same subject made in the Security Council on June 3, 1967, by the permanent representative of Israel:

The crisis in the Middle East erupted without warning on May 16 when an Egyptian general sent an ultimatum to the Commander of UNEF. At the same time as he asked for the removal of the United Nations Force, he moved his own forces into the positions held by the United Nations. The course of the events that followed is by now common knowledge and well documented in the reports of the Secretary-General.

The Secretary-General tried to prevent the crisis from getting out of hand. He failed. It was not his fault. . . .

In view of the fact that important questions have been raised before the General Assembly on the withdrawal of the United Nations Emergency Force, I wish now to inform the Assembly that it is my intention to issue within a day or two a report giving a full account of my actions on this matter.

---

8. *From Report to the General Assembly*

NEW YORK   JUNE 26, 1967

. . .

The causes of the present crisis

32. IT HAS BEEN said rather often in one way or another that the withdrawal of UNEF is a primary cause of the present crisis in the Near East. This is, of course, a superficial and oversimplified approach. As the Secretary-General pointed out in his report of May 26, 1967, to the Security Council, this view "ignores the fact that the underlying basis for this and other crisis situations in the Near East is the continuing Arab-Israel conflict which has been present all along

SOURCE: General Assembly Official Records, Fifth Emergency Special Session, Annexes, agenda item 5, document A/6730/ Add. 3.

and of which the crisis situation created by the unexpected request for the withdrawal of the Emergency Force is the latest expression.'' The Secretary-General's report to the Security Council of May 19, 1967, described the various elements of the increasingly dangerous situation in the Near East prior to the decision of the government of the United Arab Republic to terminate its consent for the presence of UNEF on its territory.

33. The United Nations Emergency Force served for more than ten years as a highly valuable instrument in helping to maintain quiet along the line between Israel and the United Arab Republic. Its withdrawal revealed in all its depth and danger the undiminishing conflict between Israel and her Arab neighbors. The withdrawal also made immediately acute the problem of access for Israel to the Gulf of Aqaba through the Strait of Tiran—a problem which had been dormant for over ten years only because of the presence of UNEF. But the presence of UNEF did not touch the basic problem of the Arab-Israel conflict—it merely isolated, immobilized, and covered up certain aspects of that conflict. At any time in the last ten years either of the parties could have reactivated the conflict and if they had been determined to do so UNEF's effectiveness would automatically have disappeared. When, in the context of the whole relationship of Israel with her Arab neighbors, the direct confrontation between Israel and the United Arab Republic was revived after a decade by the decision of the United Arab Republic to move its forces up to the line, UNEF at once lost all usefulness. In fact, its effectiveness as a buffer and as a presence had already vanished, as can be seen from the chronology given above, even before the request for its withdrawal had been received by the Secretary-General from the government of the United Arab Republic. In recognizing the extreme seriousness of the situation thus created, its true cause, the continuing Arab-Israel conflict, must also be recognized. It is entirely unrealistic to maintain that that conflict could have been solved, or its consequences prevented, if a greater effort had been made to maintain UNEF's presence in the area against the will of the government of the United Arab Republic.

The decision on UNEF's withdrawal

34. The decision to withdraw UNEF has been frequently characterized in various quarters as ''hasty,'' ''precipitous,'' and the like,

even, indeed, to the extent of suggesting that it took President Nasser by surprise. The question of the withdrawal of UNEF is by no means a new one. In fact, it was the negotiations on this very question with the government of Egypt which, after the establishment of UNEF by the General Assembly, delayed its arrival while it waited in a staging area at Capodichino airbase, Naples, Italy, for several days in November 1956. The government of Egypt, understandably, did not wish to give permission for the arrival on its soil of an international force, unless it was assured that its sovereignty would be respected and a request for withdrawal of the Force would be honored. Over the years, in discussions with representatives of the United Arab Republic, the subject of the continued presence of UNEF has occasionally come up, and it was invariably taken for granted by United Arab Republic representatives that if their government officially requested the withdrawal of UNEF the request would be honored by the Secretary-General. There is no record to indicate that this assumption was ever questioned. Thus, although the request for the withdrawal of UNEF came as a surprise, there was nothing new about the question of principle nor about the procedure to be followed by the Secretary-General. It follows that the decision taken by him on May 18, 1967, to comply with the request for the withdrawal of the Force was seen by him as the only reasonable and sound action that could be taken. The actual withdrawal itself, it should be recalled, was to be carried out in an orderly, dignified, deliberate, and not precipitate manner over a period of several weeks. The first troops in fact left the area only on May 29.

The possibility of delay

35. Opinions have also been frequently expressed that the decision to withdraw UNEF should have been delayed pending consultations of various kinds, or that efforts should have been made to resist the United Arab Republic's request for UNEF's withdrawal, or to bring pressure to bear on the government of the United Arab Republic to reconsider its decision in this matter. In fact, as the chronology given above makes clear, the effectiveness of UNEF, in the light of the movement of United Arab Republic troops up to the line and into Sharm el Sheikh, had already vanished before the request for withdrawal was received. Furthermore, the government of the United

Arab Republic had made it entirely clear to the Secretary-General that an appeal for reconsideration of the withdrawal decision would encounter a firm rebuff and would be considered as an attempt to impose UNEF as an "army of occupation." Such a reaction, combined with the fact that UNEF positions on the line had already been effectively taken over by United Arab Republic troops in pursuit of their full right to move up to the line in their own territory, and a deep anxiety for the security of UNEF personnel should an effort be made to keep UNEF in position after its withdrawal had been requested, were powerful arguments in favor of complying with the United Arab Republic request, even supposing there had not been other overriding reasons for accepting it.

36. It has been said that the decision to withdraw UNEF precipitated other consequences such as the reinstitution of the blockade against Israel in the Strait of Tiran. As can be seen from the chronology, the UNEF positions at Sharm el Sheikh on the Strait of Tiran (manned by thirty-two men in all) were in fact rendered ineffective by United Arab Republic troops before the request for withdrawal was received. It is also pertinent to note that in response to a query from the Secretary-General as to why the United Arab Republic had announced its reinstitution of the blockade in the Strait of Tiran while the Secretary-General was actually en route to Cairo on May 22, President Nasser explained that his government's decision to resume the blockade had been taken some time before U Thant's departure and it was considered preferable to make the announcement before rather than after the Secretary-General's visit to Cairo.

The question of consultations

37. It has been said also that there was not adequate consultation with the organs of the United Nations concerned or with the Members before the decision was taken to withdraw the Force. The Secretary-General was, and is, firmly of the opinion that the decision for withdrawal of the Force, on the request of the host government, rested with the Secretary-General after consultation with the Advisory Committee on UNEF, which is the organ established by the General Assembly for consultation regarding such matters. This was made clear by Secretary-General Hammarskjöld, who took the fol-

lowing position on February 25, 1957, in reply to a question about the withdrawal of the Force from Sharm el Sheikh:

An indicated procedure would be for the Secretary-General to inform the Advisory Committee on the United Nations Emergency Force, which would determine whether the matter should be brought to the attention of the Assembly (see volume III of this series, p. 509).

The Secretary-General consulted the Advisory Committee before replying to the letter of May 18, 1967, from the United Arab Republic requesting withdrawal. This consultation took place within a few hours after receipt of the United Arab Republic request, and the Advisory Committee was thus quickly informed of the decision which the Secretary-General had in mind to convey in his reply to the Foreign Minister of the United Arab Republic. As indicated in the report to the Security Council of May 26, 1967:

The Committee did not move, as it was its right to do under the terms of paragraph 9 of General Assembly resolution 1001 (ES-I), of 7 November, to request the convening of the General Assembly on the situation which had arisen.

38. Before consulting the Advisory Committee on UNEF, the Secretary-General had also consulted the permanent representatives of the seven countries providing the contingents of UNEF and informed them of his intentions. This, in fact, was more than was formally required of the Secretary-General in the way of consultation.

39. Obviously, many governments were concerned about the presence and functioning of UNEF and about the general situation in the area, but it would have been physically impossible to consult all of the interested representatives within any reasonable time. This was an emergency situation requiring urgent action. Moreover, it was perfectly clear that such consultations were sure to produce sharply divided counsel, even if they were limited to the permanent members of the Security Council. Such sharply divided advice would have complicated and exacerbated the situation, and, far from relieving the Secretary-General of the responsibility for the decision to be taken, would have made the decision much more difficult to take.

40. It has been said that the final decision on the withdrawal of

UNEF should have been taken only after consideration by the General Assembly. This position is not only incorrect but also unrealistic. In resolution 1000 (ES-I) the General Assembly established a United Nations command for an emergency international force. On the basis of that resolution the Force was quickly recruited and its forward elements flown to the staging area at Naples. Thus, though established, it had to await the permission of the government of Egypt to enter Egyptian territory. That permission was subsequently given by the government of Egypt as a result of direct discussions between Secretary-General Hammarskjöld and President Nasser of Egypt. There is no official United Nations document on the basis of which any case could be made that there was any limitation on the authority of the government of Egypt to rescind that consent at its pleasure, or which would indicate that the United Arab Republic had in any way surrendered its right to ask for and obtain at any time the removal of UNEF from its territory.

41. As a practical matter, there would be little point in any case in taking such an issue to the General Assembly unless there would be reasonable certainty that that body could be expected expeditiously to reach a substantive decision. In the prevailing circumstances, the question could have been validly raised as to what decision other than the withdrawal of UNEF could have been reached by the Assembly once United Arab Republic consent for the continued presence of UNEF was withdrawn.

42. As regards the practical possibility of the Assembly considering the request for UNEF's withdrawal, it is relevant to observe that the next regular session of the General Assembly was some four months off at the time the withdrawal request was made. The special session of the General Assembly which was meeting at the time could have considered the question, according to rule 19 of the Assembly's rules of procedure, only if two thirds, or eighty-two Members, voted for the inclusion of the item in the agenda. It is questionable, to say the least, whether the necessary support could have been mustered for such a controversial item. There could have been no emergency special session since the issue was not then before the Security Council, and therefore the condition of lack of unanimity did not exist.

43. As far as consultation with or action by the Security Council was concerned, the Secretary-General reported to the Council on the

situation leading up to and created by the withdrawal of UNEF on May 19, 1967. In that report he characterized the situation in the Near East as "extremely menacing." The Council met for the first time after this report on May 24, 1967, but took no action.

44. As has already been stated, the Advisory Committee did not make any move to bring the matter before the General Assembly, and no representative of any Member government requested a meeting of either the Security Council or the General Assembly immediately following the Secretary-General's two reports (A/6730 and S/7896). In this situation, the Secretary-General himself did not believe that any useful purpose would be served by his seeking a meeting of either organ, nor did he consider that there was any basis for him to do so at that time. Furthermore, the information available to the Secretary-General did not lead him to believe that either the General Assembly or the Security Council would have decided that UNEF should remain on United Arab Republic territory, by force if necessary, despite the request of the government of the United Arab Republic that it should leave.

Practical factors influencing the decision

45. Since it is still contended in some quarters that the UNEF operation should somehow have continued after the consent of the government of the United Arab Republic to its presence was withdrawn, it is necessary to consider the factors, quite apart from constitutional and legal considerations, which would have made such a course of action entirely impracticable.

46. The consent and active cooperation of the host country is essential to the effective operation and, indeed, to the very existence, of any United Nations peace-keeping operation of the nature of UNEF. The fact is that UNEF had been deployed on Egyptian and Egyptian-controlled territory for over ten and a half years with the consent and cooperation of the government of the United Arab Republic. Although it was envisaged in pursuance of General Assembly resolution 1125 (XI) of February 2, 1957, that the Force would be stationed on both sides of the line, Israel exercised its sovereign right to refuse the stationing of UNEF on its side, and the Force throughout its existence was stationed on the United Arab Republic side of the line only.

47. In these circumstances, the true basis for UNEF's effectiveness as a buffer and deterrent to infiltration was, throughout its existence, a voluntary undertaking by local United Arab Republic authorities with UNEF, that United Arab Republic troops would respect a defined buffer zone along the entire length of the line in which only UNEF would operate and from which United Arab Republic troops would be excluded. This undertaking was honored for more than a decade, and this Egyptian cooperation extended also to Sharm el Sheikh, Ras Nasrani, and the Strait of Tiran. This undertaking was honored although UNEF had no authority to challenge the right of United Arab Republic troops to be present anywhere on their own territory.

48. It may be pointed out in passing that over the years UNEF dealt with numerous infiltrators coming from the Israel as well as from the United Arab Republic side of the line. It would hardly be logical to take the position that because UNEF has successfully maintained quiet along the line for more than ten years, owing in large measure to the cooperation of the United Arab Republic authorities, that government should then be told that it could not unilaterally seek the removal of the Force and thus in effect be penalized for the long cooperation with the international community it had extended in the interest of peace.

49. There are other practical factors relating to the above-mentioned arrangement which are highly relevant to the withdrawal of UNEF. First, once the United Arab Republic troops moved up to the line to place themselves in direct confrontation with the military forces of Israel, UNEF had, in fact, no further useful function. Second, if the Force was no longer welcome, it could not as a practical matter remain in the United Arab Republic, since the friction which would almost inevitably have arisen with that government, its armed forces and with the local population would have made the situation of the Force both humiliating and untenable. It would even have been impossible to supply it. UNEF clearly had no mandate to try to stop United Arab Republic troops from moving freely about on their own territory. This was a peace-keeping force, not an enforcement action. Its effectiveness was based entirely on voluntary cooperation.

50. Quite apart from its position in the United Arab Republic, the request of that government for UNEF's withdrawal automatically set off a disintegration of the Force, since two of the governments

providing contingents quickly let the Secretary-General know that their contingents would be withdrawn, and there can be little doubt that other such notifications would not have been slow in coming if friction had been generated through an unwillingness to comply with the request for withdrawal.

51. For all the foregoing reasons, the operation and even the continued existence of UNEF on United Arab Republic territory, after the withdrawal of United Arab Republic consent, would have been impossible, and any attempt to maintain the Force there would without question have had disastrous consequences.

Legal and Constitutional Considerations and the Question of Consent for the Stationing of UNEF on United Arab Republic Territory

52. Legal and constitutional considerations were, of course, of great importance in determining the Secretary-General's actions in relation to the request of the government of the United Arab Republic for the withdrawal of UNEF. Here again, a chronology of the relevant actions in 1956 and 1957 may be helpful.

53. *November 4, 1956.* The General Assembly, at its first emergency special session in resolution 998 (ES-I), requested "the Secretary-General to submit to it within forty-eight hours a plan for the setting up, with the consent of the nations concerned, of an emergency international United Nations Force to secure and supervise the cessation of hostilities. . . ."

54. *November 5, 1956.* The General Assembly, in its resolution 1000 (ES-I), established a United Nations Command for an emergency international Force, and, *inter alia,* invited the Secretary-General "to take such administrative measures as may be necessary for the prompt execution of the actions envisaged in the present resolution."

55. *November 7, 1956.* The General Assembly, by its resolution 1001 (ES-I), *inter alia,* approved the guiding principles for the organization and functioning of the emergency international United Nations Force and authorized the Secretary-General "to take all other necessary administrative and executive action."

56. *November 10, 1956.* Arrival of advance elements of UNEF at staging area in Naples.

57. *November 8-12, 1956.* Negotiations between Secretary-Gen-

eral Hammarskjöld and the government of Egypt on entry of UNEF into Egypt.

58. *November 12, 1956.* Agreement on UNEF entry into Egypt announced and then postponed, pending clarification, until November 14.

59. *November 15, 1956.* Arrival of advance elements of UNEF in Abu Suweir, Egypt.

60. *November 16–18, 1956.* Negotiations between Secretary-General Hammarskjöld and President Nasser in Cairo on the presence and functioning of UNEF in Egypt and cooperation with Egyptian authorities, and conclusion of an *"aide-mémoire* on the basis for the presence and functioning of the United Nations Emergency Force in Egypt" (the so-called "good faith accord").

61. *January 24, 1957.* The Secretary-General in a report to the General Assembly suggested that the Force should have units stationed on both sides of the armistice demarcation line and that certain measures should be taken in relation to Sharm el Sheikh. On *February 2, 1957,* the General Assembly, by its resolution 1125 (XI), noted with appreciation the Secretary-General's report and considered that "after full withdrawal of Israel from the Sharm el Sheikh and Gaza areas, the scrupulous maintenance of the Armistice Agreement required the placing of the United Nations Emergency Force on the Egyptian-Israel armistice demarcation line and the implementation of other measures as proposed in the Secretary-General's report, with due regard to the considerations set out therein with a view to assist in achieving situations conducive to the maintenance of peaceful conditions in the area."

62. *March 7, 1957.* Arrival of UNEF in Gaza.

63. *March 8, 1957.* Arrival of UNEF elements at Sharm el Sheikh.

64. In general terms the consent of the host country to the presence and operation of the United Nations peace-keeping machinery is a basic prerequisite of all United Nations peace-keeping operations. The question has been raised whether the United Arab Republic had the right to request unilaterally the withdrawal "as soon as possible" of UNEF from its territory or whether there were limitations on its rights in this respect. An examination of the records of the first emergency special session and the eleventh session of the General Assembly is relevant to this question.

65. It is clear that the General Assembly and the Secretary-General

from the very beginning recognized, and in fact emphasized, the need for Egyptian consent in order that UNEF be stationed or operate on Egyptian territory. Thus, the initial resolution 998 (ES-I) of November 4, 1956, requested the Secretary-General to submit a plan for the setting up of an emergency force, "with the consent of the nations concerned." The "nations concerned" obviously included Egypt (now the United Arab Republic), the three countries (France, Israel, and the United Kingdom) whose armies were on Egyptian soil, and the states contributing contingents to the Force.

66. The Secretary-General, in his report to the General Assembly of November 6, 1956, stated, *inter alia:*

9. Functioning, as it would, on the basis of a decision reached under the terms of the resolution 337 (V) "Uniting for peace," the force, if established, would be limited in its operations to the extent that consent of the parties concerned is required under generally recognized international law. While the General Assembly is enabled to *establish* the force with the consent of those parties which contribute units to the force, it could not request the force to be *stationed* or *operate* on the territory of a given country without the consent of the government of that country (see volume III of this series, p. 347).

67. He noted that the foregoing did not exclude the possibility that the Security Council could use such a Force within the wider margins provided under Chapter VII of the United Nations Charter. He pointed out, however, that it would not be necessary to elaborate this point further, since no use of the Force under Chapter VII, with the rights in relation to Member states that this would entail, had been envisaged.

68. The General Assembly in its resolution 1001 (ES-I) of November 7, 1956, expressed its approval of the guiding principles for the organization and functioning of the emergency international United Nations Force as expounded in paragraphs 6 to 9 of the Secretary-General's report. This included the principle of consent embodied in paragraph 9.

69. The need for Egypt's consent was also stated as a condition or "understanding" by some of the states offering to contribute contingents to the Force.

70. It was thus a basic legal principle arising from the nature of the Force, and clearly understood by all concerned, that the consent of Egypt was a prerequisite to the stationing of UNEF on Egyptian

territory, and it was a practical necessity as well in acquiring contingents for the Force.

The "good faith" aide-mémoire *of November 20, 1956*

71. There remains to be examined whether any commitments were made by Egypt which would limit its pre-existing right to withdraw its consent at any time that it chose to do so. The only basis for asserting such limitation could be the so-called "good faith" *aide-mémoire* which was set out as an annex to a report of the Secretary-General submitted to the General Assembly on November 20, 1956.

72. The Secretary-General himself did not offer any interpretation of the "good faith" *aide-mémoire* to the General Assembly or make any statement questioning the remarks made by the Foreign Minister of Egypt in the General Assembly the following week. It would appear, however, that in an exchange of cables he had sought to obtain the express acknowledgment from Egypt that its consent to the presence of the Force would not be withdrawn before the Force had completed its task. Egypt did not accept this interpretation but held to the view that if its consent was no longer maintained the Force should be withdrawn. Subsequent discussions between Mr. Hammarskjöld and President Nasser resulted in the "good faith" *aide-mémoire*.

73. An interpretive account of these negotiations made by Mr. Hammarskjöld in a personal and private paper entitled *"Aide-mémoire,"* dated August 5, 1957, some eight and a half months after the discussions, has recently been made public by a private person who has a copy. It is understood that Mr. Hammarskjöld often prepared private notes concerning significant events under the heading *"Aide-mémoire."* This memorandum is not in any official record of the United Nations nor is it in any of the official files. The General Assembly, the Advisory Committee on UNEF, and the government of Egypt were not informed of its contents or existence. It is not an official paper and has no standing beyond being a purely private memorandum of unknown purpose or value, in which Secretary-General Hammarskjöld seems to record his own impressions and interpretations of his discussions with President Nasser. This paper, therefore, cannot affect in any way the basis for the presence of

UNEF on the soil of the United Arab Republic as set out in the official documents, much less supersede those documents.

Position of Egypt

74. It seems clear that Egypt did not understand the "good faith" *aide-mémoire* to involve any limitation on its right to withdraw its consent to the continued stationing and operation of UNEF on its territory. The Foreign Minister of Egypt, speaking in the General Assembly on November 27, 1956, one week after the publication of the "good faith" *aide-mémoire* and three days following its approval by the General Assembly, said:

We still believe that the General Assembly resolution of November 7, 1956, still stands, together with its endorsement of the principle that the General Assembly could not request the United Nations Emergency Force to be stationed or to operate on the territory of a given country without the consent of the government of the country. This is the proper basis on which we believe, together with the overwhelming majority of this Assembly, that the United Nations Emergency Force could be stationed or could operate in Egypt. It is the only basis on which Egypt has given its consent in this respect.

He then added:

. . . as must be abundantly clear, this Force has gone to Egypt to help Egypt, with Egypt's consent; and no one here or elsewhere can reasonably or fairly say that a fire brigade, after putting out a fire, would be entitled or expected to claim the right of deciding not to leave the house.

Analysis of the "task" of the Force

75. In the "good faith" *aide-mémoire* the government of Egypt declared that, "when exercising its sovereign rights on any matter concerning the presence and functioning of UNEF, it will be guided, in good faith, by its acceptance of General Assembly resolution 1000 (ES-I) of November 5, 1956."

76. The United Nations in turn declared "that the activities of UNEF will be guided, in good faith, by the task established for the Force in the aforementioned resolutions [1000 (ES-I) and 997 (ES-I)]; in particular, the United Nations, understanding this to correspond to

the wishes of the government of Egypt, reaffirms its willingness to maintain UNEF until its task is completed."

77. It must be noted that, while Egypt undertook to be guided in good faith by its acceptance of General Assembly resolution 1000 (ES-I), the United Nations also undertook to be guided in good faith by the task established by the Force in resolutions 1001 (ES-I) and 997 (ES-I). Resolution 1000 (ES-I), to which the declaration of Egypt referred, established a United Nations Command for the Force "to secure and supervise the cessation of hostilities in accordance with all the terms" of resolution 997 (ES-I). It must be recalled that at this time Israel forces had penetrated deeply into Egyptian territory and that forces of France and the United Kingdom were conducting military operations on Egyptian territory. Resolution 997 (ES-I) urged as a matter of priority that all parties agree to an immediate cease-fire, and halt the movement of military forces and arms into the area. It also urged the parties to the armistice agreements promptly to withdraw all forces behind the armistice lines, to desist from raids across the armistice lines, and to observe scrupulously the provisions of the armistice agreements. It further urged that, upon the cease-fire being effective, steps be taken to reopen the Suez Canal and restore secure freedom of navigation.

78. While the terms of resolution 997 (ES-I) cover a considerable area, the emphasis in resolution 1000 (ES-I) is on securing and supervising the cessation of hostilities. Moreover, on November 6, 1956, the Secretary-General, in his second and final report on the plan for an emergency international United Nations Force, noted that "the Assembly intends that the Force should be of a temporary nature, the length of its assignment being determined by the needs arising out of the present conflict." Noting further the terms of resolution 997 (ES-I) he added that "the functions of the United Nations Force would be, when a cease-fire is being established, to enter Egyptian territory with the consent of the Egyptian government, in order to help maintain quiet during and after the withdrawal of non-Egyptian troops, and to secure compliance with the other terms established in the resolution of November 2, 1956."

79. In a cable delivered to Foreign Minister Fawzi on November 9 or 10, 1956, in reply to a request for clarification as to how long it was contemplated that the Force should stay in the demarcation line area, the Secretary-General stated: "A definite reply is at present impossi-

ble but the emergency character of the Force links it to the immediate crisis envisaged in the resolution of November 2, [997 (ES-I)] and its liquidation.'' This point was confirmed in a further exchange of cables between the Secretary-General and Mr. Fawzi on November 14, 1956.

80. The Foreign Minister of Egypt (Mr. Fawzi) gave his understanding of the task of the Force in a statement to the General Assembly on November 17, 1956:

Our clear understanding—and I am sure it is the clear understanding of the Assembly—is that this Force is in Egypt only in relation to the present attack against Egypt by the United Kingdom, France, and Israel, and for the purposes directly connected with the incursion of the invading forces into Egyptian territory. The United Nations Emergency Force is in Egypt, not as an occupation force, not as a replacement for the invaders, not to clear the Canal of obstructions, not to resolve any question or settle any problem, be it in relation to the Suez Canal, to Palestine or to any other matter; it is not there to infringe upon Egyptian sovereignty in any fashion or to any extent, but, on the contrary, to give expression to the determination of the United Nations to put an end to the aggression committed against Egypt and to the presence of the invading forces in Egyptian territory.

81. In letters dated November 3, 1956, addressed to the Secretary-General, the representatives of both France and the United Kingdom had proposed very broad functions for UNEF, stating on behalf of their governments that military action could be stopped if the following conditions were met:

(*a*) Both the Egyptian and Israel governments agree to accept a United Nations Force to keep the peace.

(*b*) The United Nations decides to constitute and maintain such a Force until an Arab-Israel peace settlement is reached and until satisfactory arrangements have been agreed in regard to the Suez Canal, both agreements to be guaranteed by the United Nations.

(*c*) In the meantime, until the United Nations Force is constituted, both combatants agree to accept forthwith limited detachments of Anglo-French troops to be stationed between the combatants.

These broad functions for the Force were not acceptable to the General Assembly, however, as was pointed out in telegrams dated November 4, 1956, from Secretary-General Dag Hammarskjöld to the Minister for Foreign Affairs of France and the Secretary of State for Foreign Affairs of the United Kingdom.

82. Finally, it is obvious that the task referred to in the "good faith" *aide-mémoire* could only be the task of the Force as it had been defined in November 1956 when the understanding was concluded. The "good faith" undertaking by the United Nations would preclude it from claiming that the Egyptian agreement was relevant or applicable to functions which the Force was given at a much later date. The stationing of the Force on the armistice demarcation line and at Sharm el Sheikh was only determined in pursuance of General Assembly resolution 1125 (XI) of February 2, 1957. The Secretary-General, in his reports relating to this decision, made it clear that the further consent of Egypt was essential with respect to these new functions. Consequently, the understanding recorded in the "good faith" *aide-mémoire* of November 20, 1956, could not have been, itself, a commitment with respect to functions only determined in February and March 1957. It is only these later tasks that the Force had been performing during the last ten years—tasks of serving as a buffer and deterring infiltrators which went considerably beyond those of securing and supervising the cessation of hostilities provided in the General Assembly resolutions and referred to in the "good faith" *aide-mémoire*.

The stationing of UNEF on the armistice demarcation line and at Sharm el Sheikh

83. There remains to examine whether Egypt made further commitments with respect to the stationing of the Force on the armistice demarcation line and at Sharm el Sheikh. Israel, of course, sought to obtain such commitments, particularly with respect to the area around Sharm el Sheikh.

84. For example, in an *aide-mémoire* of February 4, 1957, the government of Israel sought clarification as to whether units of the United Nations Emergency Force would be stationed along the western shore of the Gulf of Aqaba in order to act as a restraint against hostile acts, and would remain so deployed until another effective means was agreed upon between the parties concerned for ensuring permanent freedom of navigation and the absence of belligerent acts in the Strait of Tiran and the Gulf of Aqaba. The Secretary-General pointed out that such "clarification" would require "Egyptian consent." He stated:

The second of the points in the Israel *aide-mémoire* requests a "clarification" which, in view of the position of the General Assembly, could go beyond what was stated in the last report only after negotiation with Egypt. This follows from the statements in the debate in the General Assembly, and the report on which it was based, which make it clear that the stationing of the Force at Sharm el Sheikh, under such terms as those mentioned in the question posed by Israel, would require Egyptian consent.

85. It is clear from the record that Egypt did not give its consent to Israel's proposition. The Secretary-General's report of March 8, 1957, recorded "arrangements for the complete and unconditional withdrawal of Israel in accordance with the decision of the General Assembly." There is no agreement on the part of Egypt to forgo its rights with respect to the granting or withdrawing of its consent to the continued stationing of the Force on its territory. On the contrary, at the 667th plenary meeting of the General Assembly on March 4, 1957, the Foreign Minister of Egypt stated:

At our previous meeting I stated that the Assembly was unanimous in expecting full and honest implementation of its resolutions calling for immediate and unconditional withdrawal by Israel. I continue to submit to the Assembly that this position—which is the only position the Assembly can possibly take—remains intact and entire. Nothing said by anyone here or elsewhere could shake this fact or detract from its reality and its validity, nor could it affect the fullness and the lawfulness of Egypt's rights and those of the Arab people of the Gaza Strip.

86. The Foreign Minister of Israel, in her statement at the 666th meeting of the General Assembly, on March 1, 1957, asserted that an assurance had been given that any proposal for the withdrawal of UNEF from the Gulf of Aqaba area would come first to the Advisory Committee on UNEF.

Question of the stationing of UNEF on both sides of the armistice demarcation line

87. Another point having significance with respect to the undertakings of Egypt is the question of the stationing of UNEF on both sides of the armistice demarcation line. The Secretary-General, in his report of January 24, 1957, to the General Assembly, suggested that the Force should have units stationed also on the Israel side of the armistice demarcation line. In particular, he suggested that units of

the Force should at least be stationed in the El Auja demilitarized zone which had been occupied by the armed forces of Israel. He indicated that if El Auja were demilitarized in accordance with the armistice agreement and units of UNEF were stationed there, a condition of reciprocity would be the Egyptian assurance that Egyptian forces would not take up positions in the area in contravention of the armistice agreement. However, Israel forces were never withdrawn from El Auja and UNEF was not accepted at any point on the Israel side of the line.

88. Following the Secretary-General's report, the General Assembly on February 2, 1957, adopted resolution 1125 (XI), in which it noted the report with appreciation and considered:

... that, after full withdrawal of Israel from the Sharm el Sheikh and Gaza areas, the scrupulous maintenance of the armistice agreement requires the placing of the United Nations Emergency Force on the Egyptian-Israel armistice demarcation line and the implementation of other measures as proposed in the Secretary-General's report, with due regard to the considerations set out therein with a view to assist in achieving situations conducive to the maintenance of peaceful conditions in the area; ...

89. On February 11, 1957, the Secretary-General stated in a report to the General Assembly that, in the light of the implication of Israel's question concerning the stationing of UNEF at Sharm el Sheikh, he "considered it important . . . to learn whether Israel itself, in principle, consents to a stationing of UNEF units on its territory in implementation of the functions established for the Force in the basic decisions and noted in resolution 1125 (XI) where it was indicated that the Force should be placed 'on the Egyptian-Israel armistice demarcation line.'" No affirmative response was ever received from Israel. In fact, already on November 7, 1956, the Prime Minister of Israel, Mr. Ben-Gurion, in a speech to the Knesset (Parliament), stated, *inter alia*, "On no account will Israel agree to the stationing of a foreign force, no matter how called, in her territory or in any of the territories occupied by her." In a note to correspondents of April 12, 1957, a "United Nations spokesman" stated:

Final arrangements for the UNEF will have to wait for the response of the government of Israel to the request by the General Assembly that the Force be deployed also on the Israel side of the Armistice Demarcation Line.

90. In a report dated October 9, 1957, to the twelfth session of the General Assembly, the Secretary-General stated:

Resolution 1125 (XI) calls for placing the Force "on the Egyptian-Israel armistice demarcation line," but no stationing of UNEF on the Israel side has occurred to date through lack of consent by Israel.

91. In the light of Israel's persistent refusal to consent to the stationing and operation of UNEF on its side of the line in spite of General Assembly resolution 1125 (XI) of February 2, 1957, and the efforts of the Secretary-General, it is even less possible to consider that Egypt's "good faith" declaration made in November 1956 could constitute a limitation of its rights with respect to the continued stationing and operation of UNEF on Egyptian territory in accordance with the resolution of February 2, 1957.

92. The representative of Israel stated in the General Assembly, on November 23, 1956:

If we were to accept one of the proposals made here—namely, that the Force should separate Egyptian and Israel troops for as long as Egypt thought it convenient and should then be withdrawn on Egypt's unilateral request—we would reach a reduction to absurdity. Egypt would then be in a position to build up, behing the screen of this Force, its full military preparations and, when it felt that those military preparations had reached their desired climax, to dismiss the United Nations Emergency Force and to stand again in close contact and proximity with the territory of Israel. This reduction to absurdity proves how impossible it is to accept in any matter affecting the composition or the functions of the Force the policies of the Egyptian Government as the sole or even the decisive criterion.

93. The answer to this problem, which is to be found in resolution 1125 (XI), is not in the form of a binding commitment by Egypt which the record shows was never given, but in the proposal that the Force should be stationed on both sides of the armistice demarcation line. Israel in the exercise of its sovereign right did not give its consent to the stationing of UNEF on its territory and Egypt did not forgo its sovereign right to withdraw its consent at any time.

Role of the UNEF Advisory Committee

94. General Assembly resolution 1001 (ES-I) of November 7, 1956, by which the Assembly approved the guiding principles for the organi-

zation and functioning of UNEF, established an Advisory Committee on UNEF under the chairmanship of the Secretary-General. The Assembly decided that the Advisory Committee, in the performance of its duties, should be empowered to request, through the usual procedures, the convening of the General Assembly and to report to the Assembly whenever matters arose which, in its opinion, were of such urgency and importance as to require consideration by the General Assembly itself.

95. The memorandum of important points in the discussion between the representative of Israel and the Secretary-General on February 25, 1957, recorded the following question raised by the representative of Israel:

In connection with the duration of UNEF's deployment in the Sharm el Sheikh area, would the Secretary-General give notice to the General Assembly of the United Nations before UNEF would be withdrawn from the area, with or without Egyptian insistence, or before the Secretary-General would agree to its withdrawal?

96. The response of the Secretary-General was recorded as follows:

On the question of notification to the General Assembly, the Secretary-General wanted to state his view at a later meeting. An indicated procedure would be for the Secretary-General to inform the Advisory Committee on the United Nations Emergency Force, which would determine whether the matter should be brought to the attention of the Assembly.

97. On March 1, 1957 the Foreign Minister of Israel stated at the 666th plenary meeting of the General Assembly:

My Government has noted the assurance embodied in the Secretary-General's note of February 26, 1957, that any proposal for the withdrawal of the United Nations Emergency Force from the Gulf of Aqaba area would first come to the Advisory Committee on the United Nations Emergency Force, which represents the General Assembly in the implementation of its resolution 997 (ES-I) of November 2, 1956. This procedure will give the General Assembly an opportunity to ensure that no precipitate changes are made which would have the effect of increasing the possibility of belligerent acts.

98. In fact, the February 25, 1957, memorandum does not go as far as the interpretation given by the Foreign Minister of Israel. In any event, however, it gives no indication of any commitment by Egypt, and so far as the Secretary-General is concerned it only indicates that

a procedure would be for the Secretary-General to inform the Advisory Committee which would determine whether the matter should be brought to the attention of the General Assembly. This was also the procedure provided in General Assembly resolution 1001 (ES-I). It was, furthermore, the procedure followed by the Secretary-General on the withdrawal of UNEF.

Observations

99. A partial explanation of the misunderstanding about the withdrawal of UNEF is an evident failure to appreciate the essentially fragile nature of the basis for UNEF's operation throughout its existence. UNEF in functioning depended completely on the voluntary cooperation of the host government. Its basis of existence was the willingness of governments to provide contingents to serve under an international command and at a minimum of cost to the United Nations. It was a symbolic force, small in size, with only 3,400 men, of whom 1,800 were available to police a line of 295 miles at the time of its withdrawal. It was equipped with light weapons only. It had no mandate of any kind to open fire except in the last resort in self-defense. It had no formal mandate to exercise any authority in the area in which it was stationed. In recent years it experienced an increasingly uncertain basis of financial support, which in turn gave rise to strong annual pressures for reduction in its strength. Its remarkable success for more than a decade, despite these practical weaknesses, may have led to wrong conclusions about its nature, but it has also pointed the way to a unique means of contributing significantly to international peace-keeping.

9. From Report to the General Assembly
on the Liquidation of UNEF

NEW YORK   JULY 12, 1967

1. THIS REPORT is the final one in the series of annual reports on UNEF which have been submitted by the Secretary-General to the General Assembly since the Force came into being in November 1956. It thus marks the end of a pioneering effort, of the first peace force of the United Nations and, for this reason, it may claim a special significance. This final report is an opportune time to broaden and lengthen the comments and observations usually presented by the Secretary-General in the introductions and conclusions of the annual reports on UNEF, to express some general views on United Nations peace-keeping activities and to record some of the more important lessons to be learnt from the experience with UNEF.

2. Separate reports on the decision to withdraw the Force, and covering the details of its evacuation, have been submitted previously. The experience acquired with the withdrawal of UNEF most certainly points up the desirability of having all conditions relating to the presence and the withdrawal of a peace-keeping operation clearly defined in advance of its entry onto the territory of a host country. In most instances, however, this is unlikely to prove to be practicable for the reason that the critical situation which demands the presence of the operation is likely to require that presence so urgently that time cannot be taken to negotiate agreements on detailed conditions in advance of the entry. Moreover, it remains an open question as to whether in the present stage of the development of international order, any host country would be inclined to accept formal limitations on its sovereignty with regard to the exercise of its consent for the presence of an international force. Its attitude in this regard is bound to be influenced by the knowledge that there can never be certainty

SOURCE: General Assembly Official Records, Twenty-second Session, Annexes, agenda item 21, document A/6672, part I.

about the action on a given matter such as the presence of a United Nations Force, which the Security Council or the General Assembly might take at some future date, since the decisions of these political bodies are always subject to political considerations.

3. The Force came into existence in response to General Assembly resolution 1000 (ES-I) of November 5, 1956, which established the United Nations Command. It took actual shape as a force on November 10 of that year when its first advance party, consisting of forty-five Danish military personnel, landed at Capodichino airport, Naples, the temporary United Nations staging area. Its initial deployment on Egyptian territory was on November 15, 1956, when Danish and Norwegian advance parties landed at Abu Suweir. Following the request of the government of the United Arab Republic, on May 18, 1967, for the withdrawal of the Force, which was, in fact, preceded by movements of United Arab Republic troops up to the line in Sinai for the first time in over a decade, UNEF ceased to be operational in Sinai, including Sharm el Sheikh and the Gaza Strip on May 19, 1967. The evacuation of the Force from the United Arab Republic and United Arab Republic-controlled territory, however, was completed only on June 17, 1967.

4. The Force was a highly successful peace-keeping operation, but it was costly enough by United Nations standards. In the period of its existence it suffered eighty-nine fatalities and many wounded and injured, a number of these occurring in the early period of the Force as a result of encounters with mines, often in poorly mapped mine fields. Its total cost to the United Nations over its ten and a half years of deployment was approximately $213 million, which was, by normal military standards, quite inexpensive for a force of UNEF's size. Its peak strength was 6,073 in March 1957; it had been reduced to 3,378 at the time of its withdrawal. This was a small cost by comparison with the human and financial consequences of a resumption of war in the area. The financial cost of the Force to the United Nations was, of course, considerably reduced by the absorption by the countries providing contigents of varying amounts of the expenses involved.

5. The sudden outbreak of war in the Near East, the severe crisis in the United Nations, and the disastrous shattering of peace in the area which soon followed the withdrawal of UNEF need be mentioned only in passing in this report on UNEF's final period of service. What would probably happen whenever UNEF might be

withdrawn had been pointed out by the Secretary-General in his reports on UNEF in preceding years. This likelihood was why, despite the increasing difficulties of financing the Force and his belief that no United Nations peace-keeping operation should become relatively permanent, the Secretary-General had never recommended the termination of UNEF or even its conversion into a large-scale observation operation. The risk implicit in any such action had always seemed to the Secretary-General to be much too great.

6. The recent tragic events in the Near East that followed UNEF's withdrawal, however—a withdrawal which in itself was a product of deep-seated and long-continuing Arab-Israel hostility—do not obscure, but rather underscore, the achievements of UNEF as a unique peace-keeping venture. When, in March 1957, UNEF reached the International Frontier in Sinai and the Armistice Demarcation Line in the Gaza Strip as the military forces of Israel withdrew across the line, it was deployed along what had been only four months before one of the most troubled borders anywhere in the world. With UNEF's deployment there, that line became and remained almost completely quiet. The terrorizing raids of the fedayeen across that line into Israel became a thing of the past. Infiltration across the line from either side was almost ended. Fields near the line on both sides, which for long had been left uncultivated because it was near suicidal to come into view in the open fields, were now being worked right up to the line itself and on both sides of it. Costly irrigation systems were extensively installed. Heavy investments in new citrus orchards and in other cash crops were made. A new prosperity came to the area in UNEF's decade. Above all, because of UNEF's effective buffer role, there was security as there was no longer a military confrontation between the armed forces of Israel and the United Arab Republic, and clashes between those forces practically ceased.

7. In consequence, there was throughout Gaza and Sinai an unaccustomed quiet for more than ten years. This was due, very largely, if not entirely, to the presence of UNEF.

8. It is very much to the credit of UNEF, to the wisdom and tact of its successive commanders and officers, to the understanding, the fine demeanor, and the discipline of its men, that throughout the years of its deployment in Sinai and the Gaza Strip its relations with the local population and with the local authorities continued excellent until the last few days of its presence. This was of crucial importance

because otherwise it would have been impossible for a United Nations peace-keeping operation to maintain itself and to function for very long. It is inconceivable that the personnel of such a United Nations operation could be maintained if hostile relations should develop between it and the local authorities and particularly between it and the local population.

9. The Force, in the sense of maintaining quiet and preventing incidents, was a most effective United Nations peace-keeping operation, although others have also enjoyed great success. Like the other peace forces—the United Nations Peace-keeping Force in Cyprus and the United Nations Operation in the Congo—UNEF was, however, an international force in only a limited sense. Its troops were provided as national contingents which retained their identity as such and were seldom broken up. The officers and men wore their national uniforms except for the distinctive United Nations headgear: the helmet, fieldcap, or beret of United Nations blue, and the United Nations insignia. The personal arms they carried for self-defense only were those employed and provided by their national armed forces. Each contingent marched according to its own national custom and cadence. Each contingent had its national commanding officer who gave his orders in his national language. Each contingent had its own national dishes and dietary practices. The Force as a whole, however, was under a Commander who was an international staff member, being appointed by the Secretary-General and responsible only to him. But the governments providing the contingents retained the right to withdraw their units at their pleasure. It is surprising, in retrospect, how seldom this authority has been exercised.

10. It is relevant to note some of the features which are peculiar to United Nations peace-keeping forces in general and to UNEF in particular, as compared with normal military operations. The essentially *ad hoc* nature of United Nations peace-keeping operations affects their nature and functioning from the very outset. In these operations none of the planning and preparation which are expected of normal military procedures can be counted upon. UNEF, for example, was called for in mid-emergency by a resolution of the General Assembly and had to be quickly established out of nothing, without the benefit even of its anticipation. The process of organizing, dispatching, concentrating, and deploying the Force, not to mention its logical support, had to be telescoped into a few days.

Such a procedure inevitably gives rise to all sorts of problems—organizational, administrative, and military. It particularly causes some shock at first to well-trained military men and requires a considerable adjustment on their part to very unfamiliar ways.

11. The United Nations, unlike national governments with military establishments, has no permanent logistical services or military establishment. The logistical basis of a peace-keeping operation is therefore an *ad hoc* emergency arrangement organized by the Field Operations Service with the assistance of governments and various private concerns throughout the world. Furthermore, the budgetary scale of United Nations peace-keeping operations is always at the minimum level and does not allow for logistical establishments, communications, depots, etc., of the kind which normally support national armies at home or serving abroad. Under rigid budgetary limitations, therefore, and subject to constant pressure for new economies, the Field Operations Service has to provide logistical support for such operations as best it can.

12. The circumstances of the setting up of such an *ad hoc* emergency operation make it inevitable that the Commander, his staff, his contingent commanders, and the national contingents meet each other for the first time in the area of operations and when already fully committed to their tasks.

13. The *ad hoc* nature of United Nations peace-keeping operations has other consequences. There can be no initial standardization of stores and equipment, which leads to serious problems of administration and maintenance later on. There are no standard operating procedures to begin with, but these are soon formulated. The standard of training and method of operation of contingents vary widely. The rotation of some contingents every six months also militates against continuity and whatever common standards may be hoped for. Although there is no difficulty in obtaining infantry units, adequately trained technical support elements are far less easily available.

14. While the Force Commander exercises operational command and control of the Force as a whole, the national contingents exercise responsibility over their men for such matters as discipline, punishment, awards, and promotions. Although this never caused any serious problem in UNEF, the relationship of the Force Commander with the contingents under his command was in fact quite different from,

and potentially far weaker than, the relationship of the commander of a national army with the units under his command. On the other hand, the pride of national contingents and their officers and men in being part of a United Nations Force offsets, to a very large extent, the weakness in the link of command between national and international responsibilities and produces a remarkable solidarity, *esprit de corps,* and high standard of the United Nations working languages.

15. Despite the excellent morale of UNEF, difficulties of communication among personnel and contingents did give rise to some serious problems and misunderstandings, especially when senior military officers and staff could not communicate in one or other of the United Nations working languages.

16. The UNEF military man was faced with a concept of soldiering which is entirely foreign to anything taught him in national service. The soldier is trained basically to fight. In UNEF, however, he was ordered to avoid fighting in all circumstances, and, indeed, to seek to prevent it. Though armed, he could use force only in the last resort in self-defense. He had no enemy. Under provocation he had to show discipline and restraint; his tasks had to be carried through by persuasion, tact, example, calm and soldierly bearing, but if humanly possible never by force. It is an immensely encouraging fact that the soldiers of UNEF, almost without exception, were able for over ten years to live up to these unaccustomed and exacting standards and to carry out their duties with extraordinary success and with a minimum of friction.

17. There are a number of circumstances peculiar to United Nations peace-keeping forces which can, and sometimes do, create considerable problems for the Commander of a force and also for the Secretary-General. In particular, they constitute potential weaknesses in the authority of the Force Commander. For example, most contingents of the United Nations Force maintain direct communications with their home countries. These are supposed to be used only for domestic and national administrative matters. When, however, as does happen, they are used for direct communication with the home government on matters which are strictly within the authority of the Force Commander or at times even on political matters, misunderstandings and confusion are very likely to arise.

18. It may be inevitable that, for reasons usually quite unconnected with the peace-keeping force, some contingents of a Force will

come to be viewed with more favor than others by the host government. This can also give rise to embarrassment and difficulty both in the relations among the contingents of the Force and in the task of the Commander in maintaining its unity and morale and even in its proper use and deployment.

19. On the administrative side, too, there are certain potential or actual problems. The relationship of civilian and military authorities is sometimes strained even in national establishments. In UNEF and other peace-keeping operations the entire financial and logistical set-up has to be under the supervision of a civilian, normally the ranking Secretariat member who usually is the chief administrative officer, and of United Nations Headquarters in New York. The Secretary-General has the responsibility to ensure coordination, sound administration, economy, and accounting to the Advisory Committee on Administrative and Budgetary Questions and the Fifth (Administrative and Budgetary) Committee of the General Assembly. The disbursement of United Nations funds has to be kept under United Nations control. Inevitably this distribution of functions, administrative authority, and responsibilities may lead to friction between the international Secretariat element and the Military Command and staff. In particular, the stringent economies which have to be practiced in United Nations operations may be, and sometimes have been, interpreted by the military as arbitrary and unjustified attitudes on the part of civilians which handicap the operation, while the civilians, in their turn, may feel that the military are showing little understanding for the particular administrative and other difficulties of the United Nations Operations. In only one United Nations operation, however, and in that only during one brief stage, has the misunderstanding between the military and civilian branches assumed an acute form. In that single instance, the relief of the Commander sooner than had been planned proved to be the necessary and adequate remedy.

20. Another potential source of unpleasantness on the administrative side is the difference in the reimbursable allowances stipulated by governments for their contingents. This difference in the money actually paid to individual soldiers by the United Nations, which is determined by the varying pay and allowance scales among the governments contributing the contingents, is in some cases very striking and does not fail to have an adverse effect on the relations

among the contingents of the force and on its morale. All efforts to gain an equitable scale of allowances common to all contingents have, however, so far been unsuccessful.

21. An operation such as UNEF is not an end in itself. It is, in fact, a practical adjunct to peace-making. It becomes necessary in a conflict situation, when fighting is stopped, because cease-fires, truces, and armistices are seldom self-enforcing or self-policing. Some third presence is required at least to verify and report the breaches. The true function of a peace-keeping effort is to create a climate of quiet which is more congenial to efforts to solve the underlying problems that lead to conflict. It may achieve this better climate in a number of ways, such as averting military confrontations by acting as a buffer through patrolling and policing activities, and through providing an added assurance by its very presence. It is not an enforcement agent and can expect to exercise at best only a very limited degree of authority; an authority, moreover, which, unless explicitly defined in its mandate and the consequent agreements with the host country, automatically and instantly vanishes once it is challenged by the host government.

22. It is only realistic to accept the fact that when a United Nations peace-keeping operation, whether it be an observation mission or a peace force, is no longer welcome in a country and cooperation with it is withheld, it cannot hope to continue to perform any useful function, may well soon find itself defenseless and in grave danger, and thus had best be withdrawn as amicably as the prevailing circumstances will permit. If there should be serious doubt about the wisdom of this latter course, it would be advisable to abandon altogether the notion of a voluntary peace-keeping operation and turn to consideration of enforcement-type actions under Chapter VII of the Charter. The two cannot be mixed. It should be added, however, that it is extremely doubtful that any of the peace-keeping operations thus far mounted by the United Nations would have been acceptable to the governments of the countries in which they have been stationed if they had been originally envisaged in the context of Chapter VII of the Charter. There is no room at all for doubt about this as regards UNEF.

23. Some fundamental principles clearly applicable to any United Nations peace force have been forged in the long experience of UNEF. Such an operation is entirely voluntary: the full consent of

the host country and any other parties directly concerned is the indispensable pre-condition for the stationing of the force. The contingents comprising the force are voluntarily provided by the governments of Member states, subject to conditions of service and finance mutually agreed upon by the governments and the United Nations. There must be a will on the part of the parties themselves for quiet in the area together with a recognition of the need for international assistance to this end, which is expressed in the extension of a reasonable degree of cooperation to the operation in the performance of its functions. The force must be always exclusively under United Nations command and neither the force as a whole nor any of its components shall take instructions from the host government, from any other party directly concerned, or from a government providing a contingent. The force must have assurance, by means of a formal agreement, of the rights, privileges, and immunities essential to its effective functioning, such as freedom of movement on land and in the air and exemption from customs duties for its equipment and supplies.

24. United Nations experience with such operations, and this was notably so in the case of UNEF, indicates that the success of a peace-keeping operation may, in itself, induce a false sense of security. The ability of the operation to re-establish and maintain quiet for an extended period may come to be mistaken for a solution of the basic problem. This can only increase the sense of shock when, ultimately and inexorably, it is demonstrated that problems of conflict may lie dormant even for long periods but they do not necessarily solve themselves by the passage of time, and the day may come when they will explode anew. Peace-keeping operations can serve their purpose properly only if they are accompanied by serious and persistent efforts to find solutions to the problems which demanded the peace-keeping in the first place.

25. It merits emphasis that United Nations peace-keeping operations function within the wider framework of the United Nations as a whole. Many of the frustrations, the cross-currents, the pressures, and particularly the political stresses of the Organization inevitably have a major impact on the original setting-up of a peace-keeping operation and on its day-to-day functioning as well. The present limitations of the United Nations in a world still dominated by rigid concepts of national sovereignty, by power politics, and by acute

nationalistic sentiments are also the inherent limitations of United Nations peace-keeping operations.

26. The recognition of the existence of these limitations should not lead to a passive acceptance of a situation which needs to be remedied. The Secretary-General interprets the shock and dismay produced by the withdrawal of UNEF and the renewed fighting in the Middle East as an expression of how much reliance, especially on the part of those directly concerned, had come to be placed upon the United Nations as an instrument for the maintenance of peace in some areas of the world. Clearly, an important lesson to be gained from this sobering experience is that the peace-keeping function of the United Nations should be strengthened so as better to serve the cause of world peace.

27. Before concluding these observations, the Secretary-General wishes once again to pay tribute to the governments which have provided contingents for UNEF—those of Brazil, Canada, Denmark, India, Norway, Sweden, and Yugoslavia, which provided contingents throughout the existence of the Force—and also those of Colombia, Finland, and Indonesia, which responded promptly to the initial requirement for troops for UNEF and whose contingents served in the early months of the Force. In taking part in such a novel operation, these governments willingly accepted the risks and uncertainties as well as the varying financial burdens involved and showed in a most practical manner their support of a pioneering effort of the United Nations toward keeping the peace. The Secretary-General would also wish to express his admiration and gratitude to the many thousands of officers and men from these ten countries, without whose discipline, understanding, and exemplary bearing UNEF's success would have been impossible. In addition, he wishes to express appreciation to those governments which, throughout the years, gave the financial and other support to UNEF which allowed it to continue its most valuable function for a far longer period of time than was originally foreseen.

. . .

THE SIX-DAY WAR

WITH THE OUTBREAK of the Six-Day War between Israel and her Arab
neighbors on June 5, U Thant was faced with the complex and interlocking
task of informing the Security Council of military developments, maintaining
his lines of communication with United Nations representatives in the com-
bat area, safeguarding the lives of personnel assigned to the United Nations
Truce Supervision Organization (UNTSO) and the de-activated United
Nations Emergency Force (UNEF) assembled in the Gaza sector awaiting
evacuation, and trying to arrange a cease-fire. As the following documents
will show, the information on the fighting was fragmentary and some of it
unverified because of limitations on the movements of United Nations
observers and lack of communications, but it was the best information
available to the Security Council. Thant used both written reports and
personal interventions to pass along communications from United Nations
representatives in the field and from the governments involved. On one day
alone, June 10, he made nine oral statements to the Security Council. It was
through the Secretary-General that the Council received the replies of Israel
and the Arab countries to the four cease-fire resolutions adopted between
June 6 and 11. He was seriously concerned during this period by the lack of
respect on the part of the governments concerned for the rights and safety of
United Nations personnel. Although Government House in Jerusalem was
supposedly inviolable as the headquarters of UNTSO, it was first entered by
Jordanian troops and later occupied by Israel. The Secretary-General protested strongly to the Israeli government and to King Hussein of Jordan. He
also protested to Israel against the strafing of a convoy of Indian UNEF
troops near Gaza even though the vehicles were painted white, as were all
UNEF vehicles. Despite acceptance of the Security Council's cease-fire
demands by both sides as early as June 7, fighting continued on the Israeli-
Syrian sector. It was not until June 11 that the Secretary-General was finally
able to report that the cease-fire arrangements were being observed.

1. *Statement in the Security Council*

NEW YORK   JUNE 5, 1967

MR. PRESIDENT, in response to your invitation I present to the Council all the information that I have received from United Nations sources in the Middle East on the outbreak of hostilities. Of course, the United Nations sources have no means of ascertaining how the hostilities were initiated. As usual, reports coming from the parties are conflicting, but all agree that serious military action on land and in the air is taking place at a number of points and is spreading.

I have instructed both the Chief of Staff of the United Nations Truce Supervision Organization (UNTSO) and the Commander of the United Nations Emergency Force (UNEF) to keep reporting urgently all information available to them and I shall keep members of the Council informed as new information comes in. This information is unavoidably fragmentary.

As far as information from the United Nations Emergency Force is concerned, it must be remembered that the Force is no longer on the [demarcation] line, but is concentrated in its camps and is in the process of withdrawal. The information given by the Commander of the Emergency Force is therefore, of necessity, somewhat general, and much of it has been given to the Commander by the United Arab Republic liaison service in Gaza.

General Rikhye, Commander of UNEF, reported that at 0800 hours local time today two Israel aircraft violated United Arab Republic air space over Gaza town. One of these aircraft was shot down by anti-aircraft fire and fell into the sea. The pilot bailed out and was picked up by a motor-launch. Also at 0800 hours local time, two Israel aircraft violated United Arab Republic air space over El Arish and were fired on by anti-aircraft guns. The United Arab Republic claims one Israel aircraft was shot down. Personnel of the Emergency Force in Rafah Camp reported heavy firing between United Arab Republic

SOURCE: Security Council Official Records, Twenty-second Year, 1347th meeting.

and Israel forces across the international frontier south of Rafah, starting at 0800 hours local time. United Arab Republic authorities in Gaza informed General Rikhye of a large-scale Israel air raid throughout the United Arab Republic including a raid on Cairo. I am informed that Israel has denied the report of the raid on Cairo. The United Arab Republic authorities also informed General Rikhye that at 0800 hours local time Israel forces had attacked El Qusaima in Sinai. At 0915 hours local time, United Arab Republic artillery in Gaza started firing toward Israel-controlled territory. Firing stopped at 0930 hours local time, but resumed again at 1000 hours local time. The Commander of UNEF is taking all possible steps to ensure the security of UNEF personnel still in the area.

General Bull, Chief of Staff of UNTSO, has informed me that firing in Jerusalem commenced at 1125 hours local time and was continuing. General Bull requested an immediate cease-fire at the highest local levels. The senior Jordanian delegate to the Israel-Jordan Mixed Armistice Commission accepted a cease-fire for 1200 hours local time. In a meeting between General Bull and the Israel authorities on the morning of June 5, General Bull was informed that United Arab Republic planes had crossed the border and that Israel aircraft had been sent to meet them.

At 1145 hours local time, Israel informed General Bull of its acceptance of his request for a cease-fire at 1200 hours local time. Most firing had ceased by 1210 hours local time, although a few mortar rounds continued to be fired from Jordan and near Mount Scopus. One mortar round landed in the Government House compound, which is the headquarters of UNTSO. No casualties are reported.

Since sporadic mortar firing from Jordan continued after the cease-fire, a second cease-fire was proposed for 1230 hours local time and accepted by both sides.

On the Israel-Syrian armistice demarcation line, United Nations military observers reported overflights by Syrian jet fighters between 1155 hours and 1206 hours local time on June 5 and reported air battles, anti-aircraft fire, and explosions from aircraft bombing. The senior Israel delegate to the Israel-Syrian Mixed Armistice Commission informed the UNTSO officer-in-charge at Tiberias, at 1218 hours local time, that Israel considered itself in a state of war with Syria. The Chairman of the Israel-Syrian Mixed Armistice Commission reported that Damascus airport was being attacked by Israel aircraft at 1110 hours local time.

The Commander of UNEF reported that at 1245 hours local time Israel artillery opened fire on two camps of the Indian contingent of UNEF which were in the process of being abandoned, and soon thereafter United Arab Republic tanks surrounded one of the camps which still contains one reduced Indian company. Orders have been given for the Indian personnel in both camps to be withdrawn immediately.

General Rikhye also reported that a UNEF convoy immediately south of Khan Yunis on the road between Gaza and Rafah was strafed by an Israel aircraft on the morning of June 5, although the vehicles, like all UNEF vehicles, are painted white. First reports indicate that three Indian soldiers were killed and an unknown number wounded in this attack. The Commander of UNEF has sent an urgent message through the Chief of Staff of UNTSO to the Chief of Staff of the Israel Defense Forces urging him again to give orders to Israel Armed Forces to refrain from firing on UNEF camps, buildings, and vehicles.

After hostilities began on the morning of June 5, the Chief of Staff of UNTSO drew the attention of Israel and Jordan to the inviolability of the Government House area and asked them to ensure that this inviolability would be fully respected. Both sides gave him the required assurance. However, at 1330 hours local time today approximately one company of Jordanian soldiers occupied the garden of Government House. General Bull in person protested to the Commander and asked him to withdraw his troops. He also protested in the strongest terms to the senior Jordanian delegate to the Israel-Jordan Mixed Armistice Commission against the violation of United Nations premises by Jordanian soldiers, whose withdrawal within half an hour he demanded. He also informed the Israel authorities of these developments and requested them to ensure that Israel soldiers would not enter the Government House area. By then an exchange of fire had already begun between the Jordanian soldiers in the Government House garden and Israel soldiers nearby. General Bull later informed me by an emergency message that Jordanian troops had not withdrawn and were demanding to enter Government House itself and had demanded that no telephone calls be made from Government

House. Firing was continuing and mortar shells were now landing within the Government House compound. United Nations Headquarters lost radio contact with UNTSO headquarters in Jerusalem at 0852 hours New York time, at which time Jordanian troops occupied Government House.[1] This also means that United Nations Headquarters has lost direct contact with headquarters UNEF, whose messages are routed through UNTSO.

In view of these developments I have addressed the following urgent appeal to the King of Jordan:

His Majesty King Hussein
Hashemite Kingdom of Jordan, Amman, Jordan
Your Majesty,
I have just been advised at 0900 hours local time that all communications with Government House have ended because of its occupation by Jordanian troops. This is a breach of extreme seriousness. I appeal to Your Majesty with utmost urgency to order the immediate removal of Jordanian troops from the grounds and buildings of the Government House compound in Jerusalem. As Your Majesty knows, this compound has been respected by both parties to the Hashemite Kingdom of Jordan-Israel Mixed Armistice Commission as the headquarters of the United Nations Truce Supervision Organization and therefore under the exclusive United Nations occupation and control.

U THANT
Secretary-General of
the United Nations

[1] In the interest of historical accuracy, it is to be noted that the report that Jordanian troops had "occupied" Government House was originally based on incomplete information owing to a communications breakdown caused by the events in the Government House area. On the basis of a review of events and a checking with the Chief of Staff of UNTSO, it was later determined that the actual facts as regards the reported entry of Jordanian troops into Government House on June 5, 1967, were as follows: At approximately 1445 hours local time, three Jordanian soldiers entered Government House over the protest of UNTSO, but were persuaded by UNTSO staff to leave the building after about ten minutes.

2. *Report to the Security Council*

NEW YORK   JUNE 5, 1967

1. IN VIEW OF the apparent uncertainty about the time when the Council meeting which adjourned on the morning of June 5, 1967 [1347th meeting], will reconvene, I have decided to circulate to the members the information I have received since I gave my oral statement to the Council this morning. This written statement is supplemental therefore to this morning's oral statement.

2. Direct communication with General Bull continues to be suspended for the reasons which I mentioned in my previous statement. We understand, however, that heavy firing is taking place in and around the Government House compound in Jerusalem. A cease-fire in the area was called for at 1500 hours LT [local time] but was not respected, although both delegates to the Israel-Jordan Mixed Armistice Commission agreed to the arrangement.

3. The Chairman of the Israel-Syria Mixed Armistice Commission has reported from Damascus that Damascus airport has been intermittently under air attack since 1110 hours GMT and that other locations in Syria have also been under air attack. The Mixed Armistice Commission has also received complaints from Israel that Megiddo, Eilabum and a locality south of Akko have been attacked from the air.

4. Contact has been re-established with the Commander of the United Nations Emergency Force who reports artillery firing at 1430 hours LT on the Indian Battalion main camp, with whom communications have now broken down. Snipers' fire is reported at the same time from Rafah Camp. At 1520 hours LT, artillery firing was reported near Swedish Battalion main camp and at the same time artillery and mortar fire were reported near Rafah Camp. In Rafah Camp one Brazilian soldier and two local civilians are reported lightly wounded.

SOURCE: Security Council Official Records, Twenty-second Year, Supplement for April, May and June 1967, document S/7930.

5. A later report from the Commander of the Force states that during the artillery firing on the Indian main camp referred to above, one Indian officer and one soldier were killed and one officer and nine soldiers wounded.

6. The Commander of the Force has pointed out that a contributing factor to the casualties suffered from artillery fire was the proximity of the military positions of the United Arab Republic to the camps concerned.

7. The Commander of the Force reports that only sporadic firing has been heard since 1600 hours LT, but that at 1630 hours LT two Israel aircraft attacked the Wadi Gaza bridge and are reported to have destroyed it. This is the bridge on the main road south from Gaza.

8. At 1748 hours LT the United Nations radio station in Amman, Jordan, reported that it was under air attack.

9. In my statement to the Security Council this morning [1347th meeting] I read out to the Council an urgent appeal which I had sent to His Majesty the King of Jordan relating to the occupation by Jordanian troops of the headquarters of the United Nations Truce Supervision Organization in Palestine (UNTSO) in Government House, Jerusalem. I now wish to read to the Council the text of a message which I have addressed today to the government of Israel through the permanent representative of Israel to the United Nations concerning the incident which I mentioned in my statement this morning in which a strafing attack by Israel aircraft led to the deaths of three Indian soldiers of the Force, and the later casualties caused by Israel artillery fire on the camps of the Force.

10. I regard both of these incidents as being in their different ways so serious that I have taken the unusual step of informing the Council of these two messages before having confirmation of the receipt of the messages themselves by those to whom they are addressed.

11. The message to Israel is as follows:

The Secretary-General presents his compliments to the permanent representative of Israel to the United Nations and has the honor to refer to tragic incidents involving personnel of the Indian Contingent of the United Nations Emergency Force which occurred during June 5.

In a strafing attack by Israel aircraft on a convoy of the Force immediately south of Khan Yunis on the road between Gaza and Rafah three Indian soldiers were killed and an unknown number were wounded. All vehicles in the convoy were painted white, as are all vehicles of the Force. Prior to this incident the Commander of the Force, as a result of Israel artillery fire on two camps occupied by the Indian Contingent of the Force, had, through the Chief of Staff UNTSO, requested the Chief of Staff of the Israel Defense Forces to give instructions that a strict cease-fire would be observed in the vicinity of the installations and camps of the Force. This appeal was acceded to and General Rikhye was notified that instructions had been given to the Israel forces to observe strictly the cease-fire in the vicinity of all the installations and camps of the Force. After the incident, the Commander of the Force again urged the Chief of Staff of the Israel Defense Forces to order Israel forces and especially Israel aircraft to take special care to avoid firing on personnel and installations of the Force.

At 1230 hours GMT on June 5, the main camp of the Indian battalion of the Force came under Israel artillery fire which killed one officer and one soldier and wounded one officer and nine soldiers.

The Secretary-General requests the permanent representative of Israel to the United Nations to convey to the government of Israel his strong protest against the above-mentioned acts by the Israel Armed Forces, which have led to tragic and unnecessary loss of life among Force personnel, and to request them to take urgent measures to ensure that there is no recurrence of such incidents.

12. A later report received through a non-United Nations channel, sent by the Chief of Staff UNTSO indicates that heavy firing broke out in the Government House area in Jerusalem at about 1130 hours GMT on June 5 and all communications were cut shortly thereafter. Jordanian soldiers in the compound were attacked and later driven out by Israel troops. The Israel troops then forced their way into Government House at about 1230 hours GMT. When the firing subsided temporarily at about 1400 hours GMT, the Chief of Staff UNTSO and his staff were ordered out of Government House by the Israel troops and escorted into Israel. Government House itself was heavily damaged but there were no casualties among UNTSO personnel. General Bull reported that firing was still going on in Jerusalem at 1410 hours GMT. The Chairman of the Israel-Jordan Mixed Armistice Commission and his staff are continuing to function, and General Bull is attempting to establish a temporary headquarters.

13. In view of these developments, I have sent the following cable to the Prime Minister of Israel, Mr. Levi Eshkol:

I understand that Israel forces have now displaced the forces of Jordan in the Government House Compound in Jerusalem. Whatever the circumstances leading to the Israel occupation of Government House and its grounds, its continued occupation by Israel troops is a most serious breach of the undertaking to respect its inviolability.

I therefore request the Government of Israel to restore the grounds and buildings of the Government House Compound urgently to exclusive United Nations control. When this has been done I propose to seek a formal undertaking from both sides to respect the United Nations Truce Supervision Organization's occupation of Government House in the future.

14. The Commander of the United Nations Emergency Force has reported that two Israel tanks entered the barbed wire around Rafah Camp at about 1500 hours GMT and that fire from these tanks had caused a number of casualties among the local staff of the Rafah Camp. It has been the scene throughout the day of sporadic exchanges of mortar and artillery fire. In view of the continued danger to Force personnel, the Commander of the Force has decided to move units in exposed places to bivouac areas on the beach as soon as it is possible to do so.

15. I received word late this afternoon from the Chief of Staff of the United Nations Truce Supervision Organization, again by a non-United Nations channel, that heavy firing was continuing in and around the city of Jerusalem with consequent great risk of damage to the holy places. I strongly support the idea that has been advanced that Jerusalem should be declared an open city in order to protect for all mankind its irreplaceable historical religious places which are of inestimable spiritual significance.

3. Report to the Security Council

NEW YORK   JUNE 6, 1967

1. IN VIEW OF the apparent uncertainty about the time when the Security Council will convene, I am circulating to the members information which I have received since the issuance of document S/7930 in order not to delay the availability of this information to the members.

2. The Chief of Staff of the United Nations Truce Supervision

SOURCE: Security Council Official Records, Twenty-second Year, Supplement for April, May, and June 1967, document S/7930, Add. 1.

Organization in Palestine (UNTSO) reported on the evening of June 5, 1967, as follows.

3. The situation in Tiberias and Damascus was reported quiet. The situation in Beirut was reported as quiet. The Chairman of the Hashemite Kingdom of Jordan-Israel Mixed Armistice Commission had been informed by the Israel delegate that Jordan was shelling Tel Aviv and Lydda and by the Jordanian delegate that Israel was shelling Jenin. He was further informed by the Israel delegate that Israel would bomb Ramallah and Amman if Jordan did not stop shelling Tel Aviv and Lydda. The Chairman of the Mixed Armistice Commission approached both sides in an effort to stop Jordanian shelling and the threatened retaliation by Israel. In Jerusalem heavy machine-gun and mortar fire was continuing in the general area of Mount Scopus.

4. Firing in Jerusalem continued throughout the night of June 5/6, and on June 6 heavy mortar and machine-gun firing continued in and north of the Mandelbaum Square area. At about dawn Israel forces appeared to be making a ground attack to link up with Mount Scopus, employing close air support. The Chairman of the Mixed Armistice Commission is still in his headquarters but has lost contact with the delegates of both parties.

5. The UNTSO Tiberias control center reported that heavy firing broke out at 0355 hours GMT on June 6 along almost the entire length of the Israel/Syria Armistice Demarcation Line. Artillery, tanks, aircraft, and napalm were employed. The UNTSO Tiberias control center reported that at 0528 hours GMT Syrian armed forces had launched an infantry attack from Tel el Azaziyat toward Shear. At 0552 hours the Senior Israel Delegate informed the Israel-Syrian Mixed Armistice Commission that Syrian forces had launched an armor and infantry attack toward Tell el Qadi. A cease-fire had been proposed by the Chairman of the Mixed Armistice Commission for 0600 hours GMT but the fighting continued. At 0943 hours GMT the Chairman of the Mixed Armistice Commission reported that he was still in contact with both the Syrian and Israel delegations and that the bulk of his OP's continued to be manned. Two proposed cease-fires since the fighting broke out along the Israel/Syria Armistice Demarcation Line had been unsuccessful, and in his opinion a local cease-fire was not feasible in the present circumstances.

6. Israel newcasts reported that Latrun and Jenin in Jordan had been occupied by the Israel forces.

7. In Gaza the Commander of the United Nations Emergency

Force had attempted by messages to the military authorities of both the United Arab Republic and Israel to secure a general cease-fire by both sides around camps and other concentrations of Force troops. The communications of Force HQ had been made extremely difficult by Israel artillery fire in and around the area of Force headquarters, and Force radio antennae and telephone wires were cut. The contingents of the Force had been caught during the day of June 5 in the various exchanges of fire between the two sides as reported by me on June 5. All efforts are being made to concentrate Force personnel in safe areas and to arrange for their evacuation. A Swedish ship is arriving in Gaza during the day of June 6 to evacuate the Swedish contingent, the Norwegian Hospital and various nonessential personnel. Other possibilities for evacuation are being urgently examined both at Headquarters and in the area. The Force Commander reported that urgent consideration was being given to bringing the Indian battalion to Tre Kroner Camp in Gaza on foot on June 6.

8. UNEF headquarters came under direct Israel artillery fire during the night of June 5/6. Efforts were made by the Commander to contact the Israel authorities with a view to stopping this fire. However, after two and a half hours of intensive shelling, which caused heavy damage to the headquarters buildings and damaged nearly half of its vehicles, the Commander of the Force was forced to abandon his headquarters when a direct hit completely knocked out his radio communications. During this artillery fire three Indian soldiers were killed and three Indian soldiers wounded. I am protesting to the Israel government the shelling of Force headquarters and the tragic loss of life caused by it.

9. The Commander of the Force re-established his headquarters in the Tre Kroner Camp near the beach in Gaza and re-established communications. At 1040 hours GMT he reported heavy small arms firing in the town of Gaza. He also reported that the Indian contingent was surrounded at Deir el Balah at 0700 hours GMT by Israel troops who had left them alone and proceeded toward the town of Deir el Balah where fighting continued. Rafah Camp has also been by-passed by Israel forces and is quiet. The Yugoslav contingent at El Arish reported continued exchanges of fire between the two sides. The Swedish contingent in the Tre Kroner Camp near Gaza beach are reported all safe and it is intended to evacuate them by ship from Gaza today, June 6.

10. At 1225 hours GMT the Commander of the Force reported that an Israel tank unit had entered Gaza town at 1100 hours GMT and at 1115 hours GMT had by-passed the United Nations Tre Kroner Camp and had proceeded north along the beach road. Firing in Gaza died down from about 1145 hours GMT. At 1200 hours GMT the Yugoslav contingent in El Arish reported all quiet.

11. In closing I must express to members of the Council, and particularly to the representative of India, my deep regret at the heavy casualties which the Indian contingent have suffered through no fault of their own and in a situation where they had no means of defending themselves. I ask the permanent representative of India to the United Nations to express to the government of India and to the families concerned my deep condolences and sympathy.

---

4. Statement in the Security Council

NEW YORK   JUNE 7, 1967

I RECEIVED this morning the following cable from the Foreign Minister of Jordan:

I have the honor to acknowledge receipt of your cable informing me of the Security Council resolution [233 (1967)] calling upon the governments concerned as a first step to take forthwith all measures for an immediate cease-fire and for a cessation of all military activities in the area. This cable is to inform Your Excellency that the government of the Hashemite Kingdom of Jordan has taken note of the Security Council resolution and has authorized me to convey its acceptance of the said cease-fire resolution. I would add that I was in telephonic contact with Mr. El-Farra, our permanent delegate, when the Security Council voted the cease-fire resolution unanimously. Consequently, immediate orders were issued to our armed forces to observe the cease-fire resolution except in self-defence.

AHMAD TOUKAN
Minister for Foreign Affairs

SOURCE: Security Council Official Records, Twenty-second Year, 1349th meeting.

The cable is dated June 7, 1967. I have, by telephone, informed the government of Israel of its contents through the Permanent Mission of Israel to the United Nations.

The Chief of Staff of UNTSO reports that on the morning of June 7 the Jordan-Israel Mixed Armistice Commission headquarters was occupied by Israel forces. The Chief of Staff of UNTSO lodged a strong protest with the Israel authorities, insisting that the Mixed Armistice Commission headquarters should be evacuated at the earliest possible moment by Israel troops.

I regret to inform the Council of the death of an UNTSO observer, Commandant Thomas Wickham of the Irish Army, who was killed on June 7 on the road between Kuneitra and Damascus. I wish to express my sympathy and condolences to the government of Ireland and the family of Commandant Wickham.

I have instructed the Chief of Staff of UNTSO to do whatever he can to continue with his functions and to make his good offices available to the parties whenever there is an opportunity to do so.

The Commander of UNEF reports that he is continuing his efforts to ensure the security of the remaining contingents of UNEF pending their evacuation. He reports that none of the units are at present in danger. Urgent efforts continue to find methods for their evacuation.

I also regret to have to report to the Council that the death of one Brazilian soldier of UNEF in Rafah Camp on June 5 is now officially confirmed. The Commander of UNEF has also informed me that, according to the lastest information, the casualties suffered by the Indian contingent are nine killed, twenty wounded, and twelve missing. I have expressed to the governments of India and Brazil my deep sorrow at these casualties.

In view of the occupation of the headquarters of both UNTSO in Jerusalem and UNEF in Gaza by Israel troops, I have formally approached the government of Israel to ask for their assurances that the records and documents of both of these headquarters, which are of both practical importance and irreplaceable historic value, will be preserved and protected, undisturbed and undamaged, until UNTSO and UNEF personnel return to their respective headquarters.

I have no further detailed information about the fighting, which I understand to be continuing at numerous points.

5. From Statement in the Security Council

NEW YORK   JUNE 8, 1967

. . . I HAVE JUST received the following communication from Mr. El-Kony, permanent representative of the United Arab Republic to the United Nations. It is dated June 8, 1967:

I have the honor to inform you, upon instructions of my government, that it has decided to accept the cease-fire call, as it has been prescribed by the resolutions of the Council on June 6 and 7, 1967 [233 (1967) and 234 (1967)], on the condition that the other party ceases the fire.

SOURCE: Security Council Official Records, Twenty-second Year, 1351st meeting.

6. Statement in the Security Council

NEW YORK   JUNE 9, 1967

AT THIRTY-SIX MINUTES past midnight New York time today, I received the message from the Minister for Foreign Affairs of the Syrian Arab Republic which has just been read by you, Mr. President.

The permanent representative of Israel was informed of this message by telephone at five minutes past one o'clock this morning, New York time. The President of the Security Council was similarly informed, and the message was immediately relayed to the Chief of Staff of UNTSO, with instructions to inform the Israel authorities in Jerusalem.

SOURCE: Security Council Official Records, Twenty-second Year, 1352nd meeting.

At 7:14 A.M., New York time today, I was advised by the Chairman of the Israel-Syrian Mixed Armistice Commission that he had received the following message from Syria:

In spite of our observance of the cease-fire which was communicated to you at 4 A.M. this morning we are now being subjected to an Israel attack on the whole length of the armistice demarcation line and against our towns and villages which began this morning, and continues at this moment. Different arms are being employed, aircraft, tanks, artillery, and infantry. We hold the Security Council and the international conscience responsible for this criminal aggression. We demand immediately the convocation of the Security Council, the immediate cessation of the aggression and the punishment of the aggressors. Please circulate this document to the members of the Security Council.

IBRAHIM MAKHOUS
Minister for Foreign Affairs
Syrian Arab Republic

At 0900 hours GMT—that is, 5 A.M. New York time—the Chief of Staff of UNTSO received a message from the Israel authorities strongly advising against the intention of the Chairman of the Israel-Syrian Mixed Armistice Commission to man observation posts on the Syrian side of the line as this would be a severe risk to the safety of the military observers, since there was severe shelling and shooting in the area.

General Bull was unable to contact the UNTSO Tiberias control center and then contacted the Israel authorities, recalling to them that both sides had accepted a cease-fire and expressing his deep concern about the new developments.

At 7:45 A.M. New York time, I received reports from General Bull based on reports from the Israel-Syrian Mixed Armistice Commission of artillery shelling and air bombing in the central demilitarized zone at between 0745 and 0755 hours GMT. Further bombardment and aerial activity were reported by the Tiberias control center half an hour later. The Chairman of the Israel-Syrian Mixed Armistice Commission requested headquarters, UNTSO, to contact Israel authorities.

General Bull also reported at this time that he had been informed by the Israel authorities that there was heavy shelling going on in the north near Syria, including the town of Safad, and that in the early hours of the morning some sixteen villages and towns had come under heavy artillery fire.

At 8:21 A.M. New York time, I received through commercial channels the following message, similar to that transmitted by the Chairman of the Israel-Syrian Mixed Armistice Commission, from the Minister for Foreign Affairs of the Syrian Arab Republic:

In spite of our acceptance of the two appeals in the resolutions of the Security Council for a cease-fire, which was communicated in our telegram of this morning and broadcast over Radio Damascus at the same time, Israel continues its aerial aggression over Syrian territory combined with a general attack by the Israel army and tanks. We have managed to stay calm so far. We ask immediate measures to prevent the war from breaking out afresh.

IBRAHIM MAKHOUS
Minister for Foreign Affairs
Syrian Arab Republic

At 0930 hours New York time today, I received a message from the Chairman of the Israel-Syrian Mixed Armistice Commission stating that the first confirmed bombing by Israel aircraft north and east of Lake Tiberias was at 0746 hours GMT on June 9. The message went on to say that "Bombing, napalming, and strafing have been continuous up to 1218 hours GMT. The bombing of the village of Sqoufiye now in progress. Heavy explosions also heard north of Lake Tiberias."

At 10:32 A.M. New York time today, I received the following message through the Israel-Syrian Mixed Armistice Commission in Damascus from the Minister for Foreign Affairs of the Syrian Arab Republic:

Israel attack still going on inside our territory. All enemy air and ground arms assaulting our country. Israel lying. Did not for a moment respect Security Council resolutions. We request immediate convening of Security Council and prompt compulsion for Israel to stop aggression immediately.

IBRAHIM MAKHOUS
Minister for Foreign Affairs
Syrian Arab Republic

7. *Intervention in the Security Council*

NEW YORK   JUNE 9, 1967

[THE FOLLOWING STATEMENT by the Secretary-General was made shortly after Gideon Rafael, Ambassador of Israel, told the Security Council that his government had announced it would accept the cease-fire provided the other governments involved did likewise.]

The cables to the two governments of Israel and Syria, conveying the Security Council resolution of today [235 (1967)], were dispatched immediately after the adoption of that resolution. Ambassador Adib Daoudy of Syria informed me orally at 2:15 P.M. today that he had just spoken to Damascus and relayed the latest Security Council resolution. According to Ambassador Daoudy, Syria accepts the terms of the resolution and is ready to stop immediately military operations on Syrian territory.

Just a few moments ago, I received this communication in writing from the permanent representative of Syria to the United Nations:

Concerning the information which I transmitted to your office at 2:15 P.M. this afternoon, I have the honor to inform you on instructions from my government, after a telephone conversation with my Foreign Minister Mr. Ibrahim Makhous, that he has instructed me to convey to you officially the acceptance of the Syrian Government to Security Council resolution S/7960.

(Signed) GEORGE J. TOMEH
Permanent Representative

Mr. President, I have just been informed that the response of Israel was that given by the permanent representative of Israel in his statement to the Council a moment ago.

SOURCE: Ibid.

8. *Second Intervention in the Security Council*

NEW YORK   JUNE 9, 1967

MR. PRESIDENT, I have just received a communication from the permanent representative of Israel to the United Nations. The text of the communication reads as follows:

June 9, 1967
1505 hours

I have the honor to confirm what I said in the Security Council on June 9, that I have been instructed by telephone to announce that Israel accepts the cease-fire resolution adopted by the Security Council [235(1967)], provided that Syria accepts it and will implement the cease-fire.

(Signed) GIDEON RAFAEL
Permanent Representative

SOURCE: Ibid.

THE SITUATION IN VIETNAM

IN HIS SPEECH before the Fourth World Conference of Friends on July 30, U Thant returned to the Vietnam problem with his first comprehensive comment since April. There was no mention of any new initiatives on his part. Actually he had virtually suspended his Vietnam peace efforts after the poor reception given his March 14 proposal for a standstill truce. For one thing, he felt that nothing could be done until the United States stopped bombing North Vietnam. For another, he was preoccupied with the Middle East conflict and the further deterioration of relations between the United States and the Soviet Union. In his press conference on September 16, the Secretary-General acknowledged that he had shelved his Vietnam efforts temporarily, since "the first priority is the cessation of bombing of North Vietnam." If that priority was not met, Thant did not see how he could usefully pursue his efforts toward finding a peaceful solution. He went on: "It does not mean that I have given up my efforts. I just want to stress that I have only suspended my efforts in finding a solution. At the right moment, of course, I will continue my efforts."

Although he offered no new proposals in his Greensboro speech, he did strongly challenge the correctness of the Johnson administration's contention that the United States was fighting to save Vietnam from communism. "It is nationalism," Thant said, "and not communism, that animates the resistance movement in Vietnam against all foreigners, and now particularly against Americans. Those Vietnamese who have fought and still fight against foreigners do so to win their national independence. I am convinced that the war cannot be brought to an end until the United States and her allies recognize that it is being fought by Vietnamese, not as a war of communist aggression, but as a war of national independence." The Secretary-General also took issue with Americans who deplored the magnitude of death and destruction in Vietnam but who took the position that since the United States was involved, rightly or wrongly, there was no alternative but to go ahead with the war. "It seems to me that nothing could be more dangerous," he said, "than this kind of thinking, that the only alternatives are military escalation and immediate withdrawal. I am convinced that there are other alternatives, despite the fact that Hanoi refuses to negotiate with Washington while the bombing of North Vietnam is going on, and Saigon will not negotiate with the National Liberation Front under any circumstances. I regard the continuation of the war in Vietnam as being totally unnecessary."

From Address before the Fourth World Conference of Friends

GREENSBORO, NORTH CAROLINA   JULY 30, 1967

. . .

DURING RECENT WEEKS the Middle East crisis has once again focused attention on the United Nations. This is with good reason, for the situation in the Middle East has posed one of the gravest threats to the peace of the world that has been experienced since the Second World War, and, I may say, it continues to be ominous and menacing. The communications media, and especially radio and television, have brought to the living-rooms of millions of American families the proceedings of the Security Council and the General Assembly. Without doubt, there is a better awareness today of the limitations as well as the potentialities of the United Nations in preserving peace and promoting international security, and—I hope—of the need for it.

The reactions, at any rate in this country, seem to have been mixed. At the very beginning of the crisis there was considerable comment, much of it critical, on my decision to accede to the demands of the government of the United Arab Republic for the withdrawal of the United Nations Emergency Force from Sinai and the Gaza Strip. I have explained at length, orally and in writing, the compelling reasons for this decision. I have also explained in a number of reports, both to the Security Council and to the General Assembly, the nature of the problems in the Middle East and the need for international action to solve these problems. As a result of these explanations, I believe there is now a better understanding of the fact that the conflict had a long history and deep-rooted causes. As for the withdrawal of the United Nations Emergency Force, I remain convinced that no other course would have been reasonable, sensible, and practical in the circumstances. I may also state in passing that in the course of several meetings of the Security Council since May 22,

SOURCE: UN Monthly Chronicle, vol. IV, August-September 1967, pp. 75-83.

1967, not one member of the Council expressed the view that my decision to comply with the demand of the government of the United Arab Republic was unjustified, or that a decision on the question of the withdrawal of the United Nations Emergency Force should have been taken by the Security Council or the General Assembly.

After the Security Council called for a cease-fire and after this call was accepted by the parties to the conflict, there was a little more time to take stock and ponder the crisis and its background. The recent emergency special session of the General Assembly, while it could not agree on a substantive resolution, gave an opportunity for the exposition of the various views of Member states on the crisis. The matter has now gone back to the Security Council and I am sure that the Council will wish to give attention to the deep-rooted causes of the conflict and to take appropriate measures toward ensuring a durable peace in the region.

While it may not be too difficult to analyze the causes of the conflict in the Near East, and even to agree upon an agenda for immediate action, it is less easy to see the Middle East crisis in its longer-term perspective. I would like to suggest how this might be approached. I believe we should begin with the Charter of the United Nations and the solemn commitments it contains.

The Charter expresses the determination of the peoples of the United Nations "to establish conditions under which justice and respect for the obligations arising from treaties and other sources of international law can be maintained." It also proclaims that the purposes of the United Nations are "to maintain international peace and security." To this end all Member states have bound themselves to "refrain in their international relations from the threat or use of force against the territorial integrity or political independence of any state, or in any other manner inconsistent with the purposes of the United Nations."

These are not mere words. They are, as I said, solemn undertakings. Too often, however, they are forgotten or conveniently overlooked. The attempt is then made to blame the ills of this world, and they are indeed many, on the Charter of the United Nations. We are told that the Charter requires strengthening, that teeth should be put into the Charter, and so forth; and there seems to be a somewhat naïve belief that by structural changes brought about by amending the Charter, we can strengthen the United Nations, and indeed turn it into a supra-national authority, with the power to come down heavily against the aggressor and to protect the rights of the victims of aggression.

I have explained on earlier occasions my view that it is not the Charter that has failed the international community, it is the international community that has failed to live up to its responsibilities under the Charter. I have also repeatedly stressed that the United Nations can be only as strong as its Member governments permit it to be. As long as governments jealously guard their sovereignty rights and as long as they are unwilling to surrender any part of their sovereignty to serve the common good of the international community, it would be futile to expect the United Nations to develop into a supra-national authority. It is well to remember that the Charter does impose a considerable degree of limitation on the dogma of absolute sovereignty of nation-states; but they are reluctant, in practice, even to that extent, to reconcile the concept of national sovereignty with the idea of international authority.

In the context of the United Nations action or lack of action in regard to serious situations of crises in several parts of the world, one often hears the charge that the United Nations has failed. Yet, to speak of the failure of the United Nations seems to me to be a contradiction in terms. If Member states are united in the pursuit of the purposes of the Charter, it is impossible that they should ever fail. The plain fact is that the nations are not united in the pursuit of the purposes of the Charter.

In maintaining international peace and security, the basic assumption underlying the Charter was that the five permanent members [of the Security Council] would act in concert. The United Nations was the offspring of the wartime coalition, which was expected to keep peace in concert even as it had won the war. Unfortunately, soon after the signing of the Charter the tensions and conflicts between the superpowers began to show up and to dominate international relations. The reality of a divided world became apparent and began to impede the successful working of the United Nations. Alignments and alliances were formed and there was nothing that the United Nations could do, under the terms of its Charter, to prevent nations from belonging to hostile camps.

When nations follow divided loyalties, and when alignments are formed around the superpowers, the apparatus established by the

United Nations inevitably comes to be utilized as a forum not so much for harmonizing the actions of Member states as for propagating the rival viewpoints of the protagonists in the cold war. The conflicts and the rivalries which characterized their division began to affect the working of the United Nations, and they continue to do so.

It is now plainly seen that the United Nations cannot go very far toward keeping international peace and security if the superpowers do not cooperate toward that end. Such is the constitution of the United Nations that it has no effective authority over the superpowers, or indeed over any other state. In effect the United Nations can be an effective instrument for keeping the peace, provided the superpowers are willing to let it keep the peace, either by throwing their weight on its side, or by refraining from active opposition.

This aspect of the problem is related to the larger question of international cooperation with a view to fashioning a new world. It is obvious that there cannot be true international cooperation if its scope is relegated merely to the level of satisfying regional or ideological interests. Global problems and tensions can be tackled on an adequate scale only by the international community acting in concert. At this stage, however, the international community can act only through nations, and the reality is that these nations, for reasons of self-interest, are not willing to abide by the principles and purposes of the Charter where their vital interests are involved.

Therefore, what needs to be stressed is the fact that "we the peoples of the United Nations," in the language of the Charter—and not "we the governments of the United Nations"—are the primary source, and therefore the ultimate authority, of the Charter of the United Nations. They, the peoples, have to be made conscious of the role that is expected of them, in influencing their governments to act according to the Charter of the United Nations. Established attitudes and traditional concepts have to give way to new concepts and new attitudes to problems.

I realize, of course, that old habits of thought die hard. We need a major educational effort to persuade the peoples as well as Member states that in the long run their true interests would be better protected, and no nation's essential authority would suffer, by their fulfilling their obligations under the Charter. I also realize that while one of the primary purposes of the United Nations is to serve as a center for harmonizing the actions of nations in the attainment of their common ends, as laid down in the Charter, the United Nations is also an instrument of multi-lateral diplomacy which the governments of Member states are entitled to use to protect and even to promote their national interests.

All that I am trying to explain at this point is that whenever the national interest, usually the short-term national interest of a Member state, clashes with the larger interest of the international community, there is a special need to invoke the harmonizing function of the United Nations, so that the national interest and the overall international interest may be reconciled. This is true of both political and economic interests.

Unfortunately we are still very far indeed from the goals I have outlined thus far. In the pursuit of their political interests, governments seem to have egocentric impulses which convince them that they should pursue a policy of "everyone for himself." Similarly, in the pursuit of their economic interests, governments seem to feel that it does not matter what disadvantages their economic policies may entail for other nations as long as such policies benefit their own country.

These attitudes overlook a thesis which has been stated many times, and which governments readily accept in principle, that there is a close relationship between prosperity and peace and that both are in a very real sense indivisible. We cannot have certain countries continuing to make great economic and technological progress and have the rest of the world wallowing in poverty, suffering from chronic hunger, disease, and ignorance. These conditions are a fertile ground for national unrest and for international insecurity.

What worries me even more is the increasing failure on the part of governments to observe the fundamental Charter injunction to refrain in their international relations from the threat or use of force against the territorial integrity or political independence of any state. Too many governments seem to feel that this commitment applies only to "the other fellow." This is wrong in itself. What makes it worse is that the uninhibited use of force to obtain political ends in one part of the world produces repercussions elsewhere. The standards of international morality are eroded in the process. The mass media of communications are pressed into service to obscure the truth and to justify actions however unjustifiable. Before long, a credibility gap develops and all too soon it becomes difficult to distinguish truth from propaganda.

The dangers inherent in the process can be illustrated by the war in Vietnam as well as by the recent conflict in the Middle East. The war in Vietnam has been progressively intensified during the last two and a half years. During this period the number of men and the amount of war material involved in the actual fighting has immensely increased. The savagery of the war has steadily escalated and the casualties on the part of all parties involved in the fighting have reached frightening proportions and continue to mount. This is even more true of innocent civilians not directly involved in the fighting who are the helpless victims of the war. There seems to be no end in sight and yet, according to published reports, progress is claimed, which the facts belie.

In the attempts that are made to justify this tremendous waste of human resources, the issues are oversimplified as much as are the proposed solutions for the problem. I have, on several occasions, expressed my own views on the war in Vietnam, and presented certain ideas on how it might be brought to an end.

I have repeatedly stated how wrong it is to regard the war in Vietnam as a kind of holy war against a particular ideology. I have expressed the view that the motivating force on the part of those who are being charged with this ideology is really a strong sense of nationalism, a desire to win their national independence and establish their national identity. It is nationalism, and not communism, that animates the resistance movement in Vietnam against all foreigners, and now particularly against Americans. Those Vietnamese who have fought and still fight against foreigners do so to win their national independence. I am convinced that the war cannot be brought to an end until the United States and her allies recognize that it is being fought by the Vietnamese, not as a war of communist aggression, but as a war of national independence.

It is sometimes argued that those who fight against foreigners in Vietnam constitute a small minority of the Vietnamese people. History is replete with instances where the freedom fighters often constituted a minority. The rest of the populace were indifferent to change or preferred the continuation of the status quo. Is it not a fact, to take but one example, that during the American Revolution, the colony of

New York recruited more troops for the British than for the Revolution? As for popular support, is it not a fact that the Revolution could claim that of less than one third of the people? Is it not also a fact that thousands of rich American Tories fled for their lives to Canada? It is far from my intention to draw a parallel between the American Revolution and the Vietnam conflict, but I just want to illustrate my point that freedom fighters throughout history constituted a minority.

As for the solutions, there are those who claim that military victory is feasible and that all that it requires is the application of more manpower and more military power. At the other extreme are those who believe that the only solution is the immediate withdrawal of the United States and its allies from the conflict. In between there are a substantial number of people who share the viewpoint of a very well-meaning and knowledgeable American whom I met recently. His view may be summed up as follows: "Rightly or wrongly, we are in Vietnam. We deplore the magnitude of death and destruction but we must deal with the situation that exists. No doubt we have become increasingly involved against our original intentions but we have no alternative." I believe this is the general view held by the majority of American people who are at heart peace-loving.

It seems to me that nothing could be more dangerous than this kind of thinking, that the only alternatives are military escalation and immediate withdrawal. I am convinced that there *are* other alternatives, despite the fact that Hanoi refuses to negotiate with Washington while the bombing of North Vietnam is going on, and Saigon will not negotiate with the National Liberation Front under any circumstances.

I regard the continuation of the war in Vietnam as being totally unnecessary. I have analyzed the public statements of the objectives on both sides, and if the task of diplomacy is only to realize the objectives which are explicit or implicit in these statements, I believe this would be possible and an honorable peace could be brought about in Vietnam. The first task is to end the fighting and to bring the problem to the conference table. This first task requires certain first steps and I regard it as a great tragedy that it has not been possible to get the parties concerned to take these first steps.

Meanwhile, as the war goes on, there are two other aspects of it, interacting upon each other, which I find increasingly disturbing. The first is the repercussions which the war in Vietnam is having on other

situations of crisis elsewhere in the world. I am also deeply concerned at the fact that so many people are willing to turn a blind eye,
or at best become hardened, to the sheer human suffering involved in
the continuation of this conflict. The Preamble to the Charter recalls
the determination of the peoples of the United Nations to "reaffirm
faith in fundamental human rights, in the dignity and worth of the
human person." To ignore human suffering is not only to fail in this
duty, but also to provide fuel for one crisis after another.

We have seen this happen clearly enough in the Middle East. One
of the chronic and underlying causes of the conflict, and one to which
no solution has been found for nineteen years, is the situation of the
Palestine refugees. This problem has not only remained unsolved but
has become much graver as a result of the recent military conflict. I
am glad to say that in the recent meetings of the Security Council and
the emergency special session of the General Assembly on the Middle
East crisis, when there was disagreement on so many other aspects of
the problem, there was agreement on the principle of humanitarian
assistance for the innocent victims of the conflict.

I believe that both in Vietnam and in the Middle East there will be
no solution to the problem if the human factor is ignored, and the
problem will become susceptible of solution only if the interest of
human beings involved is kept in mind. I have just referred to the case
of the Palestinian refugees. There is imperative need for making a
fresh search for peace in the Middle East so that the rights of all
countries in the area may be respected, because the various countries
are inhabited by human beings, and their rights as nationals of Member states are as important as the sovereign rights of the states
themselves. If this simple fact were accepted it would become easier
to agree upon solutions which would produce a durable peace in the
Middle East and put an end to the cycle of threats and counterthreats
leading to actual armed conflict which has three times during the last
twenty years produced so much suffering for the unfortunate people
involved.

Another regrettable aspect of both the war in Vietnam and the
conflict in the Middle East is the effect that they have had on the
relations between the two superpowers. It seems to me that, if these
conflicts can be resolved, there may be a resumption of the détente
between East and West which was developing until the recent escalation of the Vietnam conflict. There are a number of global problems

for which solutions cannot be found except on the basis of a closer cooperation between the two superpowers. This is also true of such problems as disarmament, the conclusion of a treaty for the nonproliferation of nuclear weapons, and the ending of the arms race between the two superpowers. It seems to me that the superpowers already recognize that they have a common interest in solving these problems but they seem to be very wary about making any positive approach for reasons which are well known.

I realize, of course, that a détente between the two superpowers cannot by itself bring about peaceful conditions over the rest of the world. However, it is an indispensable first step and I believe that it would immediately produce a congenial climate for cooperation in the United Nations itself.

I also believe that such cooperation should eventually include the People's Republic of China. China has recently joined the nuclear club and the progress that it has made in the development of nuclear weapons has surprised qualified observers in this country and elsewhere. It bodes little good for the interests of world peace and security to perpetuate the isolation of China and keep her cut off from normal contact with the rest of the world. I believe that the time must come when China can play its part as a member of the international community on equal terms with others, and the sooner this happens the better.

. . .

From Statement at Opening Meeting of
United Nations Council for South West Africa

NEW YORK   AUGUST 10, 1967

THE GENERAL ASSEMBLY met in special session on April 21, 1967, to take steps to implement its decision of October 27, 1966, under which the United Nations would assume responsibility for the administration of South West Africa. Its task was complicated by the fact that the *Ad Hoc* Committee, established by the Assembly in the October resolution, had been unable to agree on how to accomplish its aim. On May 19, however, the Assembly finally adopted a resolution creating an eleven-nation Council for South West Africa to administer the former League of Nations mandate until it reached independence. The Council was to be based in South West Africa and was directed to enter immediately into contact with the government of South Africa to work out procedures for the transfer of the administration to the United Nations. June 1968 was set as the target date for independence. This resolution was adopted by a vote of 85 to 2, with 30 abstentions. The negative votes were cast by Portugal and South Africa. The latter contended that the Assembly's action terminating the mandate and all related actions were illegal. South African officials made it clear that they would not cooperate in any way with the newly created Council. In addressing the opening session of the Council, Thant did not refer specifically to South Africa's defiance of the United Nations but this was what he meant when he mentioned "the difficulties which confront the council" in carrying out its assigned tasks.

. . . THIS IS AN important occasion; for the coming into operation of this Council constitutes an important step toward the assumption by the United Nations of its responsibilities under General Assembly resolution 2145 (XXI) of October 27, 1966, which terminated South Africa's mandate in South West Africa and made that Territory a direct responsibility of this Organization. By that decision the General Assembly, after twenty years of fruitless negotiations, "reaffirmed that the provisions of its resolution 1514 (XV) are fully applica-

SOURCE: UN Press Release SG/SM/787.

ble to the people of the mandated Territory of South West Africa''
and that the people of the Territory "have the unalienable right to
self-determination, freedom and independence in accordance with
the Charter. . . .''

Having taken this almost unanimous decision the United Nations
has now to arrange for the transfer of the administration of the
Territory and the setting up of the necessary governmental
machinery. In its resolution 2248 (S-V), adopted at its fifth special
session on May 19, 1967, the General Assembly charged this Council,
among other things, with the tasks of negotiating that transfer with
the least possible upheaval and of administering South West Africa
until independence with the assistance of a United Nations Commissioner. The Council was instructed to ensure the maximum possible
participation of the people of South West Africa in the administration
of their country and to do all in its power to enable the Territory to
attain independence by June 1968.

We all recognize the difficulties which confront the Council in
fulfilling these tasks. That is why the General Assembly in its resolution 2248 (S-V) appealed to all states to extend their wholehearted
cooperation and to render assistance to the Council. As the General
Assembly noted with deep concern, and as I have pointed out on past
occasions, the world community is confronted in southern Africa
with an explosive situation which, if unresolved, could undermine the
very basis of cooperation between the races in Africa for many years
to come. For this reason the work of this Council, which is concerned
with an important aspect of that problem, is of great importance. For
it offers a fresh point of departure, a new possibility of reconciliation,
a chance to stem the growing racial hostility in that part of the world.
Let us hope that all Member states will heed the General Assembly
appeal and cooperate to the full in making effective the decision of
October 27, 1966, which they so overwhelmingly endorsed.

It is not my intention to comment in detail on the numerous specific
tasks which have been assigned to this Council. I wish only to
emphasize the importance of your work and the grave responsibilities
which you bear. May I wish you every success and assure you of my
whole-hearted cooperation and that of my colleagues in the Secretariat. . . .

DIPLOMATIC PRIVILEGES AND IMMUNITIES

AT THE END of June 1967, during the fifth emergency session of the General Assembly on the Middle East situation, U Thant found himself facing a potentially dangerous dispute involving diplomatic privileges and immunities. The dispute began on June 26 when the Foreign Minister of Guinea, Béavogui Lansana, and the permanent representative of Guinea to the United Nations, Achkar Marof, were arrested after their Royal Dutch Airlines plane made an unscheduled stop at Abidjan, Ivory Coast, as they were returning home from the Assembly meeting. This was a clear violation of the Convention on the Privileges and Immunities of the United Nations to which the Ivory Coast had acceded. Under this convention representatives of members of United Nations bodies were guaranteed immunity from arrest while traveling to and from the place of meetings. The United Nations was further involved by the detention of an official of the Universal Postal Union from Guinea, Joseph Montlouis, and his family who were en route to Conakry on the same plane. There was no doubt in the mind of the Secretary-General that his personal intervention was required because of the special responsibilities of the United Nations to see that the privileges and immunities set forth in the convention were respected. In this case, he also had the backing of the Organization of African Unity (OAU) and of several African states individually.

On June 30, Thant handed the Foreign Minister of the Ivory Coast, Arsène Assouan Usher, an *aide-mémoire* urging the release of the Guinean personalities. He also informed the foreign minister he had requested the Liberian government to have its ambassador in Abidjan visit the Guineans and check on their well-being. Usher readily agreed to the latter request, but it soon became apparent that the release of the detained individuals was closely linked to the prior arrest of several nationals of the Ivory Coast by Guinean authorities and to the seizure of a fishing boat, flying the Ivory Coast flag, in February 1967, together with its crew of twenty-two. A detailed account of Thant's efforts and those of his personal representatives is contained in his August 14 report to the Security Council. Although he did not say so it was apparent that further mediation efforts would be useless. Guinea had decided to take its case to the General Assembly and the Security Council. On August 14, President Sékou Touré requested the Secretary-General to inscribe the question on the agenda of the two United Nations organs. In letters of August 14 and 16, the Guinean government also informed Thant that it had decided to boycott all meetings of specialized agencies until the release of Lansana and Achkar. The day after the Assembly opened its twenty-second session on

September 19, the Secretary-General requested the inscription of an agenda item entitled: "The situation which has arisen between Guinea and the Ivory Coast involving section 11 of the Convention on the Privileges and Immunities of the United Nations." The deadlock was broken before the General Committee could act on the inscription of the proposed item. On September 25, the Secretary-General received an official communication from the Ivory Coast announcing the release of the detained Guineans. On the following day, Guinea informed Thant it had released the Ivory Coast nationals on September 22. While this ended the dispute between Guinea and the Ivory Coast, Thant believed that important questions of principle had been raised concerning both the Convention on Privileges and Immunities and Article 105 of the Charter, which deals with diplomatic privileges. On his own initiative, he proposed the inscription of an agenda item entitled "Reaffirmation of an important immunity of representatives of Member states to the principal and subsidiary organs of the United Nations and to conferences convened by the United Nations." This was inscribed and referred to the Sixth (Legal) Committee of the General Assembly, along with a similar item proposed by the United States entitled "Measures tending to implement the privileges and immunities of representatives of Member states to the principal and subsidiary organs of the United Nations and to conferences convened by the United Nations as well as the obligations of states concerning the protection of diplomatic personnel and property." At the conclusion of the Sixth Committee's debate, Constantin Stavropoulos, Legal Counsel of the United Nations, speaking on behalf of the Secretary-General, said it seemed elementary that the rights of representatives should be protected by the Organization and not left entirely to the bilateral action of the states immediately involved. He added that the Secretary-General, therefore, would continue to feel obligated to assert the rights and interests of the Organization on behalf of representatives of Member governments whenever the need arose. The Assembly finally completed action on December 18 by approving a resolution which made no mention of the dispute between Guinea and the Ivory Coast but which deplored "all departures from the rules of international law governing diplomatic privileges and immunities. . . ." The vote was 101 to none, with one delegation (Colombia) abstaining. The resolution urged all Member states, which had not already done so, to accede to the Convention on Privileges and Immunities and called on all Member states to take every measure to see that the privileges and immunities accorded in Article 105 of the Charter were implemented.

Report on Efforts to Liberate Nationals of Guinea and the Ivory Coast Detained by the Other Country

NEW YORK   AUGUST 14, 1967

---

1. THE SECRETARY-GENERAL, having in mind the provisions of Article 34 of the Charter of the United Nations and in order to keep the Security Council fully informed of matters which might lead to international friction or give rise to a dispute, has deemed it desirable to submit the present report to the Security Council. The report concerns the situation which has arisen between Guinea and the Ivory Coast as the result of the detention in the Ivory Coast of Mr. Béavogui Lansana, Minister for Foreign Affairs of the Republic of Guinea, and Mr. Achkar Marof, permanent representative of the Republic of Guinea to the United Nations; of a Universal Postal Union (UPU) official from Guinea, Mr. Joseph Montlouis, and members of his family; and another Guinean citizen, Mr. Cissé Ausomany. It also outlines the efforts of the Secretary-General to obtain the release of the above-mentioned Guinean nationals detained in Abidjan, as well as his endeavors, in exercise of his good offices, to obtain the release of a number of nationals and residents of the Ivory Coast detained by the government of Guinea.

2. On June 28, 1967, the *Chargé d'affaires* of the Permanent Mission of Guinea to the United Nations transmitted to the Secretary-General a formal protest from his government against the arrest of the Guinean nationals mentioned in the previous paragraph. Also on June 28 the Administrative Secretary-General of the Organization of African Unity (OAU), asked the Secretary-General to intervene with the government of the Ivory Coast to obtain the release of Foreign Minister Béavogui Lansana and Mr. Achkar Marof.

3. On June 29, at their request, the Ministers for Foreign Affairs of Algeria, Mali, Mauritania, and the United Republic of Tanzania,

SOURCE: Security Council Official Records, Twenty-second Year, Supplement for July, August, and September 1967, document S/8120.

together with the permanent representative of the Republic of the Congo (Brazzaville) to the United Nations, met with the Secretary-General and requested him to approach the government of the Ivory Coast in order to secure the release of Mr. Béavogui Lansana and Mr. Achkar Marof.

4. On June 30, the President of the Republic of Guinea, Mr. Sékou Touré, addressed a telegram to the Secretary-General drawing his attention to the special responsibility of the United Nations in this matter and registering the strongest possible protest against the action of the government of the Ivory Coast.

5. The Secretary-General replied to this cable by a telegram dated July 3 informing President Touré of his efforts in this respect.

6. At a meeting on June 30 the Secretary-General presented to Mr. Arsène Assouan Usher, Minister for Foreign Affairs of the Ivory Coast, an *aide-mémoire* appealing to him for the release of the Guinean personalities detained in Abidjan. The Secretary-General also informed Foreign Minister Usher that he had requested the Liberian government to ask its Ambassador in Abidjan to visit the detained persons and to ascertain their well-being. Foreign Minister Usher assured the Secretary-General that the Liberian Ambassador would receive the full cooperation of the authorities of the Ivory Coast to this end.

7. Earlier on June 30 the Secretary-General had met with the *Chargé d'affaires a.i.* of the Permanent Mission of Liberia to the United Nations and presented to him the request referred to in paragraph 6 above.

8. Mr. Usher requested a meeting with the Secretary-General, which took place on July 3, and presented to him an *aide-mémoire* in reply to the Secretary-General's *aide-mémoire* of June 30. The Ivory Coast *aide-mémoire* confirmed that a group of Guinean nationals, including in particular Mr. Béavogui Lansana, Foreign Minister, and Mr. Achkar Marof had been under detention in Abidjan since June 26. This detention, however, according to the *aide-mémoire,* was a consequence of the prior arbitrary arrest of several nationals and residents of the Ivory Coast in the Republic of Guinea. For two years, Mr. François Kamano, Director of the Family Allowances Equalization Fund of the Ivory Coast, had been detained at Conakry by the Guinean authorities and had been tortured in order to force him to implicate himself in a plot which the Ivory Coast was alleged to have

contrived against Guinea, with the aim of overthrowing President Touré. The Guinean government had rejected various approaches made at the request of the government of the Ivory Coast by certain friendly states, such as Mali, in order to obtain the release of Mr. Kamano.

9. Furthermore, in February 1967, a fishing boat flying the Ivory Coast flag, which found itself in distress off the Guinean coast, was apprehended, together with its entire crew of twenty-two persons. In this case, too, the Guinean government had rejected approaches made in order to obtain the release of the crew and the return of the trawler.

10. In concluding, the government of the Ivory Coast requested the Secretary-General to use his good offices with the government of Guinea with a view to settling the problem of the nationals and residents of the Ivory Coast arrested in Guinea, so that the government of the Ivory Coast might be able to accede to the Secretary-General's appeal for the release of the Foreign Minister, Mr. Béavogui Lansana, Mr. Achkar Marof, and the other Guineans detained in Abidjan.

11. The Secretary-General stated to Mr. Usher that he could not link the detention of the Guinean personalities with the imprisonment of Mr. Kamano and the seizure of the fishing trawler and subsequent arrest of its crew. The detention of the Guinean personalities was in contravention of international agreements to which the government of the Ivory Coast was a signatory and had provoked international repercussions and even affected the responsibilities of the Secretary-General. For example, in General Assembly resolution 2202 A (XXI) the Secretary-General was called upon to consult urgently with Mr. Achkar Marof, Chairman of the Special Committee on the Policies of *Apartheid* of the Government of the Republic of South Africa, in connection with a seminar on *apartheid* which was scheduled to take place from July 24 to August 4, 1967.

12. While the Secretary-General was willing to use his good offices in regard to Mr. Kamano and the crew of the fishing trawler, he reiterated his pressing appeal to Mr. Usher for the immediate release of Mr. Béavogui and Mr. Achkar.

13. By letter of July 3 the *Chargé d'affaires a.i.* of the Permanent Mission of Liberia to the United Nations, transmitted to the Secretary-General a telegram he had received from Mr. J. Rudolph Grimes,

Secretary of State of Liberia, informing him of the efforts made by the government of Liberia in connection with the persons detained, respectively, by the governments of the Ivory Coast and Guinea.

14. At a meeting on July 4, the Secretary-General expressed to the Foreign Minister of the Ivory Coast that, as he had explained in their previous meetings, it was not possible for the Secretary-General to link the two cases. However, in response to the request for good offices contained in the Ivory Coast *aide-mémoire* of July 3, the Secretary-General was prepared to send a personal representative to Guinea for the purpose of discussing all aspects of these matters with the government of Guinea, including the release of the nationals and residents of the Ivory Coast detained by the Guinean authorities. It would facilitate the task of the Secretary-General and his personal representative if the government of the Ivory Coast would release Mr. Béavogui and Mr. Achkar, as well as Mr. Montlouis and his family, prior to the sending of the representative.

15. Mr. Usher hoped that the Secretary-General would not await the release of the Guinean personalities before approaching the government of Guinea on the case of the nationals and residents of the Ivory Coast. While he could not commit his government at this stage, the Foreign Minister said his government might be prepared to release Mr. Achkar in order to facilitate the discharge of the Secretary-General's responsibilities. He was afraid, however, that it would not be possible to release the other Guineans until assurances were given by the government of Guinea concerning the release of the nationals and residents of the Ivory Coast. Mr. Usher informed the Secretary-General that he hoped to leave the same evening for Europe where he would join the President of the Ivory Coast, Mr. Félix Houphouët-Boigny and convey to him the Secretary-General's appeal.

16. It was agreed that the Secretary-General would remain in touch with the Foreign Minister through the Permanent Mission of the Ivory Coast to the United Nations.

17. On July 6, the permanent representative of Ghana to the United Nations, on behalf of his government, transmitted to the Secretary-General a note from the Ministry of External Affairs of Ghana on the subject of the seizure by the Guinean authorities of the fishing trawler *Kerisper*. The note of the Ministry of External Affairs of Ghana stated, *inter alia,* that the trawler which was owned by the

Société indépendante maritime des pêches ivoiriennes and registered in Abidjan under No. AN496, had left Abidjan on February 12 for the usual fishing trip of fifteen days when it was seized off the coast of Guinea. The crew of the trawler was composed of two Frenchmen, one Ivory Coast national, two Malians, eleven Ghanaians, two Togolese, and two Upper Volta nationals. The members of the crew had all been engaged at Abidjan Harbour and were resident in and about Abidjan.

18. The government of Ghana refuted as completely unfounded the allegation of the Guinean authorities that the trawler was on a mission to Guinea to kidnap former President Kwame Nkrumah, now residing in Conakry.

19. The government of Ghana appealed to the Secretary-General to use his good offices to obtain the release of the Ghana nationals and all other members of the crew of the *Kerisper*. Should the government of the Republic of Guinea intend to put the fishermen on trial, the government of Ghana appealed for the intervention of the Secretary-General for permission to be granted the government of Ghana to secure counsel for its nationals.

20. In a letter of July 6 addressed to the Secretary-General, President Touré gave an account of the developments which had taken place. The Guinean delegation, which had participated in the fifth emergency special session of the General Assembly and was therefore covered by diplomatic privileges and immunities as well as by the provisions of the Vienna Convention on Diplomatic Relations, had been detained by the government of the Ivory Coast when it was proceeding to Conakry aboard a regular KLM flight. Against this illegal and arbitrary action, the government of Guinea had only one immediate recourse against KLM and, as a result, against the Netherlands government on which this Company depended, bearing in mind the obligations which KLM had contracted of transporting the Guinean delegation to safe port (Conakry). Even if account were taken of the explanations offered by KLM concerning the reasons for the unscheduled landing in Abidjan, the fact was that the aircraft found itself in Abidjan as a result of *force majeure*. Another Guinean, Mr. Joseph Montlouis, an official of UPU, had been arrested with his family at the same time and under the same circumstances as the Guinean delegation.

21. President Touré recalled that this was not the first time that

Guinea had had to face such a situation; the Guinean ministerial delegation traveling to attend a session of the Council of Ministers of the OAU was arrested in Ghana last October. At the time, Guinea had made its position clear: the OAU, having called the meeting to which the Guinean delegation was traveling, was responsible for ensuring respect for its charter by obtaining the liberation of the Guinean delegation. Concerning the civil aspect of the question, Guinea had placed responsibility for this arrest on Pan American Airways, the carrier in whose aircraft the Guinean delegation was being transported and, consequently, on the United States government, which covered the activities of the airline. As a result, by acting against the United States government, whose citizens on Guinean territory were immediately arrested, and by suspending Guinea's participation in the OAU meetings, Guinea was able with the assistance of friendly countries to obtain the release of the delegation.

22. In the view of President Touré, the Abidjan affair was but a repetition of the Accra events. Guinea held the United Nations responsible, since it was the United Nations which had called the emergency special session from which the Guinean delegation was returning. Therefore, Guinea was awaiting the result of United Nations action before considering concrete measures that might have to be taken in order to have Guinea's dignity respected.

23. President Touré also dealt with the so-called "matters in dispute" between the Ivory Coast and Guinea. He referred first to a plot against Guinea in 1965 followed by the arrest of an Ivory Coast citizen, Mr. François Kamano, and stated that Guinea had formally accused the Head of State of the Ivory Coast of having instigated the plot; in this instance, Guinea had informed the President of Liberia, who had always shown much interest in the development of friendly relations between the Ivory Coast and Guinea and who had intervened with both President Houphouët-Boigny and President Touré, that if the Head of State of the Ivory Coast expressed his regrets and committed himself to no further interventions in the internal affairs of Guinea, Guinea would then release Mr. Kamano and again re-establish relations between the two countries on a new basis. Such a commitment need not be made in public.

24. A second matter was that of the arrest in Guinean territorial waters, eight kilometers from Conakry, of an Ivory Coast trawler. An inquiry was under way, and the matter had been referred to the

revolutionary tribunal. However, after the personal intervention of President William Tubman, the proceedings had been suspended. A new meeting was scheduled to take place after the return of President Tubman from Europe in order to find an amicable solution. Guinea had no doubt that such a meeting would have resulted, in accordance with the wishes of President Tubman, in a broader meeting with President Houphouët-Boigny, President Tubman, and President Touré, which might have succeeded in ending all "matters in dispute" between the two countries. President Touré added that, concerning the matter of the trawler, if the Ivory Coast had dealt directly with Guinea in this affair and expressed regrets for the presence of the ship in Guinean territorial waters, the trawler and the crew would have been released, whatever charges Guinea had against it.

25. Finally, President Touré referred to an incident in April 1966 in which troops of the Ivory Coast penetrated twelve kilometers into Guinean territory in the region of Beyla and seized five Guinean police and customs guards who were still detained by the authorities of the Ivory Coast.

26. Guinea stated that since the illegal detention by the Ivory Coast of the Guinean delegation was a clear violation of international law, it was not in the interest of Member states of the United Nations that Guinea accept the procedure advanced by the Ivory Coast; this would give any government having difficulties with another the possibility of arresting personalities of that government as a means of pressure and of negotiation.

27. In concluding, President Touré stated that the detention of the Guinean Minister, Mr. Béavogui, was not sufficient to sacrifice the Guinean revolution. Even if it were the Chief of State of Guinea himself who had been arrested by the Ivory Coast authorities, it would have been treason and a crime against the nation and people of Guinea and against Africa to accept discussions with the Ivory Coast on the basis laid down by that country.

28. Confirming a request made to the Secretary-General on July 7, 1967, the *Chargé d'affaires* of the Permanent Mission of the Netherlands to the United Nations addressed to the Secretary-General a letter dated July 10, 1967, with various attachments soliciting the latter's good offices in connection with the arrest in Conakry of the representative of KLM and his three assistants.

29. In telegrams of July 10, the Secretary-General informed Presi-

dent Touré of the Republic of Guinea and President Houphouët-Boigny of the Republic of the Ivory Coast that he had designated Mr. José Rolz-Bennett, Under-Secretary for Special Political Affairs, as his personal representative for the purpose of discussing with both governments ways and means of settling the difficulties which had recently arisen between the two countries.

30. The Secretary-General's personal representative arrived at Conakry on July 12, and delivered to President Touré a letter dated July 10 from the Secretary-General. At a meeting held on July 13, President Touré outlined the position of the government of Guinea, along the lines of the letter which the President had addressed to the Secretary-General on July 6. In the view of the government of Guinea, the detention of the Guinean personalities in Abidjan was a flagrant violation of the principles of the United Nations and of international agreements concluded under its auspices. Therefore, it was the responsibility of the United Nations to obtain the immediate release of the persons who were under detention. Guinea was the victim; its rights as a Member of the United Nations had been violated. The United Nations and its Secretary-General, therefore, bore the sole responsibility in this affair. On the civilian side, Guinea had no doubt that KLM was responsible. Knowing the prevailing difficulties between Guinea and the Ivory Coast, the KLM aircraft, in view of its declared inability to land in Conakry owing to bad weather, could have landed in Sierra Leone, or in Dakar or Bamako, in order to let the Guinean passengers disembark there. There was no question, furthermore, of linking this matter with the detention in Guinea of Mr. Kamano and of the trawler *Kerisper* and its crew. Both Mr. Kamano and the *Kerisper* and its crew had been detained as a result of violations of Guinean laws, and their cases could in no circumstances be equated to the arbitrary detentions of the Guinean personalities by the authorities of the Ivory Coast. Later on the same day, July 13, in reply to a personal message from the Secretary-General transmitted orally to him by the personal representative, President Touré said that in maintaining his position of principle firmly, he would, nevertheless, after the release of the Guinean personalities detained in Abidjan, place himself at the disposal of the Secretary-General regarding the persons detained in Guinea.

31. The Secretary-General's personal representative met with President Houphouët-Boigny and Foreign Minister Usher in Paris on

July 16 and 17, and handed President Houphouët-Boigny a letter dated July 10 from the Secretary-General. The position of the government of the Ivory Coast was explained at length by President Houphouët-Boigny and Foreign Minister Usher to the personal representative, the main points having already been stated to the Secretary-General in the Ivory Coast *aide-mémoire* of July 3. It was a matter of deep regret to the government of the Ivory Coast to have had to detain the Foreign Minister of Guinea and the permanent representative of Guinea to the United Nations, as well as other Guineans traveling on the KLM plane, but no other course seemed to be open for the purpose of obtaining compliance by the government of Guinea with its international obligations and with elementary human rights. It was a matter of record that the government of Guinea had refused all approaches made to it for the liberation of the nationals and residents of the Ivory Coast which it had arbitrarily arrested. For the government of the Ivory Coast, this was a matter not only of law but also, fundamentally, of concern for human dignity. There was mounting indignation in the Ivory Coast against the repressive measures taken by the government of Guinea against nationals and residents of the Ivory Coast and both the party and the government of the Ivory Coast were under increasing pressure to take adequate measures to guarantee the safety and obtain the release of the prisoners unlawfull held by the Guinean authorities. The government of Guinea should awaken to its responsibilities and realize that it could not continue its arbitrary and high-handed conduct against its neighbors, particularly against the Ivory Coast.

32. The Ivory Coast was a peaceful country and one which took pride in its record of respect for international commitments and of development of friendly relations with its neighbors. Its sole concern was to provide better living standards for its people and to contribute to peace and stability in the area. The accusations leveled by the government of Guinea against the government of the Ivory Coast, and more specifically against its President, of organizing a plot to overthrow President Touré, were totally unfounded and designed only to poison the relations between the two states.

33. The detention of the Guinean personalities in Abidjan could not be considered in isolation from the long list of arbitrary and illegal actions committed against the Ivory Coast by the government of Guinea. President Houphouët-Boigny emphasized that he viewed the

arrest of the nationals and residents of the Ivory Coast by the Guinean authorities as a human problem, involving the well-being and even the lives of innocent people who had committed no crime whatsoever and yet had been deprived of their liberty and subjected to maltreatment. The government of the Ivory Coast, for its part, was giving the most considerate treatment to the Guineans detained in Abidjan and had no desire whatsoever to keep them for a single moment more after the release of the Ivory Coast nationals and residents detained in Guinea. In its desire to cooperate with the Secretary-General, the government of the Ivory Coast wished to submit a proposal envisaging the following steps: *(a)* the release by the government of the Ivory Coast of the Guinean personalities detained in Abidjan and their transport to Bamako, Mali, at an agreed date and hour; *(b)* the release on the same date and at the same hour by the government of Guinea of Mr. Kamano and the crew of the fishing trawler and their transport to Monrovia, Liberia. The Ivory Coast hoped that the Secretary-General would carefully consider this proposal which, in its view, constituted a fair and equitable solution.

34. After reporting to the Secretary-General about his discussions with the governments of Guinea and the Ivory Coast, the personal representative, upon instructions of the Secretary-General, departed again for Paris, where he met with President Houphouët-Boigny and Foreign Minister Usher. The Secretary-General requested Mr. I. S. Djermakoye, Under-Secretary for Trusteeship and Non-Self-Governing Territories, to accompany the Personal Representative in his discussions with President Houphouët-Boigny and Foreign Minister Usher.

35. A letter dated July 20 from the Secretary-General was handed to President Houphouët-Boigny, in which the Secretary-General submitted certain suggestions designed to solve the differences between the two countries. The procedure suggested by the Secretary-General envisaged the following steps: (i) the Ivory Coast would undertake on its own initiative, or in response to an appeal by the Secretary-General, to release the personalities detained, at a given date, and would let them proceed to Conakry; (ii) at the time of the release, Mr. José Rolz-Bennett would be in Conakry as personal representative of the Secretary-General to discuss with the government of Guinea various matters concerning the United Nations, such conversations to last not more than forty-eight hours; (iii) the President of Guinea

would undertake, on his own initiative or in response to an appeal by the President of Liberia or by the Secretary-General, to release the prisoners before the end of Mr. Rolz-Bennett's stay in Conakry and to have them sent to Monrovia; (iv) all sides would agree that the sequence of unrelated events would take place as described above and would commit themselves to take the required actions to that effect.

36. The government of the Ivory Coast made the following counter-proposals: (i) Mr. José Rolz-Bennett would be in Conakry as personal representative of the Secretary-General to discuss with the Guinean government various questions of interest to the United Nations; these discussions would not last more than twenty-four hours; (ii) on the same date, Mr. I. S. Djermakoye would be in Abidjan as personal representative of the Secretary-General to discuss with the government of the Ivory Coast various questions of interest to the United Nations; these discussions would not last more than twenty-four hours; (iii) the Ivory Coast would undertake on its own initiative, or in response to an appeal by the Secretary-General to release the Guinean personalities detained in Abidjan on a given date, and to transport them to Monrovia; (iv) Guinea would undertake, on its own initiative, or in response to an appeal by the Secretary-General, to release all nationals and residents of the Ivory Coast detained in Guinea, and on the same date to transport them to Monrovia; (v) the personal representative of the Secretary-General in Conakry would accompany the Guinean nationals to Guinea while the personal representative of the Secretary-General in Abidjan would accompany the Ivory Coast nationals to the Ivory Coast; (vi) all sides would agree that the sequence of unrelated events would take place as described above and would commit themselves to take the required actions to that effect.

37. On July 24, the personal representative of the Secretary-General held discussions in Conakry with President Touré and outlined to him the Secretary-General's suggestions. President Touré reiterated that the clear separation between the two questions was a matter of principle on which it was not possible for Guinea to compromise and, therefore, any procedure which envisaged either simultaneous or nearly simultaneous release by both sides could not be accepted by Guinea. In its desire to cooperate with the Secretary-General, President Touré was prepared to accept a procedure whereby, one week

after the release by the Ivory Coast of the Guinean personalities, the government of Guinea would be prepared to respond favorably to any appeal by the Secretary-General for the release of the crew of the trawler *Kerisper* and of the vessel itself. President Touré gave to understand that the case of Mr. Kamano might have to be dealt with separately.

38. After further discussions in Paris with Mr. Usher, who found the procedure that was acceptable to the government of Guinea unacceptable to his government, the personal representative of the Secretary-General and Mr. Djermakoye returned to Headquarters on July 27 to report to the Secretary-General.

39. On July 28 the Secretary-General addressed a letter to Mr. Usher formally requesting the immediate release of the members of the Guinean delegation to the fifth emergency special session of the General Assembly, as well as the release of the UPU official and the members of his family detained by the Ivory Coast. The Secretary-General further stated that by ignoring the diplomatic immunities enjoyed by the persons detained in Abidjan, the government of the Ivory Coast had established a grave precedent. If the situation were to continue, the Secretary-General would have no other choice but to raise a firm protest and consider other means open to him to remedy a situation contravening the Convention on the Privileges and Immunities of the United Nations as regards the Guinean delegation to the General Assembly, and on the privileges and immunities of the specialized agencies as regards Mr. Montlouis, the UPU official and his family. The Secretary-General reiterated his willingness to continue his efforts to obtain the release of the nationals and residents of the Ivory Coast detained in Guinea and expressed his confidence that their release would be favorably considered by the Guinean government within a brief lapse of time following the release of the Guinean citizens in Abidjan.

40. On August 11, the permanent representative of the Ivory Coast to the United Nations handed to the Secretary-General the text of his government's reply, dated August 10, to the Secretary-General's letter mentioned in the preceding paragraph. According to the government of the Ivory Coast, the legal arguments adduced by the Secretary-General, based on the Convention on Privileges and Immunities of the United Nations and the Vienna Convention on Diplomatic Relations, did not seem relevant. For the government of

the Ivory Coast the situation was that a gross violation of its law on transit had been committed by Guinean diplomats who, whatever the circumstances which may have brought them to Abidjan airport and precisely because of the situation prevailing between Guinea and the Ivory Coast, should have taken all the necessary steps to avoid breaking the laws of the Ivory Coast during their transit through Abidjan. According to the Ivory Coast law on air transit, the members of the Guinean delegation had two courses of action open to them: either wait in the aircraft or in the transit waiting room of the airport until they could take the airplane to their final destination, or ask at the airport for a transit visa valid only for the interval until they were able to continue their journey. It was highly regrettable that the persons concerned should have chosen a third course: that of leaving the transit waiting room and entering the territory of the Ivory Coast without a transit visa, an outright infringement of the Ivory Coast legislation on the entry and stay of aliens, whatever their status, in the national territory. The fact that the Guineans in question were holders of diplomatic passports in no way exempted them from the formalities of obtaining a transit visa. The letter went on to refer to several instances of what it described as flagrant violations of international law and practice by the Guinean government. It concluded by stating that the government of the Ivory Coast, while deeply regretting not being able to accede to the Secretary-General's request to release the Guinean delegation, very much hoped that a humane solution may be found in regard to the persons detained in the Ivory Coast and Guinea. To that end and despite the violation of the law committed in the Ivory Coast by members of the Guinean delegation, the government of the Ivory Coast repeated its offer to release these persons as soon as the Guinean government had agreed to take similar measures with regard to Mr. François Kamano, the crew of the *Kerisper,* and the vessel itself.

THE SITUATION IN THE MIDDLE EAST

THE FIFTH EMERGENCY SESSION of the General Assembly debated the Middle East problem from June 17 to July 5 and again from July 12 through July 21 but the Members were so sharply divided that no resolutions were adopted except two on the status of Jerusalem and one on refugees. The basic questions of Israeli troop withdrawals, national security, innocent passage of ships through the Strait of Tiran and the Suez Canal, and the future of the one million Palestinian refugees were left unresolved partly because of differences over timing and methods of procedure. Much of the debate was devoted to partisan attacks on one side or the other. Thus, at the time U Thant issued the Introduction to his Annual Report on September 15 the situation was much the same as it had been on June 10 when the Six-Day War ended. In this document and in a press conference on September 16, the Secretary-General gave his views on the problem. He noted that the United Nations had been involved in the Middle East for twenty years and had often restored quiet by mediation, cease-fires, truces, and armistice agreements, but added that over the years there had been "no enduring, persistent effort by any United Nations organ to find solutions" to the basic issues. He called for urgent and determined effort by the Organization to bring about conditions essential to peace in the area. "I am bound to express my fear," he said, "that, if again no effort is exerted and no progress is made toward removing the root causes of conflict, within a few years at the most there will be ineluctably a new eruption of war."

Both in the Introduction and in his press conference Thant expressed the view that international involvement, primarily the United Nations, would be essential, since direct negotiations between Israel and the Arab countries seemed unlikely at the moment. He suggested that one helpful step would be authorization for the designation by the Secretary-General of a special representative for the Middle East, who could serve "as a reporter and interpreter of events and views for the Secretary-General and as both a sifter and harmonizer of ideas in the area." Thant first advanced this idea during his Cairo visit the previous May. A similar proposal for a special representative had been incorporated in one of the resolutions which failed to obtain the necessary majority for adoption by the Assembly at the fifth emergency session. This was the so-called seventeen-power resolution sponsored by Afghanistan, Burundi, Ceylon, the Congo (Brazzaville), Cyprus, Guinea, India, Indonesia, Malaysia, Mali, Pakistan, Somalia, the United Republic of Tanzania, Yugoslavia, and Zambia.

The Secretary-General acknowledged that there was disenchantment with the United Nations as an aftermath of the Middle East and that the feeling bordered on hostility in some quarters toward its presence in the area. The

Arabs, he said, felt the United Nations had not done enough and Israel felt the Organization was no longer needed and that it was in the way. "Such attitudes, of course, are both misguided and short-sighted," he said. He commented further: "I have no doubt whatever that the impartial United Nations presence there continues to be helpful to both sides, is needed now as much as ever, and that the time will come when this will once more be understood and appreciated by all parties concerned."

---

1. From Introduction to the Twenty-second Annual Report

NEW YORK   SEPTEMBER 15, 1967

I. General

1. DURING THE PERIOD under review the international political situation has not only not improved; it has in fact deteriorated considerably. It was only recently that I noted how the war in View-Nam has been progressively intensified during the last two and a half years, how the number of men and the amount of war material involved in the actual fighting have immensely increased, how the savagery of the war has steadily escalated, and the casualties on the part of all parties involved in the fighting have reached frightening proportions. In addition, the flare-up in the Middle East in June of this year, which was sudden though not surprising, has led to a further deterioration of the international scene. The war in the Middle East has tended to overshadow the situation in Cyprus, which has shown no great improvement during this period.

2. I shall refer to these issues in somewhat greater detail in subsequent sections of this introduction. At the present time I must note that only limited progress has been made in other areas of activity such as disarmament, outer space, economic and social development, decolonization and human rights.

SOURCE: General Assembly Official Records, Twenty-second Session, Supplement No. 1A (A/6701/Add. 1).

3. The frustrations to which I referred in my introduction to last year's annual report in respect of such long-standing problems as the situation in South Africa, South West Africa and Southern Rhodesia continue, although in respect of both South West Africa and Southern Rhodesia the General Assembly and the Security Council respectively have, during the period under review, taken certain definite steps which may help in time to improve the situation.

4. In regard to one area with which the United Nations is concerned—West Irian—I am glad to report that the Indonesian Government has assured me that it will comply fully with the remaining responsibilities deriving from the Agreement signed on August 15, 1962, between the Republic of Indonesia and the Kingdom of the Netherlands. The act of self-determination in West Irian will take place in 1969, at a date to be decided upon in due course, and, as called for in the Agreement, one year before the date of the consultation I shall appoint a United Nations representative "to advise, assist and participate in arrangements which are the responsibility of Indonesia for the act of free choice."

5. I should also like to report that, upon the notification on November 2, 1966, by the Government of Indonesia that it wished to resume participation in the Fund of the United Nations for the Development of West Irian, the Fund was reactivated and the Administrator of the United Nations Development Programme assumed full responsibility for its operation.

6. Within the Organization itself, I again find it necessary to report with regret that the financial difficulties are no nearer solution than they have been in the past. The Special Committee on Peace-keeping Operations, in spite of its best efforts, has been unable to evolve and formulate certain well-established ground rules and guidelines which are essential for the successful conduct of future peace-keeping operations. The problem received detailed consideration at the last regular session of the General Assembly and several ideas and suggestions were submitted for overcoming the impasse that had been reached. The Special Committee on Peace-keeping Operations, which was asked by the Assembly to continue its work, established two working groups, one to study the various methods of financing peace-keeping operations and the other to study matters relating to the facilities, services and personnel which Member states might voluntarily provide for a United Nations peace-keeping operation.

The Committee and its working groups held a number of meetings but failed to arrive at any generally acceptable conclusions. This is a matter of deep regret to me, especially as recent events have shown very clearly the need to agree on basic guidelines for the conduct of peace-keeping operations, and I express the hope that this problem will receive the urgent attention it deserves. I am also constrained to report that in spite of the unanimous agreement reached two years ago on overcoming the financial difficulties through voluntary contributions by Member states, such contributions have not been forthcoming, and the Organization's financial difficulties remain. I appeal once again to all Member governments, and especially those that have decided in principle to make voluntary contributions, to do so at an early date as a gesture of confidence in the United Nations and as a token of their abiding interest in the Organization's effective functioning and financial stability.

II. Disarmament

7. Despite the menacing international situation, and perhaps in some measure because of it, the past year has been marked by increasing activity and some important progress in the field of disarmament. In accordance with the resolutions adopted by the General Assembly at its twenty-first session, the Conference of the Eighteen-Nation Committee on Disarmament has met in almost continuous session to deal with the tasks assigned to it and has concentrated its efforts on reaching agreement on a treaty for the non-proliferation of nuclear weapons; the Preparatory Committee for the Conference of Non-Nuclear-Weapon States has been engaged in considering the arrangements for convening the Conference; and a group of consultant experts appointed by the Secretary-General has been assisting in the preparation of a report on the effects and implications of nuclear weapons.

8. In January 1967, the Treaty on Principles Governing the Activities of States in the Exploration and Use of Outer Space, including the Moon and Other Celestial Bodies, was signed. Article IV of the treaty provides that outer space and celestial bodies should be free of nuclear weapons and other weapons of mass destruction, and prohibits the establishment of military bases, installations and fortifica-

tions, the testing of any type of weapons and the conduct of military manoeuvres on celestial bodies.

9. The Treaty for the Prohibition of Nuclear Weapons in Latin America, which was signed in February at Mexico City, marks an important milestone on the road to disarmament. It provides for the creation, for the first time in history, of a nuclear-free zone in an inhabited part of the earth. It is the first treaty in the field of disarmament which establishes an effective system of control under a permanent supervisory organ. The safeguards system of the International Atomic Energy Agency is to ensure that atomic energy is not diverted from peaceful to military purposes and, in addition, a system of special inspection to guard against violations has been provided for, in cases where there is suspicion of clandestine activities outside the Agency's safeguards system. This treaty, which was conceived and negotiated throughout by the states of Latin America themselves, is of importance not only to Latin America; it may provide an example and a stimulant for progress in other disarmament measures of world-wide as well as of regional significance.

10. When these two treaties enter into force, they will mark significant steps towards preventing the spread of nuclear weapons to areas of our universe and our planet and thus help to contain and reduce the dimensions of the problem of the proliferation of nuclear weapons.

11. The question of non-proliferation has remained at the top of the agenda for international disarmament discussions during the course of the year. Intensive negotiations have taken place among the main nuclear powers and their allies, both inside and outside the Eighteen-Nation Committee, in a major effort to work out an agreed text of a treaty, and definite progress has been made.

12. The tabling by the Soviet Union and the United States of separate identical draft treaties on non-proliferation, on August 24, 1967, was an event of great significance. It marked the culmination of years of patient efforts to narrow and remove the differences between them. The importance of the success they have achieved in agreeing on the principal provisions of a treaty is diminished to some extent by their failure to agree on the article dealing with safeguards. I am, however, confident that the overriding necessity of their reaching agreement if there is to be a treaty will lead the sponsors of the draft treaty to reconcile their differences.

13. The non-nuclear countries in the Eighteen-Nation Committee, aligned and non-aligned, have understandably raised a number of serious questions regarding the provisions and effects of a treaty on non-proliferation. They are concerned that the treaty should encourage and not limit the fullest utilization of the peaceful applications of atomic energy, including peaceful explosions of nuclear devices when these become technologically and economically feasible; they desire to avoid any discrimination as regards peaceful uses of atomic energy or in the operation of a system of safeguards and controls; they wish to ensure that the treaty will provide a real beginning for the reduction and elimination of nuclear weapons by the nuclear powers and will embody an acceptable balance of mutual responsibilities and obligations of the nuclear and non-nuclear powers. Above all, they are concerned, and this applies particularly to the non-aligned countries which are not under the "nuclear umbrella" of any nuclear power, as to how their security can be assured if they renounce the right to acquire nuclear weapons as a deterrent against either nuclear or conventional attack on them. These and other aspects of the question of non-proliferation have been considered in detail in the Eighteen-Nation Committee. For their part the nuclear powers have endeavoured to reassure the non-nuclear powers regarding all of these questions, which, of course, will be given the most thorough consideration in the General Assembly.

14. Although differences of opinion remain, the atmosphere in the Eighteen-Nation Committee and the relations among its members continue to be good. The members of the Committee are on the whole cautiously hopeful of early agreement on a treaty. I am convinced that if the spread of nuclear weapons is to be prevented, this can only be done by treaty. No other way can be effective for any length of time. I regard the successful conclusion of a treaty for the non-proliferation of nuclear weapons as an indispensable first step towards further progress on disarmament. In fact it is difficult to conceive of any agreement in the foreseeable future on any other measure of disarmament if it is not possible to reach agreement on a treaty to prevent the spread of nuclear weapons.

15. The preoccupation of the non-nuclear countries with questions of their security, in the context of either the proliferation or the non-proliferation of nuclear weapons, was demonstrated by the adoption of General Assembly resolution 2153 B(XXI), which provided for the

convening of a conference of non-nuclear-weapon states not later than July 1968. The Preparatory Committee for the Conference of Non-Nuclear-Weapon States has been actively considering the scope of the Conference and the question of the association of nuclear states with its work. The main items on the agenda of the Conference deal with: (1) methods of assuring the security of non-nuclear-weapon states; (2) the implications of the acquisition of nuclear weapons by non-nuclear-weapon states; (3) the prevention of the proliferation of nuclear weapons through cooperation among non-nuclear-weapon states; and (4) programmes for the peaceful uses of nuclear energy. All these are extremely important problems, the successful solution of which will pave the way for the cessation of the nuclear arms race and the establishment of conditions that will ensure the maintenance of peace and security.

16. Increased attention has also been devoted to the question of non-dissemination of conventional armaments. The problem of the limitation, reduction and control of conventional armaments has occupied the United Nations and the Conference of the Eighteen-Nation Committee on Disarmament to a greater or lesser extent for many years. The problem has once again been brought to the fore by the recent military conflict in the Middle East, and the discussions in the General Assembly at its fifth emergency special session and in the Eighteen-Nation Committee have stimulated renewed attention to various aspects of the question. For political and economic as well as military reasons it is obviously desirable that the balance of conventional armaments which antagonistic states maintain as a deterrent should be kept at the lowest possible level.

17. The question of a comprehensive test ban continues to be one of the main subjects of consideration in the Eighteen-Nation Committee. France and the People's Republic of China have continued to conduct nuclear weapons tests in the atmosphere and appear to be reaching the thermonuclear stage. The Soviet Union and the United States seem to have accelerated the rate of underground testing. The non-nuclear powers, and particularly the non-aligned states, have for their part continued to press for a halt to all testing in all environments, but thus far without success. The nations carrying out tests in the atmosphere seem intent on improving their nuclear capability and arsenals. Those conducting underground tests are still divided over the question of the need for on-site inspection, despite improvements

in the instrumentation and techniques for detecting and identifying seismic events. Fears have been voiced that they may wish to continue underground testing in order to seek new and improved offensive and defensive missiles.

18. The small measure of success that has been achieved in controlling the arms race, in bringing about the reduction and elimination of nuclear weapons and in making progress towards general and complete disarmament has led to a growing sense of concern and disquiet regarding both the nuclear and the conventional arms races. I believe we have reached a critical period when there is an imminent danger of proliferation of nuclear weapons as more and more countries acquire the technological know-how that would permit them to make nuclear weapons and are in a position to acquire the plutonium as a by-product of nuclear-power reactors. The spread of nuclear weapons to additional countries poses an incalculable threat by increasing the mathematical probability of the outbreak of nuclear war by accident, miscalculation or design. At the same time there is a very grave danger that the nuclear arms race may be pushed to unimaginable levels by a new race for anti-missile missiles, anti-anti-missile missiles and the whole new armoury of weapons and counter-weapons associated with the concept of ballistic missile defences and the means to overcome such defences. A new round in an unending nuclear arms race could upset the delicate balance of stability that exists at the present time between the nuclear super-powers, and could give rise to new fears and tensions which would offset the small but hopeful progress that has been made towards a détente and disarmament. While it is true that the threat of nuclear war poses the main danger to humanity, the arms race in the field of conventional weapons and the dissemination of such weapons by the larger to the smaller powers also create dangers and tensions which can lead to local or regional conflicts. The nuclear powers can easily become involved in such conflicts with all the attendant risks of precipitating a global nuclear war.

19. In the introduction to my last annual report, I referred to the desirability of undertaking a comprehensive study of the consequences of the invention of nuclear weapons. It was a matter of deep gratification to me that the General Assembly at its last session took up this suggestion and authorized me to prepare, with the assistance of qualified consultant experts, a report on the effects of the possible

use of nuclear weapons and on the security and economic implications for states of the acquisition and further development of these weapons. The work on this report is proceeding satisfactorily and I hope to make the report available before the Assembly begins the debate on the various items of its agenda relating to problems of disarmament.

. . .

IV. Peace-keeping

27. The events of 1967 have brought both the practice and the theory of United Nations peace-keeping to an important milestone—and perhaps even to a crossroads. For some years now there has been, both within and outside the Organization, a protracted and wide-ranging controversy about many aspects of peace-keeping, and especially about its constitutional and financial aspects. The fact that the concept of peace-keeping as such is not mentioned in the Charter has contributed to this controversy. The withdrawal of the United Nations Emergency Force and the events which followed upon it have abruptly brought the United Nations and the world face to face with the realities of that aspect of the United Nations peace effort which has come to be known as peace-keeping, and with the great usefulness as well as with the intrinsic fragility of such operations

28. The first reality of United Nations peace-keeping is its voluntary nature. Peace-keeping efforts must be accepted voluntarily by all parties to a conflict if they are to be effective at all—and, as we have seen recently, the time may come when that voluntary acceptance can be suddenly and unexpectedly withdrawn. When that happens, the usefulness of a peace-keeping operation almost automatically comes to an end. It must be emphasized that peace-keeping, in the sense of the operations thus far conducted by the United Nations, has no relation to enforcement action as provided for in Chapter VII of the Charter, nor can there ever be any question of peace-keeping forces being used in such a way as to appear to be occupation forces. The effectiveness of peace-keeping depends above all on the willingness of the parties to a conflict to accept, however grudgingly, a peaceful alternative to violence, even if they have no real will to peace in a solid and enduring sense.

29. The voluntary principle pervades all other aspects of peace-

keeping. Military personnel are made available voluntarily by governments, which can withdraw them at any time. In practice over the years, there have been surprisingly few instances of such withdrawals, whether for political or other reasons. The men engaged in a peace-keeping operation can carry out their duties only with the voluntary cooperation of the authorities and people of the host country and in some cases of other parties directly concerned. The financing of the only major peace-keeping force still operating, the United Nations Force in Cyprus, is on an entirely voluntary basis, with quite disturbing indications of a tendency towards financing future peace-keeping operations in a similar way. This is indeed a fragile and undependable foundation for operations which are usually vital to international peace and security.

30. The lack of progress in the establishment of a more durable framework for peace-keeping operations, with agreed and authorized guidelines and ground rules for setting them up, conducting and financing them, undoubtedly diminishes the confidence with which the United Nations can face the probable conflict situations of the future. It is not to the credit of the United Nations that after nineteen years of peace-keeping efforts each operation has still to be improvised for lack of measures of a general preparatory nature by the appropriate organs. While it seems to be agreed that the United Nations must have some capacity to act effectively in time of danger, it has still not been possible to agree on methods by which that capacity might be increased and made more reliable, especially in the periods between crises. This deficiency stems from the fundamental differences among the Members in their interpretation of the Charter with regard to United Nations activity in behalf of peace.

31. In this uncertain situation, the decision of a number of Member states to earmark elements of their armed forces for standby service in United Nations peace-keeping operations is a welcome step. It would be helpful in connection with such forward-looking action if Members could at least agree that the General Assembly would study such questions as the standardization of training and equipment for standby forces, the relationship of the United Nations to governments providing such forces, and the constitutional and financial aspects of employing them. This could be done either by a committee specially appointed for the purpose or by the Secretary-General himself who would be authorized to carry out the necessary studies.

Such a study would give some impetus to the development of the peace-keeping concept and technique and would provide useful practical ideas. The Secretary-General has now gone as far as he can properly go in this direction without specific authorization.

32. These are the basic elements of the United Nations peace-keeping problem—its voluntary nature, its inability to operate if any party is determined on violence, and the lack of agreement in the United Nations on the legitimate basis for peace-keeping, present and future. There are other less fundamental difficulties which are sometimes cited—perhaps because the real basic obstacles seem so intractable—as principal causes of the lack of progress or improvement in United Nations peace-keeping. It is often said, for example, that the lack of military staff and the lack of planning in the Secretariat are an important source of weakness. The proponents of this position, who mistakenly equate United Nations peace-keeping operations—which are only semi-military in their functioning—with normal national military operations, never make clear what they would expect even a limited military staff at United Nations Headquarters to do. It is all too obvious that contingency military planning by the Secretariat for specified future operations would be, to put it mildly, politically unacceptable. Apart from anything else, such planning would depend upon the gathering of political intelligence which it would be out of the question for the United Nations to attempt.

33. It has also been said that the preparation of all sorts of standing operational procedures would greatly improve the quality of United Nations peace-keeping performance. The fact is that such procedures do exist and have been compiled routinely for each peace-keeping operation. These are used as a basis when a new operation is mounted, but experience has shown that instructions and procedures have to be adapted specifically to each operation since, so far at any rate, the various peace-keeping operations have differed widely in scope, nature, composition and function.

34. The Secretariat has at the present time neither the authorization nor the budget to engage in widespread planning, staff work, recruitment or training activities such as are common to national military establishment; nor, indeed, in present circumstances would such activity have much practical utility. A plan for the training of officers for United Nations peace-keeping duties was elaborated in detail some years ago, but has never been implemented for lack of

authorization and financing. In the political circumstances prevailing at the United Nations it is hard to see how a United Nations military staff, even if authorized by the competent organs, could justify its existence and actually improve very much the quality either of existing operations or of hypothetical future ones.

35. The hard and frustrating fact remains that the principal obstacles in the way of an improvement in United Nations peace-keeping are primarily political and constitutional, and only secondarily military and financial. The crossroads which we seem to have reached in peace-keeping is marked by a political and constitutional impasse. Member states today have the choice of two main directions. They could, despite all the difficulties, frustrations and disappointments, pursue and develop the possibilities of United Nations peace-keeping as a rational and civilized method of seeking to mitigate conflict while basic solutions are sought. They could, on the other hand, decide that the conditions of the contemporary world are too complex and too violent to allow reasonable and peaceful regulation and that the United Nations has no useful active role at present in helping to keep the peace or in developing a potential for future action of that nature. The latter course seems to me to be unthinkable for, should it be adopted, the dangers of the present and the risks of the future would surely not be slow in developing to a critical and disastrous stage. Whatever may be the short-comings of the United Nations and whatever its failures in finding durable solutions or in maintaining peace, its achievements both at the conference table and in the field have already demonstrated the essential worth of the peace-keeping concept.

36. The United Nations cannot begin to justify the hopes placed in it unless it is enabled by its Members to meet the challenge of the increasingly dangerous situations in many parts of the world by improved methods and new initiatives. It is worth repeating that the pioneering efforts in peace-keeping have not been matched by new and imaginative initiatives in the process of peace-making involving the peaceful settlement of disputes. The capacity of the United Nations to settle disputes or promote constructive and peaceful solutions to disputes is as much in need of study as the problems of peace-keeping—perhaps more so. The tendency for peace-keeping operations, originally set up as temporary expedients, to assume a semi-permanent character because no progress is made in settling the basic

causes of conflict is a serious reflection on the capacity of the United Nations to settle disputes even when these disputes have been brought to the Organization by the parties directly concerned.

37. The United Nations Force in Cyprus, during the past year, has continued to perform its essential function of preventing a recurrence of fighting and, as necessary, contributing to the maintenance and restoration of law and order and a return to normal conditions. The underlying assumption in this activity has been that, by helping to keep the peace and by promoting normalization, the Force would create the conditions in which a political settlement, which necessarily is mainly the responsibility of the parties, could better be sought.

38. The main effort towards a solution has been in the dialogue, recently resumed, between Greece and Turkey. United Nations mediation has been long blocked by the impasse over the selection of a mediator between the governments of Cyprus and Turkey. My special representative in Cyprus, under his broadened responsibilities, has been able, in the prevailing circumstances, to do no more towards a solution than to establish useful official contacts with the governments in Ankara and Athens in addition to his regular contacts with the Cyprus government and the Turkish Cypriot leadership.

39. To the best of my knowledge—I have to say with regret—there has been no significant progress towards a solution of the Cyprus problem. All the parties concerned, of course, wish the United Nations peace-keeping force to remain on the island. Thus, I have felt obliged to recommend to the Security Council the extension of the mandate of the Force in Cyprus. It seems all too clear that, in the absence of a solution to the Cyprus problem, the withdrawal of the Force will lead to renewed hostilities and a consequent threat to peace and security in the Eastern Mediterranean.

40. In my view, however, it should not be expected that the Force can remain on the island indefinitely, if only because of unsatisfactory and inadequate financial support. In any case, a United Nations force, as I see it, should not be called upon to maintain indefinitely an obviously unsatisfactory status quo.

41. In welcome contrast to the tragic events of 1965, the situation in Jammu and Kashmir during the past year has been quiet and the United Nations Military Observer Group in India and Pakistan has reported few cease-fire violations, none of them of serious military or political significance. Such minor difficulties or incidents as have

occurred were resolved readily with the cooperation of the parties and through the good offices of the Observer Group. However, following last year's promising development at Tashkent, there has been no serious effort on the part of the United Nations to contribute to an ultimate solution of the problem.

V. *The Middle East*

42. The eruption of full-scale war in the Middle East early in June of this year came as a terrific shock, but hardly as a surprise. This 1967 outbreak was the third war between Arabs and Israelis in that area within a score of years, each threatening the general peace. That is more than enough war in any one area.

43. For eighteen of those twenty years the sole barriers against continuous war were the four armistice agreements concluded by means of United Nations mediation in the spring and summer of 1949 and the United Nations peace-keeping machinery in the area—the United Nations Truce Supervision Organization in Palestine and later the United Nations Emergency Force. Those agreements, as is made explicit in each of them, were considered at the time of their negotiation as only a step towards peace, and not as a basis for a more or less permanent way of life in the Middle East. They are not peace treaties and, although they were firm and voluntary undertakings by the signatory governments and were entered into in good faith, they did not represent any fundamental changes in attitude on the part of governments or peoples. On the other hand there has been no indication either in the General Assembly or in the Security Council that the validity and applicability of the armistice agreements have been changed as a result of the recent hostilities or of the war of 1956; each agreement, in fact, contains a provision that it will remain in force "until a peaceful settlement between the parties is achieved." Nor has the Security Council or the General Assembly taken any steps to change the pertinent resolutions of either organ relating to the armistice agreements or to the earlier cease-fire demands. The agreements provide that by mutual consent the signatories can revise or suspend them. There is no provision in them for unilateral termination of their application. This has been the United Nations position all along and will continue to be the position until a competent organ decides otherwise.

44. The suspicions, fears and animosities which have character-ized the relations between Arabs and Israelis since the resolution on the partition of Palestine have been ever-present and always appar-ent. Dangerous tensions have never ceased nor greatly eased, and United Nations peace-keeping personnel have had to be constantly on the alert for incidents of fighting. There have been periods of relative quiet, but there was never real peace or the prospect of real peace. The threat of war was ever present. Finally—and, it seems, inevitably in the historical circumstances—in June, once again all-out war came to the area.

45. There is a profound lesson to be derived by this Organization from recent developments in the Middle East. United Nations peace-keeping and peace-making activities had their genesis in Palestine. They have been more prolonged, more intensive and more varied in that area than in any conflict situations elsewhere. It may be regis-tered here that the United Nations has had considerable success over these twenty years in stopping fighting in the area by means of mediation, cease-fire, truce and armistice agreements, in restoring quiet along acutely troubled lines and generally in containing explo-sive situations. But the basic issues which provoke the explosions remain unsolved and, indeed, except for a few sporadic and inconclu-sive debates over the years, largely untouched by the United Nations. There has been no enduring, persistent effort in any United Nations organ to find solutions for them. In my view, the failure of the United Nations over these years to come to grips with the deep-seated and angrily festering problems in that area has to be consid-ered as a major contributing factor to the war of last June, although, naturally, primary responsibility rests inescapably with the parties involved. I am bound to express my fear that, if again no effort is exerted and no progress is made towards removing the root causes of conflict, within a few years at the most there will be ineluctably a new eruption of war.

46. There is a desperate need for a determined, immediate and urgent effort by the United Nations to help bring about the conditions essential to peace in the Middle East. That effort should be constant and unrelenting until those conditions have been achieved.

47. This summer, at the fifth emergency special session of the General Assembly, the basic issues of the Middle East were dis-cussed fully, but unhappily without conclusive results, except for the

two resolutions on Jerusalem and one on the humanitarian aspects relating to refugees, displaced persons and prisoners of war. The Security Council, of course, took prompt cease-fire actions and also adopted a resolution on humanitarian aspects. On each of the basic issues, if taken separately, there could be agreement by a large number of the Members on a reasonable solution; on some, the support would be very great. But because of the nature of the issues, complicating considerations of priority, timing and simultaneous decision intrude, and thus far have blocked United Nations action. There is the immediate and urgently challenging issue of the withdrawal of the armed forces of Israel from the territory of neighbouring Arab states occupied during the recent war. There is near unanimity on this issue, in principle, because everyone agrees that there should be no territorial gains by military conquest. It would, in my view, lead to disastrous consequences if the United Nations were to abandon or compromise this fundamental principle. But in the context of the current problems of the Middle East, the issue of withdrawal loses sizable support when taken alone by separating it from other vital issues and particularly that of national security. The unwillingness of the Arab states to accept the existence of the state of Israel, the insistence of some on maintaining a continuing state of belligerency with Israel—although those maintaining belligerency may themselves refrain from committing belligerent acts—and the question of innocent passage through the Strait of Tiran and the Suez Canal are also fundamental issues which present hotly controversial problems and sharp division, even though there is much agreement on the principles involved. The problem of the more than a million Palestinian refugees has persisted with little effort at solution since the summer of 1948, and now that problem has been enlarged by the substantial increase in the number of refugees as a result of the recent war. Another serious problem for which no solution had been found at the time of the outbreak of hostilities in June was that of the El Fatah-type sabotage and terrorist activities across the borders into Israel, with resultant retaliation.

48. The United Nations may again be able by new peace-keeping endeavours and strengthened machinery to achieve a measure of quiet in the Middle East—for a time—but it should now be fully clear that this is not good enough and that more must be done in order to avert another round of hostilities later on. A determined effort is

needed now to find solutions to the issues which have thrice in the past led, and no doubt will again in the future lead, to war between Arabs and Israelis. Naturally, it would be most encouraging if it seemed likely that Arabs and Israelis could themselves undertake to try to find the way to solution of the issues between them, but I am aware of no sign that this is in the realm of present possibility. It seems to me certain, therefore, that international effort, assistance and concerted action will be indispensable to any move towards solutions and away from a new recourse to battle. One helpful step that could be taken immediately would be an appropriate authorization for the designation by the Secretary-General of a special representative to the Middle East. Such an appointee could serve as a much needed channel of communication, as a reporter and interpreter of events and views for the Secretary-General and as both a sifter and a harmonizer of ideas in the area.

49. It seems to me also that there are certain fundamental principles which have application to the issues of the Middle East and which no one would be disposed to dispute as to their intrinsic worth, soundness and justness, at least when taken separately. It is indispensable to an international community of states—if it is not to follow the law of the jungle—that the territorial integrity of every state be respected, and the occupation by military force of the territory of one state by another cannot be condoned. Similarly, every state's right to exist must be accepted by all other states; every state is entitled to be secure within its own borders; people everywhere, and this certainly applies to the Palestinian refugees, have a natural right to be in their homeland and to have a future; and there should be free and unimpeded navigation for all through international waterways according to international conventions. The fact is that the parties themselves are firmly and solemnly committed to these principles. In the armistice agreements, for example, they have undertaken scrupulously to respect the Security Council injunction against resort to military force in the settlement of the Palestine question; they agreed that no aggressive action by the armed forces of either party would be undertaken, planned or threatened against the other party; they agreed to respect fully the right of the other party to security and freedom from fear of attack by the armed forces of the other and they agreed that no warlike or hostile act would be committed by one party against the other.

50. Similar commitments have been undertaken by the parties in their membership in the United Nations and in their acceptance of its Charter provisions, which in Article 2, paragraphs 3 and 4, require that "all Members shall settle their international disputes by peaceful means in such a manner that international peace and security, and justice, are not endangered" and that "all Members shall refrain in their international relations from the threat or use of force against the territorial integrity or political independence of any state, or in any other manner inconsistent with the purposes of the United Nations."

51. It would be difficult but, I believe, definitely possible to work out in detail a blueprint for the solution of the major Arab-Israel problems in the Middle East which would go some way towards meeting the demands of justice, reason and practicability. However, the real and stubborn obstacle to solutions and to peace is, unmistakably, the unwillingness of the parties for their own reasons to give consideration to any proposals unless they conform very closely to their long-established and rigidly held positions. These attitudes are backed by strong emotions. The essential pre-condition for an advance towards peace in the Middle East is an end to incitement to hatred, the achievement of calm and a recourse to reason.

52. In the Middle East today, as an aftermath of the recent war, there are expressions of disappointment with the United Nations, in some quarters even bordering on hostility towards its presence in the area. On the one hand, there is the feeling among Arabs that the United Nations has not done enough and is not to be relied upon. On the other hand, there seems to be a decided feeling in some quarters in Israel these days that a United Nations presence there is no longer needed, that it tries to do too much and is in the way. Such attitudes, of course, are both misguided and shortsighted. However faulty or selective the memories of government and peoples may be, the record stands indelibly that the United Nations in its twenty years of intensive effort to achieve and maintain quiet and ultimate peace in the Middle East, has rendered invaluable services to both sides in that area, and has saved countless lives and endless destruction there. That effort has been very costly to the United Nations in both men and money. In this regard, Count Bernadotte gave his life, the Truce Supervision Organization has suffered twenty-one fatalities (eight civilian and thirteen military) and the Emergency Force had eighty-nine fatal casualties. The record also shows that governments and peoples in the area, Israelis and Arabs alike, have at various times in

the past not only welcomed but acclaimed in glowing terms the United Nations presence in the area and its helpful actions, by means of mediation—the United Nations Truce Supervision Organization and the United Nations Emergency Force, as well as the United Nations Relief and Works Agency for Palestine Refugees in the Near East and the Technical Assistance Board, now merged in the United Nations Development Programme. I have no doubt whatever that the impartial United Nations presence there continues to be helpful to both sides, is needed now as much as ever, and that the time will come when this will once more be understood and appreciated by all parties concerned.

53. The role of peace-keeper is never likely to be continuously popular with any of the parties to a conflict. By the very nature of its status and its moderating functions, a peace-keeping operation can never espouse the cause of any of the parties. There thus tends to be an underlying element of dissatisfaction and frustration in the relations of the United Nations with the parties to a conflict. This condition may even at times border on a breakdown in those relations. This, however, does not signify that the peace-keeping work of the United Nations has served no purpose, nor that it would be in the interest of the parties to a conflict to do without the assistance which the Organization alone can give them. Quite apart from its more positive functions, the United Nations provides an invaluable repository and a safe target for blame and criticism which might otherwise be directed elsewhere. The Organization has, during all its years and in many situations, performed a vital function as an international lightning rod, as, in fact, it is now doing in the Middle East. These are facts of international life which should not be lost sight of when the effectiveness and the future of the peace-keeping function are being considered. The basic problem, now as always, lies in the acceptance by governments of international decisions and machinery and the degree of their realization that the wider interests of international peace may in the long run also coincide with their own best interests. We are today, I need hardly add, very far, in general, from such a realization.

VI. Problems of Economic and Social Development

54. Financial considerations continue to affect United Nations activities in the economic and social field and, again this year, have

caused the rejection or postponement of some world-wide projects. Three quarters of the way through the United Nations Development Decade, the resources made available, either bilaterally or multilaterally, to meet the major requirements of the developing countries are still far from being satisfactory. Nevertheless, the world community may find some grounds for encouragement in certain recent achievements and some new prospects.

55. The increasing tendency to adopt a comprehensive approach to the problems of development is particularly worthy of note. The United Nations work programme is concerned more and more, both conceptually and in practice, with the major elements of national development, and there is a better understanding of the interrelationship of its economic and social aspects.

56. The emphasis now placed on population problems confirms this trend. Population control is seen not only as a means of overcoming economic difficulties but also as a way to social and human progress in modern societies. In its resolution 2211 (XXI) of December 17, 1966, the General Assembly reiterated its interest in the question of population growth and economic development, and in July 1967 I invited governments, non-governmental organizations and private individuals to contribute to a new trust fund for population activities, which will be in addition to the financial resources provided for this purpose under the regular budget of the United Nations and the various United Nations technical assistance programmes. The response has been gratifying and it is my belief that contributions to the trust fund will very soon reach the level of $5.5 million, which I have cited as necessary for a five-year programme of action. United Nations expenditures in the population field have thus far been relatively small, given the importance of the problem in the development process. The new resources will permit the Organization to double its activities in the field of population as a whole and treble them at regional and country levels, where action is particularly urgent.

57. Another illustration of the global approach to development is to be found in the continuous momentum of planning policies. The increasing use of planning as a rational and pragmatic instrument of action is slowly beginning to yield results, and there is a better understanding of the need for a correct definition of objectives, measures for bringing about social and mental change, and plan implementation in developing countries. The Committee for Develop-

ment Planning can give a new impetus to these efforts; it has particularly stressed the importance of the domestic front in the drive for progress and the mobilization of human and natural resources as a principal concern of integrated policies for development.

58. The experience gained in development planning will be of considerable value in the preparatory work for the second development decade. Much work remains to be done before specific guidelines and proposals can be formulated; however, on a preliminary basis, it has been proposed that the United Nations might adopt a charter for the second development decade which should identify certain targets to be attained by combined action on the part of the nations of the world. The Committee for Development Planning has felt that the target for over-all growth of the economy needs to be defined more precisely and in greater detail than that set for the present Decade. Minimum objectives might be set for other economic and social areas such as per capita food consumption, standards of health, education and employment.

59. The concept of "development decade" should become the framework for substantive co-ordination, as distinct from formal administrative co-ordination. For instance, the work of the Advisory Committee on the Application of Science and Technology to Development, with its attempt to evolve a world-wide plan for the development of scientific institutions, would fit into this framework. The Committee has recently prepared an important study on the production and consumption of edible protein, which is the first in a series of reports that will deal with specific problems meriting concerted attack by the international community.

60. Increasing the food supply in order to meet nutritional requirements all over the world will take a long time and will call for an intricate system of measures, both in the agricultural and industrial fields. For many years to come, planned international food aid will be needed, whatever the institutional arrangements, and I am quite certain that the General Assembly will continue to consider and review, as it decided to do in resolution 2096 (XX) of December 20, 1965, policies designed to meet these needs.

61. It is anticipated that food aid will remain an important component of international aid, in cash and in kind. Again this year, I am constrained to express my great concern regarding the loss of momentum in international aid and its adverse effects on the results

of the current Development Decade. Sustained and persistent efforts are needed through trade and aid measures in order to supply the developing countries with the external resources that they require to reinforce their own endeavours. The Kennedy Round of negotiations has been a noteworthy success, but it must be recognized that the new agreements do not give much satisfaction to the developing countries, especially in the agricultural sector. The establishment, with the assistance of the United Nations Development Programme, of an export promotion programme involving the four regional economic commissions, the United Nations Conference on Trade and Development, the United Nations Industrial Development Organization, the Food and Agriculture Organization of the United Nations and the General Agreement on Tariffs and Trade is certainly a step towards a more balanced system of international trade relationships.

62. The Economic and Social Council devoted a good deal of attention at its forty-third session to the means designed to encourage the flow of private capital to the developing countries, and I am convinced that there is scope at present for an increase of this flow. Private capital is, however, not suitable for many projects of a non-commercial nature, such as the provision of economic infra-structure and of educational facilities. The continuing need for international public financing is a recognized fact.

63. In the coming months two issues will, I hope, give further proof that the principle of solidarity between Member states remains alive. The first is the question of replenishing the resources of the International Development Association. The situation of the Association is of particular concern, as the contributions provided in 1965 are nearly exhausted. The type of loans granted by the Association play an irreplaceable role in the development of certain sectors of the economy, especially the infra-structure, of developing countries. I urge the principal governments involved to make every effort to ensure the replenishment of funds for this vital institution.

64. The second issue will be the establishment of the United Nations Capital Development Fund, which has been formally decided by the General Assembly. It seems to me that, in the present circumstances, serious consideration should be given to the possibility of using for the management of the new Fund, under some suitable arrangement, the experience and knowledge gained by the United Nations Development Programme. I have already drawn attention to

the constantly growing scope and flexibility which the Programme has proved capable of acquiring. I have also pointed out that, with its present size and diversity, the United Nations Development Programme cannot be considered simply as a bank for pre-investment projects; rather it should be viewed as a central development agency reaching in many directions, highly adaptable to new requirements, and capable of linking its action closely with that of financial institutions such as the new regional banks.

65. Special mention should be made of the increasingly vital contribution made by the regional economic commissions to the United Nations efforts directed towards the economic and social development throughout the world, particularly the developing countries. The regional economic commissions are providing the essential leadership in the quest for cooperation within the respective regions they serve by their practical and operational programmes which have hastened the building up of regional institutions. Developed as well as the developing countries, members of the regional economic commissions have, as on the recent occasions of the twentieth anniversary commemoration of the Economic Commission for Europe and the Economic Commission for Asia and the Far East, reiterated their determination to intensify their efforts and cooperate more closely to narrow the growing gap between the rich and the poor nations.

66. In the past year questions of cooperation and coordination among members of the United Nations family have assumed increasing significance. I decided, therefore, in agreement with the Advisory Committee on Administrative and Budgetary Questions, to establish the position of Under-Secretary for Inter-Agency Affairs.

67. In response to the recommendations of the *Ad Hoc* Committee of Experts to Examine the Finances of the United Nations and the Specialized Agencies there has, in the past year, been much inter-agency consultation in the administrative and budgetary fields. This consultation has been concerned first and foremost with the proposal to set up a joint inspection unit, and I look forward to its establishment early next year. On the question of the implementation of the *Ad Hoc* Committee's recommendations as a whole, I am presenting a special report to the General Assembly.

68. I welcome the increasing concern in the whole United Nations system with various aspects of what may broadly be described as evaluation. Evaluation of technical cooperation activities is being

undertaken in accordance with decisions of the Economic and Social Council. Special rapporteurs will soon be appointed in the realm of social development, to make an appraisal of field activities in this area. In a broad sense the joint inspection unit soon to be established may also be engaged in activities which are related to evaluation. The same holds true for the Committee for Programme and Co-ordination of the Economic and Social Council.

69. With a highly developed international system, what is most needed now, I believe, is patient effort by the appropriate inter-governmental bodies and the Secretariat—each in its own area of competence—to make the present structure of institutions within the United Nations family function more effectively.

70. The United Nations Conference on Trade and Development has in the past year further developed and consolidated its activities and a general advance has been made in the identification and examination of the main problems faced by the world trading community in the fields of commodities, manufactures, financing, invisibles and shipping, as well as on the broad levels of trade policy in general and of development assistance. The United Nations Conference on Trade and Development is thus now fully in operation as a mechanism for evolving an integrated trade and development policy, continuing the historical process that brought about the Geneva Conference of 1964, which gave birth to this new instrument for international economic cooperation.

71. It is also my duty to record, however, that, in the period under review, progress made towards the fulfilment of the aims and objectives set forth in 1964 has been alarmingly slow, and that no significant breakthrough has been registered in either trade or development financing from the point of view of the developing countries. It is true that a great number of important trading nations have participated, under the aegis of the General Agreement on Tariffs and Trade, in the Kennedy Round of negotiations, and that the successful conclusion of those negotiations has represented a very important step which will contribute to further growth in world trade. It is also true, on the other hand—and it has been widely recognized—that this growth can be expected to be particularly marked in the trade of developed countries among themselves, and that most developing countries are likely to reap much smaller benefits from the agreements reached in

the Kennedy Round. Developing countries are still facing basic difficulties which need urgent attention in order to avoid a further widening of the gap between the developed countries and the developing world. There is no doubt that the domestic policies of developing countries will be decisive in determining whether this gap will continue to widen or whether it can be narrowed; this does not detract, however, from the convergent importance in this regard of international measures in the field of trade and development.

72. While the permanent machinery of the United Nations Conference on Trade and Development will continue to be fully geared to these problems, it is my fervent hope that the second session of the Conference, to be held at New Delhi from February 1 to March 26, 1968, will offer an opportunity for concerted practical action by the world community, in a spirit of shared responsibility, towards the achievement of accepted common objectives, at least on specific issues where concrete progress does not appear to be out of reach. Among such issues, reference has often been made in the recent past to the liberalization of primary commodity trade; the establishment of a general system of preferences for manufactures and semi-manufactures in favour of developing countries; a scheme for supplementary financing; the financing of buffer stocks; measures for trade expansion, economic cooperation and integration among developing countries, with supporting action on the part of developed countries; and trade relations between countries having different economic and social systems. As I stated in the introduction to my annual report last year, however, there is no doubt that the political will of governments of Member states will remain the main factor which will determine the extent to which the United Nations Conference on Trade and Development can constitute an effective mechanism for the adoption of concrete solutions.

73. With regard to one of the issues mentioned above, the establishment of a general system of preferences, I should like to stress the significance to be attached to the declaration made on April 13, 1967, by the President of the United States of America, at the meeting of American Chiefs of State held at Punta del Este, to the effect that his government was ready to explore "the possibilities of temporary preferential tariff advantages for all developing countries in the markets of all the industrialized countries." This attitude has considerable potential economic significance for the developing countries.

74. What we should expect from the second session of the United Nations Conference on Trade and Development on these major issues of trade and development are basic political decisions which may allow the permanent machinery of the Conference to pursue many of its tasks in operational terms. A series of convergent follow-up measures could then be envisaged, aiming at concrete agreements and practical results within a certain set time. When I referred, in addressing the Economic and Social Council recently, to the need for the Kennedy Round to be followed by a "New Delhi Round," I had in mind the emergence from the New Delhi Conference of such a process of continuing action-oriented international cooperation. The successful pursuit of such convergent measures would call for the joint and sustained cooperative efforts of both the developed and the developing world.

75. On the institutional plane, in order that these efforts of the United Nations in the field of trade and development may be further developed for the maximum benefit of governments, it is necessary to enlist the support of all organizations and bodies which are in a position to make a positive contribution to international action, and some noteworthy steps have been taken in this respect. The harmonious development of such efforts is bound to depend largely upon the existence of an appropriate distribution of functions. It would consequently seem desirable for the central role vested in the United Nations Conference on Trade and Development by the General Assembly in the field of trade, including invisibles, to be reaffirmed and strengthened.

76. The establishment of new United Nations machinery for industrial development takes on particular significance in the light of disappointments with the rate of economic growth of the developing countries in recent years. By its nature as well as in its terms of reference, the United Nations Industrial Development Organization reflects a growing awareness of the crucial importance of a modern industrial sector. The developing countries are increasingly looking towards accelerated industrialization as the only alternative to the chronic stagnation of their economies and the widening of the economic gap that separates their populations from the benefits of contemporary industrial society.

77. The high hopes inspired by the establishment of a central

United Nations machinery for industrialization must not, however, obscure the magnitude and complexity of the underlying tasks. So far, almost 95 per cent of the world's industrial output has come from countries with less than one third of the world's population. The creation of a better balance by opening comparable possibilities for the vast populations of the developing countries, whose industrial output has so far been limited to only 5 per cent of the world's production, will require massive efforts. The United Nations Industrial Development Organization may have an important role to play in the achievement of genuine international cooperation in this field. But there can be no doubt that the goal of accelerated industrialization for the developing countries will require vast resources.

78. The building up of industrial complexes and the establishment of manufacturing plants for a large variety of industrial products, in an effort to ensure the fullest utilization of their natural resources, is likely to become the single most important task of the developing countries in the next decade or two. There is little likelihood that their basic social and political problems will be amenable to solution in a stable environment without the establishment of an autonomous productive capacity based on modern technology. Only the prodigious possibilities of applied technology hold out the hope of effectively providing productive employment and higher incomes for the expanding populations of the developing countries.

79. Though neither the United Nations Industrial Development Organization nor any other existing United Nations machinery has at its disposal the vast resources required, the organization may nevertheless play a strategic role in promoting the mobilization of international efforts and in seeking new ways of dealing with the protracted problems of development. If the ultimate goal is to be taken seriously and industrialization of the developing countries is to be significantly accelerated, new approaches will have to be found for effective international action. An adequate strategy for industrial development is now considered an important requirement in the long-range development policies of individual countries. At the same time, more attention will have to be devoted to evolving an international strategy for the promotion of cooperation with a view to achieving the goals of industrial development.

80. Examples of action of strategic significance in respect to these goals are the cooperative programmes that are being developed for

the promotion of export-oriented industries and the high priority that must be accorded to the development of industries producing agricultural requisites. In another area, the renewed emphasis on food aid programmes is intended to meet immediate shortages, but an adequate level of food supplies will depend, in the long run, on the capacity of the developing countries to produce or pay for the bulk of their own requirements. Their agricultural development is hampered at present by the lack of fertilizers, insecticides, pesticides, tractors, agricultural implements, and other farm requirements whose availability in adequate supply in the developing countries depends ultimately on the existence of industries capable of producing them where they are needed.

81. At the International Symposium on Industrial Development, which will be held late in 1967, the broad policy questions of industrialization and appropriate measures for constructive cooperation at an international level will be considered. The agenda of the Symposium includes a general survey of world industry as well as the consideration of the particular problems and prospects of the main industrial sectors. An industrial promotion service will be organized in conjunction with the Symposium, to provide an opportunity for people from the developed and developing countries to discuss specific industrial development projects.

---

82. The past year has been one of swift evolution in the operational effectiveness and potential of the United Nations Development Programme. Its Governing Council, its Administration and the executing and participating agencies have taken significant steps to raise the quality of assistance under the Programme and to speed its delivery. The United Nations—through many of its inter-governmental bodies, the Secretariat, its regular programme of technical assistance, the funds-in-trust operations and, with respect to field work, especially the resources of the United Nations Development Programme—has played an active role in this forward movement.

83. New programming procedures for the United Nations Development Programme have been recommended to permit approval of requests for technical assistance as and when the need occurs and to commit financing for the duration of the projects. This greater flexibility and responsiveness would further improve not only the plan-

ning of programmes, but also the implementation of national and regional technical assistance furnished through the Programme.

84. Meanwhile, other measures have already been applied to make assistance under the Programme increasingly strategic. There is a more intimate collaboration between the governments and the Programme in the delineation of priority needs, as well as in the integration of projects, large and small. The agencies, at their headquarters and in the field, have joined whole-heartedly in this effort to add greater thrust and coherence to our development cooperation efforts. This is particularly appropriate at a time when new interdisciplinary and miltipurpose projects are being sought by the governments of developing countries.

85. The scope of the United Nations Development Programme as an inter-governmental and inter-agency cooperative endeavour has been broadened through a continually growing collaboration with the regional economic commissions and various United Nations bodies, as well as with regional and bilateral assistance programmes, both private and public.

86. The network of consultative relationships between the Programme and financing institutions is also expanding. These are producing results on many levels. They are facilitating investment follow-up of pre-investment work—investment which some estimates put at over $1,800 million. At the same time, these closer relations are serving to orient more of its work in directions which will stimulate further investment.

87. The United Nations Development Programme is also providing financial and technical support to national and regional lending institutions. The African Development Bank is one example. Through direct initiatives, the Administrator has supported the creation of new financing institutions when they appeared to be required. An example of this is the promising effort to create a Caribbean Development Bank. The Programme is also prudently expanding its portfolio of development investments. It is doing this by making short-term loans from its cash reserves which are committed but not immediately required. These loans, placed in association with other financing agencies, including regional banks, are dedicated to development projects.

88. At the same time, the Programme is efficiently administering the provision of technical and capital assistance under the reactivated

Fund of the United Nations for the Development of West Irian.
Thirty million dollars have been pledged to the Fund by the Netherlands. Additional contributions are expected from Indonesia on the
completion of a master plan for development now in preparation. This
performance suggests the ability of the Programme to administer,
with suitable adaptations, and additional funds-in-trust arrangements
which governments might wish to assign to it in other areas of
regionalized or specialized development assistance.

89. This dynamic evolution of the Programme is, I am certain, a
source of great satisfaction to the more than 130 participating governments, that is to say, the governments of nearly all the developed and
developing countries in the world. It is one further reward for the
confidence they placed in the Programme by voluntary pledging
finance for the current programme whose cost, exclusive of the West
Irian fund, has reached the impressive total of $1,761 million, of
which $781 million is to come from the central resources of the
Programme and $980 million as contributions of the developing coun-
tries directly concerned.

90. The United Nations Development Programme is a striking
demonstration that multilateral technical cooperation works, and
works efficiently. Yet we must face the fact that its contribution
remains modest—limited not by structural deficiencies, which are
energetically being overcome, but by the limited funds placed at its
disposal.

---

91. We are not winning the war on want. The opportunity gap for
many, if not most, individuals and nations in the world is growing
wider. Inequality is increasing. Each week more and more people
suffer the degradation of an economic and social injustice which is
needless, and they know it.

92. The responsibility for combating poverty more effectively lies
heavily upon developing and developed countries alike. The emerging nations are far from doing all they honestly could and all that they
must. The industrialized nations, for their part, must awaken from the
apathy accompanying their affluence to the realities of the world
around them, to the epochal ferment in which they are inevitably
involved. They can help the developing world to reach the stage of
self-sustaining growth or leave it in its present stage of under-devel-
opment; the choice rests heavily with them, for the use they make of

only a small part of the annual increase in their technical and physical wealth will determine to a large extent the tide of human progress.

93. We are near the point of no return. Unless all countries are prepared to do more, much more than they have been doing, the world will not solve the food problem. The lives of hundreds of millions of young people in rural areas will be wasted. The swelling migration to the cities will make living in urban centres in developing countries almost intolerable. Violence will become the rule rather than the exception.

94. It is not too late to open a new age of responsibility. This will call for a radically new ethos for survival, involve a bolder dimension of world partnership for development, and demand certain sacrifices. Measured by ability and reward, the sacrifices are small indeed. They are required now. Assistance from the advanced nations to the developing nations should be increased without delay, doubled, then tripled in as few years as possible.

. . .

X. Financial Situation of the United Nations

136. The Organization's financial position and prospects continue to give little cause for optimism. The high hopes that emerged following the consensus reached at the nineteenth session of the General Assembly remain unfulfilled. The patient and persistent efforts of the Special Committee on Peace-keeping Operations have, as already noted, yielded disappointing results. The searching examination of United Nations finances undertaken in 1966 by an *ad hoc* committee of experts has left unresolved the basic problems posed by the Organization's short- and long-term indebtedness. The generous example of twenty-three countries in voluntarily contributing approximately $23.6 million to assist the United Nations out of its financial difficulties has failed to inspire others to follow suit despite repeated assurances that such support would soon be forthcoming. Fortunately, the Organization's cash position has been such during the past twelve months as to enable it to meet its immediate obligations without recourse to further borrowing. Nevertheless, the current situation, while not immediately critical, is precarious.

137. The *Ad Hoc* Committee of Experts to Examine the Finances of the United Nations and the Specialized Agencies reached the

conclusion, in March 1966, that the Organization's minimum net deficit as of September 30, 1965, was $52 million, towards which $20.1 million of voluntary contributions has been paid or pledged as of the time the Committee reported. Thus, in the judgement of the Committee, additional contributions of not less than $31.9 million were needed in order to restore solvency. On the basis of certain alternative assumptions, mainly with respect to sums to be credited or repaid to Member states from the "surplus accounts" for the United Nations Emergency Force and the United Nations Operation in the Congo, the estimated deficit and the resulting additional voluntary contributions required would need to be increased—according to the Committee's analysis—by $21.4 million to a total of $73.4 million and $53.3 million, respectively.

138. In the almost two years that have elapsed since the *Ad Hoc* Committee began its examination, the situation, while showing improvement in some respects, has deteriorated in others. In particular, because of the positions of principle of some governments, there has continued to be a cumulative shortfall in the collection of contributions to the regular budget for the financial years 1966 and 1967 and to the budget of the United Nations Emergency Force for 1966. In the net result and in the light of the Secretariat's best judgement as to the extent to which assessed contributions and other income will in fact be received for 1967 and prior years, and of expenditures and obligations incurred since September 30, 1965, the minimum deficit, estimated by the *Ad Hoc* Committee at $52 million, should now be considered as having risen to some $60 to $62 million. In the meantime, voluntary contributions paid or pledged to the special account that has been established for the purpose of liquidating this deficiency together with interest earned thereon have amounted to $23.6 million. The additional voluntary contributions now needed on the basis of the *Ad Hoc* Committee's estimates can therefore be considered as falling within a minimum range of some $36.5 million to $38.5 million. These requirements relate solely to the regular budget and the Working Capital Fund and to special accounts of the United Nations Emergency Force and the United Nations Operation in the Congo— that is to say, to the United Nations activities which have been financed wholly or in part by assessed contributions as apportioned by the General Assembly. They do not provide, for example, for the needs of the United Nations Force in Cyprus which, under a Security

Council decision, has been financed from the outset on a strictly voluntary basis. As I have repeatedly had occasion to point out, this method of financing United Nations peace-keeping operations has proved equally uncertain and unsatisfactory, as evidenced by the fact that when the currently authorized mandate of the United Nations Force in Cyprus expires on December 26, 1967, the account of the Force will show an estimated deficit of approximately $9 million in the absence of further pledges of financial support.

139. It is, of course, to be expected that past and present financial difficulties notwithstanding, and with prudent husbanding of its net liquid assets, the United Nations will continue for some time to come to meet its more pressing obligations. Obviously, however, as the Organization's chief administrative officer, I cannot face with equanimity a situation of continuous and growing deficits, especially when these represent, in large part, debts due to individual Member states for reimbursement of extra and extraordinary costs they have incurred in providing men and matériel for the various peace-keeping operations in which the United Nations has been or is now engaged. Failure to meet these obligations within a reasonable period of time can only result in those countries that have consistently responded to United Nations needs for troops and logistical support having also to bear a wholly disproportionate share of the financial costs involved. In such an event, moreover, the promptness and effectiveness with which the Organization can be expected to cope in future with similar situations is bound to be impaired.

140. As regards the longer-term outlook, the problems to be resolved are perhaps less financial than political in origin and character. They are the consequence, for the most part, of basically divergent views, particularly among the large contributors, as to the kind of organization the United Nations should be, the type of activity in which it should or should not engage, and the manner in which certain of its activities should be authorized, directed and financed. All attempts to resolve these problems through administrative and budgetary means have so far, understandably, proved futile. The *Ad Hoc* Committee of Experts, for example, could do no more than call attention to the fact that the non-participation of some Members in the financing of certain assessed items of expenditure, notably the servicing of the United Nations bond issue, and the payment, in some instances, of their *pro rata* share of appropriations for the regular—

as distinct from the voluntarily financed—programme of technical assistance, have led to a cumulative deficit in the regular budget.

141. Thus, as matters now stand, the situation is one of gradual but steady deterioration. If this trend is to be arrested, as it must be, fresh and determined efforts will be needed to liquidate the legacy of past peace-keeping indebtedness; to devise ways and means whereby future operations involving relatively large expenditures by United Nations standards are financed on a firmer and more reliable basis than in the past; and to reach accommodations that will arrest the regular budgetary shortfall and thereafter safeguard the integrity of the Organization as an expression of collective financial responsibility.

. . .

XII. Concluding observations

148. The picture given above of what I regard as the most significant developments in the United Nations during the last twelve months is, on the whole, a discouraging one. I have already referred briefly to the situation in Viet-Nam. It is a subject on which I have expressed myself with frankness in many public statements and I have nothing new to say. I continue to feel that it is within the bounds of possibility, provided certain first steps could be taken, to bring this problem to the conference table. I also feel that, on the basis of the stated objectives of all the parties concerned, it is possible to secure an honourable peace. I must reiterate my conviction that without these first steps I see no end to the continuing conflict and the human suffering involved on the part of combatants and non-combatants alike. In this connection I would like to draw attention to resolution XXVIII of the twentieth International Conference of the Red Cross in regard to the protection of civilian populations against the dangers of indiscriminate warfare.

149. Both the conflict in Viet-Nam and the recent fighting in the Middle East have inevitably affected the whole climate of international relations, including of course the relations between the two super-powers. What worries me even more is the continuing and possibly increasing tendency which colours so much of international relations and of human life in general today—the recourse to violence

and threats of violence throughout the world. It is all too clear that the civilized and reasonable approach to international disputes, of which peace-keeping has been a part, cannot long survive if there is increasingly a resort to violent solutions and to more and more widespread exhortations to violence in the name of one cause or another. This problem is relevant to a far wider subject than United Nations peace-keeping—it is, in fact, relevant to nothing less than the question of human survival.

150. Twenty-two years ago we saw the end of the most violent and destructive war in history. The shock of that war and what it made men do to each other produced a reaction in favour of peace and order—an atmosphere in which acts of violence when they occurred engendered revulsion. That mood, alas, especially among those who hold the reins of power, soon began to evaporate. We now again see violence, threats, incitement, intimidation and even hatred being used as weapons of policy in increasingly numerous areas of the world.

151. When unbridled use of force is accepted and intimidation and threats go unchallenged, the hopes of a world order such as the one outlined in the Charter become dim and hollow. When prejudice and hatred dominate the relations of nations or groups of nations, the whole world takes a step backward towards the dark ages. When violence is highlighted and even glamorized by mass media, thus instilling in society, and particularly in the young, an appetite for solving problems by force, the turbulences of today are dangerously fanned and the seeds of larger and deeper troubles at national and international levels are sown for the future. When force and military competitiveness displace cooperation, negotiation, law and diplomacy as the natural elements of the relations between states, the nightmare of a third world war comes steadily nearer to the world of reality.

152. And even though, by some kind fate, the world may escape the ultimate catastrophe, fear and violence debase the whole coinage of human intercourse and poison the atmosphere of international relations as surely as the various forms of pollution in daily life with which modern man has afflicted himself. Violence erodes the spirit of law, order and international morality. Violence and the spirit of violence, if unchecked, will soon wither the tender growth of world

order which has been fostered since the Second World War. In that event, the world would inevitably return to the sort of international chaos which produced two world wars within thirty years.

153. There is but one true answer to violence, duress and intimidation among states; the answer must be found in a resolute rejection of violence and a determined resistance to it by that vast majority of men and women throughout the world who long to live in peace, without fear. This would be a movement of mankind to save mankind. But to be effective, such a popular movement must be coupled with a determined effort by governments to put to work the instruments of international order which they already have on hand in the common interest of peace and the advancement of man.

154. The pioneering experiments in United Nations peace-keeping are a promising aspect of the grand effort to build a world community based on peaceful and reasonable methods and practices. But if that effort is to go forward to success, the tide of violence and the trend towards violent solutions must be stemmed by a massive effort of governments and peoples alike. That effort must include more persistent and vigorous attempts to find just and peaceful solutions to the many problems throughout the world which give rise, through despair, to the resort to violence.

155. In these circumstances I have asked myself what could be done, in addition to peace-keeping operations, to help resolve international conflicts even before they become a threat to international peace and security. I believe it is necessary to draw attention to the urgent need for states to have wider recourse, in their relations with other states, to the various means for the pacific settlement of disputes. By Article 33 of the Charter, Member states have bound themselves to seek, first of all, a solution to any disputes, the continuance of which is likely to endanger the maintenance of international peace and security, by negotiation, inquiry, mediation, conciliation, arbitration, judicial settlement, resort to regional agencies or arrangements, or other peaceful means of their own choice. In this connection, I cannot fail to draw attention to the availability of the International Court of Justice, as a principal organ of the United Nations, for the settlement of legal disputes. Prompter and wider recourse to the Court might well have settled issues which have remained unresolved in the hope that political solutions might be found for them. I am aware that criticism of the Court was expressed at the last regular

session of the General Assembly as a result of the disappointment of many Member states at the outcome of the South West Africa cases; however, I regard it as essential that the independence of the Court should be fully protected and that it should not be subjected to political pressures in the course of its work or as a result of a particular case. It is in the interests of every Member state to ensure that the principles of the Charter are paramount, and that the Court is able to discharge its responsibilities free of political considerations. I hope that, in the years immediately ahead, the Court will play an increasingly useful role in regard to the peaceful settlement of disputes. If this hope is to be realized, I would suggest that it would be opportune for states at this time to review their position regarding the acceptance of the compulsory jurisdiction of the Court under Article 36 of its Statute. At present only forty-three of the 125 parties to the Statute of the Court have accepted such jurisdiction, and then subject in some instances to wide reservations. Both as regards the number of acceptances of compulsory jurisdiction, and as regards the reservations in some of those acceptances, the situation can hardly be regarded as satisfactory in the present condition of world affairs.

156. In the introductions to previous annual reports I have also had occasion to refer to a number of situations where governments have requested the assistance of the Secretary-General in seeking to resolve outstanding problems between them, although no principal organ other than the Secretariat has been formally seized of those problems. One such instance, mentioned in the report for 1963–1964, related to Cambodia and Thailand where, at the request of the governments concerned, I appointed a special representative to assist them in seeking solutions to their difficulties. Another instance arose this year between Guinea and the Ivory Coast as the result of the detention in the latter of the Minister for Foreign Affairs of Guinea to the United Nations while they were returning to Conakry from the fifth emergency special session of the General Assembly. In view of the possible repercussions of this situation, I thought it my duty to report on it, and on the use of my good offices to obtain the release of certain nationals and residents of the Ivory Coast detained by the government of Guinea, to the Security Council as well as to the general membership. In so doing, I did not have in mind the Secretary-General's discretion, under Article 99 of the Charter, to bring to the attention of the Council any matter which in his opinion might

threaten international peace and security, but rather the right of the Security Council, under Atricle 34 of the Charter, to investigate, if it so wishes, any dispute or any situation which might lead to international friction or give rise to a dispute. In the light of this right of the Council, I feel it is my duty to notify it of any situation where my good offices have been invoked to which it would appear to me that Article 34 of the Charter would be applicable. In this connection, I would suggest that Member states, whether or not they are directly involved in a dispute or in a situation which might lead to international friction or give rise to a dispute, should give further study and thought to the opportunities provided by Article 34 of the Charter for the Council to inquire at an early stage into such situations or disputes.

157. I should also like to make one other suggestion in the same context. One of the preoccupations of the founders of the United Nations in 1945 was to remedy what were considered to be the failings of the League of Nations, while preserving its useful features. Provision was made at San Francisco in Article 28, paragraph 2, of the Charter, for periodic meetings of the Security Council at which each of its members might, if it so desired, be represented by a member of the government or by some specially designated representative. Further provision appears in the rules of procedure of the Security Council for the holding of such periodic meetings twice a year.

158. The above-mentioned provisions have not so far been implemented, although suggestions to this effect were made by both my predecessors in 1950 and 1955, respectively. On a number of occasions the General Assembly has also suggested to the Council that it convene meetings under Article 28, paragraph 2, of the Charter and in 1958 certain members of the Council itself made formal proposals, subsequently withdrawn, to this end.

159. It appears to me that previous efforts to implement the relevant provisions on periodic meetings of the Security Council failed not on their merits but on the basis of the prevailing atmosphere at the times when they were made. A further effort to put these provisions into effect would seem opportune at the present time, when there would appear to be a more general willingness to discuss at a high level matters of concern to the international community as a whole. I have in mind a modest beginning to test the value of such meetings, an ideal opportunity for the first of which might be provided by the

opening of the twenty-second session of the General Assembly at which many Foreign Ministers will be present. Personally I have little doubt that, once initiated, such periodic meetings will provide an outstanding opportunity for a general review of matters relating to international peace and security which are within the competence of the United Nations and for seeking a consensus approach to such matters. While periodic meetings, to permit the possibility of the fullest and frankest discussion, should probably be informal and closed, a public meeting might also be convened at the end of a particular series to announce any results achieved and to permit members of the Council so wishing to elaborate publicly thereon if they so wished.

160. If there should appear to be a general willingness to initiate a periodic meeting of the Council during the early days of the twenty-second session of the General Assembly, I would be prepared to suggest a tentative agenda for such a meeting well in advance so that agreement might be reached upon it. On the basis of the experience gained at such meetings, a decision could be arrived at on when a future meeting should be held and on whether full effect should be given to the provision in the rules of procedure of the Council that such meetings should be held twice a year.

161. I have often referred to the desirability and need for the United Nations to achieve universality of membership as soon as possible because I share the common and widely held belief that no organization with the comprehensive aims of the Charter can be successful unless all the diverse peoples, cultures and civilizations of modern life are represented in it. Furthermore, outstanding international problems, such as the crisis in Southeast Asia and disarmament, would seem to stand a better chance of settlement through the attainment of universality of membership of the United Nations. Political difficulties that appear to stand in the path of this objective will, I hope, be measured against the long-term advantages that universality entails.

162. I believe it is necessary to note that, while universality of membership is most desirable, like all concepts it has its limitations and the line has to be drawn somewhere. Universality, as such, is not mentioned in the Charter, although suggestions to this effect were made, but not adopted, at San Francisco, and the Charter itself foresees limitations on United Nations membership. Under Article 4

of the Charter not only must a state be peace-loving, but it must also, in the judgement of the Organization, be able and willing to carry out the obligations contained in the Charter.

163. In making this observation I have in mind those states which have been referred to as "micro-states," entities which are exceptionally small in area, population and human and economic resources, and which are now emerging as independent states. For example, the Trust Territory of Nauru, which is expected to attain independence in the immediate future, has an area of 8.25 square miles and an indigenous population of about 3,000, while Pitcairn Island is only 1.75 square miles in extent and has a population of eighty-eight.

164. It is, of course, perfectly legitimate that even the smallest territories, through the exercise of their right to self-determination, should attain independence as a result of the effective application of General Assembly resolution 1514 (XV) on the granting of independence to colonial countries and peoples. However, it appears desirable that a distinction be made between the right to independence and the question of full membership in the United Nations. Such membership may, on the one hand, impose obligations which are too onerous for the "micro-states" and, on the other hand, may lead to a weakening of the United Nations itself.

165. I would suggest that it may be opportune for the competent organs to undertake a thorough and comprehensive study of the criteria for membership in the United Nations, with a view to laying down the necessary limitations on full membership while also defining other forms of association which would benefit both the "micro-states" and the United Nations. I fully realize that a suggestion of this nature involves considerable political difficulties, but if it can be successfully undertaken it will be very much in the interests both of the United Nations and of the "micro-states" themselves. There are already one or two cases where the states concerned have realized that their best interests, for the time being at least, rest in restricting themselves to membership in certain specialized agencies, so that they can benefit fully from the United Nations system in advancing their economic and social development without having to assume the heavy financial and other responsibilities involved in United Nations membership. The League of Nations had to face the same issue over

the question of the admission of certain European states which were then referred to as "Lilliputian" states. Although the League of Nations was unable to define exact criteria, it prevented in due course the entry of the "Lilliputian" states.

166. As already mentioned, a necessary corollary to the establishment of criteria on admission to full membership is the definition of other forms of association for "micro-states" which would not qualify for full membership. As members of the international community, such states are entitled to expect that their security and territorial integrity should be guaranteed and to participate to the full in international assistance for economic and social development. Even without Charter amendment, there are various forms of association, other than full membership, which are available, such as access to the International Court of Justice and membership in the relevant United Nations regional economic commissions. Membership in the specialized agencies also provides an opportunity for access to the benefits provided by the United Nations Development Programme and for invitation to United Nations conferences. In addition to participation along the foregoing lines, "micro-states" should also be permitted to establish permanent observer missions at United Nations Headquarters and at the United Nations Office at Geneva, if they so wish, as is already the case in one or two instances. Measures of this nature would permit the "micro-states" to benefit fully from the United Nations system without straining their resources and potential through assuming the full burdens of United Nations membership which they are not, through lack of human and economic resources, in a position to assume.

167. This latter suggestion of observer status for the "micro-states" naturally brings to mind the question of observer status in general. While the question of observers from non-member states was raised by Mr. Trygve Lie in a report on permanent missions submitted to the General Assembly at its fifth session, and while I have referred to it for a number of years in the introductions to my annual reports, the institution is one which rests purely on practice and which has not been set on any firm legal basis through discussion and decision in the General Assembly.

168. In my introduction to last year's annual report as well as in previous years, I have already expressed my strong feeling that all

countries should be encouraged and enabled, if they wish to do so, to follow the work of the Organization more closely by maintaining observers at the Headquarters of the United Nations, at Geneva and in the regional economic commissions. They will thus be exposed to the impact of the work of the Organization and the currents and cross-currents of opinion that prevail within it, besides gaining opportunities to contribute to that exchange. However, I have also explained that I have felt obliged to follow the established tradition—which, as already noted, has no firm legal basis—by which only certain governments have been enabled to maintain observers. I would like to repeat the suggestion I made last year that this question may be further examined by the General Assembly so that the Secretary-General might be given a clear directive as to the policy to be followed in the future. Were the Assembly, perhaps on the initiative of a Member state, to study the questions involved, I am sure that it would be possible formally to establish the status of observer and to draw up legal rules permitting non-members to follow items of interest to them in the United Nations.

169. In the above observations I have endeavoured, as frankly and as objectively as I can, to draw the attention of the Organization to the serious problems which it has to tackle if the effectiveness of the United Nations is to be maintained and improved. This is not the first time in its history that the United Nations is facing a "crisis" of confidence, and I am sure it will not be the last. At the same time, this "crisis" is itself an index of the high hopes that Member states have come to place in the Organization, and their faith that these serious problems can and should be solved by determined efforts and a spirit of cooperation on the part of the governments of Member states. The United Nations is an instrument of multilateral diplomacy which has some special advantages when dealing with problems involving the reconciliation and harmonization of the interests of several Member states. Like all tools, its utility will depend upon the skill and tenacity of those who have the occasion and the need to use it. I hope that this instrument will be put to more effective use in the coming months, so that a climate of confidence will be established—confidence in the ability of the Organization to weather the storms, to build bridges of reconciliation, to re-establish lost lines of communication and to prove once again its capacity to promote peace and progress.

2. From Transcript of Press Conference

NEW YORK   SEPTEMBER 16, 1967

THE SECRETARY-GENERAL: Mr. Raghavan[1] and friends, the last time we met was on the eve of grave events in the Middle East which erupted four months ago. In my Introduction to the Annual Report, which is scheduled to be published on Monday, I have dealt at some length with that problem. Then, there is the Vietnam war, and we are all familiar with the cruel facts, the increasing casualties on all sides and the continued destruction of Vietnam.

The international outlook on the eve of the coming twenty-second session of the General Assembly is far from encouraging. Since I am sure that many governments are aware that it would be very dangerous to pursue a policy of drift, I am hopeful that new peace initiatives, based on the principles of the Charter, will be considered very seriously by all Members of the United Nations.

MR. RAGHAVAN: Mr. Secretary-General, may I say at the outset how happy we all are to meet with you again, and so soon after your rather strenuous trip to Kinshasa. We are also grateful to you for acceding to our request to advance the timing of the conference to meet the European and Asian deadlines. I am sure that I am also reflecting the sentiments of all my colleagues here when I say we wish we could meet with you more often, perhaps monthly.

I should now like to put a question. You, yourself, have said that the situation in the world outlook is not at all encouraging, and you referred to Vietnam and the Middle East. Yesterday, you said that there is frustration all around. Many persons outside fear that this Organization politically is increasingly becoming like its habitat: an air-conditioned glass house, cut off from the realities of the world. Do

SOURCE: UN Press Release SG/SM/807.

[1]Chakravanti Raghavan, President, United Nations Correspondents Association.

you have any thoughts on the subject or remedies for altering the situation?

THE SECRETARY-GENERAL: I do not subscribe to the view that the United Nations has developed into a mere forum for debates and discussions because of its inability to function effectively in serious crisis situations in many parts of the world. The United Nations, as you know, is just a reflection of the entire membership; it just holds up a mirror to the human situation today. If the United Nations fails, it is a failure of the entire membership. If the United Nations succeeds, it is a success of the entire membership. I do not feel that there is no future for the United Nations vis-à-vis its peace-keeping functions. If only some conditions are met, then the United Nations will develop into a really effective instrument for peace. Among those conditions is the need for better understanding and better cooperation between the big powers, which is the essence of the Charter. Without the agreement of the big powers on basic problems involving war and peace, the United Nations will be just impotent to deal with those basic problems. So, I am not pessimistic about the future of this Organization.

QUESTION: Would you give us your views on the Vietnam situation today, and do you intend to take any further initiative for negotiation?

THE SECRETARY-GENERAL: As I have indicated through a United Nations spokesman last month, I have, for the moment, suspended my efforts toward a settlement of this problem, because of the simple fact that I have all along defined priorities toward its settlement, and the first priority is the cessation of bombing of North Vietnam. If that priority is not met, I do not see how I can usefully pursue my efforts toward finding a peaceful solution. It does not mean that I have given up my efforts. I just want to stress that I have only suspended my efforts in finding a solution. At the right moment, of course, I will continue my efforts.

QUESTION: Mr. Secretary-General, there is a report that a Soviet military mission has gone to China, presumably to firm up cooperation between China and the Soviet Union in increasing help to North Vietnam. Do you have any information on that or about any increased help to North Vietnam by those two powers?

THE SECRETARY-GENERAL: To my knowledge, there are indications that Hanoi is receiving increasing aid, both military and economic, from countries friendly to Hanoi. According to reports, which are, of course, not confirmed, an agreement has been reached between Hanoi and some of its sympathizers regarding the provision to Hanoi of volunteer technicians, particularly air crew, such as pilots, gunners and engineers.

QUESTION: In the light of the decisions taken by the Arab heads of state at Khartoum, compared to the stated position of the Israeli government, with reference to the Middle East and Jerusalem, do you see any possible role for the United Nations in this situation? If so, do you envisage the possibility of a new second sort of United Nations Emergency Force (UNEF) in the area?

THE SECRETARY-GENERAL: Regarding the Middle Eastern situation, I believe that a United Nations role is essential; it is imperative. I think in the question of the Arab-Israeli dispute, third-party involvement will be necessary for a long time to come. When I say "third-party involvement" I mean primarily the United Nations. I cannot think of any other organization or agency which can perform the functions of the third party more efficiently and more effectively than the United Nations. So I do not see how the United Nations can wash its hands of the Middle Eastern crisis.

Of course, I understand the motivations of some of the parties primarily involved to negotiate directly without any third-party involvement. But I do not think it is a practical proposition in the existing circumstances. It would be ideal, of course, if the contestants in any dispute, for instance Arabs and Israelis, could negotiate directly. It would be ideal, for instance, for the United States and Cuba to negotiate directly, for the Ivory Coast and Guinea to negotiate directly, or for Thailand and Cambodia to negotiate directly. But in the existing circumstances, those are not practical propositions. Therefore, I still maintain the view that third party involvement will be necessary for some time.

QUESTION: Mr. Secretary-General, you have set down a program of priorities for a possible solution of the conflict in Vietnam. Do you have any such recommendations in terms of priorities or suggestions or initiatives for the latent conflict in the Middle East?

THE SECRETARY-GENERAL: The Middle Eastern crisis is before the two deliberative organs of the United Nations, the Security Council and the General Assembly. Since that item is before those two organs, I do not think I should venture any program or formula setting up priorities, as in the case of Vietnam. In the case of Vietnam, none of the deliberative organs of the United Nations has come out with any formula or resolution, and I have therefore been expressing my own views in the context of the Charter provisions as I understand them. With respect to the Middle Eastern crisis, I have made some observations in my Introduction to the Annual Report which, as I have said before, will be released to the Press on Monday.

QUESTION: Is there any possibility that you will visit the Middle East in the near future?

THE SECRETARY-GENERAL: I do not see any usefulness or desirability of my visiting the area in the near future. Of course, if at any moment a visit by me should be deemed to be helpful, I shall be prepared to go any time. But I do not see any prospect of my visit in the very near future.

QUESTION: Aden and South Arabia is an area rapidly becoming a cockpit. The United Nations seems stalemated there, and yet the situation continues to deteriorate every day. Can you suggest what can be done to stop the situation from sliding downhill into a new Middle East crisis?

THE SECRETARY-GENERAL: As far as Aden is concerned, as you are all aware, the United Nations Special Mission on Aden, comprising three members, is functioning. Yesterday, on my return from the Congo, Ambassador Shalizi,[2] one of the members of the Mission, saw me and explained to me that the Mission expected to submit its report by the end of this month. At the present moment, the Chairman of the Mission, Ambassador Perez Guerrero,[3] and another member, Ambassador Keita,[4] are not in New York. I have been assured that the report on the findings of the Mission will be published by the end of this month. I should like to express one fervent hope on this question: that with unity and the cooperation of all nationalist elements in the territory, an early independence in conditions of peace will be achieved, which is the primary objective of the relevant resolutions of the General Assembly.

QUESTION: Mr. Secretary-General, you said that your first priority on Vietnam was the cessation of bombing, and you had said previously, I believe, that you felt that within three or four weeks negotia-

[2]Ambassador Abdul Satar Shalizi of Afghanistan.
[3]Ambassador Manuel Perez Guerrero of Venezuela.
[4]Ambassador Moussa Leo Keita of Mali.

tions could be under way. I have two questions: Do you still think so, and do you have any idea of what the objective of such negotiations might reasonably be, for instance, a neutral and independent South Vietnam?

THE SECRETARY-GENERAL: Last January, I volunteered the opinion I was convinced that, after the cessation of the bombing of North Vietnam, meaningful talks would take place in a matter of three to four weeks. I repeated that statement on subsequent occasions. To my knowledge, Hanoi has never refuted or denied this. Not only has Hanoi not refuted this, but Hanoi came out with the statement that there would be meaningful talks only after the cessation of the bombing of North Vietnam. As I have said on a previous occasion, the term "permanent cessation" has no meaning. "Permanent" does not necessarily mean that the cessation of bombing must be for one year or for ten years. It is only a matter of nuance. I am convinced, and many leaders of governments friendly to Hanoi are also convinced, that once the bombing of North Vietnam is stopped, there will be meaningful talks between Hanoi and Washington. But that is only the first step. In the last analysis the problem of Vietnam must be solved by the people of Vietnam themselves, without outside interference. The meeting between Washington and Hanoi can only create conditions to facilitate the participation of the people of Vietnam in fashioning their own future. In other words, the meeting between Washington and Hanoi should pave the way toward the implementation of the Geneva Agreements of 1954. One of the twin objectives of those Agreements was the creation of a nonaligned and independent Vietnam.

QUESTION: Did your visit to Kinshasa [Congo] add to your hope or expectation that the Republic of South Africa may eventually accept United Nations control over South West Africa and the ultimate independence of that country?

THE SECRETARY-GENERAL: No, I am sorry that I did not have that impression. Of course, the matter will be taken up by the Council of Eleven on South West Africa formed by the General Assembly, and that Council has to report its findings to the coming session of the General Assembly. I see no indication of South Africa's complying with the decisions of the General Assembly.

QUESTION: Can you identify the countries that are sending air crews to North Vietnam?

THE SECRETARY-GENERAL: No, I am not in a position to identify those countries. But according to the reports available to me, some sort of agreement has been reached between Hanoi and some of its sympathizers regarding the provision of volunteer technicians.

QUESTION: Mr. Secretary-General, you have received a petition from the Buddhist community in Europe, and some of the items seem interesting to me, particularly items 4, 5 and 7. Item 4 reads:

The whole machinery of the balloting was in the firm hands of the police, of Colonel Loan, who alone with his men controlled the 8,824 polling stations throughout the country, and therefore can put into the boxes as many ballots as they want.

Item 6 reads:

Do the Johnson observers know that before some of them reach a polling place that they wanted to inspect, innumerable security measures under the supervision of Loan's men were taken long before they arrived, giving ample time to the secret agents to arrange the polling places and clear them of any opposition to the régime?

Finally, item 7 reads:

The most elementary thing that the observers should have known is that the pressure on the people was tremendous. When you say to those poor peasants that they will have to vote and have their identification cards stamped by the secret police, because if they don't vote they will not have the stamp of the police on their cards and therefore will lose their right to buy food, milk and rice, it is expected that few people would choose starvation.

May I ask your comments on that?

THE SECRETARY-GENERAL: Yes, I received the communication from a Buddhist organization some time ago and a United Nations spokesman had also announced it in one of the Press briefings, about ten days ago, I believe. Regarding the substance of this letter, I do not think that I am competent to comment on it. From published accounts, everybody knows that elections were conducted on September 3. There were 8,824 polling stations. Of course, I have no means of knowing who supervised those polling booths and who counted the votes. Those are factors which are not very clear. As far as the United Nations is concerned, as you know, I was asked by the government in Saigon to send observers to observe the elections on September 3. I replied to the government that I am not competent to send observers without the proper authorization of a deliberative organ.

In the past, as you know, the United Nations was involved in observing elections in certain Trust Territories like the Cameroons, for instance, and for the United Nations to observe the elections in the Cameroons, a long process had to be followed. First of all, the matter was taken up in the Trusteeship Council. The Trusteeship Council recommended to the General Assembly that observers should be sent and the General Assembly decided to send observers, and those observers were sent many weeks ahead of the actual elections to see that the polling registers were correct, that everybody who was eligible to vote was on the list, that all the candidates were satisfied that the voting would be proper and fair, that all the parties primarily involved in the elections were able to send observers to every polling booth, and that they could observe even the counting of votes. So the United Nations was involved in observing such elections.

If the United Nations is to be involved in any election of any country, I think that there is a general agreement here that either the General Assembly or the Security Council must decide on a course of action authorizing me to send observers. So in the circumstances, I have no means of knowing about the correctness of the allegations made in that document.

QUESTION: Mr. Secretary-General, recently there have been new initiatives, I believe, in harnessing the efforts of the Security Council to go into the question of Vietnam. Some time ago you had maintained the position that this was not feasible. Do you still hold that position? You spoke of initiatives by the General Assembly. Do you still hold the position that the Security Council at this stage would not be the effective organ for taking that initiative?

THE SECRETARY-GENERAL: Regarding prospective United Nations involvement in the Vietnam problem, I have made my position known during the last three years or so, because of the difficulties I had enumerated on previous occasions. But let me say this: I would be the happiest man if the Security Council were in a position to contribute toward the settlement of the Vietnam problem. Let me say that I would be the happiest man. Of course, it is up to the Security Council to decide either to act or not to act if there is a request by a Member state for Security Council involvement.

But the plain fact is that in matters of that nature involving peace-keeping, the Security Council will not act and cannot act in the face of the opposition of one permanent Member. That has been the experience of the United Nations in the last twen*y-two years. To cite one example, the United Nations could not be effectively involved in an operation of a peace-keeping character in the Dominican Republic crisis because of the opposition of one big power. So I do not see any prospect of effective Security Council involvement in the Vietnam situation in the face of the opposition of at least two big powers. The answer is as simple as that.

But let me repeat: I would be the happiest man if the Security Council were in a position to contribute toward the settlement of the Vietnam problem.

QUESTION: Do you think the Arab leaders have become more realistic after the last war with Israel? Do you think a call from you to the Arab countries to renounce their belligerency and to recognize Israel would be of help?

THE SECRETARY-GENERAL: I think that that is before the General Assembly and the Security Council, and I do not think I should venture an opinion on this aspect of the problem.

QUESTION: You have spoken of the role of the Security Council and what it can and cannot do in the case of Vietnam. If the situation were reversed—instead of bringing this issue as it was brought in January 1966 to the Security Council with the simultaneous announcement of the resumption of bombing—do you see any possibility of the General Assembly's making some contribution to a solution?

THE SECRETARY-GENERAL: I am sure that most of the Chairmen of delegations to the forthcoming session of the General Assembly will make some observations on the Vietnam problem whether the item is before the Assembly or not. You will remember that last year the majority of the delegations, to my knowledge, had expressed their desire to see an end to the bombing of North Vietnam. So it seems to me that the need for the cessation of the bombing of North Vietnam is a viewpoint shared by the vast majority of the Members of the United Nations—whether the item is inscribed in the agenda or not.

QUESTION: Mr. Secretary-General, do you foresee or expect any movement toward the representation of Red China in the United Nations at the coming session?

THE SECRETARY-GENERAL: I do not see any indication of any change on the part of the General Assembly regarding its attitude toward that item, particularly because of the fact that Peking's statements and actions confuse even many of its sympathizers. So, as far as I am concerned, I do not see any change in the attitude of the General Assembly toward this item in its forthcoming session.

QUESTION: Mr. Secretary-General, what importance do you attach to yesterday's reports through the French news agency to the effect that perhaps Hanoi is now taking a new interest or a new initiative on getting peace talks into action?

THE SECRETARY-GENERAL: I do not think Hanoi's statements in recent days represent a new initiative. To my knowledge, that is the traditional attitude that has been held by Hanoi all along: to have meaningful talks, the first requisite is the cessation of bombing. So I do not think it is a new attitude or a new definition of an attitude. Even on August 30, Premier Pham Van Dong, made a statement in Hanoi reiterating the traditional line taken by Hanoi, and the one essential phrase in that statement is:

If the American side really desires conversation, it should first cease unconditionally the bombings and every other act of war against the Democratic Republic of Vietnam.

Of course, the word "unconditionally" might confuse some observers, but to my way of thinking it means that if Hanoi is asked to do something, to have some reciprocal action as a price for the cessation of bombings, Hanoi will not pay that price.

I think that has been understood by all the parties primarily concerned. I have explained to you on previous occasions, if we come down to brass tacks, that the facts are the following: In South Vietnam, according to some official estimates, there are at present 50,000 North Vietnamese regulars. Of course, Hanoi has never admitted either the presence of the North Vietnamese regulars in the South, nor the number involved. But that was the estimate: 50,000 North Vietnamese regulars in the South. Also, there are official statements to the effect that there are approximately half a million United States and allied armed forces in South Vietnam. So the fact is that the United States allied armed forces constitute ten times the number of reported North Vietnamese regulars in the South. Of course, there are hundreds of thousands of indigenous armed forces both under the government of Saigon and under the National Liberation Front.

Therefore, the position is this: If Hanoi is asked to withdraw these 50,000 regulars from the South, I am afraid Hanoi will not comply with this. Or if Hanoi is asked to cut off all supplies and reinforcements to its men in the South, I do not think Hanoi will comply with such a demand. It would be tantamount to asking Hanoi to leave its men in South Vietnam to their fate. So that is the difficulty. At the same time, the bombing of North Vietnam has not produced the desired results, as has been admitted by many top officials in Washington.

So my point is: If we really desire peace, the earlier the better. And for the creation of conditions for peace, why not take a limited risk of stopping the bombing for three or four weeks? I think this risk is worth taking in the context of the possible results to be achieved.

. . .

QUESTION: Mr. Secretary-General, as I understood your comment on the previous question, you said, if we really desired peace, why not take a risk of ending the bombing for three or four weeks. Would that satisfy Hanoi when it has asked for an unconditional end of the bombing? Do you think that talks could begin in three or four weeks if the bombing were stopped for three or four weeks?

THE SECRETARY-GENERAL: I am convinced of it. There will be meaningful talks.

QUESTION: Four weeks?

THE SECRETARY-GENERAL: Yes.

QUESTION: Do you mean by that that an announcement should be made in Washington that the bombing is being stopped for three or four weeks, or did you mean that the bombing should be stopped unconditionally with silent determination to let it go on at least three or four weeks?

THE SECRETARY-GENERAL: No, I do not think it will be necessary for Washington to announce publicly that it will stop for three to four weeks. I do not think it is the idea behind Hanoi's insistence on the cessation of bombing. [The Secretary-General wishes to emphasize that the intent of his reply to this question is that what is important is a decision in Washington to stop the bombing of North Vietnam unconditionally, and not an announcement of a pause.—Note added by United Nations Office of Public Information.]

QUESTION: Mr. Secretary-General, did you have any suggestion from Hanoi, directly or indirectly, that it would in fact sit down to talk after a bombing pause of three or four weeks?

THE SECRETARY-GENERAL: In the circumstances, I do not think Hanoi will come out publicly or privately and say to anybody that it would talk with Washington on such and such a condition. But it is the assumption of those governments which have very friendly relations with Hanoi that Hanoi will definitely come to the conference table in three to four weeks after the unconditional cessation of bombing.

As you will recall, even Premier Kosygin reiterated this belief. But I do not think Hanoi will come out even privately and say that it will do this or that if certain conditions are met.

. . .

QUESTION: Mr. Secretary-General, you were quoted yesterday as denying a story that you had threatened to resign because of unhappiness with the lack of cooperation between the two big powers. Can you comment on your feeling about whether you are unhappy that you accepted reappointment, and on the prospects you see for any increased cooperation between the big powers at the forthcoming session?

THE SECRETARY-GENERAL: On my return from the Congo yesterday morning, I was asked by some correspondents at the airport whether it was true that I had decided to resign. I was taken by surprise. It was the first time I had ever heard of it and I told them that there was absolutely no foundation to that rumor. Of course, the entire membership has asked me to serve another term of five years. It would be ridiculous on my part to announce my intended resignation every six or eight months. If and when the time comes for me to decide, I can assure you that you will be among the first to know.

. . .

Statement in the Security Council concerning the Stationing of United Nations Observers on the Suez Armistice Line

NEW YORK   OCTOBER 25, 1967

U THANT WAS seriously handicapped in the days following the six-day Middle East war by the absence of United Nations machinery to supervise and report on implementation of the cease-fire along the Suez Canal. The Security Council resolutions of June 6 and 7, which were applicable to the Egyptian-Israeli sector, made no provision for United Nations observers, as did the later resolutions of June 9 and 11 which dealt with the Israeli-Syrian sector. At the end of June, 110 observers manned sixteen observation posts on both sides of the Israeli-Syrian armistice line, while token observation machinery was in operation along the Jordanian and Lebanese borders. At a meeting of the Security Council on July 8, the Secretary-General reported that he had approached the governments of Israel and the United Arab Republic on his own initiative with a proposal for the stationing of United Nations observers in the Suez area. He said that Lieutenant-General Odd Bull, Chief of Staff of the United Nations Truce Supervision Organization (UNTSO), had estimated that a minimum of twenty-five observers would be needed. These could be provided by UNTSO temporarily pending the arrival of replacements. The Council approved the Secretary-General's proposal by means of a consensus of the members' views, read by the President. Thant reported on July 11 that both Israel and the United Arab Republic had accepted his proposal and that he was proceeding with arrangements to set up observation posts. By the time arrangements were completed on August 10, a revised estimate had increased the number of observers needed from twenty-five to forty-six. They were to man three observation posts on the United Arab Republic side of the line and four on the Israeli side. This was a far cry from the 3,378 men in the United Nations Emergency Force (UNEF) at the time of its withdrawal, but it did re-establish the United Nations presence on the Egyptian-Israeli border. On October 25, Thant made a statement before the Security Council proposing a major expansion of the observer operation to a strength of ninety, an increase in the number of observation posts to eighteen, and the purchase of four small patrol boats and four helicopters, with operational and maintenance personnel. The proposed expansion was approved by the Council in a consensus read by the President on December 8.

I HAVE TAKEN particular note of the expressions in the course of the current debate relating to the possible strengthening of the United Nations Observer Operation in the Suez Canal sector. I too have been giving some thought to this matter for some time because, in view of the number and serious nature of the breaches of the cease-fire— which has been called for by the Security Council—since the observers have been stationed in the sector in pursuance of the Security Council's consensus of July 9/10, 1967, it has become increasingly apparent that the operation needs strengthening in certain ways.

At present there are forty-three United Nations observers stationed in the canal sector. They man nine observation posts and engage in limited patrolling in jeeps. They have no means of observing by air or sea and their mobility is limited. The canal itself is about eighty-eight miles long and the observers must be deployed on both sides, on its east and west banks.

I am in the process of consulting with General Bull, the Chief of Staff of UNTSO, on means of enabling the Observer Operation in the canal sector to become more fully effective in maintaining the cease-fire. It is immediately apparent that steps along the following lines are necessary if proper effect is to be given to the Council's consensus.

(1) To increase the number of observers to ninety in order to increase substantially the patrolling function and the number of observation posts. Such an increase, of course, would require expanding, in consultation with the parties, the national distribution of the observers.

(2) To double the number of observation posts on each bank of the canal, which means increasing the present total from nine to eighteen.

(3) To acquire and make use of possibly as many as four small patrol crafts for United Nations observers patrolling in the waters of the canal, the Bitter Lakes, and adjacent waters.

(4) To acquire and use four small helicopters with operational and maintenance personnel for the purpose of increasing the mobility of the observers and for aerial observation, two to be stationed on each bank of the canal.

SOURCE: Security Council Official Records, Twenty-second Year, 1371st meeting.

More specific requirements and details will result from the consultations now under way with the Chief of Staff and will be reported in due course. All such measures, of course, would relate exclusively to the Security Council's cease-fire resolutions and its consensus, and therefore would necessarily be of a provisional and temporary nature. The strengthening of the Observer Operation in the Suez sector along the lines thus indicated would entail, of course, a substantial increase in the cost of the operations beyond the estimated cost set out in my report of October 4. The estimated financial implications will be submitted to the Council as soon as the necessary calculations are completed.

Because the observers in the Suez sector have on several occasions been caught in exchanges of fire between the two sides it is being contemplated, on the suggestion of the Chief of Staff, General Bull, that body armor to protect the upper torso, in addition to the steel helmets already in use, should be provided to the observers. The cost for that item would not be great.

May I take this occasion also to call to the attention of the members of the Council that in the absence of any Security Council action, such as its resolution 236 (1967) adopted on June 12, relating to the Syrian sector and its consensus of July 9/10 relating to the Suez Canal sector, there is no United Nations observation operation beyond token representation in the Israel-Jordan and Israel-Lebanon sectors. Thus for those sectors there is at present no machinery to assist in implementing the Security Council's cease-fire resolutions 233 (1967) and 234 (1967) of June 6 and 7 which apply to all sectors.

Naturally I shall seek and expect the full cooperation of the parties in these measures to strengthen the cease-fire operation and make it more effective.

REORGANIZATION OF THE SECRETARIAT

As HE BEGAN his second term as Secretary-General, U Thant became more and more convinced that a reorganization of the top echelon of the Secretariat was long overdue. It had been more than a decade since the last reorganization and with the passage of time had come new operations and expanded responsibilities. The proliferation of under-secretaries and other staff positions of equivalent rank had created inequities which especially disturbed him. He felt the single-level structure was unfair to key senior officials who bore the heaviest responsibilities. This was the thinking behind his proposal, put forward in the October 18 note, for a return to the concept of two levels in the top echelon of the Secretariat which existed before the reorganization of 1955. At that time Dag Hammarskjöld had decided to create a new title of under-secretary which would be given to the eight assistant secretaries-general and a number of top-ranking directors. At the time of his death in 1961, Hammarskjöld was considering the re-introduction of the two-level concept. Thant's proposal provided that the top officials would have the title of Under-Secretaries-General and the second level would become Assistant Secretaries-General. He listed eleven posts which would be graded initially at the higher level. These were: Chef de Cabinet and Under-Secretary-General for General Assembly Affairs; two Under-Secretaries-General for Special Political Affairs; Director of Administration (combining functions of Director of Personnel and Controller); Under-Secretary-General for Political and Security Council Affairs; Under-Secretary-General for Trusteeship and Non-Self-Governing Territories; Under-Secretary-General for Economic and Social Affairs; Under-Secretary-General for Conference Services; Executive Director of the United Nations Industrial Development Organization; Secretary-General of the United Nations Conference on Trade and Development; and Director-General of the United Nations Office at Geneva.

Thant suggested that some other agencies within the United Nations (like UNICEF), supported mainly by voluntary contributions, might place their top official in the first level if their executive boards so decided. The proposals in the October 18 note related only to the reorganization of the top echelon. He said, however, that he would appoint a committee of experts to make recommendations to him on reorganization of the Secretariat at other levels. He first spoke of a small team of four or five, but in a statement before the Fifth (Administrative and Budgetary) Committee on December 14 he said he had decided to expand the group to seven. This committee, named on April 8, 1968, consisted of the following: Louis Ignacio-Pinto (Dahomey), Bernard de Menthon (France), Platon D. Morozov (USSR), Manuel Perez Guerrero (Venezuela), A. A. Stark (United Kingdom), Wilbur Ziehl (United States), and C. V. Narasimham (India).

1. *Note by the Secretary-General*

NEW YORK   OCTOBER 18, 1967

1. FOR SOME TIME I have been giving thought to the question of reorganization of the Secretariat. It will be recalled that I have made more than one public reference to the need for such a reorganization. As I said in my statement of September 1, 1966:

I believe that, within its limitations, the Secretariat has performed well and that, with further organizational improvements, it is capable of doing even better.

In my acceptance speech of December 2, 1966, I also stated:

. . . All the organizational or other administrative improvements that are necessary will be undertaken with the assistance of my colleagues so that all Members may continue to rely upon the efficiency, competence, and integrity of this body of dedicated servants of the Organization.

2. The last reorganization of the Secretariat was undertaken in 1955 and I believe that, in view of the vastly expanded responsibilities of the Secretariat in the interval, the time is opportune for a new look at the present setup and its possible improvement. In this connection I have studied the proposals which were made in the summer of 1961 and which are contained in documents A/4776, of June 14, 1961, and A/4794, of June 30, 1961. I do not believe that these proposals are entirely appropriate at the present time in view of the changed circumstances.

3. In this paper I am concerned mainly with the top echelon of the Secretariat. Member governments are aware that, when the Secretariat was first set up, there were eight Assistant Secretaries-General and a number of top-ranking Directors. In 1955, Mr. Hammarskjöld decided to promote the top-ranking Directors to the rank of Under-Secretary and in the process he down-graded, to some extent, the Assistant Secretaries-General to the same level. It is on the basis of

SOURCE: General Assembly Official Records, Twenty-second Session, Annexes, agenda item 74, document A/C.5/1128.

this reorganization that the top echelon of the Secretariat has been functioning for the past twelve years.

4. It is relevant to note that, in the 1961 proposals to which reference was made above, both the Committee of Experts on the Review of the Activities and Organization of the Secretariat and Mr. Hammarskjöld thought in terms of reintroducing two levels within the top echelon.

5. At present, in the Secretariat at Headquarters, there are four-teen Under-Secretaries, excluding those Under-Secretaries who are in charge of or concerned with programs essentially financed by voluntary contributions (e.g., UNDP, UNICEF, and UNITAR). The figure of fourteen, however, includes the Secretariat officials in charge of organs of the General Assembly which are part of the Secretariat proper, such as the Secretary-General of UNCTAD and the Executive Director of UNIDO. The former has his main office in Geneva and the latter in Vienna. In Geneva there are also the Direc-tor-General of the United Nations Office at Geneva and the United Nations High Commissioner for Refugees. There is also the Commis-sioner-General of the United Nations Relief and Works Agency for Palestine Refugees in the Near East, with headquarters in Beirut. Then there are the four Executive Secretaries of the regional eco-nomic commissions. I must also mention in this connection the heads of the various special missions, some of which have continued over long periods and will presumably continue for some time to come, such as the United Nations Truce Supervision Organization in Pales-tine and the United Nations Military Observer Group in India and Pakistan. A list of these posts as of today appears in annex I below.

6. Considering the varying levels of responsibility of these offi-cials, all of whom are now of the same rank in the Secretarist of the United Nations, it is, I think reasonable to conclude that this equation of rank is somewhat unreal, and less than fair to some of the senior officials on whom a heavy load of responsibility rests.

7. In regard to the programs financed by voluntary contributions, the present position is equally unreal since it places at the same level the Administrator of UNDP, with vast responsibilities, both substan-tive and financial, and the heads of other agencies within the United Nations listed in annex I.

8. So far as the activities of the United Nations in the economic and social fields are concerned, annex II contains a note which

compares the present position in the United Nations and in the specialized agencies. A study of this statement leads me to the conclusion that in these fields it is essential that the key officials of the United Nations should have an appropriate status, not only in relation to their inherent responsibilities, but also in relation to their opposite numbers in the specialized agencies with whom they regularly do business.

9. Taking all these factors into account, I have come to the conclusion that it would be proper and opportune to reintroduce the concept of two levels in the top echelon of the Secretariat, with proper geographical distribution at both levels. While, of course, the placement at either of the two levels of officers already in service will not prove an easy task, I believe that in the long-term interests of the Organization this has to be undertaken.

10. Annex III contains a list of the positions I believe should be graded at the higher level. The consideration that has guided me in reclassifying these posts at the higher level is mainly the responsibility that goes with them, although equitable geographical distribution has also been taken into account in determining the number of posts involved.

11. It will be seen that I have kept the present structure of the Secretariat unchanged except in regard to the combination of the posts of Controller and Director of Personnel. I believe that it would be an advantage if there were one official, at the higher level within the top echelon, in charge of the joint offices, assisted by two officers at the lower level of the top echelon, in charge of the present offices of the Controller and the Director of Personnel. I have in mind for this official the designation of Under-Secretary-General in charge of Finance and Management.

12. In classifying the official in charge of the Office of Conference Services at the higher level, I have taken into account the vastly increased work-load of the conference program and the consequent increase in the responsibilities of the post.

13. I have given some thought to the appropriate designation of the two levels within the top echelon. Keeping in mind the reference to the post of Assistant Secretary-General in the Convention on the Privileges and Immunities of the United Nations, I intend to designate the officials in the higher level of the top echelon as Under-

Secretaries-General and officials in the lower level of the top echelon as Assistant Secretaries-General.

14. It is my intention that the officials at the higher of the two levels should receive a salary that exceeds that of the officials at the lower level by a net amount of $2,000 ($3,500 gross) per year. The financial implications of these proposals, as far as the Secretariat proper is concerned, will be approximately $43,250 gross per year, or $27,000 net per year.

15. As regards the heads of those agencies within the United Nations listed in annex I whose programs are supported mainly by voluntary contributions, I feel that the Executive Director of UNICEF can justifiably be placed at the higher level. This is, however, primarily a matter for the consideration of the Executive Board of UNICEF.

16. In addition to the proposals made above, I believe that the Administrator of UNDP should receive a different treatment. In view of the level of his responsibilities, to which I have already drawn attention, I consider that his post should be equated with the head of a major specialized agency. The other senior officials in the UNDP headquarters set-up could then be given appropriate ranks in due course, this readjustment being made by the Administrator of UNDP in consultation with me.

17. It will be observed that these proposals only relate to the top echelon. I propose to appoint a small team of four or five experts to consider the problem of reorganization of the Secretariat at other levels and to make appropriate recommendations to me. I shall pursue this matter further as soon as the present proposals have been implemented.

18. I hope that the General Assembly will take note of these proposals which, subject to necessary budgetary action, I intend to implement with effect from January 1, 1968.

[ANNEXES OMITTED.]

2. Statement in the Fifth (Administrative and Budgetary) Committee

NEW YORK   DECEMBER 14, 1967

I AM GLAD to have this opportunity to make a short statement before the Fifth Committee on the question of the reorganization of the top echelon of the Secretariat. As you are aware, the proposals I made were evolved after very careful consideration in the light of my personal experience of the working of the Secretariat over a period of five to six years. In proposing two levels at the top echelon I was reverting to the earlier arrangement which had prevailed from the beginning of the United Nations Secretariat until sometime in 1953. You will also recall that, in 1960, when he himself had over seven years experience as Secretary-General of the United Nations, my distinguished predecessor, Mr. Hammarskjöld, had also come to the conclusion that the reorganization of the top echelon in two categories was desirable.

In evolving these proposals I have taken into consideration the comments and suggestions made by the Chairman and members of the Advisory Committee on Administrative and Budgetary Questions in the course of my informal consultations with them.

I have also noted the various suggestions and comments made in the Fifth Committee on this question, in the course of the debate on agenda items 75 and 83. I believe it is extremely desirable that the proposals that I have made should come into effect from January 1, 1968, as I had intended.

As the Controller has already pointed out, the financial implications of the proposal in regard to two levels in the top echelon are small, and for 1968 no special appropriation will be needed.

As I have stated in document A/C.5/1128, it is my intention to apply

SOURCE: UN Press Release SG/SM/882. The summary record is given in General Assembly Official Records, Twenty-second Session, Fifth Committee, 1225th meeting.

the principle of equitable geographical distribution to both levels of the top echelon.

In document A/C.5/1128 I have also stated that it was my intention "to appoint a small team of four or five experts to consider the problem of reorganization of the Secretariat at other levels and to make appropriate recommendations to me." After further consultations I have come to the conclusion that it would be desirable to appoint a Committee of seven members with wide geographical distribution, which will enable me to secure the assistance and advice of people of recognized competence from the various parts of the world, including two or three members who have experience of both the work of the permanent missions to the United Nations and the work of the Secretariat.

As for their terms of reference, I have in mind that they should undertake a review of the most important aspects of the present organization of the Secretariat of the United Nations, including the offices in Geneva, the Secretariats of UNCTAD, UNIDO, and the regional economic commissions, with a view to ensuring the most efficient functioning of the Secretariat with the optimum use of available resources. The Committee may also consider the division of responsibilities, under the authority of the Secretary-General, of the various units and their interrelationship, in order to improve the functioning of the Secretariat as a whole. I also believe that, within the available time, the Committee might devote some attention to the management procedures of the Secretariat and propose detailed studies, if considered necessary. On all these matters, I hope the Committee will make valuable recommendations to me, and I shall give them my urgent and earnest consideration.

It would also be my intention to request the Committee to take a look at the organization of the top echelon of the Secretariat in the light of the comments made in the Fifth Committee at the present session. Whatever recommendations the Committee may have to make on this subject will be received by me with an open mind and I shall make further proposals to the General Assembly at its twenty-third session if, on the basis of the recommendations of this Committee, I feel that some minor changes may be desirable.

I understand that on certain assumptions, a paper on financial implications in regard to the working of this Committee has already been prepared, and I hope it will be considered and approved by the Fifth Committee.

Mr. Chairman, I hope that the statement I have made will help the Fifth Committee in the consideration of this question.

Statement on the Role of Religious Convictions
at the Third International Teach-in

TORONTO   OCTOBER 22, 1967

U THANT's statement before the Third International Teach-in at Toronto on October 22 was devoted entirely to an explanation of the principles of Buddhism and the effect that his religious convictions had had on his work at the United Nations. He had touched on this subject frequently in previous speeches, but never in such a comprehensive way. At Toronto he spoke more directly of his own faith and of its parallel to the principles of the United Nations Charter, particularly those dealing with tolerance and nonviolence. His remarks confirmed publicly what his friends and associates had already known: that he was an intensely religious man.

I HAVE BEEN requested by the students of the University of Toronto to participate in the "Faith and Peace" session of the third international teach-in to be held in Toronto from Friday, October 20, to Sunday, October 22, 1967. I have been asked to make a brief statement mainly on the effect that my faith, which is Buddhism, has had on my work at the United Nations and also on the role that men of all faiths can play in bringing morality into the conduct of international relations.

A specific question has been posed: "To what extent have your religious convictions motivated your concern for peace and human well-being?" Normally I would be unwilling to discuss in public my religious faith and the manner in which it may have affected my way of living and my approach to my work. However, in the special circumstances of the Toronto teach-in I felt that it would be proper for me to respond to the invitation to discuss this specific question.

As is commonly known, I am a Buddhist. As a religion, Buddhism has some unique features and also some basic principles which are of relevance to the theme of this teach-in. In my statement to follow I shall deal briefly with some of the cardinal principles of Buddhism

SOURCE: UN Press Release SG/SM/822, October 20, 1967.

which seem to me to have a direct relationship to the state of the world today.

The doctrine taught by Gautama Buddha, which is called Dhamma, or universal principle of truth, is at once philosophy, science, ethical teaching, and the supreme way to spiritual perfection. It is all these things and more. It is different from the other religions of the world, as it has features not to be found in any of them, while at the same time it is independent of many ideas that are commonly thought to be essential to religion (for instance, the idea of a creator-God and the principle of the soul). Such concepts do not find any place in Buddhism.

Buddhism offers to the world absolute truth; a rational explanation of the mysteries of life, of good and evil and the problem of suffering; and a way by which the ultimate reality—Nirvana—can be reached. It teaches, above all, a universal compassion, to be extended to all living beings, irrespective of their status, race, or creed. All sentient beings are involved in suffering; all are struggling in a dark ignorance that blinds them to the truth of their own nature and the laws that govern their existence. It is through the ignorance of the law of Karma that men do evil to one another, and thus to themselves. If each of us were to realize that whatsoever he does to another he does in effect to himself, through the law of reciprocal action, this world would become a happy and peaceful place. There would be no more crime, no more injustice, no more wars, and no more hatred between one nation and another. But it is in the nature of Samsara that we shall never be able to produce a perfect paradise on earth; all we can do is to mitigate the suffering wherever possible, strive to make our fellow men a little happier—no matter how bad their Karma may be—and at the same time seek to purify and ennoble ourselves. This is the only certain way to happiness, in this life and in lives to come.

I believe that it is only in the Dhamma (the absolute truth) that we can hope to find a solution to the problems that beset us. It is only there that we can find a justification for our inherent belief in a moral order in the world—and a basis for right action, inspired by love and compassion in our relations with our fellow men. The Dhamma teaches us that violence will not resolve any of our conflicts. Similarly hatred and greed will only breed more hatred and greed.

One of the doctrines of Buddhism has a direct relevance to present-day conditions. It is the doctrine of selflessness or nonegoism. To be egoistic is to be blind to the needs, and the reality, of others. In addition, egoism is bad for oneself because it does not exist for long by itself. It becomes, in course of time, the parent of the twin sins of pride and prestige. If there is one lesson that history teaches us, it is that wealth and power, pride and prestige, are not only transitory but even illusory.

Another doctrine of Buddhism is the universal principle of Metta— unbounded love and compassion for all living creatures. Buddhism teaches that the principle of nonviolence should extend not only to other human beings but to all living things.

I have dwelt very briefly on some important principles of Buddhism which I believe are relevant to the human condition today. The universal principle of truth is obviously the most basic of them. So many of the problems that we face today are due to, or the result of, false attitudes—some of them have been adopted almost unconsciously. Among these is the concept of narrow nationalism—"my country, right or wrong." It is lack of truth in international relations that leads to the conscious or unconscious adoption of double standards. It is therefore essential that, in international relations as in human relations, we should practice, as we preach to others, the universal principle of truth.

The doctrine of Karma, the principle that every action has a reaction, obviously has a direct application to international relations. The [United Nations] Charter calls on us to practice tolerance and live together in peace with one another as good neighbors. This is the practical application of the principle of reciprocity.

The principle of nonviolence is also a basic concept of the Charter. One of the most fundamental principles to which Member states have committed themselves is to refrain in their international relations from the threat or use of force. History teaches us that no durable solution can be found for any human problem except by persuasion and by common consent. The use of violence is double-edged, as violence is bound, by the doctrine of reciprocal action, to provoke violence in turn. Before long, we find that the rule of law has given place to the law of the jungle. We have therefore to go back to first principles and to observe the Charter commitment regarding the nonuse of violence or the threat of violence in international relations.

The doctrine of nonegoism is equally important in international relations. Today we have in the world two superpowers, a number of major powers, and a very large number of smaller nations. It is understandable that the major powers should pursue objectives which seem to them to be in their own national interests; but they should not be blind to the existence of a larger goal, the common interest of all countries, large and small, in the survival of the human race. They should, at least occasionally, pause to reflect on the course of history, which has seen the rise and fall of so many great empires. Generations to come will judge the conduct of those in positions of authority today by the effect that their actions had on the course of human peace and progress. If they wish to have an honored place in human history they must appear as men of peace and not as mere victors in war.

The law of love and compassion for all living creatures is again a doctrine to which we are all too ready to pay lip service. However, if it is to become a reality, it requires a process of education, a veritable mental renaissance. Once it has become a reality, national as well as international problems will fall into perspective and become easier to solve. Wars and conflicts, too, will then become a thing of the past, because wars begin in the minds of men, and in those minds love and compassion would have built the defenses of peace.

APPOINTMENT OF A SPECIAL
REPRESENTATIVE TO THE MIDDLE EAST

UP TO NOVEMBER 1967, the United Nations had been unable to agree on a resolution dealing with such basic issues as the withdrawal of Israeli troops from positions they occupied during the six-day Middle East war, the right to innocent passage of shipping through the Suez Canal and the Strait of Tiran, and guarantees for secure boundaries between Israel and her Arab neighbors. The General Assembly at its fifth emergency session had failed to act because of a rigid division between Israeli and Arab supporters which prevented rival resolutions from getting the required majority. On November 9, the Security Council met at the request of the United Arab Republic to consider what it called the dangerous situation prevailing in the Middle East as a result of Israel's refusal to withdraw its forces from territory occupied during the June war. Between then and November 22, the Council held seven meetings on the complaint. It seemed to be faced by the same division that had deadlocked the Assembly. On November 16, however, the United Kingdom introduced a compromise resolution which met the basic objections of both Israel and the Arab countries. This resolution, which eventually became known widely as resolution 242 (1967), was approved unanimously on November 22. Since this document has served as the basis for subsequent negotiations, we are reproducing the text here:

The Security Council,
Expressing its continuing concern with the grave situation in the Middle East,
Emphasizing the inadmissibility of the acquisition of territory by war and the need to work for a just and lasting peace in which every state in the area can live in security,
Emphasizing further that all Member states in their acceptance of the Charter of the United Nations have undertaken a commitment to act in accordance with Article 2 of the Charter,
1. *Affirms* that the fulfillment of Charter principles requires the establishment of a just and lasting peace in the Middle East which should include the application of both the following principles:
(i) Withdrawal of Israeli armed forces from territories occupied during the recent conflict;
(ii) Termination of all claims or states of belligerency and respect for and acknowledgment of the sovereignty, territorial integrity and political independence of every state in the area and their right to live in peace within secure and recognized boundaries free from threats of acts of force;

2. *Affirms further* the necessity

(a) For guaranteeing freedom of navigation through international waterways in the area;

(b) For achieving a just settlement of the refugee problem;

(c) For guaranteeing the territorial inviolability and political independence of every state in the area, through measures including the establishment of demilitarized zones;

3. *Requests* the Secretary-General to designate a special representative to proceed to the Middle East to establish and maintain contacts with the states concerned in order to promote agreement and assist efforts to achieve a peaceful and accepted settlement in accordance with the provisions and principles in this resolution;

4. *Requests* the Secretary-General to report to the Security Council on the progress of the efforts of the special representative as soon as possible.

Thant had anticipated the requests contained in the final paragraphs and was ready to name his special representative immediately. On November 23, he sent a note to the Council informing it that he had selected Gunnar Jarring of Sweden for the post. On December 22, one month after the adoption of resolution 242 (1967), Thant informed the Council that Jarring had already visited the capitals of the various Middle East countries involved in the war and had been "received with the utmost courtesy and with expressions of willingness to cooperate with his mission." He also reported that Jarring would make his headquarters in Cyprus and that he would start a new round of visits on December 26 with a trip to Jerusalem.

---

1. Note on the Selection of Gunnar Jarring

NEW YORK   NOVEMBER 23, 1967

RESOLUTION 242 (1967), adopted by the Security Council on November 22, 1967, in its operative paragraph 3, "*Requests* the Secretary-General to designate a special representative to proceed to the Middle East to establish and maintain contacts with the states concerned in order to promote agreement and assist efforts to achieve a peaceful

SOURCE: Security Council Official Records, Twenty-second Year, Supplement for October, November and December 1967, document S/8259.

and accepted settlement in accordance with the provisions and principles in this resolution.''

This provision of the resolution, on the one hand, requires careful consideration and, on the other, must be implemented expeditiously. Since last May, at the time of my visit to Cairo, when I first advanced the notion of a special representative of the Secretary-General to the Middle East, I have given much thought to the question of who, in the light of all the necessary qualifications, might best be sought to carry out the heavy responsibilities of this challenging assignment, and I have engaged in a number of informal consultations on the matter with interested parties. Consequently, I am happy to be able now to inform the Council that I am inviting Ambassador Gunnar Jarring of Sweden to accept the designation for this vital task and I have reason to believe that he will be willing to do so, I am confident that Ambassador Jarring will do all that can be done in carrying out the assignment.

In pursuance of the above action I am, on November 23, 1967, addressing the following note to the governments of Israel, Jordan, Lebanon, Syria, and the United Arab Republic:

The Secretary-General of the United Nations presents his compliments to the permanent representative of ——— to the United Nations and has the honor to refer to resolution 242 (1967) adopted by the Security Council at its 1382nd meeting on November 22, 1967. In that resolution the Security Council '*Requests* the Secretary-General to designate a special representative to proceed to the Middle East to establish and maintain contacts with the states concerned in order to promote agreement and assist efforts to achieve a peaceful and accepted settlement in accordance with the provisions and principle in this resolution.'

The Secretary-General of the United Nations presents his compliments to the permanent representative of ——— to inform his government that he is designating Ambassador Gunnar Jarring of Sweden as his special representative in pursuance of the Security Council resolution. Ambassador Jarring is at present serving as the Ambassador of Sweden to the Union of Soviet Socialist Republics. The government of Sweden has agreed to make Ambassador Jarring available for the United Nations assignment in the Middle East.

Prior to his present post, Ambassador Jarring served at various times as Swedish Minister to India, to Ceylon, to Iran, to Iraq, and to Pakistan. He was Director of the Political Division of the Swedish Ministry of Foreign Affairs from 1953 to 1956 and was permanent representative of Sweden to the United Nations from 1956 to 1958, during which time he served on the Security Council from 1957 to 1958. After leaving the United Nations,

Ambassador Jarring served for a period as Swedish Ambassador to the United States of America.

Ambassador Jarring will be proceeding to the Middle East very soon. The exact date and time of his arrival in the area will be communicated later.

The Secretary-General takes this opportunity to express his earnest hope and his confidence that each of the governments concerned will extend to Ambassador Jarring its full cooperation and will afford him all facilities necessary for the effective discharge of the important task entrusted to him.

---

2. Progress Report to the Security Council

NEW YORK   DECEMBER 22, 1967

---

1. IN PURSUANCE OF paragraph 4 of Security Council resolution 242 (1967) of November 22, 1967, I am submitting the following report on the progress of the efforts of the special representative to the Middle East.

2. On November 23, 1967, I reported to the Council [S/8259] that I had invited Mr. Gunnar V. Jarring of Sweden to accept the designation as the special representative mentioned in paragraph 3 of the Council's above-mentioned resolution. Mr. Jarring accepted this designation and arrived at United Nations Headquarters on November 26.

3. While at United Nations Headquarters, Mr. Jarring had discussions concerning his mission with me and with some of my colleagues in the Secretariat. He also consulted with the permanent representatives of Israel, Jordan, Lebanon, the Syrian Arab Republic, and the United Arab Republic, and with some others, regarding his mission.

4. While Mr. Jarring was at United Nations Headquarters he decided, after consultation with the parties concerned and with the concurrence of the government of Cyprus, that he would set up the headquarters of the United Nations Middle East Mission in Cyprus.

5. Mr. Jarring left New York for Cyprus on December 9, 1967,

SOURCE: Security Council Official Records, Twenty-second Year, Supplement for October, November and December 1967, document S/8309.

arriving there on December 10. From Cyprus, Mr. Jarring embarked upon a first round of visits to interested governments mainly for the purpose, as described by Mr. Jarring, of getting acquainted. He visited Beirut from December 12 to 14, Jerusalem from December 14 to 16, and Amman from December 16 to 18. He visited Cairo from December 18 to 20, returning on the latter date to his headquarters in Cyprus. During each of these visits he met the head of state and other high officials.

6. Mr. Jarring reports that in all the countries he visited he was received with the utmost courtesy and with expressions of willing-ness to cooperate with his mission. He further reports that all the governments visited welcomed the prospect of his early return to continue the conversations. He has, therefore, indicated his intention to proceed to Jerusalem on December 26, and subsequently to visit the other capitals.

7. Mr. Jarring also reports that each of the governments visited agreed that the details of the conversations with him should be kept confidential.

8. During the course of Mr. Jarring's mission, I shall be reporting to the Council from time to time in order to keep the members informed of Mr. Jarring's efforts and progress.

THE SITUATION IN CYPRUS

IN MID-NOVEMBER 1967, the situation in Cyprus began deteriorating rapidly. Fighting broke out at several points on November 15 between Cypriot National Guard troops and Turkish Cypriot contingents. The situation was all the more serious because the National Guard manhandled personnel of the United Nations Force (UNFICYP) and deliberately damaged UNFICYP equipment during the fighting. By November 18, the fighting had spread to the Limnitis area. On November 20, members of a UNFICYP patrol were beaten and disarmed by Turkish Cypriot fighters. Turkish jet aircraft repeatedly flew over Cypriot territory. Turkey and Greece appeared to be on the brink of war.

From the beginning of the outbreak, U Thant and his special representative in Cyprus, Bibiano F. Osorio-Tafall, made continuous attempts to effect a cease-fire. On November 22, the Secretary-General sent an urgent appeal to the President of Cyprus and the Prime Ministers of Greece and Turkey, calling on them to use the utmost restraint. He also dispatched Jośe Rolz-Bennett, Under-Secretary for Special Political Affairs, to Athens, Ankara, and Nicosia—with the approval of the three governments concerned—to help ease the growing tension. Two days later Thant sent a new appeal to the three governments, proposing that they agree at once on a phased reduction of all non-Cypriot armed forces other than those of UNFICYP from the island. This was a reference to Greek and Turkish troops, whose presence was a major factor in the rise in tension. The Secretary-General offered his personal good offices and the assistance of UNFICYP in efforts to bring about such a reduction and ultimately the complete withdrawal of the Greek and Turkish forces. The Security Council, after a two-day debate on November 24 and 25, authorized its President of the Council to read a consensus noting "with satisfaction the efforts undertaken by the Secretary-General to help maintain peace in the region" and calling upon the parties to refrain from any acts which might aggravate the situation.

By the time Thant submitted his periodic report to the Council on December 8, asking for an additional extension of the mandate of UNFICYP, the fighting had ceased but the political issues remained unresolved. The Secretary-General again reminded the parties that his good offices continued to be available and urged them "to seize the opportunity emerging from the recent crisis and to display the statesmanship and goodwill which is essential to resolve this complex and long-standing question." In his report Thant had left it to the Council as to whether the stay of UNFICYP should be extended for three months or six months. In its resolution, which was adopted unanimously on December 22, the Council fixed the extension at three months. The resolution did not deal with the substance of the Cypriot controversy or with the Secretary-General's suggestion that the mandate of UNFICYP be enlarged to include supervision of disarmament and authority to help devise practical arrangements to safeguard internal security. As shown in the statement made by Thant after the vote, he was not completely happy with the results of the Council debate. Noting the sharply divergent views of the three parties on the issues to be raised in future discussions, the Secretary-General said, "I would have welcomed clear guidance by the Council on the basic points which have been the subject of much negotiation with the parties during the drafting of the resolution. The weight of the Council's views would have been invaluable to me in the exercise of my good offices and in its absence I deem it my duty to forewarn the Council of the difficulties that lie ahead."

---

1. From Report to the Security Council

NEW YORK   DECEMBER 8, 1967

. . .

155. THE RECENT EVENTS in the island and their very serious repercussions have shown how precarious the situation regarding Cyprus remains and how easily and rapidly, in spite of the best efforts of the United Nations Force, relatively small incidents can develop into an imminent threat to international peace.

156. I have already reported to the Council the three appeals which I made to the parties during the recent crisis and their replies to them, as well as the efforts of my personal representative, Mr. Jośe Rolz-Bennett [S/8248/Adds. 3–9]. These appeals included a call to avoid all acts of force or the threats of recourse to force; a particular plea to the governments of Greece and Turkey to take immediate measures to end any threat to the security of either one by the other as well as of Cyprus and, as a first step, to carry an expeditious withdrawal of those of their forces in excess of their respective contingents in Cyprus. I also said that such reductions, which would need to be in stages, should envisage the ultimate withdrawal from the island of all non-Cypriot armed forces, other than those of the United Nations. This would make possible the

SOURCE: Security Council Official Records, Twenty-second Year, Supplement for October, November, and December 1967, document S/8286.

positive demilitarization of Cyprus and would be a decisive step toward securing peace on the island. I further stated that, with regard to any further role, that it might be considered desirable for the Force to undertake, I gathered that this could involve, subject to the necessary action by the Security Council, enlarging the mandate of the Force so as to give it broader functions in regard to the realization of quiet and peace in Cyprus, including supervision of disarmament and the devising of practical arrangements to safeguard internal security, embracing the safety of all the people of Cyprus. The response of the parties to these appeals was encouraging and does, I believe, provide a basis for the parties and the Security Council to consider the various issues involved, leading toward further positive steps in the search for a durable solution of the Cyprus question.

157. Throughout the recent crisis regarding Cyprus, the world lived through very anxious days, witnessing a chain of events that seemed to be leading inexorably to an armed conflagration. It was possible, at the eleventh hour, to stem the tide but it is of the utmost urgency now to act with speed and determination in the search for a lasting solution to the Cyprus question. While the mediation effort required by the Security Council in its original resolution of March 4, 1964 [186 (1964)] has been inoperative for some time because of the impasse, with which the Council is well acquainted, following the submission of Mr. Galo Plaza's report of March 26, 1965 [S/6253], neither the parties nor the Security Council can afford to allow the situation regarding Cyprus to stumble from crisis to deeper crisis and from danger to graver danger. I wish to urge all concerned, therefore, to seize the opportunity emerging from the recent crisis and to display the statesmanship and goodwill which is essential to resolve this complex and long-standing question. I wish to reiterate that my good offices continue to be available to the parties and to the Security Council to this end.

158. The renewal of the mandate of the United Nations Force is one obvious step for the maintenance of peace in Cyprus, and I recommend to the Council that it extend the Force for another period, whether of six or of three months. What steps over and above this extension can be taken by the Council in consultation with the parties is, of course, for the Council itself to determine.

159. I would conclude this report by drawing attention once again to the continuing precariousness of the situation regarding Cyprus and by expressing the hope that the parties and the Council will proceed with

urgency to intensive consideration of ways and means of preventing a recurrence of conflict and of finding a basis for the settlement of the Cyprus problem.

---

2. Statement in the Security Council

NEW YORK   DECEMBER 22, 1967

THE RESOLUTION just adopted by the Security Council provides for the extension of the stationing of the United Nations Peace-keeping Force in Cyprus for a further period of three months ending on March 26, 1968. I am immediately requesting the governments of the states providing contingents for the Force to cooperate by continuing to make their contingents available.

I take this opportunity to express once again my deep appreciation to the governments of Australia, Austria, Canada, Denmark, Finland, Ireland, Sweden, and the United Kingdom for their wholehearted and unfailing contribution to this important United Nations peace-keeping operation, which has discharged the mandate defined for it by the Security Council with impartiality, restraint, and a high sense of duty.

May I also express gratitude to those states which have shown their active concern for the effectiveness of the Organization by making the generous voluntary financial contributions which have made possible the continuing existence of the United Nations operation in Cyprus.

The resolution invites the parties to avail themselves of the good offices proffered by the Secretary-General and I wish to assure the parties that I am immediately available to them, that I will do all within my power to help them find a way to resolve their differences, and that I hope they will respond to the invitation of the Security Council without delay. Bearing in mind the sharply divergent views of some of the parties in regard to the issues that may be raised during their forthcoming discussions with me, or my representatives, I would have welcomed clear guidance by the Council on the basic points which have been the

SOURCE: Security Council Official Records, Twenty-second Year, 1386th meeting.

subject of much negotiation with the parties during the drafting of the resolution. The weight of the Council's views would have been invaluable to me in the exercise of my good offices and in its absence I deem it my duty to forewarn the Council of the difficulties that lie ahead. The members of the Council will understand, therefore, why I regard it as necessary now to reiterate in the strongest possible terms the call which I made to the parties concerned in my report to the Council of December 8, 1967, namely, to display the statesmanship and goodwill which is essential to resolve this complex and long-standing question.

Statement at Presentation of Declaration on
Population Growth

NEW YORK   DECEMBER 8, 1967

BY 1967 BOTH the United Nations and U Thant had come a long way from their first cautious exploration of possible international action in the field of population control. In his statement to the summer session of the Economic and Social Council, the Secretary-General noted the changed world attitude toward the population problem. Because of the psychological breakthrough, he said, the United Nations could "now embark on a bolder and more effective program of action in this field." He announced that he himself, as Secretary-General, had decided to establish a trust fund, to be raised through voluntary contributions of governments and institutions, with the purpose of establishing training centers and pilot projects to help countries which wanted to tackle the population problem. The Secretary-General discussed the problem again in the Introduction to his Annual Report, declaring that population control was seen "not only as a means of overcoming economic difficulties but also as a way to social and human progress in modern societies.' ₁n the following statement, made at a ceremony at which he received the "Declaration on Population Growth" from John D. Rockefeller III, Chairman of the Board of both the Population Council and the Rockefeller Foundation, Thant took the position that "any decision with regard to the size of the family must irrevocably rest with the family itself, and cannot be made by anyone else." He went on, "But this right of parents to free choice will remain illusory unless they are aware of the alternatives open to them. Hence the right of every family to information and to the availability of services in this field is increasingly considered as a basic human right and as an indispensable ingredient of human dignity."

I AM VERY PLEASED to receive this Declaration on population growth and human dignity and welfare. I want to express my particular appreciation to Mr. John D. Rockefeller III, Chairman of the Board both of the Population Council and of the Rockefeller Foundation, for his untiring efforts to secure ever wider acceptance of the Declaration. This document has now been signed by twenty-five heads of state or government.

There are important links between population growth and the imple-

SOURCE: UN Press Release SG/SM/874.

mentation of the rights and freedoms proclaimed in the Universal Declaration of Human Rights. It is therefore wholly appropriate that the date chosen for this ceremony should be followed so closely by Human Rights Day.

It is also appropriate because, nowadays, population planning is seen not only as an integral part of national efforts for economic and social development but also as a way to human progress in modern society.

We observe today rapidly changing attitudes toward the population problem, particularly in the developing countries where the rates of population increase are usually so high. There now exists in many countries an express desire to limit the size of families, as illustrated by the fact that highly dangerous and illegal means are increasingly used for this purpose. The desire to limit the size of the family is not surprising. With an ever higher percentage of newborn children assured of healthy and productive lives, parents do not, as in the past, see the need for a very large family to be assured of good care in their old age.

The Universal Declaration of Human Rights describes the family as the natural and fundamental unit of society. It follows that any choice and decision with regard to the size of the family must irrevocably rest with the family itself, and cannot be made by anyone else. But this right of parents to free choice will remain illusory unless they are aware of the alternatives open to them. Hence, the right of every family to information and to the availability of services in this field is increasingly considered as a basic human right and as an indispensable ingredient of human dignity.

The work of the United Nations itself in the population field has so far been relatively limited, given the importance of the problem. Against this background, I invited, in July of this year, governments, nongovernmental organizations, and private individuals to contribute to a new trust fund for population activities. I renew this invitation today. Our aim is to expand our work in those countries where it is more needed and which request our help.

We are concerned with the number of human beings on earth. We bear an immense responsibility for the quality of human life in future generations. I have no doubt that we can succeed. Man has shown increasing ability to master his environment. He is now acquiring the knowledge, as well as the means, to master himself and his own future. It is his duty to do so—for his own sake and for the sake of succeeding generations to whom we must bequeath a life worthy of human beings.

Letter to Pope Paul VI

NEW YORK   DECEMBER 20, 1967

U THANT's December 20 letter to Pope Paul VI reflects, as did a number of earlier communications, his desire to encourage peace efforts by religious leaders. In January he had supported the Pope's appeal for an extension of the Tet truce in Vietnam and at the time of the Six-Day War in the Middle East he had endorsed the Roman Catholic leader's proposal that Jerusalem be declared an open city.

I AM MOST GRATEFUL to Your Holiness for having sent me the text of Your message calling for the observance of a "Day of Peace" on the first day of the year 1968 and of every year thereafter. The deep spiritual inspiration of this message cannot but command the greatest respect and the most devoted attention. At this time in history, when nations and individuals are called upon for the very survival of humanity to understand and accept increased responsibilities in a world becoming ever more complex and interdependent, it is indeed appropriate that we should direct our serious attention on the first day of each year to the steps that must be taken in mankind's imperative search for a lasting peace. Such an effort could serve both as a reminder and as an inspiration with regard to the imposing task of building a better world, a task in which every human being, however high or humble his position may be, has a worthy role to play. It is of the utmost importance, as well, for the great religions to reaffirm their pledge of devoting their energies to the cause of peace so that with their aid and by virtue of their example, nations and peoples may advance in their respect for each other and in the strengthening of understanding and cooperation, which are essential if we are to move from a state of fear and anxiety to an era of just and stable peace.

Allow me to assure Your Holiness, once again, that I share Your deep concern regarding the achievement of peace in our troubled times.

Accept, Your Holiness, the reiteration of my profound respect and highest consideration.

SOURCE: UN Press Release SG/SM/885.

Index

Index by Lisa McGraw

341.2308
C79p
v.7

89433

Cordier, Andrew W., ed.
Public papers...United Nations

DATE DUE

DEMCO 38-297

CALDWELL COLLEGE LIBRARY
CALDWELL, NEW JERSEY